Personal Finance

Abraham M. Bertisch

Personal Finance

Abraham M. Bertisch

Professor of Economics and Finance
State University of New York (SUNY)–
Nassau Community College

The Dryden Press

Harcourt Brace College Publishers

Fort Worth Philadelphia San Diego New York Orlando Austin San Antonio
Toronto Montreal London Sydney Tokyo

Acquisitions Editor: Rick Hammonds
Developmental Editor: Bill Teague
Project Editors: Charlie Dierker/Matt Ball
Art Director: Bill Brammer
Electronic Publishing Supervisor: Michael Beaupré
Production Manager: Kelly Cordes
Photo & Permissions Editor: Shirley Webster
Director of Editing, Design, & Production: Diane Southworth
Publisher: Elizabeth Widdicombe

Copy Editor: JaNoel Lowe
Text Type: 10/12 Sabon

Cover Image: Ben Britt
Interior Illustrations: Lamberto Alvarez/Lamberto Alvarez III

Address for Editorial Correspondence
The Dryden Press, 301 Commerce Street, Suite 3700, Fort Worth, TX 76102

Address for Orders
The Dryden Press, 6277 Sea Harbor Drive, Orlando, FL 32887
1-800-782-4479, or 1-800-433-0001 (in Florida)

ISBN: 0-03-097737-1

Library of Congress Catalog Card Number: 93-72065

Printed in the United States of America

4 5 6 7 8 9 0 1 2 3   032   9 8 7 6 5 4 3 2 1

The Dryden Press
Harcourt Brace College Publishers

*To my wife Sara and to my children,
Rochelle, Jason, Benjy, and Michelle*

Amling and Droms
Investment Fundamentals

Berry and Young
Managing Investments: A Case Approach

Bertisch
Personal Finance

Boyet
Security Analysis for Investment Decisions: Text and Software

Brigham
Fundamentals of Financial Management
Sixth Edition

Brigham and Gapenski
Cases in Financial Management
Second Edition

Brigham and Gapenski
Cases in Financial Management: Module A
Second Edition

Brigham and Gapenski
Cases in Financial Management: Module B
Second Edition

Brigham and Gapenski
Cases in Financial Management: Module C
Second Edition

Brigham and Gapenski
Financial Management: Theory and Practice
Seventh Edition

Brigham and Gapenski
Intermediate Financial Management
Fourth Edition

Brigham, Gapenski, and Aberwald
Finance with Lotus 1-2-3
Second Edition

Chance
An Introduction to Options and Futures
Second Edition

Clauretie and Webb
The Theory and Practice of Real Estate Finance

Cooley
Advances in Business Financial Management: A Collection of Readings

Cooley and Roden
Business Financial Management
Third Edition

Curran
Principles of Corporate Finance

Dickerson, Campsey, and Brigham
Introduction to Financial Management
Fourth Edition

Evans
International Finance: A Markets Approach

Fama and Miller
The Theory of Finance

Gardner and Mills
Managing Financial Institutions: An Asset/Liability Approach
Third Edition

Gitman and Joehnk
Personal Financial Planning
Sixth Edition

Greenbaum and Thakor
Contemporary Financial Intermediation

Harrington
Case Studies in Financial Decision Making
Third Edition

Hayes and Meerschwam
Financial Institutions: Contemporary Cases in the Financial Services Industry

Johnson
Issues and Readings in Managerial Finance
Third Edition

Kidwell, Peterson, and Blackwell
Financial Institutions, Markets, and Money
Fifth Edition

Koch
Bank Management
Second Edition

Kohn
Money, Banking and Financial Markets
Second Edition

Lee and Finnerty
Corporate Finance: Theory, Method, and Application

Maisel
Real Estate Finance
Second Edition

Martin, Cox, and MacMinn
The Theory of Finance: Evidence and Applications

Mayo
Finance: An Introduction
Fourth Edition

Mayo
Investments: An Introduction
Fourth Edition

Pettijohn
PROFIT+

Reilly
Investment Analysis and Portfolio Management
Fourth Edition

Reilly
Investments
Third Edition

Sears and Trennepohl
Investment Management

Seitz
Capital Budgeting and Long-Term Financing Decisions

Siegel and Siegel
Futures Markets

Smith and Spudeck
Interest Rates: Principles and Applications

Stickney
Financial Statement Analysis: A Strategic Perspective
Second Edition

Turnbull
Option Valuation

Weston and Brigham
Essentials of Managerial Finance
Tenth Edition

Weston and Copeland
Managerial Finance
Ninth Edition

Wood and Wood
Financial Markets

THE HARCOURT BRACE COLLEGE OUTLINE SERIES

Baker
Financial Management

When I began teaching Personal Finance, I sought a book that would present students with a life cycle approach to personal money management. I wanted something that was practical and down to earth as well as sophisticated and analytical. Needs and interests are changing. None of the books on the market addressed certain topics that have become important financial issues for consumers. (Students need a book that is up to date and functions as an information resource to help them address their current as well as future financial concerns.) In addition, I wanted a book that would offer true value to the students, both for the short term and the long term.

Personal Finance does all of these things. It utilizes a comprehensive life-span financial approach. It encompasses a lifetime of personal finance, showing students of all ages how to gain and maintain control of their financial lives. Most topics discussed may be of immediate concern to some students, while other topics will be of interest only to others, especially younger students, from a future perspective.

For example, Chapter 4 on financing a college education is of obvious and immediate or short-term interest to younger college students. More mature students may be concerned with the long-term goal of financing their children's education. This chapter explores the financial aid resources and savings and investment plans available for meeting college costs from a student's, as well as a parent's, perspective.

The book is also as practical and down to earth in tone as possible. I have been careful to write at the level of sophistication appropriate for students at the college and university level. Where appropriate, I have used humor and wit (including frequent cartoons) to stimulate student interest. At the same time, the book is sophisticated and analytical in the way it covers topics. The choice of topics given chapter treatment indicates this analytical approach. (See the Coverage section, following.) It can also be seen in detail by the care taken to provide background and context for financial issues. The world of personal finance involves more than short-term consumer decisions, and students need to see beyond the price tag to bigger issues.

The main message of a personal finance textbook is the need for a lifetime of judicious and methodical planning. Proper retirement planning should begin with the first day that a young person starts a career job search. Benefit plan considerations should be an integral part of the career/company search process. This book endeavors to provide young people with foresight rather than hindsight. Its purpose is to avoid the "if only I had…" syndrome frequently heard in later years. Therefore, even such topics as preparing for retirement and estate planning apply to young people.

As for short-term value, the publisher has found ways to maintain high production values while finding ways to cut costs and pass savings on to the student. The principle savings is in the decision to publish this book with a paperback cover. The art program is restricted to two colors rather than using expensive four-color photographs. Original art and figures have been commissioned wherever possible to maximize the impact of the two-color design.

Also mindful of future value, I have written the book to be a valuable addition to the students' permanent library. Under the heading of Information Resources, many public and private sources of financial information are provided. The generous glossary includes terms found throughout the world of personal finance, and is not limited solely to terms discussed within the book. I hope that students will keep *Personal Finance* on their bookshelves as a reference manual after the course is successfully completed.

Let me tell you more about this book including its features, coverage, flexibility, pedagogy, and helpful ancillary package.

Features

In summary form, here are the most important reasons why *Personal Finance* is a better book for instructors and students:

1. When students are able to purchase a book that provides low cost and high value, they start on the right foot for making future financial decisions.

2. The book takes a *life cycle approach*, covering the major financial events of a lifetime. It familiarizes students with the major financial institutions and instruments that they will encounter in the course of their lives.

3. New topics, not adequately covered in most personal finance texts, are provided here to help students meet the changing needs of the financial world.

4. Level and tone are appropriate for the general college student; coverage is sophisticated and analytical in focusing on the most important issues, in context.

5. The book enables students to evaluate and analyze the various financial institutions and instruments and to determine how, if, and when to incorporate them into their personal financial lives.

6. Case studies, examples, questions for thought, and suggested projects are presented in each chapter to help students review and master the material.

Coverage

Some personal finance textbooks cover such elementary topics as how to write a check or how to open a checking account and how to purchase household appliances. These topics have not been included in this text. I believe these subjects are neither in the purview of finance nor on a college level. This book has a more academic or sophisticated touch to it. For example, Chapter 2, The World of Banking, provides analytical and historical coverage of banking in addition to practical hands-on coverage. This methodology provides students with a better understanding of the banking system and the problems the banking industry has experienced. This understanding is critical to students' choices of banks for checking and other accounts. Many students leave home at the beginning of their college years and this issue becomes of immediate interest.

Mindful of the importance of automobiles in students' lives, Chapter 3, Credit, Credit Cards, and Personal Bankruptcy, discusses the financial aspects of purchasing a car, among many other credit topics. The strategy behind Chapter 3 is to put all the credit information (except for home mortgages) into one chapter.

Some competing textbooks have as many as four chapters on the topic of planning and budgeting. Obviously, this issue is important. Students need to know how to get their financial records and papers in order. They also need to understand the concepts of budgeting and planning. However, my experience has indicated that hardly any students will go through life with a pencil and paper itemizing their expenses and incomes. Textbooks that devote two to four chapters to planning and budgeting are very likely overdoing this subject. A single, but comprehensive, chapter on this topic should be sufficient.

By not expanding coverage to some of the above issues, I have made room for new and more relevant issues. Four chapters are unique: Chapter 4, Financing a College Education; Chapter 10, The Computer as a Personal Finance Tool; Chapter 11, Reading Economic Indicators; and Chapter 17, Marriage and Divorce: Tying and Untying Financial Knots.

Chapter 4 provides students with a practical discussion of what is to most of them their current primary financial concern: financing their postsecondary education. Another practical discussion is found in Chapter 10 which presents a thorough overview of how a PC can be used to enhance and foster many of our personal financial activities, such as budgeting, banking, investing, and tax preparation.

Chapter 11 is for students lacking a background in economics or for those who need a refresher in some of the basic concepts of economics. It discusses such household economic terms as the business cycle, Federal Reserve, fiscal policy, monetary policy, GNP, unemployment rate, consumer price index, the Dow Jones averages, yield curves, economic indexes, and financial indicators. Students having a fundamental grasp of basic economic concepts stand a better chance of making intelligent personal financial decisions.

Chapter 17 covers divorce, unfortunately a very prevalent phenomenon. I believe that any course that intends to prepare students to cope with their current and future financial affairs must examine and analyze the financial aspects of marriage and divorce. In addition to these topics, the chapter examines prenuptial contracts and the financial aspects of unwed couples who live together. This text, as a life cycle guide to financial management, implicitly discusses marriage. Unfortunately, however, the financial aspects of divorce are neglected in other personal finance textbooks. Statistically, divorce is a factor in nearly one of two marriages in the United States today. The financial consequences of divorce often result in a severe lowering of standard of living of mothers with dependent young children. This financial issue, although admittedly unpleasant, must be thoroughly understood by young people so they will be prepared to address it if they experience a divorce.

Flexibility

As mentioned, this text covers all the essential chapters for a personal finance lifetime (cradle-to-grave) perspective. I hope that the reader will find this book to be comprehensive. In fact, it may be criticized for containing more chapters than can comfortably be taught in a one-semester course.

I recognize that different instructors and courses have various objectives and interests. Instructors teaching this course usually have a variety of backgrounds. Some come from the finance department; others are from economics, accounting, business, or home economics departments. Not all of the 19 chapters need to be covered in any one semester. The nonstandard chapters—Chapters 4, 10, 11, 17—are optional and should serve as enrichment to meet the needs of the diverse interests of instructors and students alike. The text provides the instructor with the opportunity to select and choose a variety mix of chapters. It contains enough wealth of materials to enable the instructor to select the material most suitable for his or her particular audience.

For example, the section on investments—Chapters 12 to 14—discusses investments in considerable detail. Those who teach Personal Finance from an investment perspective should find that this book covers these subjects in a very comprehensive manner. Instructors who do not orient this course toward investments need not cover these chapters in their entirety and can assign them as optional readings.

Another block of chapters (complete with a unique foreword) includes Chapters 7 to 9 on insurance issues. Instructors who do not wish to cover this material in class can present the material to the students as optional readings.

Pedagogy

Each chapter presents topical material using the following items of pedagogy:

- **Learning objectives** to help the student focus on the lesson ahead.

- **Boxes** on special issues, ranging from checklists to financial formulas, from interesting financial history to worked examples, and from case studies to amusing anecdotes.

- A handsome program of **illustrations**, including technical graphs and charts designed for easy readability; original art work, to open each chapter and focus attention; miscellaneous small cartoons; and various financial quotations, many drawn from the real-world financial press.

- **Lively cartoons** on issues of personal finance as culled from *The Wall Street Journal* and other periodicals.

- **Chapter summaries** that review the most important points covered.

- **Key terms** intended to aid student review.

- **Review questions and problems** to direct the student in reviewing the chapter.

- **Computer problems**, noted by a disk symbol, which are always quantitative in nature. They can be solved using *The Spreadsheet as a Personal Financial Tool* package or manually, if the student prefers.

- **Suggested projects** to get students out and doing the kind of direct research they will need to muster when dealing with their own financial decisions.

- **Information resources** listing suggested readings that expand the student's understanding of material in the chapter and names, addresses, and telephone numbers of institutions charged with providing current financial information to consumers upon request.

A few items of pedagogy complete the book:

- **The Glossary** that defines most financial terms the student will discover in the world beyond the classroom. The listing is not limited to those items discussed in the textbook.

- **Appendices** that provide quick reference for looking up present and future values.

Ancillaries

Instructor's Manual and Test Bank

The Instructor's Manual and Test Bank has been prepared by Ken Mark, Kansas City Community College; Debra Berg, Oakton Community College; and Sue Beck Howard, University of North Florida. It supports instructors with the following items:

- Teaching guidelines, including
  Suggested lecture outlines
  Questions for class discussion
  Topics requiring additional student review
  Difficult topics
- A full test bank of objective questions, identified by level of difficulty, including
  Fifteen true/false questions per chapter
  Ten multiple choice questions per chapter
- Answers to the computer problems as solved by the spreadsheet package, *The Spreadsheet as a Personal Financial Tool*.

Computerized Test Bank

The printed test bank is also available in computerized form as *ExaMaster Plus*. With this powerful software package, available for IBM PCs and compatibles, as well as the Macintosh, instructors can individualize and customize tests as needed. The publisher also supports adopters with the Request-a-Test service, under which the publisher will print tests for instructor convenience. More information on this service appears in the Instructor's Manual.

The Spreadsheet as a Personal Financial Tool

To support the use of personal computers in the student's financial plans, adopters of the book will receive *The Spreadsheet as a Personal Financial Tool*, programmed by Kent Finkle. This software package consists of a large, integrated collection of spreadsheet templates, keyed to topics within the textbook by the computer symbol, or disk icon. The spreadsheet templates will allow the student to test different financial options easily and quickly, leaving the burden of calculation to the computer. Moreover, each chapter contains one or more homework problems designed to be solved using the spreadsheet package. To run the spreadsheet template, *Lotus 1-2-3* (release 2 or higher) is required, as well as a 3½-inch, 720K or higher disk drive. The software is also available on two 5¼-inch, 360K diskettes, but the user would need to run the templates from a hard disk drive for satisfactory use.

Study Guide

I have also written a study guide that contains chapter outlines, discussion questions, crossword puzzles, and self-tests consisting of both multiple choice and true and false questions.

Acknowledgments

I would like to express my gratitude to my wife Sara, who tirelessly and meticulously typed, edited, and reviewed the entire manuscript from its inception to completion. I consider her to be the book's co-author and could not possibly have completed this project without her input and encouragement.

I also thank Mr. Abraham Wachsman of the Social Security Administration for his kind technical assistance and suggestions.

I also express my appreciation to the following colleagues for their comments and ideas, which were invaluable in preparing the manuscript:

Professor Debra Berg
Oakton Community College

Professor Louis Buda
State University of New York (SUNY)–
Nassau Community College

Professor Barret Burns
Houston Central Community College

Professor Bill Childress
Lansing Community College

Professor Robert Herman
SUNY–Nassau Community
College

Professor Arlene Holyoak
Oregon State University

Professor Sue Beck Howard
University of North Florida

Professor Robert F. Kegel, Jr.
Cypress College

Professor Marie Kratochvil,
Chairperson, Economics and Finance
SUNY–Nassau Community College

Professor John Landro
Wisconsin Technical College

Professor Jan Lazur
Lansing Community College

Professor Phil Levine
Rutgers University

Professor Kimberly McCollough
Santa Fe Community College

Professor Ken Mark
Kansas City Community College

Professor Jack Parker
Manchester Community College

Professor Carl H. Pollock, Jr.
Portland State University

Professor Warren St. James
SUNY–Nassau Community College

Professor Herbert Schlager
Essex County College

Professor Robert Strain, Jr.
SUNY–Nassau Community College

Professor Joe Weintraub
Joint Council of Economic Education

Professor Mari S. Wilhelm
University of Arizona

Professor Se Woo
SUNY–Nassau Community College

Any comments by reviewers of this textbook will be most welcome.

Finally, I would like to thank the book team at The Dryden Press for their efforts and support: Rick Hammonds, Acquisitions Editor; Bill Teague, Developmental Editor; Charlie Dierker and Matt Ball, Project Editors; Kelly Cordes, Production Manager; Bill Brammer, Art Director; Michael Beaupré, Electronic Publishing Supervisor; and Shirley Webster, Literary Rights Editor.

Abraham M. Bertisch

Abraham M. Bertisch is Professor of Economics and former Chairman of the Economics Department at the State University of New York–Nassau Community College campus. He received his Ph.D. degree from New York University. Professor Bertisch has been a visiting lecturer at St. John's University, New York University, Hofstra University, Adelphi University, and the City University of New York (CUNY). In addition to writing for major journals and participating in grant and research studies, he travels widely throughout the world, presenting lectures on economics and personal finance and appearing on radio and television programs, discussing these topics. He recently conducted a lecture series at the Touro International School of Business and Management in Moscow, Russia.

BRIEF CONTENTS

CONTENTS

Chapter Seventeen

Marriage and Divorce: Tying and Untying Financial Knots   **593**

Chapter Eighteen

Preparing for Retirement   **611**

Personal Finance

Abraham M. Bertisch

CHAPTER ONE

Few people plan to fail but most people fail to plan.
(anonymous)

Financial Budgeting and Planning: Getting Started

LEARNING OBJECTIVES

- To appreciate the importance of developing and of organizing financial records as a prerequisite to personal financial planning

- To learn how and why to set up a personal or a family budget

- To illustrate how to construct a financial statement and a net worth statement

- To comprehend how budgeting is a basic component of setting financial goals and of setting personal financial planning

- To understand the meaning and the importance of financial planning

- To list the elements common to most financial plans

- To clarify the factors that should be considered when establishing a financial plan

- To identify the basic steps in selecting a competent professional planner

Getting Organized

Money and what to do with it is a problem everyone should have—because there is a solution. This book will help develop such a problem and assist you in solving it.

You cannot seem to get your financial act together? You or your parents are earning a handsome salary, but your spending seems even greater? "Disorganized" is the kindest word for your financial records? You have wonderful plans for a graduate degree program, for a house, for investments, for retirement, for saving, for reducing your tax bracket, but you or your family hardly has time to balance a checkbook? If you answer yes to these questions, you need an organized and systematic strategy, known as a *financial plan*, to achieve your goals.

This chapter outlines the basic strategy involved in financial planning. Each topic described here will be discussed in detail in later chapters. With a plan, you can approach life in an organized and efficient manner. You will need to think about your financial life as an integrated, long-range construct. The first step toward setting up a financial plan is to get your records and documents organized.

Record Keeping

Establishing an efficient financial record keeping system should be your first priority. A well-organized record keeping system is indispensable. While you can save and invest without proper files, you almost certainly will lose time and money in the process. Good records will also help minimize your tax obligations (discussed further in Chapter 5). Keeping poor records leads to confusion, and confusion leads to waste. Good organization, planning, and record keeping are important keys to financial success because they help you make the right decisions.

If you or members of your family are like many people, your financial documents are scattered about in numerous places. If key information about your family finances is stored only in your head, your spouse's, or your parents', and if you, your spouse, or your parents alone know the secrets of your filing system, then you and your family have a problem. If pulling together your tax records each April is an annual nightmare, you are not alone. And if the prospect of reconstructing your financial affairs after a burglary or a fire throws you into a panic, you are in good company. Most people do not have their financial files well organized. They do piling instead of filing.

Now and in the future, you want to have enough assets to keep your family financially secure. As you plan and save, you acquire bank accounts, various insurance policies, IRAs, stocks, bonds, pension annuities, a will, a house or an apartment, and so on. You have planned for each and every contingency as much as possible to protect your family. But what would happen if you, your spouse, or your parents suddenly died or became incapacitated? Would anyone know where to find all those financial documents necessary to protect the family? If anything should suddenly happen to you, your spouse, or your parents, would the family have the tax records necessary for filing its income tax return by next April? Who will know when to pay the various insurance premiums, the mortgage on the house, and other loans? Where are the receipts and records of payment?

Personal or Family Financial Checklist

Organizing your important financial files and documents will take some effort because of their vast number. The following personal or family financial checklist includes the items generally needed in your files.

Documents
1. Stock certificates and broker's statements
2. Real estate deeds
3. Bank accounts, bank certificates of deposit, IRAs
4. Bonds
5. Guarantees, warranties
6. Sales receipts (for major and costly items)
7. Birth certificates
8. Life insurance policies and payment receipts
9. Wills
10. Marriage certificate (and divorce papers, if any)
11. Social Security card
12. Military discharge papers
13. Citizenship papers and passport
14. Adoption papers
15. Contracts
16. Auto registration and title
17. Burial plot certificate
18. Employee group insurance coverage
19. Accident and disability policies
20. Homeowners policy
21. Auto policy
22. Additional liability policy
23. Safe-deposit box (location of the bank box number and location of the keys)
24. Pension contract papers
25. Health records
26. List of credit cards
27. Videotape or photos of valuables

Files and Records

Monthly bank statements; canceled checks; tax returns; Tax (including W-2 statements, charitable contributions, medical bills, property tax records, or copies of tax returns); budget; net worth statement (explained later in this chapter); list of names, addresses, and phone numbers of your banker, lawyer, stockbroker, accountant, life and property insurance agent, tax preparer, employee benefits counselor, and financial planner.

To keep yourself from wading through too many papers from past years, separate your back and current files.

Preparing a Family Finanical Checklist

If you, your spouse, or your parents have difficulty answering these questions, then prepare a personal or family financial checklist. Such a document should list all the family's assets and liabilities, their location, and instructions as to how they work, payments due, dividends, renewal or maturity dates, and location of keys for safe-deposit boxes. Provide clear instructions to tell surviving relatives how to claim benefits so that financial affairs can be managed quickly in any emergency. Your financial checklist should guide your survivors not only to important documents but also to important people who handle your business affairs.

List everyone who helps manage your family's money, including your family's banker, broker, lawyer, accountant, and insurance and real estate agents, as well as the employee benefits counselor at work. Organizing a family financial file or check-list may take a few hours of work—searching, probing, and telephoning for all the data—but once having gathered this information, you have taken the first step. In getting your family's financial checklist together, you are beginning to get control over your financial affairs.

You do not need a home computer to do the job well, but using one could make it easier. After making a computer printout, you can save the information on your disk for next year. Then you can update dollar amounts and make other changes without retyping the entire document.

Now that you have organized your data, you are prepared for the next step, establishing a family budget.

Family Budget

The **family budget** is a plan for use of expected income and other resources for spending, saving, and investing. It serves to balance outgo with income and helps families figure out what they want and how to pay for it. Everyone can use a budget, not just those who feel that they cannot make ends meet financially. Virtually every business uses budgets to define priorities, and so should households.

No matter what their age, most people will discover that security lies in the judicious management of their limited resources. This means that they are able to meet daily expenses and the reasonable requests of family members. Then there must be enough for future needs. Ultimately, it's not what you earn that gives you financial security, but what you save. You need sufficient savings for emergencies as well as the big expenses, such as college tuition, the down payment on a home, purchasing a car, and saving for retirement. Though tough to put together and even harder to follow, a family budget supplies the foundation of a well-made financial program.

Like "diet," the word "budget" can raise unpleasant images of self-denial. But this should not be the case. Budgeting deserves to be viewed more favorably and positively.

Although putting a budget together involves lots of effort, diligence, time, and patience, a solid budget also provides financial ease of mind. It sheds light on one's spending habits, aids in tax planning, and helps correlate wants and resources. It can help anyone capture money that just seems to trickle away and can free up dollars for savings and investments. Most people who do not have a budget often wonder how their money vanishes. Therefore, even if you have a healthy surplus, you should examine your spending patterns to make sure your money is going toward your goals.

How to Set Up a Budget   Ironically, creating a family budget can be more challenging than putting together a business budget. You have to map the many directions your money has taken without the help of an office staff, a mainframe computer, or even a single Harvard MBA. You will have to enlist the cooperation of your parents or your spouse and children for this project without being able to threaten or fire them.

Keep your budget simple. If it becomes too complicated, it will never be used. But if it is easy to work with, within just three months you can reduce your overhead, free up dollars for savings, and even set aside money for splurging.

Begin your budget by listing all sources of income, such as wages, pensions, and any other regular income (e.g., alimony and child support). When listing your salary, disregard taxes withheld, Social Security deductions, and other payroll deductions. You do not have use of that money. People often have sources of spendable income beyond their paychecks or business earnings, such as the interest on saving and checking accounts, money market funds, dividends from stocks, rental income, and so on. Before listing such items as interest and dividends, try to ascertain your tax bracket and subtract that percentage from these incomes. For instance, if you are in the 28 percent tax bracket and earned $3,000 in taxable interest and dividends this year then you should list $2,160 ($3,000 minus 28 percent). This would maintain your consistency of listing only after-tax income and not mixing after-tax and pre-tax income.

Organizing your spending records takes longer. In order to examine how you have spent your income in the past, you have to wade through back bills, credit card statements, and checkbooks. Monitoring your expenses and income for six months usually picks up all the routine monthly costs as well as those lump sum or irregular payments such as insurance and tuition.

Start with your checkbook. Take six blank sheets of paper, each labeled with the appropriate month. Then set up expense categories. Record each check under an appropriate expenditure category (shelter, food, clothing, recreation, education, health, miscellaneous). Then assemble bills from department stores and credit card companies and place each purchase in the proper budget category. Try to estimate the cash expenditures for which you have no receipts. Table 1–1 shows a typical budget that can be used as a guide.

How to Monitor a Budget   Now comes the moment of truth. You must compare your expenditures for the past six months with your total net income for this period. By monitoring how close actual expenses come to budgeted ones, you can see what you can realistically afford. Next tally up all the items in each category and divide the totals by the total income for the six months. This tells you what percentage of your income goes to which budget items and helps you to identify trouble spots.

If your total income exceeds your total expenses, you will have a surplus. If expenditures exceed income, the result will be a deficit. If there's often too much month left at the end of the money, try to understand why. Are your mortgage and car payments too high for your salary? Are you repaying a loan for education or for some medical bills? Do you buy more clothes than you wear? Are you paying too much for life insurance? Are you too free with your charge cards? At this point, it is useful to differentiate between "fixed" expenses and "variable" expenses. Fixed expenses are those payments that do not vary from month to month and over which you have

TABLE 1–1	Budget Outline

BUDGET

Expenses	Month 1	2	3	4	5	6	7	8	9	10	11	12
Food												
Groceries												
Delivered goods												
Snacks												
Expenses												
Work lunches												
School lunches												
Shelter												
Rent/Mortgage												
Utilities												
Heat												
Property taxes												
Water												
Garden supplies												
Telephone												
Property insurance												
Maintenance/Cleaning												
Garbage collection												
Condominium fees												
Transportation												
Car payments												
Gasoline												
Maintenance/Cleaning												
Car insurance												
Bus/Taxi/Tolls/Parking												
Clothing												
Personal												
Spouse												
Children												
Maintenance/Cleaning												
Education												
Lessons												
Tuition												
Books												
Supplies												
Installment Payments												
Credit union												
Credit cards												
Department stores												
Student loans												
Other												
Savings												
Credit union												
Education												
Company savings plan												
IRA												
Other												

TABLE 1–1	Budget Outline (continued)

Expenses	Month 1	2	3	4	5	6	7	8	9	10	11	12
Family												
Life insurance												
Child care												
Allowances												
Gifts												
Pets												
Other												
Donations												
Church/Synagogue												
Political												
Charitable												
Other												
Personal												
Barber/Beauty shop												
Toiletries												
Postage												
Tobacco												
Alcohol												
Newspapers/Magazines												
Other												
Health												
Medications												
Insurance												
Doctor												
Dentist												
Exercise classes/Equipment												
Recreation												
Vacations												
Meals out												
Movies/Plays/Music												
Spectator sports												
Sports equipment												
Television/Cable/Public TV												
Miscellaneous												
Union/Other membership dues												
Taxes: Social Security												
Income, federal												
State												
Local												
Unreimbursed business expenses												
Other												
Total Expense												
Income												
Paychecks												
Dividends												
Interest												
Social Security												
Pension												
Gifts												
Other												
Total income												
Total surplus or deficit												

little control. Examples of fixed expenses are rent or mortgage payments, health insurance costs, interest costs on previous loans, or the cost of commuting to work. Variable expenses are flexible expenses that change from month to month and over which you have much more control. Food, clothing, recreation, gifts, donations, and utility bills are common examples of variable expenses. There may not be much you can do about your fixed expenses or even some of your variable expenses, but at least you will know what is happening with your finances, where your weak spots are, and what, if anything, should be done about it. If any budget items consume what you consider to be too high a percentage of your income, then construct a "revised" or proposed budget for the next six months.

After three to six months of recording monthly expenses, your ledger page will have become a spreadsheet, which is a simple mathematical model of your finances over time. You can follow rows across the page to see how particular categories of spending vary over time. You can also calculate average amounts for certain expenses.

At this point, you can enlist the aid of a home computer and software packages specifically designed for budgeting. Although you will still have to get yourself organized and follow the procedures described above, a computerized program can make the record keeping easier and give you faster and superior results. For example, with a spreadsheet program or money management program, you can ask your financial model "what if" questions, instantly manipulating income and spending categories to analyze different approaches. (This subject is further discussed in Chapter 10.) However, if you do not have a computer, you can accomplish the same results with paper, pencil, and a pocket calculator.

Budget experts claim that if more than 15 percent of your after-tax income goes to pay for old and new consumer debts (such as credit card and car payments), you are too heavily in debt. Allocate as much as you possibly can, a set amount each month, for debt repayment. Consumer debt payments should not be stretched out more than 12 months (except for car loans). Once safely out of debt, you will have to be strict with yourself about purchases on credit.

There is no set formula for a budget, no ideal percentages to spend on such items as housing, food, education, investments. Everyone's life is different and so is everyone's budget. It is like a puzzle. And therein lies the secret of setting a budget you can live with: do it your own way, the way that suits you and your family. How you spend and save reflects your personality. Just as there are no right or wrong personalities, there is no absolutely correct way to handle money. Any method you use is reasonable as long as it works for you and meets your objectives.

Setting a family budget is a matter of deciding on priorities in life and then managing finances to achieve them. Someone in the family will have to keep records or enter data into your computer program for a few months to see that your new proposed and revised budget stays on target and that everyone in the family is adhering to it. With enough juggling, you should be able to produce a budget that gives you the operating surplus you are looking for.

Net Worth Statement

A budget tells you whether you are saving money, how you are spending your money and on what, and whether you are running up a deficit. Now that you know this information, you should also know the amount of your total net worth. Just as a medical doctor would require you to undergo a comprehensive examination before discussing your state of health, it is necessary to create a budget as well as a personal financial report or net worth statement to establish your financial health.

Net worth is the difference between what you own and what you owe, your assets minus your liabilities. By constructing a list of what you own and what you owe and subtracting the second from the first, you can learn exactly what your net worth is.

The net worth statement tells much about your financial condition. It details the estimated current value of assets and the estimated current amount of liabilities. It may be more or less than you thought. It may even be a negative sum, and this means you are insolvent. That is acceptable if you are a student or just starting out. If, however, you are 38 and your net worth is "in the red," you should get busy setting up a strategy, which is a financial plan to remedy the situation. Start by paying off debts and building up an asset reserve to see you through emergencies and help you reach long-range goals. A personal financial report or net worth statement can be prepared for an individual, a husband and wife, or a family.

The net worth statement should be updated at least once a year or as major changes occur in your financial situation. It is an essential step in developing a personal financial plan. An analysis of your net worth can reveal how close you are to achieving your short- and long-range goals and whether the assets you have acquired will help you reach them.

It is useful to have the numbers available for other purposes as well. An application for a college loan (discussed in Chapter 4) or a home mortgage (discussed in Chapter 6) or an IRS audit (discussed in Chapter 5), for example, will ask you to disclose assets as well as debts. Net worth is also useful in determining your insurance needs (discussed in Chapter 8).

Let's Start Planning

Constructing a Net Worth Statement

Using Table 1–2 as a guide, start by itemizing cash on hand, in checking and money market accounts, and in savings accounts. Next list personal property, the most important being your house or apartment (if you own one). Include anything that has market value—jewelry, furniture, cars, antiques, furs, stamps. List any real estate that you own, and then list all your financial assets—stocks, bonds, money vested in a pension fund.

It is helpful to divide your assets into two categories, **liquid and nonliquid. Liquid investments** are those that you can quickly convert into cash without paying sizable penalties or receiving less than they are worth. Bank accounts, stocks, and bonds are liquid investments. Use the most recent quote in the newspaper to calculate their worth. Liabilities as well should be presented in order of liquidity and maturity. Loans are presented at their outstanding values. Funds in IRAs (explained in Chapter 18), for example, are listed under **nonliquid investments** because a 10 percent penalty must be paid on any withdrawals before age 59½.

TABLE 1–2	The Net Worth Statement

Assets	Monetary Value	Owner of Asset
1. Liquid Assets		
Current Assets		
Checking account balance	$_____	_____
Savings account balance	$_____	_____
Savings bonds	$_____	_____
Money market funds	$_____	_____
Certificates of deposit	$_____	_____
Treasury bills	$_____	_____
Cash	$_____	_____
Total current assets	$_____	_____
Securities		
Stocks	$_____	_____
Bonds	$_____	_____
Mutual funds	$_____	_____
2. Nonliquid Assets		
Long-Term Financial Assets		
Insurance, cash value	$_____	_____
Annuities	$_____	_____
Equity in pension funds	$_____	_____
Profit-sharing plans	$_____	_____
IRA and Keogh plans	$_____	_____
Business interest	$_____	_____
401(K) plans	$_____	_____
Other	$_____	_____
Personal Property		
Home furnishings	$_____	_____
Antiques	$_____	_____
Automobiles	$_____	_____
Coins/stamp collection	$_____	_____
Furs/jewelry	$_____	_____
Clothing	$_____	_____
Real Estate		
Residence	$_____	_____
Vacation property	$_____	_____
Income property	$_____	_____
Total Assets	$_____	_____

continued

TABLE 1–2	The Net Worth Statement (continued)

NET WORTH

Liabilities	Monetary Value	Owner of Asset
Debt and Installment Loans		
(List only the unpaid principal balance.)		
Automobile loans	$_____	_____
Home improvement loans	$_____	_____
Education loans	$_____	_____
Margin loans	$_____	_____
Bank loans	$_____	_____
Check overdraft	$_____	_____
Credit card balance	$_____	_____
Other (alimony, child support, etc.)	$_____	_____
Current Liabilities		
Current bills	$_____	_____
Medical and dental	$_____	_____
Real estate (mortgage) balances		
Residential	$_____	_____
Recreational	$_____	_____
Income property	$_____	_____
Unpaid Taxes		
Capital gains	$_____	_____
Personal property	$_____	_____
Real estate	$_____	_____
Estimated federal	$_____	_____
State	$_____	_____
Total Liabilities	$_____	_____
The Bottom Line		
Total Assets	$_____	_____
(minus) Total Liabilities	$_____	_____
Your Net Worth	$_____	_____

Realistic Assessment of Value

Be realistic when assessing property and collectibles. If you have stamps, coins, diamonds, or art to sell, you are very likely to receive less than a dealer's posted sale price (discussed in Chapter 16). Dealers sell at retail but buy at wholesale.

When calculating personal assets such as clothing, appliances, furniture, stereos, books, and other effects, you can only approximate. Tour the house with a pencil and paper, and list what you think these items are worth. It is often a judgment call; most used items do not have much market value. Estimate what you think could realistically be fetched in today's market if you had to sell them within a week (at a tag sale). Check a reference book (such as the Blue Book) to pin down the worth of motor vehicles. To assess the current value of your home or other real estate, check the classified section of a newspaper or a local real estate agent. Likewise, list all liabilities—money you owe others, mortgages, student loans, car loan, credit cards, bank loans.

The Bottom Line

Now comes the final step. Combine everything you own, and deduct all you owe. The result is your net worth, the accounting term for the difference between assets and liabilities. Your net worth should increase over the years. It need not increase each week or month, but a primary goal and measure of your financial progress should be a steady increase in your net worth over the long run.

Obviously, your net worth is a function of your budget. If your expenses equal income or worse, exceed it, you should make a serious effort to increase your income or reduce spending or both. There will be years when a person's net worth may seriously decline for unavoidable and even desirable reasons. Running a deficit is all right for a while. A four- to eight-year stint through college and graduate school, for instance, will invariably reduce your net worth. But this was made possible by your parents or your own planning in previous years. There will undoubtedly be some abnormal years in your life when you cannot avoid spending more than you earn. But over your lifetime these years should be the exception rather than the rule.

Building Assets: Starting to Save

Now that you have a good set of financial records, a personal financial checklist, a budget, and a net worth statement, your next step is to build your assets. You have to save, of course. How much you actually save and where you invest it are at least theoretically less important than establishing the initial pattern. Once your financial life is organized so that you save regularly, a foundation is established upon which you can build your financial security.

Pay Yourself First A good budget should include a category for savings as shown in Table 1–1. Savings should not be an afterthought. If you want to save, adhere stubbornly to the concept of "paying yourself first." Build savings into your budget instead of treating them as what is left over after you have spent to your heart's content. Do not put off starting until you are earning "enough." Earning more money does not always provide freedom from budget constraints; it is not just poor people who have problems. You cannot grow financially unless you earn more than you spend, and save and invest more than you borrow.

Building an estate is an extremely flexible process. The most important step is to make savings a regular monthly expense. There are numerous ways to build assets steadily and relatively painlessly. Put a fixed percentage of your paycheck into long-term savings or investments each month. Pay out money to savings as regularly and faithfully as you pay your monthly rent and utility bills. Here are some ways to go about this:

1. Join a payroll deduction plan, which ensures a regular contribution that is automatically invested in a company profit sharing stock purchase or savings plan.

2. Seek out a bank that offers automatic monthly transfers from your checking account into a money market or mutual fund.

3. Buy the stocks of companies that allow you to reinvest your dividends in new shares without paying commissions and to purchase additional shares at discount prices (see Chapter 12).

4. Invest in stocks of utility companies that qualify for tax-deferred dividend reinvestment (see Chapter 12).

5. Purchase an insurance policy that builds cash value (discussed in Chapter 9).

6. Set up an IRA or Keogh plan (discussed in Chapter 18).

Naturally, prior to undertaking any of these activities, you should read the appropriate chapter in this textbook.

These and other suggestions for long-term savings and asset building are discussed throughout this book. How much should you save? The standard answer is 7 to 10 percent of your after-tax income. Try 5 percent as an initial deduction, adjusting it up or down as your cash needs change. Take the opportunity to get rich slowly.

Emergency Fund   Your first savings priority should be an emergency fund. Before you do anything else, set up a relatively liquid **emergency savings fund,** such as a bank money market fund, from which to draw in case of unemployment, illness, or some other major unanticipated need. Money market accounts (discussed in Chapter 14) are good vehicles for an emergency fund, since your money is safe and accessible immediately while earning interest at competitive market rates. An adequate emergency fund should contain three to six months of your net income. Additionally, you should have insurance against catastrophes (discussed in Chapters 7 to 9).

Once you have saved enough to cover emergencies, think about investing your surplus funds. You have cash for an emergency. You are earning the money you need for basic expenditures. You have become accustomed to saving a part of your paycheck. Now it is time to put your savings to work for you. The earnings on your investments can make some of your goals real now. But what are your goals?

Setting Goals

Before you do anything else, you need to establish some financial goals. Keep them realistic. Just as you did with your budget, first consult your spouse and the teenagers (if any) in your family. Getting everyone to agree will not necessarily be easy. So start focusing upon **long-range goals** that will take years to achieve—providing for retirement, buying a house, providing for the kids' education.

Next, take **short-range goals,** those objectives you hope to reach in six months to five years. Expect some divergence of opinions, but try to arrive at a family compromise. You and your family need to decide where you want to be and what you want to have—next year, 5 years from now, 10 years down the road, when you retire. Defining and setting realistic goals is part of financial planning. Put it all down on paper, and have everyone agree to it. This needs to be done at least once a year.

Goals are going to change throughout one's life and therefore ought to be reevaluated constantly. It is essential to set attainable goals and keep adjusting them.

Your goals tell you where you are heading, where you want to be, and when you want to get there. Your budget frees up cash to help you meet your goals. Your net worth statement tells you the total resources you have to work with. Now that you have established some goals, you are ready for financial planning, because now the question is, How do I get there from here? In other words, how much and where do you need to start saving and investing to arrive at the goals you have set?

What Is Financial Planning?

Financial planning can be defined as the careful preparation and coordination of plans necessary to prepare for future financial needs and goals. It is not investment analysis. It involves mapping strategies to achieve your defined goals. Calculating

---

Financial Ratios

Your budgeting process can be analyzed by utilizing some financial ratios. Financial ratios provide an indication of changes in one's financial condition. One financial ratio is the **debt ratio.** This is derived by dividing liabilities by net worth.

$$\text{Debt Ratio} = \frac{\text{Total Liabilities}}{\text{Net Worth}}$$

The lower your debt ratio, the more favorable your financial condition. Suppose your total liabilities are $60,000 and your assets $120,000. Then, your debt ratio is

$$\frac{\$\,60,000}{120,000} = .5$$

In this case your net worth is twice as great as your debts, or expressed differently, your debts are half as much as your net worth.

   A higher debt ratio would be less favorable. Suppose your net worth is $150,000 but your liabilities are $300,000. Then your debt ratio is $300,000/$150,000, or 2. This is a far less favorable financial position.

   Another helpful financial ratio is **current ratio.** This is derived by dividing liquid assets by current liabilities.

$$\text{Current Ratio} = \frac{\text{Liquid Assets}}{\text{Current Liabilities}}$$

This indicates how well-prepared you are to make your debt payments. For example, if you have $9,000 in liquid assets and $3,000 in current liabilities, then your current ratio is equal to $9,000/3,000, or 3. This means that you have $3 in liquid assets available to pay every dollar in current liabilities. The lower this ratio, the more likely you are to run into problems meeting your debt obligation. Therefore, the higher your current ratio, the more favorable your financial situation.

future financial needs as exactly as possible can provide a psychological advantage; most people find it easier to invest and save when they have definite purposes for the money.

You may wonder why budgeting is not a sufficient means of achieving financial security. A sound budget is no substitute for a financial plan, for without a plan of what you hope to accomplish, budgeting becomes a meaningless exercise.

Without realizing it, most people take many of the basic steps that are part of financial planning. They buy insurance, save money, invest in stocks, and write a will, all because they know there are risks in everyday living, such as death, disability, and unemployment. There are dreams and aspirations of life, too, such as education, marriage, children, retirement, homes, travels, and vacations that require financial preparation and coordination. This is what planning is for.

The aim of a good **financial plan** is to help you establish, organize, and then achieve those dreams. What is your highest priority—educating your children, building a comfortable retirement fund, or buying a new dream home?

Unpleasant financial surprises are sure to occur at various points in our lives. "Why wasn't I prepared for this?" is a refrain often heard from those hit by such surprises. Long-range planning can lessen the impact of these financial crises. Although we have little control over many events that affect us, being financially prepared for all eventualities makes life that much easier.

Financial planning is a growth industry. An estimated 10 million Americans are now using financial planners, and the pool of capital they influence is several hundred billion dollars deep. Plans are available from such large firms as Sears, E. F. Hutton, Merrill Lynch, Prudential-Bache, as well as from small firms and individual advisers. Their prices range from $25 to $30,000. It is sometimes possible to find low-cost financial planning services for individuals. For instance, Price Waterhouse, the accounting firm, will prepare a personal financial analysis that covers net worth tax strategies, investment strategies, projections for education and retirement savings, insurance evaluation, stock options advice, and some estate planning. Included in the $325 cost is follow-up advice, via a toll-free number.

Do-It-Yourself Planning

Although everybody needs financial planning, not everybody needs a financial planner. Planners do not have a monopoly on the basic information needed to set up a proper financial plan. With a little discipline and study, you can be your own competent planner, managing your own finances, with occasional assistance from specialists in the various financial areas. You can also get information from many widely available publications. One worth checking out is *Consumer Reports Books—Complete Guide to Managing Your Money*. If you have a personal computer, some software programs on the market can help you generate your own constantly updated financial plan. (See Chapter 10 for some suggested programs and further discussion.)

A thorough reading of this book should provide you with the basics to handle your own finances. Taking a personal finance course and reading this text are therefore good starts to becoming your own financial planner, if you so choose. This course and the text should familiarize you with the financial tools you require to take control of your financial life. After reading this text and keeping abreast of periodic financial literature, you should be able to handle most of the personal finance decisions that arise.

For more complex problems, many books and software on the market should provide assistance, or you can consult an attorney or an accountant.

The do-it-yourself approach is especially valid for a family with a household income of less than $50,000 a year and little net worth. The investment and asset management strategies that many planners develop may be impractical unless you have more cash coming in and a wider base of savings and investments than most people are able to accumulate on a middle-income salary. At that level you can often do for yourself many things for which planners would charge you. Many financial planners will nevertheless assist individuals of modest resources and income in constructing plans and budgets for reasonable fees.

Financial planners have traditionally advised the affluent—the successful men or women with too little time for managing their financial affairs. But in recent years, financial planning has been trickling down to a broader audience. Increasingly, middle- and upper-income Americans are overwhelmed by the complexity of their finances and are turning to professional planners to help sort things out: How much to save? How much to invest? How much to put away for retirement? How to prepare for the 3-year-old's college tuition down the line? Many people are also turning to planners to restructure their investment portfolio, change insurance policies, and establish tax shelters.

What Is a Financial Planner?

The term "financial planner" has been loosely applied to such financial advisers as brokers, insurance salespeople, accountants, and attorneys. But in the past few years the meaning has become more specific. It now describes the approximately 200,000 professionals who concern themselves with a person's comprehensive finances, not just a single aspect of them.

Although they should be familiar with tax law and estate planning as well as investing, insurance, banking, and real estate, financial planners are not necessarily accountants or lawyers. What they do is take a holistic approach to your financial situation. They are the general practitioners of the money advice world. Since financial planning as a profession is less than 20 years old, many practitioners came to it from other pursuits—mainly accounting, law, or the selling of insurance, stocks, or tax shelters. A planner's background identifies his or her specialty as well as possible biases. A good financial planner is informed about the economy, can predict trends fairly accurately, asks his or her clients in-depth questions, and is knowledgeable about existing and upcoming tax laws and tax-savings methods, budgeting, and estate planning.

What Can You Expect from a Good Planner?

A competent planner will look at your family's present situation and future goals and then devise a plan that will make all your financial bits and pieces fit together. The details should be laid out in a written plan of 10 pages or so, unless your holdings are complex.

The planning process usually starts with an analysis of a person's present situation—net worth, cash flow, income taxes, and financial goals. The planner will devise a workable budget if you do not have one, or evaluate the budget you are already using. The plan should present several ways to meet your goals. In addition, a planner should be able to coordinate any specialized help you may need from other professionals such as accountants, lawyers, brokers, and insurance agents.

The person best qualified to do that is a skillful generalist who knows the rudiments of household money management, insurance, investing, retirement, and estate planning. Planners would, therefore, help people to calculate what their children's education is likely to cost, as well as when they plan to retire and how high they expect their monthly expenses to run. On the income side of the ledger, pension plan payouts and inheritances can also be estimated. In addition, inflation must be taken into consideration.

You can expect a planner to estimate the current income your family would require should you die or become disabled and to tell you how the recommended policies would provide for those needs. Finally, the planner will present specific suggestions to carry out your plan.

Selecting a Planner

How do you find a highly trained, competent, and qualified planner, and which one should you hire? Extreme caution is necessary because under the current law, anyone—from competent professional to incompetent opportunist—can set up shop as a financial planner.

Be on guard for people offering one-product solutions to all financial needs. Salespeople often call themselves financial planners to disguise their true calling. Also be on the alert for undisclosed conflicts of interest. A planner's education, credentials, and professional certificates, such as licenses in stock or real estate brokerage, are a good sign but also a possible signal indicating the planner's biases. A real estate broker may push you toward real estate while you may want to concentrate in mutual funds, CDs, and bonds. Planners sometimes claim to be independent when in fact they are employed by a company with a basket full of products to sell. Some planners pretend to give objective advice and present elaborate computer projections of glittering wealth if the advice is followed, merely to sell a particular line of financial products.

While no path in finance is absolutely certain, a competent planner will try to help you build a solid, safe, balanced, and diversified portfolio which will slowly but steadily enable you to achieve economic security. It is not a quick fix or fast buck approach.

Planners' Credentials: Your Financial Physician May Not Have a License

Financial planning remains an essentially unregulated business. There is no such thing as a financial planning license yet. In recent years many states have been debating bills that would require planners to post bond, pass a written test for a license, and disclose more information about themselves, such as educational background and business affiliations. But until these laws are passed, planners, unlike attorneys or accountants, are not required to complete an academic degree program or pass a certifying examination before hanging up a shingle. Neither are financial planners governed by a self-regulatory organization like the National Association of Security Dealers (NASD), which can clamp down on any securities broker who violates securities laws. In 1993 there were 18,600 people registered with the Securities and

SOURCE: Roger Roth.

Exchange Commission (SEC) as investment advisers or financial planners. (See Figure 1–1.) These advisers do not have to pass tests, as do brokers. The above mentioned NASD and SEC are regulatory agencies that perform a broad role in regulating financial markets and transactions. These functions are discussed in chapters 12, 13, and 14. The SEC, likewise, has little regulatory control over this growing group of practitioners.

Many planners go through the voluntary certification programs available for financial planners. The two main courses of study which most candidates take by mail are the **certified financial planner** (CFP) program offered by the International Board of Certified Financial Planners (IBCFP) and the **chartered financial consultant** (ChFC) curriculum of the American College, a school for insurance professionals in Bryn Mawr, Pennsylvania. To earn either set of initials, a planner must pass a series of rigorous written exams.

The above two colleges' fiercest competitors for status in the planning field are the more than 40 "mainstream" colleges and universities that offer undergraduate or graduate degrees in planning or that prepare students to take the CFP exam. Among them are Baylor University, Georgia State University, San Diego State University, the University of South Carolina, and New York University.

A CFP, ChFC, or mainstream planners degree does not by itself signify competence, but it does show at least some serious commitment to financial planning. A preferred choice would be a CPA or law degree as well as a CFP or ChFC certificate.[1]

Another source for finding a planner is the Atlanta-based International Association for Financial Planning (IAFP). Membership in such a financial planning trade group is the most common planning credential. The IAFP has established a registry

---

[1] You can get a list of the CFPs in your area by writing to the Institute of Certified Financial Planners, 3443 S. Galena, Suite 190, Denver, CO 80231.

of 24,000 financial planners which can be obtained by writing to the International-alAssociation for Financial Planning, 2 Concourse Parkway, Suite 800, Atlanta, GA 30328, or phoning (404) 395-1605.

Planners' Fees

There is no standard fee system or scale for planners. Some planners work on a fee basis while others operate entirely on commissions. Most planners depend on a combination of fees and commissions. We will look at each of these three payment methods from the customer's viewpoint.

Fee-Only Planners   The fee-only structure, it could be argued, offers the best protection since it presents the fewest possible conflicts of interest. The fee-only planner may only make recommendations and leave it up to you to contact your own broker, insurance agent, or lawyer to implement the plan. Some claim that fee-only planners are not tied to any particular financial product or financial broker and thus can provide an objective service. In a sense, the fee-only planner is like a doctor

| FIGURE 1–1 | The Growing Number of Registered Investment Advisers |

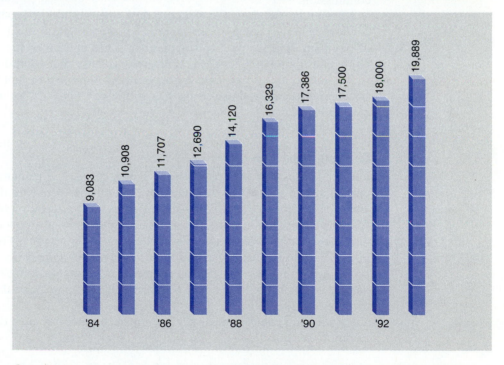

Over the last 10 years, the number of registered financial planners has roughly doubled.

SOURCE: Securities Exchange Commission.

who prescribes specific medications but has no financial relationship with the local pharmacy. But "fee only" tends to be expensive. Fees can run to several thousand dollars. A computer-generated plan can be considerably less costly if the client does not need extensive individual counseling. Finding a fee-only planner may be problematic since only about 10 percent of all planners are fee only.

Commission-Only Planners Because of the high cost of fee-only planners, many middle-income-bracket people will rely on advisers associated with some financial product. **Commission-only planners** are open to the charge that they may be more interested in generating commissions than in looking after their clients' welfare. This is especially true of nonindependent planners, such as brokers. Unethical planners can use their proposed plan merely to generate sales of life insurance, pensions, tax shelters, and other investments that yield them high commissions. It would be prudent to ask for an accounting of any commissions your planner will receive on products he or she recommends.

Fee and Commission Planners **Fee and commission planners** charge an initial fee and also receive commissions. They claim that many people do not have a stockbroker or an insurance agent and want an adviser who will offer them full financial services. Such a planner provides not only the financial plan but also the implementation to carry it through to specific financial investments which they sell for a commission.

Ultimately, the choice of a financial planner should be based more upon one's confidence in the person and in his or her professional standing than on the method of payment. The fee paid to the planner could end up as the smaller expense of implementing a financial plan. Wills, trusts, and other legal documents will have to be drafted by an attorney. An accountant will need to be consulted to handle tax arrangements, and brokerage fees will have to be paid for any investments the plan calls for.

Structure of the Plan

Financial plans vary in sophistication, scope, detail, and magnitude. A plan may be presented as a sophisticated 50-page document, complete with detailed records, tax analyses, and objectives, listing a family's entire financial picture and outlining a course well into the future. Or it may be no more than a simple list of assets, liabilities, income and expenses, and general goals for next year. But whatever form it takes, it should be an organized statement clarifying a family's current finances, pointing out areas that need extra attention, and specifying how to achieve the defined goals. It should also be a plan that you understand and that clearly helps you to achieve those goals.

Quality and completeness vary from plan to plan, but most contain a number of common elements:

1. *Net worth statement* Assets, such as equity in your home, cash value on life insurance, and stocks and bonds are compared against your mortgage and other debts to present a picture of your overall net worth.

2. *Family budget*   This reveals your family's ability to save and achieve any goals set out in the plan.

3. *Life insurance*   Estimating your family's expenses upon your death—such as legal and burial costs, plus living expenses—and comparing them to any income available for the survivors helps determine whether additional insurance is required.

4. *Disability insurance*   The plan determines how much income you would have if you were disabled and how much additional disability insurance you should purchase, if any.

5. *Investment strategies*   Guidelines are given on the types of investments that are best for you, given your tax bracket and age.

6. *Tax estimate*   A rough estimate of the coming year's federal tax liability is computed, based on information from last year's return.

7. *Cash flow analysis*   The plan evaluates your debt ratio and determines whether you have enough cash reserves.

8. *Long-term accumulation plans*   Savings needs are projected for specific goals.

9. *Retirement income*   The plan estimates your retirement income needs, Social Security, and pension benefits. By factoring in your expected life span, a planner can project the amount you must accumulate by retirement age. Working back from that sum, he or she can figure out how much you need to set aside every year and how to find the money in your budget.

Once these specifics are determined, the cost estimates must be attached to them. The first part of the plan should tell you where you are; the second part should dictate options for getting where you want to go, giving the pros and cons of each option. All these elements must be shaped into a program designed to achieve your particular goals. A good personal financial plan is specific, personal, and practical. Individuals, even in the same tax bracket, have dramatically different needs that require different financial planning decisions.

A financial plan should include explanations for all assumptions made, such as the inflation rate used to estimate your retirement needs, your estimated tax bracket in future years, and the expected rate of return assumed on your investments and your tolerance for risk. The planner should then pinpoint any trouble spots in your financial picture, such as tax problems, insufficient insurance, poor returns on investments, or too much risk.

Finally, your planner should be able to project how much wealth you can hope to accumulate over the next 5, 10, 20, or 40 years, or longer. Systematic financial planning involves considering one's financial situation from a lifetime perspective. It is an attempt to preserve one's present assets, increase wealth, and build financial security.

Personal Factors of a Plan

Financial planners recommend that people consider seven factors when establishing a financial plan:

1. Age

2. Diversification

3. Children

4. Liquidity

5. Taxes

6. Risk

7. Estate planning

These will all be reflected in your plan.

Age Most plans should contain a variety of different types of assets often referred to as **asset mix**, depending on the age of the investor. Your financial goals will not remain static. At age 24, saving for retirement may be the furthest thing from your mind. Twenty years later, however, you might feel it is imperative that you be able to afford to retire at age 55. Periodically, you need to reevaluate your goals and the amount of money you are committing to them.

Age will often determine the kind of investments people will make. As they enter their thirties, young adults traditionally take on responsibility for spouses and children and adopt a more earnest fiscal stance. Once people know how much money they will need and when, they decide where to invest. There are two basic choices: debt-based or lending assets, and equity-based or ownership assets.

Debt-Based Assets With a **debt-based asset**, the investor, in effect, lends money by making a bank deposit, taking out an annuity (see Chapter 18), or buying a note, bill, or bond of a government or corporation. In its simplest form, a debt-based asset pays interest regularly and repays the original sum at maturity. If the asset must be sold before maturity, its market value can fluctuate with interest rates, and so debt-based assets that mature in no more than 10 years are generally recommended.

Equity-Based Assets By contrast, **equity-based assets** represent ownership, with the owner assuming the risks and rewards. The most common are stocks in corporations; but real estate, precious metals, and commodities all fall into this category. No return is certain on these assets, and their market value can fluctuate over a much greater range than debt-based assets. The potential for appreciation is usually much greater, as is the potential for loss.

A prudent plan for a younger working person, whose work life can still be measured in decades, would be to invest one-third in relatively low-risk debt-based assets, one-third in stock mutual funds that seek growth, and one-third in an assortment of other assets, including real estate, tax shelters, and perhaps some precious metals. But for someone, for example, only five years away from retirement, 60 to 65 percent of the portfolio should be in conservative debt-based assets while the rest could go into stock mutual funds that seek both income and growth.

As you get older, you should emphasize safer income-producing securities, corporate bonds, and bank certificates of deposit. Evaluate your asset mix periodically. You usually get better returns if you invest for the long run, ignoring minor price fluctuations both in individual holdings and in the markets as a whole.

Diversification   One age-old precaution against the economy's and market's whims is to put some diversity into a portfolio. Portfolio diversification is the art of distributing an investor's funds among stocks, bonds, real estate, and other investments to achieve good returns while limiting risk. Since different types of investments will perform well at different times, diversification helps you offset the volatility of a single type of investment. The chances that you will suffer a simultaneous loss over many different investments is less likely than if you invest in any single one.

A diversified plan should balance assets among different investments so that total return will be reasonably stable despite market or interest rate fluctuations. One type of product should not exceed 25 percent of your portfolio. On the other hand, a plan should also not look like a shopping list of every known investment product. This will create confusion and will be difficult to manage efficiently. Many other investments that will be discussed in the following chapters can help you stay ahead of inflation and build assets.

Children   Raising a family is among life's greatest and also most expensive joys. Parenthood calls for not only a large measure of emotional maturity but also a high degree of financial planning. There are endless uncertainties in child raising, but one thing is certain: kids will lighten your pockets for years to come. A study for the National Institute of Child Health and Human Development found that an average family spends about a quarter of its aggregate income to raise a first-born child to age 22; two children will use up about 40 percent of their parents' income.

Potential parents need not necessarily let financial considerations get in their way if they are planning a family provided they properly prepare and plan ahead. Nevertheless, in order to continue living in an affluent style, many young couples are having smaller families and postponing them until their careers and finances are more firmly established. During these years, careful budgeting and planning are essential. New parents may be overwhelmed by the expense, but babies are almost a bargain compared with the cost of teenage and college years.

Newborns are quite expensive. Hospital bills, obstetricians' and pediatricians' fees, infant formula, baby food, and diapers can run over $5,000 for the first year. But, as will be discussed in Chapter 4, the most expensive part of child rearing is paying for four or more years of a college education. Even with widespread financial assistance, paying for college is no easy task, and it will not get easier. All but the most financially burdened parents must dig into their own resources before a college will award aid. Throughout the 1980s and early 1990s, college costs outpaced inflation. Freshmen entering college in the fall of 1993 were looking at four-year bills totaling nearly $70,000 at private schools and $34,000 at public institutions (see Table 4–1 on page 131).

The early child-rearing years are the time to begin a steady savings plan to pay for college education. Otherwise, your little darling may have to work at McDonald's for two years before entering college. It may once have seemed like over-compensation to start saving and investing for college as soon as possible after a child is born, but that is no longer the case.

For many families, one of the biggest financial hurdles is building up equity for a child's college days. Paying for college will continue to be the ultimate test of their ability to plan effectively. Although kids certainly do cost a fortune, one need not be intimidated. Most parents would readily agree that although they pay a small fortune to raise their children, they are getting a bargain.

Liquidity   **Liquidity** is another important investment consideration. It is defined as the convertibility of assets into cash on short notice with no loss of principal. A checking account at a bank can provide liquidity almost instantly, while real estate, artwork, collectibles, and other nonliquid assets can take months or even years to sell. To ensure at least minimum liquidity, a plan should generally include a money market account. Such an account (discussed in Chapter 14) is easily accessible for emergencies yet pays a market rate of interest. If you structure a plan with large investments in long-term certificates of deposit, bonds, annuities, or other products that cannot be cashed in without large losses or stiff penalties for early withdrawal, you are not flexible when you suddenly need the money.

REAL

Taxes   Taxes and how they affect investments are often the immediate concern of those setting up a financial plan. Investors need to develop a wariness of taxes that can compromise their ability to achieve their goals. The higher peoples' tax bracket, the more they need to consider the tax consequences of their maneuvers. Suppose that you are 25 years old, earning $50,000 a year, and planning to retire at age 65. Assuming 6 percent average annual raises, by the time you reach retirement age, you will have earned over $8 million in gross income. That is a lot of money to work with and to shield from taxes.

Suppose also that you are married and file jointly, in the 31 percent bracket, and are considering putting money into a taxable account paying 10 percent a year. The IRS will take 31 percent of your 10 percent earnings—3.1 percent, leaving you a 6.9 percent after tax return. If you believe that inflation will be roughly 4.5 percent as it was in recent years, you will have about 2 percent left after taxes and inflation. That may not sound like much, but it is a respectable real after-tax income. Evaluating investments in terms of real after-tax returns is the only way to be sure of making progress toward your goals.

A financial plan should be structured so as to maximize after-tax earnings. For a more thorough examination of taxes, see Chapter 5.

Risk   The amount of risk you are willing and able to take is a most important consideration because the return on an investment generally increases with the risk taken. Unfortunately, risk is a complicated factor: the true risk of an investment is often difficult to assess, and many people have trouble assessing their taste for risk.

To some people, security means taking no risks at all with their money. However, there are no absolutely secure, risk-free investments. All financial decisions involve some element of risk. Risk must be calculated, managed, and controlled but will always be present in any financial decisions. Suppose you decide not to take any risks and place all your money ($10,000) in the vaults at Fort Knox. Have you avoided risking it? If inflation next year hits 12 percent, you will lose $1,200 of purchasing power. Is your money really safe in the safest vault? Is its value protected? Obviously not.

Opportunity Cost One way to better understand the concept of risk is to understand and use the concept of **opportunity cost**. The amount of other products that must be foregone or sacrificed to obtain some amount of any given product is called the *opportunity cost* of that good. Consumer resources, namely time and money, are limited. Opportunity cost recognizes that when you spend money or time on any product or activity, you are giving up the opportunity to spend that same time or money on some other product or activity. Therefore, the opportunity cost of spending money or time on a certain product or activity is measured by the value of time or money. For example, the opportunity cost of your studying five hours this weekend for your upcoming personal finance course is the five hours that you could have used to study for your upcoming calculus exam. Opportunity cost teaches us that nothing is free and all of life's decisions involve costs.

PURCHASING

When money market funds paid 17 percent in the late 1970s and the inflation rate was 12 percent, some people insisted on keeping their money in savings accounts yielding 5¼ percent because they considered them to be risk free. But the opportunity cost of keeping money in a savings bank account earning 5 percent per year interest while inflation raged at an annual rate of 12 percent meant foregoing the opportunity of earning 17 percent and that the funds "saved" were shrinking by 7 percent a year. If you had $100,000 saved in such an account, your buying power would be shrinking by $7,000 annually. Therefore, a key element of any financial plan is making your money grow. This means that it must more than match the rate of inflation.

Probe your financial personality. You need to determine how much risk you are willing to take with money. This should be governed by your age, family responsibilities, current and potential income, and savings, as well as tolerance for risk. A younger person can afford more risk than an older person. If you have a large family, you will probably be more conservative with your money than, say, a single person or couple without children. You would likely put most of your financial assets in investments that guarantee steady but hardly spectacular returns and let you be highly liquid. To a great extent, the mix in your portfolio should reflect the degree of risk you are willing to run.

Estate Planning: Wills Finally, a will (discussed in detail in Chapter 19) is an essential part of your plan. Without it you will have no control over how your property is distributed. If you and your spouse do not have wills (two-thirds of all Americans don't), the state decides not only how to dispose of your property but also who will be the guardian of your minor children if you and your spouse both die before your child turns 18. Under some state laws, some distant relative you have never heard of may walk away with a portion of your assets.

Estate planning can make a difference in terms of the future harmony of your family even when only modest sums of money are involved. Although the thought of writing a will, especially when you are young, may seem morbid and depressing, it's

"You know you've arrived when they stop calling you a 'yuppie' and start calling you a 'fat cat'...!"

SOURCE: "Pepper...and Salt," *The Wall Street Journal,* April 27, 1988, 27. Reprinted by permission of Cartoon Features Syndicate.

just another form of protection and consideration you leave your family in the event of your untimely demise. It should be an integral part of your personal financial plan.

Updating and Evaluating Your Plan

No matter how sophisticated, comprehensive, and well-organized your financial plan is, it will never be final. Even if your finances stay the same, the rest of the world will not. To work, your plan must withstand the swirling currents of a volatile economy. Booms, recessions, interest rate fluctuations, new tax laws, and inflation may necessitate a change in your plans. Therefore, a financial plan is just a starting point that will call for periodic revisions, additions, and updating. It is a process, not a one-time decision. It requires the commitment of a certain amount of time and must be reviewed regularly.

What will happen after you establish your financial plan? You need to know what to do or, if you have a planner, what your planner will do when circumstances change. For most people, a yearly update is sufficient. But the birth of a child, a job change or promotion, a recent inheritance, a major illness, or the sale of a home can undo the best financial plan overnight.

Evaluate your plan a year after it is written. If you have met your original short-term goals, if you are making progress toward your long-term ones, and if your net worth is rising at least as fast as inflation, then you have a winner. But if, after a year, you are disappointed by the results, then you need to revise your plan or, if you are using a planner, start looking for another one.

SUMMARY

Effective planning is essential to the successful management of personal finances. The first step is to establish an efficient financial record keeping system. This will enable you to prepare a family financial statement listing all of the family's assets and liabilities in a clear, concise, and organized manner.

Next, construct a family budget, the plan for use of expected income and other resources for spending, saving, and investing. It will help you define priorities and analyze your spending patterns and needs.

Then, write a net worth statement. Net worth, is your assets minus your liabilities, measures your financial condition and is a function of your budget. An important goal and measure of your financial progress is an increase in your net worth over the years. To achieve any financial goals, you must establish a pattern of saving and investing on a monthly basis Record keeping, budgeting, net worth, saving, and investing can all be pulled together and channeled in a specific direction and for a specific purpose through the use of financial planning. Planning is the preparation and coordination necessary to prepare for future financial needs and goals.

Although with some training most people could prepare their own plans, many middle- and upper-income earners are turning to professional planners to structure and implement one for them. The planner's mandate is broad, an invitation to become immersed in all aspects of a client's financial life. Selecting a trained, competent, and qualified financial planner is difficult because there are no national standards or licensing procedures for this profession. Many planners are really disguised insurance agents or salespeople for financial services such as mutual funds. Some planners charge a fee for preparing a plan, some charge a commission for the products they recommend you buy in the plan, and others charge both a fee and a commission.

Financial plans vary greatly in scope, magnitude, focus, and level of sophistication. A plan should include such basic elements as a balance sheet, a life insurance and disability insurance package, investment strategies, a tax estimate, a cash flow analysis, and a retirement income plan. Before adopting a plan, people must consider and weigh seven factors that will determine the nature and strategies of the plan. These factors are age, diversification, children, liquidity, taxes, risk, and estate planning.

Financial planning is a lifetime job. As a person moves through the life cycle, plans and goals will have to be changed to reflect the new circumstances.

KEY TERMS

Certified financial planner (CFP)	Fee-only planner
Chartered financial consultant (ChFC)	Family budget
Commission-only planner	Family financial statement
Current ratio	Financial plan
Debt-based assets	Financial planner
Debt ratio	Financial planning
Diversification	Liquid investments
Emergency savings fund	Liquidity
Estate planning	Net worth
Equity-based assets	Nonliquid investments
Fee and commission planner	

REVIEW QUESTIONS AND PROBLEMS

1. Define and explain the following: (a) a budget, (b) family financial statement, (c) net worth statement, (d) financial plan.
2. Describe several ways in which you can safeguard your records.

3. What are the benefits of an organized method of record keeping?
4. What are the purpose and value of a net worth statement?
5. What is meant by the "pay yourself first" philosophy of saving?
6. What is personal financial planning?
7. What personal factors affect a family's financial planning?
8. Describe the structure of a financial plan and the elements contained therein.
9. Who needs a professional planner, and who does not?
10. "Financial planning is essentially an unregulated industry."
    A. Discuss the meaning of this statement.
    B. How does this create difficulty in selecting a competent and qualified planner?
    C. What credentials should a person look for in a planner, and what do these credentials signify?
11. "Beware! Some planners may be disguised salespeople." What is meant by this phrase?
12. What is the difference between debt-based assets and equity-based assets? Give examples of each.
13. Describe how financial goals and plans will change as people move through different stages in their lives.
14. What is meant by portfolio diversification? How does it limit risk?
15. Why is liquidity an important consideration for every investor?
16. "There are no absolutely secure, risk free investments." Explain the logic behind this statement.

17. (REAL) For an investor in the 33 percent tax bracket, what must a taxable account pay to generate a real after-tax return of 12 percent, if the inflation rate is 5 percent?

18. (PURCHASING) An investor wishes to increase her buying power from $10,000 to $12,000 in one year, facing an inflation rate of 8 percent. What interest rate must she earn?

SUGGESTED PROJECTS

1. A. Follow the instructions in this chapter for organizing your financial records.
   B. Prepare a personal or family financial statement. Use the checklist provided earlier in this chapter.
   C. After you have completed the family statement, explain why and how this enables you to get a better "handle" on your personal finances.
2. A. Prepare a personal or family budget. Use Table 1–1 as your guide.
   B. After you have finished entering the figures for the first month, try to analyze your budget. What has the budget made you aware of that you weren't aware of before?
   C. Have you spotted any problem areas in your budget? Explain.
   D. How do you think you should go about rectifying any problems in your budget?
   E. What do you plan to do with your surplus and how will you finance any budget deficits?
   F. How are you now in a better position to make plans? Explain.

     G. Follow your budget over several months, and try to analyze any emerging patterns that you detect.

     H. Calculate your debt ratio and current ratio and analyze your findings.

3. Prepare a net worth statement as shown in Table 1–2.

     A. Does the bottom line (assets minus liabilities) surprise you?

     B. Follow your net worth statement over time to see if your net worth is growing or declining.

4. Interview your friends and relatives, and find out their major financial problems and concerns. Discuss with them the concepts of record keeping, budgeting, financial statements, net worth statements, and planning. See if any of these can be useful in overcoming some of their financial problems. Report your findings to the class.

5. List three or four of your long-range personal financial goals. In general terms explain how you plan to achieve those goals.

INFORMATION RESOURCES

Abramson, E. M. "Mastering Your Money." *Modern Maturity*, October–November 1990, 66–71.

Emshwiller, John. "Costly Counsel." *The Wall Street Journal*, October 20, 1989, R-5.

Giese, William. "Do Your Investments Fit Your Goals?" *Changing Times*, February 1991, 51–54.

Giese, William. "Go Ahead, Take a Chance." *Kiplinger's Personal Finance Magazine*. January 1993, 61–64.

Hallman, G. V., and Rosenbloom, J. S. *Personal Financial Planning*. 4th ed. New York: McGraw-Hill, 1987.

Henderson, Nancy. "Weeding Out Your Home Files." *Changing Times*, January 1991, 41–43.

Institute of Certified Financial Planners. 3443 S. Galena, Suite 190, Denver, CO 80231.

International Association for Financial Planning. 2 Concourse Parkway, Suite 800, Atlanta, GA 30328 (404/395-1605).

O'Reilly, Brian. "Picking the Right Financial Planner." *Fortune*, February 25, 1991, 144–147.

Phillips, Carole. *The New Money Workbook for Woman: A Step by Step Guide to Managing Your Personal Finances.* New York: Brick House, 1988.

Pond, Jonathan. *Jonathan Pond's Guide to Investment and Financial Planning:* New York Institute of Finance, 1992.

Quinn, Jane Bryant. *Making the Most of Your Money*. New York: Simon and Schuster, 1992.

Richmark, Louis S. "How to Protect Your Financial Future." *Fortune*, January 25, 1993, 58–60.

Rosefsky, Bob. *Money Talks*. New York: McGraw-Hill, 1989.

Schultz, Ellen. "Is a Financial Planner Really Necessary?" *The Wall Street Journal*, May 31, 1991, C-1.

Siegel, Joel G., and Shim, Jae K. *The Personal Financial Planning and Investment Pocket Guide*. New York: McGraw-Hill, 1989.

Sloane, Leonard. "Do It Yourself, or Go to a Pro?" *The New York Times*, March 3, 1991, F-19.

Van Caspel, Venita. *Money Dynamics for the Nineties*. New York: Simon and Schuster, 1988.

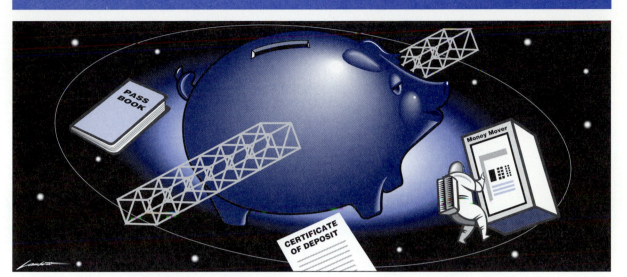

CHAPTER TWO

What the World of Banking Offers You

- To understand the various types of financial institutions offering savings and checking accounts
- To identify and to compare the various types of savings and checking instruments that are available to consumers
- To trace the origins of the new financial services industry
- To survey the services offered by financial supermarkets
- To comprehend how compound interest makes deposits grow over time and how effective yield is determined
- To evaluate the relative safety of money invested with various financial institutions
- To discuss the factors to consider when selecting a financial institution

This chapter discusses the full range of banking services available to a depositor or saver and tells how to select the services most suitable for our needs. It discusses the latest developments and changes in the banking industry and how they affect us all.

Banking has indeed become a bewildering new business in the past few years. Added conveniences and services as well as unbridled competition have resulted from rapid technological and regulatory changes. The proliferation of savings options in recent years has made it possible for consumers to earn higher yields on their money but also has created confusion. Gone are the days when your main banking decision was selecting the color of your checkbook. Like computer shoppers, bank shoppers can be overwhelmed by the abundance of new products and reluctant to make choices for fear that something better will come along next month.

Deciding where to bank can now be a considerable challenge. There are wide choices of **financial institutions** with which to deposit savings—from banks, savings and loan associations (S&Ls), and credit unions to nonbank financial services companies. A financial institution is an institution that uses its funds chiefly to obtain financial assets as opposed to tangible assets. Such institutions serve to bring together borrowers and lenders, making available loanable funds to those willing to pay for their use. In economics, a distinction is made between **tangible assets** and **financial assets.** Tangible assets are resources that have physical or material substance such as factories, buildings, machinery, equipment and land, yielding services in production or directly to consumers. Financial assets are nonmaterial property rights, which include money, notes, bonds, equities, and claims or titles of received income or value received from others.

Financial institutions are subdivided into depository institutions (including commercial banks and savings and loan associations) and nondepository institutions (such as mutual funds, money market mutual funds, life and property insurance companies, and pension funds).

Depository institutions obtain funds from the receipt of money deposits from savers who seek a very safe, low-risk insured savings vehicle. In contrast, nondepository institutions obtain funds from premiums, investment earnings, and other nondeposit sources from investors. These generally involve some element of risk. The financial services mega-industry already embraces more than 90,000 business entities, including:

14,500 commercial banks
5,000 savings and loan associations
1,000 mutual savings banks
16,000 credit unions
1,000 investment banks
5,000 broker-dealers
1,000 mutual funds
1,000 mortgage banks
3,000 pension funds (other than banks and insurers)
2,000 life and health insurance companies
3,000 property casualty insurance companies
3,300 insurance brokerage agencies

plus numerous factoring companies, leasing companies, credit card and traveler's checks issuers, and finance companies.

An array of new savings and checking instruments, offering a variety of interest rates and conditions, is now available. The variety of choices is perplexing or unknown to many consumers and is forever changing. Some have chosen to stay with the product they know best, the traditional passbook savings accounts or checking accounts. But whether you will stay with the traditional passbook savings account or grab every new financial gadget and innovation the banks offer you, knowing and understanding the basics of banking will help to make your choice more informed. This chapter provides the foundation necessary for an intelligent and informed approach to banking. Let's begin by defining the different banking institutions and the services they offer.

Banking Institutions

The variety of services and fees differs dramatically among commercial banks, savings and loan associations, and credit unions, the three types of institutions loosely called "banks." Choosing the one for your checking, borrowing, saving, and investing requires you to assess particular banking needs and preferences. All three types of institutions offer various types of checking accounts and savings accounts and are capable of making loans.

Commercial Banks

Commercial banks are institutions that accept demand deposits (checking accounts), make a wide range of commercial and industrial loans, and engage in many other financial activities (discussed further on). Commercial banks dominate the financial industry in terms of the amount of assets they hold, and they have the widest range of accounts and services for both individuals and businesses. Commercial banks include federally chartered national banks as well as state chartered banks.

There are some 14,500 commercial banks, also called *regular banks,* with 63,000 main and branch offices around the country. They used to have unique rights and privileges, such as a monopoly on checking accounts, which ended with the bank reform legislation in 1982.

Savings and Loan Associations (S&Ls)

There are 5,000 **savings and loan associations (S&Ls),** also known as *thrifts.* Counting branches, the total number of S&L offices tops 25,000. Until recently, thrifts simply accepted deposits from the public and made loans for the purchase of homes and other durable goods. This was their original purpose—to encourage family thrift and home ownership. Their financial fortunes rested upon the spread between the interest rate paid to depositors and the rate earned on their mortgage portfolios.

The major banking reform legislation affecting S&Ls, which lifted restrictions that applied to them, was the Garn–St. Germain Depository Institutions Act of 1982.The law made it possible for S&Ls to offer a wide variety of accounts. It also increased the amount that thrifts could lend for nonresidential real estate ventures.

Since bank reform and deregulation, thrifts have been undergoing very rough times. Hundreds have collapsed, and hundreds more are slated to close. Those that survive are operating more like commercial banks, providing a wide range of financial services, such as checking accounts, commercial loans, telephone bill-paying accounts, credit cards, and networks of automated teller machines. They have undergone far-reaching changes. Many thrifts have even exorcised the words "thrift," "savings," or "savings and loan" from their titles. A number of S&Ls have changed their charters and names to "federal savings bank," indicated by the initials FSB. The usual reason for such a change is cosmetic, to get the word "bank" on the sign. (The thrift crisis will be discussed later in this chapter.)

The distinction between what banks and thrifts do is becoming blurred in the minds of many people, including bankers. Commercial banks and thrifts are aggressively marketing themselves in areas that used to belong almost exclusively to the other. With their expanded powers, thrifts can and often do offer essentially the same banking services as commercial banks. But there are a few real differences between commercial banks and thrifts. The law requires that at least 70 percent of the loans made by federally chartered thrifts be used for home mortgages. Their mortgage rates tend to be more competitive, and they consistently offer higher returns on savings instruments and accounts. Commercial banks generally have more capital and more experience with a range of financial products.

Credit Unions

You may find that you do not need the services of a bank or a thrift institution at all. Your financial services may be handled very satisfactorily at a credit union instead. A **credit union** is a not-for-profit cooperative association of people who pool their savings and lend money to one another. Generally, the members have a "common bond," such as working for the same company, living in the same community, or belonging to the same house of worship, club, fraternal group, or trade union. Whatever the bond, members in effect pool their resources for their financial common good.

Credit unions' small scale, their structure as cooperatives, and their nonprofit status give them several advantages that banks lack. They often pay above average interest on savings and charge less than commercial lenders. Their fees and minimum required account balances tend to be lower as well. With minimum overhead and a federal tax exemption, credit unions can provide credit cheaply for their members. Loan terms are as a rule comparatively liberal, and branch offices are often located at the workplace.

Each member is a part owner and has one vote, regardless of how much the member may have in savings. The members elect a board of directors that sets policy. A credit committee consisting of members acts on loan applications, a process that tends to be speedy because the applicants are generally well known, at least in the smaller organizations.

Besides offering basic services, the largest credit unions have in recent years begun staking out territories that had been monopolized by the more sophisticated financial institutions. Many credit unions offer such products and services as savings certificates, credit and debit cards, automated teller machine services, discount brokerage, pooled stock purchases, IRAs, money orders, payroll deduction plans, traveler's checks, interest-bearing checking accounts, money market fund equivalents, mortgage loans, and financial counseling. Such advantages, plus their conveniences, make credit unions enormously popular.

Credit unions are attracting a growing number of consumers angered by rising bank transaction fees and minimum balance requirements. There are nearly 16,000 of these member-run cooperatives, with 58 million people using credit unions for basic financial services. Total assets more than doubled from $69 billion in 1980 to $195 billion by 1989. These numbers are still small when compared with those of commercial banks and thrifts. But some of the larger credit unions are getting more and more competitive in their products and services.

As for safety, since most credit unions are federally insured and invest in member loans and government-backed securities, they are relatively risk free.

Here is a point to consider: If you depend on canceled checks for financial record keeping, you will need to get accustomed to a new method called truncated checking (discussed further on). Since some credit unions do not return checks, your record is the carbon copy attached to each check you write.

Financial Integration

Banks and credit unions are no longer alone in offering banking services, nor are banks offering only banking services. Until recently, commercial banks, savings and loan associations, securities firms, and insurers have each provided distinct services and have competed only within their own types of firms. But as the traditional barriers separating financial industries have begun to erode, if not disappear altogether, firms have started to offer an integrated range of products. In the future, consumers may likely have one household "operations" account, similar to the cash management account offered by Merrill Lynch and others. Such an account would consolidate payments for and investment in a wide range of services from mutual funds to home insurance to gas and electric bills. (This topic will be discussed later in this chapter.)

The Upheaval of Deregulation
Many of the regulatory barriers that existed from the 1930s to the 1980s in the financial world came in response to the Stock Market Crash of 1929 and its 9,000 bank failures, when overconcentrated financial power helped lead to disaster. Yet today, the public tends to view large business entities as economically efficient and safer, and as sources of innovation that benefit consumers. This belief, coupled with the Reagan administration's strong philosophy of deregulation, led in the early 1980s to the biggest upheaval in financial services since the 1930s.

Nonbank Banks and Interstate Banking
The trumpet blast of legislation also caused the walls restraining interstate banking to tumble. A commercial bank cannot legally open a branch outside its home state unless the other state allows entry. However, deregulation permitted nonbank institutions to offer many of the traditional services previously offered only by banks. Thus, banks and other companies have been legally hurdling the interstate barriers by setting up so-called **nonbanks**, also known as *consumer banks* (see Figure 2–1).

FIGURE 2–1   **Advertisement Countering Nonbanks**

SOURCE: American Banker's Association, 1985.

The emergence of nonbank banks has added to the confusion in the banking industry. This double-speak nickname simply reflects the fact that nonbanks do not meet the statutory definition of a bank and are therefore not subject to banking regulations and restrictions. Federal law defines a bank as an institution that handles regular checking accounts and makes commercial loans. Nonbanks are institutions that are allowed to offer checking accounts **or** commercial loans but cannot do both, thus escaping the legal definition of a bank. By sacrificing one of these services, usually the lending power, nonbanks escape the 1927 McFadden Act, which bars banks from crossing state lines unless state law permits.

A couple of dozen nonbanks that technically do not meet the government's definition of a bank have been set up by large banks as a way to circumvent restrictions on interstate banking. But the U.S. Court of Appeals ruled in January 1985 that the intent of the law was to bar such institutions, and so the court ordered new nonbank banks to close down.

In May 1985, the Supreme Court ruled in its *Dimension* decision that the Federal Reserve Board cannot restrict the activities of nonbank banks. The court stated: "If the Bank Holding Company Act falls short of providing safeguards desirable or necessary to protect the public interest, that is a problem for Congress ... to address."

What is the importance of the above court decisions? As a result of these, there are no services unique to banks anymore. General Motors makes consumer loans, and General Electric offers home mortgages, while both Sears, Roebuck and Control Data Corporation accept federally insured deposits through financial subsidiaries. The future of nonbank banks may have to be decided by Congress, which has not yet accepted the courts' invitation to act.

Interstate banking is also spreading in other ways. For example, there are over 60,000 automatic teller machines (ATMs) across the country, and more than a third belong to ATM networks such as PLUS and CIRRUS, which enable depositors to obtain quick cash away from home. This is a form of interstate electronic banking. In addition, since 1982, commercial banks have been allowed to buy failing out-of-state savings and loans. Also since 1982, nearly 20 states have passed laws letting in out-of-state banks. Interstate banking is usually restricted to neighboring states through so-called regional compacts, and such arrangements were upheld by the Supreme Court in June 1985.

In a historic accord, California and New York bankers, in March 1986, agreed to an interstate banking deal. As of 1990, New York banks are free to acquire banks in the fast-growing California market. California banks will be free to do the same in New York. This agreement is important in pushing the whole concept of interstate banking.

The Fees Squeeze

Perhaps the most profound change to have occurred in recent years as a result of federal deregulation was the elimination of ceilings on interest for savings and checking accounts. Until deregulation, banks were not allowed to pay any interest on checking account balances; this meant that banks got to use depositors' money for free while they lent it out at market interest rates. Banks were also restricted to paying only 5.25 percent on most passbook savings accounts. Deregulation cost banks a lot of money. With interest ceilings lifted and nonbanking financial institutions blossoming, banks and S&Ls had to fight hard for depositors by offering market-related competitive interest rates.

Deregulation plunged banks into a highly competitive free-market environment which they were not fully prepared to deal with. A few institutions resorted to making lucrative but ultra-risky loans so that they could pay those premium rates. This was to lead several years later to a rash of bank failures. An immediate problem arose: the increased cost of paying competitive interest rates while coping with encroachment from nonbank financial institutions.

To solve this problem, large regional banks tried to improve profits by becoming less dependent upon their shrinking interest earnings. They charged more for basic banking services. Since 1980, federally insured banks and thrifts have raised fees and have required higher minimum balances. Bankers insisted that higher fees were necessary to compensate the banks for the loss of the savers' subsidy that occurred when Congress, in 1980, began taking off the ceiling on savings rates and letting the institutions pay market rates of interest.

Deregulation also spawned the need for discouraging small, unprofitable accounts. Because large banks had to pay out more money to attract deposits, they began charging for services that once were free. At most large banks, small balance depositors pay even for the most mundane services, such as checks and money orders. This practice is known as *market segmentation.*

Market Segmentation

Market segmentation means that banks have singled out a segment of the banking public as their target customers and are lavishing most of the perks on this select few. Not surprisingly, the target group is the affluent, for today's bank profits lie with customers who have sizable, stable deposits and the resources to purchase and benefit from an array of financial services and products that the banks can sell them. Banks claim that they can no longer afford to serve all customers equally. They therefore offer inducements to their target customers.

Stricter account balance requirements and penalties are among the most discouraging banking developments for small depositors. Large depositors, on the other hand, are beneficiaries of priority services, a package of free banking privileges. Among them are the attentions of a personal account officer; private tellers; the use of a special customer service number, where bank personnel stand ready to answer any banking question 24 hours a day, seven days a week; banking by appointment; and personal overdraft notification by phone.

The cost of basic banking in the early 1980s doubled, leaving many customers claiming that they could not afford it. After several members of Congress introduced bills to protect poor constituents, the American Banker's Association encouraged its members to come up with "voluntary" solutions. The solutions differed from bank to bank. Some banks offer free checking if a $100 minimum is maintained. The depositor is permitted to write only 8 to 10 checks per month and must make all but two withdrawals and deposits per month on automatic teller machines. For full service, many banks charge $3 to $5 a month and 20 to 50 cents per check.

Other banks discovered that $200, or so-called "cheapie" accounts, known as *lifeline banking,* have actually been good for business. These accounts have attracted college students, who presumably will move on to more profitable accounts after they graduate. Eventually banks may be able to sell other services, such as car loans, to these customers. The higher rates and fees that banks charge have more than off-set the higher rates they have had to pay to depositors. But generally deregulation has skewed the market in favor of individuals with large accounts and with the need for the more sophisticated, fee-related services.

The benefits of modern banking are not being spread evenly. The winners are those who are wealthier, who have big balances, and who can make full use of the new services. The banking world has become more harsh for those without sub-stantial balances.

The New Financial Services Industry: Banks Bank on New Fields

Besides charging higher fees, bankers decided to go into new financial service fields. Banks are now offering a wide variety of products to the public, having added home banking, discount stock brokerage service, and retirement accounts, among other services, to traditional checking and savings accounts. Some states have broadened the scope of banks' activities even further, allowing them to sell insurance and oper-ate mutual funds.

Banks, which used to help you save money, are now eager to help you invest it. Many banks and savings and loan associations have, during the past few years, either bought a stock brokerage house or became affiliated with one.

Bank stock brokerage represents a radical change from the past. For 50 years, banks had been prohibited from doing much more than attracting depositors and lending out their money. In 1982, deregulation allowed banks to add brokerage to their financial services.

As a result of technology and deregulation, the whole concept of consumer bank-ing is changing. Banks are trying to leave such traditional tasks as taking deposits and cashing checks to machines, freeing their employees for more challenging jobs, such as selling the variety of products they now offer.

The Parade of Products

The products and services being offered by most banks today constitute an impres-sive array of choices:

1. Checking accounts

2. Passbook savings accounts

3. Certificates of deposit

4. Automated teller machines

5. Home banking

6. Financial supermarkets

7. Asset management accounts

8. Credit cards

9. Debit cards

Let's examine each of these nine basic service categories that banks now offer.

Checking Accounts

A personal checking account is essential for managing your finances. When you decide to open a checking account, it may appear that all you need to do is ask the bank's customer service representative at the new accounts desk for information about opening the account. Sounds simple? It isn't. You will probably be asked if you want a **regular checking account**, a **money market account**, a **NOW account**, or a **super NOW account**. These types of accounts differ in three major ways: the charges depositors pay, the minimum balance required, and the interest (if any) depositors receive.

One of the fruits of deregulation was supposed to be the opportunity to earn interest on a checking account. But a barrage of fees has turned checking into a battlefield littered with a variety of charges. In many banks, high fees eat up the interest earned unless depositors maintain an uncommonly high balance in their checking account.

Despite the plethora of names, there are only four types of checking accounts available to depositors: regular checking, money market deposit accounts (MMDAs), NOW accounts, and super NOW accounts. Let's examine each.

Regular Checking   Depositors may pay a fee or may get "free" checking. The cost depends upon the number of checks written or the size of the balance they keep on deposit. There are four basic fee structures for **regular checking accounts**:

1. "Free" (if a minimum balance is maintained)

2. Charge per check

3. Monthly maintenance or service charge

4. Monthly maintenance or service charge, plus a per-check fee.

The regular checking account is "free" if the required minimum balance is maintained, but there are monthly maintenance charges if the balance drops below the minimum. There is generally no charge per check. This account is attractive to those who write many checks and can maintain the required minimum balance, without earning interest, to avoid maintenance charges. But a "free" account costs depositors in the form of forgone interest. For example, assume that you must maintain $3,000 in the account. If money market accounts are currently yielding 6 percent, you are forgoing more than $180 interest annually, or $15.33 per month. This may be more expensive than an account that charges, say, $5 per month and has no minimum balance requirements. However, for many people who consistently maintain low balances, a checking account that pays no interest but charges no fee is often more rewarding than an account that pays a few dollars of taxable interest but costs $5 or so in monthly service charges. Otherwise, the interest you earn for the few days after you deposit your paycheck may be more than offset by service charges as you pay bills and slide down below the minimum.

A "charge per check" account may be advantageous if you keep less than the required minimum balance for "free" accounts and write few checks per month. A "monthly maintenance or service charge" account could be most economical if your average balance is usually small but you write many checks per month. Choice number 4 (above) is generally not a recommended fee structure for consumers.

When gathering information from different banking institutions, depositors should be sure to ask how minimum balances are calculated. One bank may levy a charge if the balance in the checking account ever dips below a certain amount during the course of a month. Another bank may have higher fees but apply them only if the average monthly balance falls below a specified level. Most banks, for example, slap a $1 to $10 monthly fee plus 15 to 50 cents a check on accounts that fall below a $1,000 daily minimum or $2,000 monthly average balance. At many banks with graduated fee scales, the lower the balance falls, the higher the fees a depositor will be charged.

But comparison shopping makes a difference. Bank fee structures vary dramatically, even between banks right across the street from each other. Depositors need to investigate savings and loan, brokerage house, and credit union alternatives. Before opening a new account, they should understand exactly how fees are assessed and what triggers extra charges. Those who cannot keep enough cash in their checking accounts to escape fees (or those who do not want to) should consider so-called no-frills accounts offered by some banks. Here depositors pay a flat monthly fee no matter what their balance, but they also have to live with restrictions on the number of checks they can write each month or how often they can make deposits or withdrawals at a teller's window instead of at an automatic teller machine.

Check Clearing Almost 40 billion checks are processed in the United States each year. All of them must "clear." The checks, and the funds they represent, must shuttle

"It's not fair! Bankers can write all kinds of poems without you caring a bit—but let a poet write one lousy bad check...."

SOURCE: "Pepper...and Salt," *The Wall Street Journal,* December 3, 1991, A-15. Reprinted by permission of Cartoon Features Syndicate.

between the banks where they are deposited and the banks on which they are drawn. In most cases, the checks clear without problems. About 1 percent, though, are returned, usually for insufficient funds.

When trying to decide which of several competing banks should get your checking accounts, ask how quickly each promises to clear any checks you deposit and make the money available for withdrawal. Choosing the fastest one lets you accumulate more interest on your balance if you have a NOW or super NOW account. When banks count the number of business days for check-clearing purposes, they exclude the day the deposit is made. If you deposit a check on Monday and the check has a one-day hold on it, the money will be available for your use at the start of the banking day on Wednesday. Saturdays and Sundays do not count, even if the bank is open for business. Therefore, an eight-day hold on a Monday deposit means that funds do not become available until Friday morning of the following week.

The Expedited Funds Availability Act of 1988

In response to protests that banks profit unfairly from the **float**, the interest banks collect by investing depositors' funds that are frozen during the check-clearing period, Congress passed the Expedited Funds Availability Act in 1988. Banks and thrifts may no longer sit on a depositor's money for weeks before the depositor can draw against a check he or she had deposited. Under federal banking rules that took effect September 1, 1990, depositors have access to local checks on the second business day following deposit and to nonlocal checks on the fifth day. In either case, depositors can withdraw the first $100 on the next business day, even if it is the full amount of the deposit.

The act further mandates that funds deposited in the form of cashier's checks, certified checks, and government checks must be available to depositors on the next business day. Some institutions go beyond the legal minimums and offer instant credit. Some banks give immediate cash status for any check deposited, as long as depositors have a savings account at the bank with a balance larger than the check amount. Many banks do this by putting a "hold" on your savings account for the amount. If the check is eventually returned as uncollectible, the bank dips into your savings to reclaim its money.

You can hasten the clearance process by not depositing a check at a credit union or small mutual savings and loan association. Most need a day or two just to forward it to a commercial bank that's in the Federal Reserve clearing system. That bank takes another day to send it to a Fed branch, which electronically credits the check amount to the depositing institution, usually within 48 hours. If you deposit a lot of out-of-town checks, you may want to shop around for the bank in your area that has the shortest holding period. You can get a copy of the bank's policy from a bank officer or teller.

An alternative way to cash a check and avoid the check-clearing delay may be to deposit your check into your savings account where there may be no need for instant access, simultaneously transferring an equivalent amount of money from your savings account to your checking account for instant access.

Money Market Deposit Accounts (MMDAs)   First made available in late 1982, **MMDAs** have drawn billions of dollars from other savings instruments. They offer current money market interest rates and easy access through check-writing privileges. There are no restrictions on withdrawals or penalties as long as a minimum balance, usually at least $1,000, is maintained in the account.

Money market deposit accounts are not actually checking accounts, since depositors are limited to three checks and three preauthorized transfers (such as automatic mortgage payments) per month. But MMDAs generally pay the highest rates of any bank account on which depositors can write checks. If you expect to keep, say, $10,000 in a liquid account, the difference in interest between the money market deposit account and the lower-paying super NOW should steer you to the MMDA. If the minimum is not maintained, the interest rate drops to the NOW account rate or even lower. This type of account is ideal for one's emergency liquid cash fund, assuming the minimum balance can be met.

NOW Accounts   **NOW** (negotiable orders of withdrawal) **accounts** are interest-bearing accounts that provide unrestricted check-writing privileges. Depositors are required to keep a specified minimum average monthly or daily balance which usually varies between $1,000 and $1,500 among most banks. Should the balance fall below the minimum, a monthly service charge and per check charge are imposed, and no interest is paid on the balance. No charges are usually levied and interest is paid when the balance is at the minimum or above. NOW accounts pay interest at rates generally no higher than those of passbook savings accounts.

Before opening a NOW account, consider carefully whether it's worth keeping $1,000 or more in an account earning a usually low rate of interest when higher rates are often available elsewhere, such as in CDs or money market mutual funds.

Super NOW Accounts   **Super NOW accounts** combine features of NOW accounts and money market deposit accounts. Like the former, there are no restrictions on check writing and telephone transfers. But like MMDAs, an average minimum monthly balance of $2,500 is usually required to earn a market interest rate higher than that of savings passbooks, but lower than that paid on MMDA. The average super NOW interest yield has in the past trailed that of MMDAs by 1 to 2 percentage points. With the present environment of low interest rates, the gap between rates on NOWs, Super NOWs, and MMDAs has narrowed.

Some Super NOW accounts have monthly per check and per deposit fees. If the balance falls below $2,500, the maintenance fees are often higher than those of NOW accounts. Because they usually pay below market rates, NOW and super NOW accounts should be treated as checking accounts. The funds that are deposited should be sufficient only to maintain minimum balances and write checks.

Compare Costs   Comparing costs at dozens of banks and S&Ls and credit unions is a tedious task. But there are two general rules when shopping for low-cost checking: S&Ls offer better deals than banks and credit unions often offer better deals than S&Ls. In addition, old-fashioned, non-interest-bearing accounts are cheaper to maintain than NOW accounts. Traditional bank accounts as well as savings and loan NOWs allow lower monthly balances to avoid checking fees than bank NOW accounts do.

Truncation   Many banks store canceled checks only on microfilm. This practice—called check "safe keeping," "truncated checking," or "truncation"—is spreading as an option to trim checking costs. The account holder does not receive his or her canceled check. A bank may offer depositors a discount of $1 to $2 a month on checking fees in exchange for truncation. If a depositor later needs proof of payment, the bank can produce a copy of a check in a day or two.

Checking Account Privileges   Time-conscious investors should take advantage of the many checking account privileges their bank provides, including:

1. *Overdraft checking*   The overdraft account, or preapproved credit line, adds a line of credit to your checking account that will be activated whenever you write a check that overdraws your balance. If you qualify for this type of account, a credit line of $1,000, $2,000, or more will be added to the checking account you already have. The fee structure will still be determined by the basic account. As with other forms of credit, there are finance charges on any unpaid balance. While the interest or finance charge is high, the loan term need not be long.

2. *Direct payment deposit*   Another checking service quite commonly available from many banks is direct paycheck deposit. Most large companies allow employees to designate one of several banks to receive salary deposits directly. Depending on bank policies, customers can often write checks against those sums on the day of the transfer.

3. *Automatic bill paying*   Also known as elecronic funds transfer (EFT) or automatic funds transfer (AFT), many institutions permit customers to authorize the automatic monthly payment of bills such as mortgage or loan installment debts through this process. The transfers, paid directly to the creditor, are deducted automatically from their checking accounts and are listed on their monthly statement. After the initial authorization, no paperwork is required until they wish to change the terms.

Passbook Savings Accounts

Passbook savings accounts were traditionally offered mainly by savings and loan associations. Today they are available at commercial banks as well. These fixed rate accounts are generally the least attractive options because they offer low rates without providing the ability to write checks. They are considered outdated, no longer a viable means of saving. The future belongs to money market deposit accounts paying variable market interest rates, which are generally higher than those of passbook savings accounts. Millions of people have therefore switched to money markets and other more attractive forms of saving.

What used to be called the passbook account is more likely to be referred to these days as "regular" savings or **"day of deposit, day of withdrawal" accounts.** But their new names don't add any real appeal to them. Although the 5.5 percent interest ceiling on these accounts was removed in April 1986, many of them continued to pay interest at or near the 5.5 percent rate. During the early 1990s they often paid between 2 and 4 percent interest. Nevertheless, savings accounts have some allures. They provide instant access to your money, liquidity, predictability, simplicity, and no withdrawal penalties, and they permit small deposits or withdrawals. They also qualify a depositor, in many places, for free checking.

Certificates of Deposit (CDs)

Certificates of deposit (CDs) are time deposits which pay a fixed or variable interest rate approximating the prevailing market rate. Traditionally, the appeal of CDs has been safety. When buying a CD, savers are depositing money at a banking institution for a specific period of time, most commonly 30 days to five years. Consumers who shop around will discover a variety of CD options. Deregulation has removed the old strictures on the types of CDs that banks can offer, and diversity now reigns. Minimum deposits and maturities vary widely, but to earn the maximum rate, either a $2,500 minimum must be maintained or the maturity must exceed 31 days.

With yields averaging around 4 percent for short-term CDs and under 6 percent for the five-year variety, CDs became an out-of-favor investment during the early 1990s. Yet they still appeal to people who place a premium on safety and simplicity.

Depositors generally find that the longer the maturity, the higher the rate earned. As with all investment advantages, there is an offsetting disadvantage to a long maturity date. Depositors must agree to tie up these funds for the time of the deposit. Should they decide to cash in the CD before its maturity date, the bank will assess an interest penalty for early withdrawal. If the interest that has accrued on a CD is not enough to cover the penalty, the bank may dip into the depositor's principal to make up the difference. CDs are therefore attractive only to those who can tie up their money for the entire deposit period. They therefore do not make a good emergency fund.

Fixed or Variable-Rate CDs Interest rates may be fixed at the same rate for the length of the account, or they may vary, indexed to some other fluctuating rate. In terms

SWITCH

Switch or Stay Put?

You invested $10,000 in a two-year CD six months ago at 6.25 percent and are now bombarded with ads proclaiming that current 18-month CDs pay 7 percent. What should you do?

To decide, you will need to determine three things: the interest remaining if you hold the CD to maturity; the reinvestment interest the funds would earn in a higher rate CD for the time remaining on the original CD; and the penalty for early withdrawal. The objective is to see if putting the funds into a new CD gives you more or less total earnings than you would get by staying put.

With monthly compounding, the money in the original two-year, 6.25 percent CD would earn $1,328 over the 24-month period. You have already accrued $317 in interest, leaving $1,011 for the remaining 18 months. The original $10,000 would earn $1,103 invested in a new 7 percent CD for the next 18 months. After forfeiting three-months of interest as a penalty, at about 0.52 percent per month, or $157, you are left with $946. The question then becomes, Is $1,011 less than $1,103 minus $157? Obviously not, and so it is best to keep that 6.25 percent CD for the remaining 18 months.

of the principal invested, a **variable-rate CD** is as secure as a **fixed-rate CD,** but it is considerably riskier in the stability of its income. As its name implies, the interest rate on a variable-rate CD can change during its term, usually in line with changes in interest rates generally. The change occurs periodically, usually every month but occasionally every week.

If you believe that interest rates are going to rise in the future, a variable-rate CD is a better bet than a fixed-rate CD. Alternatively, you could stay with fixed-rate maturities of less than one year. If you believe that interest rates are going to fall, a fixed-rate CD is the better bet. It would be wise to lock in current higher yields as long as possible. If you will not need the money for a while and want to lock in present rates, it might be prudent to consider buying several CDs of varying maturities. By doing so, if rates rise, some of the principal can be reinvested without the penalties most banks impose on early withdrawals. The penalties that apply to early sale of fixed-rate CDs apply equally to early sale of variable-rate CDs.

A fixed-rate short-term CD is as close as savers can come to a risk-free investment. While a CD is not very liquid, the money is insured up to $100,000 and it earns the interest stated until the end of its term.

Five hundred dollars is enough to buy a CD in many banks and S&Ls. There are no rate ceilings on certificates that run longer than 31 days. Deregulation has resulted in intense bank competition for deposits. This means that the depositor faces a mishmash of terms, rates, and minimum deposits. This can all be quite bewildering, and comparison shopping is an obvious necessity.

CDs have both an interest rate and an effective annual yield. The common denominator used to compare CDs is the **effective annual yield,** which takes into account the effects of when and how interest is compounded (see Tables 2–2 and 2–3). Unlike bond interest which is usually paid semiannually, CD interest usually compounds quarterly; that is, interest is earned on the interest that has already built up. Depositors receive the principal and all the interest when the CD matures.

Money market account and CD rates are commonly listed in most major newspapers. Figure 2–2 shows a weekly survey of these rates in leading banks nationwide. The jumbo rates referred to in Figure 2–2 are for CDs of $100,000, which generally receive a preferential rate of interest.

Brokered CDs One option for people with $1,000 or more to deposit is to use brokers who accumulate deposits into $100,000 packages and place them in banks around the country. **Brokered CDs** are therefore bank-issued certificates of deposit sold by brokerage houses. Led by Merrill Lynch, which pioneered the concept in 1982, many brokers now make a market in CDs. Buying a CD from a brokerage firm permits a saver to tap into the national CD market. Instead of phoning banks and thrifts around the country to determine the best deal in CDs, a saver can get a list of high-yielding CDs in a single call or visit to a broker. Brokers' fees usually amount to about a quarter of 1 percent of the interest.

These CDs, like certificates obtained at a bank or savings and loan, generally have the backing of the FDIC and frequently pay higher yields than bank CDs. Not all brokered CDs are federally insured. Under a law that went into effect during the summer of 1992, brokered CDs are covered by FDIC insurance only at well-capitalized institutions.

FIGURE 2–2 | **Sample Listing of Savings Rates**

TOP SAVINGS RATES

SMALL SAVERS RATES		JUMBO RATES	
Institution / Rating	**% Yield**	**Institution / Rating**	**Rate**
MONEY MARKET ACCOUNTS	**4.41%**	**MONEY MARKET ACCOUNTS**	**2.63%**
First Dep Natl Bk, Tilton, NH (3)	3.31%	Chevy Chase Svgs, MD (0)	3.45%
First Signature B&T, Portsmouth, NH (3)	3.28	New So. Fed Svgs, Birmingham, AL (3)	3.42
Colonial Natl Bank, Wilmington, DE (3)	3.25	Equitable Fed Svgs, Wheaton, MD (0)	3.40
New So. Fed Svgs, Birmingham, AL (3)	3.17	Columbia First Bank, Arlington, VA (1)	3.40
Key Bank USA, Albany, NY (3)	3.14	First Signature B&T, Portsmouth, NH (3)	3.31
6-MONTH C.D.'S	**2.81%**	**6-MONTH C.D.'S**	**4.41%**
Southern Pacific T&L, Culver City, CA (3)	3.98	1st Dep Natl Crdt Card, Concord, NH (3)	4.00%
First Dep Natl Bk, Tilton, NH (3)	3.80	Southern Pacific T&L, Culver City, CA (3)	3.98
MBNA America, Wilmington, DE (3)	3.61	CommerceBank, Newport Beach, CA (2)	3.80
Colonial Natl Bank, Wilmington, DE (3)	3.60	First Dep Natl Bk, Tilton, NH (3)	3.80
J C Penney Natl Bk, Harrington, DE (3)	3.55	MBNA America, Wilmington, DE (3)	3.61
1-YEAR C.D.'S	**3.08%**	**1-YEAR C.D.'S**	**3.17%**
MBNA America, Wilmington, DE (3)	4.28%	MBNA America, Wilmington, DE (3)	4.28%
Southern Pacific T&L, Culver City, CA (3)	4.08	1st Dep Natl Crdt Card, Concord, NH (3)	4.11
Cal. Thrift & Loan, Santa Barbara, CA (3)	4.00	Southern Pacific T&L, Culver City, CA (3)	4.08
Guaranty Bank, Milwaukee, WI (2)	3.96	Cal. Thrift & Loan, Santa Barbara, CA (3)	4.04
J C Penney Natl Bk, Harrington, DE (3)	3.95	First Dep Natl Bk, Tilton, NH (3)	4.00
2½-YEAR C.D.'S	**3.66%**	**2½-YEAR C.D.'S**	**3.71%**
Am Fed Svgs Bank, Rockville, MD (0)	4.90%	First USA Bank, Wilmington, DE (3)	4.65%
JC Penney Natl Bk, Harrington, DE (3)	4.60	Cal. Thrift&Loan, Santa Barbara, CA (3)	4.55
Cal. Thrift & Loan, Santa barbara, CA (3)	4.52	Eastern Svgs Bank, Baltimore, MD (0)	4.39
Eastern Svgs Bank, Baltimore, MD (0)	4.39	Key Bank USA, Albany, NY (3)	4.39
Key Bank USA, Albany, NY (3)	4.39	New So. Fed Svgs, Birmingham, AL (3)	4.37
5-YEAR C.D.'S	**4.75%**	**5-YEAR C.D.'S**	**4.78%**
MBNA America, Wilmington, DE (3)	5.91%	MBNA America, Wilmington, DE (3)	5.91%
Am Fed Svgs Bank, Rockville, MD (0)	5.75	Eastern Svgs Bank, Baltimore, MD (0)	5.54
Colonial Natl Bank, Wilmington, DE (3)	5.55	Cal. Thrift & Loan, Santa Barbara, CA (3)	5.41
Eastern Svgs Bank, Baltimore, MD (0)	5.54	Family Savings Bank ,L.A., CA (1)	5.25
Continental Svgs of Am, S.F., CA (0)	5.40	Chevy Chase Svgs, MD (0)	5.20

Rates in gray bands are national averages. Small savers yields, reported by 100 Highest Yields, are based upon account-opening minimums: jumbo rates are based upon $100,000 deposit and are not compounded. Effective yield is for first year. Figures in parentheses rate financial strength, on a scale of zero to three the strongest, as determined by Veribanc Inc. based on reports filed with regulators. A u indicates no rating, usually due to insufficient information. Rates as of Wednesday.

SOURCE: *The New York Times*, September 26, 1993, Sec. 3, 15. Copyright © 1993 by the New York Times Company. Reprinted by Permission.

Brokers usually act as intermediaries for bank and S&L certificates. They scour the country for institutions unable to raise the funds locally, purchase enormous blocks of certificates, and then resell them to the public in units as small as $1,000. Brokers also provide information about the issuing bank or thrift and its financial health.

Brokered CDs offer another advantage: liquidity. Should savers need to cash in their CD, they can do so without incurring the usual early withdrawal penalty. Because brokers make a secondary market in the CDs they offer, they are generally willing to buy them back. But savers should not assume that they will always receive full face value. If interest rates have risen since the certificate was issued, CD owners will take a loss. In such an event, the principal (or face value of the CD) will be reduced by an amount sufficient to make the yield (interest paid as a percentage of the CD's current price) competitive with rates on newly issued CDs.

Suppose you had $10,000 in brokered CDs yielding 6 percent and due to mature in one year. If you decided to sell after six months, when prevailing rates on comparable certificates had risen to 7 percent, you would lose one-half of 1 percent, or $50. This is less than the one to three months of interest penalty (of at least $100) that you would incur if you withdrew early from a $10,000 certificate at a bank. If interest rates have fallen, you may even sell at a profit.

But the biggest advantage of brokered CDs is the one-stop shopping convenience, especially for those who have a sizable amount to deposit. Savers can diversify their CDs with staggered maturities and different institutions and keep track of them all in one account.

Out-of-State Bank CDs A CD broker offers convenience by handling the paperwork. But if savers want to earn the most, they can do even better by dealing directly with a bank. If they do not mind giving up the convenience of dealing with a local institution, they can bypass brokers and bank by mail. Higher-yielding institutions are often in economically depressed areas, or fast-growing ones, and must offer above average rates to attract deposits. They actively solicit funds from out-of-state savers.

When savers realize that out-of-state banks offer substantially higher rates of interest, many put their money where their mailboxes are. The *Wall Street Journal* and the *New York Times* carry ads for obscure savings and loans in tiny far-flung towns. Therefore, although banks are still legally prohibited from having branches outside their home states, savers and borrowers are able to seek out banking bargains wherever they exist, by phone and mail. What draws customers to faraway banks are higher rates.

Savers can readily consult the Thursday or Friday business pages of daily newspapers, which often carry a listing of the highest yields around the country. The *Bank Rate Monitor* publishes a weekly list of the 100 highest yields for federally insured CDs nationwide. At least two other publications scan the market for the top yields and issue the changing results weekly (*100 Highest Yields*, Box 402508, Miami Beach, FL 33140, 800/327-7717 and *Savers Rate News*, Box 143520, Coral Gables, FL 33114).

In general, the smaller, more aggressive institutions feature the best rates. The highest-yielding CDs tend not to be in major money centers such as New York or San Francisco, because the larger banks there do not have to work as hard to attract savings. But depositors should not let high interest rates blind them to the risks. The more aggressive an out-of-state bank is, the greater the suspicion should be about its motives for offering such high rates. The bank may be making excessively risky loans or having a run on its local deposits and going outside to cover its costs. Savers who opt for long-distance investing need to ascertain that the institution is insured by the FDIC.

Automated Teller Machines (ATMs)

New technologies have radically changed the way Americans handle their money, and even more changes are on the way. Citibank pioneered the **automated teller machine (ATM)** concept in 1977, and now it is hard to find a bank of any size without them. ATMs now do most transactional business. They can give depositors 24-hour access to their checking and savings account and enable them to deposit checks and transfer funds between accounts without ever talking to a teller.

While an ATM cannot as yet open a new account or issue a car loan, in the next few years machines may very likely provide these services as well. These advanced ATMs will eliminate the need for many branch personnel. Some banks are currently experimenting with microbranches that have a number of ATMs but only a single bank employee to answer questions and perform special functions.

As automatic teller machines and regional ATM networks continue to grow, depositors are able to get to their account from more locations and from nearby states. Networks of interlinked systems such as CIRRUS, TYME, MAC, NYCE, and PLUS give depositors access to their home bank account from ATMs across the country. CIRRUS has about 33,000 ATMs and the network has been expanding worldwide. While you are vacationing in Wyoming, you can still have access to your account in Maine. Or if you are a student with a bank account near your college in Ohio, you can let your parents know when you are running low on funds so that they can deposit money into your account at their bank in California. You will be able to withdraw the money the next day if the banks are on the same network.

The ATM, plus the 800 telephone number and direct mail, is expected to transform interstate banking. The need for personal services and bank buildings will be sharply reduced. Customers will send checks through the mail and transact big-ticket financial business over the phone. (They may also use their home computers for these transactions, as we will see in Chapter 10.) Thus, the banks are less likely to pay fancy prices to buy local banks in other states, when that becomes legally possible. They will probably have offices in every locale but not on every street corner.

Financial Supermarkets

Do you still need your old bank? A bank used to be where you went if you wanted a checking account, a savings account, or a loan. A brokerage house was the place you went to for stocks and bonds. But now, in the new world of deregulation, bankers are trading stocks and brokers are making loans and accepting deposits. Nearly every institution that moved into the financial supermarket field wants to offer you everything from checking accounts to a full line of investing services. As banks expand the range of their services and move more aggressively into investments and insurance, and as regulators continue to interpret the laws separating banking and securities more liberally, consumers are becoming more accustomed to a separate area in their branch devoted solely to these kinds of products.

What makes the business so attractive is the sheer complexity of the financial lives of people with even a moderate income. Most have a checking and savings account as well as a money market fund. As home buyers, they require home insurance and mortgages, often large ones. Most people finance car purchases and cannot drive without insurance. There is clearly room for consolidation among these services.

The buzzword in financial services marketing these days is "life cycle." Ordinarily, consumers first buy banking, insurance, and credit card services, and then a home. Only as they age do they buy high-profit items such as stocks and bonds. Market research indicates that people do not like to change suppliers of financial products. Thus, catching consumers early is critical if a company wants to sell them a full line of financial products throughout their lives.

Dubbed "financial supermarkets," these giant money stores can consolidate a consumer's finances. An upper-middle-income American family, according to a survey, uses, on the average, 38 financial products as disparate as car insurance, stocks, and mortgages, sold by 20 different companies. **Financial supermarkets** are poised to offer one-stop shopping for every financial need, from savings and investing to insurance and mortgages.

In recent years, giant new financial institutions have been emerging, acquiring one another, and expanding the lines of products and services that they sell in one location. Sears is one of the pioneers in this field; the owner of Allstate Insurance is now a place to buy stocks as well as stockings, houses as well as housewares, since it acquired the Dean Witter brokerage firm and Coldwell Banker real estate. Kroger is selling frozen food in its store aisles as well as hot deals in mutual funds, annuities, and insurance.

Prudential-Bache Securities, BankAmerica, American Express, Citicorp, Merrill Lynch, Travelers, TransAmerica, Aetna, Security Pacific, and other financial supermarkets can already serve customers in most of the five major financial areas (banking, insurance, brokerage, investments, pensions), and they are all working to extend their reach and penetration. These financial conglomerates have come along much faster than expected because of profound changes in insurance, banking, and securities wrought by the interplay of high interest rates, technology, and deregulation in the early 1980s. Thus, the next decade promises many new developments in the business of financial services. A huge American industry, fragmented until now, is consolidating and entering a new age.

Even though savings and checking accounts are insured by the FDIC, investment and insurance products are not. Therefore, banks and financial supermarkets try to separate the two categories in their branches as much as possible to avoid some inevitable confusion. Moreover, federal and state laws and regulations require banks to establish distinct subsidiaries of affiliates for their brokerage activities. As a result, even though there may be one-stop shopping, customers must deal with different people in a different part of the bank when discussing deposits and loans, on the one hand, and stocks and insurance on the other.

Asset Management Accounts

An outgrowth of the financial supermarket is the **asset management** or **sweep account**. Banks are touting programs known as "sweep" or "central asset management" or "universal accounts" or "cash management services." This kind of automated money market checking account is offered nationwide by many banks and large supercompanies or brokerage firms.

Such single accounts pull together much of their financial business—stocks, bonds, checking, money market accounts, credit and debit cards—into one place, keeping track of everything on a single statement. There is no more dealing with shoe boxes full of scraps of paper. Asset management accounts also eliminate the delay between receiving dividends (or interest collected on investments or the proceeds from the sale of securities) and depositing them in the bank so that they can earn money right away.

On the cash management side, depositors can pay bills or write their own loan with a central asset account and dine out and get cash with the account's bank card. The bank covers the checks depositors write by transferring the exact amount from their money market balance to their checking account, leaving the rest to earn interest, dividends, or capital gains. Depositors can have paychecks deposited automatically into the account and bills paid the same way.

On the investment side, depositors can use the bank's facilities not only to trade securities at discounted rates but also for financial planning, management of real estate investments, and trust and estate planning. Uninvested cash is automatically swept into the money market fund of the depositor's choice.

The Sweeping Process Sweep accounts function like standard checking accounts, except that all balances above a minimum level needed to compensate the bank for its services are automatically invested by the bank for the depositor's benefit. Instead of sitting idle, funds earn interest until they are released to cover checks written on the account. Because the sweep is made daily after all checks have been processed against the account, the money is invested whenever it can earn money for the account holder, even overnight and on weekends. The cash earns interest from the minute the depositor gets it until the day it is withdrawn.

Some asset management accounts offer a daily sweep of accumulated funds only when they reach $1,000; then the entire amount is swept. Amounts less than that are swept weekly. Others sweep every idle dollar every day. There are other differences as well. Some universal accounts return canceled checks, and others merely list check transactions on the monthly statement.

The account's monthly statements give the account holder an overview of his or her finances, including the number and the amount of checks written, details of each month's securities transactions, dividends paid in stocks held on the money market fund, and charges on the debit or credit card. A well-structured statement will give you a monthly snapshot of your financial situation. Sweeps can be tied in with debit or credit cards, personal credit lines, and discount brokerage services.

The sweep feature offered as a cash management service by many banks is attractive because it shifts responsibility for investment from the account owner to the bank. Account holders do not have to remember to invest the money. It is all done by the bank's computers, which ensure that their customer's money is at all times in relatively high yielding investments.

Are These Accounts for You? While investors can, of course, open checking and money market accounts on their own, arrange for brokerage services, and get a credit card from their bank, all for substantially less than the asset management account fee, the universal account saves time and energy, which are worth money. The accounts are not recommended if you do not need to consolidate a portfolio of securities. But if you have, say, at least $25,000 in money market funds, savings accounts, stocks, mutual funds, or bonds and are tired of waiting in bank lines to cash dividend and interest checks, you may be a prime candidate for a central asset account.

The overriding question that investors must answer before opening a universal account is whether it is worth its price. Most of these accounts charge annual fees of $50 to $100. Minimum deposits in cash and securities range from $5,000 to $25,000. Asset management accounts have not yet gained widespread acceptance among the average consumer, but are likely to do so in the future.

Debit Cards

Like all industries, banks are cutting costs. A primary villain in their cost structure is the blizzard of paper, from deposit slips and withdrawal and transfer forms to checks. Americans write 40 billion checks a year, and the number is rising.

One weapon in the bank's battle against paper is the local and national **debit card** (also known as a *cash card*), which immediately deducts money from consumers' checking accounts when they make a purchase. Merchants accepting debit cards thus receive immediate payment with consumers' funds, and consumers do not receive monthly bills. Banks have already laid the groundwork for debit cards by issuing more than 191 million plastic cards for use at automated teller machines. These cards also act as debit cards at a small but growing number of businesses.

The card you put into a bank's automated teller machine (ATM) is actually a debit card. It "debits" (withdraws) money from your account. When you use it to buy goods, it becomes a retail card, a sort of electronic check that allows you to use cash instead of credit. This system is the next generation of plastic competing for space in American wallets. It is currently taking its place next to checks, cash, and credit cards as an accepted form of payment. During the early 1990s, VISA's Interlink and MasterCard's Maestro debit clearing networks were fighting a heated battle to sign up banks to issue their debit cards. (Credit cards are discussed in Chapter 3.) Banks and S&Ls now form networks to share ATMs in a state or region, or nationwide. This gives flexibility and avoids branching and interstate banking restrictions.

A debit card requires that all purchases and sales of goods and services be processed by **point-of-sale (POS)** terminals connected on line with a bank's computer. Payments for goods and services are made at the checkout counter by debiting the buyer's bank account and crediting the seller's. A gasoline station is an example of how a POS works. First, the customer inserts the ATM card into a terminal near the pumps and punches in his or her personal identification number (PIN). That connects the customer with the bank, verifies that he or she has enough money in a checking or savings account to cover the transaction, and authorizes the customer to use one of the pumps connected to the system. When the customer finishes pumping the gas, the purchase is debited from his or her bank account and the machine delivers a receipt to remind the customer to enter the withdrawal in a checkbook. No attendant is necessary; the customer can buy gasoline even after the station closes for the night, or even if the gas station is thousands of miles away from the bank.

A point-of-sale transaction is similar to using cash. But if you are short of cash, a debit card can see you through a place that does not take credit cards or personal checks, such as gas stations and fast food restaurants.

As a method of payment, the debit card still has some disadvantages. The retailer's gain is the consumer's loss because consumers cannot earn interest on the float while a check is clearing. Neither can a consumer postdate a check. The money has to be there when the consumer makes the purchase. Debit cards may look and imprint like credit cards, but there is a big difference. The true credit card works like a loan, an interest-free loan if you pay the creditor back fast enough, usually within 30 days. But the debit card works like an electronic check, written against your bank balance, that clears instantly. There are no interest charges because you get no credit.

There is an additional crucial difference between a credit card and a debit card. With a credit card consumers get bills that they either pay or do not pay if they have a disagreement with the issuer. With a debit card, however, the moment the purchase is made, the money disappears from the consumer's bank account. If there is an error, that money has to be reinstated into the consumer's account. Another disadvantage concerns liability for bogus charges if a card is lost or stolen. Debit card liability may run as high as $500 and, in rare cases, the full amount charged to the card holder's bank account. So treat your debit card as cash, not plastic. Since debit cards offer fewer advantages to consumers than credit cards, their growth and acceptance has been sluggish. Most cash card systems are sponsored by banks that limit use of their cards to participating stores in a single state or a handful of adjacent states. A true national system awaits a major marketing campaign by the two big bank-card organizations, VISA and MasterCard. They have already issued a joint cash card called "Entree." If it becomes widespread and universally accepted, then it may eventually replace cash.

Deposit Insurance

One thing that worries depositors is the safety of the bank. We have all seen headlines and heard news coverage concerning closures, defaults, and losses at S&Ls and other banks. How safe is your deposit? How much of a risk are you taking by depositing that money? What would happen if the bank should default?

Federal deposit insurance is a legacy of the New Deal and the Great Depression. It was instituted to prevent the contagion of bank runs by protecting the small depositors, restoring stability and public confidence at the grass roots level. The government's goal was to bolster confidence in banks and prevent runs that often led to bank failure and financial panic. The Glass-Steagall Act of 1933 established the **Federal Deposit Insurance Corporation (FDIC)**, which insures deposits at 98 percent of the nation's commercial banks and savings and loans. The FDIC was to amass billions of dollars in reserves to protect depositors. These funds were to come from premiums paid by member banks. A year later, the **Federal Savings and Loan Insurance Corporation (FSLIC)** was set up to do the same for those institutions. As of 1980, both guaranteed up to $100,000 per account in nearly 15,000 commercial and savings banks. The **Financial Institution Reform, Recovery and Enforcement Act of 1989 (FIRREA)**, a law enacted by the U.S. Congress, effectively abolished the FSLIC and transferred its responsibilities to the FDIC. The Savings Association Insurance Fund, with the optimistic-sounding acronym SAIF, was also created. It replaced the FSLIC and is administered by the FDIC, which previously insured only commercial banks. Separate insurance funds have been established for the S&Ls (under SAIF) and commercial banks (under BIF, the new Bank Insurance Fund). By keeping the two funds separate, the FDIC hopes to insulate the commercial banks from the S&L problems. Although the bureaucracy has changed, the government's promise remains the same. The FDIC insures deposits and any interest due up to $100,000. About 93 percent of the nation's credit unions are insured by **NCUSIF,** the **National Credit Union Share Insurance Fund,** set up by Congress in 1970 and backed by the U.S. Treasury. Like federal depositors' insurance at other financial institutions, the fund protects accounts for up to $100,000.

The FDIC has a mandate to maintain confidence in the commercial banking system and to provide stability through its regulatory and insurance functions. In addition, it is empowered to preserve that confidence and stability through the quick and efficient resolution of bank failures.

The S&L Crisis

At first glance, the banking system does not appear to be too sound. Bank failures reached a postdepression high in the mid-1980s. As shown in Table 2–1, from 1986 to 1992 more than 1,140 banks failed. The FDIC fund, which stood at $18.3 billion in 1986, has been battered by these failures, costing it more than $26 billion. Consequently, in 1991 the FDIC had a deficit of $7 billion and was compelled to borrow from the Treasury. Giant as well as small banks are tottering as a result of huge interest rate swings, enormous loan defaults, and hypercompetitive pressures accompanying deregulation. In 1991 the Bank of New England, a $22 billion asset commercial bank, went bankrupt and was seized by the FDIC. It was the third largest bank failure in U.S. history.

While the problems in commercial banking are serious, the situation in the savings and loan industry is critical. Historically, S&Ls attracted deposits by offering interest rates on savings accounts that were higher than those permitted in commer-

TABLE 2–1	A Decade of Failures

The Number of Banks Closed Because of Financial Difficulty in the Last 10 Years.

Year	Number
1981	10
1982	42
1983	48
1984	79
1985	120
1986	138
1987	184
1988	200
1989	206
1990	169
1991	124
1992	120 (estimated)

SOURCE: Federal Deposit Insurance Corporation.

cial banks. S&Ls typically paid 5.5 percent interest while commercial banks paid 5 percent on savings accounts and no interest on checking accounts. This interest rate advantage ensured S&Ls of a stable pool of savings that could be used for mortgage lending. Deregulation of the banking industry weakened the competitive position of S&Ls. It eliminated interest rate ceilings on commercial banks and permitted all types of banks to provide essentially identical services. The result was that S&Ls had to compete more aggressively for a pool of savings. This meant paying higher interest rates to attract deposits and offsetting those higher costs by making riskier loans.

Fraudulent, mismanaged, or unlucky institutions have lost more than $500 billion of our deposits and interest, or $5,000 for every American household. After simmering for five years as a financial crisis, the S&L problem intensified as a political issue in 1990 when President Bush's own son, Neil, was implicated in the fraudulent mismanagement of a failed S&L in Colorado.

A wary depositor might contemplate shopping around among banks, hoping to monitor their soundness. Unfortunately, that has proved difficult even for experts and bank regulators because outsiders rarely have access to a bank's loan portfolio. In recent years, a new service was formed for depositors who want to verify the financial soundness of a bank. The Veribanc Corp., P.O. Box 461, Wakefield, MA 01880, offers consumers a safety rating on most banks. For a safety rating, consumers can call Veribanc at 800/442-2657. It costs $10 (charged to a VISA or MasterCard) plus $5 for each additional bank or S&L you ask about in the same phone call.

The State of Our Banking System: It's Bad but Not All That Bad

Despite all the buffeting, there is no need to rush to your bank with a shopping bag to withdraw every cent you have on deposit. The banking system is not about to collapse. If we are going to lose money because of banks' financial problems, it will not be as depositors but as taxpayers, since the government will have to help the FDIC bail out many collapsing banks. The news of bank troubles must be viewed in its proper context. There are about 15,000 banks, 3,150 S&Ls, and 18,300 credit unions. About 15 percent of the banks may have some financial troubles, but the other 85 percent are financially healthy. We must distinguish between the disappearance of some percentage of thrifts and commercial banks and the collapse of our monetary system in general. Most of the troubled banks are concentrated in the energy and agricultural states—Texas, Louisiana, Oklahoma, Florida, California, and Illinois. In fact, the vast majority of the more than 600 banks shut down or bailed out by the FDIC between 1981 and 1988, at a cost of nearly $10 billion, were located west of the Mississippi, mainly in Texas and California, where state thrift regulations were loose and local economies had booms and severe recessions.

Despite years of expansion during the 1980s by the U.S. economy as a whole, many banks and savings and loan associations were racked by troubles in the farm belt, depressed conditions in the oil patch, and unwise real estate ventures all over the country. As mentioned, many of the industry's problems can be traced to the early 1980s when both state and federal regulation was reduced and savings institutions were permitted to enter a broad array of new businesses. Hoping to benefit from the Texas oil boom, many institutions began lending heavily and almost indiscriminately to high-risk businesses, particularly real estate ventures, in the hope of making huge profits. Many Texas thrift owners pumped money into energy ventures in 1983, when oil sold for $29 per barrel, only to see their collateral collapse in value when oil prices plummeted below $10 in 1986.

When the economy declined in the Southwest, savings and loan institutions found themselves saddled with billions of dollars in loans for real estate that was worth only a fraction of the loans. In addition, failing loans to foreign borrowers, mainly in Latin America, threatened even greater losses. The weakest institutions are in such bad shape that they threaten to exhaust the multibillion dollar government insurance funds that protect depositors. If that happens, taxpayers again will have to come to the rescue.

But How Safe Is the FDIC?   Obviously, if every bank failed at the same time, the FDIC could not pay off all the depositors. Depositors therefore should not look to FDIC insurance alone to protect their deposits. FDIC insurance may be considered as an additional safety net. Deposit insurance is not intended to match every dollar on deposit with a dollar of insurance. It is there in case of a crisis. No insurance in the world can cover every deposit. Although the number of bank failures broke recent records in 1982, 1983, 1987, 1988, and 1990, the FDIC still managed to pay off depositors of the failed thrifts and banks. However, the FDIC became increasingly threatened with illiquidity.

President Bush signed into law the Financial Institutions Reform, Recovery, and Enforcement Act (FIRREA) on August 9, 1989, the most important legislation to affect savings institutions in 55 years. Under this legislation, taxpayers and S&Ls would share the cost of salvaging the S&L industry. By 1991 the administration had already spent $80 billion on the bailout, not counting temporary borrowing and interest costs. This law, better known as the Thrift Bailout Bill, is estimated to cost as much as $500 billion during the next 40 years. The new law reorganizes and enlarges government regulation of the S&Ls, provides funds for bailing out failed S&Ls, and seeks to restore confidence in the thrift industry.

A new bailout agency known as the Resolution Trust Corporation (RTC) was given responsibility for dealing with savings institutions placed in receivership, including the sale of $300 billion of real estate owned by failed institutions. The RTC is additionally borrowing money. It sold $45 billion in bonds in 1990 alone and is scheduled to issue much more in years to come. Over these bonds' 40-year life, taxpayers will have to pay the interest on them. The RTC has grown into one of the biggest financial institutions in the country and the largest seller of real estate.

Both commercial banks and thrift institutions are facing higher insurance premiums to offset the program's cost. New capital requirements mandated by FIRREA are designed to provide a cushion of private investment to fortify thrifts against problem loans. Many thrifts will not be able to meet these new standards and it is estimated that as many as two-thirds of the country's 2,900 thrift institutions may ultimately be shut down or merged. The thrift industry will forfeit to commercial banks its dominant share in mortgage lending.

You Can Bank On Federal Deposit Insurances   The ultimate soundness of FDIC insurance rests on the U.S. Treasury. Congress has passed resolutions stating that the full faith and credit of the United States will stand behind deposit insurance. The deposit insurance agencies can borrow from the Treasury in the event of an emergency. In addition, Congress reaffirmed, in 1982, the federal government's commitment to back up these agencies by acting as the insurer of last resort, meaning that it would pay off deposits up to $100,000 per account should the agencies' funds be exhausted. There are currently proposals in Congress to limit deposit insurance to $100,000 per person.

Before investigating savings rates anywhere, you should determine what premium you place on the safety of your cash. Friendly service is no substitute for insurance on your deposit. Whether you have $100 in your account, the maximum amount of $100,000, or something in between, you want to be certain that your deposit is insured. If you do not have federal protection, you may be taking an unnecessary risk. You may be getting a higher rate on your savings, but there is always the chance you could end up with nothing.

All forms of deposits are insured, from checking accounts to bank money market funds to certificates of deposit. The vast majority of America's banks, S&Ls, and credit unions are federally insured. Each institution displays a sign declaring its membership in either BIF, SAIF, or NCUSIF. All SAIF–insured S&Ls are required by law to display a sticker of an American eagle surrounded by the words "backed by the full faith and credit of the United States Government." Some even print these words right on the front door or front cover of your passbook. If they have it, they usually flaunt it. If you do not see such a sign, make sure to ask if deposits are insured.

About 900 banks and S&Ls are not federally insured, most notably some Maryland S&Ls and Massachusetts savings banks. These institutions, which usually decline federal insurance because of the red tape that comes with it, often insure themselves by pooling money in a fund. Like federal deposit insurance, such insurance funds typically cover depositors up to $100,000. Obviously, this insurance is not as strong and as safe as federal insurance.

If Your Bank Fails   If your insured bank or S&L were to fail, at worst, you would not have access to your funds for a week and would have to forfeit the interest payments during that period. Savers with amounts that exceed the $100,000 insurance limit may recover only part of their money, depending on how regulators handle the failure.

"Good Morning. Thank you for calling whatever the name of this savings and loan is today."

SOURCE: "Pepper…and Salt," *The Wall Street Journal,* October 22, 1990, A-15. Reprinted by permission of Cartoon Features Syndicate.

Strangely enough, if your bank or S&L fails, you might not know it at first. Often, instead of closing a troubled bank and paying off depositors, the FDIC may choose to merge the bank with a healthy one. Between 1934 and February 1989, the FSLIC closed (rather than merged) only 112 institutions, triggering deposit insurance in the process. In most cases, the FDIC arranged a takeover for an insolvent bank, and the new bank opened on the same spot. The FDIC sold all the deposits of the failed institution to a healthy institution and service to customers was uninterrupted. Typically, the defunct bank or S&L would close Friday evening and reopen Monday morning under new ownership. Insured accounts were transferred intact to the new institution. It was like marrying off a poor person to a wealthy spouse at a shotgun wedding. The FDIC often gave the acquiring bank a dowry of an undisclosed infusion of cash.

If another institution took over the closed bank or thrift, all deposits would be transferred to the new institution and no one would lose any of their principal or interest. But if a marriage partner could not be found regulators would pay depositors up to the federally insured limit of $100,000, or transfer them to another institution. In that case, uninsured depositors would usually have to wait to recover part of their funds as the FDIC liquidated the institution's assets.

Depositors may be further impacted by a failure of an insured bank by suffering a reduction of interest. The FDIC guarantees deposits, not the interest rate being paid on them. Thus, CD holders may find their high-yielding 10 percent certificate suddenly earning only 5 percent if their accounts are transferred to another institution by the FDIC. The new institution could simply renege on the interest rate commitment given to CD owners by the defunct bank.

In December 1991 President Bush signed new banking legislation into law known as the **Federal Deposit Insurance Corporation Improvement Act (FDICIA)**. This law requires the FDIC to shut down insolvent banks at the lowest possible cost. This actually increases your chances of losing money in a failed bank or S&L. Rather than transferring both insured and uninsured deposits to another institution as the FDIC did in the past, the agency will now increasingly transfer only the insured deposits up to a $100,000 limit. That means that individuals with more than $100,000 in a failed bank are likely to suffer losses. In 1992 about 50 percent of bank failures resulted in loss to uninsured depositors, up from about 15 percent in previous years. An uninsured depositor typically can lose 15 to 20 cents on the dollar, but sometimes as much as 50 cents on the dollar when a bank closes. The amount of the loss depends upon how much the FDIC can recover by selling assets of the failed bank. The purpose of FDICIA is twofold—to provide funding for Federal Deposit Insurance and to reduce taxpayers' exposure to losses when depository institutions fail.

Too Big to Fail   The banking law passed in 1991 makes it more difficult for regulators to decide that a bank is "too big to fail" because of its importance to the economy. However, the big banks are still likely to offer extra protection to businesses and institutions that cannot avoid deposits over $100,000 or to foreign depositors. That is because regulators still have the power after special reviews and approvals to rescue a big bank on the grounds that its failure could create a chain reaction which might collapse the financial system. Thus, one additional safeguard for individuals is to place their money in the nation's biggest banks.

What If You Have More Than $100,000?   The first step you should take to safeguard your deposits is to verify that your accounts are insured in full. The basic unit of deposit insurance provided by the FDIC's Bank Insurance Fund (BIF) or Savings Association Insurance Fund (SAIF) is $100,000 per person at any one bank or S&L. That means all checking accounts, savings accounts, and CDs held by an individual at one bank (including all its branches) are lumped together for $100,000 of coverage.

Among the banking customers who must make some decisions are those with more than $100,000 to put in the bank. These depositors have a number of ways to keep their money safe. Perhaps the simplest form of protection for people with more than $100,000 to deposit is to open accounts at several different banks, each with a balance of no more than $100,000. In reality, you should limit your deposit to about $90,000 per account per institution since the federal insurance ceiling applies to both principal and interest. Interest earnings that swell your account balance above $100,000 would not automatically be protected in the event of a bank failure.

For those who prefer to stick with one bank, there are several tactics. You can get more than $100,000 in coverage from the same institution through certain combinations of accounts. By setting up different accounts in the names of different family members, a family could have substantially more than $100,000 in fully insured funds in a single institution. The limit applies, in the words of the law, to all accounts owned by an individual "in the same capacity and the same rights." In effect, depositors can get more than $100,000 of insurance by opening different accounts "in different capacities and rights" in the same bank. For example, a married couple, or any two or more persons, could stretch their coverage to $500,000 in one bank if they maintain a joint checking account, separate checking accounts, and separate accounts in trust for each other. However, all of a couple's joint accounts at the same bank are considered as one. For instance, if a husband and wife have two joint accounts in the same bank, one with his name preceding hers and one with her name preceding his, they are not both insured up to $100,000 by the FDIC.

Also, funds in other types of bank accounts, such as IRAs and Keoghs, are insured separately when held by the bank in a trust or custodial capacity, up to a maximum coverage of $100,000 per account. Each depositor, therefore, can have at least two fully insured accounts, one for ordinary deposits and the other for an IRA.

Changes in your life might affect your FDIC coverage. For instance, death or

Jointly Insured

On joint accounts owned by different combinations of individuals, the insurance works this way: Assume that there are two joint accounts, one owned by husband Harry and wife Beatrice with a balance of $110,000 and another owned by husband Harry and daughter Sue with a balance of $70,000. The $110,000 account is insured up to $100,000 ($50,000 for each owner), leaving $10,000 uninsured. The $70,000 in the other account is prorated ($35,000 each between Harry and Sue). Thus, Harry has an insurable interest totaling $85,000 in both accounts, while his wife Beatrice and daughter Sue have insurable interests of $50,000 and $35,000, respectively.

Insured Banks Offer Uninsured Products

Insured banks may offer uninsured products and need not indicate which products are insured and which are not.

Banking Products Which are Typically Insured	Banking Products Which are *Not* Typically Insured
1. Checking accounts	1. Annuities
2. Savings accounts	2. Mutual funds
3. NOW accounts	3. Life insurance
4. Christmas club accounts	4. Corporate securities (stocks & bonds)
5. Certificates of deposit	5. Treasury bills, bonds, and notes
6. Money market deposit accounts	6. Commercial paper
7. Trust fund accounts	7. Shares of bank stock

(These various financial instruments will be defined and discussed in following chapters.)

divorce could convert your joint account to an individual account and put you over the $100,000 limit. Savers will also have to reevaluate their protection if and when Congress changes deposit insurance rules.

Changes in you life might affect your FDIC coverage. For instance, death or divorce could convert your joint account to an individual account and put you over the $100,000 limit. Savers will also have to reevaluate their protection if and when Congress changes deposit insurance rules.

Consumer Complaints As directed by Congress, the FDIC has established a division of consumer affairs to receive and take appropriate action upon complaints with respect to unfair and deceptive practices by banks. This office has jurisdiction over all federally insured banks and will enforce compliance with regulations defining such unfair or deceptive acts or practices. Depositors who have a complaint and have been unable to resolve the problem directly with the bank involved should phone the FDIC consumer hot line 800/934-3342 or write to the following address: Office of Bank Customer Affairs, Federal Deposit Insurance Corporation, Washington, DC 20429.

Totten Trusts Individuals may also open trust accounts that are considered separately for insurance purposes. **Totten trusts** are one such example. They are easy to open. The depositor merely asks his or her bank to open the trust in favor of a spouse, a son or daughter, or a grandchild, the only beneficiaries eligible. No lawyers are required. Once the account is open, the individual who established it can use it as an ordinary bank account, the only difference being that when the depositor dies, the balance of the account goes to the person named as beneficiary. Each trust is insured up to the $100,000 limit.

Understanding Interest

Now that you have decided to place your savings in a safe FDIC–member bank, should you choose the one with a money market account that pays 7.75 percent interest compounded daily or the one that promises an 8 percent annual yield? Which is better, a certificate of deposit offering 6.5 percent compounded daily on a 360-day basis or one that uses a 365-day basis?

As you may remember from high school, the account paying 7.75 percent is superior because daily compounding produces an annual yield of 8.17 percent. When the interest on a CD is calculated on a 360-day basis, this generally means that you will receive 1/360 of the annual percentage rate daily, which is greater than receiving 1/365 of the annual rate daily.

"Interest" is the money that financial institutions, state and federal governments, businesses, and individuals pay you for the use of your money. The amount of interest offered is generally expressed as a percentage figure called "annual interest rate." This figure tells you that your annual interest rate will be equal to a certain percentage of your balance. There are numerous ways to calculate interest. Methods of compounding and rules for rounding off vary from bank to bank.

To understand how to calculate interest, we need a firm grasp of such concepts as the time value of money, future and present value, and simple and compounded interest.

Time Value of Money

The **time value of money** involves calculating the feasibility of paying or receiving sums of money over future periods of time. It consists of two major elements: future value and present value. **Future value,** the result of *compounding,* is the amount to which a current sum will increase at a specified future date based on a certain interest rate. **Present value** is the current value of a future sum based on a certain interest rate and period of time.

Both future value and present value computations are based on basic interest rate calculations. The future values of different investments are essential to many financial decisions. Most financial planning illustrations use the compound method of interest calculation.

Simple and Compounded

Your bank can use either a simple or a compounded method to calculate interest. **Simple interest** is computed on your deposit balance. It is the annual percentage rate, without any compounding. Simple interest assumes that interest earned in each period is withdrawn, not reinvested. The formula used to calculate simple interest is

$$\text{Simple Interest} = \text{Principal} \times \text{Rate of Interest} \times \text{Time}$$

or

$$SI = P \times r \times t.$$

Using this formula we can calculate simple interest on a $10,000 deposit earning 8 percent annual interest over four years as ($10,000) × (0.08) × 4 = $3,200.

Compound interest is computed on your balance, plus any interest you are paid and leave in your account. In other words, you earn interest on your previously earned interest as well as on your original deposits. Invest $100 at 10 percent compounded annually and at the end of the first year, you have $110 ($100 plus $10). That $110 earns interest the second year. You end the second year with $121 ($110 plus $11), and so on. By contrast, with simple interest you earn only on your original investment. Thus, you end year 1 with $110, year 2 with $120 and so forth, adding just $10 each year. Compounding increases the interest you earn, and therefore you should know if interest is compounded and how often.

For example, a balance of $10,000 earning 5.25 percent simple interest will give you an annual yield of $525. A balance of $10,000 earning 5.25 percent interest compounded daily will earn a yield of 5.47 percent, or $547, over the course of a year. **Yield** is the actual interest your account will earn. It is defined as the annual return on an investment calculated as a percentage of its current price. When choosing an investment or bank account, be aware of how the interest is computed. Although the difference in this example is not astounding, over many years or when you are investing larger sums, the difference can become substantial.

Table 2–2, provides an example of a **future value table.** This table illustrates the future value of an investment, such as a CD, if the earnings are permitted to accumulate and earn interest compounded annually over the years. It shows the future value of $1 invested for a specified number of periods and at a specified interest rate each period. To use the table, simply multiply the future value of $1 by the number of dollars you intend to invest. For example, the future value of $1 (principal plus accumulated interest) invested at 9 percent over 10 years will be $2.367. This means that every dollar invested at 9 percent will be worth $2.36. A $10,000 CD invested at 9 percent will therefore be worth $23,670.

See if you can follow the chart on your own. How much will $10,000 invested at 10 percent annual compounded interest be worth after 12 years? Look at the chart under 10 percent and you will find that the future value factor of $1 (principal plus accumulated interest) at 12 years is $3.138. This means that every dollar will be worth $3.13, or a $10,000 CD will be worth $31,380. A more complete future value table appears as an appendix at the end of your book.

Future value or compound interest can also be calculated by means of the following future value formula:

$$FV = P \times (1 + r)^t$$

FV is the future value amount you will have at the end of a certain amount of time. *P* is the beginning amount, or principal. The interest rate is *r* and the number of time periods for computing is the exponent *t*. An exponent tells you how many times to multiply a number times itself. Thus,

$$2^3 = 2 \times 2 \times 2$$

The effects of compound interest are considerations which are of prime importance to most financial decisions. The compound interest formula is the basis for future value as well as present value calculations of all types.

TABLE 2–2	Yearly Compound Interest Rate (Future Value)

Future Value of $1—Principal Plus Accumulated Interest Compounded Annually

FUTURE

Number of Years	4.00%	5.00%	6.00%	7.00%	8.00%	9.00%	10.00%	12.00%
1	1.040	1.050	1.060	1.070	1.080	1.090	1.100	1.120
2	1.082	1.103	1.124	1.145	1.166	1.188	1.210	1.254
3	1.125	1.158	1.191	1.225	1.260	1.295	1.331	1.405
4	1.170	1.216	1.262	1.311	1.360	1.412	1.464	1.574
5	1.217	1.276	1.338	1.403	1.469	1.539	1.611	1.762
6	1.265	1.340	1.419	1.501	1.587	1.677	1.772	1.974
7	1.316	1.407	1.504	1.606	1.714	1.828	1.949	2.211
8	1.369	1.477	1.594	1.718	1.851	1.993	2.144	2.476
9	1.423	1.551	1.689	1.838	1.999	2.172	2.358	2.773
10	1.480	1.629	1.791	1.967	2.159	2.367	2.594	3.106
11	1.539	1.710	1.898	2.105	2.332	2.580	2.853	3.479
12	1.601	1.796	2.012	2.252	2.518	2.813	3.138	3.896
14	1.732	1.980	2.261	2.579	2.937	3.342	3.797	4.887
16	1.873	2.183	2.540	2.952	3.426	3.970	4.595	6.130
18	2.026	2.407	2.854	3.380	3.996	4.717	5.560	7.690
20	2.191	2.653	3.207	3.870	4.661	5.604	6.727	9.646
22	2.370	2.925	3.604	4.430	5.437	6.659	8.140	12.100
24	2.563	3.225	4.049	5.072	6.341	7.911	9.850	15.179
26	2.772	3.556	4.549	5.807	7.396	9.399	11.918	19.040
28	2.999	3.920	5.112	6.649	8.627	11.167	14.421	23.884
30	3.243	4.322	5.743	7.612	10.063	13.268	17.449	29.960

Note: For a more complete future value table on amounts compounded annually, see Appendix A.

Using our example above, assume that you invest $10,000 in a 10-year certificate of deposit that pays 9 percent interest compounded annually. Because 9 percent can also be written as 0.09, the formula looks like this:

$$FV = \$10,000 \times (1 + 0.09)^{10}$$

Using a calculator, we find that 1.09^{10} equals 2.367. Because $FV = \$10,000 \times 2.367$, we find that the above $10,000 investment will grow to $23,670 over the course of 10 years.

If the 9 percent interest were compounded monthly instead of annually, the r in this example would be 0.09 divided by 12, or 0.0075, and the t would be 10 multiplied by 12, or 120. Our formula would look like this

$$FV = \$10,000 \times (1 + .0075)^{120}$$

or

$$\$24,510 = \$1,000 \times (0.0075)^{120}$$

We can also find the answer to the above problem by using Table 2–3. If we look at the 9 percent column, we find the future value factor for 120 months to be 2.451. If we multiply $10,000 by our future value factor of 2.451, we derive $24,510.

This shows that monthly compounding results in $843 more over 10 years than annual compounding.

The above formula is built into financial calculators. But compound interest can easily be calculated by using the above formula in conjunction with any calculator that figures exponents. Compound interest can therefore be calculated either by use of tables such as Table 2–2 or by the above formula.

Present Value

Present value is the inverse of future value. Rather than calculating the value of a present amount of money at some future date, present value is concerned with finding the current value of a future sum. It determines the current monetary value of a sum of money that will be available at some future date. It is defined as the number of dollars that must be invested today at a specified rate of return to increase to an anticipated dollar amount at a specified future date.

Suppose you are offered an investment that will pay you $1,000 five years from today. If you could earn 8 percent on other investments, how much is the above investment worth to you now?

The following formula can be used to derive your answer:

$$PV = \frac{FV}{(1+i)^t}$$

(PV = present value; FV = future value; i = interest, and t = the number time periods before the cash is to be received.)

TABLE 2–3	Monthly Compound Interest Rate (Future Value)							
Future Value of $1—Principal Plus Accumulated Interests Compounded Monthly								
Number of Months	4.00%	5.00%	6.00%	7.00%	8.00%	9.00%	10.00%	12.00%
12	1.041	1.051	1.062	1.072	1.083	1.094	1.105	1.127
24	1.083	1.105	1.127	1.150	1.173	1.196	1.220	1.270
36	1.127	1.161	1.197	1.233	1.270	1.309	1.348	1.431
48	1.173	1.221	1.270	1.322	1.376	1.431	1.489	1.612
60	1.221	1.283	1.349	1.418	1.490	1.566	1.645	1.817
84	1.323	1.418	1.520	1.630	1.747	1.873	2.008	2.307
120	1.491	1.647	1.819	2.010	2.220	2.451	2.707	3.300
240	2.223	2.713	3.310	4.039	4.927	6.009	7.328	10.893
360	3.313	4.468	6.023	8.116	10.936	14.731	19.837	35.950

Note: For a more complete future value table on amounts compounded monthly, see Appendix B.

Future Value of a Single Amount

Suppose you are offered a $10,000 investment that will return you $13,500 in principal and interest at the end of five years. Is that an attractive investment if you think you could earn 9 percent annual interest on a competing investment? To answer the question, we must calculate the future value of $10,000 invested elsewhere. To do this we can use Table 2–2. We find that a 9 percent investment over five years compounded will have a multiplier factor of 1.539. If we multiply $10,000 × 1.539, we get $15,390. This is the future value of $10,000 invested at 9 percent compounded over five years. In this light our investment offer above which promises a future value of $13,500 on a $10,000 investment is hardly attractive.

We could have obtained the same results by using the formula

$$FV = P \times (1 + r)^{t64}$$

Substituting, we get $15,390 = $10,000 × (1 + .09)^5.

CASE 1

Peter Johnson deposits $1,000 in an account paying 4 percent interest per year compounded annually. What is the future value of his account and the interest earned after five years?

Answer: Here P = $1,000; r = 4%; and t = 5; thus

$$
\begin{aligned}
\text{Future Value} &= \$1,000 \times (1\,1\,0.04)^5 \\
&= \$1,000 \times 1.045 \\
&= \$1,000 \times 1.04 \times 1.04 \times 1.04 \times 1.04 \times 1.04 \\
&= \$1,216.65
\end{aligned}
$$

$$
\begin{aligned}
\text{Interest earned} &= \$1,216.65 - \$1,000 \\
&= \$216.65
\end{aligned}
$$

CASE 2

Linda Taylor deposits $2,500 in an account paying 3 percent interest annually compounded monthly (12 times yearly). What is the future value of her investment after five years?

Answer: The compounding is done monthly. Therefore, the interest rate must be a monthly rate. A 3 percent annual interest rate is equivalent to an interest rate of 3 percent divided by 12, or 0.25 percent monthly. Two years are equivalent to 24 monthly periods. Therefore, r = .025 percent and t = 24.

$$
\begin{aligned}
\text{Future Value} &= \$2,500 \times (1 + .25)^{24} \\
&= \$2,500 \times (1.25)^{24} \\
&= \$2,655
\end{aligned}
$$

We can obtain the same answer by using Table 2–2. We find that a 3 percent investment over 24 months compounded will have a multiplier factor of 1.062. If we multiply $2,500 by 1.062, we get $2,655.

Therefore, solving the equation for *PV*, we get:

$$PV = \frac{\$1,000}{(1 + .08)^5} = \frac{\$1,000}{1.4693} = \$680.59$$

We can also find the answer to this problem by using Table 2–4, Annual Present Value Factors. Look at the 8 percent interest column on the table. You will find that the PVF (present value factor) for five years is .681. Multiply $1,000 by .681 and you get $681.

If the time element in the above problem was stated in terms of months rather than years, we would use Table 2–5 to find the PVF for a given number of months.

The above formula or table can also be used if you want a certain amount of money in the future and need to know how much must be invested now so that you will have that amount in the future. The amount which must be invested now is called the *present value*. The amount needed in the future is the future value. The basic issue of present value boils down to the question, How much would you have

TABLE 2–4	Annual Present Value Factors							

PRESENT

Present Value of $1 Received at the End of Each Period for a Given Number of Years

Number of Years	4.00%	5.00%	6.00%	7.00%	8.00%	9.00%	10.00%	12.00%
1	0.962	0.952	0.943	0.935	0.926	0.917	0.909	0.893
2	0.925	0.907	0.890	0.873	0.857	0.842	0.826	0.797
3	0.889	0.864	0.840	0.816	0.794	0.772	0.751	0.712
4	0.855	0.823	0.792	0.763	0.735	0.708	0.683	0.636
5	0.822	0.784	0.747	0.713	0.681	0.650	0.621	0.567
6	0.790	0.746	0.705	0.666	0.630	0.596	0.564	0.507
7	0.760	0.711	0.665	0.623	0.583	0.547	0.513	0.452
8	0.731	0.677	0.627	0.582	0.540	0.502	0.467	0.404
9	0.703	0.645	0.592	0.544	0.500	0.460	0.424	0.361
10	0.676	0.614	0.558	0.508	0.463	0.422	0.386	0.322
11	0.650	0.585	0.527	0.475	0.429	0.388	0.350	0.287
12	0.625	0.557	0.497	0.444	0.397	0.356	0.319	0.257
14	0.577	0.505	0.442	0.388	0.340	0.299	0.263	0.205
16	0.534	0.458	0.394	0.339	0.292	0.252	0.218	0.163
18	0.494	0.416	0.350	0.296	0.250	0.212	0.180	0.130
20	0.456	0.377	0.312	0.258	0.215	0.178	0.149	0.104
22	0.422	0.342	0.278	0.226	0.184	0.150	0.123	0.083
24	0.390	0.310	0.247	0.197	0.158	0.126	0.102	0.066
26	0.361	0.281	0.220	0.172	0.135	0.106	0.084	0.053
28	0.333	0.255	0.196	0.150	0.116	0.090	0.069	0.042
30	0.308	0.231	0.174	0.131	0.099	0.075	0.057	0.033

Note: For a more complete present value table on amounts compounded annually, see Appendix C.

TABLE 2–5	Monthly Present Value Factors

Present Value of $1 Received at the End of Each Period for a Given Number of Months

Number of Months	4.00%	5.00%	6.00%	7.00%	8.00%	9.00%	10.00%	12.00%
12	0.961	0.951	0.942	0.933	0.923	0.914	0.905	0.887
24	0.923	0.905	0.887	0.870	0.853	0.836	0.819	0.788
36	0.887	0.861	0.836	0.811	0.787	0.764	0.742	0.699
48	0.852	0.819	0.787	0.756	0.727	0.699	0.671	0.620
60	0.819	0.779	0.741	0.705	0.671	0.639	0.608	0.550
84	0.756	0.705	0.658	0.613	0.572	0.534	0.498	0.434
120	0.671	0.607	0.550	0.498	0.451	0.408	0.369	0.303
240	0.450	0.369	0.302	0.248	0.203	0.166	0.136	0.092
360	0.302	0.224	0.166	0.123	0.091	0.068	0.050	0.028

Note: For a more complete present value table on amounts compounded monthly, see Appendix D.

to deposit or invest today into an account paying x percent interest in order to equal a given sum to be received y years in the future? For instance, assume you have a goal 10 years from now of obtaining $10,000. Banks are offering 8 percent on certificates of deposit. You would like to know how much you need to invest today in a CD in order to attain your objective of $10,000 after 10 years. Using the same formula

$$PV = \frac{FV}{(1+i)^t}$$

we get

$$PV = \frac{\$10,000}{1+(.08)^{10}} = \frac{\$120,000}{2.1589} = \$4,632.$$

The interest rate used in finding present value of a future sum of money is called the discount rate. The **discount rate** is the rate at which future dollars are traded for present dollars. Present value will depend on two factors: the interest rate and how far into the future the payments are. The higher the discount rate and the further into the future the payments are received, the less valuable are future dollars compared to present (or current) dollars. For many, formulas can be cumbersome. However, you can easily determine the present value using a business calculator or one with an exponential function or a computer. Moreover, present value and future value charts, such as those found at the end of this book, are available to show various equivalent compounding rates for certain time periods.

There are various ways of figuring compound interest. Interest, for example, may accrue "daily," "continuously," "quarterly," "semiannually" or "annually." **Accrued daily** means that the bank figures the interest on your balance each day and adds it to your balance daily. Your balance plus the day's interest are the basis for the next day's calculation. **Continuous interest** means that the bank figures the interest on your balance each day. At the end of the month, the daily interest is totaled and added to your ending balance. The interest is the basis for next month's calculation. **Quarterly** or **semiannual interest** means that the daily interest accrued is totaled and added to your balance every three or six months. **Compounded annual interest** means that the daily interest accrued is totaled and added to your balance at the end of each year.

Which is in your best interest? Obviously, the more frequently the interest on your money is compounded, the higher the yield, since additional interest is generated each time. Table 2–6 shows the effect of compounding schedules at several interest rates.

Effective Yield

It is virtually impossible for a consumer who is just looking at bank advertisements to tell how much real yield he or she is getting from an account. There are a number of important differences in the way various banks calculate your return, but the biggest question centers on compounding, that is, how frequently the interest rate is applied to the current balance in an account.

It is important to read the fine print on any ad or brochure about a specific offering. Check to see if the institution pays a simple or a compounded interest rate, and if compounded, how often. For example, as Table 2–6 shows, a $100,000 deposit at 9 percent simple annual interest earns $9,000 per year. But you would earn $9,200 if the interest were compounded semiannually, $9,310 if the interest were compounded quarterly, $9,380 if compounded monthly, and $9,420 if compounded daily. The larger the deposit, the more substantial the differences. And so, when you are shopping around for rates on your CDs or IRAs, look at the figure called "effective yield" because it takes compounding into account.

Day of Deposit, Day of Withdrawal

Your account balance, which serves as the basis for figuring interest (and service charges), is also determined in several ways. Most advantageous is **day of deposit to day of withdrawal**, combined with daily compounding of interest. The basis for calculating interest is either from the day of deposit or "something else." The

| TABLE 2–6 | Effective Annual Yields | | | | |

Quoted Interest Rate	Annually	Semi-annually	Quarterly	Monthly	Daily
8.0%	8.0%	8.16%	8.24%	8.30%	8.33%
9.0	9.0	9.20	9.31	9.38	9.42
10.0	10.0	10.25	10.38	10.47	10.52
11.0	11.0	11.30	11.46	11.57	11.63

Compounding Periods

Check Your Interest

Question: What is the present value of $25,000 to be received in eight years if the discount rate is 7 percent?

Answer:

$$PV = \frac{\$25{,}000}{(1+.07)^8} = \frac{\$25{,}000}{(1.07)^8} = \frac{\$25{,}000}{1.718} = \$14{,}550$$

We can derive the answer another way. Look at Table 2–4. Find the 7 percent PVF column and notice that the PVF for eight years is .582. If you multiply $25,000 by the PVF of .582, you also get $14,550.

---

something else may be that the dollar amount is added to your account on the day the check clears. Many banks assume a 10-day period for collecting funds from the bank whose check you deposited.

Playing the Rate-Chasing Game

Here are some rules for playing the new rate-chasing game. When evaluating the rates splashed on full-page ads in your local newspaper, what you see is not necessarily what you get. Make a special point of avoiding institutions using a "low balance" method of computing interest because it can cut yields on passbook accounts by more than half. A fraction of a percentage point over a period of time can mean a difference of hundreds or thousands of dollars in interest.

EFFECTIVE YIELD

How Effective Yield Is Calculated

Suppose you put $10,000 in a one-year CD with an 8 percent interest rate compounded quarterly. That means 2 percent interest quarterly, or $200 interest on $10,000 in the first quarter. In the second quarter, interest is paid on $10,200, bringing the total value of your investment to $10,404. Interest paid in the third quarter brings the total to $10,612.08. At the end of a year, the $10,000 investment has become $10,824.32, for an effective **annual yield** of 8.24 percent.

A more accurate way to state the true return on investments of more than one year is by measuring **average annual yield**. This is because effective annual yield is based on the return in the first year only. If your $10,000 were invested in a five-year CD, also paying 8 percent compounded quarterly, there would be $14,859.46 in the account at the end of five years. Dividing your $4,859.46 total return by 5, the average annual return would be $971.89, or 9.71 percent.

---

1. *Compare annual yields* In shopping among banks and S&Ls, compare annual yields. Unlike the "simple" interest rate, the annual yield takes into consideration the methods of compounding and computing, which may vary the interest earned by several percentage points on passbook savings and by several tenths of a point on other accounts. You may want to "shop" as carefully for the best place to put your savings as you would shop for a car.

    A good way to compare rates is to ask competing institutions variations on this question: If I were to place $1,000 into such and such an account at the beginning of the year, how much would I have, taking into account all the fees, at the end of the year? As of March 1993, all banks and S&Ls are required to use a uniform method for figuring yield and present it as the annual percentage yield, or **APY.** This is provided under the Truth in Savings Law of 1993. Banks can still compound interest however they like. But no matter how interest is calculated, the APY lets you compare apples to apples. If $1,000 goes into an account with an APY of 4.5 percent, you will have $1,045 after a year; if the APY is 5.3 percent, you will have $1,053. The APY shows the actual return on a $100 deposit for a 365-day year.

2. *Penalties for premature withdrawal* Since you may plan on putting away some savings for a specified length of time, it is important to consider the new penalties for drawing them out before the period ends. For example, the penalty for early withdrawal of a CD varies from bank to bank. The minimum penalty for a certificate of less than one year is one month's interest. For certificates maturing in a year or more, early withdrawal will cost at least three months' interest.

3. *Beware of interest rate hype* Interest rates advertised by banks often sound too good to be true. While the banks do not lie outright, their claims can be thoroughly misleading and expensive. An error in reading what the banks really pay can be a compounding one. It can translate into thousands of lost dollars over the life of the account. The problems start with simple advertising hype— 10 percent returns on IRAs, for example, splashed across a full-page newspaper ad that turn out to be in effect only for the first two or three months and decrease after that. But at least such facts can usually be uncovered by reading the small print. Disbelieve every high rate ad until you have studied all the terms. What the big black type giveth, the spidery type may taketh away. For example, suppose you put $4,000 into an account offering 5.5 percent on deposits up to $1,500 and 7 percent for larger amounts. Some banks will pay the top rate on your whole $4,000 deposit. But others will chisel you a little by paying 7 percent only on that portion of your money that exceeds $1,500, while the rest gets the lower, 5.5 percent rate.

4. *Pay attention to interest rate fluctuations* When rates are on the rise, invest in money market accounts whose rates of return fluctuate, too. Conversely, when you think interest rates have peaked, lock in your savings in long-term, fixed rate CDs.

5. *Watch the real or positive rate of interest* An increase in interest rates does not really make you richer if that extra interest is drained off by a rise in the cost of

living. If you are earning, say, 8 percent a year and prices climb at that same rate, your investment is growing at a zero real growth rate. In fact, you are losing ground because you are paying taxes on the interest income. Savers should constantly be mindful of the spread between nominal interest rates and inflation. This provides the real rate of interest.

6. *Finally, shop around*   To the banks' chagrin, savings and loans, credit unions, and brokerage houses have invaded their turf and offer better interest rates for savers almost across the board.

Shopping for the Right Bank

Banks, savings and loans, credit unions and other kinds of depository institutions compete intensively in order to attract new business. To compound the quandary of many customers, banks and savings institutions are advertising for their business and offering a wide variety of products to the public. This is a high-stakes game in which you are the prize. Change is the hallmark of the banking industry today, and so it pays to keep abreast of the new products and services that are constantly introduced.

Bank customers have to make more choices than ever before, and one of the first is whether to spread their business among several different banks or do one-stop banking, which many banks encourage. Some banks offer lower fees or lower interest rates to customers who use a number of the bank's services, for example, a preferred mortgage rate for those who maintain checking accounts. By consolidating all your cash reserves at one financial institution, you automatically increase your clout and qualify for the waivers or services you want.

Since the federal government's October 1983 deregulation action allowed banks to set their own investment terms and interest rates, banks can offer whatever terms they see fit. Savers, therefore, have to ask a lot of questions and should ask more than one bank before depositing or investing their money. Finding the right bank has become intimidating for many customers who do not have the time to study all of them.

Every financial institution has an entire menu of services and fees. It pays to comparison shop for a bank that fills your specific need at low cost or for no charge. Comparison shopping can be done most conveniently by phone, but request brochures and other printed materials to ensure that information communicated verbally is accurate. The problem is that banks often offer little help. Brochures featuring bank services are mainly promotional, frequently failing to specify the size of service fees and when they are imposed. Before opening a new checking account, ask several local banks for their service charge brochures so that you can compare costs.

Take a few weeks to survey interest rates offered on the product you think you might need. You do not need to scout a dozen bank lobbies for brochures. A few phone calls will do. Look for the costs of services you may need in the future, such as a mortgage, as well as the costs of services you use now. You will have to compare one institution's accounts and services with another's, one at a time. And when you do, you are bound to run into a blizzard of charges and fees that obscure the true cost of what it is you're buying.

If it is an interest-paying checking account you want or a line of credit or a savings account with flexible rates or an asset management account, you can look for them all at one institution or spread your business among competing institutions in your area. Depositors need not feel restricted to their local savings and loan. Savers can even bypass local financial institutions entirely and do business by mail with a more distant bank or S&L that offers a bit more on deposits, charges less for credit, or addresses their banking needs in some other way that local institutions do not.

All this can make choosing a place for your savings a more difficult job than ever. But before going out on the hunt, you must decide what makes you feel comfortable. Are you willing to trade the personal relationship with a local banker for higher yields from an institution operated by people you know nothing about? A 1983 banking industry survey indicated that 40 percent of depositors chose their bank primarily because it was nearby and convenient.

To help you decide which bank is right for your deposits and accounts, here is a guide to the things you should consider.

Checklist for Choosing a Bank

1. *Safety*   How safe is my deposit? Is it insured by an agency of the federal government or by some other agency?

2. *Liquidity*   To what extent are my funds available for withdrawal? Is there a penalty for early withdrawal? Am I limited as to the amount or number of times I can make withdrawals?

3. *Yield*   How much do I earn on my deposit? Is the yield set at a fixed rate, or does it fluctuate with market rates?

4. *Minimum deposit*   What is the minimum deposit required to open and maintain the account? What is the minimum required to earn the maximum yield and avoid charges?

5. *Convenience*   How much trouble is it to open, maintain, and close the account? Can this be done by phone, correspondence, or bank machine?

6. *Charges*   Are there one-time or periodic service charges? Am I charged for each deposit or withdrawal?

7. *Check-writing privileges and transfers*   Does the account provide additional benefits such as check-writing privileges or the ability to transfer funds between accounts?

8. *Problem solving*   If you ever have a problem, will you have easy access to someone to resolve it quickly and courteously?

9. *Quick crediting of deposits*   In this age of electronic transactions and check clearing, will you have almost immediate access to routine deposits? You should be able to use money from a local or government check right away the next day.

10. *Clarity of explanatory materials*   Can you understand the bank's handouts and applications? They should describe in readable fashion the account rules and the way rates and prices change as your balance rises and falls.

11. *User friendly*   Drop in at the branch you're considering to see how it handles customers during the peak lunch-hour rush, particularly on Fridays. Is there a single line that moves people quickly and efficiently to the next available teller? Are there enough tellers? Is there an express line for customers with simple deposits or withdrawals?

12. *Convenient hours, services, and facilities*   Can the bank accommodate direct deposits of your paycheck? Does it offer evening and weekend hours and a link to a statewide or national network of cash machines?

13. *Crediting of interest*   How is my interest credited? Is it simple interest or compounded? If compounded, is it compounded daily, monthly, quarterly, semi-annually, or annually?

As you have seen in this chapter, banking has become a dynamic, innovative, rapidly changing, and increasingly competitive industry that already operates in the electronic age. This chapter described the basic institutions of banking, the instruments used, and the newest trends and developments. But banking will continue to evolve. You will need to keep constantly abreast of the newest developments in banking to make sure that your savings are earning the highest returns at a level of risk that best suits your needs, requirements, and lifestyle.

SUMMARY

There is a variety of financial institutions available to serve customers. Various types of savings instruments are available to consumers. Savings and checking accounts are the two basic kinds of accounts offered by depository institutions. Other instruments include certificates of deposit and money market accounts.

The banking industry is undergoing rapid changes. The deregulation trend of the 1980s has resulted in increased competition among such financial institutions as commercial banks, savings and loan associations, mutual savings banks, credit unions, money market mutual funds, and the newly emerged financial supermarkets.

Rapid change has also resulted in increased bank failures and losses. Federal deposit insurance protects the accounts (up to $100,000) of most commercial banks, savings and loan associations, and credit unions. The banking industry is still considered a safe place for a consumer to save money, but a clear understanding of banking insurance is necessary in order for depositors to get the safest and maximum insurance protection for their savings.

KEY TERMS

Accrued daily interest

Asset management accounts

Automated teller machines (ATMs)

Average annual yield

Brokered CDs

Certificates of deposit (CDs)

Check clearing

Commercial banks

Compound interest

Compounded annual interest

Continuous interest

Credit unions

Day of deposit, day of withdrawal account

Debit card

Effective annual yield

Federal Deposit Insurance Corporation (FDIC)

Federal Savings and Loan Insurance Corporation (FSLIC)

Financial institutions

Financial integration

Financial supermarkets

Fixed-rate CDs

Float

Money market deposit accounts (MMDAs)

National Credit Union Share Insurance Fund (NCUSIF)

Nonbank banks

NOW accounts

Passbook savings accounts

Point of sale (POS)

Quarterly or semiannual interest

Regular checking accounts

Savings and loan associations (S&Ls)

Simple interest

Super NOW accounts

Sweep accounts

Totten trusts

Truncation

Variable-rate CDs

Yield

REVIEW QUESTIONS AND PROBLEMS

1. Discuss factors that should be considered in choosing a bank.
2. Identify and explain the following items: (a) truncation, (b) ATM, (c) EFTS, (d) super NOW accounts, (e) certificates of deposit, (f) credit unions.
3. Distinguish between a checking account and a NOW account.
4. What factors and criteria should be considered in selecting an institution to deposit your money?
5. What are the three main categories of banking (depository) institutions?
6. What is a credit union? What types of services does it offer? How does it differ from other financial institutions?
7. What federal corporations insure which depository institutions? Explain the role federal deposit insurance plays in the banking system.
8. Explain the advantages and disadvantages of an asset management account.
9. How safe is money invested in various financial institutions?

10. Discuss the effect of compound interest on your savings account.

11. Your parents wish to invest a sum of money now in a certificate of deposit in order to have $20,000 in five years from now when your kid sister will be ready for college. If interest rates are currently 8 percent, how much will they have to invest now? (*Hint:* Use present value formula.)

12. Suppose you invested $2,000 in a 2½-year certificate of deposit that pays 8.5 percent interest compounded annually. How much would your principal and interest be at the end of the 2½-year period? *(Hint:* Since this example uses 2½ years and 8.5 percent, Table 2–3 may not be useful. However, with the future value formula, the answer can easily be derived. You may also refer to Appendix D.)

13. Explain how effective yield is calculated.

14. Define, differentiate between, and discuss the various types of accounts and services offered by commercial banks and S&Ls.

15. Harvey and his wife, Pat, have $550,000 that they would like to deposit in the form of bank CDs or bank money market accounts. They have one child: a daughter, Karen, age 9. How can Pat and Harvey arrange their accounts so that the entire amount is fully covered by federal deposit insurance?

16. How has the Expedited Funds Availability Act of 1988 reformed the check-clearing process? What are the law's provisions?

17. (SWITCH) Interest rates are down to 4 percent, and six months ago you deposited $20,000 for three years at 8 percent. How much would interest rates have to rise on CDs of the same maturity to make it pay to switch?

18. (FUTURE)
    A. Twenty years ago, Sally's uncle deposited enough money at 5 percent compound interest to accumulate $14,965 today. How much did he deposit?
    B. Sally needs to accumulate $100,000 by age 40. Her current age is 25. She has inherited $14,965 from her uncle. What annual compound interest rate must she earn to reach her goal?

19. (PRESENT)
    A. You are offered an investment that requires an upfront payment of $10,000 and which would pay you $15,000 in eight years. If you can borrow money at 5 percent, would this be profitable?
    B. You are offered a choice between two investments. The first pays you $15,000 in eight years, while the second pays you $16,000 in nine years. If you can borrow money at 5 percent, which is the better investment?

20. (EFFECTIVE YIELD) An account generates an effective annual yield of 12 percent. What is the annual interest rate, given quarterly compounding?

SUGGESTED PROJECTS

1. Visit your bank and inquire about the various types of checking accounts it offers. Enter them on the list below.

Account	Minimum Balance	Fees & Charges	Services Provided
A.			
B.			
C.			
D.			
E.			

Compare the services and costs of each account. Explain which of the above accounts is best suited to your needs and why.

2. Visit several local banks and discuss investing $1,000 in a CD. Ask each bank to explain to you precisely how it calculates interest on this account. Ask for a printout showing how much you will have in your account one year from today. After having visited several (preferably five) banks, write a report explaining the different ways that banks compute interest and which one you would recommend as the best for the depositor. Present your findings to your class.

INFORMATION RESOURCES

"Bad Deals in High Yields." *Changing Times,* June 1989, 63–67.

Bodnar, Janet, and Kevin McManus. "What If Your Bank Fails?" *Changing Times,* February 1991, 27–35.

Brumbaugh, R. Dan, Jr. *Thrifts under Siege.* Cambridge: Ballinger Publishing, 1989.

Davis, Kristin. "Bank Savings: Finally, What You See Is What Your Get." *Kiplinger's Personal Finance Magazine,* June 1993, 32–34.

Giese, William. "Brokered Accounts That Do It All." *Kiplinger's Personal Finance Magazine,* May 1992, 69–72.

"Home Banking Is Here—If You Want It." *Business Week,* February 29, 1988, 108.

"Increase Approved in Fees Banks Pay to Insure Deposits." *The New York Times,* May 13, 1992, 1.

Office of Bank Customer Affairs, Federal Deposit Insurance Corporation, Washington, DC 20429.

100 Highest Yields. P.O. Box 402508, Miami Beach, FL 33140 (800/327-7717).

McCormally, Kevin. "Why Yields Aren't Always What They Seem." *Kiplinger's Personal Finance Magazine,* November 1992, 89.

Quinn, Jane Bryant. "The Era of Debit Cards." *Newsweek,* January 2, 1989, 51.

———"How to Keep Money Safe." *Newsweek,* March 25, 1991, 49.

———"S&Ls: After the Crackup." *Newsweek,* February 27, 1989, 56.

Quint, Michael. "Banks Directors Face Rising Risks." *The New York Times,* March 26, 1992, LD-1.

———"Mastercard and Visa in a Debit-Card Battle." *The New York Times,* May 5, 1992, D-1.

———"U.S. Shift on Deposit Insurance." *The New York Times,* March 26, 1992, LD-1.

Rudolph, Barbara. "Finally, the Bill Has Come Due." *Time,* February 20, 1989.

Savers Rate News. P.O. Box 143520, Coral Gables, FL 33114.

Updegrave, Walter L. "Just How Safe Is That Guaranteed Investment?" *Money,* March 1989, 123–132.

Veribanc Corp., P.O. Box 461, Wakefield, MA 01880 (800/442-2657).

"Ways to Get the Most from Your Bank." *Money,* March 1988, 96–115.

White, Lawrence J. "The Reform of Federal Deposit Insurance." *Journal of Economic Perspectives,* (Fall 1989): 11–29.

"Who Can Raid Your Checking Account?" *Kiplinger's Personal Finance Magazine,* March 1992, 28.

Woolley, Suzanne. "The Dawn of the Debit Card." *Business Week,* September 21, 1992, 55.

CHAPTER THREE

Credit, Credit Cards, and Personal Bankruptcy

LEARNING OBJECTIVES

- To acquire a basic understanding of the purposes, techniques, and problems of obtaining credit

- To discuss how to obtain and use credit in order to achieve personal financial goals

- To recognize the benefits and dangers associated with borrowing

- To explore the types of consumer credit available and the procedures for obtaining loans, credit lines, and credit cards

- To examine the basic consumer legislation passed to protect the rights of borrowers

- To understand the methods used to determine interest costs, interest charges, and the true cost of credit

- To consider steps to take if you get into financial trouble and cannot meet your credit obligations

The famous adage, "Only people who don't need credit can get it," is not quite accurate. Indeed, at some point in life, virtually everyone needs credit and most people are able to get it.

It's bound to happen. At various stages in life, you will borrow for a variety of reasons. Credit in the form of student loans (discussed in Chapter 4) may have made it possible for you to go to college. And after graduation, credit will likely continue to play a role in your life. Your broker calls with a great investment opportunity, your child has just been accepted by a private college, or your furnace conks out in the dead of winter and your money is already frozen in your home's equity or your IRA.

Borrowing is one answer. When consumers use credit cards instead of cash to make purchases, they are in effect borrowing for short periods of time. When households finance purchases of homes, they often borrow for periods of up to 30 years. The question, however, is where to borrow, how to borrow, and what to watch out for. The key is to choose the amount and form of credit that fit into your financial plans while not overspending your budget merely because credit is available.

This chapter will discuss how to handle credit, your credit record, applying for credit, understanding interest charges, and the bewildering variety of loan and credit options available. The chapter deals primarily with consumer loans. Mortgage loans to buy real estate are discussed separately in Chapter 6. In addition, this chapter discusses the issue of personal bankruptcy, which occurs when one gets hopelessly mired in excessive debt.

Needless to say, one is not obligated to use credit. It is a personal choice. You, as a consumer, must decide whether you want to save up to pay cash for an item or use credit and pay an interest or financing cost. In both cases, you are reducing current income. If you pay cash, you have to put aside money each month or week until you are finally able to afford the item. This may reduce your present amount of savings or the money you are able to spend currently on other items. Using credit does not make a borrower richer. A borrower merely uses future income now. If consumers use credit, they have already made the purchase but are paying for it currently and in the future, including the interest charge, which may reduce their future savings and spending ability.

However, few Americans have any choice but to borrow, at least for certain purchases. The price of a decent dwelling runs well over 20 times what most people can expect to save in a year. For many car buyers, too, borrowing is the only reasonable recourse. Many Americans resort to borrowing to pay for their everyday purchases.

Credit also has its disadvantages. It can provide a false sense of security. By purchasing with credit, borrowers may become overextended. This can be avoided through an honest and disciplined attitude toward borrowing. Credit has to be managed. Keeping credit under control and paying off major debts gives individuals the freedom to make changes and choices that cannot possibly be made by people burdened with oppressive monthly debt payments.

Calculating Your Credit Capacity

There is no reason to be debt plagued. Calculating the amount of credit you can comfortably handle is quite simple. All that is required is a self-administered cash flow analysis and an honest assessment of your risk of becoming a debt junkie. You need not take some creditor's word for how much debt you can handle. Often lenders are overeager to lend, especially if you have collateral waiting to be repossessed.

"That three year loan you gave me must be defective. It only lasted three months."

SOURCE: United Features Syndicate. Frank & Ernest reprinted by permission of NEA, Inc.

The Cash Flow Statement

You can conduct your own credit test by first estimating your current annual disposable income from all sources. Table 3–1 demonstrates a sample cash flow statement. It is similar to the budget illustrated in Table 1–1. If filled in, it can show the amount of money you have available for increased spending on credit payments. If any money is left in line 6 of Table 3–1, divide it by 12 (months). That is the most you can devote each month to any additional installment payments. This method helps determine how much additional debt you can manage.

Debt-to-Income Ratio

Another way to manage credit and to test debt endurance is to be very aware of your debt-to-income ratio. For creditors, the bottom line is the size of a borrower's financial obligations relative to his or her ability to pay. They call this the **debt-to-income ratio.** A rough guideline for debt-to-income ratio is 20 to 80. In other words, individuals carry too much credit if they spend more than about 20 percent of their take-home pay for credit obligations. Note that we are using take-home pay, not gross pay, in this ratio. To derive take-home pay, we need to subtract taxes, Social Security, union dues, and any other deductions from our gross pay when figuring debt-to-income ratio.

Credit analysts start marking borrowers as default risks once they reach this 20 to 80 ratio. They are generally not eligible for more credit unless their income increases or they clear old debts. However, the percentage can vary with income. For example, 20 percent may be appropriate for a $30,000 income but too low for a $200,000 income. Another factor to consider in determining your debt capacity is the adequacy of your financial reserves. If you suddenly lost your job, could you pay off your debts? How secure is your job? Are there one or two incomes in the family? A second income can serve as a cushion in the event of a sudden job loss.

Obtaining a Loan

The credit business is no longer limited to banks. Savings and loans, credit unions, finance companies, brokerage firms, even Sears, Roebuck and General Motors are all offering loans. As a result, consumers in the market for anything from a small

TABLE 3–1	Cash Flow Statement

CASH FLOW

1. Annual Income
- 1a. Salaries and bonuses $ _____
  (include scholarships and grants)
- 1b. Interest and dividends _____
- 1c. Child support or alimony received _____
- 1d. Pensions, annuities, and Social Security _____
- 1e. Rents, royalties, and fees _____
- 1f. Total annual income _____

**2. Annual Taxes (income and property)
and Social Security deductions** _____

3. After-Tax Income (line 1f minus line 2) _____

4. Annual Expenses
- 4a. Rent or mortgage payments and utilities _____
- 4b. Food and clothing _____
- 4c. Child care _____
- 4d. Furniture, appliances, and home improvements _____
- 4e. Recreation and entertainment _____
- 4f. Car payments, repairs, and gasoline _____
- 4g. Medical, legal, and financial expenses _____
- 4h. Insurance premiums _____
- 4i. Educational expenses _____
- 4j. Student and other loan payments _____
- 4k. Other _____

**5. Total Annual Living Expenses
(sum of lines 4a through 4k)** _____

**6. Funds Available for Savings
and Investments (or for increased
interest payments on loans)
(line 3 minus line 5)** _____

personal loan to a six-figure home mortgage have many more choices but also face much more confusion. To be sure of getting the best terms, consumers need to know how to work their way through the maze of lenders and the variety of deals they offer. Borrowers need to do their homework before applying for credit.

Before applying for a loan, a borrower should examine his or her credit report. This can be accomplished by phoning the lending institution, inquiring as to which credit bureau the lender uses, and then contacting the credit bureau. For a small fee, credit bureaus will send consumers their report (more about this later). This should be done no matter how clean one thinks his or her record is. If the credit record is found to be accurate, then the borrower can safely and confidently schedule an appointment.

It is essential to arrive at the loan appointment prepared. Preparation means two things: understanding what you want and providing the necessary backup documentation to prove that you qualify for the loan. You should be ready to answer these fundamental questions.

1. How much do you want to borrow?

2. Why do you want this loan?

3. Over what period of time would the loan be repaid?

4. From what sources would it be repaid?

Borrowers simplify the lender's evaluation process by bringing along supporting documentation, such as appraisals of valuable assets, recent savings or brokerage statements to verify liquid assets, pay stubs, income tax returns, credit card bills, mortgage records, and the like. Anything that demonstrates a borrower's credit-worthiness should be brought to the loan interview.

Of all the information that loan applicants provide a lender on the application, two items transcend the others: the purpose of the loan and the applicant's gross annual income. Most banks will assume that the loan request is reasonable if it does not exceed the aforementioned debt-to-income ratio of 20 percent (of the borrower's after-tax salary). If a loan is for something important, rather than for a frivolous impulse, it stands to reason that the loan will mean more to the borrower, its benefits will be lasting, and the borrower will be more likely to repay it on time.

Nevertheless, certain categories of information count heavily with most creditors. Knowing what these categories are can help applicants fill out at least some sections of their credit application in a way that improves their odds of getting the loan approved. The way in which applicants are evaluated and the questions asked can vary from lender to lender and from city to city. There may be many questions or only a few. As people differ, so do lenders.

Borrowers are awarded points for each of their answers to key questions on the credit application. After the score on the application has been tallied, most lenders will add or subtract points from the total, based upon information they get from the credit bureau report.

The Four Cs of Credit

Lenders will generally try to ascertain basic financial facts about you from their credit application. They rely on what they call the **four Cs**: capacity, capital, collateral, and character.

1. *Capacity* Sufficient income to be able to repay.
   A. Earning power—Is your income sufficient to meet credit payments? Also required is some indication that your employment will remain unchanged at least until the proposed loan has been repaid.

    B. Current credit commitments—How many other credit commitments do you have? Will another credit obligation strain your budget? They also want to know your expenses: how many dependents you have, whether you pay alimony or child support, and the amount of your other obligations.

2. *Capital*   The applicant's overall financial situation.
    A. Net worth—Your accumulated assets minus debts.
    B. Financial resources—What is the value of your life insurance, car, home, savings account, stocks, bonds, IRA, and the like? The creditor wants to know your total financial situation.

3. *Collateral*   Property to sell if the borrower defaults on the loan. What do you have of value that can be used as security for the loan in the event you do not meet your obligations? The focus here will be on liquid assets. An applicant's net worth may be high, but if it is in such things as pension, equity, or other nonliquid assets, it does not provide the liquid collateral the lender is seeking.

4. *Character*   The willingness to repay a loan. Will you repay the debt? The credit report tells the potential creditor a lot about your character. Creditors want to know how much you owe, how often you borrow, whether you pay bills on time, and whether you live within your means. They also are interested in how long you have been at your current job and how long you have been living at your present residence.

    We may add a possible fifth "C" or factor of credit for lenders, *condition* (economic conditions). Although economic conditions are beyond the control of individual credit applicants, they are important factors that affect the ability of borrowers to repay their loans. Lenders are more likely to approve a loan application during a booming high-growth economy than during a period of economic sluggishness and high unemployment.

Fitting a Computer Model

Many lenders resort to computer models in evaluating loan applications. Computer models are fashioned like actuarial tables, which are derived from an insurance company's past experience with people who have similar characteristics. In designing a model, a creditor selects a random sample of credit customers, usually a certain number of people who repay their debts and a certain number of people who do not. The company also selects the characteristics by which it will judge each applicant. The information for those characteristics comes from answers to questions on credit applications.

    A computer matches the number of payers versus the number of nonpayers who have each characteristic. For example, the computer might find that 75 percent of the payers own a home while only 20 percent of nonpayers are homeowners. A computer program determines how well each characteristic predicts who will pay and who will not. If people with a particular characteristic are found more likely to repay than those without it, that characteristic is said to be "predictive." Once the computer determines that a characteristic is predictive, that characteristic is assigned points according to how well it predicts. Home ownership is generally more predictive than car ownership, for example, and would be assigned more points. The specific characteristics and the exact number of points each is assigned are usually closely guarded secrets of each lending institution.

Your Credit Record

A loan applicant's credit record, therefore, is just one of the factors involved in whether or not he or she will get the loan. A squeaky clean record does not guarantee that an application will be approved. The credit grantor might decide, for example, that although you have been paying off other obligations satisfactorily, the new loan you are applying for could push you over the limit. Alternatively, a creditor might overlook past problems in your credit history because other factors suggest that you are a good risk for the credit you currently want.

A credit file, nevertheless, serves as the final piece of the puzzle that persuades a bank or merchant to extend or reject an applicant's credit. A surprising number of organizations collect, process, store, and exchange information about individuals and groups. About 2,000 **credit bureaus** in cities and towns across the nation serve as clearinghouses for information about consumers' debts and their bill-paying habits. Banks, finance companies, merchants, and other creditors continuously feed information to the bureaus, showing when and how much credit has been extended to a consumer and whether he or she is paying it off as scheduled.

Each month when you pay a credit card bill on time, for example, that fact and any outstanding balance on your account are reported to a bureau and added to your file. If you miss a payment, that is recorded, too. The same with your other debts, although some creditors do not report every month. You may want to request your lender to report your payments of debt since not all lenders always do so. In addition to reports from creditors, the computerized files include public record information about bankruptcies, lawsuits, judgments, tax liens, arrests, and convictions, for example, that could affect an applicant's creditworthiness, as well as one's employment history and income. Such information is available on line via computer networks to thousands of credit-granting subscribers.

Although a perfect credit record may not always guarantee an applicant a loan, establishing a solid credit background is vital. Your creditworthiness will affect not only your ability to borrow money or purchase goods and services on credit but also the price you have to pay for money, your ability to obtain charge cards, and even your employment. Many employers require a credit bureau report as a condition of employment.

On your credit file will be a record of your accounts, though not in detail; it will contain notations such as "on time," "satisfactory," or if you have been careless or forgetful, "30 days late on Account no. 8." If sickness or trouble was the cause, and you explained your problem frankly to the lender who arranged postponement or new terms, this will be noted and your good credit will not be harmed.

Periodic Credit Checkups

If you are an active credit seeker or just a vigilant consumer, you should periodically review your file even if you haven't had a credit application rejected or even applied for credit. The fee is usually $5 to $10. To find your local credit bureau, check the yellow pages under "Credit Reporting Agencies." The three major credit reporting bureaus are Equifax, Trans Union, and TRW. TRW, Inc., of Orange, California, maintains files on more than 133 million Americans.

Some advisers recommend that consumers check their file each year to be sure no errors have slipped in. Other advisers believe that this is not necessary. Most people know how efficiently they pay their bills. They have a good idea of what's in their credit record and do not need to check it unless they are turned down for a loan. It may be prudent to check your record, though. If you have had a dispute with a creditor, you may want to check what the creditor is saying about you to the credit bureau. Under federal law, a creditor cannot report you as overdue on paying your bills while you are involved in a billing dispute. However, to get that protection, you have to follow set procedures that include sending a notice to the creditor indicating that the unpaid bill is in dispute.

Coping with a Credit Rejection

Rejection is never easy to deal with, whether it is from a boyfriend, girlfriend, spouse, peer group, or loan officer. No matter how rational, a rejection almost always arouses the angry response, What's wrong with me? Loan applicants should not take a credit rejection as personal or irreversible. Instead, they should learn how to cope with it rationally and rectify it.

If a loan application is rejected, the lender must give the applicant the reasons at the time of rejection. The reasons must be the actual ones used in the creditor's decision. This disclosure requirement, mandated by the Federal Reserve Board, is designed to help consumers spot discrimination and correct deficiencies in their credit history so that their future applications will have a better chance of acceptance.

Reasons for Credit Denial What may be wrong is your profession; you may be a self-employed artist or cab driver instead of a surgeon. It may be that your car is too old. You may have too many children or wives (past and present) to support, or a host of other reasons.

Before the computer age, lending officers judged applicants by considering the traditional four Cs of credit and consulting credit bureau reports. Today, computer models and statistical schemes often replace a loan officer's judgment. The four Cs of credit are hidden in many pieces of personal information fed into the computer. Whether you get credit depends on how well your characteristics fit the model. A lender may turn you down without even considering your credit report.

Some of the most common reasons for credit denial are:

1. Bad credit history

2. Insufficient income

3. Irregular or temporary employment

4. Too short a period of employment

5. Lack of credit references

"...but on the bright side, you might get a spot on 'America's Funniest Credit Applications.'"

SOURCE: "Pepper...and Salt," *The Wall Street Journal,* February 23, 1993, A-21. Reprinted by permission of Cartoon Features Syndicate.

Reversing a Rejection   If a loan application has been rejected, whether because of a troubled credit history or insufficient resources, the rejection should never be viewed as final. A rejection can be reversed by:

1. Talking with companies that reported the delinquent accounts to see how matters can be cleared up

2. Adding to your credit record an explanation for a period of delinquency, such as a prolonged illness, a layoff, or financial disarray due to divorce

3. Applying elsewhere

4. Modifying the loan application (applying for less money or a longer-term loan with smaller monthly payments)

5. Trying to get a cosigner to guarantee the loan

Correcting a Faulty Credit Report   If a credit report was a factor in a lender declining your loan application, you have the legal right to be told the name and address of the credit bureau that provided the information. This is required by the **Fair Credit Reporting Act** of 1970 and is enforced by the Federal Trade Commission. Then you may request information from the credit bureau by mail or in person. You will not get an exact copy of the file, but you will get a summary of it.

The credit bureau must provide credit records free to anyone who has been denied credit in the past 30 days and must also help interpret the data, which may take experience to analyze. Considering the huge volume of information, literally billions of reports flowing into credit bureau files, there are sure to be mistakes. If you find or suspect any incorrect or outdated information in your credit report, demand that the credit bureau investigate and correct the report. If it can not substantiate the accuracy of the item, the information must be deleted from your file.

By law, the bureau must investigate any errors you discover in your report. Then it must drop any information that turns out to be mistaken and must notify any lender who received the report within the past six months that the erroneous material has been removed from your file. All these lenders must be sent an updated report. If there is a dispute that the credit bureau's investigation does not resolve, you are entitled to add to your file a short 100-word statement telling your side of the story. Future reports to prospective lenders must include your explanation.

Before a credit agency will change its records, a person must usually clear any problem with the source that reported it. The credit-reporting agency must then be notified of the change, and the borrower should ask for written confirmation of the correction. Corrections are usually obtained by paying off an account that was in default. If that is not possible, a borrower can add a letter to the credit record explaining the reason for the delinquency, while making an effort to start paying off the balance. Such explanations may help considerably, especially if the credit record clearly shows that the delinquencies centered around a single difficult period.

The intervention of a lawyer, accountant, broker, or any other intermediary with insight into the person's situation can add weight to the appeal. Federal law also requires that most unfavorable reports be purged after 7 years (10 in the case of bankruptcy), so that past financial problems will not haunt someone for life. Creditors are generally most interested in the last few years or so.

Outside agencies that have helped consumers resolve credit bureau complaints include local Public Interest Research Group offices (U.S. PIRG, 215 Pennsylvania Avenue SE, Washington, DC 20003), Bankcard Holders of America (560 Herndon Parkway, Suite 120, Herndon, VA 22070), and some state attorneys general. The Federal Trade Commission (Bureau of Consumer Protection, Division of Credit Practices, Room S–4429, 6th Street and Pennsylvania Avenue NW, Washington, DC 20580) collects complaints but cannot help resolve individual cases.

Credit and Discrimination The **Equal Credit Opportunity Act** says that race, color, age, marital status, sex, religion, or national origin may not be used to discriminate

Setting the Record Straight

Complaints about credit bureaus have become the largest category of consumer grievances at the Federal Trade Commission. The FTC and 19 states sued TRW, the largest credit-reporting agency, for not maintaining reasonable procedures to ensure accuracy. In December 1991, TRW settled with the FTC and state attorneys general, agreeing as of 1992 to accept consumers' documentation in disputes over errors, to increase its efforts to reduce inaccurate credit files and recurring errors, and to report annually to the FTC on its progress for the next five years. In addition, as of 1992, TRW began offering consumers one free copy of their credit report each year and set up a consumer phone line (214/235-1200) for questions and problems. Equifax (800/685-1111) and Trans Union have agreed to lower their charges to $15 per report. Reports continue to be free at all three bureaus for 60 days after you have been turned down for credit.

against borrowers in any part of a credit dealing. It is illegal to turn a woman down for a loan on the assumption that she might become pregnant and leave her job. It is likewise illegal for creditors to ask a woman about her childbearing plans. It is illegal even to discourage a woman from applying for a loan just because she is of childbearing age.

Women who are divorced or widowed may not have separate credit histories if past credit accounts were listed in their husbands' names. But under the Equal Credit Opportunity Act, creditors must consider the credit history of any account that women have held jointly with their husbands. Married women are entitled to get credit in their own names if they can qualify. Creditors must also look at the record of any account held only in the husband's name if a woman can prove that it also reflects her own creditworthiness. For example, a widowed or divorced woman should point out that she handled all accounts properly when she was married and that bills were paid by checks from her own account. If the record is unfavorable, if a former husband was a bad credit risk, she can try to show that the record does not reflect her own reputation.

Establishing New Credit Students and other new entrants to the work force may have difficulty getting credit. It's somewhat of a Catch 22 situation, whereby you can not get credit until you have established a good credit record, but you can not establish a reliable credit record without getting credit.

However, the situation is not exactly hopeless. Students can start by obtaining and using credit at a gas station or local department store to establish a credit records. Many gas companies and even VISA will extend credit to college students. Banks prefer a borrower to have worked at one job for at least six months and may insist at first on a cosigner. The cosigner, usually a relative or friend, agrees to be liable for the debt in case the borrower does not meet his or her obligations; however, the borrower's name goes on the account, and he or she thus begins to establish a credit history. Another relatively easy way to obtain credit is to take a savings-secured loan or passbook loan. This loan is secured by the borrower's balance in his or her passbook or savings account. Once a credit rating is established, it becomes a matter of record at one or more credit bureaus around the country. The record lists all accounts for the past seven years and indicates whether payments have been made on time.

Bear in mind that creditworthiness is subjective and standards vary widely. Applying to a number of banks simultaneously is not recommended because multiple inquiries in a short period of time are reported to credit bureaus. Before submitting an application, talk to a loan officer to see whether you meet that bank's credit criteria.

Interest Rates: The Price of Using Credit

Everything has a price, and the use of someone else's money is no exception. The interest rate is the annual amount that a borrower must pay for the use of a dollar for a year. If the interest rate is 10 percent, a borrower must pay 10 cents per year for the use of a dollar for a year. The actual rate of interest (the price of money) is determined in the marketplace where money is borrowed and lent. Like other prices, they are affected by the fundamentals of supply and demand. Both borrowing and lending involve risks and uncertainties which are reflected in the level of interest rates. Not being repaid, receiving only partial payment, or receiving payment while the money's purchasing power has diminished are some of the concerns that preoccupy lenders and the credit market.

Since a borrower repays the principal and interest in money, inflation over the course of the loan will make the amount the lender receives worth less in terms of the goods and services the money can buy. Lenders typically estimate an expected rate of inflation and try to protect themselves against the money's loss in value by requiring a premium related to their expectation. This premium will be in addition to what lenders require as compensation for making loans. The greater the inflationary expectations in the credit markets, the greater the premium borrowers will have to pay to obtain funds.

These and other factors, which determine the amount of money borrowers and lenders are willing to exchange at different interest rates, are varied and complex. Rather than focusing on these underlying factors, let us concentrate on how consumers can find and determine the best "price" for their money.

Most consumers do not bother to "shop" for small loans. On $5,000 for five years, the difference between 12 and 14.5 percent is about $6 a month, which to many borrowers appears as a trifle, although over five years it amounts to over $360. Obviously, an informed borrower needs to check the market for the lowest rate. Rates will vary not only with where the loan is obtained but also according to the type of loan. Lenders usually charge less interest for a secured loan, where borrowers put up collateral such as real estate or securities, than for an unsecured loan, where they rely for repayment on a borrower's income and credit record. Rates are often lower for installment loans whereby the consumer makes a larger down payment. Variable rate loans generally carry a lower initial rate than fixed rate loans.

No single institution is likely to have the lowest rate for every type of borrowing. That is why borrowers need to canvass a number of lenders when looking for money. The best place to start is where you keep your checking and savings accounts. Many banks charge people who already have accounts as much as two percentage points less than their rate for noncustomers. Customers with all their checking, money market, and IRA deposits at the same financial institution can often better the standard deal simply by pointing out their loyalty.

The interest costs on consumer credit were tax deductible until 1990. The Tax Reform Act of 1986 phased out interest costs gradually and as of January 1, 1990, it can no longer be deductible except through a home equity loan, which is discussed later.

The Truth in Lending Law

The federal **Truth in Lending Law** of 1968, governing consumer borrowing, requires lenders to disclose the true cost of consumer credit by providing a clear explanation of all charges involved. Credit costs vary. There are several ways of computing and of quoting interest rates. Two loans with the same interest rate do not always cost the same.

By remembering two terms, you can compare credit prices from different sources. Under the Truth in Lending Act, the credit agency must tell you in writing and before you sign any agreement the total finance charge and the annual percentage rate (APR). This mandatory truth in lending statement accompanies your loan agreement. The law requires that all interest be quoted in a uniform manner, enabling consumers to compare the rates of various loans.

The **total finance charge** is the total cost of the loan, which must be quoted in dollars. It is the dollar amount paid yearly to use credit. It includes interest costs and sometimes other costs, such as service charges, loan fees, finder's fees, points, and investigation fees. For example, borrowing $100 for a year might cost $9 in interest. If there is also a service charge of $1, the total finance charge would be $10.

The **annual percentage rate (APR)** is the actual rate of interest, because it takes into account all loan fees, charges, and costs, as well as interest. It is the percentage cost of credit on an annual basis. It also includes a vital but often overlooked factor: the amount of money the borrower can use at any time. This is the key for measuring and comparing the cost of credit, regardless of the amount of credit or how long the borrower has to repay it. It is the most accurate way to compare lending rates.

Suppose you borrow $100 for one year and pay a total finance charge of $10. If you can keep the entire $100 for the whole year and then pay it all back at once, you are paying an APR of 10 percent. But if you repay the $100 principal and $10 total interest (or *add-on interest*) in 12 equal monthly installments, you do not get to use the $100 for the whole year. Each month you get to use less and less of the $100, but have paid $10 for this use. In effect, you have use of about half the original $100 amount on average for the full year. In this case, the $10 add-on interest charge for credit amounts to an APR of 18 percent.

Most loans are self-amortizing; that is, by the time you complete all the scheduled payments, you have paid all the principal and all the interest. All creditors must state the true cost of their credit in terms of the finance charge and the APR before borrowers sign a credit contract. The Truth in Lending Law does not set interest rates, but it does require their disclosure so that borrowers can make an intelligent choice.

Add-On Interest

Suppose you take a $1,000 loan at a 10 percent annual interest rate, to be repaid in 12 months.

How much will you have to pay monthly to pay off the loan? The lender will want the present value of the future payments to equal the loan amount. If you have a loan amount and an interest rate, you can find the monthly payment by first summing the monthly present value factors associated with the interest rate and then dividing that sum into the loan amount. This can be derived by use of Table 3–2. In Table 3–2 we find the present value factor sum associated with 10% and 12 months is 11.375. Therefore, $1,000/11.375 = $87.91 as a monthly payment.

Total interest paid, or the **add-on interest**, is equal to ($87.91 $\times$ 12) − $1,000 or $54.94.

You could easily (and mistakenly) view your interest rate as being only equal to $54.92/1,000, or 5.49 percent.

This add-on interest does not reflect the true interest rate of 10 percent because each monthly payment includes the same repayment of principal and, as stated earlier, the borrower does not have full use of $1,000 for the entire loan term.

TABLE 3–2	Monthly Present Value Factor Sums

Annual Interest

Number of Months	8.00%	9.00%	10.00%	11.00%	12.00%	15.00%	18.00%
12	11.496	11.435	11.375	11.315	11.225	11.079	10.908
24	22.111	21.889	21.671	21.456	21.243	20.624	20.030
36	31.912	31.447	30.991	30.545	30.108	28.847	27.661
48	40.962	40.185	39.428	38.691	37.974	35.931	34.043
60	49.318	48.173	47.065	45.993	44.955	42.035	39.380
84	64.159	62.154	60.237	58.403	56.648	51.822	47.579
120	82.421	78.942	75.671	72.595	69.701	61.983	55.498
240	119.554	111.145	103.625	96.882	90.819	75.942	64.796
360	136.283	124.282	113.951	105.006	97.218	79.086	66.353

Note: See Appendix D for a table of Monthly Present Value Factors.

Borrowers should look for both the total finance charge and the APR on all credit forms before they sign on the dotted line. These features can be used as a basis for comparison when evaluating credit offers.

Despite legal safeguards, borrowers still have to be on the alert. The Truth in Lending Law protects only consumer loans, not business loans. Business loans are not governed by truth in lending or by state rate ceilings. For this reason, borrowers should be on guard for lenders who encourage them to take out a business loan when it is really for personal use.

The Loan Prepayment Penalty: Rule of 78

Another issue that borrowers need to consider often is whether they should repay the loan on time or repay it earlier than scheduled if the opportunity arises. Most credit agreements specify that if consumers pay off a loan before its scheduled maturity, their refund of interest charges will be determined by the so-called rule of 78. The **rule of 78** is a method of determining interest charges in which relatively high interest is charged during the early period of the loan.

The name "rule of 78" derives from the fact that the sum of the number of months in a one-year loan equals 78. In other words,

$$12 + 11 + 10 + 9 + 8 + 7 + 6 + 5 + 4 + 3 + 2 + 1 = 78.$$

Thus, you pay $\frac{12}{78}$ of the total interest charge the first month, $\frac{11}{78}$ the second month, $\frac{10}{78}$ the third month, and so on until you reach the final payment, which is equal to $\frac{1}{78}$ of the loan. If you total all these payments, you get $\frac{78}{78}$, which is equal to the total interest charge of your loan.

The rule of 78 becomes the rule of the sum of the digits involved for any number of equal installment payments for which a loan was contracted. For example, if you make an early repayment on a two-year loan with 24 equal installments, you would use the rule of 300.[1]

If you repay the entire loan after one month, you will owe 24/300 of the total amount of interest. This means that you will pay 8 percent of the total, as opposed to the pro rata distribution of interest that would equal 1/24, or 4.17 percent. In a three-year contract, the denominator is 666 and the first month's interest is 5.4 percent.

The rule is best illustrated using a simple example. Assume that you enter into an installment loan agreement in which you receive $3,000 and are to repay the principal and the finance charge in 12 equal monthly installments. After making six monthly payments, you decide to repay the loan fully. How much do you still owe?

If you had paid six installments, the supposition is that you owe exactly one-half of the remaining principal and have also repaid half of the interest due. But using the rule of 78 (see Table 3–3), the lender calculates that you have paid 73 percent

$$\frac{12}{78} + \frac{11}{78} + \frac{10}{78} + \frac{9}{78} + \frac{8}{78} + \frac{7}{78} = \frac{57}{78},$$
$$\text{or}$$
$$0.1539 + 0.1410 + 0.1282 + 0.1154 + 0.1026 + 0.0897 = 73 \text{ percent}$$

of the interest owed and only 50 percent of the balance. Clearly, early payment of a loan based on the rule of 78 is expensive. Although you prepaid six months in advance (50 percent early), you still pay 73 percent of the total interest payment. If you decide now to prepay the loan and pay off the other 50 percent of principal owed ($1,500), you will end up having paid 73 percent of the annual interest costs while only having used the money for half a year.

While the rule of 78 penalizes borrowers who prepay their loans, it allows lenders to earn interest at a quicker pace, because a large portion of the total interest is allocated to the early months. Lenders do not have to calculate what borrowers owe in this step-by-step manner because they use prepaid tables like the one shown in Table 3–3.

The Loan Menu

The variety of loans available is considerable. Let us examine the various kinds of loans and their distinguishing features and characteristics.

Variable-Rate Loans

Another option borrowers are often confronted with when applying for credit is choosing between a rate of interest that remains unchanged throughout the loan period, known as a **fixed-rate loan,** or a loan whose interest rate may vary during the loan period, a **variable-rate loan.** Many people unwittingly run the risk of stretching out their payments by choosing variable-rate installment loans. The rate

---

[1] We derive 300 by adding:

$24 + 23 + 22 + 21 + 20 + 19 + 18 + 17 + 16 + 15 + 14 + 13 + 12 + 11 + 10 + 9 + 8 + 7 + 6 + 5 + 4 + 3 + 2 + 1 = 300.$

TABLE 3–3	Monthly Interest Payment Credits		
Payment	**Percent of Total Annual Interest Paid Each Month**		
1	$\frac{12}{78}$	=	0.1539
2	$\frac{11}{78}$	=	0.1410
3	$\frac{10}{78}$	=	0.1282
4	$\frac{9}{78}$	=	0.1154
5	$\frac{8}{78}$	=	0.1026
6	$\frac{7}{78}$	=	0.0897
7	$\frac{6}{78}$	=	0.0769
8	$\frac{5}{78}$	=	0.0641
9	$\frac{4}{78}$	=	0.0513
10	$\frac{3}{78}$	=	0.0385
11	$\frac{2}{78}$	=	0.0256
12	$\frac{1}{78}$	=	0.0128
78	$\frac{78}{78}$		1.0000

of interest paid on a variable-rate loan may change periodically, depending on fluctuations in the interest rate index selected by the creditor. This index is typically pegged to the yields on three-month Treasury issues, the prime lending rate, or certificates of deposit.

Variable-rate or "floating-rate" loans worry consumers, who fear that a sharp rise in interest rates might increase their monthly payments to a level they can not afford. To deal with this built-in uncertainty, banks have structured repayment of loans in two ways.

Variable Term Option: Fixed Monthly Payments The first system established a fixed monthly payment for the entire term of the loan. Instead of altering the monthly payments, however, the bank extends the loan term if rates go up and shortens it if rates drop. Under this variable term arrangement, the monthly payment is calculated using the current interest rate at the time the loan is established. If average interest rates during the term of the loan are higher than the rate used to calculate the monthly payment, the borrower will have to make extra payments at the end of the original loan expiration date. If average interest rates drop, the borrower will owe less money and will be able to pay off the loan earlier. The big advantage of this fixed monthly payment system is that it simplifies budgeting and helps borrowers plan their monthly payments.

Variable Payments Option: Interest Freezes and Caps Those who choose variable payments have the payment amount adjusted periodically depending on how much and which way interest rates move. The bank may establish a fixed period of time during which the interest rate does not change. This may be for three months, six months, or longer, depending upon the type of loan. The bank may also set a "cap," a maximum guideline which limits the amount by which the interest rate can increase.

Interest Rate Roulette

Assume that you are taking out a 48-month variable-term automobile loan for $10,000 and the initial interest rate is 14 percent. That puts your monthly payment at $273.27. If your rate goes up 0.5 percent a year, you will owe one additional monthly payment. If it goes up 1 percent every year, you will stretch your payments two more months. But if it goes up 5 percent soon after the loan is taken out, you will have to make four additional monthly payments. Of course, the opposite could happen. If rates dropped 1 percent each year, you would make only 45 monthly payments. In reality, a variable-rate loan is much like playing a game of interest rate roulette, and the longer the term of the loan, the higher the stakes.

Some banks offer variable rate loans at a slightly lower starting rate than that set for fixed rate borrowings because this type of lending transfers the risk that interest rates will rise from the lending institution to the borrower.

If you are offered a variable-rate loan, judge it by the incentive offered to forgo the certainty of a fixed rate and by what you think will happen to interest rates in the next few years. Borrowers often get to choose whether changes in the rate will be reflected in the amount of the monthly payment or in the term of the loan. Most variable loan customers choose the fixed monthly payment option, meaning that their 48-month notes might actually be paid off in 47 to 49 months.

Banks promote variable rates because they protect lenders against getting stuck with low interest loans on their books. Variable rates can be a good deal for customers, too, but only if rates drop or hold steady.

Personal Unsecured Loans

One broad category of credit is the **personal unsecured loan**. Such a loan is issued primarily based upon the borrower's good credit rating, steady job, and so on. It does not require any collateral or lien on borrowers' assets. This is available from banks, finance companies, and employee credit unions. Typically, it takes the form of a checking account overdraft, which allows depositors to cover the checks they write even when they exceed their cash balance.

Banks and other lenders are aggressively offering unsecured **lines of credit** that typically give depositors access to funds ranging from $2,000 to $25,000. A line of credit is an agreement between a bank and a customer whereby the bank agrees to lend the customer funds up to a previously agreed upon maximum amount. The actual amount depositors qualify for depends upon their income, and they can draw on the line simply by writing a check. The advantage of the overdraft privilege is that it represents a line of credit that may be tapped as needed. You can arrange for a credit line to be linked to your personal checking account to protect you from the embarrassment and expense of an overdraft. With a credit line, you are covered for the exact amount of the overdraft up to your line of credit. There is generally no charge for the service and interest is charged only on the amount borrowed until it is repaid.

Secured Loans

A loan backed by a borrower's or cosigner's assets is known as a **secured loan**. A borrower can secure a loan by having a creditworthy relative, friend, or employer cosign the loan. By so doing, the cosigners guarantee payment on the loan. By merely vouching for the borrower's character, a cosigner assumes full liability for the loan if the borrower does not pay, plus any late fees or collection costs. Cosigners have the same legal obligation for repayment as the original borrower and the lender may move against either signer. A creditor can legally collect the debt from the cosigner without first attempting to collect from the borrower. Being a cosigner is therefore an onerous responsibility. Cosigners are asked to take a risk that a professional lender is unwilling to take.

Even when the borrower never misses a payment, cosigners can encounter credit problems if they later apply for a loan of their own. A cosigned loan will very likely show up on a cosigner's credit report because the cosigner is potentially liable for the debt. This can prevent the cosigner from qualifying for his or her own loan.

Lenders may, however, charge a lower rate of interest or offer a longer repayment period for loans secured by collateral or a cosigner. One popular kind of loan that may be secured is for homeowners who want to make improvements; another is for the purchase of a car.

Borrowers typically receive a secured loan backed by the equity in their home. If borrowers do not have equity in a home or are reluctant to dip into it, they can get a loan collateralized by other assets like a savings account, bonds, stocks, or certificates of deposit. Individuals can borrow against the amount in their savings accounts, for instance, a method that will result in their paying out more interest than they accrue but may help to ensure that they will put the money back. This is known as a **passbook loan**. Let's examine some of these and other common secured loans.

Passbook Loans   Many banks and thrift institutions still make loans secured by passbook accounts and charge two to three percentage points above the rate depositors are earning. During times when market interest rates on savings accounts and certificates of deposit seem disappointingly low, borrowers may be able to turn them to their advantage if they need a low-cost loan. If, for example, you are earning 5 percent on your passbook savings account and borrow against it by obtaining a passbook loan at 8.5 percent, your net cost of credit is only 3.5 percent. That is considerably less than the national average of 16 to 19 percent on credit card loans. You could use the money to pay off expensive credit card debt while continuing to earn interest on your savings.

Passbook loans have one serious drawback: depositors cannot get access to the money securing their loan as long as the debt is outstanding. If you have money in a passbook account, you could avoid a loan altogether simply by withdrawing the funds. You thereby avoid paying interest on what is, in effect, a loan of your own money. What you are really paying for is the discipline of repaying a loan rather than trusting yourself to replenish your savings account once it has been depleted.

CD Loans   Banks will also lend against a CD and generally charge 2 to 4 percent above the rate they are paying on it. Getting a loan against a CD has fewer disadvantages, since the money is tied up for the term of the deposit anyway and the depositor would have to pay a penalty if he or she made an early withdrawal. With either kind of loan, the bank would deduct both the principal and interest from the borrower's savings if he or she failed to repay the debt.

Second Mortgage Loan   When borrowers need a substantial sum of money, want to pay it back over a long period, and would like the security of a fixed rate, they may resort to a **second mortgage.** This type of installment loan, usually from a bank or savings and loan, puts a lien on the equity in a borrower's house (its market value minus the unpaid balance of the first mortgage). Because the holder of the first mortgage has first rights to the home if the borrower defaults, the second mortgage holder charges a higher interest rate than for a first mortgage and the terms are usually 15 years or less.

Most second mortgage lenders will let you borrow as much as 80 percent of your equity. Such a loan is usually economical only if you need $5,000 or more, since initial expenses make smaller loans prohibitive. Second mortgages, like first mortgages, impose closing costs. Banks typically charge 3 points or 3 percent of the loan as a closing cost. On a $20,000 second mortgage, those up-front costs would total

---

Diving Into a Second Mortgage

Marge and Henry Phillips would like to take a second mortgage loan to build a swimming pool in their back yard. They bought their home 10 years ago for $200,000. They paid $40,000 in cash and received a mortgage of $160,000 to pay for the balance of the house. Today, the assessed market value of their home is $270,000.

The Phillips apply for a second mortgage against the equity in their home. The current balance remaining on their first mortgage is $128,000. The bank will offer them only 80 percent of the equity in their home.

Question: How much of a second mortgage can Marge and Henry qualify for?

Answer: Their equity is equal to the current market value minus their first mortgage balance.

	Current Market Value	$270,000
−	First Mortgage Balance	128,000
=	Current Home Equity	142,000

The bank will lend them 80 percent of their current home equity.

$$\begin{array}{r} \$142,000 \\ \times\ .80 \\ \hline \$113,000 \end{array}$$

Naturally, the Phillips may not need such a large sum for their swimming pool but can borrow up to that amount if they wish to do so.

$600. Bankers are often eager to refinance original first mortgages, that is, to make new, larger loans reflecting the higher market value of the house. The owners then pay off their old first mortgage and have money left to spend or invest as they please. The interest payments on second mortgages are tax deductible.

Because borrowers are putting up the equity of their homes as collateral, the eligibility requirements for second mortgages are more liberal than those for most other types of loans. But second mortgages are another form of debt and should not be used frivolously. They are much too expensive to be used to meet short-term expenses.

Home Equity Loan   Many consumers do not understand home equity loan lending. Home equity loans are essentially a newer and cheaper variation on second mortgages. Once considered as desperate a measure as pawning a wrist watch, borrowing against one's home has gained new respectability and almost any homeowner can do it. Lenders have helped do away with any remaining stigma by giving this form of borrowing a felicitous new name: **home equity loan.** This is a form of a large-denomination consumer loan, which in reality is a credit line secured by the equity in a borrower's home.

People who have built up equity in their homes can reap benefit from this increasingly popular mortgage-secured line of credit. Many banks, large brokerage firms, S&Ls, finance companies, and credit unions now offer lending plans designed to allow borrowers access to this equity without disturbing the home's existing financing. Inflation during the 1970s and a booming housing market during the 1980s pushed up the median price of American houses, giving average homeowners considerable equity.

According to the Federal Home Loan Mortgage Corp., almost $3 trillion is locked in the equity of homes in the United States. Banks and brokerage houses throughout the country are attracted by the profits to be made by unlocking this enormous equity. Home equity lines of credit are usually a lender's safest product. Delinquencies are traditionally very low because people pay mortgages before other obligations and go to great pains to avoid defaulting.

The 1986 tax reform act helped make home equity loans a hot item. A wide loophole allowed homeowners to escape the phaseout of the deduction for consumer interest. Because this kind of borrowing is secured by the borrower's home, it is considered deductible mortgage interest rather than nondeductible consumer interest. A home can therefore serve as the source of deductible interest debt for college

A Home Equity Sail

If, for example, you financed 80 percent of a $100,000 yacht purchase with a 10-year consumer loan at 11 percent, you could not write off any interest. But if you borrowed $80,000 with an 11 percent home equity loan for 10 years, you could deduct $8,800 interest the first year, for a tax saving of $2,240 if you are in the 28 percent bracket. You would have a tax savings each year throughout the 10-year period.

tuition, cars, vacations, home improvements, or even grocery bills, as long as home-owners do not borrow any more than the original cost of their home plus the cost of improvements. The interest is fully tax deductible provided that homeowners do not use the equity loan to invest in stocks or bonds.

The interest qualifies for the mortgage deduction only up to the first $100,000 of debt. Homeowners cannot (as of October 14, 1987) deduct more than the interest on a $100,000 home equity loan. They can deduct the interest payments on all home mortgages that total up to $1 million on no more than two homes. But beyond that total, there is a separate $100,000 cap on the home equity loan.

Equity lines have become strong rivals of the government's nondeductible loan programs for financing college educations. They can be prudently tapped to pay off higher-priced debt on credit cards or auto loans.

The idea of converting a home into cash without actually selling it is being aggres-sively promoted by lenders. If you have owned a house for a number of years, you are very likely bombarded with tantalizing offers and teaser rates to help you tap its appreciated value.

A Rose by Any Other Name... In fact, stripped of its bells and whistles, a home equity loan is just a second mortgage with a twist. The particular appeal of a credit line, as opposed to a straight second mortgage, is its flexibility. A borrower of a second mortgage receives all the funds at once and begins paying back principal and pay-ing interest on the entire amount on a monthly schedule. A second mortgage gives borrowers access to a lump sum of cash, but those who need only a handful at a time might consider the home equity credit accounts an attractive loan option.

Home equity loan vendors offer a line of credit to draw against, sometimes tapped by credit card, rather than the fixed loans typical of a mortgage. Once they qualify as borrowers and their line of credit has been established, borrowers are guaranteed a maximum amount of credit available any time they want. A minimum credit line is typically $10,000. It is not activated until they need the funds and draw on the amount needed. When borrowers need a loan, they "access" their account by sim-ply writing a check, making a phone call, or using a credit card. Interest is paid only on the funds actually borrowed, not on the untapped portion of the credit line. It works like an overdraft checking account but with a much larger line of credit.

Once their credit line has been established, homeowners can borrow and repay on whatever schedule they like. The lender may set the duration of the line of credit at five years or longer or may even extend it indefinitely. Once the line is on the books, homeowners can take out advances up to the maximum of the line, though some lenders specify a minimum amount per withdrawal.

Interest Rates Because there is a dwelling as collateral, these secured loans are offered at lower interest rates than most ordinary consumer credit, including credit card bor-rowing. But the interest rates on home equity lines do fluctuate. Most are variable rates, pegged two or more percentage points above the average prime rate, and are adjusted monthly.

The big difference between home equity loans and most other forms of revolving credit lies in the magnitude of the sums lent. Depending upon the size of their income, homeowners can borrow into the six figures. This is also the only type of sizable credit line available to most consumers for long time periods, sometimes up to 10 years.

EQUITY

The Loan-to-Value Ratio

While equity credit lines features vary by state and lenders, the concept is basically the same. Here is how a typical line works. You apply for a revolving line of credit secured by the value of your home. What matters is how much your home is currently worth, not what you paid for it. The lender agrees to extend a line of credit based on a percentage, generally 70 to 80 percent of the appraised current market value of your home, minus any remaining balance of any first mortgage or other liens against your property. This is often called the **loan-to-value ratio**. For instance, if your home is appraised at $200,000 and a lender will go up to 80 percent of the value, you would be eligible for a $160,000 line of credit. But if you still had $60,000 to pay on your first mortgage, you would qualify for only a $100,000 credit line.

Problem: Let's say you own a house appraised at $150,000 and have an outstanding mortgage balance of $80,000. Lenders informed you that their loan limit is 75 percent of the appraised current value of your home. How much of a home equity loan can you expect to receive?

Answer:

	Appraised Value	$150,000
		× 75%
		$112,000
−	Mortgage Balance	80,000
=	Maximum Line of Credit	32,500

The Hazards and Risks of Home Equity Loans

Like most deals that sound too good to be true, home equity loans have some pitfalls:

1. Even before homeowners borrow their first cent, they will be subjected to some considerable closing costs. Borrowers must pay all the expenses associated with a traditional second mortgage: title search, title insurance, appraisal and application fees, attorney's fees, origination fees (points), mortgage insurance, recording fees, credit report, and annual charges for maintaining the account. These can total as much as 5 percent of the approved line of credit.

2. Money borrowed on a home equity line of credit represents another lien against the property. Moreover, once the line of credit is used, the bank has a lien on the home that secured it and can foreclose if the borrower fails to repay. If you start floundering financially, you do so at the risk of the roof over your head. Lenders prefer equity loans because the bankruptcy law regarding unsecured personal loans tends to leave them high and dry. Loan officers need not be too choosy about approving applicants for such secured loans.

   The trend toward easier access to home equity is attracting unsavory lenders to the business and causing alarm among debt counselors and legitimate lenders.

Some of these loan shops actually advertise that they make no income or credit check. All they really care about is your home equity, which they can foreclose on if you default. That is the bottom line in home equity loans. You are betting your house against your ability to repay. If you are laid off, disabled, or compelled to take early retirement, you might not have enough money to meet the payments.

3. Another potential risk is that someone who fails to meet required payments on the equity financing could lose more than a home. This is because the credit received is based on the current value of the house, and if that value declines, the borrower could be required to turn over additional assets to meet the obligations.

4. The longer homeowners hold off using their credit line, the less time they may have to repay any borrowings. The lifetime of these lines often begins the minute you open them, and so if you wait to take a loan until the fourth year of a five-year line, you are going to be handling much larger monthly payments. This is considered one of the major problems with home equity credit lines.

5. A further drawback of home equity loans is that on a borrower's credit record, the total amount of a credit line is treated as if it were an outstanding loan, even if the borrower has not yet borrowed against it. This could keep a borrower from getting credit somewhere else. He or she might, for example, be turned down for lower-interest dealer financing on a car because of a $20,000 open credit line.

    Borrowers who pay off the principal and interest due in order to close out their credit line need to notify the lender that they want to terminate the account. Otherwise, the institution will assume that they plan to keep the full credit line for future use. Consequently, the lender will not take the necessary action to remove the lien against the borrower's house.

6. Another danger in home equity loans is deceptively low monthly payments. Some lenders require borrowers to pay only the interest and suggest no amortization schedule. Whatever remains at the end of the maximum term is covered with a lump-sum payment. The day of reckoning may not come for five or more years, but when it does, you risk losing your home unless you have disciplined yourself to save a repayment fund.

7. The variable interest rates, usually two percentage points above the prime rate, often have no cap, or ceiling. This means that if the prime rate goes to 21 percent, as it did in the early 1980s, the bank would be charging a borrower 23 percent for a loan that once seemed so attractive at 10 percent.

Giving It a Second Thought

People considering a home equity loan should be disciplined consumers who have a reliable cash flow in their household, are in stable financial shape, and can keep a tight rein on borrowing.

Potential borrowers need to give the idea careful thought before opening one of these accounts. This powerful credit tool should be used safely and carefully. Parents with college-bound children may find this an attractive alternative for financing tuition over a four-year period. It is also suitable as a home improvement loan. If you are tempted to sign up but do not expect to be borrowing more than a few thousand dollars, consider this first: a lot of banks also offer revolving credit lines that may cost a little more in interest but do not require you to remortgage your property. There is no reason to put a new lien on your house to get a slightly better rate on what is essentially a small personal loan.

Installment Loans: Financing Your Car

When you take an **installment loan,** you sign a contract to repay the balance, plus interest and service charges, in equal installments over a specified period. The most common example of an installment loan is an auto loan, although this type of lending arrangement is also a popular way of financing consumer durables. Installment loans are available with fixed or variable interest rates.

Buying a car is one of the most complex and costly financial dealings most people face, second only to purchasing a home. In addition to selecting from a bewildering array of domestic and imported models and negotiating over price and options, most car buyers also need to arrange a loan to buy a new car. The variety of financing options available can make deciding where to borrow and what terms to seek as complicated as deciding what model car to buy.

Car buyers who need to arrange auto financing should not just check with their bank. Dealers and many other financial institutions offer especially attractive car loan rates and terms. The only way to be sure of getting the best deal is to comparison shop. Car buyers should treat the car purchase and its financing as two entirely different transactions.

Consumers need to shop for car financing as much as they shop for automobiles. When purchasing a car on credit, the real concern is more often not the price of the car but the cost of the car. First go to your bank and find out the rates. Then telephone several lenders in your area to check on their annual percentage rate (APR) for new car loans.

Generally speaking, credit unions, which are nonprofit organizations, charge less than banks do for auto loans. Bank loans, in turn, are usually less costly than financing supplied through dealers by the auto companies' financing subsidiaries, such as General Motors Acceptance Corporation or Ford Motor Credit. But those shopping for financing for a new car may sometimes discover that they can drive a better bargain on the showroom floor than at the bank.

Interest rates are not always the only consideration in comparison shopping for auto financing. People unable to get large enough bank loans to buy the cars of their dreams might qualify at a finance company, particularly if it is affiliated with an automaker. They are often more liberal than the banks since they are eager to promote sales of their cars. Auto dealers sometimes offer buyers the choice of a cut-rate loan or a price cut, the amount of which is essentially the price of special financing.

Car buyers searching for the best interest rate should not inadvertently ignore other parts of the car deal. Table 3–4 can be used to determine the monthly payments on auto loans at the interest rates shown. If you need a $10,000 loan, for example, at 10 percent APR, your monthly payments on a four-year note would be approximately $254. Your monthly payment on the same loan at 12 percent APR would be $263. The 2 percent difference in your interest rate results in a $9 difference in monthly payment. This means that each 1 percent difference in interest rate should cost only $4.50 extra per month on a $10,000 loan.

TABLE 3–4	Monthly Payments and Interest Costs

This table shows the approximate monthly payment and total interest cost of auto loans with selected annual percentage rates (APRs) and loan durations of two to five years. Figures are rounded to the nearest dollar. Actual amounts may vary slightly.

APR	Loan Amount	2 Years Monthly Payment	2 Years Total Interest	3 Years Monthly Payment	3 Years Total Interest	4 Years Monthly Payment	4 Years Total Interest	5 Years Monthly Payment	5 Years Total Interest
7%	$ 4,000	$179	$298	$124	$ 446	$ 96	$ 598	$ 79	$ 752
	5,000	224	373	154	558	120	747	99	940
	6,000	269	447	185	669	144	897	119	1,128
	7,000	313	522	216	781	168	1,046	139	1,317
	8,000	358	596	247	893	192	1,195	158	1,505
	9,000	403	671	278	1,004	216	1,345	178	1,693
	10,000	448	745	309	1,116	239	1,494	198	1,881
8%	$ 4,000	$181	$342	$125	$ 512	$ 98	$ 687	$ 81	$ 866
	5,000	226	427	157	641	122	859	101	1,083
	6,000	271	513	188	769	146	1,031	122	1,300
	7,000	317	598	219	897	171	1,203	142	1,516
	8,000	362	684	251	1,025	195	1,375	162	1,733
	9,000	407	769	282	1,153	220	1,546	182	1,949
	10,000	452	855	313	1,281	244	1,718	203	2,166
9%	$ 4,000	$183	$386	$127	$ 579	$100	$ 778	$ 83	$ 982
	5,000	228	482	159	724	124	972	104	1,228
	6,000	274	579	191	869	149	1,167	125	1,473
	7,000	320	675	223	1,014	174	1,361	145	1,719
	8,000	365	771	254	1,158	199	1,556	166	1,964
	9,000	411	868	286	1,303	224	1,750	187	2,210
	10,000	457	964	318	1,448	249	1,945	208	2,455
10%	$ 4,000	$185	$ 430	$129	$ 646	$ 101	$ 870	$ 85	$1,099
	5,000	231	537	161	808	127	1,087	106	1,374
	6,000	277	645	194	970	152	1,304	127	1,649
	7,000	323	752	226	1,131	178	1,522	149	1,924
	8,000	369	860	258	1,293	203	1,739	170	2,199
	9,000	415	967	290	1,455	228	1,957	191	2,473
	10,000	461	1,075	323	1,616	254	2,174	212	2,748
12%	$ 4,000	$188	$ 519	$133	$ 783	$105	$1,056	$ 89	$1,339
	5,000	235	649	166	979	132	1,320	111	1,673
	6,000	282	779	199	1,174	158	1,584	133	2,008
	7,000	330	908	233	1,370	184	1,848	156	2,343
	8,000	377	1,038	266	1,566	211	2,112	178	2,677
	9,000	424	1,168	299	1,761	237	2,376	200	3,012
	10,000	471	1,298	332	1,957	263	2,640	222	3,347

This example shows that for each $1,000 you borrow on a four-year loan, each point you negotiate off the interest rate will save just 45 cents a month on payments. Therefore, car shoppers must consider and compare deals as complete packages, including:

1. The price of the car

2. The trade-in amount

3. The APR on the loan

4. The required down payment

5. The size of the loan

6. The term

7. The monthly payments

8. The total finance charge

If offered a choice between a cash rebate or a trade-in and cut-rate financing, you need, with the help of a financial calculator, to run the numbers for both deals, the smaller loan at the higher rate and the larger loan at the lower rate. Often a combination of a dealer trade-in and someone else's loan is the best choice.

Rates often vary with the size of the down payment and length of time for repayment. A larger down payment or shorter loan term may translate into a lower rate because it reduces the lender's risk. A person putting 25 percent down on a four-year loan can expect to pay a higher rate of interest than someone who puts 50 percent down and borrows for a three-year period. Higher car prices have prompted many lenders to offer loans for longer than the usual 48 months. Loans of 60 months have become routine in some regions, and 72- and 84-month loans are entering the scene.

Test Drive Your Car's Finances

It's time to buy your $12,000 dream car. Dealer *A* offers you $4,000 for your trade-in and will finance the $8,000 balance at 10 percent annual interest for four years. Dealer *B* offers you $4,500 for your trade-in but charges 13 percent interest on the $7,500 balance. Which deal is better? If you check the interest tables (Table 3–4), you will notice that deal *A* will cost you $1,739 in interest and deal *B*, $2,158. (The $2,158 figure is derived by averaging the total interest cost for $7,000 and $8,000 at 13 percent. The average of $2,014 and $2,302 is $2,158.) Deal *A* saves you $419 in interest, but this is not quite enough to make up for the $500 lower price tag that comes with deal *B*. The deal *A* bargain interest rate would cost you $81 more.

are entering the scene.

The longer the loan, the lower the monthly payments, but you will pay more over the life of the loan. For example, if you take a $10,000 loan at 12 percent interest, the monthly payments on a 60-month loan would be $222; on a 72-month loan, $195; and on an 84-month loan, $176. But that 80-month loan will cost you over all $1,464 more in interest than the 60-month loan. Shortening the length of a loan will therefore increase the monthly payments but decrease your total finance charge.

Car Leasing

Prompted by rising car prices and the phaseout in the tax deduction for interest payments, more people are leasing automobiles for long terms. **Leasing** is an alternative form of financing where ownership is vested in the hands of the lender instead of the borrower. It is a contractual agreement under which you make monthly payments for the use of a car over a set period of time, usually between three to five years.

When you lease a vehicle, you are paying only for that portion of the car's value that will be used up during the contract. At the end of the lease term, you return the automobile to the leasing company. Leasing deals, often heavily subsidized by automobile manufacturers, are a viable alternative to buying a car for cash or on credit. Leases gen-

LEASE

Leasing versus Buying on Credit

Here is a comparison of a typical lease and financing arrangement for a 1994 compact car. The actual purchase price is $16,000. If financed, the interest rate would be 12.75 percent. The cash saved by leasing would have been invested to earn taxable interest of 8 percent. Both the lease and the loan would have been for five years. Note that the difference in final cost between purchasing and leasing is relatively minor.

	Purchase (via Loan)	Lease
Down payment	$ 1,182	$ 0
Refundable security deposit	0	325
Monthly payments	355	271
× 60 total +	21,300	16,260
Fee at lease termination	0	100
Total outlay including interest	22,482	16,360
Estimated resale value of car	− 7,650	0
Net cost	14,832	16,360
Interest on cash saving (after tax)	0	− 952
Final cost	14,832 +	15,408

SOURCE: Bank Lease Consultants

What $319 for 48 Months Really Means

Manufacturers who trumpet low–monthly –payment leases can squeeze the pride tag in a number of ways: by subsidizing the interest rate built into the deal, just as they offer cut–rate loans to buyers; by cutting the price of the car, either directly or through offsetting rebates; or by hiking up the residual—the value they assume the car will be worth at the end of the lease—so you pay for less depreciation while you drive.

To get the payment down to $319 a month on the four–year Acura Vigor lease detailed below, American Honda cut the price of the Acura to $2,482 below suggested list price and built a bargain–rate interest factor (3.9%) into the lease. You may not find that kind of information in leasing ads, but you will see a lot of small print. To help you understand it, review this slightly abbreviated annotated version of the footnote in the Vigor ad. We've broken out the important clauses and distilled the legalese.

What It Says:

1. Available through April 30, 1993, at participating Acura dealers to qualified lessees approved by American Honda Finance Corporation.
2. Subject to availability. Advertised lease rate of $319/month is for a 48–month closed–end lease for the Vigor GS automatic with MSRP of $28,065, including destination charges.
3. Taxes, title, license and registration, insurance, and optional equipment and services not included.
4. Advertised rate based on a consumer payment of $1,000 as a prepaid rental reduction down payment.
5. and a dealer–capitalized cost reduction of $2,482.30; condition of dealer participation may affect actual rate.
6. Consumer's $1,000 down payment, first month's lease payment, refundable security deposit equal to one month's payment rounded to the next highest $25 increment, title, license and registration fee, and tax to the extent applicable are due at lease signing.
7. Total of monthly payment is $15,312 plus tax as applicable..
8. Option to purchase at end of lease for purchase price is $12,067.95 plus applicable tax and official fees except in Mississippi, New York and South Dakota, where no purchase option is available.
9. Lessee pays for maintenance, insurance, repairs and service, any and all taxes related to the vehicle or the lease, registration renewals, and excessive wear and tear and use.
10. Mileage charge of $1.5/mile over 15,000 miles per year.
11. A disposition fee of no more than $400 is due if vehicle is not purchased at the end of the lease term.

continued

What $319 for 48 Months Really Means (continued)

What It Means:

1. There's no guarantee you can get this deal. Dealers don't have to participate—although most Acura dealers do—and you must have a good credit record. Honda says 80% or more applicants qualify.

2. If this exact car isn't available, the dealer doesn't have to order it for you. Switching to a car with a different list price would affect the monthly payment.

3. These costs vary greatly around the country and can be steep. In Los Angeles County, for example, sales taxes would add $26.32 to the monthly payment, bringing it to $345.32. License, registration and other required fees for the Vigor would cost $662.46.

4. You must make a $1,000 down payment to get the $319–a–month lease. Spread over the four years, that's another $21 a month. Down payments are often the key to "low" monthly payments.

5. If the dealer won't give up that much profit, you'll pay more per month; if you can negotiate a bigger discount, you'll pay less. Honda says most dealers will go along with the suggested cut.

6. The cost will vary depending on where you live. The total for someone in Los Angeles County would be $2,440; That's a $1,000 down payment plus $82.50 in sales taxes on it; $662.46 in title, license and registration fees; $345.32 for the first payment, including sales tax; and a security deposit of $350.

7. Typically, sales taxes are added to each lease payment. If you state rate is 4%, for example, about $13 would be added to each $300 payment. This means you pay tax on less than the full value of the car and spread out the bill over the term of the lease.

8. The right to purchase the car at this price isn't available in these three states because Honda believes offering the option in an advertisement would trigger additional disclosure requirements. Other leases do allow end–of–lease purchases in these states.

9. You're responsible for all these costs, just as if you had purchased the car. Excess–wear–and–tear charges could total several hundred dollars.

10. This charge applies if you drive the care more than 60,000 miles.

11. This is an extra fee if you don't buy the car at the end of the lease. It is not negotiable but may be lower if state law requires.

to pay the full cost of the car. A sizable part of it, usually between 33 and 50 percent, is left at the end of the term and covered by returning the car in good condition.

A key number in the lease is the **residual value**. For instance, if an automaker determines that a $16,000 car will be worth $8,000 after three years, payments on a three-year lease would be based on only $8,000. This is the amount the leasing company thinks the car will be worth at the end of the lease period. To figure the payments, a leasing company starts with the price of the car and subtracts its residual value. The difference is the depreciation the lessor pays for. It is divided by the number of months of the lease. To that is added what amounts to an interest (finance) charge to compensate the leasing firm for financing the car to the lessor.

In the past, finance companies sold **open-end** leases that held the consumer responsible if the car's actual value at the end of a lease was lower than the target set at the agreement's start. However, most leases offered by auto makers in recent years have been **closed-end** leases in which residual value is fixed. That means lessors have no further obligation after they return the car at the end of the fixed lease term, unless it has been driven more than the mileage limit or given more than normal wear and tear. Some leasing contracts often limit the amount of mileage that a lessor can put on a car. For example, on a three-year Cadillac lease, General Motors charges 10 cents for every mile beyond 45,000.

As stated, the residual value is a key factor in determining the leasing costs. The higher it is, the less depreciation you pay for and therefore the lower the monthly payments. The fact that you pay for only the part of the car that depreciates automatically means that cars that retain more of their value longer will offer more attractive leases.

Most lease contracts allow lessors to purchase the car at the end of the lease for a set price known as the **option price**. The option price may be the residual value or another amount, such as the market price for similar models of this car. All leases should state clearly who pays for maintenance and repairs.

The main argument against leasing is that at the end of the lease you have nothing to show for all that money. Leasing, however, may be more feasible under the following circumstances:

1. If you lack money for a down payment

2. If you do not want to tie up your cash

3. If you plan to keep the car for four years or less

4. If you are more concerned about lower monthly payments than equity in your car.

Balloon Note

One of the newer developments in car financing is the **balloon note**. In some ways it resembles a lease and works much like a balloon mortgage (see Chapter 6). Borrowers make monthly payments for a set period, say a three- or four-year term. The bank, in effect, charges for the deterioration of the car. When the term ends, the consumer may keep the car by paying off the note with a balloon (a lump sum), refinance it, or turn in the car to the lender.

In balloon note financing, the bank estimates what a particular model car will be worth when the loan period ends. The lender then guarantees the customer that it will buy back the car at that price, provided the vehicle has been well maintained and the ceilings on mileage have been observed. The lender subtracts this guarantee buyback price from the car's sticker price to arrive at a residual price. The customer pays principal and interest on the residual, plus interest on the guaranteed value. The balloon comes at the end, when the customer must pay the entire guaranteed value in one installment or give up the car.

BALLOON

Does Your Balloon Float?

To see how a balloon note works, take a car carrying a sticker price of $10,724. You make a 10 percent down payment, leaving a balance of $9,652 to be financed. The bank charges a 12.95 percent interest rate. The bank also assumes 54 percent depreciation on the car and then guarantees to buy it back for $4,900 (about 45 percent of the sticker price) when the loan ends in 36 months. This $4,490 is the car's residual value. To figure your monthly payment, the lender subtracts from the price both your down payment and the car's expected residual value at the end of the loan term. The bank collects principal and interest on the car's anticipated depreciated value ($9,652 minus $4,900) of $4,752 and only interest on the residual $4,900.

At the end of the loan term, you face a $4,900 balloon payment in order to keep the car. If you do not have the cash, you have three options: one, forget the debt and turn the keys over to the bank; two, sell the car and pay the amount in cash, possibly making a profit; or three, refinance the $4,900 as a used car loan, which will carry a higher interest rate.

Your monthly payment is lower than it would be if you financed the entire $9,652 ($10,724 minus $1,072) conventionally. You also gamble on what interest rates will be at the end of the term if you plan to refinance. You would be financing at used car rates, which are generally between three and five percentage points higher than new car rates.

The potential advantages of a balloon note depend upon a customer's situation. In some cases, no down payment is required. Lower monthly payments let customers afford a more expensive car or one with more options. The balloon loan, however, remains something of a gamble. Borrowers could come out ahead if the actual market value of the car at the end of the loan is more than the lender anticipated, enabling them to sell the car, pay off the loan balance, and pocket the difference. If the car is in satisfactory condition but not worth as much as the lender said it would be, the borrower may simply choose to drop the keys on the lender's desk and walk away.

In summary, a balloon loan can make a new car possible for buyers on tight budgets because monthly payments are lower. It can also be useful to people who decide to buy a car that they could not otherwise afford. It is actually a hybrid between a lease and a loan. It works like a loan but has the advantages of a lease.

Margin Loans

The first place you probably think of when you want to take out a loan is your bank. But consider an alternative source for loans. If you have a stock portfolio at a brokerage house, you can borrow against your securities by opening a margin account with your broker.

Margin loans (also known as *broker loans*) are usually associated with investors who borrow to buy more securities, a sophisticated leverage strategy that can increase both risk and return (see Chapter 12). But consumers can borrow against their securities for any purpose. Many customers have discovered margin loans as a good source for low-cost credit.

In order to obtain margin loans, borrowers have to first place stocks and bonds in a special margin account as collateral. Under Federal Reserve Board regulations, individuals can generally borrow up to 50 percent of the market value of the common and preferred stocks listed on the American and New York Exchanges and on the over-the-counter (OTC) market, up to 70 percent of the market value of corporate bonds, and up to 95 percent on U.S. government securities.

Once a lender has received a margin loan, the equity balance in the account (the value of securities minus the loan) must generally not drop below 30 percent of the total account portfolio. The New York Stock Exchange requires a minimum of 25 percent, but brokerage houses usually require a higher balance. If the securities decline below that margin maintenance requirement, borrowers will be asked to deposit additional cash to bring the equity in their account up to the required level. If they cannot come up with the cash, the brokerage house will be forced to sell some of their securities. Borrowers can reduce the chances of having to add additional securities or cash by not borrowing the maximum permitted.

Rates are generally at least 1 or 2 percentage points below what banks usually charge for a consumer loan and are considerably less than the costs of many types of short-term financing. But a broker loan is a variable-rate loan with all its inherent risks. Because of the interest rate risk involved with this type of loan, most people should view margin account borrowing only as an alternative to traditional short-term financing. This means that borrowers should plan on paying back the loan within six months, or a year at most, to avoid fluctuating interest rates.

Although margin loans are generally issued by brokerage houses, consumers can borrow up to 70 percent of the market value of their stocks and bonds at most banks as well, in the form of a secured loan.

IRA Loans

When the government gave IRA (Individual Retirement Account) holders a 60-day grace period to transfer their accounts or roll over lump-sum distributions (see Chapter 18), it created, in effect, a source for low-interest, short-term loans.

Although borrowers may not offer an IRA as collateral for a secured loan, nothing prevents them from using their IRA money during the 60-day grace period. The direct cost is nil, since you pay no one interest for the use of your own money. The only cost is the interest that you would have earned if the funds had been kept in the IRA during this period. As you may recall from Chapter 1, this is known as the opportunity cost. The important thing to remember is that borrowers cannot exceed the 60-day period, or their low-interest loan could become one of the highest-priced loans imaginable. First, they will be charged a 10 percent penalty fee on the entire amount of the IRA, and then it will be taxed as current income for that year.

Life Insurance Loan

The cash surrender value of a life insurance policy can be tapped in the form of a low-interest loan at any time and for any reason. The overpayments made by the policyholders of a whole life insurance policy are accumulated by the life insurance company as a form of savings known as cash surrender value. Policyholders may keep the loan outstanding for as long as they choose and pay only the interest. They forfeit the return on the investment portion of their policy, and the amount of coverage is reduced by the amount of the outstanding loan until the loan is repaid. (This is discussed in greater detail in Chapter 9.)

Credit Life Insurance

It is easy to feel nervous when signing on the dotted line for a loan. A borrower typically should ask himself or herself: Could I afford the monthly payments if my spouse died? And if I die, could my spouse make the payments without me? Many lenders have an answer—**credit life insurance**, which repays the entire loan balance on the death of either spouse. Many lenders promote it for mortgages as well as for auto loans, personal loans, and other types of debt.

But credit insurance is actually a prohibitively expensive form of life insurance and is probably best avoided. Instead, borrowers who want insurance for their loan can buy an inexpensive term policy directly from an insurance company. This is much cheaper than a credit life policy. By law, a lender cannot require a borrower to buy credit life as a condition for granting a loan, but some include it in the loan contract unless the borrower requests otherwise.

Credit Cards: America's Biggest Card Game

Credit cards are not only a way of life among consumers but an increasingly important part of the nation's financial system. About 100 million Americans hold more than 700 million credit cards, of which some 310 million are MasterCard and VISA cards. The typical adult in the U.S. has eight credit cards, according to the Bankcard Holders of America, a nonprofit consumer group. Every day more than 200 million credit cards slide in and out of charge machines across the United States. Hundreds of billions of dollars in sales are transacted with these cards each year.

Advertising has made charge cards appear attractive and enticing. But when we strip away their gold plating and allure, major charge cards are really little more than a revolving line of credit loan. To clarify a few terms:

A **revolving line of credit** is a fixed dollar amount available to a borrower which allows the borrower to purchase goods and services without cash at any time. As the credit is paid off, it becomes available to the borrower again, thus the term "revolving." Revolving credit is sometimes compared to a wheel that can roll, say, 15 feet, but no further. To get the wheel rolling again, you must first push it back toward the starting point by paying off all or part of the debt balance. Since it rolls back and forth in the same place, it may be better described as a treadmill.

A **credit card** gives the cardholder a revolving line of credit. One does not have to pay the full amount owed each month, but there is a finance charge on any unpaid balance. With a **charge card** or charge account, there is usually no assigned line of credit. You therefore must pay the full amount owed when you are billed.

"As soon as I receive a confirmation notice on your credit card I'll pronounce you 'husband and wife.' "

SOURCE: "Pepper...and Salt," *The Wall Street Journal,* April 3, 1989, A-15. Reprinted by permission of Cartoon Features Syndicate.

Overdraft checking adds a line of credit to a checking account that is activated whenever the individual writes a check for more than the account balance. A home equity credit line, as discussed previously, also offers a large line of credit to qualified homeowners.

Credit and charge card issuers are not doing you a favor by giving you a card. Credit cards are a very profitable business. These issuers earn tens of billions of dollars profit annually in the form of annual fees as well as interest charged on outstanding consumer revolving credit. On top of that, merchants who accept these cards are charged 1 to 6 percent of the dollar value of each transaction. For years, credit cards have been one of the banks' main profit centers, helping offset damage from bad loans and competitive incursions by other lenders. Between 1983 and 1988, credit cards earned three to five times more than the ordinary banking rate of return, according to a study by Professor Lawrence Ausubel of Northwestern University.

Visa and MasterCard

Two organizations, VISA International and MasterCard International, provide banks with advertising and computer record keeping services. They do not issue any cards. The cards are issued by some 15,000 individual U.S. banks, S&Ls, and credit unions. Each bank sets its own credit terms, interest rates, grace periods, and penalty fees within the limits of state law. Some aggressively sell across state lines, while others deliberately restrict themselves to in-state or regional customers. Other major credit card sponsors are American Express, Discover, and Diners Club. In addition to these general purpose credit cards, many department stores and other merchants issue single-purpose cards that can only be used for buying something in a particular store or chain of stores.

TABLE 3–5	Different Billing Systems		
	Adjusted Balance	**Previous Balance**	**Average Daily Balance**
Monthly interest rate	1.5%	1.5%	1.5%
Previous balance	$400	$400	$400
Payments	$300	$300	$300 (paid on the 15th day)
Interest charge	$1.50 ($100 × 1.5%)	$6.00 ($400 × 1.5%)	$3.75 (average balance of $250 × 1.5%)

Playing Your Cards Right

Americans spend $32 billion a year just to use general-purpose credit cards—for fees, interest and other charges. Sixty-nine percent of cardholders carry balances on their bank cards. The average balance in 1993 was $1,644. At an interest rate of 18 percent, that $1,644 cost about $300 a year. Consumers could save much of these expenses by tailoring their cards to their spending habits. When evaluating credit card offers, applicants should look carefully at the fine print before signing up. The following are some key features to carefully check.

Interest Costs (Finance Charge)   Despite the common perception that all major charge cards are the same, there are major differences between bank cards, particularly in the interest rates charged, and a number of issuers use adjustable rates that float up and down with the market. This means that consumers have a wide variety of choices. If one bank charges too high an interest rate, consumers can get a credit card at a bank that offers better rates. They can take advantage by shopping around in what has rapidly become a nationwide marketplace for charge cards.

The **transaction date** is the day on which a cardholder uses his or her card for a purchase or a cash advance. A record of the transaction is sent to the cardholder's bank, which enters it in his or her account on the **posting date**. If cardholders do not pay their balances on time, they are charged interest or a finance charge on the average daily balance starting from the posting date. The monthly finance charge is one-twelfth of the bank's annual interest rate. Therefore, a card charging a seemingly modest 1.75 percent monthly finance charge is actually charging a 21 percent annual rate of interest.

Truth in lending requires that credit card issuers tell cardholders the method of calculating the finance charge. Creditors use a number of different systems to calculate the balance on which they assess finance charges. Some creditors add finance charges after subtracting payments made during the billing period. This seldom used system is called the **adjusted balance method**. Other creditors give no credit for payments made during the billing period. This is called the **previous balance method**. This is the most expensive method of computing finance charges. Not many companies use this method anymore. The most commonly used method is the **average daily balance method**. Creditors using this method add the balances for each day in the billing period and then divide by the number of days in the billing period.

TABLE 3–6	Major Credit Card Providers	

Annual fees and interest rates on unpaid balances can vary greatly.

	Annual Fee	Interest Rate
American Express*	$55–$300	16.25**
AT&T	$0–$40	17.9–18.9**
Bank of New York	$0–$25	14.4–17.9**
BankAmerica	$18–$48	17.0–19.0**
Chase Manhattan	$20–$50	16.8–19.8
Citicorp (U.S. only)	$20–$60	16.8–19.8
Discover (Sears)	$0	19.8
First Chicago	$0–$100	18.9–19.8**
M&N Corp	$20–$40	16.9–18.9
Manufacturers Hanover	$20–$40	17.8–19.8
Wells Fargo	$18–$48	17.0–19.0**

Note: Information was current as this book went to press.

* American Express also issues the Optima card under these terms.

** One or both of the percentages are based on variable rates.

As the table shows, the finance charge varies considerably for the same purchases and payments. Consumers could pay three or four times as much interest on one card as on another, even though both charge the same annual percentage rate (APR). Banks and other issuers of credit cards are obliged by law to explain the math, but their explanations are often clear only to a CPA.

Those who tend to operate with high monthly balances should seek a card on which interest rates fall as balances rise. To encourage heavier use of their cards, some banks charge two different interest rates, known as **tiered rates,** depending on the size of your balance. The initial rate of say, 16.8 percent, typically applies to charges of up to $2,000. Above that amount the interest rate is reduced by one or two points. Although such cards are relatively rare, they permit cardholders to pay a lower rate of interest by putting all of their charges on one card instead of splitting them up.

The Grace Period Other crucial features to look for are factors affecting borrowing costs, specifying the method of calculating the finance charge. . The first item to check is the interest-free **grace period,** the time between the date of the credit card purchase and the date the bank starts charging cardholders interest on the loan. Some banks have no grace period—the interest meter starts ticking the day the purchase was made—while most extend 25 to 30 days' grace. Even banks with grace periods cancel them if cardholders fail to pay off their balance in full each month. The difference can add up, especially on large purchases.

Suppose you make $250 worth of purchases during a monthly billing cycle and pay your bill in full. At a bank with a 30-day grace period, you would owe no interest. If your card had no grace period and a standard 16.5 percent interest rate, you would pay as much as $3.50 in interest.

About 25 percent of all banks now start charging interest on the purchase date. A 25- to 30-day grace period during which cardholders can pay their bill in full and not incur an interest charge is the next best thing to free money. If you time your purchases just after the "posting date" (the last date on which purchases will show up on your next bill), and if you pay every bill in full just before the finance charge accrues, you can get at least six weeks, and maybe as much as two months, of free credit. The financial advantage is even greater if you maintain an interest-paying checking or money market account and earn interest until the bill is paid.

Annual Fees   More than 95 percent of all banks charge an annual fee on their credit cards. Charges range from $0 to $300, as can be seen in Table 3-6, with $20 to $25 common for the regular VISA and MasterCard accounts with credit lines of $500 to $3,500. Nearly 400 banks in 1991 offered a variety of no-fee cards. However, an advertised free card may not be a bargain. A "free" card might not be free at all:

1. It might offer no grace period. You will always be charged interest from the day a purchase is posted to your account, even though you pay in full by the end of the month.

2. When you use your card for cash advances, there is rarely a grace period. But some institutions charge a 2 to 4 percent fee for cash advances on top of the regular interest rate.

3. There could be "transaction fees" of $1 to $2.50 a month for using the card or for rolling over balances. That amounts to the same as an annual fee, but the ad or brochure might forget to mention it.

Since cardholders are not likely to find a truly free card with no annual fee and very low rates, they need to let their payment habits determine their choice. Cardholders who are a "revolvers," the bank's term for someone who continuously allows unpaid balances to revolve into the following billing cycle, should opt for cards with the lowest interest rate. Cardholders who pay off their balances in full each month are known as **convenience users.** They generally have a 25-day grace period to pay before interest rates accrue and can afford the luxury of basing their choice of a card on something other than interest rates. The best card in that case may often be one with no annual fee.

Cardholders who generally run a high balance should, however, be wary of the trade-off between low annual fees and high interest rates. "No-fee" cardholders who

---

Bargain Cards

The Bankcard Holders of America (BHA) features a toll-free number (800/327-7300) for consumers to order its list of 47 banks that offer relatively low-rate and no-fee cards. The list costs $4 and is also available by writing to BHA, 560 Herndon Parkway, Suite 120, Herndon, VA 22070.

pay 20 percent interest on a $1,000 outstanding monthly balance, for example, would save money by paying a $15 annual fee and interest of 15 percent or less.

Cardholders should, however, refrain from switching to another bank every time they become aware of a better offer. Switching does not always make sense. To find out how much, if anything, you would save by switching banks, first analyze how you use your credit card. If your monthly balance averages $100, for example, the savings would be $8.30 a year by switching from a card charging 19.8 percent to one charging 11.5 percent. But much of that could be eaten up by additional costs, such as late payment charges or higher annual fees than you are currently paying. Switching to a lower rate card, therefore, is beneficial for users who habitually carry over large balances. Some credit card issuers offer a "balance transfer" feature under which the new cardholder can transfer balances outstanding on other, higher interest rate credit cards. Under a balance transfer program, cardholders typically receive several checks that can be used to pay off these balances. The amount of the check written is then added to the balance of the lower interest card that issued the checks.

The number and type of establishments accepting each card is another factor to consider. VISA, MasterCard, Discover, and American Express are by far the most universally accepted of the major cards. Both are accepted at about 4 million locations in about 160 countries worldwide. Credit card companies are currently continuing their efforts to win acceptance as a form of payment in new industries such as supermarkets and hospitals. There are also travel and entertainment cards, popularly known as T&E cards, which include such leading issues as American Express, Diners Club, and Carte Blanche. These require that you pay off the entire balance when your bill arrives. There is normally no interest charge, but there is an annual fee for use of the card. Some T&E cards offer certain credit options.

Secured Credit Cards

People who apply for collateral, backed, or **secured credit cards** are those who generally cannot get the cards any other way. These cards are targeted mainly to consumers with credit problems. Citibank launched a secured-card program in June 1991. To qualify, customers must make a deposit, usually a minimum of $500 to $3,000, with the institution issuing the card. They then get a credit line equal to the deposit. The bank can draw on the deposit if payments are delinquent for more than 60 to 180 days.

However, these cards have some disadvantages. Banks find that people with poor credit histories are so anxious to get credit that they are willing to pay interest rates as high as 22 percent, nonwaivable annual fees ranging from $20 to $75, and application fees as high as $65. Additionally, cardholders have to put up with relatively low interest or no interest on their deposits. Secured cards are not a good choice for people with positive credit histories since they have to agree to put the deposit out of reach for the life of the card. For more information on banks that offer secured credit cards, individuals can call Bankcard Holders of America (BHA) at 800/237-1800.

Card Tricks: Premium Cards

With so many cards currently in the pockets of Americans, card issuers have been vigorously competing to get you to use their card. Their technique, similar to that used by the breakfast cereal, soda, beer, or detergent producers, is known as "product differentiation." The credit card issuers are rushing to differentiate themselves from one another by offering a panoply of services.

Card issuers try to convince consumers that their product is unique or different. The difference may be real or imaginary. The important thing to card issuers is that consumers buy it. VISA and MasterCard, for example, have introduced cards with higher credit lines. They also tout such extras as frequent flier miles, travel insurance, and special hotel services. American Express has added access to health spas around the world to the list of extra benefits offered to its gold card members.

Several banks offer "frequent spender" programs in which cardholders can build up points that allow them to buy merchandise at a discount. Wells Fargo and Citibank offer "Wells Dollars" and "Citidollars" for users of their VISA cards and MasterCards. For each purchase made with the card, the cardholder receives a certain amount of scrip money—glorified Green Stamps—which can be applied to reducing the cost of watches, briefcases, and other items appearing in Wells Fargo and Citibank shopping catalogs. The General Electric Capital Corporation's GE Rewards card has a similar program.

MasterCard also has a travel bonus program. If cardholders use their gold card to charge any airline ticket, rental car, or hotel room, they get bonus points with American Airlines, National Rental Cars, or Sheraton hotels, respectively. With the American Express card and many others, holders earn a free travel mile for every dollar they charge. Typically, these cards carry high annual fees and interest rates, but some consumers fly so often that they more than recoup the upfront costs. Others commonly offer a credit card registration fee that will report lost or stolen cards and provide cash and airline tickets in emergencies.

Most of the major card issuers have introduced **premium cards** in recent years. These so-called premium cards offer services that may justify the fee for big spenders or frequent travelers, such as a 24-hour toll-free travel service, customized billing privileges, check-cashing services, $500,000 of travel accident insurance, membership in an international network of private clubs, and preferential treatment in reserving luxury hotel rooms and limousines. And, as the American Express Company puts it in its promotional literature, its premium "platinum" card confers on the holder "unparalleled prestige worldwide." Most people, however, have little use for unparalleled prestige worldwide and may just be paying for a lot of unnecessary frills. For the vast majority of credit card holders, a basic card provides all the credit and services they need.

The high credit limits on premium cards may appear useful. But is it advantageous for cardholders to borrow large sums of money at charge card rates? Borrowing

Lost of Stolen Cards

The Truth in Lending Act limits a cardholder's loss from unauthorized use of a credit card to a $50 account in the event of a card being stolen or lost. It is the cardholder's responsibility to contact the card issuer immediately if the card is stolen or lost. If a cardholder notifies the card issuer before the card is used, he or she is not liable for anything.

SOURCE: *Time*, March 31, 1986. Reprinted by permission of Michael Witte.

$500 at 18 percent is expensive enough; borrowing $20,000 at that rate would be foolish. Cardholders would be better served with a personal or installment loan from a bank at substantially cheaper rates.

With so many cards and so many options, a cardholder would be welladvised to look beyond the flattering brochures and enticements. The way you use your card will determine which deal will cost you the least. Cardholders should weigh how much they would use the benefits against the extra cost of a premium card.

Credit Card Abuse

Credit cards that require bills to be paid in full each month can be efficient instruments for record keeping and for purchasing budgeted items. But they can also contribute to impulse buying, excessive buildup of debt, and abuse of the credit card as a loan instrument. The cards should be used for their convenience in purchasing items that you can afford. The card generally gives the consumer an interest-free loan for a month. The consumer should have the funds on hand to pay the bill before interest is due. Otherwise, credit card loans become a very expensive form of borrowing. Their finance charges are relatively high. Abusing a credit card can turn a consumer into a credit card "addict"—one who constantly builds up debt to the card's limit and makes only the minimum required payment.

Smart Cards

The millions of cards floating around in American wallets are becoming electronic keys, capable of unlocking a dizzying array of services. Credit has become only one of many services offered by the cards. Special out-of-town business arrangements, money machines, computer services, insurance, and financial management accounts are among the many other services now available through credit cards. These and other new uses will be possible because of the advent of **smart cards**, which have a tiny microchip embedded in them. The chip will provide credit limits and ratings that can be read by a store computer, approval for a cash advance, or an electronic replica of the cardholder's signature to ensure that the card is not stolen.

For many people, the chief attraction of smart cards may be their promise of lightening the load of plastic in their wallet. Soon we may need only a single smart card to withdraw money from our bank accounts, make retail purchases, and record information about our stock holdings and insurance coverage. And, smart cards used as debit cards may lead us to a cashless (electronic funds transfer) society. (The topic of debt cards and cashless society is discussed further in Chapter 10.)

Personal Bankruptcy

Credit can be very tempting. Our mail boxes are stuffed with come-ons for credit cards, prestige cards, and affinity cards. Homeowners are being deluged with solicitations for home equity lines of credit and unsecured loans. Bank computers spew out "very special invitations" to millions of potential borrowers. Others advertise "guaranteed credit approval" or "car sale—no money down!" Some lenders make their invitations to borrow sound like a sweepstakes pitch, "If someone handed you $10,000, how would you spend it?"

This frenzy of solicitation makes credit seem easy, inviting, and accessible. Some people succumb to the temptation and overindulge. Too much of this good thing can result in bankruptcy.

Bankruptcy is no simple matter, and its use as a tool for debt relief should be considered only as a last resort. It was not designed as an easy way to evade paying our debts. But for those who are mired in bills and no longer have the means

You Have Plenty of Company

Some of the celebrities who filed for personal bankruptcy during recent decades are:

Director Peter Bogdanovich *(Paper Moon)*
Rocker Mick Fleetwood
Singer Isaac Hayes
Actor Chris Robinson ("General Hospital")
Author Clifford Irving
Evangelist Sun Myung Moon
Former U.S. Secretary of Agriculture Earl Butz
Pitcher Gaylord Perry
Former Texas governor John B. Connally
Heart surgeon Denton Cooley
Former billionaire brothers Nelson and Herbert Hunt
Singer Wayne Newton
Actress Kim Basinger

to fulfill their debt obligations, bankruptcy has been provided by the law as a means to absolve those debts and allow the debtors to reenter the system and get a fresh start.

As Figure 3–1 shows, an increasing number of Americans saddled by debt take bankruptcy as the one clear road out of indebtedness. In 1985, nearly 340,000 debtors filed for personal bankruptcy, seeking protection under the Federal Bankruptcy Law, the primary vehicle for personal relief. Even during periods of prosperity such as the years 1985 to 1988, filings for personal bankruptcies surged at double-digit annual rates and topped 718,100 in 1990. In 1991, there were 811,000 personal bankruptcy cases filed in the United States, a 188 percent increase over the previous year and a record.

Many bankruptcy filings involve low- and middle-income wage earners undone by relatively small amounts of unsecured debt, such as unforeseen medical expenses or a few thousand dollars in credit card bills, often coupled with a job loss. However, a profile of bankrupts revealed that some 80 percent of them held jobs. Those filing for bankruptcy were not confined to a financial underclass but instead represented a cross section of Americans, including some prominent celebrities.

| **FIGURE 3–1** | **The Rising Tide of Personal Bankruptcy** |

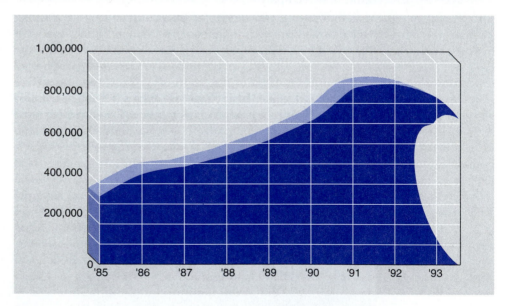

Filings for personal bankruptcy have more than doubled over the last eight years.

SOURCE: Administration Office of U.S. Courts. Data for 1993 are estimated based on filings through June of 1993.

Avoid It If at All Possible

Despite its increasing acceptability, bankruptcy should be avoided if at all possible. First, take stock of your finances. Individuals who spend more than they earn, who develop lines of credit without any cohesive design, are liable to become credit "junkies" and headed for trouble. Credit should be used for the purchase of fixed assets such as a car, furniture, and home improvements. When consumers begin to use it for everyday purchases and stop paying it back in full, they are courting a financial crisis and must curtail their growing appetite for debt.

If debt pressures continue to mount, consumers should seek help. For some people, cutting up their credit cards may be a first and helpful step in the direction of controlling their urge for credit. Many cities have counseling services that teach debtors how to budget and help them negotiate informal arrangements with creditors. The Consumer Credit Counseling Service, a nonprofit organization sponsored by the National Foundation for Consumer Credit in Silver Spring, MD, offers free or low-cost assistance at each of its more than 700 offices nationwide. (To locate the office nearest you, call 800/388-2227.) Credit counselors generally help you work out a budget and a repayment plan aimed at allowing you to live comfortably and still resolve your credit problems. Consumers should note that credit counseling agencies have a bias against filing for bankruptcy, because large lender groups provide most of their support.

If you find yourself in an unbearable debt crisis and the solution offered by such an agency is not to your satisfaction, you may have to consider filing for bankruptcy. But before hiring a lawyer and starting this serious procedure, it would be wise to make every effort to settle your debts by other means. Don't hide from your creditors. Arrange a meeting and try to work out a mutually reasonable and acceptable repayment arrangement. Creditors are generally much more flexible and reasonable than most debtors expect.

No one really wants to go into bankruptcy court. For the credit companies, court suits mean legal costs that eat into their profits. They would rather negotiate with debtors to let them stretch out their payments and recover the whole sum than sue in court and collect only part of what is owed them.

Declaring Bankruptcy

If all else fails, then a debtor could resort to bankruptcy. The bankruptcy process itself is fairly simple for most debtors. Usually, it involves no more than an initial interview with an attorney, during which the facts of the individual's financial situation are determined, and a brief court appearance in which the bankrupt person testifies under oath as to the truth and validity of his or her petition.

The **Federal Bankruptcy Reform Act** of 1978 cleared up the confusion surrounding the issue of bankruptcy and also made it easy for many Americans to declare themselves bankrupt. The law replaced the panoply of state laws and regulations with a set of uniform standards. It created a checklist of items that debtors could use to protect themselves from creditors.

The federal district courts have overall authority for bankruptcy laws and cases and hand them over to bankruptcy judges. Federal bankruptcy laws provide two methods by which individuals can file for bankruptcy: Chapter 7 or Chapter 13. Before filing for protection, a debtor must determine which chapter to use.

Chapter 7   The more drastic course is **Chapter 7**. If you are in deep debt and your income is not consistent, you may be better off filing under Chapter 7. You must pay a filing fee (usually under $100), make a comprehensive list of your assets and liabilities, and submit the list to the judge. The judge will determine what you can retain and will ask a trustee to dispose of the rest among the creditors. Once that is done, your slate is clean of all obligations except "nondischargeable" debts such as alimony, child support, income taxes, government-insured student loans, and (under most state statutes) parking tickets. These debts cannot be discharged under bankruptcy statutes.

The court will not confiscate and auction off all of a debtor's assets. Debtors are permitted to keep such necessities as clothing, basic furniture, and dishes, which usually have very little resale value anyway. Exempted property varies from state to state. The court, however, will generally order such items as stereo equipment, motorboats, and any other nonessentials with market value to be sold off. Most bankruptcy judges will permit individuals to keep any item that has a value of $200 or less. Married couples may keep jointly owned goods worth up to $400 each. But the total value of all belongings of the debtor cannot exceed $4,000. In addition, individuals can retain up to $10,000 in real estate home equity. There is also a $1,200 exemption for a car and $500 for jewelry.

The bankruptcy law discourages **loading up**, the practice of amassing large amounts of debt by consumers who intend to file for bankruptcy. Debtors cannot walk away from debts incurred by the purchase of a luxury item such as a sportscar, jewelry, or yacht within 40 days of the filing. Nor will the court discharge a debt arising from a cash advance of $1,000 or more drawn on a credit line within 20 days of the filing. Credit card purchases above $1,000 in the 20 days before filing for bankruptcy must be repaid. This is to discourage a last buying spree before filing for bankruptcy. Drunk drivers also cannot use bankruptcy to escape debts arising from damage awards to accident victims.

Chapter 7 would be suitable where there is no steady income, or the income is so low that after paying normal expenses, there is nothing left to fund a repayment plan. Individuals whose financial records indicate that they have income to cover necessities and at least part of their obligations can be prohibited from using Chapter 7. This decision can be made only by the bankruptcy judge.

The law gives federal bankruptcy judges the discretionary power to discharge Chapter 7 bankruptcy petitions if they think these represent an abuse of the system. When someone seems to be abusing the law, a judge can throw the case out of Chapter 7, leaving the debtor to file under Chapter 13. The law permits one Chapter 7 filing every six years.

Chapter 13   Debtors who have a steady and stable source of income that is insufficient to pay off all creditors would be good candidates for **Chapter 13**, often termed the "wage-earner" plan. The plan is available to self-employed persons as well as the unemployed, as long as they have a source of income. Chapter 13 allows the filer to consolidate nearly all debt, including taxes, and to propose a trustee-supervised plan to repay at least part of the debts over three to five years.

In turn, under Chapter 13, debtors are allowed to keep and manage their own assets while conforming to the payback arrangement approved by the bankruptcy court. When an individual works out a repayment under court supervision, lenders can get a court order assigning all of a borrower's income for three years to repay the debts, after allowance for food and other basic needs. This is known as **garnishment** of wages. The debtor is protected from creditors' lawsuits, demands for payment, and other harassments. There is no limit on the number of Chapter 13 filings.

Your Future Creditworthiness

If you ever contemplate a declaration of bankruptcy, be aware of its implications. On the positive side, the declaration keeps creditors at bay. No one can foreclose on your home or repossess your car while you are in bankruptcy proceedings. This may offer some relief from the financial and mental pressure to which debtors are usually subjected.

But declaring bankruptcy has its price. For one thing, it makes reestablishing credit extremely difficult since in either case, Chapter 7 or Chapter 13, credit reporting agencies will record the filing. Even though you can file for bankruptcy every six years, the bankruptcy filing stays on your credit record for a full 10 years, whether or not you have managed to settle your financial problems before that time.

For the next 10 years it will be extremely difficult to borrow money, receive credit, or take out a mortgage. Mortgages, car loans, and unsecured personal lines of credit are virtually unobtainable unless you put down a 30 percent deposit or get someone with a good credit history to cosign. It will likewise be almost impossible to obtain standard credit cards. The only form of credit card available would be a secured credit card, in which you deposit with the bank a sum of money, which then becomes the credit limit for the card. The bank can seize your deposit if you do not pay your bills.

Although Chapter 13 filers try to repay some debts, they may have no better chance at reestablishing credit than people who file under Chapter 7. Getting credit after declaring bankruptcy is difficult but possible. While people who declare bankruptcy must list all debts when they file, chances are that creditors which they have paid regularly will not learn of their bankruptcy and thus will not revoke their privileges. If they keep up their payments, they can still build up an acceptable credit history. The law bars an employer from firing an employee who files for bankruptcy, but it does not prevent a prospective landlord from turning down a prospective tenant if he or she runs a credit check and is scared off.

SUMMARY

Credit is a tool that can serve your financial goals and enable you to obtain and achieve things that you couldn't otherwise afford. Used carefully and intelligently, it can become an indispensable part of your financial life. You need to know how to buy it, compare it, use it, and avoid abusing it. If abused, credit can turn into a burden that can play havoc with a person's financial life.

KEY TERMS

Add-on interest	Life insurance loans
Adjusted balance method	Line of credit
Annual percentage rate (APR)	Loading up
Average daily balance method	Loan-to-value ratio
Balance transfer feature	Margin loans
Balloon note	Open-end lease
Chapter 7 bankruptcy	Option price
Chapter 13 bankruptcy	Overdraft checking
Charge card	Passbook loan
Closed-end lease	Personal unsecured loan
Credit bureau	Posting date
Credit card	Premium cards
Credit life insurance	Previous balance method
Debt-to-income ratio	Residual value
Equal Credit Opportunity Act	Revolving line of credit
Fair Credit Reporting Act	Rule of 78
Federal Bankruptcy Reform Act	Second mortgage loan
Four Cs	Secured credit cards
Garnishment	Secured loan
Grace period	Smart cards
Home equity loan	Tiered rates
Installment loans	Total finance charge
IRA loans	Transaction date
Leasing	Truth in Lending Law

REVIEW QUESTIONS AND PROBLEMS

1. Discuss the pros and cons of using consumer credit.
2. Explain the "four Cs" of credit, and give an example of each.
3. What personal information do lending institutions consider significant on a loan application?
4. Explain the difference in true interest rates between an installment loan and a single payment loan.
5. Discuss the various sources of credit available to a borrower.
6. A. Discuss the circumstances under which a debtor should declare bankruptcy under Chapter 7 and under Chapter 13.
   B. Which type of personal bankruptcy offers the most protection for the debtor?

7. Is it better to save now and buy later or to buy now and go into debt?
8. What is an installment loan?
9. Define *revolving credit*.
10. Explain the difference between simple interest rate and the APR.
11. What is the purpose of allowing people to declare bankruptcy?
12. Give examples of "debts" that cannot be discharged through bankruptcy. Suggest reasons for these exceptions.
13. What two items of credit-cost information must lenders report according to the Truth in Lending Law?
14. What advantages accrue to the credit card user from the "grace period"?
15. Of what value is a person's credit rating? Explain how it is established.
16. What is the law as it applies to a wife when she applies for credit in her own name?
17. Discuss the pros and cons of a home equity loan.
18. How can a credit card be helpful to an individual? How can it be detrimental?
19. What is a secured loan, and why does it cost less than an unsecured loan?
20. Discuss the pros and cons of taking a passbook loan.
21. When shopping for a loan, what types of information should you collect?

22. (EQUITY) Prices of homes in your area have risen lately. The last time your home was appraised, the value was $175,000. The percentage of market value used is 80 percent. Remaining balance of first mortgage/liens is $30,000. The bank tells you that your maximum credit line, before your mortgage is considered, is now $180,000. What is your qualified credit line, net of mortgage? What is the appraised current market value of your home?

23. (BALLOON) The sticker price of the auto you are interested in is $20,000. The down payment required is 10 percent. The buy-back percentage is 40 percent. The down payment is $2,000. What is the lender's assumed depreciation on the car?

SUGGESTED PROJECTS

1. Imagine that you needed a $10,000 loan for two years. Conduct a survey in your area of the various sources of credit available. Construct a chart or table showing the different institutions that offer you credit. Record their interest charges, terms of repayment, fees, and the like. Explain which loan offer is the best and why.
2. If there is a commercial or savings bank or credit union with a small-loan department near you, arrange an interview with the manager and gather information on:
   A. How the bank investigates and determines a loan applicant's creditworthiness.
   B. What the loss experience of the bank has been on small loans.
   C. What fees, if any, the lender charges on a small loan in addition to the stated interest.
   D. What security or collateral the lender requires.
   E. What collection procedures the bank follows if the borrower is late in meeting payments.
3. Visit a local automobile dealership. Select the car of your dreams and find out what the finance charge and the annual percentage rate would be if you made the minimum down payment permitted and paid the balance in equal monthly

installments over a four-year period. Also find out what the dealer would offer you for your old car (if you have one) on a trade-in. Then visit your local bank and find out what the finance charge and the annual percentage rate would be if you borrowed an amount equal to the balance you would owe on the car, to be financed over the same period of time. Compare your rates, and present your conclusion as to which deal would be preferable.

INFORMATION RESOURCES

Anrig, Greg, Jr. "How to Cope with Lending Rate Gloom." *Money*, May 1989, 70–81.

Asinof, Lynn. "Card Issuers Aren't Dealing Out Low Rates." *The Wall Street Journal*, 7 March 1991, C-1.

Bankcard Holders of America, 560 Herndon Parkway, Suite 120, Herndon, VA 22070.

"Best Ways to Pay for Your New Car." *Changing Times*, October 1988, 93–96.

Barnhill, N.W. "Wrong Way Loans. *AARP Bulletin*, April 1993, 2.

Bodnar, J., and K. McCormally. "Living Debt Free." *Kiplinger's Personal Finance Magazine*, May 1992, 38–43.

Brunette, William Kent. *Conquer Your Debt*. Englewood Cliffs, NJ: Prentice-Hall, 1990.

"Charge It Your Way." *Time*, July 1, 1991, 50–51.

"Credit Card Come-ons." *Consumer Reports*, November 1988, 720–22.

Davis, Kristin. "Bankruptcy: The 10-Year Mistake." *Kiplinger's Personal Finance Magazine*, October 1991, 89–92.

Davis, Kristin. "Choosing a Credit Card You'll Love." *Kiplinger's Personal Finance Magazine*, August 1991, 35–40.

Davis, Kristin. "Credit Bureaus: Will They Get It Right?" *Kiplinger's Personal Finance Magazine*, March 1992, 82–85.

Elias, Stephen. *How to File for Bankruptcy*. Nolo Press, 1990.

Federal Trade Commission, Bureau of Consumer Protection, Division of Credit Practices, Room S-4429, 6th Street and Pennsylvania Avenue NW, Washington, DC 20580.

"Getting the Kinks Out of Your Credit Report." *Business Week*, May 25, 1992.

Giese, William. "Which Credit Card Is Just Right for You? *Kiplinger's Personal Finance Magazine*, February 1993, 55–59.

Henry, Ed. "Buy the Car or Lease It?" *Kiplinger's Personal Finance Magazine*, May 1993, 88–93.

Hilder, David B.,and Peter Pae. "Rivalry Rages among Big Credit Cards," *The Wall Street Journal*, May 3, 1991, B-1.

Hodge, Marie. "Get an Extra Charge Out of Your Credit Cards." *50 Plus*, February 1988, 27.

Kehrer, Daniel M. "How to Cut Out Debt." *Changing Times*, April 1988, 23–27.

Leonard, Robin. *Money Troubles: Legal Strategies to Cope with Your Debt*. Nolo Press, 1990.

McCormally, Kevin. "What to Know When You Lease a Car." *Kiplinger's Personal Finance Magazine*, August 1991.

McCormally, Kevin. "When Debt Pays." *Kiplinger's Personal Finance Magazine*, July 1991, 40–43.

Pae, Peter. "Many Will Find Charging a Lot Cheaper as Citicorp Reduces Some Key Card Rates." *The Wall Street Journal*, April 17, 1992, B-1.

Pae, Peter. "Watching for 'Traps' on Lower Card Rates." *Wall Street Journal*, February 21, 1992.

Public Interest Research Group, U.S. PIRG, 215 Pennsylvania Avenue SE, Washington, DC 20003.

"Pushing Plastic is Still One Juicy Game." *Business Week,* September 21, 1992, 52–54.

Quinn, Jane Bryant. "It's All on the House." *Newsweek*, January 27, 1992, 43.

———"Leasing Your Wheels." *Newsweek*, May 22, 1989, 85.

———"Let Them Eat Credit." *Newsweek*, November 18, 1991.

Quint, Michael. "Mastercard and Visa in a Debit-Card Battle." *The New York Times*, May 5, 1992, D-1.

Razzi, Elizabeth. "How to Find the Right Home Equity Loan." *Kiplinger's Personal Finance Magazine*, March 1993, 83–84.

Schultz, Ellen E. "Consolidating Debt Can Be a Costly Cure." *The Wall Street Journal*, September 4, 1991, C-1.

"Someone's Got a File on You." *Changing Times*, July 1988, 41–45.

What You Should Know before Declaring Bankruptcy. Free booklet available from the American Financial Services Association, 1101 14th Street NW, Washington, DC 20005.

"Where to Find Lower Credit Card Rates." *The Wall Street Journal*, November 14, 1991, C-1.

Credit Laws: Summary

The following credit laws were all intended to protect and promote the interests and rights of consumers. Consumers should be familiar with these laws in order to know what their legal rights are and to be able to be alert for any violation of their legal rights.

Truth in Lending Act of 1968 (Effective July 1, 1969)

The Truth in Lending Act is essentially a disclosure law, which applies to any institution or business that regularly offers credit. It requires disclosure of specific, meaningful, and uniform information by lenders for each credit offer. Creditors are required to state the full cost of credit in plain language on credit purchase agreements and loan applications. The law requires creditors to truthfully advertise their charges in a uniform way. Lenders must report both the total finance charge in dollars and the annual percentage rate (APR) of interest. The total finance charge in dollars includes all interest and fees that must be paid in order to receive the loan. The APR is the true rate of interest paid over the life of the loan and must be calculated in a manner prescribed by the law. The APR permits borrowers to compare credit costs regardless of the dollar amount of these costs, or the length of time over which the payments are to be made. Both the total finance charge and the APR must be prominently displayed on the form used to secure credit. Consumers may sue creditors for damages if they fail to disclose credit information or provide inaccurate information. It also grants the consumer-borrower a right of rescission (cancellation) for certain credit contracts. It entitles credit customers to request an itemization of the amount financed if the creditor does not automatically provide it. It requires creditors to refrain from issuing unrequested credit cards. It limits a cardholder's liability for unauthorized uses of a stolen or lost credit card to $50 per card.

Civil Rights Act of 1968

This act prohibits discrimination because of race, color, religion, national origin, or sex when creditors apply to obtain financing for their homes or other loans.

Federal Garnishment Law
(Effective July 1, 1970)

This law is part of the Truth in Lending Act (Consumer Credit Protection Act). It limits the portion of an employee's wages that can be garnished. Garnishment means any legal procedure through which the earnings of an individual are required to be withheld for payment of any debt. The law provides that the maximum portion of the aggregate disposable earnings of an individual for any workweek which is subject to garnishment may not exceed 25 percent of his or her disposable earnings for that week, or an amount by which disposable earnings for that week exceed 30 times the federal minimum hourly wage, whichever is less. The act prohibits firms from firing an employee because of a wage garnishment.

Fair Credit Reporting Act
(Effective April 24, 1971)

This law requires credit-reporting agencies to supply information that is equitable and fair to the consumer. It provides protection against credit reports that contain inaccurate, incomplete, or obsolete information about the personal and financial situations of credit applicants. This law provides recourse when a credit-investigating agency gives a consumer a bad rating. It requires lending agencies to disclose to consumers the name and address of any credit-reporting bureau which supplied reports used to deny credit, employment, or insurance. It requires credit-reporting bureaus to disclose the file's contents and reveal its sources of information. It grants consumers the right to inspect their credit file. If a consumer proves any of the information incorrect, inaccurate, or unverifiable, the credit bureau must promptly delete or modify it and notify creditors of the past six months and the potential employers of the last two years. It requires credit-reporting agencies to send the consumer's version of a disputed item to certain creditors and businesses. Any negative information about consumers can be part of their files for no longer than 7 years, with the exception of bankruptcy, which may be reported for 10 years.

Equal Credit Opportunity Act
(Effective October 28, 1975)

This act makes it illegal for a creditor to discriminate on the basis of sex, marital status, color, race, age, or receipt of public assistance when considering a credit application. Such factors cannot be used in credit-scoring formulas. The law requires that credit should be granted on the basis of creditworthiness. No inquiries about the sex or marital status of a prospective borrower may be made by the lender. The act requires that the same acceptance criteria be applied to both males and females. Questions about childbearing plans are off limits. Married women do not have to disclose their husband's income when applying for credit. A spouse cannot be asked to cosign or endorse a loan unless he or she is going to share equally in the proceeds of the loan. Whether they are married or not, women have the right to apply for credit in their own name. Credit applicants are entitled to receive a response from a creditor within 30 days after submitting their application, indicating whether the request was approved or denied. A credit denial must be in writing and must explain the reason for the denial or indicate the applicant's right to an explanation. Consumers who can prove that a creditor has discriminated against them may sue for actual damages plus punitive damages of up to $10,000.

Fair Credit Billing Act (Effective October 28, 1975)

This bill was passed to ensure that billing disputes are resolved fairly and within a reasonable length of time. It established procedures for dealing with billing errors and billing disputes. Credit card companies are required to periodically mail to consumers a statement specifying their conflict resolution procedures. Credit card companies have 30 days to acknowledge a billing error complaint and 90 days to resolve the problem. Credit card companies are required to credit customer accounts promptly and to return overpayments if requested. Consumers who made a credit card purchase of a defective product or service for over $50 can withhold payment until the problem has been resolved. Creditors who fail to comply with the rules applying to the correction of billing errors automatically forfeit the amount owed on the item in question, up to a total of $50, even if the bill was correct. Bills must be mailed to cardholders at least 14 days before payments are due. This act allows merchants to give cash discounts of up to 5 percent to customers who pay by cash instead of using credit.

Fair Debt Collection Practices Act (Effective March 20, 1978)

This legislation was passed to regulate the professional and ethical practices of collection agencies that collect debts arising out of purchases, on behalf of a third party. It entitles borrowers to be treated fairly by debt collectors. Borrowers are entitled to a written notice from the debt collector, describing their debt in detail, and what to do if they believe that they do not owe the money. Borrowers have 30 days from receipt of the written notice to respond to the debt collector and to deny the debt. This act restricts unfair techniques used by debt collectors. Debt collectors cannot use abusive language, threats, or harassment, or attempt to collect the debt through misrepresentation or deceptive means. Collection agencies cannot telephone at unusual hours or make repeated telephone calls during the day. The act also prohibits calls to a debtor's place of work without permission and forbids collectors from disclosing the nature of their calls to anyone except debtors. The Federal Trade Commission is responsible for enforcing this act, which limits the damages and penalties that can be recovered for violation.

CHAPTER FOUR

CLASS OF 1994
This shirt cost
my family $71,000.

Financing a College Education

LEARNING OBJECTIVES

- To evaluate the need for planning to meet ever-rising college tuition costs

- To examine the high cost of college education and the need for advance planning to meet these costs

- To identify the sources of tuition assistance

- To clarify the process of applying for financial aid and meeting eligibility requirements

- To explore how the government and colleges determine eligibility for aid

- To discuss self-financing plans that parents can use to prepare for their children's college years, such as tax shelters and prepayment plans

As a college student, you are already familiar with the challenging task of paying for college tuition. This chapter will explore this issue in detail from both a parental and a student's perspective. Undoubtedly, college students and their parents will find this issue to be one of the most important and challenging problems they will face together.

Parents of teenagers are suffering from a new American affliction: tuition shock. When they see tuition bills, they are experiencing the same kind of sticker shock that they get when browsing through new-car showrooms. Indeed, a year at a prestigious private college these days can cost as much as a luxury car. Paying for a college education is the second biggest investment most families make, after buying a home. In fact, financing a B.A. degree increasingly resembles buying a house. It requires a long-term commitment to saving, borrowing, and paying off debt. According to a report by the Student Loan Marketing Association, almost three-quarters of postsecondary expenditures for tuition fees and room and board are financed by parents and students from earnings, savings, sales of assets, and private credit.

College Is a Good Investment

Few quarrel with the statement that a quality college education is the best investment young people can make in themselves. To many Americans, especially poorer ones, a college education is a ticket to a good job and a better life. After 11 to 15 years of work experience, the average college graduate earns almost 60 percent more than a high school graduate. (See Figure 4–1.) Over their lifetimes, college graduates receive some $600,000 more than high school graduates. Therefore, college remains a sound financial investment even without factoring in cultural and other advantages. The problem with a college education is that the costs are paid up front, while the benefits are received slowly over a lifetime.

Tuition Trauma

The most important decision in the lives of many teenagers is choosing a college. But for many, that decision will come down to money. Fewer and fewer can afford college costs, and for many the debt burdens are becoming unbearable. In an age of skyrocketing college costs, an acceptance letter from a college is often meaningless unless it is followed by a financial aid award that can transform the dream into reality. Even then, youthful visions of a medical, legal, or other professional career are often tempered by thoughts of five-figure student loans, 20 hours a week of busing tables in the student cafeteria, and a second mortgage on the family home.

Campuses once seethed with student unrest, but today's centers of educational protest are off campus, among parents facing college bills. No wonder. The total cost—tuition, room, board, fees, and travel—of a year at an average private university was about $15,968 in the 1993–94 school year (see Table 4–1). That was more than half of what the median U.S. family earned that year. Even the annual cost in 1993–94 at a public university, $7,881, was threatening when multiplied by four years times three or four college-age children.

Throughout the 1980s and early 1990s, students and parents watched the cost of college rise nearly 10 percent per year, twice the rate of inflation (see Table 4–2). And as Table 4–1 projects, the spiral seems likely to continue. If we total the tuition for the years 1993, 1994, 1995, and 1996 in Table 4–1, we find that the 1993 freshman class faced an average cost of $34,000 for four years at a public university, and approximately $69,000 for a private school. With an assumed tuition inflation rate of just 5 percent, the parents of an April 1991 newborn can expect to have

FIGURE 4–1	The Financial Benefits of Higher Education

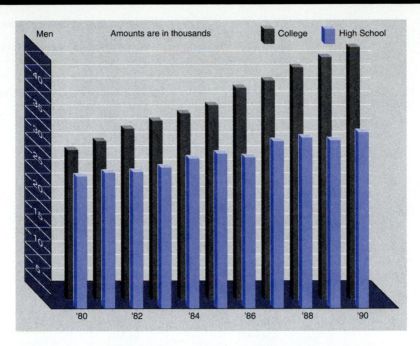

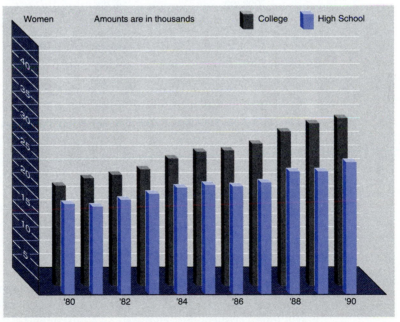

These graphs compare the median income (in thousands of dollars) of college-educated men and women with that of high school-educated men and women.

SOURCE: U.S. Bureau of the Census.

TABLE 4–1	The Price of Knowledge

Projected Annual College Costs

(Covers tuition, room, board, fees, and travel at a college; assuming a 5 percent average tuition inflation rate)

Year	Public University	Private University
1992–93	$ 7,506	$ 15,207
1993–94	7,881	15,968
1994–95	8,275	16,766
1995–96	8,689	17,604
1996–97	9,123	18,484
1997–98	9,579	19,409
1998–99	10,058	20,379
1999–00	10,561	21,398
2000–01	11,089	22,468
2001–02	11,644	23,591
2002–03	12,226	24,771
2003–04	12,837	26,009
2004–05	13,479	27,309
2005–06	14,153	28,675
2006–07	14,860	30,109
2007–08	15,603	31,614
2008–09	16,384	33,195
2009–10	17,203	34,854
2010–11	18,063	36,597
2011–12	18,966	38,427
2012–13	19,914	40,348

SOURCE: Basic data from U.S. Department of Education, American Council on Education, Education Department.

confronted a $150,226 tuition by the time their son or daughter finishes four years of a private college in the year 2013.

More than half the high school graduates in the United States go to college. Some families will be in the enviable position of covering college costs solely from their own resources, but most of them, in fact, cannot afford it. Even if they have been saving for some time, the cost can seem overwhelming. Couples, perhaps like your parents, who bore children in their late thirties and face tuition bills in their late fifties may be reluctant to pillage their home equities so close to retirement.

The result is a budget squeeze that has left many middle-income families feeling newly impoverished. (See Figure 4–2.) Consequently, if you are now in college or if your children are headed for college in the future, you have a compelling reason to school yourself about how to finance higher education. It may become vital to educate yourself on important and pertinent tax laws, preplanning, and investments.

This chapter explores the various forms of aid available to parents and students in financing a college education. It should make you aware of the process of seeking out

TABLE 4–2	Education Inflation Patterns

TUITION

How average annual percentage increases in tuition and fees at four-year colleges nationwide compared with increases in the Consumer Price Index.

	% Increase at Public Colleges	% Increase at Private Colleges	% Increase In the CPI
1977–78	0	6	6.5
1978–79	5	7	7.6
1979–80	6	9	11.3
1980–81	4	10	13.5
1981–82	16	13	10.3
1982–83	20	13	6.2
1983–84	12	11	6.3
1984–85	8	9	4.3
1985–86	9	8	3.6
1986–87	6	8	1.9
1987–88	6	8	3.6
1988–89	5	9	4.1
1989–90	7	9	4.8
1990–91	7	8	6.1
1991–92	12	7	4.6

SOURCE: College Board, U.S. Bureau of Labor Statistics.

and finding various forms of financial assistance, and how and where to apply for it. It discusses the pros and cons of loans, grants, work-study programs, and prepayment as well as savings plans.

Availability of Aid

Relief is available—sometimes in fuller measure than you might think. It comes in the form of financial aid, grants, scholarships, loans, and student part-time jobs. Before you start ruling out schools because of cost, bear in mind that 63 percent of all students at private colleges and 31 percent at public colleges receive some form of aid. Fifty-one percent of all students receive some kind of federal assistance. Billions of dollars of assistance are still available—not only for low-income families—despite much-publicized cutbacks in federal aid programs.

Student loans are playing a bigger part in financing higher education as can be seen by the two graphs in Figure 4–3.

The first step toward getting your share of benefits is to learn the basics of the financial aid system. Parents and students should contact financial aid offices for

FIGURE 4–2	The Financial Benefits of Higher Education

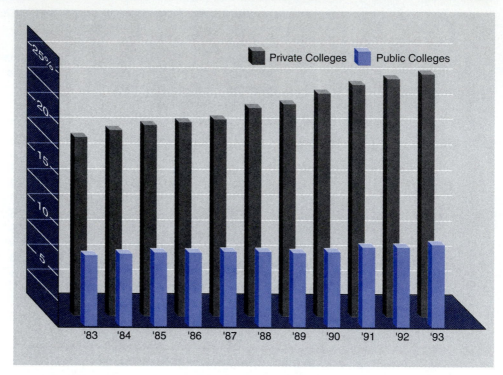

It's not just the costs of tuition and fees that spiral higher each year; the percentage of median family income devoted to college education is rising, too.

SOURCE: College Board and U.S. Bureau of the Census; 1993 data estimated.

information and apply for aid early and earnestly. Financial aid supposedly goes to the students who need it the most. In practice, it is apt to go to those who best understand how and where to apply for it, a process that has recently become more complicated.

The Financial Aid Process

Schools award financial aid on the basis of either need or merit. Unless you are an outstanding student with superior grades, you will most likely apply for a need scholarship. Need is not solely a matter of total income. Each year thousands of parents of collegians and high school seniors toil over a 1040-like document used by almost all U.S. colleges and universities. This system, designed to help standardize the allocation of aid, subjects a student's family's finances to a process called **need analysis** and records his or her family size, income, assets, debts, household expenses, and other information.

| FIGURE 4–3 | More Dollars in Student Loans, More Students with Loans |

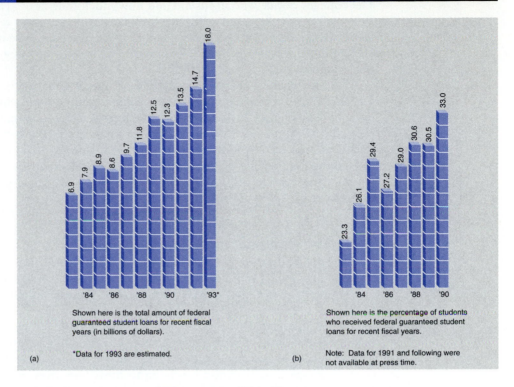

(a) Shown here is the total amount of federal guaranteed student loans for recent fiscal years (in billions of dollars).

*Data for 1993 are estimated.

(b) Shown here is the percentage of students who received federal guaranteed student loans for recent fiscal years.

Note: Data for 1991 and following were not available at press time.

SOURCE: U.S. Census Bureau and U.S. Department of Higher Eductation.

The Aid Form

Most schools use the College Scholarship Service's **Financial Aid Form (FAF)** and the American College Testing Program's **Family Financial Statement (FFS)** to determine eligibility for need-based scholarships. Using a complicated formula, both arrive at virtually the same reckoning of a key figure known as your **family contribution:** the amount of money they deem that you can reasonably afford to pay out of pocket for a year of college. Chances are you won't find this amount so reasonable.

The aid forms ask for financial information from a student's immediate family only, not grandparents, aunts, or uncles. Applicants have to disclose only their financial assets such as cash, stocks, and bonds, as opposed to personal property such as boats, cars, and airplanes. As of 1993 the need-definition formula for federal financial aid excluded the equity value of the family home among the assets available to pay for college. This switch greatly expanded middle-class eligibility for aid.

The government requires that every applicant for federal aid fill out a standard aid form for the school to which he or she is applying. Many schools also request the most recently filed federal income tax form to determine the student's eligibility for federal grants and loans and for aid awarded out of the university's own funds. These forms should be filed as early in the new year as possible.

Criteria for Aid

The colleges decide who needs aid and how much they need. That decision varies from college to college, but qualifying for financial aid generally rests heavily on such factors as family income and assets, family size, how many parents work, age of the oldest parent, number of family members in college at the same time, and the cost of attendance.

While each school has its own method of assessing family financial capabilities, it typically uses a formula to determine what amount a family has left after paying basic living expenses. It then applies a progressive rate, ranging from 20 to 50 percent of this disposable income, to represent the expected contribution from income to college expenses. In addition, schools expect from 5 to 8 percent of family assets to be contributed annually. Parental assets are protected to a greater extent than income because typically a family's major assets are their home and personal belongings.

The Family's Demonstrated Financial Need

Exceptional students, in the classroom or on the sports fields, may receive generous scholarships; but for most, the key to receiving aid is showing need. Students should not assume that they are too well off to qualify. Thousands of families who qualify for support fail to apply because they mistakenly assume that their income is too high. Even a family with a $75,000 income might qualify for some loan aid, although colleges expect families with above-average income and assets to give until it hurts.

Even if they live at home, students are expected to contribute their share to college costs. Colleges usually expect freshmen to contribute from $700 to $1,000 a year from summer or part-time job earnings, plus 35 percent of their savings or other assets, such as stocks or bonds. The summer or part-time job contribution is expected even if the student did not work.

Adding the parents' and students' contributions gives a student or a parent an idea of what colleges expect from the family. For example, if you are a 45-year-old breadwinner and your income was $42,000 before taxes, you may be expected to come up with $3,120. If your young scholar is asked to contribute $1,200 ($800 from a summer job and $400 from other assets or gifts), that brings the total expected family bill to $4,320 for the academic year. Subtracting that sum from the total cost of attending college, let's say $10,000, gives the crucial number—$5,680—your family's demonstrated financial need, or demonstrative need.

The **demonstrated financial need** is therefore the difference between the annual cost of attending a particular school, which includes tuition, fees, room, board, books, supplies, and other related expenses, and an amount the student and the family are expected to contribute. Thus, the demonstrated financial need is the amount the family can officially apply for in aid.

The Aid "Package"

There are two basic types of aid: **grants** and **scholarships,** which need not be repaid, and **loans,** which must be repaid with interest. Grants are preferable to loans and are also harder to get. Grants and loans can be secured from four different sources: the federal government, state and local governments, individual universities, and other institutions (foundations, companies, funds).

Financial aid at one time meant a money grant. Nearly half of the average awards are still so-called gift aid, grants or scholarships that can amount to a sizable discount on a college's sticker price. Colleges are increasingly offering aid in the form of an **aid package,** consisting of a combination of loans, on-campus part-time jobs, scholarships, grants, revolving loans from endowments, tuition installments, and prepayment plans that guarantee level costs. Some colleges arrange deals with local banks to provide loans to students at favorable rates. The aid package is usually custom-tailored to bridge the gap between what it will cost a family to send a student to the college and what college administrators decide the family can pay for itself.

Although loans are assuming growing importance, scholarships still provide significant amounts of student aid. **Merit scholarships,** those awarded without regard to a student's financial need, are increasing as colleges compete for a declining population of high school seniors. The highly competitive National Merit Scholarship Program is well known, and eligibility is determined by test scores. This has prompted concern that some needy applicants could lose out to students with higher academic achievement who do not really need scholarship funds. Financial need, nevertheless, remains the basis for the majority of scholarships.

Sources of Aid

The U.S. government is by far the largest source of financial aid to students. Federal financial assistance in 1991 to 1992 was nearly $18.4 billion. The U.S. Department of Education offers seven major student financial aid programs:

1. PELL grants

2. Supplemental Educational Opportunity Grants (SEOG)

3. Guaranteed Student Loans (GSL)

4. Parent Loans for Undergraduate Students (PLUS) and Supplemental Loans for Students (SLS)

5. Perkins loans (formerly National Direct Student Loans [NDSL])

6. College Work-Study (CWS) program

7. Health Education Assistance Loan (HEAL)

Most federal financial aid funds are actually awarded to universities and colleges, which in turn award them to their students as part of the aid packages. These are known as campus-based programs. The SEOG, CWS, and Perkins loans are all

campus-based programs. This means that they are administered by the financial aid administrator at each participating school and are awarded as part of an aid package. The other federal programs—PELL grants, GSL, PLUS, and HEAL—require students to apply on their own to the government or a lender. A financial aid package may contain aid from one or more of these programs.

An applicant must be at least a half-time student to qualify for most federal grants and loans. Different schools define "half time" differently. If part-time students want to qualify for aid, they may have to take one more course each semester. They also have to earn a C average to maintain eligibility. There are no age-specific federal or state scholarships or grants. The law prohibits discrimination on the basis of age, which effectively puts 18-year-old and 65-year-old students in the same category.

Bear in mind that the rules, amounts, and requirements for federal aid programs change practically every year. Students need therefore to make sure to get the latest information regarding these aid programs.

Grants

Pell Grants   The **PELL grant** program provides up to $3,700 per year in grant money to qualified undergraduates (for the 1993-94 academic year). Normally, PELL grants go to students whose families have an annual income of less than $42,000. For many students, PELL grants provide a foundation of financial aid, to which aid from other federal and nonfederal sources may be added. Unlike loans, grants do not have to be paid back. Students may receive a PELL grant for each year of undergraduate study. The deadline for applying for PELL grants is May 1 of each year.

Supplemental Educational Opportunity Grant (SEOG)   If you need more money, you can apply for a **Supplemental Educational Opportunity Grant (SEOG).** A SEOG is an award earmarked for undergraduate students with greater financial needs than a PELL grant can fulfill. Priority is given to PELL grant recipients. Students can get up to $4,000, depending upon their demonstrated need. The funds come from the government but are distributed by individual colleges. It is one of the largest college-based grant programs.

The campus-based SEOG program differs somewhat from a PELL grant. The Department of Education guarantees that each participating school will receive enough money to pay the PELL grants of its students. But each school receives a set amount of money for SEOGs, and when that money is gone, there are no more SEOGs for that year. It is therefore important for students to meet the school's financial aid application deadlines. Each school sets its own deadline. But most deadlines are quite early in each calendar year.

Loans

Guaranteed Student Loan (GSL) (STAFFORD LOAN)   Each April, high school seniors nervously check the mail for the thick envelopes that announce acceptance at college. Most envelopes also contain award letters outlining the college's aid package. Once the family's share is assessed, you can figure out the remaining need, which will determine whether you qualify for a **GSL** (also known as a *Stafford Loan*) and how much you can borrow. The arithmetic is simple: the cost of attending college minus your family contribution and any other aid from scholarships, campus aid, work-study, or veterans' benefits. The remainder is the amount of money you can borrow under the GSL. The GSL program, the largest federal student aid effort, is an entitlement program, which means that everyone who is eligible can get a loan.

Freshmen can borrow up to $2625 and sophomores can borrow up to $3,500 (as of July 1, 1993) while juniors and seniors may borrow as much as $5,500 per year for the next three years. The total GSL debt that a student can have outstanding as an undergraduate is $23,000. Graduate students can receive up to $8,500 per year and no more than $54,750 in all, including any loans made at the undergraduate level.

The loans are issued by banks or thrift institutions directly to the student at a fixed, below-market interest rate. They are insured by a guarantee agency of the student's state and reinsured by the federal government. Students are charged an origination fee of 5 percent to be deducted before they get the loan. Borrowers also may have to pay an insurance premium of up to 1 percent of the loan's outstanding balance per year.

Stafford loans allow students to spend more time on their studies because they are not overwhelmed by expenses during school or as they begin their careers. The government pays the interest until the student leaves school. The interest rate is equal to the 90-day Treasury bill rate plus 3.1 percentage points adjusted annually, with a 9 percent cap. Loan repayment actually begins 6 to 12 months after the student leaves school, at 8 percent interest, with a minimum annual payment of $600. Students have at least 5 years and as long as 10 years to complete repayment. If a student falls below half-time student status, he or she is considered to have left school and must start repaying 6 to 12 months later. Payments can be deferred until six months after finishing military service or overcoming a physical or mental disability. Payments can also be deferred for one year if the student can prove economic hardship.

Table 4–3 shows the typical monthly payments and total interest charges for 8 percent loans of varying amounts, with typical repayment periods.

TABLE 4–3	GSL Typical Repayment Plans			
Total GSL Charges	Number of Payments	Monthly Payments	Total Interest Charges	Total Indebtedness Repaid (Loan Principal plus Interest)
$ 2,500	60	$ 50.70	$ 541.46	$ 3,041.46
5,000	60	101.39	1,082.92	6,082.92
10,000	120	121.33	4,559.31	14,559.31
12,500	120	151.67	5,699.14	18,199.14
25,000	120	303.33	11,398.28	36,398.28

SOURCE: Massachusetts Higher Education Assistance Corporation.

Parent Loans for Undergraduate Students (PLUS)

PLUS loans are for parents who want to borrow to help pay for their children's education. Parents or independent students do not have to demonstrate financial need to borrow up to $4,000 a year. This federal loan program carries a maximum of $20,000 over five years for each dependent undergraduate child, in addition to a Stafford loan. The variable interest rate is based on the 52-week U.S. Treasury bill rate plus 3.1 percent, with a 10 percent interest rate cap. The rate adjusts each July. Parents have up to 10 years to repay the unsecured loan, starting 60 days after the last loan disbursement, and can defer repayment of principal until after their child leaves school. Like Stafford loans, these loans are made by local banks and thrift institutions.

Further information regarding Stafford loans and PLUS loans can be obtained from the U.S. Department of Education, 800/562-6872

Supplemental Loans for Students (SLS)

Under **SLS,** independent undergraduate and graduate students may borrow up to $4,000 per year, to a total of $20,000 over five years. This is in addition to the Stafford limits. PLUS loans are for parent borrowers; SLSs are for students. Both loans provide additional funds for educational expenses. Unlike Stafford loans, repayment begins soon after the loan is made. Like Stafford loans, PLUS and SLS loans are made by a lender such as a bank, credit union, or savings and loan association. The interest rate is a variable rate, tied to movement in the 52-week Treasury bill, but it will never exceed 12 percent. The interest rate is recalculated on June 30 of each year. Unlike Stafford borrowers, PLUS and SLS borrowers do not have to show need.

Perkins Loans (formerly National Direct Student Loans [NDSL])

Under the **Perkins loans,** unusually needy first-time borrowers can get $4,500 for freshmen and sophomores and up to $13,500 thereafter, through graduate school, for a total of $18,000, all at a bargain rate of 5 percent. Repayment begins six months after graduation and can be spread over a maximum of 10 years.

The amount of each payment depends on the size of your debt and on the length of your repayment period. Usually, you must pay at least $30 per month. In special cases—for example, if you are unemployed or ill for a long period time—your school may allow you to make payments that are less than $30 per month or may extend your repayment period.

Table 4–4 shows typical monthly payments and total interest charges for three different 5 percent loans over a 10-year period.

The loans are made through a school's financial aid office. Most students borrow from one of two programs, the GSL or the Perkins. Both carry subsidized interest rates. While the student is in school, the government pays the interest.

Health Education Assistance Loan (HEAL)

Medical and nursing students are eligible for all the regular federal aid programs, plus an alternative or supplement for students going into medical fields, called the **HEAL** loan. But it is hardly cheap. The interest rate is pegged at 3.5 percent above the 90-day U.S. Treasury bill rate. The interest on HEALs compounds while the student is in school.

This loan enables medical and dental students to borrow up to $20,000 per academic year from banks or state agencies with the maximum total reaching $80,000.

| TABLE 4–4 | Sample 5 Percent Loans over 10 Years |

Total Loan Amount	Number of Payments	Monthly Payments	Total Interest Charges	Total Repaid
$ 4,500	120	$ 47.73	$ 1,227.60	$ 5,727.60
9,000	120	95.46	2,455.20	11,455.20
18,000	120	190.92	4,910.40	22,910.40

SOURCE: U.S. Department of Education.

There is no "need" test for a HEAL loan, but it is costly borrowing and should be kept to a minimum. Repayment for M.D. candidates usually begins two or three years after graduation from medical school.

Loan Repayment   Both GSL and Perkins loans require borrowers to start paying back the money six months after completion of studies, whether or not they are gainfully employed. Students working toward a graduate degree part-time can defer repaying their loans for several years.

Loan Deferment and Cancellation   Some government loan programs offer deferments or even outright loan forgiveness to students who enter the military or public service agencies, such as the Peace Corps, or teach after graduation.

If, for example, a new graduate teaches handicapped persons or is a full-time teacher in an elementary or secondary school serving low-income pupils, 15 to 30 percent of a Perkins loan will be canceled annually over a five-year period. Working in a Headstart Program produces a 15 percent cancellation for each year of service. The initial repayment of both Perkins and GSLs can be deferred, with no interest charge, for up to three years if the borrower serves in the Peace Corps, Public Health Service, or VISTA. Under the Army's Loan Repayment Program, the Defense Department will pay off the Perkins and Stafford or federally insured student loans at a rate of 15 percent a year if the borrower enlists in the National Guard, or 33 percent yearly if he or she enters an active branch of the armed services, for a maximum benefit of $55,000.

Students can receive further information on any of the federal financial aid programs by phoning the Federal Student Aid Information Center (301/984-4070) or United Student Aid Funds (800/428-9250).

Loan Consolidation   Another way to lift some of the financial burden from the shoulders of a college graduate just starting a business career is to look into a **loan consolidation program.** A consolidation program involves taking out one new larger loan to pay off a variety of older smaller loans. The Student Loan Marketing Association (a government-chartered company known as Sallie Mae, discussed in Chapter 13), has a plan called *Smart Loan* that enables borrowers who owe at least $5,000 on eligible loans to consolidate the debt into a single new loan. **Smart Loan** offers extended repayment terms ranging from 10 to 25 years, flexible payment schedules, and (for most borrowers) lower interest rates. The individual can choose several methods of repayment, reduce the size of the monthly payments, and stretch out the period over which payments will be made. One option allows students to make interest-only payments for the first four years, graduated payments for the next two years, and fixed-level payments for the seventh year through the remainder of the term.

Defaulting on Loans When you take a loan, you sign a legal document known as a *promissory note*. By signing it, you are agreeing to repay according to the terms of the note. This note is a legally binding document. This commitment to repay means that you will have to pay back the loan even if you do not complete your education or are not able to get a job after completing school. Think about what this obligation means before you take a loan (see Figure 4–4). If you do not pay back your loan on time or according to the terms in your promissory note, you may go into default. If you do, your school or lender can require you to repay immediately the entire amount you owe. It can sue you to collect that amount, and it can ask the federal government for help in collecting from you. Consequently, joining the ranks of those

FIGURE 4–4	Loans in Default

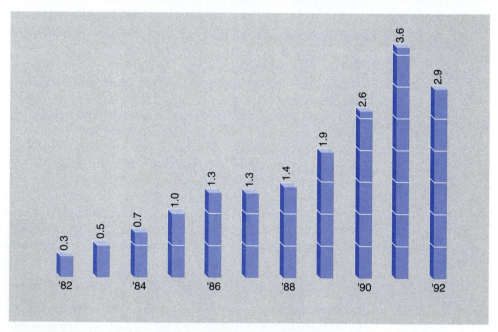

Shown is the total default cost for the Federal Guaranteed Student Loan program for recent years (in billions of dollars).

SOURCE: U.S. Department of Education.

"Professors, parents, friends, fellow debtors…!"

SOURCE: "Pepper…and Salt," *The Wall Street Journal*, May, 1992, A-15. Reprinted by permission of Cartoon Features Syndicate.

causing the high default rate (about 11 percent) on Perkins is not a sound alternative to repayment. It's inherently wrong, of course, and there are some good reasons to dissuade the prospective graduate who claims to "know" this guy who just walked away from his loans and nothing happened to him.

If there are siblings whose college years are still ahead, a blemished credit record in the family will make it hard for them to get loans. More directly, a loan default notice to a credit agency may prevent a young person from obtaining credit cards, charge accounts, or a car loan. Moreover, the Justice Department has been busy filing thousands of lawsuits against defaulters. And the IRS impounds any tax refunds due to student loan defaulters. During the spring of 1989, the IRS forwarded more than 300,000 student loan defaulters' refund checks worth $181 million to the Department of Education. It was the fourth year in a row that the IRS intervened in this way, and it plans to accelerate its crackdown on the 2.2 million graduates who are not keeping up with their government-backed student loan payments.

Excessive Borrowing Both parents and students should be careful not to get in over their heads. Excessive borrowing may make students comfortable during their school years but may place a heavy burden on them afterward. In addition to considering present needs before borrowing, students should realistically project their ability to repay a loan after graduation. They should consider their future career plans when deciding how much debt they can handle. A future surgeon can afford to borrow more than a future social worker. Students should consider the effect a large debt burden will have on their lifestyle. In partial recognition of this problem, some schools are putting a limit on the number of loans a student may assume.

College Work-Study (CWS)

The **CWS program** offers undergraduate and graduate students with very limited funds a chance to earn money to help pay their educational expenses. All of the

"Good day, madam. I'm working my son's way through college."

SOURCE: Drawing by Handelsman, (c) 1974
The New Yorker Magazine, Inc.

students' earnings are applied to college tuition and room and board. Colleges provide jobs on campus, such as clerking or cafeteria work or contract with outside businesses to hire students. Salaries are funded jointly by the federal government and the college. Students must earn at least the current federal minimum wage and may earn more, depending upon the skill required. Students can apply for CWS jobs at the college aid office, but they must demonstrate financial need. The school sets the student's work schedule. In arranging a job and assigning work hours, the financial aid administrator takes into account the student's class schedule, health, and academic progress.

Cooperative Education

A more specialized form of **earning and learning** is **cooperative education,** which blends classroom instruction with related on-the-job experience. Cooperative programs, which were originally geared for engineering students, have since the mid-1970s expanded to almost all other disciplines.

It often takes five years to get a degree since many co-op students either alternate semesters between being a full-time student and a full-time worker, or work half days and attend classes half days. For them, the work experience and the chance to pay off a substantial part of their college bills are worth the longer wait for a degree.

Other Sources of Financial Aid

While federal government loans and work-study programs are very helpful, many students will need even more funding to cover their education costs. The increased systemization of the financial aid process requires an equally systematic approach from families.

Next to Uncle Sam, the biggest providers are the colleges and universities themselves, which supplement the federal programs by distributing vast amounts of scholarships, loans, and jobs from their own funds. It is often the college that provides middle-income families with their greatest financial assistance. Because of soaring costs, schools have devised innovative programs to help students pay the price. For instance, the University of Pennsylvania has its Penn Plan, a 10-year easy-payment system of bank loans administered by the university and secured by its endowment funds.

If the college cannot help enough, families should investigate scholarship alternatives from such sources as employers, state and municipal governments, corporations, labor unions, community groups, foundations, and other outside sponsors. There are thousands of scholarship funds, memorials, trusts, and foundations nationwide, contributing billions of dollars in the form of grants, scholarships, and interest-free loans. They should not be overlooked.

The nonprofit National Merit Scholarship Corporation runs the largest private college award competition. To qualify, students must take the PSAT/NMSAT exam, a preliminary version of the Scholastic Aptitude Test (SAT) early in their junior year of high school. Each year nearly one million students take this test of which eight to ten thousand win money from the National Merit Scholarship Corporation or one of the 205 colleges and 390 private companies that support it.

Students can learn about lenders in their state by contacting their state guarantee agency. To obtain the state guarantee agency's address and phone number, and to receive more information about borrowing, call the Federal Student Aid Information Center, 800/333-INFO.

Many programs are open only to students who fall into some specialized field or category. Eligibility may depend on where a student lives, his or her proposed career, race, religion, artistic talents, or even special interests.

High school guidance counselors and local libraries have much information about foundations, religious and community organizations, town or city clubs, civic groups, chambers of commerce, and employers that offer scholarships. Aid administrators generally do not recommend companies that do specialized computer searches for scholarships tailored to students and their interests. These companies usually charge students for information about federal, state, military, and private aid, however the information is also available also free from each source.

College financial aid offices are the best source of information about financial aid, and most try to direct students to both public and private funds. It may also be very profitable to obtain guides to college scholarships, available in all school and public libraries, and to search for scholarships for which you qualify. Students who are members of an ethnic or racial minority may contact the school's financial aid office or its office of minority affairs, if it has one, and ask for information on financial aid for minority students.

Every state provides some form of financial assistance to qualified residents. Most awards are based on need, although some are based upon other criteria, including academic performance. Generally, recipients of awards or loans must be legal residents of the state and must be enrolled in a college or university within the state. A few states have reciprocity agreements.

Self-Financing: Planning for College Costs in Advance

A savings cushion is still the best defense against tuition shock. Parents who want their children to enjoy the benefits of a college education may have to choose between saddling them with debt when they are young adults or planning and building an education fund in advance. For parents who have both the foresight and the capital to set aside money soon after a child is born, the problem is lessened. Money invested at regular intervals will grow into a surprisingly large nest egg by the time the child reaches college age. But for parents of young children, the message is clear: start saving for college early! Saving for college should be no different from investing for any other long-term goal.

Parents should set a target and begin making systematic payments to a college fund. The simplest way for parents to make sure they will have enough cash is to make equal monthly or annual deposits in an interest-bearing account. Parents do not have to save enough to fund four full years, since they will almost certainly have loan options once their child starts college. Therefore, those who can set aside only enough to finance just a year or two of future college costs should not be discouraged.

The American Association of State Colleges and Universities proposes that parents save at least $1,000 a year per child ($83.33 monthly) to build a college fund. This is a savings goal within reach of middle-income parents. Assuming that the investments are in the child's name from birth and earn 8 percent a year for 18 years, this would produce an after-tax accumulation of about $39,000, reasonably close to the cost of attending four years of college at a public institution. This assumes that education costs will rise by the same rate at which they increased at public institutions during the past 20 years.

Tax-Exempt Educational Nest Egg

Thanks to the magic of compound interest—especially if it is sheltered from taxes—there are steps parents can take to make college tuition bills manageable.

To accumulate a nest egg large enough to pay out $190,000 over four years of college, parents have to start saving about $5,000 at 8 percent in tax-exempt municipal bonds annually, from the year the child is born (see Table 4–5B). Optimists who think that a $140,000 nest egg will be sufficient will have to save $3,800 a year at 8 percent tax-exempt (see Table 4–5A). If the funds are kept in taxable investments and earned 8 percent before taxes, then parents would have to save substantially more each year.

Table 4–5A demonstrates the growth year by year of an annual contribution of $3,800, compounded and tax exempt.

Table 4–5B demonstrates the growth year by year of an annual contribution of $5,000, compounded and tax exempt.

TABLE 4–5A	Your Growing Nest Egg		

NEST EGG

Year	Annual Contribution	Average Interest Rate	Accumulated End-Year Total
1	$ 3,800	8%	$ 3,800
2	3,800	8%	7,904
3	3,800	8%	12,336
4	3,800	8%	17,123
5	3,800	8%	22,293
6	3,800	8%	27,876
7	3,800	8%	33,906
8	3,800	8%	40,419
9	3,800	8%	47,452
10	3,800	8%	55,048
11	3,800	8%	63,252
12	3,800	8%	72,113
13	3,800	8%	81,682
14	3,800	8%	92,016
15	3,800	8%	103,178
16	3,800	8%	115,232
17	3,800	8%	128,250
18	3,800	8%	142,310

TABLE 4–5B	Your Growing Nest Egg		

NEST EGG

Year	Annual Contribution	Average Interest Rate	Accumulated End-Year Total
1	$ 5,000	8%	$ 5,000
2	5,000	8%	10,400
3	5,000	8%	16,232
4	5,000	8%	22,530
5	5,000	8%	29,333
6	5,000	8%	36,679
7	5,000	8%	44,614
8	5,000	8%	53,183
9	5,000	8%	62,437
10	5,000	8%	72,432
11	5,000	8%	83,227
12	5,000	8%	94,885
13	5,000	8%	107,476
14	5,000	8%	121,074
15	5,000	8%	135,760
16	5,000	8%	151,621
17	5,000	8%	168,751
18	5,000	8%	187,250

Tax-Sheltered Scholarships

Current tax laws permit some limited strategies that may gradually increase the size of a family's college fund. Basically, they involve investing money in the child's name, rather than in the parent's. Shifting income to a child as a tax maneuver is not a new idea. But there are several ways of doing it, and each method has its own advantages and disadvantages. Parents should naturally consult a lawyer, tax accountant, or financial adviser to figure out the best way to do this.

Some popular tax-sheltered savings methods are discussed below.

Transferring Funds to Kids: Uniform Gifts to Minor Accounts (UGMA)   The effectiveness of custodial accounts, used to shift income from parent to child, has been curtailed by the 1986 tax reform but is still viable although less attractive. Currently, anything over the first $1,000 of income on gifts to children under 14 is taxed at the parents' top rate. That $1,000, however, is better than nothing. Children 14 and older pay tax at their own rate on all unearned income.

It therefore still pays for parents to keep at least some money in each child's name. Parents may still put as much as $10,000 a year ($20,000 if they give jointly) in a **UGMA** for each child. A child under 14 can earn up to $600 in interest or dividends tax free. The next $600 is taxed at the child's 15 percent bracket, lower than the parents' probable 28 or 31 percent bracket. On anything above $1,200, the parents' tax rate applies. This means that it would pay to put, for example, a $20,000 CD earning 5 percent interest ($1,000 a year) in a child's name as a tax shelter. Kept in the parents' name, that money could be taxed at 28 or 31 percent. All that is needed to set up a UGMA is a Social Security number for each child. Parents may act as custodians for the account, which most banks and brokerage firms will set up.

Zero

A Zero for Your Education

How much should you invest today in zero coupon bonds for each $1,000 you want when your child is ready for college? With 7 percent zeros, a $290 investment will grow to $1,000 by the time today's newborn is 18. You could guarantee a $60,000 college fund with an investment of just $17,400. The reason the cost of zeros rises with the child's age, of course, is that there is less time for the bond to grow to $1,000.

For Every $1,000 You Want When Your Child Is 18, Invest This Much Today in Zero Coupon Bonds Yielding

Age of Child	6%	7%	8%	9%	10%	12%
Newborn	$345	$290	$244	$205	$173	$123
5 years	464	409	361	318	281	220
10 years	623	577	534	494	458	394
15 years	839	816	794	772	751	711

Another commonly recommended tactic is to transfer the funds to assets that defer taxable income until a child turns 14 to take advantage of his or her lower tax bracket. Once the child turns 14, all the accounts' earnings, as mentioned, will be taxed at his or her rate.

Shifting income from parents to children, while very tempting taxwise, can also backfire. College financial aid formulas require a much larger percentage contribution to tuition costs from student assets than from parental assets.

Home Equity Loans   Since the 1986 tax reform, interest charges for student loans are no longer tax deductible. The Tax Reform Act left only one itemized deduction that homeowners may use to help finance a college education: the **home equity loan.**

Under the tax law, interest is deductible as long as the loan is secured by the residence. Parents can therefore consolidate their tuition and consumer debt and pay it off with funds from a second mortgage or home equity loan. The interest on such loans is fully deductible, provided the loan does not exceed the original purchase price of the house plus permanent home improvements. Interest on debt in excess of a house's purchase price may still be deductible if used for educational or medical expenses. See Chapter 3 for a discussion of home equity loans.

U.S. Savings Bonds   A new way to shelter taxes and build savings for a child's college tuition is to buy Series EE U.S. Savings Bonds. As of 1990, parents with joint incomes under approximately $95,000 receive tax exemptions on income from these bonds used to pay for a child's college tuition. (This is discussed in detail in Chapter 13.)

Zero Coupon Bonds   Another, often tax-deferred or tax-exempt investment getting a lot of attention lately is **zero coupon bonds.** These are discussed in detail in Chapter 13. Zero coupon bonds sell at deep discounts, and, as their name suggests, pay no interest during their term. To compensate for the missing payments, all the interest is paid in a lump sum when the bond matures at face value. Parents can time their maturities to coincide with their child's college years. Because they are available for relatively small sums, as little as $200, zero coupon bonds are among the most attractive college investments. A $1,000 zero yielding 7 percent and maturing in 18 years, for example, costs just $290 today (see the accompanying box). If parents put about $17,400 worth of such bonds into a newborn's account, it would grow to the more than $60,000 needed to pay for four years at a public university starting in 2012.

Although the bonds do not pay interest, the IRS taxes owners as though payments were received periodically instead of all at once at maturity. This tax treatment is not a serious problem if parents purchase tax-exempt zero coupon municipal bonds. However, although they are tax exempt, zero coupon municipal bonds have the disadvantage of bearing very low interest rates. (Municipal bonds are discussed in Chapter 13.)

Baccalaureate Bonds   Zero coupon bonds especially created to help parents save for their children's college tuition are known as **baccalaureate bonds.** These tax-exempt municipal bonds, customized for parents of tomorrow's scholars, are winning favor among state lawmakers. At least 23 states (California, Connecticut, Delaware, Florida, Hawaii, Illinois, Indiana, Iowa, Kansas, Maryland, Michigan,

Missouri, New Hampshire, North Carolina, North Dakota, Oregon, Tennessee, Texas, Vermont, Virginia, Washington, Wisconsin, and Wyoming) have already offered such bonds.

The zero coupon bonds are sold at a big discount on their face value, making them accessible to many middle-income parents. Some states pay holders a cash bonus at the bond's maturity if their child attends a state college.

Zero coupon bonds (or baccalaureate bonds), which can be bought in relatively small denominations but can yield triple or quadruple the original investment when they reach maturity 18 years later, offer a promising method for building a college fund. They are a predictable investment that yields a known result.

Tuition Prepayment Plans: Pay Now, Study Later

Families who qualify for little or no financial aid, but cannot easily dip into liquid assets and come up with thousands of dollars year after year, have a problem that colleges are no longer ignoring. Institutions may not be able to cut costs for such families, but many are trying to make the bills easier to pay.

Some schools offer **tuition prepayment plans,** such as letting parents finance four years at the freshman rate by paying the entire amount at once. Students can avoid any year-to-year increases by paying four years' tuition up front. Colleges offering such plans will usually refund most of the unused tuition money if the student drops out or transfers.

Early Prepayment Plan

Duquesne University in Pittsburgh is credited with being the first institution (in 1985) to offer an early prepayment plan, originally restricted to alumni. Under Duquesne-type plans, parents pay a flat one-time sum pegged to the age of their young child. In return, they get a guarantee that all tuition costs will be covered when the youngster starts college, regardless of how much the price has risen. The younger the child when the plan is initiated, the lower the prepayment.

Prepayment Calculations

Like everything else in life, this offer is a gamble. The cash you pay in advance has future value. Before committing to a prepayment plan, some calculations are necessary. If you anticipate future tuition inflation to be greater than your anticipated after tax earnings (interest and dividends) on the money for the next four years, it may be worthwhile to prepay. If you believe that interest rates will be higher than tuition increases, then pay year by year. If you took a loan to make the prepayment, you still would have to compare the interest rate you are paying on the loan with your estimate of college tuition increases for the next four years or more. For example, if the college offers you a 12 percent loan to prepay the tuition, does it pay for you to take the loan? If you think college costs will increase at more than 12 percent a year, it is obviously worthwhile. If not, don't prepay.

Under this program, parents buy a tuition option or futures contract with a lump-sum payment that will cover four years at the school for a child 2 to 18 years away from enrollment. The college, for its part, gets a pool of students likely to attend and an ample sum of capital to invest.

The pay now, study later tuition plans offered by some private colleges have spread to public universities. Most are patterned after a program set up in Michigan, which is similar to the Duquesne plan.

In 1988 Michigan created the Michigan Education Trust (MET), which allows parents to buy a future college education for a one-time investment (of $6,756) for a newborn. It guarantees four years' worth of undergraduate tuition at any Michigan state college, even if costs increase at a faster pace than originally projected. It allows students to choose among Michigan's 15 public four-year colleges and universities and 29 community colleges. In addition, students can have payments applied to tuition costs at private colleges. The state invests the money, expecting that it will grow enough to cover undergraduate tuition. Several other states, such as Florida and Indiana, have implemented programs similar to the Michigan Education Trust. However, during the fall of 1991, Michigan put its program on hold and did not permit any more families to buy in. The reason given was that the price of the Michigan Education Trust contracts was below tuition at the time of purchase and tuition costs were rising faster than Michigan's investments could handle. Consequently, the future of such trusts is in question.

But even if they do continue, these plans contain other risks as well. If the child does not enroll or fails to meet entrance requirements or does not attend that school for any other reason or decides not to go to college at all, the programs vary on how much of the investment is refunded. At some schools, parents can get back only their original investment without any of the earnings it has accumulated over the years. And if the student fails to maintain acceptable grades, the prepayment can be forfeited altogether.

None of the available programs offer a panacea. If college costs continue to increase faster than inflation and college financial aid programs, then other, more drastic, approaches will be needed. These could include taking out a second mortgage on the family home or having a nonworking spouse return to the labor force. Many parents may have to scale back expectations and send a child to a public institution rather than a private one.

SUMMARY

Parents and students can cope with soaring college costs by using financial aid, advance planning, or both. Financial aid comes in the form of grants and loans as well as work-study programs. The largest source of financial aid is the U.S. government. It is imperative that families be familiar with the various aid programs and know how to demonstrate financial need.

Some tax-exempt savings programs remain for parents who want to save years in advance of their child's college years. Tuition prepayment programs are a growing and relatively new approach to containing inflationary college costs. These new programs may mark a turning point in tuition finance. In the future, middle-income families, squeezed out of need-based scholarships and cut-rate government loan programs, will have to rely more on planning and savings than on financial aid.

KEY TERMS

Aid package

Baccalaureate bonds

Campus-based programs

College Work-Study (CWS) program

Cooperative education

Demonstrated financial need

Earning and learning

Family contribution

Family Financial Statement (FFS)

Financial Aid Form (FAF)

Grants

Guaranteed Student Loan (GSL)

Health Education Assistance Loan (HEAL)

Home equity loan

Loan consolidation program

Loans

Merit scholarships

Need analysis

Parent Loans for Undergraduate Students (PLUS)

PELL grants

Perkins loans

Scholarships

Smart Loans

Stafford loans

Supplemental Educational Opportunity Grants (SEOG)

Supplemental Loans for Students (SLS)

Tuition prepayment plans

Uniform Gifts to Minor Account (UGMA)

Zero coupon bonds

REVIEW QUESTIONS AND PROBLEMS

1. Define and explain the following terms: (a) financial aid form, (b) demonstrative need, (c) need analysis, (d) family contribution.
2. How do colleges and universities decide who needs financial assistance? Discuss some aid criteria that enter into their decision.
3. Discuss the major characteristics of (a) PELL grants and (b) Supplemental Educational Opportunity Grants (SEOG).
4. How do you qualify for a Guaranteed Student Loan (GSL), and what determines the amount you are eligible to receive?
5. What are PLUS and SLS loans? Compare and contrast these two loans.
6. Under what circumstances can federal loans be canceled or deferred?
7. Besides federal financial aid, what other sources of financial assistance could a student search for? What are some helpful sources of information to find private and public funds?
8. Parents can still use their children as a tax shelter. Explain how, under what conditions, and how much money parents can shelter under a child's name.
9. What are some drawbacks of tuition prepayment plans?
10. Explain how baccalaureate bonds can help build a college fund.

11. (TUITION) You read in the paper that the current four-year tuition at a public university is high and going up. The article goes on to say that in 20 years the future tuition will probably be twice as much. What assumed inflation rate is the author using?

12. (NEST EGG) You would like to accumulate $100,000 in 10 years. You think that you can earn 12 percent in a growth mutual fund. How much must you save each year to reach your goal?

13. (ZERO COUPON BONDS) You have $15,000 and you want to use zero coupon bonds to produce $25,000 in 10 years. What effective interest rate must be earned?

SUGGESTED PROJECTS

Visit your college financial aid office. Discuss your general financial situation with a financial aid counselor. Try to get as much literature on financial aid as possible. Ask your counselor if there are any loans or grants that you may be eligible for but have never applied for. Make a list of these loans and grants. Then carefully prepare a list of arguments—pro and con—for you to use in deciding whether to apply for these loans or grants. Present your decision (to apply or not apply for aid) to your class, and get the reaction of classmates.

INFORMATION RESOURCES

"Anxious Parents Flock to Tuition Schemes." *The Wall Street Journal,* March 9, 1989, C-1.

Chany, Kalman and Geoff Martz. *The Student Access Guide to Paying for College.* NJ: Princeton Review, 1993.

"College Bonds: The Yields, the Allure, the Drawbacks." *Changing Times,* April 1991, 76-78.

Davis, Kristin. "Winning the College Aid Game." *Kiplinger's Personal Finance Magazine,* January 1993, 79–85.

Dennis, Marguerite. *Dollars for Scholars.* New York: Barron's, 1992.

"Do Colleges Collide on Financial Aid?" *The Wall Street Journal,* May 2, 1989, B-1.

Henderson, Nancy. "Here Come the College Bills." *Changing Times,* November 1990, 63–68.

"How to Pay a $150,000 Tuition Bill?" *Changing Times,* October 1989, 88-92.

Krefetz, Gerald. *How to Pay for Your Children's College Education.* New York: Macmillan, 1988.

Leider, Robert and Anna. *Don't Miss Out: The Ambitious Student's Guide to Financial Aid* (latest edition). Octameron Press, P.O. Box 3437, Alexandria, VA 22302. ($7.75, including shipping and handling)

Mitchell, Jacqueline. "Michigan Flunks Its Tuition Trust Fund." *The Wall Street Journal,* March 20, 1992, C-1.

1993 College Money Handbook. Princeton: Peterson's Guides.

Perry, Nancy J. "Planning Now for College." *Fortune,* February 25, 1991, 128.

Putka, Gary. "Arithmetic on College Aid Varies Widely." *The Wall Street Journal,* May 11, 1993, B-1.

Putka, Gary. "Tuition Trauma." *The Wall Street Journal,* October 20, 1989, R-34.

Schiffres, Manuel. "College Savings Plans that Work." *Kiplinger's Personal Finance Magazine,* April 1992, 65–69.

"Starting the Baby's College Fund." *Working Woman*, September 1988, 95–99.

"Tuition-Saving Strategies for Middle-Income Parents." *The Wall Street Journal*, December 3, 1991, C-1.

U.S. Department of Education. *The Student Guide 1993–1994*.

CHAPTER FIVE

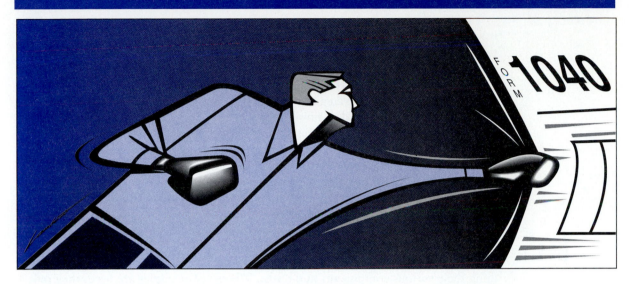

Coping with Federal Taxes

LEARNING OBJECTIVES

- To examine the terminology of federal income taxation
- To determine who must file a federal personal income tax return
- To define the different classes of filing status
- To become familiar with the major federal personal income tax forms
- To underscore the importance of tax records
- To identify the steps and calculations involved in completing a federal personal income tax return
- To know how to use such items as tax deductions, exemptions, exclusions, and tax credits for one's maximum tax benefit
- To study what a tax audit means and to learn how to cope with one

"Taxes," wrote Justice Oliver Wendell Holmes, "are what we pay for civilized society." But many Americans are wondering whether civilized society is now being sacrificed for taxes. Enormous federal budget deficits are prompting new rounds of tax increases. Many taxpayers are irked by what they consider a maddeningly complicated tax structure that the nation has devised for itself.

Imagine what autumn would be like if the people in charge of the tax laws had control of the football rules. Confusion would reign on the gridiron. Coaches would be tearing their hair out, the players would be stumbling over one another, and referees' flags would be flying all over the field.

Unfortunately, the tax game is not just a spectator sport. When the folks on Capitol Hill decide to change the rules, as they do almost every year, the hair-tearing confusion and penalties fall on us. However, we cannot pick up the ball and go home; we have to go on playing by Uncle Sam's rules. Keeping up with tax regulations is no simple task. It's up to taxpayers to learn the new rules and regulations and figure out how to blend them into strategies to keep their tax bills as low as possible.

This chapter is designed to familiarize you with the process of filing and paying income taxes. This process involves planning, record keeping, and professional assistance. A general knowledge of the tax system and its deductions, exclusions, regulations, and limitations is essential to obtain maximum tax benefit.

This chapter is not a guide to filing your tax returns. The tax laws as well as rules, regulations, and court rulings change almost every year. Thus, any step-by-step guide to tax preparation would be out of date in a year or two. There are many current tax manuals and guides on the market, as well as professional tax advisers and preparers to consult, as we shall see later on.

Therefore, this chapter will be limited to the broader issues of income taxes, examining their various components and terms. Whenever examples are used, they reflect the rules as they were in 1993. Some of these rules may very likely have changed by the time you read this chapter, but the principles underlying them will remain the same.

This chapter likewise discusses only income taxes. Taxes on wealth, such as inheritance, estate, and gift taxes, are discussed in subsequent chapters.

Today the chief source of federal revenue is the income tax. It was originally introduced as a means of helping to finance the Civil War but in its modern form dates only from 1913. In that year, the states ratified the 16th Amendment to the U.S. Constitution, which granted Congress the power to tax personal income. It authorized the U.S. government to "lay and collect taxes on incomes, from whatever source derived." The first permanent individual income tax in the United States became effective on March 1, 1913.

The **Internal Revenue Service (IRS)**, a branch of the U.S. Treasury Department, is responsible for collecting taxes owed by the general public, enforcing federal tax laws, and providing taxpayers with information and documents for the preparation of their tax reports.

Tax Reform

In 1981, with the Economic Recovery Tax Act (ERTA), Congress passed the largest tax cuts in U.S. history. These cuts, which were implemented over three years, reduced individual federal income taxes by 23 percent. It likewise reduced the effective gift and estate tax.

When President Reagan subsequently signed the **Tax Reform Act of 1986** into law, even the name of the law under which we figure and pay our taxes changed. The Internal Revenue Code of 1954, as amended, became the **Internal Revenue Code of 1986**. For 32 years Congress made amendments to the old law, changing both the rates and the rules from time to time, but this new name reflected the magnitude of

FIGURE 5–1 | **A Frequent Refrain**

President Reagan was not the first, nor only, president to promise tax cuts, as this Bush-era advertisement shows.

SOURCE: Reprinted by Dryfus Corporation.

the reform. The 1981 ERTA Law, as well as the Tax Reform Act of 1986, made sweeping changes in our tax system. Many of these changes are discussed throughout this chapter.

Tax reform is a perennial political issue. Each administration and Congress tries to improve the tax system and get it "just right." This is likely to continue in the future. The advertisement shown in Figure 5–1 underscores society's ongoing preoccupation with tax reform.

At the heart of the 1986 Tax Reform Act was a drastic reduction of tax rates and a compression of **tax brackets.** The old steeply graduated 15-bracket rate structure, with rates ranging from 11 to 50 percent, was squeezed into what was widely hailed as a two-bracket 15 and 28 percent system. (The Bush Administration in 1991 changed it to three basic tax brackets, 15 percent, 28 percent, and 31 percent. In 1993 President Clinton added two more brackets, 36 percent and 39.6 percent.) However, the slashed tax rates did not necessarily slash tax bills. The thrust of the Tax Reform Act of 1986 was tax reform, not tax relief, illustrated by Figure 5–2.

| **FIGURE 5–2** | **The Tax Burden** |

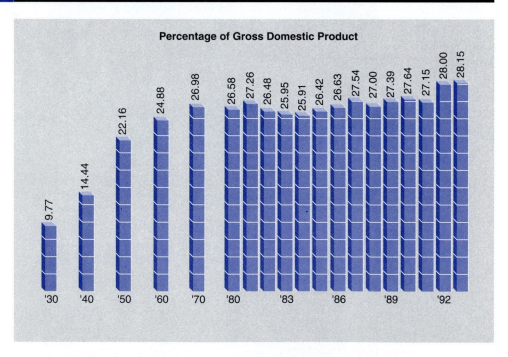

In recent history, the total of federal, state, and local taxes exceeds 25 percent of the gross domestic product. The Tax Reform Act of 1986 did not lessen this percentage.

SOURCE: U.S. Department of Commerce, 1986; and U.S. Department of Commerce, *Survey of Current Business,* various years (Tables 1.1, 3.2, 3.3, and 3.6). Figures for 1991 to 1993 are estimated.

The trade-off for lower rates was "base broadening," letting the Internal Revenue Service apply the tax to more income. This was accomplished by eliminating many tax loopholes and shelters and crimping some old and established deductions. Overall, it provided for a more equitable system. But the reforms also introduced new heights of complexity.

Tax Avoidance: Don't Cheat (Yourself) on Taxes

There are two kinds of tax cheaters: those who cheat the government and those who cheat themselves. If you try to cheat the IRS, you may get yourself into legal problems. But if you shortchange yourself by failing to take advantage of legitimate tax deductions, credits, and exemptions, no one will come after you.

Another famous American jurist, Judge Learned Hand (1872–1961), once wrote: "Over and over again the courts have said that there is nothing sinister in so arranging one's affairs as to keep taxes as low as possible. Everybody does so, rich or poor, and all do right, for nobody owes a public duty to pay more than the law demands. Taxes are enforced extractions, not voluntary contributions."

Coming from a federal judge, that famous endorsement of tax planning is authoritative and encouraging. This statement should cause you to ask yourself, Am I arranging my financial affairs to keep my taxes as low as legally possible or am I making voluntary contributions to the IRS because of ignorance, negligence, or oversight?

Successful tax planning demands year-round tax thinking. That does not mean dwelling on financial matters and fretting about the IRS all the time. But taxpayers do need to keep their mind's eye open to possible tax ramifications as they go about their personal and professional business. As a taxpayer, you should get in the habit of asking yourself how a planned action—buying or selling investments, switching jobs, or getting married, for example—might affect your tax bill and consider steps that will minimize your tax obligations.

If the avoidance of taxes is indeed the only intellectual pursuit that still carries any reward, as economist John Maynard Keynes quipped, now is the time to get out your thinking cap.

Marginal versus Average Tax Rates

When discussing tax brackets, we should differentiate between marginal and average tax rates. **Marginal tax rate** is the term used to describe the rate at which a taxpayer pays tax on his or her last dollar of income or, alternatively, the rate at which the taxpayer saves on his or her last dollar of deductions. In other words, it refers to the highest tax rate at which, given a particular level of income, any additional income is taxed. The **average tax rate** is the actual percentage of each taxable dollar paid in taxes.

The marginal tax rate is more important than the average tax rate for financial planning purposes. The average tax rate has limited usefulness for decision-making purposes. The taxpayer is more interested in how his or her decisions will affect his or her tax liability at the margin—that is, the last dollars earned or last dollars saved from deductions. The marginal rate is the appropriate rate to consider for investment decision-making purposes. It determines the tax effect of additional income or deductible items. Figure 5–3 shows the marginal tax rate for various income levels for 1993 for single and married taxpayers.

MARGINAL

For an example of how changes in income can affect taxes paid, assume that Larry Baker, a single taxpayer, has a total taxable income of $15,000. His marginal tax rate is 15 percent. Larry is paying $.15 in taxes on every dollar he earns. Now suppose Larry suddenly gets a promotion and his income rises to $28,000. For any income above $22,100, Larry moves into the 28 percent bracket. His taxes will be a combination of marginal rates and amounts:

$$(.15 \times \$22,100) \; + \; (.28 \times [\$28,000 - \$22,100]) =$$

$$\$3,315 \; + \qquad\qquad (.28 \times \$5,900) =$$

$$\$3,315 \; + \qquad\qquad\qquad \$1,652 = \$\,4,967 \text{ tax}$$

FIGURE 5–3	Income Levels within Marginal Tax Rates

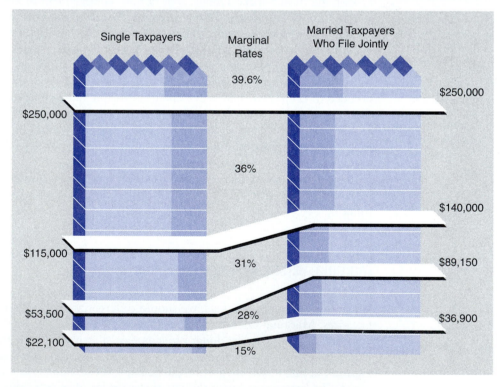

The marginal tax rates take effect at different income levels for single taxpayers and married taxpayers who file jointly.

SOURCE: Internal Revenue Service.

Dividing his tax by total income ($4,967 ÷ $28,000) we see Larry's tax is 17.7 percent of his income. This is his average tax rate. But from now on, every additional dollar up to $53,500 Larry earns will be subject to a 28 percent tax. Therefore, his marginal tax rate is 28 percent. If he earns above $51,900, his marginal rate becomes 31 percent. This is the rate he would use in any investment considerations or other financial decisions. If Larry is offered overtime next week, which means $100 extra income, he would base his decision on the fact that he would have an after-tax net additional earnings of $72 next week.

Tax Witholding: The W-4 Form

On your first day at work, you will probably be asked to complete a simple document, the **W-4 form, Employee's Withholding Allowance Certificate**. It is your introduction to **tax withholding**, also called *payroll withholding*, the federal government's easy method to ensure that taxes are collected.

There are two methods for paying income tax in a timely fashion. Wage earners generally have taxes withheld from their paychecks. The IRS requires an employer to deduct an amount for federal income tax from an employee's pay and send it to the government. People who will owe more than $500 in tax on other income typically make estimated tax payments on Form 1040ES four times a year.

Payroll withholding is based on income, family size, and status, as well as a number of other factors. The W-4 form gives an employer the information to determine how much tax to withhold from an employee's salary. The number of W-4 allowances claimed does not change the actual tax liability, but how much tax the employee pays out in installments each payday. The value of one allowance equals the value of one personal exemption (discussed further on) on your income tax return. Each allowance tells your employer to ignore $2,350 (in 1993) of salary (or $728.50 in federal income taxes for someone in the 31 percent bracket) when deciding how much to take out of each of your paychecks for the IRS.

A change in one's personal situation may require a withholding checkup. Getting married, having a baby, buying a home, and turning 65—all can justify lower withholding. Often people who hold two jobs at once and couples in which both spouses work have too little tax withheld if their W-4s do not take both jobs and both incomes into account.

But it would be unwise to get carried away and claim too many allowances. Taxpayers generally face a penalty if their withholding tax totals less than 90 percent of their liability, or 100 percent of last year's tax liability. Ideally, the amount of tax withheld during the year should come close to matching the tax owed when a taxpayer completes the tax return early in the following year. Any other result means that you let the U.S. Treasury use your money for free or risk a penalty for underwithholding.

The W-2 Form

At the end of the year, the law requires employers to mail their employees a **W-2 form** (see Figure 5–4), which reports a worker's annual earnings and the amounts that were

---

FIGURE 5–4 **Sample W–2 Form**

1 Control number	22222	For Official Use Only ▶ OMB No. 1545-0008	

2 Employer's name, address, and ZIP code	4 Statutory Employee ☐ Deceased ☐ Pension plan ☐ Legal rep. ☐ 942 emp. ☐ Subtotal ☐ Deferred compensation ☐ Void ☐

7 Allocated tips | 8 Advance EIC payment

9 Federal income tax withheld | 10 Wages, tips, other compensation

| 3 Employer's identification number | 4 Employer's state I.D. number | 11 Social security tax withheld | 12 Social security wages |

| 5 Employee's social security number | | 13 Social security tips | 14 Medicare wages and tips |

19a Employee's name (first, middle initial, last) | 15 Medicare tax withheld | 16 Nonqualified plans

17 See Instrs. for Form W-2 | 18 Other

19b Employee's address and ZIP code

| 2c | 21 | 22 Dependent care benefits | 23 Benefits included in Box 10 |

| 24 State income tax | 25 State wages, tips, etc. | 26 Name of state | 27 Local income tax | 28 Local wages, tips, etc | 29 Name of locality |

Copy A For Social Security Administration   Cat. No. 10134D   Department of treasury—Internal Revenue Service

Form **W-2 Wage and Tax Statment**

For Paperwork Reduction Act Notice and instructions for completing this form, see separate instructions.

SOURCE: Internal Revenue Service.

---

deducted for federal income tax, Social Security (Federal Insurance Compensation Act, or FICA), and (if applicable) state and local income taxes. A copy of your W-2 form must be filed with your tax return to document your earnings and the amount you have already paid in taxes.

Record Keeping

Annual tax-filing trauma is over by April 15 for most Americans, but the hassles of keeping tax-related records never end. Each year many taxpayers go through the unnerving experience of having their personal income tax returns examined by the IRS. In many cases, the documentation that was used on their tax return causes problems.

Clear, well-organized records of itemized deductions—along with canceled checks, receipts, and other supporting information—can save taxpayers tax dollars and tax preparation dollars, too. An accountant's or tax preparer's time is not cheap, and the expense will be greater if taxpayers just dump the proverbial shoe box of jumbled checks, receipts, and account statements in their tax preparer's lap. Before sitting down to do your own taxes or meeting with a tax preparer, you should orga-

Some Record Keeping Recommendations

Record keeping can be a simple process if you start with a system that is comfortable for you. Here are five useful guidelines:

1. To preserve legitimate business tax deductions, keep pen and paper handy. Start maintaining records on a daily, weekly, or monthly basis, depending on the number of documents or transactions involved.

2. Keep essential records where they will be protected from fire and theft. Small vaults or safes for the home can be bought for this purpose, or a safe-deposit box can be rented at a local bank.

3. Keep duplicate copies of essential documents in a separate place. Original documents should be protected in a safe-deposit box and photocopies used for routine reference. Maintain photocopies of your tax return and all attachments, in case the IRS loses it and asks you to file again.

4. Keep a list of important documents, indicating the location of each. Some might be in the files of your attorney or accountant, for example. Indeed, many taxpayers have realized that they needed more folders than ever in the home file cabinet because of the 1986 tax overhaul. New on 1987 returns, for instance, was Form 8606 for reporting nondeductible contributions to individual retirement accounts (IRAs). The IRS requires taxpayers to save those forms until all funds are withdrawn from the tax-deferred savings plan. That could mean 50 years or more of filing for people in their 20s.

5. After completing your taxes each year, file away in one package a photocopy of the return and all the receipts, wage statements, and other papers that support your income and deduction items. The package has to be kept at least three years, the IRS's statute of limitation for examining a return. The statute runs six years if the IRS finds a taxpayer has omitted an item accounting for more than 25 percent of reported income, and it is extended indefinitely in cases of fraud or in which no return was filed.

nize your records and try to calculate total income, deductions, expenses, and capital gains or losses yourself.

The IRS Loves Good Records

We have had this dream, many of us, in which we are walking into a classroom for the final exam and we realize that we have not been in class all semester, we haven't read the text, we aren't prepared, and we haven't a prayer. When we get older, this nightmare may be replaced by a new one: we're walking into an IRS office for an audit with no records, no supporting documents, nothing. We haven't a prayer.

You can avoid such nightmarish problems if you have adequate records for the year under examination. The key is to be organized right from the beginning of each year.

Income tax regulations require taxpayers to keep adequate records that will enable them to establish the amount of gross income, deductions, and credits to include on their income tax return. Maintaining proper records is the taxpayer's responsibility. No uniform method is required, but failure to maintain proper records and documentation may mean that some of your deductions are disallowed when the IRS examines your return. The inability to substantiate a deduction because of inadequate record keeping has been included in the definition of negligence. The penalty is 5 percent of the total additional tax due.

Taxpayers should avoid the habit of waiting until they are up against the deadline to start accumulating tax records. If you update your records as you pay for expenses, there is less chance of forgetting various deductible expenses than if you throw your records together hastily just before preparing your tax return. Paying tax-deductible items by check provides an automatic record of these expenditures.

Record Categories

The following are just a few of the areas in which better records could translate into annual tax savings:

1. *Charitable contributions*   Ask for a receipt when donating cash or property (such as used clothing and furniture). Keep a log of your expenses traveling to and from volunteer activities.

2. *Work-related expenses*   Deductions can be taken for such diverse expenditures as business use of a home computer and luggage or a briefcase purchased for the job. Maintain records of business publication subscriptions, dues to professional associations, the costs of looking for a new job in the same field, and a job-related move. Retain pay stubs that show deductions for union dues.

3. *Travel on the job*   Taxpayers who incur business-related travel and entertainment (T&E) expenses must keep adequate records. Tax deductions are not allowed for such expenditures on the basis of estimates or taxpayer testimony. For adequate T&E records, taxpayers need receipts or paid bills as well as a diary or similar record made near the time of the expenditure to establish the business purpose for the expense. The diary or receipt should name the persons entertained, the place, date, business relationship, and nature of business discussed. For travel expenses, the diary should state the destination, when, why, and how much it cost, with a breakdown of travel fare, cabs, lodging expenses, phone bills, meals, and the like.

4. *Business use of car*   Maintain daily records of any business use of your car. Keep a log showing the date of each trip, the mileage driven, and the business purpose. Also keep supporting evidence, such as a signed contract or gasoline credit card slips.

5. *Computer use*   To deduct the expenses of a home computer, it is necessary to keep track of all the time it is used. The only way to know what percentage of the cost qualifies as a business expense is to know how business use compared with total use. When recording business use, the specific project involved must be noted.

6. *Real estate*   Taxpayers who own residential property must maintain records of the original purchase price, including related fees such as title search. The cost of major improvements must be recorded in a record book. All canceled checks and invoices for improvements should be kept in a file. Improvements increase the "basis" of the home and therefore reduce the tax that will be owed when the home is sold. The most valuable and irreplaceable home documents should be stored in a safe-deposit box or a fireproof safe or filing cabinet.

7. *Securities*   Taxpayers who own securities (stocks, bonds, mutual funds) should keep a separate file on each security, or at least a columnar work sheet with a listing for each security. All purchase confirmations should be recorded indicating the name of the security, in whose name it is registered, number of shares, date of acquisition, and the original cost. When securities are sold, the specifics of the transaction should be entered on the work sheet. The sales confirmation slip should be stapled to the purchase confirmation slip so that the gain or loss on the transaction can be determined easily for that year's income tax return.

8. *Medical and dental expenses*   Only medical bills that amount to more than 7.5 percent of your gross income qualify for an itemized deduction (these are described later in more detail). The cost of traveling to the doctor and pharmacist can also be deducted. A log of taxi bills, bus fares, tolls, parking fees, or auto mileage (deductible at actual costs or 9 cents a mile in 1992) should be maintained. Keep pay stubs that show salary deductions for medical insurance.

9. *Real estate taxes and state income taxes*   Discussed later.

10. *Home mortgage interest*   Discussed later.

Filing Your Tax Return

Who Must File

Penalty

Whether U.S. citizens or residents must file tax returns depends upon their gross income, their filing status, their age, and whether they are blind. Figure 5–5 shows the minimum gross incomes for various categories of people that needed to file in 1993. People who fail to file their taxes are subject to two penalties, the late-filing penalty and the late-payment penalty. The late-filing penalty is 5 percent of the tax due for each month a return is late with a maximum 25 percent penalty. If you owe $5,000, this would cost you $250 each month until you file. The late-payment penalty is 0.5 percent per month, or $25 on a $5,000 delinquency. In addition, you would have to pay 8 percent interest annually on any late payment.

Taxpayers who are not required to file a tax return should file to receive refunds on any withheld interest or other withheld income.

Do-It-Yourself Tax Filing

According to the IRS, roughly 50 percent of the over 100 million Americans who pay taxes prepare the returns themselves. You should be able to do it yourself if

FIGURE 5–5 **Sample Chart Showing Who Must File (For Most Taxpayers)**

To use this chart, first find you marital status at the end of 1992. Then, read across to find your filing status and age at the end of 1992. (Being blind does not change your filing requirement.)

You must file a return if your gross income was at least the amount shown in the last column.

Marital Status	Filing Status	Age*	Gross Income
Single (including divorced and legally separated	Single	under 65 65 or older	$5,900 $6,800
	Head of household	under 65 65 or older	$7,550 $8,450
Married with a child and living apart from your spouse during the last 6 months of 1992	Head of household	under 65 65 or older	$7,550 $8,450
Married and living with your spouse at end of 1992 (or on the date your spouse died)	Married, joint return	under 65 (both spouses) 65 or older (one spouse) 65 or older (both spouses)	$10,600 $11,300 $12,000
	Married, separate return	any age	$2,300
Married, not living with your spouse at the end of 1992 (or on the date your spouse died)	Married, joint, or separate return	any age	$2,300
Widowed before 1992 and not remarried in 1992	Single	under 65 65 or older	$5,900 $6,800
	Head of household	under 65 65 or older	$7,550 $8,450
	Qualifying widower(er) with dependent child	under 65 65 or older	$8,300 $9,000

*If you were age 65 on January 1, 1993, you are considered to be age 65 at the end of 1992.

This chart, updated yearly by the IRS, shows who must file according to marital status, filing status, age, and income level.

SOURCE: Internal Revenue Service, Your Federal Income Tax: 1992 Tax Guide for Individuals (1992), 7.

1. Your income is mostly salary.

2. Your deductions are easy to compute.

3. You do not own any limited partnership units.

4. You have not sold your home or any investments this year.

5. You keep up with the latest tax-planning strategies.

Obtaining Tax Information

For taxpayers intent on filling out their own tax forms, the place to start is the basic 1040 booklet, which explains how to fill out the 1040 return and where to get additional, more detailed information. When in need of an answer to a tax question, the last source you would probably think to consult is the huge bureaucracy that wants your money. But you may be pleasantly surprised to discover that the IRS provides information that is accurate, reasonably clear, and (most important) free. The IRS provides over 100 publications on various topics without cost to taxpayers to help them understand the tax laws. These publications are revised annually and are available during the filing period. Most taxpayers should be able to meet the requirements of the tax laws by using these publications as well as films, taxpayer education programs, and library resources.

Taxpayers who have a question about a particular subject can phone **Tele-Tax**. This IRS service provides recorded information on about 140 common federal tax questions. For specific or technical questions, you can call an IRS tax adviser for help. This toll-free assistance is available nationwide; the phone numbers are listed in the Form 1040 instruction booklet. But taxpayers should not expect too much in the way of precise information over the phone. Many of the workers are part-timers, trained to handle only the most common questions. More difficult queries require more experienced and knowledgeable advisers. A caller may have to be persistent to reach someone who is knowledgeable on a particular or complicated subject. The taxpayer is ultimately responsible for any errors in his or her tax return, regardless of any misinformation received from IRS tax advisers.

Private Letter Rulings

A taxpayer can get a personal ruling or judgment on a complicated matter directly from the IRS before filing taxes. The taxpayer can simply request an individual letter from the IRS saying that the deduction would be approved. Each year, from its headquarters in Washington, DC, the IRS issues about 30,000 of these letters, called **private letter rulings**. These rulings are "private" because they are supposed to apply to only one individual taxpayer and one particular set of facts.

Most requests, not surprisingly, come from tax lawyers and accountants, and involve technical questions on stock options, partnerships and trusts, gifts to minors, estate planning, and the like. But since it can cost $5,000 to $20,000 to have an accounting firm file a request for a private letter ruling, each year several thousand individuals send in their own. These involve everything from wills and pensions to student benefits, child care, and medical deductions. For example, if your doctor prescribes swimming as part of a cure or therapy, can you deduct the cost of swimming as a medical expense? The IRS has sent out different rulings in different letters on this one. And so there is yet no clear answer. But you can try your luck and request a ruling on your specific case.

The steps for filing for a letter ruling are laid out in Revenue Procedure 86-1 published in the *Internal Revenue Bulletin*. The bulletins are available at every IRS district office.

Tax Guidebooks

Taxpayers seeking opinions other than those provided by the IRS should check with local libraries or bookstores for instruction manuals that cover regulations, laws, and cases. Updated paperback tax return guides perennially appear in the stores around December.

A tax preparation guide may easily pay for itself by steering you to a money-saving tip. It may save you time, help you avoid a blunder, or simply reduce anxiety about tax breaks you might be missing. These **tax guidebooks** are aimed at the more than 50 million American taxpayers who tackle their own returns and know that otherwise negotiating a 1040 form can be a confusing experience.

The first guide to consult is the IRS's *Your Federal Income Tax* (publication 17). This is available from any local IRS office or can be obtained free of charge by phoning 800/TAX-FORM. Some leading commercial guides are listed at the end of this chapter under "Additional Resources." Before buying one, test it on a specific tax question, ideally one that you already know something about so that you can assess the clarity and accuracy of the information. When selecting a guide, start at the end. Check the index. The key test of a tax guide's value is how easily you can find what you are looking for, how much information is provided, and how clearly the book presents itself. It is also important to check how well it explains changes in the tax laws.

Using a Professional Tax Preparer

As stated above, the two factors critical to deciding whether to seek professional advice in preparation of your return are the complexity of the return and whether there have been significant changes in your lifestyle or your financial situation. The list of "life events" that may necessitate professional help at tax time includes retirement and divorce or death of a spouse, a large inheritance, the sale of a home, and moving from one state to another. Owning a business also creates complications of its own.

Nearly half of all taxpayers pay someone else to fill out their tax returns each filing season. Many others consult paid professional tax advisers all year round.

It is important to bear in mind that even if you pay someone to prepare your return, you are legally responsible for the information in it and for any additional tax, interest, or penalty.

Anyone can hang out a shingle offering tax preparation services. No national educational or professional requirements have been established. Consequently, the help can range from highly skilled to highly incompetent. Therefore, it takes research to select the right preparer. Find out about the preparer's experience, operating procedure, willingness and ability to represent clients in an audit, and turnaround time for the return. Some independent firms set up shop early in the year and vanish after April, offering no help if you later have a problem with your return. Others offer year-round service. Let us examine some of the major categories of tax advisers available to taxpayers.

Commercial Tax Preparers Commercial tax preparation services are the most popular and generally least expensive. **Commercial tax preparers** may work for big firms, such as H&R Block, smaller firms, or independently. H&R Block, which processed 14 million returns in 1990, is the nation's single largest commercial tax preparer. It employs about 60,000 tax preparers during tax season in 9,000 outlets open nationwide during the January through April filing season and regional offices open throughout the year if any problems arise. Its average charge in 1991 was $55. There are many commercial preparers besides those who work for Block. Commercial preparers are likely to have the least professional education and training, and cannot represent taxpayers before the IRS. If you consider one, ask about the preparer's experience doing returns and training to keep up with the changing tax law.

It is important to seek a professional who offers tax and financial planning advice throughout the year, not just at tax time. Tax preparers who promise a refund before seeing your financial information, ask you to sign a blank form, or say that they have a friend at the IRS should be avoided.

Accountants   Another option is to choose an accountant. Accountants are likely to be full-time year-round tax advisers, but they have not passed the exam or met the experience requirements demanded of CPAs.

Enrolled Agents   **Enrolled agents**, perhaps the least known classification of the tax preparer, are so named because they have been granted enrollment by the Treasury Department to represent taxpayers at any level of the IRS. Enrolled agents do so by either passing a demanding two-day IRS exam on technical tax matters, demonstrating their competence, or having worked for the IRS as revenue agents for at least five years. CPAs can also represent clients before the IRS, but accountants and commercial tax preparers cannot. These tax specialists generally charge less than CPAs but more than commercial preparers and accountants. Their preparation fee is between $100 and $300.

Certified Public Accountants (CPAs)   Finally, taxpayers may choose a **certified public accountant** (**CPA**). These state-licensed professionals generally handle the most complicated returns. They must have college degrees, pass a four-part national exam in accounting practices, and take annual college-level refresher courses. Such pros are best for people who invest regularly or are self-employed. It is important to select a CPA who specializes in taxes; not all do. Since CPAs provide a variety of tax services from tax return preparation to financial planning to bookkeeping, the first step in choosing a practitioner is to identify your needs. CPAs normally bill their clients on an hourly basis, generally $75 or more an hour. If your taxes are simple and straightforward, then hiring a CPA may be an extravagance. A much less expensive tax preparer should be sufficient.

Selecting the Right Tax Adviser   An important question is whether you need more than tax preparation. Depending upon your income and the complexity of your financial life, you might benefit handsomely from the year-round tax help offered by accountants, certified public accountants, and enrolled tax agents. Such professional help may be especially important if last year involved a move to a new state, a divorce, an investment in real estate, the start of a new business, or retirement.

Year-Round Tax Planning   Once you sit down to do your return, it's too late for most of the tax-saving maneuvers that a tax preparer, CPA, or other tax professional might suggest. However, tax-return time can be the perfect time to begin a relationship with a tax expert. Doing your return will give the tax adviser a detailed look at where you stand. Once the pressure of the April 15 rush is over, you and your tax adviser should sit down to map strategy for the rest of the year. The tax professional should discuss plans and strategies that can help reduce your tax bill next year.

Filing Late

Procrastinators, take heart. If you are behind in preparing your taxes and are afraid of not meeting the April 15 filing deadline, you need not panic. The IRS can be sympathetic if taxpayers are unable to complete the tax return on time and offers fairly easy ways to put off the day of reckoning as long as the right procedures are followed.

Your First Extension

Just fill out the brief 4868 form and mail it to your IRS service center by April 15. The IRS will extend your deadline to August 15, no excuses asked. If you send in your 1040 form late without filing for a **tax-filing extension**, the IRS loses compassion and imposes a penalty of 5 percent a month plus interest on the amount owed.

The Second Extension

Before the first extension expires, you may submit Form 2688 to ask for up to two additional months. But a detailed explanation of the reason for the extension must be provided. Any reasonable explanation will usually do: serious illness that kept you in the hospital, for example, or simply "additional time needed to file a complete and accurate return." You will get a copy back from the IRS marked to show if the request is approved. This extra extension is granted by the IRS on a case-by-case basis.

The IRS developed a new APEX (Automated Processing of Extension) system that became operational in 1992. APEX is a paperless system that will grant a four-month extension to file if the taxpayer has paid either 100 percent of the tax for the year for which the return is being filed or 100 percent of the previous year's liability by April 15. The determination of whether these tests are met will be made after the Form 1040 is filed. In other words, a taxpayer who files by August 15 will not be penalized if he or she meets either test.

An additional two-month extension (equating to Form 2688) may be obtained by paying 100 percent of the current liability by August 15 (assuming the option of using the previous year's liability had been used to request the initial four-month extension).

You Can Push Off If You Pay Up   The IRS is willing to wait past April 15 for a return, but not for any money due. To be valid, Form 4868 must show the proper estimate of tax liability, and any unpaid portion of the estimate must be submitted with the form. If you pay less than 90 percent of what is due, your extension may later be ruled invalid and you could retroactively be subject to interest plus penalties.

States generally follow the federal rules on extensions, but taxpayers need to check locally on what forms should be filed.

Amended Returns: You've Sent It, Now You Can Change It

Being a punctual taxpayer and filing your return before April 15 does not mean that you cannot still tinker with it if you later discover that you failed to claim a deduction or other tax break. All you have to do is file an **amended return** on Form 1040X. This form and its instructions are available from the IRS (800/829-3676).

Revising a return is also a way to get to the IRS before it gets to you if you over-looked some income you should have declared on your return or if you now realize that you wrongly took a write-off or other benefit. Clearing up the error can cut the interest or penalty you might face later if the IRS catches up with it. Taxpayers generally have three years from the due date of the return in which to file an amended version.

The Tax Forms

The standard tax-filing form is the **1040**, which is designed for the average family. But not everybody has to file a 1040.

The 1040EZ Form

In 1982 the IRS introduced the **1040EZ form,** which is used by about 15 million taxpayers. The one-page 1040EZ (Figure 5–6) has only 11 numbered lines compared with almost 70 on the standard 1040 form. There are no supplementary forms to file with the EZ, and the instructions fit on the back of the single-page form.

The 1040EZ may be sufficient if taxpayers satisfy a fairly short list of requirements. They:

1. Must be single

2. Must be under age 65

3. Cannot claim dependents

4. Cannot itemize deductions

5. Must have less than $50,000 of taxable income consisting solely of wages and tips

6. Must have earned no more than $400 of taxable interest

The 1040A Form

For nonsingles and others who cannot use a 1040EZ but dread the prospect of a 1040, the 1040A is a step up from the EZ in complexity. It consists of two pages, with an additional two-page schedule. Taxable income must be under $50,000 and come only from wages, tips, interest, dividends, or unemployment compensation. The 1040A was revised in 1990 to allow more people to use it. You can now use the 1040A, for example, if you report pension income, credits for the elderly or disabled, or taxable Social Security benefits. You cannot use this form if you report capital gains, self-employment earnings, or alimony.

The IRS estimates that it takes about 30 minutes on average to complete a 1040EZ and may take an hour or so for many 1040As. This is in contrast to the approximately 6 hours and 41 minutes that the IRS estimates it would take an individual to file his or her own regular 1040 form. One-third of all taxpayers file the 1040A or 1040EZ forms.

| FIGURE 5–6 | Sample of 1040EZ Form |

Department of the Treasury—Internal Revenue Service

Form 1040EZ

Income Tax Return for Single Filers With No Dependents

OMB No. 1545-0675

Name & Address

Use the IRS label (see page 10). If you dont have one, please print.

L A B E L
Print your name (first, initial, last)
Home address (number and street). If you have a P.O. box, see page 10. Apt. no.

H E R E
City, town or post office, state, and ZIP code. If you have a foreign address, see page 10.

Please print your numbers like this:

9 8 7 6 5 4 3 2 1 0

Your social security number

Please see instructions on back. Also, see the Form 1040EZ booklet.

Presidential Election Campaign (See page 10.) Do you want $1 to go to this fund?

Note: *Checking "yes" will not change your tax or reduce your refund.*

Yes No

Dollars   Cents

Report your income

Attach Copy B of Form (s) W-2 here.
Attach tax payment on top of form(s) W-2.

Note: *You must check Yes or No.*

1 Total wages, salaries, and tips. This should be shown in box 10 of your W-2 form(s). Attach your W-2 form(s) 1

2 Taxable interest income of $400 or less. If the total is more than $400, you cannot use Form 1040EZ. 2

3 Add lines 1 and 2. **This is your adjusted gross income.** 3

4 Can your parents (or someone else) claim you on their return?
☐ **Yes.** Do worksheet on back; enter amount from line E here.
☐ **No.** Enter 5,900.00. This is the total of your standard deduction and personal exemption. 4

5 Subtract line 4 from line 3. If line 4 is larger than line 3, enter 0. This is your **taxable income.** 5

Figure your tax

6 Enter your Federal income tax withheld from box 9 of your W-2 form(s). 6

7 **Tax.** Look at line 5 above. Use the amount on **line 5** to find your tax in the tax table on pages 22-24 of the booklet. Then, enter the tax from the table on this line. 7

Refund or amount you owe

8 If line 6 is larger than line 7, subtract line 7 from line 6. This is your **refund** 8

9 If line 7 is larger than line 6, subtract line 6 from line 7. This is the **amount you owe.** Attach your payment for full amount payable to the "Internal Revenue Service". Write your name, address, social security number, daytime phone number, and "1992 Form 1040EZ" on it. 9

Sign your return

Keep a copy of this form for your records.

I have read this return. Under penalties of perjury, I declare that to the best of my knoledge and belief, the return is true, correct, and complete.

Your signature

X

Date

Your occupation

For IRS Use Only — Please do not write in boxes below.

For Privacy Act and Paperwork Reduction Act Notice, see page 4 in the booklet. Cat. No. 11329W Form 1040EZ

SOURCE: Internal Revenue Service, *Your Federal Income Tax*, Table 1–1, 7.

Taxpayers who itemize should use the standard 1040 form. (They itemize if their deductible expenses exceed their standard deduction. This is discussed later in the chapter.)

Let's Examine the 1040 Form

Since most people still itemize and take deductions and exemptions, let us examine a 1040 form as it appeared at presstime and see how it works. See Figure 5–7. The form for this current year may vary somewhat, but the basic structure should be the same.

The Importance of Status

Notice that the Form 1040, lines 1 through 5, provides for taxpayers to select their appropriate status. Taxpayers must indicate their filing status by checking only one of the boxes on the 1040 or 1040A forms. There are no boxes for filing status on Form 1040EZ because only single people are eligible to file that form.

A taxpayer's **filing status** is used in determining his or her filing requirements, standard deduction, and correct tax. It is also important in determining whether he or she is eligible to claim certain deductions and credits.

Married Filing Jointly or Separately   Probably the most obvious tax effect of joining together in wedded bliss is that most newlyweds will be filing a **joint return**. The tax law provides that marital status be determined as of the last day of the tax year. Therefore, even if their wedding day is December 31, the couple may report all of their income and deductions on a joint return, as if they were married the entire year, regardless of which one of them received the income or incurred the deductions. Married persons also have the option to elect **married filing separately return** status. This option may benefit married people who want to be responsible only for their own taxes or if this method results in less tax than a joint return. Those who file a joint return will generally pay less tax.

Head of Household   Taxpayers may be eligible to file as a **head of household** if they were unmarried or were considered unmarried on the last day of the year. They must have paid more than half the cost of keeping up a house that was the principal home for more than half the year for them and any children or relatives.

If you qualify as a head of household, you may figure your tax by using the special tax rate schedule for this category. It is a lower rate than singles or married filing separately but higher than marrieds filing jointly. Many single people simply check "single," unaware that they may qualify for the more beneficial "head of household" status. Single taxpayers who were never married or are legally separated, divorced, or widowed and who do not provide a home for other dependents qualify for single status.

Exemptions

Regardless of their age, the **exemptions** you claim for yourself and your **dependents** (on lines 6a through 6e) are worth $2,350 (in 1993). This means that you are

FIGURE 5–7 **Page 1 of the Sample 1040 Form**

Form **1040** Department of the Treasury—Internal Revenue Service
U.S. Individual Income Tax Return **1992** (5) IRS Use Only—Do not write or staple in this space.

For the year Jan. 1–Dec. 31, 1992, or other tax year beginning , 1992, ending , 19 OMB No. 1545-0074

Label
(See instructions on page 10.)

Use the IRS label. Otherwise, please print or type.

Your first name and initial Last name

Your social security number

If a joint return, spouse's first name and initial Last name

Spouse's social security number

Home address (number and street). If you have a P.O. box, see page 10. Apt. no.

City, town or post office, state, and ZIP code. If you have a foreign address, see page 10.

For Privacy Act and Paperwork Reduction Act Notice, see page 4.

Presidential Election Campaign (See page 10.)

Do you want $1 to go to this fund? Yes No

If a joint return, does your spouse want $1 to go to this fund? Yes No

Note: Checking "Yes" will not change your tax or reduce your refund.

Filing Status
(See page 10.)
Check only one box.

1 Single
2 Married filing joint return (even if only one had income)
3 Married filing separate return. Enter spouse's social security no. above and full name here. ▶
4 Head of household (with qualifying person). (See page 11.) If the qualifying person is a child but not your dependent, enter this child's name here. ▶
5 Qualifying widow(er) with dependent child (year spouse died ▶ 19). (See page 11.)

Exemptions
(See page 11.)

6a ☐ Yourself. If your parent (or someone else) can claim you as a dependent on his or her tax return, **do not** check box 6a. But be sure to check the box on line 33b on page 2

b ☐ Spouse

c Dependents:
(1) Name (first, initial, and last name) | (2) Check if under age 1 | (3) If age 1 or older, dependent's social security number | (4) Dependent's relationship to you | (5) No. of months lived in your home in 1992

If more than six dependents, see page 12.

No. of boxes checked on 6a and 6b

No. of your children on 6c who:
• lived with you
• didn't live with you due to divorce or separation (see page 13)

No. of other dependents on 6c

d If your child didn't live with you but is claimed as your dependent under a pre-1985 agreement, check here ▶ ☐
e Total number of exemptions claimed

Add numbers entered on lines above ▶

Income

Attach Copy B of your Forms W-2, W-2G, and 1099-R here.

If you did not get a W-2, see page 9.

Attach check or money order on top of any Forms W-2, W-2G, or 1099-R.

7 Wages, salaries, tips, etc. Attach Form(s) W-2 | 7
8a Taxable interest income. Attach Schedule B if over $400 | 8a
b Tax-exempt interest income (see page 15). DON'T include on line 8a | 8b
9 Dividend income. Attach Schedule B if over $400 | 9
10 Taxable refunds, credits, or offsets of state and local income taxes from worksheet on page 16 | 10
11 Alimony received | 11
12 Business income or (loss). Attach Schedule C or C-EZ | 12
13 Capital gain or (loss). Attach Schedule D | 13
14 Capital gain distributions not reported on line 13 (see page 15) | 14
15 Other gains or (losses). Attach Form 4797 | 15
16a Total IRA distributions | 16a | b Taxable amount (see page 16) | 16b
17a Total pensions and annuities | 17a | b Taxable amount (see page 16) | 17b
18 Rents, royalties, partnerships, estates, trusts, etc. Attach Schedule E | 18
19 Farm income or (loss). Attach Schedule F | 19
20 Unemployment compensation (see page 17) | 20
21a Social security benefits | 21a | b Taxable amount (see page 17) | 21b
22 Other income. List type and amount—see page 18 | 22
23 Add the amounts in the far right column for lines 7 through 22. This is your **total income** ▶ | 23

Adjustments to Income
(See page 18.)

24a Your IRA deduction from applicable worksheet on page 19 or 20 | 24a
b Spouse's IRA deduction from applicable worksheet on page 19 or 20 | 24b
25 One-half of self-employment tax (see page 20) | 25
26 Self-employed health insurance deduction (see page 20) | 26
27 Keogh retirement plan and self-employed SEP deduction | 27
28 Penalty on early withdrawal of savings | 28
29 Alimony paid. Recipient's SSN ▶ | 29
30 Add lines 24a through 29. These are your **total adjustments** ▶ | 30

Adjusted Gross Income

31 Subtract line 30 from line 23. This is your **adjusted gross income.** If this amount is less than $22,370 and a child lived with you, see page EIC-1 to find out if you can claim the "Earned Income Credit" on line 56 ▶ | 31

Cat. No. 11320B Form **1040** (1992)

SOURCE: Internal Revenue Service, *1040 Forms and Instructions* (1992).

allowed to reduce your gross income by $2,350 for each of your dependents, including yourself. Your dependents cannot be claimed on anyone else's tax return as an exemption. Nor can they claim themselves (if they file separately) if you can claim them. As of 1991, personal exemptions have been phased out for upper-income taxpayers. The threshold in 1993 was $162,700 for married taxpayers filing jointly and $108,450 for single taxpayers. The exemption drops 2 percent for each $2,500 by which adjusted gross income exceeds the threshold.

Income

Lines 7 through 23 determine a taxpayer's gross reportable income. In determining gross income, a taxpayer need not report all income received. Some types of income need not be reported or included as income for filing purposes, as shown below.

Exclusions from gross income for tax purposes

1. Welfare benefits

2. Veterans disability benefits

3. Workers compensation benefits

4. Child support

5. Gifts, money, or other property you inherited

6. Life insurance proceeds received because of a person's death

7. Scholarships received for tuition and course-related expenses

"Now, let's turn to page two of the 1040 form..."

SOURCE: "Pepper...and Salt," *The Wall Street Journal,* March 21, 1990, A-15. Reprinted by permission of Cartoon Features Syndicate.

In addition to the items listed on lines 7 through 23, there are **other incomes** that need to be reported, usually on line 22: other incomes. The following kinds of income should be reported on Form 1040 or on related forms and schedules:

1. Amounts received as a scholarship for room and board and travel and any other amounts received for expense other than tuition and course-related expenses

2. Amounts received in place of wages, from accident and health plans (including sick pay and disability pensions) if your employer paid for the policy

3. Bartering income (fair market value of goods and services received in return for your services)

4. Business expense reimbursements you received that are more than you spent for these expenses

5. Gains from the sale or exchange of real estate, securities, coins, gold, silver, gems, or other property

6. Gains from the sale of a personal residence

7. Prizes and awards (contests, raffles, lottery, and gambling winnings)

8. Embezzled or other illegal income

9. Unemployment benefits

Interest on state and local bonds is usually free of U.S. tax (unless deemed non-public interest issues), but the IRS, on line 8b, now wants to know how much you received. It can be a clue to hidden assets or illegal deductions for interest on loans to buy tax-exempt bonds.

Line 23 now shows your (unadjusted) total income, or gross income. Gross (or total) income is all income received during the year except income that is tax exempt.

Adjustments to Income Filling in lines 24 through 30 determines your **adjusted gross income (AGI)**. Adjusted gross income is total income minus any allowable adjustments to income. Allowable adjustments to income include the deductions for reimbursed employee business expenses, qualifying contributions to an IRA or Keogh plan (discussed in Chapter 18), the penalty paid for early withdrawal of savings, and alimony payments. At last you come up with line 31. You have determined your AGI.

After determining (line 31) adjusted gross income by subtracting (line 30) adjustments to income from (line 23) gross income, the next step is to determine (line 37) **taxable income** (see Figure 5–8). Taxable income is AGI minus itemized deductions (or the standard deduction) and minus exemptions. Taxable income is the part of your gross income that is subject to taxes.

FIGURE 5–8   Page 2 of the Sample 1040 Form

Form 1040 (1992)   Page **2**

Tax Computation

(See page 22.)

32	Amount from line 31 (adjusted gross income)	32
33a	Check if: ☐ **You** were 65 or older, ☐ Blind; ☐ **Spouse** was 65 or older, ☐ Blind. Add the number of boxes checked above and enter the total here ▶ 33a	
b	If your parent (or someone else) can claim you as a dependent, check here . ▶ 33b ☐	
c	If you are married filing separately and your spouse itemizes deductions or you are a dual-status alien, see page 22 and check here . . . . ▶ 33c ☐	
34	Enter the larger of your: Itemized deductions from Schedule A, line 26, OR Standard deduction shown below for your filing status. **But if you checked any box on line 33a or b,** go to page 22 to find your standard deduction. **If you checked box 33c,** your standard deduction is zero. • Single—$3,600 • Head of household—$5,250 • Married filing jointly or Qualifying widow(er)—$6,000 • Married filing separately—$3,000	34
35	Subtract line 34 from line 32	35
36	If line 32 is $78,950 or less, multiply $2,300 by the total number of exemptions claimed on line 6e. If line 32 is over $78,950, see the worksheet on page 23 for the amount to enter	36
37	**Taxable income.** Subtract line 36 from line 35. If line 36 is more than line 35, enter -0-	37
38	Enter tax. Check if from **a** ☐ Tax Table, **b** ☐ Tax Rate Schedules, **c** ☐ Schedule D, or **d** ☐ Form 8615 (see page 23). Amount, if any, from Form(s) 8814 ▶ **e**	38
39	Additional taxes (see page 23). Check if from **a** ☐ Form 4970 **b** ☐ Form 4972	39
40	Add lines 38 and 39 ▶	40

If you want the IRS to figure your tax, see page 23.

Credits

(See page 23.)

41	Credit for child and dependent care expenses. Attach Form 2441	41	
42	Credit for the elderly or the disabled. Attach Schedule R .	42	
43	Foreign tax credit. Attach Form 1116	43	
44	Other credits (see page 24). Check if from **a** ☐ Form 3800 **b** ☐ Form 8396 **c** ☐ Form 8801 **d** ☐ Form (specify)	44	
45	Add lines 41 through 44		45
46	Subtract line 45 from line 40. If line 45 is more than line 40, enter -0-		46

Other Taxes

47	Self-employment tax. Attach Schedule SE. Also, see line 25	47
48	Alternative minimum tax. Attach Form 6251	48
49	Recapture taxes (see page 25). Check if from **a** ☐ Form 4255 **b** ☐ Form 8611 **c** ☐ Form 8828	49
50	Social security and Medicare tax on tip income not reported to employer. Attach Form 4137	50
51	Tax on qualified retirement plans, including IRAs. Attach Form 5329	51
52	Advance earned income credit payments from Form W-2	52
53	Add lines 46 through 52. This is your **total tax** ▶	53

Payments

Attach Forms W-2, W-2G, and 1099-R on the front.

54	Federal income tax withheld. If any is from Form(s) 1099, check ▶ ☐	54	
55	1992 estimated tax payments and amount applied from 1991 return	55	
56	**Earned income credit.** Attach Schedule EIC	56	
57	Amount paid with Form 4868 (extension request)	57	
58	Excess social security, Medicare, and RRTA tax withheld (see page 26)	58	
59	Other payments (see page 26). Check if from **a** ☐ Form 2439 **b** ☐ Form 4136	59	
60	Add lines 54 through 59. These are your **total payments** ▶		60

Refund or Amount You Owe

Attach check or money order on top of Form(s) W-2, etc., on the front.

61	If line 60 is more than line 53, subtract line 53 from line 60. This is the amount you **OVERPAID.** ▶	61
62	Amount of line 61 you want **REFUNDED TO YOU.** ▶	62
63	Amount of line 61 you want **APPLIED TO YOUR 1993 ESTIMATED TAX** ▶ 63	
64	If line 53 is more than line 60, subtract line 60 from line 53. This is the **AMOUNT YOU OWE.** Attach check or money order for full amount payable to "Internal Revenue Service." Write your name, address, social security number, daytime phone number, and "1992 Form 1040" on it	64
65	Estimated tax penalty (see page 27). Also include on line 64 65	

Sign Here

Keep a copy of this return for your records.

Under penalties of perjury, I declare that I have examined this return and accompanying schedules and statements, and to the best of my knowledge and belief, they are true, correct, and complete. Declaration of preparer (other than taxpayer) is based on all information of which preparer has any knowledge.

Your signature	Date	Your occupation
Spouse's signature. If a joint return, BOTH must sign.	Date	Spouse's occupation

Paid Preparer's Use Only

Preparer's signature	Date	Check if self-employed ☐	Preparer's social security no.
Firm's name (or yours if self-employed) and address		E.I. No.	
		ZIP code	

SOURCE: Internal Revenue Service, *1040 Forms and Instructions* (1992).

Jack and Jill Fetch an Exemption

Jack and Jill have a dependent child, Jane. Jane is a full-time college student who works during the summer. Since Jack and Jill can claim Jane as an exemption on this year's tax return, Jane cannot claim herself as a personal exemption on her own return. Jack and Jill, however, can exempt three times $2350, or $7,050, of their income from taxes by taking themselves and Jane as tax exemptions (they will deduct the $7,050 on line 36).

Deductions

The law permits several expenses, known as **itemized deductions,** to be subtracted. Typical deductions are medical expenses, local taxes, charity contributions, casualty and theft losses, employee educational expenses, and certain expenses connected to your job, such as union dues, books, uniforms, and so on. The law also permits what is known as a **standard deduction,** an estimate of all deductions that may be taken by a taxpayer. On lines 33a through 35 you must decide whether to itemize deductions or to take a standard deduction. The standard deduction in 1993 was $3,700 for a single person, $6,300 for married couple filing jointly, or qualifying widow(er). If your itemized deductions exceed the standard deduction for your filing status, then obviously it pays to itemize deductions. Those who itemize deductions are required to fill in Schedule A (see Figure 5–9).

Taxpayers should itemize their deductions only if the total of their itemized deductions is more than their standard deduction. The government permits you to deduct certain expenses from your gross income before it takes a certain percent for your taxes. Therefore, if you are, say, in the 28 percent tax bracket and are able to write off an extra $1,000 of deductions above and beyond the standard deduction from your gross income, you will save $280 in taxes.

There are many categories of deductions. Most of the IRS publications and private tax guides enumerate and analyze the deductions in great detail. What qualifies as a deduction and the amount that can be deductible often change from year to year.

Some broad categories of deductions most often itemized by taxpayers cover the following areas:

1. Medical and dental expenses

2. State and local real estate taxes, income taxes, and personal property taxes

3. Interest payments on a home mortgage

4. Charitable contributions

5. Casualty losses

6. Moving expenses

7. Miscellaneous itemized deductions

FIGURE 5–9 | **Sample Schedule A**

SCHEDULES A&B	**Schedule A—Itemized Deductions**	OMB No. 1545-0074

(Form 1040)

(Schedule B is on back)

19 92

Department of the Treasury
Internal Revenue Service (5) ▶ **Attach to Form 1040.** ▶ **See Instructions for Schedules A and B (Form 1040).**

Attachment
Sequence No. **07**

Name(s) shown on Form 1040

Your social security number

Medical and Dental Expenses		**Caution:** *Do not include expenses reimbursed or paid by others.*	
	1	Medical and dental expenses (see page A-1)	**1**
	2	Enter amount from Form 1040, line 32 . **2**	
	3	Multiply line 2 above by 7.5% (.075)	**3**
	4	Subtract line 3 from line 1. If zero or less, enter -0- . . ▶	**4**
Taxes You Paid (See page A-1.)	5	State and local income taxes	**5**
	6	Real estate taxes (see page A-2)	**6**
	7	Other taxes. List—include personal property taxes · ▶	**7**
	8	Add lines 5 through 7 . . . . ▶	**8**
Interest You Paid (See page A-2.)	9a	Home mortgage interest and points reported to you on Form 1098	**9a**
	b	Home mortgage interest not reported to you on Form 1098. If paid to an individual, show that person's name and address. ▶	
Note: Personal interest is not deductible.			**9b**
	10	Points not reported to you on Form 1098. See page A-3 for special rules	**10**
	11	Investment interest. If required, attach Form 4952. (See page A-3.)	**11**
	12	Add lines 9a through 11 . . . . ▶	**12**
Gifts to Charity (See page A-3.)		**Caution:** *If you made a charitable contribution and received a benefit in return, see page A-3.*	
	13	Contributions by cash or check	**13**
	14	Other than by cash or check. If over $500, you **MUST** attach Form 8283	**14**
	15	Carryover from prior year	**15**
	16	Add lines 13 through 15 . . . . ▶	**16**
Casualty and Theft Losses	17	Casualty or theft loss(es). Attach Form 4684. (See page A-4.) . . . . . . ▶	**17**
Moving Expenses	18	Moving expenses. Attach Form 3903 or 3903F. (See page A-4.). . . . . . ▶	**18**
Job Expenses and Most Other Miscellaneous Deductions (See page A-5 for expenses to deduct here.)	19	Unreimbursed employee expenses—job travel, union dues, job education, etc. If required, you **MUST** attach Form 2106. (See page A-4.) ▶	**19**
	20	Other expenses—investment, tax preparation, safe deposit box, etc. List type and amount ▶	**20**
	21	Add lines 19 and 20	**21**
	22	Enter amount from Form 1040, line 32 . **22**	
	23	Multiply line 22 above by 2% (.02)	**23**
	24	Subtract line 23 from line 21. If zero or less, enter -0- . . . . . . ▶	**24**
Other Miscellaneous Deductions	25	Other—from list on page A-5. List type and amount ▶ .... ▶	**25**
Total Itemized Deductions	26	Is the amount on Form 1040, line 32, more than $105,250 (more than $52,625 if married filing separately)? • **NO.** Your deduction is not limited. Add lines 4, 8, 12, 16, 17, 18, 24, and 25. • **YES.** Your deduction may be limited. See page A-5 for the amount to enter. **Caution:** *Be sure to enter on Form 1040, line 34, the* **LARGER** *of the amount on line 26 above or your standard deduction.*	**26**

For Paperwork Reduction Act Notice, see Form 1040 instructions.   Cat. No. 11330X   Schedule A (Form 1040) 1992

SOURCE: Internal Revenue Service, *1040 Forms and Instructions* (1992).

Medical and Dental Expenses   Taxpayers who itemize their deductions can deduct certain unreimbursed medical and dental expenses that they paid for themselves, their spouses, and their dependents. Taxpayers cannot deduct elective cosmetic surgery.

There is a severe limitation, however, with medical deductions. Only medical expenses that exceed 7.5 percent of an adjusted gross income can be deducted. If you have $6,000 in unreimbersed medical bills and your AGI is $50,000, only $2,250 will be deductible. The first 7.5 percent of $50,000, which amounts to $3,750, is not deductible. Subtract $3,750 from $6,000 and you get $2,250.

State and Local Taxes   Any state and local real estate taxes, income taxes, and personal property taxes paid during the year may be deducted. State and local sales taxes are not deductible.

Interest Expenses   The interest deduction is severely limited. There is a limit on the amount of certain mortgage interest that is deductible and a limit on the amount of investment interest that is deductible. The amount of interest that can be written off depends not only on how much interest you pay but on what you are borrowing for. Interest payments on home equity loans discussed in Chapter 3 are still tax deductible.

As of 1991, **personal interest** is no longer deductible. If you borrow to buy a car or take a trip or if you run up a credit card balance, that is considered "personal" interest and cannot be deducted.

Interest on mortgages for a principal residence and one other house, and on business loans, is still 100 percent deductible. If you borrow to buy stocks or bonds, you can deduct all this "investment" interest only if you earn that much or more on investment income. Mortgage interest is deductible on up to $1 million of total debt incurred to buy, build, or improve your main residence and one other home, such as a summer retreat. A home is therefore likely to be one of the biggest and best tax deductions most taxpayers have.

Charitable Contributions   While tax benefits may not be the primary reason for donating to charity, the charitably inclined will find that knowledge of the tax laws will lower the cost of giving. Taxpayers may deduct any verifiable monetary or nonmonetary contribution to a recognized charity, including mileage driven while performing voluntary charitable activities. Uncle Sam also encourages gifts to charity of appreciated property, such as stocks. If the appreciation is considered a long-term capital gain, you get to write off the current value of the gift and do not have to pay tax on the appreciation that built up while you owned it.

The IRS, however, is often suspicious of noncash charity contributions. If you claim a deduction for more than $500 worth of clothing, furniture, artwork, or other noncash gifts, you must fill out another form (8283). If the donated property is worth over $5,000, you may need an appraisal to document its value and must also have the charity confirm the gift by signing the form. This is part of a growing crackdown on values that suddenly jump only when someone gives something away.

Casualty Losses   Casualty loss covers uninsured nonbusiness theft losses of property or casualty due to vandalism, fire, storms, car accidents, or other mishaps. A taxpayer may claim a loss resulting from fire, theft, natural disasters, and certain other occurrences only if the amount of loss, less any insurance reimbursement, exceeds 10 percent of adjusted gross income. There is also a kind of "deductible" amounting to $100 per occurrence. Thus, a taxpayer who had one casualty loss in a particular year and who had an adjusted gross income for that year of $50,000 could claim losses only in excess of $5,100. Casualty loss deductions deal only with the uninsured portion of your losses.

Verifying that the casualty loss actually occurred is essential and must often be done by obtaining police or fire department reports, insurance documents, and witness affidavits.

Moving Expenses   To be deductible, moving expenses generally have to be employment related. Taxpayers must also meet a time test and a distance test. In other words, they must demonstrate that the new residence is closer to their place of employment and that they worked after the move for at least 39 weeks.

Miscellaneous Items   A broad category of write-offs is known as *miscellaneous itemized deductions*. These mainly consist of unreimbursed employee expenses, expenses of producing income, and other qualifying expenses. Expenses that fall into this category include paying for help in preparing your taxes (as well as the cost of tax guides and tax preparation software). Some other miscellaneous deductions are:

1. Professional society dues

2. Employment-related educational expenses

3. Home office expenses

Home Mortgage Limitations

The law permits interest to be deducted on first or second mortgages and on home equity lines of credit, with no restriction on the use of the money as long as the total borrowed does not exceed the original purchase price plus the cost of improvements.

Here is an example of the practical effect of the limitation. Assume that you bought a home a few years back for $100,000 and added a deck that cost $10,000. Thanks to appreciation, the home is now worth $180,000. Suppose that your current mortgage amount is $70,000. The law will permit you to borrow another $40,000 against the home, for whatever purpose, and still deduct the interest. That $40,000 plus the $70,000 left on the first mortgage equals the $110,000 price-plus-improvement amount. If you borrow more, interest on the excess will be classified as nondeductible personal interest.

There are three exceptions to the limitation. Interest on additional borrowing is deductible if the money is used for home improvements or to pay for medical or educational expenses. (For more details on this topic, see the section on home equity loans in Chapter 3.)

4. Expenses associated with looking for a new job

5. Professional books, magazines, journals, and periodicals

6. Work clothes and uniforms

7. Union dues and fees

8. Unreimbursed business-related meal and entertainment expenses

9. Safe-deposit box rental

10. Cost of work-related small tools and supplies

11. Investment counsel fees

12. Investment management expenses

13. At least part of the cost of a home computer used to manage investments

For many people, the above deductions are meaningless because the total of miscellaneous itemized deductions is deductible only to the extent that it is more than 2 percent of AGI. For example, if your miscellaneous deductions amount to $800 and your AGI is $45,000, then the first $900 of miscellaneous deductions (2 percent of $45,000) does not count and therefore you cannot deduct the $800 of expenses. If you had $1,200 in miscellaneous deductions, you can deduct only $300 ($1,200 minus $900).

Deducting Employment-Related Educational Expenses   One of the most confusing areas of tax law and one that specifically concerns students is the deductibility of educational expenses. Generally, employees may take a deduction for expenses to maintain or improve skills in their present job or to meet legal or employer requirements to keep that position. Deductible expenses include tuition, books, supplies, laboratory fees, and correspondence courses. But you cannot write off these costs if your studies are intended to meet the minimum educational requirements of your current occupation or to qualify for a new profession. If you cannot convince the IRS that the courses you are enrolled in will enhance your performance and improve the skills needed in your current job, you will be taxed on what you thought was a miscellaneous itemized deduction.

Deducting Home Office Expenses   Taxpayers who are self-employed and work at home can claim **home office deductions** if it is their principal place of business and is used exclusively for business. However, taking this deduction increases one's chances of being audited by the IRS. Anyone who rents an apartment may deduct that portion of the rent that is attributable to that area set aside as a home office. In a privately owned home, say a seven-room house with one room used as a home office, one-seventh of the mortgage interest and real estate taxes can be deducted. Also deductible for home offices are prorated shares of utilities, maintenance, and home insurance premiums. Wholly deductible are costs related solely to a home office, such as paint, furniture, and depreciation of office machinery and furnishing.

Employees taking work home from the office may win the boss's praise but should not expect applause from the IRS. If you deduct depreciation and other expenses for an area at home where you do the work, the IRS is likely to argue, first, that your home office fails a requirement that it be your principal place of business and, second, that the office is for your convenience and not required.

The Internal Revenue Code provides a set of specific rules dealing with home office expenses. Generally, no deduction is available for business use of a home unless it is used *exclusively* on a regular basis as a principal place of business. This IRS position was reinforced in a Supreme Court ruling in 1993 in the case of *Commissioner vs. Soliman*.

The exclusive use requirement is the first stumbling block. It means that working on a report at the kitchen table or reading in that comfortable recliner in the den will not get you any deduction. It is not necessary to have a completely separate room set aside as an office, but whatever "separately identifiable" area you do use must avoid the taint of everyday activity. Thus, a desk and file cabinet in the bedroom can qualify as long as they are not also used for routine personal matters.

Assuming that you can satisfy the exclusive use test, the next hurdle is the "principal place of business" requirement. The IRS generally takes the view that *principal place of business* means the employer's office or other work location where the employee earns a livelihood. Under this approach, an executive's principal place of business is in the corporate suite and a teacher's place is in the classroom. This issue has been fought in the tax courts, and some taxpayers who proved that it was an absolute necessity to also have a home office have won this deduction. If you claim a home office deduction, expect the IRS to challenge the deduction and closely examine your return.

Deducting Expenses of Looking for a New Job

Job-hunting expenses may be deductible if you are looking for a new job in the same occupation or field as your present job. This deduction can be taken even if you do not succeed in landing a new job. The cost of transportation, food, and lodging on such a trip can qualify as a deductible expense, just like the cost of printing and mailing resumes and employment agency fees. However, the cost of looking for a first job does not count, nor do expenses involved in making a career switch.

Deducting Computer Use   A computer at home may ease a taxpayer's tax "byte." Taxpayers can write off the cost of a personal computer if they need it in their business or to manage investments. As previously mentioned, they need to keep a record of all the time it is used. If they let their children play computer games half the time, they get only half the write-off.

Business Trips   Expenses incurred during traveling on business trips can be deducted as business write-offs. Furthermore, you can take your spouse along and extend your stay for a few days of fun in the sun. As long as you can demonstrate that the primary purpose of the trip was to attend a business convention, for instance, you can still write off the cost of getting to and from the resort, as well as expenses for food and lodging during the convention. Your spouse's costs, however, as well as yours during the extra days, would not be deductible. When figuring the business part of lodging costs, you need not count just half of the double room rate. The deductible amount is what it would have cost you to stay in a single room. The IRS also permits a standard mileage rate deduction when using your automobile for business travel.

Deducting Meals   Taxpayers are allowed to deduct 80 percent of their meal and beverage expenses if they establish that the expenses were directly related to the conduct of their trade or business. No deductions for meal and beverage expenses are allowed unless business is discussed during, directly before, or directly after the meal, except when the taxpayer is traveling away from home on business and claims a deduction for meals.

Investment Management Expenses   Costs incurred in managing one's investments can be deducted on Schedule A. These deductions include phone calls, postage, messenger services, subscriptions to financial periodicals, investment advisory fees, charges for safe-deposit box rentals if used to store securities, and out-of-pocket travel expenses (mileage, meals, and in some cases airfare and hotel bills for trips to look after rental property).

Deriving Your Taxable Income

The result of subtracting itemized deductions (or the standard deduction) and exemptions from adjusted gross income is taxable income. The next step in figuring your taxes is to determine the amount of tax on your taxable income.

Individuals with taxable income of less than $100,000 use the **tax table**. The amount of tax shown in the tax table reflects the various rates applied to the amount of income in the different brackets. Individuals with taxable income of $100,000 or more use a tax rate schedule. The tax table is found in the back of the IRS 1040 instruction booklet mailed annually to every taxpayer (see Figure 5–10.)

Credits

Certain **tax credits** (lines 41 through 47) may be subtracted from the tax amount found in the tax table or tax rate schedule. These include the credit for child and dependent care expenses, the credit for the elderly or for the permanently and totally disabled, the foreign tax credit, and other credits.

Credit for Child and Dependent Care Expenses   A credit may be taken on line 41 for payments made for child care (for children under age 13) and for disabled dependent care while you (and your spouse if you are married) worked or looked for work. A special form, 2441, is needed to calculate the amount of the credit.

Credit for the Elderly or for the Permanently and Totally Disabled   Taxpayers who were 65 or over or totally and permanently disabled may take this credit to reduce their taxes. The amount of this credit is derived from Schedule R.

Foreign Tax Credit   A taxpayer can claim a foreign tax credit for taxes imposed and paid on income earned from activities conducted in foreign countries.

Basic Framework for Calculating Taxable Income

Gross Income
− Exemptions
− Deductions
───────────────
= Taxable Income
− Income Taxes
───────────────
= Net Income

Other General Business Credits Taxpayers can take a business credit (line 44) if they meet certain requirements, such as hiring people who are members of special targeted groups, using or selling straight alcohol as a fuel in their business, conducting research and experiments at their business, owning low-income rental housing, or incurring expenses to make their business accessible to the disabled.

The sum of the credits is subtracted from the tax liability (subtract line 45 from line 40). Then you add any other taxes you may owe (lines 47 through 53). Line 53 is the total amount of taxes owed. Now subtract all the taxes already withheld or paid during the year (lines 54 through 60), and you arrive at lines 61 through 65, which show how much you still owe or will be refunded for overpayment. Presto! You're finished.

The Alternative Minimum Tax (AMT)

Notice that line 48 has provisions for payment of an **alternative minimum tax (AMT)**. The tax laws give special treatment to some kinds of income and allow

FIGURE 5–10   **1992 Tax Table (Abridged)**

If line 37 (taxable income) is—		And you are—			
At least	But less than	Single	Married filing jointly	Married filing separately	Head of a household
			Your tax is—		
77,000					
77,000	77,050	19,532	16,913	20,253	17,916
77,050	77,100	19,548	16,927	20,269	17,931
77,100	77,150	19,563	16,941	20,284	17,947
77,150	77,200	19,579	16,955	20,300	17,962
77,200	77,250	19,594	16,969	20,315	17,978
77,250	77,300	19,610	16,983	20,331	17,993

SOURCE: Internal Revenue Service, *1040 Forms and Instructions* (1992), Section 7.

special deductions and credits for some kinds of expenses. Taxpayers who benefit from these laws have to pay at least a minimum amount of tax through an additional tax. This additional tax is called the alternative minimum tax.

The AMT is essentially a tax on tax deductions. The goal of the AMT is to make sure that taxpayers with a lot of income pay at least a reasonable tax. The AMT is the least amount the government will accept from taxpayers if their income is at certain high levels, even though they seem to have enough deductions or credits to pay no tax at all.

Handling the complex calculations that determine whether a taxpayer pays the AMT is a task for an accountant. Accountants will generally figure a tax bill twice, first by regular methods with all the deductions. In the second calculation, the adjusted gross income gets increased by all investment-related tax items. The taxpayer may then reduce the income figure, but by only a handful of IRS deductions such as casualty losses, some interest expense, and medical expenses exceeding 10 percent of adjusted gross income.

The final step in calculating AMT is to deduct an exemption—$40,000 for families and $30,000 for singles—and multiply by 24 percent. Is the number greater than the regular tax? If so, you have to pay up. If taxable income exceeds $310,000 for families or $232,500 for singles, the exemption is lost.

Though the AMT rate (24 percent) is lower than the regular rate, people subject to it pay more than they would under the regular tax rules because so few deductions and adjustments are allowed.

Earned Income Credit Taxpayers whose earned income was less than a certain amount (less than $23,370 for 1992) and who have a child are entitled to a special refundable credit (see line 56).

Capital Gains

Capital gains, the profits from sales of assets including stocks and real estate, are taxed at a maximum of 28 percent as part of the taxpayer's regular income. Capital losses remain deductible, first against gains and then up to $3,000 against other income.

Tax Shelters: Shelters from April's Showers

Tax shelters are investments designed to reduce taxes by temporarily generating losses or by using noncash deductions such as depreciation and depletion to offset taxable income. Taxpayers could thereby use deductions from one activity to offset income from any other activity. Some classic shelters were real estate, oil and gas drilling, and equipment leasing.

For years the IRS watched benignly as investors participated in these classic tax shelters. But in recent years, the agency has cracked down on abusive shelters where the tax savings far exceed the amount invested, such as the financing of greatly inflated artwork and worthless movies.

Passive Activity Congress determined that extensive tax shelter abuses contributed to public concerns that the tax system was unfair. Therefore, the 1986 tax reform law cut

Determining Taxes Due

Arrange the list below in proper format, then compute the tax amount due.

Single Person

1993 wage income	$55,000	
IRA	2,000	
Mortgage interest	10,000	
Real estate taxes	3,000	
Charitable deductions	2,500	
One exemption (for 1993)	2,350	(use current year's amount)
Medical expenses	3,000	

back tax shelters drastically through various new restrictions and stipulations. In this process, the law created a new category in the tax lexicon known as *passive activity*.

Whether a loss or credit can be used to offset other income or tax now depends upon the nature of the activity that generated it. Tax reform eliminated the use of losses from passive investments to offset ordinary income, such as using paper losses generated by a limited partnership to wipe out part of the tax bill on one's salary or portfolio income. These passive losses may be used only against income from similar passive investments.

A **passive investment** is defined as an activity involving the conduct of any trade or business in which the taxpayer does not materially participate, including all limited partnerships. The test is a tough one, demanding that you be regularly and substantially involved in the business on a year-round basis. If, for example, Scott Campbell owns a 25 percent interest in a race horse, does not perform any work, and does not participate in any of the decisions related to the race horse activity, then this, for Scott, is a passive activity because he does not materially participate. He can deduct losses derived from owning the race horse only against any income derived from the race horse this year. If his losses were $10,000 and his reported earnings were $2,000, he can deduct only $2,000 in losses.

Investments in stocks, bonds, and mutual funds do not fall into the passive category, and therefore any losses are not subject to the same restrictions. All investments in rental properties, however, are considered passive activities. As of 1993, however, investors can deduct their rental real estate losses against regular income if they can demonstrate that they are actively engaged for more than 50 percent of their annual work time (and more than 750 hours a year) in a "real property or business."

Passive losses are not rendered worthless, however. Any deductions taken for passive investment-related expenses, such as interest payments or depreciation, will continue to offset income from that investment. Only when expenses exceed income do you slip into the passive loss category. That loss can still be used to shelter income from other similar activities, such as a profitable rental or partnership. Any leftover passive loss can be suspended until future years when you do have passive income to offset.

Abusive Shelters   As of 1984, the IRS gave each shelter a registration number, which the promoters must supply to investors for inclusion on their tax returns. The 1984 rules impose a 20 percent penalty for those who participate in what the IRS determines to be an **abusive shelter**.

Capital Gains Tax on Home Sales

Homeowners over the age of 55 who sell their home are eligible for a one-time exemption of $125,000 capital gains. This provision exempts $125,000 from capital gains taxes and can be done only once in a person's lifetime. Homeowners under age 55 can sell their primary home and pay no federal tax on the gain provided they buy a new primary residence that costs at least as much as what they got for the old one. They can purchase the new house any time during a four-year period, from two years before they sell the old home until two years after.

The profit can be reduced by the original acquisition cost, which includes title company charges, attorney's fees, recording fees, and the cost of a survey. To this can be added the selling expenses, which include the real estate broker's commission, attorney's fees, advertising costs, any mortgage satisfaction charges, and state and local transfer taxes. Taxpayers can also deduct capital improvements, which could be the addition of a new room, a finished basement, central air conditioning, new plumbing, a new central heating system, a new roof, the rewiring of the electrical system, landscaping, a swimming pool, storm windows and screens, a patio, or any other structural improvements.

The above exemptions and deferment of federal taxes apply only to the sale of a home that is a taxpayer's primary residence. Although you might think that you can decide which of your residences is "primary," the IRS and the various states insist that certain criteria are met. For the IRS, it boils down to where you spend most of your time. In the event of an IRS challenge, the taxpayer , not the IRS, must prove primary residence.

The Kiddie Tax

KIDDIE

The **"kiddie tax"** is a special set of tax rules that apply to children under 14 who have investment income. Though popularly known as the "kiddie tax," it is far from child's play. As of 1987, the IRS has collared a new class of freeloaders: children. They don't clean their rooms; they hate to wash dishes, do homework, take showers, or mow the lawn; and they have ducked their fair share of the income tax burden.

Now children must pay their fair share of taxes just like grownups. In the past, some children had been used by their parents as walking tax shelters for large amounts of money. Parents would shift income-producing assets to their children who, because they were in a lower tax bracket, usually escaped tax altogether. To short-circuit such tax-dodging maneuvers, the law basically ignores them. A child's investment income over $1,200 (as of 1992) is added to the parents' taxable income, and the tax bill is figured on the new total. The tax includes all interest, dividends, capital gains, rents, trust income, or other unearned income over $1,200 held by a child under age 14.

The law also forbids dependent children to claim personal exemptions. If a dependent child has an investment income and his or her total income exceeds $600, a return must be filed. Under tax reform, a child can earn up to $3,400 tax free—as long as he or she has no unearned income, such as interest or dividends. But as soon as the child has a dollar in savings account interest or any other unearned income, then at least some tax is owed on any combination of earned and unearned income

Taxing Questions

If you are challenged regarding your primary residence, here are some typical questions you may likely need to answer in order to prove your case:

1. What are all your current addresses and former addresses?
2. How long have you owned your homes and what are their costs?
3. Have you moved furniture from one house to the other?
4. Have you rented either home during absences?
5. Where are you registered to vote and where have you voted in the past?
6. Where do your children attend school?
7. What local charities and organizations do you support?
8. Where are you licensed to drive?
9. Where has your car been registered?
10. What are the locations of your bank accounts and other investments?
11. Where have you previously filed "resident" tax returns?

over $600. If, for example, a child earned $1,000 and had interest and dividends of $2,000, the $1,000 would be tax free, $1,200 of the interest and dividends would be taxable at 15 percent and $800 at the parents' rate.

If the same $3,000 was counted as the parents' income and taxed in the 28 percent bracket, the tax would amount to $840. If it is considered the child's income, then the child pays 15 percent on only $800, which equals to $120.

This law played havoc with traditional methods of family tax planning. Gone are the days when income placed in trusts was taxed at the child's rate. The law says that the grantor of a trust established after March 1, 1986—parent, grandparent, or anyone—pays taxes on any income.

How to Survive an Audit

The Discriminant Function System

A computer is humming away in West Virginia at this very moment, checking out the billions of numbers entered on last year's tax returns. If it hasn't already, the machine will soon find your figures, scrutinize them every which way, and ponder how the picture that they paint of your financial life compares with what it knows about other taxpayers.

Every return is screened through a highly complex computer program, the **Discriminant Function (DIF) System,** which is designed to rate the likelihood of an audit producing additional taxes.

The Residency Game

If you own a ski chalet in New Hampshire and rent an apartment in New York where you work, the IRS may challenge your claim to primary residency in New Hampshire. Since the IRS does not always audit such sales, the temptation to try to get away with claiming the second home as a primary residence can be great. But it can be easy to lose at the residency game if challenged, especially if you have young children who do not attend local schools. And if you lose your dispute with the IRS, the interest on back taxes can mount up fast, as (then Vice President) George Bush found out in 1984. His claim that income from the sale of his Houston home, reinvested in another residence in Maine, was not immediately taxable was rejected by the IRS. He had to pay $144,000 in taxes and $54,000 in interest on the $590,000 gain on the home. The IRS insisted that Washington, DC, was his primary residence. That was where his job was located.

The point of all this sophisticated ciphering is to determine whether or not you should be called in for an audit. The DIF picks out returns that do not conform to normal patterns of income and deduction levels. The exact criteria applied in the DIF are a tightly guarded secret. Generally, the higher your income and the more complex your return, the greater your chance of being audited. A taxpayer in the $50,000-plus income group in 1990 stood about a 1.8 percent chance of being audited. However, the chances of being audited are also increased if a return shows any of the following:

1. Only modest income from a business or profession that typically generates much more income

2. Unusually high itemized deductions relative to your income

3. Dependency exemptions claimed for persons outside your immediate family

4. Office at home deductions, especially if your occupation is one that is normally carried on outside the home

In addition, if a previous return was audited within the last few years and you had to pay additional tax as a result, you may find yourself under scrutiny again.

The IRS currently audits less than 1 percent of taxpayers, about 1.2 million returns a year out of approximately 115 million filed. An audit notice does not necessarily mean that the IRS thinks you have filed a dishonest or fraudulent return. The IRS may simply think something is amiss with your 1040 form and would like you to clarify or substantiate your claims.

The IRS computers may select your Form 1040 for an examination if you claim itemized deductions that are well above the average amounts claimed by other individuals in the same category in your geographic area. Such a 1040 may still sidestep an examination if it is accompanied by a written explanation of sizable deductions or of other unusual items. For instance, someone with large medical expense deductions for elective plastic surgery may avoid an audit by attaching a note explaining that

IRS Forms and Schedules

Here is a brief description of various IRS forms and schedules that may be needed when filing your taxes. These forms are available from tax preparers, the IRS, and many post offices and banks throughout the country:

Form 1040EZ: Simplified return
Form 1040A: Simplified return
Form 1040: Main individual return
Form 1040-ES: Estimated tax computation
Schedule A: Itemized deductions
Schedule B: Interest and dividend income
Schedule C: Business income or loss
Schedule D: Capital gains or losses
Schedule E: Rents, royalties, trusts, and partnerships
Schedule F: Farm income
Schedule R: Credit for the elderly or disabled
Schedule SE: Self-employment tax
Form 2106: Employee business expense
Form 2119: Sale of home
Form 2210: Underpayment of tax penalty
Form 2441: Child care credit
Form 3468: Investment credit
Form 3800: General business credit
Form 3903: Moving expenses
Form 4255: Investment credit recapture
Form 4562: Depreciation
Form 4684: Casualty or theft loss
Form 4797: Supplemental gains or losses
Form 4952: Investment interest expense
Form 4972: Averaging for lump-sum distribution
Form 5695: Energy credit carryforward
Form 6251: Alternative minimum tax
Form 6252: Installment sales
Form 8582: Passive activity loss
Form 8598: Home mortgage interest
Form 8606: Nondeductible IRA
Form 8615: Kiddie tax

insurance did not cover the payments to doctors or hospitals, along with copies of the bills. Taxpayers with legitimate above-average deductions would be ill-advised to pass them up just to reduce their probability of an audit. If you have incurred deductible expenses, you are legally entitled to take them as long as you can substantiate them.

Generally, the statute of limitations on tax returns is three years. After that time, the IRS cannot audit a return or attempt to increase the tax. The one exception is a fraudulent return, which has no statute of limitations.

Preparing for an Audit

Even if your deductions are in line with the averages, you may still be audited. What should you do if you get an invitation to an IRS audit? Throw up your hands? Seek divine guidance? Rush to a palm reader? Or turn to a paid preparer?

If you get an ominous-looking letter from the IRS announcing your audit, don't panic! The chances are good that it is the simplest and most common variety, a **correspondence audit**. This audit (called a CP2000) generally stems from a mismatch of information on your tax return, with information reported to the IRS from a third party. It requires only that you mail in additional supporting documentation, such as checks and receipts, to verify a specified claim on your return. Another form of audit is a **field audit**. This entails an IRS agent coming to your home or place of business to go over your records. This extensive on-site affair is usually reserved for corporations and small business owners. Most common is the **office audit**. It means getting yourself and your papers to the local IRS office. Generally, the IRS carries out this type of audit when its questions are too involved to be handled through the mail. Self-employed filers with home offices and businesspeople with large travel and entertainment expenses are commonly called.

The notice will identify the items on the return that are being questioned, usually broad categories such as employee business expenses or casualty losses, and will outline the types of records required to clear up the matter. Office audits are usually, but not necessarily, limited to two or three issues. Taxpayers are therefore not expected to bring in all their records and prove every entry on their return.

The first decision to make is whether to go to the audit in person or be represented by a tax professional. Taxpayers have the legal right to be represented by a lawyer, certified public accountant, enrolled agent, or actuary, and the auditor must generally suspend the meeting if a taxpayer states a desire to consult with a representative. Is it advisable to hire a tax expert to handle the audit? It depends on what is at stake. If the IRS is merely asking you to substantiate deductions claimed on the return, you may be able to handle the audit without professional help. But if the issues are more complicated or involve interpretation of the tax laws, it makes sense to have a tax professional do the talking for you.

The IRS may request thorough documentation of any and all information provided on a tax return. That "request" can be upgraded to a legal summons. A summons may be used to unearth additional information from certain third parties, such as a bank, a broker, a credit card company, an accountant, an attorney, a casino, a telephone company, or a consumer credit reporting agency. In the course of an audit, the IRS may require your bank to produce photocopies of your statements, canceled checks, deposit slips, and trust agreements.

The easiest way to survive an audit is to prepare for it when you originally fill out your tax return. Even though you do not expect your return to be audited, work on the assumption that it will be. Don't rely on your memory; often an audit may not be started until a year or more after the return is filed.

If you receive an audit notification, first get a copy of the return that is being challenged. Copies of past returns can be obtained from the IRS by submitting Form 4506. The cost is $4.25 per return, including copies of schedules and other attachments.

The essential factor for audit success is the quality and organization of the documentation that supports your entries.

1. Try to reconstruct any missing records. Get copies of canceled checks from the bank, for example, duplicates of receipts, or written statements from individuals who can back up your claims. Keep in mind that although you may pay an accountant or tax professional to prepare your return, the contents of the return and their substantiation are your responsibility. Good documentation is your best defense.

2. Organize your records so that you can present your case clearly and quickly.

3. Answer all correspondence with the IRS promptly and courteously. Save yourself a possible temper tantrum by not trying to break through the busy signals on the IRS's telephone lines. Write a letter instead, and keep a photocopy. If you have to write a second letter, address it to the IRS's efficient **Problem Resolution Program**. Attach copies of every previous letter you wrote and of every notice you received from the IRS in case your local office lost them.

4. Do your homework before any meeting with an IRS agent and, if necessary, discuss any questions with the person who prepared your tax return.

5. Consider hiring an accountant or lawyer to represent you if you find the process intimidating or are uncertain about specific items on your return.

Appealing the Auditor's Verdict

If you agree with the auditor's findings, you will be asked to sign a form saying so and within a few weeks will get a bill for the extra tax plus interest and any penalty that was imposed, if any. Most audits end this way.

If you disagree, you should tell the auditor so and not sign. You will receive in the mail a report explaining the proposed adjustments to your return. At this point, you may want to seek professional advice. If, on reflection, you decide you might as well settle for the proposed amount, you can do so by signing an agreement form.

But if you are definitely not satisfied with the outcome of the audit, you have several choices if you want to keep fighting. You can ask for another meeting with the auditor to present new evidence, for example, or you can appeal informally to the auditor's supervisor, who will review the case and come to his or her own conclusion. If still unhappy, you have 30 days to ask that the case be turned over to the IRS regional appeals division. If you're still not satisfied with the appeals officer's verdict, you can take your case to the U.S. Tax Court.

"We don't have many openings left—how'd you like to be the Patron Saint of IRS auditors?"

SOURCE: "Pepper...and Salt," *The Wall Street Journal*, March 11, 1991, A-15. Reprinted by permission of Cartoon Features Syndicate.

If you appeal an audit in court, be advised that this route is slow and the legal fees can be expensive. The U.S. Tax Court lets you file a petition without first paying what the IRS insists you owe. But the court is no pushover. In 1989 individuals won complete victories in less than 5 percent of their tax court cases. Your odds (as shown in Figure 5–11) improve if you appeal instead in the U.S. District Court or the U.S. Claims Court. But there you must first pay the taxes that the IRS says are due and then hope that the court will overrule.

Most tax disputes are settled in the U.S. Tax Court, although you can also take your case to the U.S. District Court for your area or to the U.S. Court of Claims in Washington, DC. The U.S. Tax Court, which hears cases at sites around the country, has less formal procedures for cases in which the disputed amount is $5,000 or less. You can represent yourself in a small tax case.

The small tax case, unlike regular tax court cases and those in the district courts and court of claims, has two drawbacks. First, the decision is final and cannot be appealed to a higher court—by you or by the IRS. Second, each case is considered on its own. Even if a judge has previously considered a tax issue similar to yours and has ruled in favor of the taxpayer, that decision need not bind the judge in your case.

FIGURE 5–11	Who Wins in Appeal?

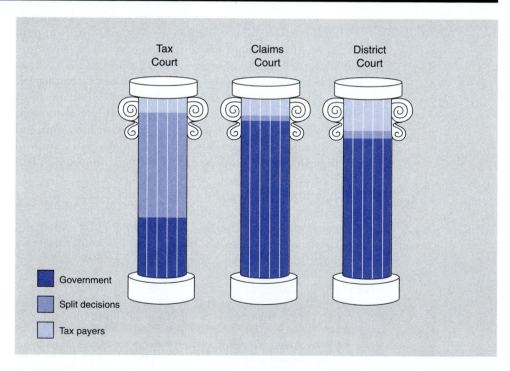

Even in District Court, where the taxpayers' chances are best, decisions wholly in favor of the taxpayer occur in less than 20 percent of the cases. Data shown are for 1989.

SOURCE: Internal Revenue Service.

If you lose the appeal or court trial, then don't refuse to pay in anger. If you fail to pay your personal taxes, the IRS can put a lien on your bank account, credit union account, stocks, bonds, or even your IRA or Keogh plan.

Unreported and Underreported Income

Did you report all of your interest income, part-time jobs, and dividends on your tax return? If not, you have a problem. The IRS document matching program is in high gear, and interest income and dividend payments reported on Form 1099 by financial institutions are now fed into IRS computers and matched up with your tax return. When the IRS catches unreported earnings, it produces a notice of unreported income, the additional tax due, interest on the tax, and penalties. Negligence penalties are 5 percent of the additional tax and 50 percent of the amount of the interest due on the underpayment. The IRS makes a presumption of negligence that can be overcome only by "clear and convincing" evidence to the contrary.

The IRS additionally imposes a 25 percent penalty for "substantial" understatement of a tax liability. It applies if you underreport your tax liability by 10 percent or $5,000, whichever is greater. When the IRS computer detects the discrepancy, the IRS automatically imposes the penalty. However, by law, the fine does not apply if a taxpayer can show that his or her calculation was based upon a reasonable interpretation of the tax code.

Since 1985, the IRS has been using **optical character recognition (OCR)** equipment to ensure that figures supplied by financial institutions are being reported by taxpayers. The OCR system is part of the service's Underreported Program, designed to identify taxpayers who have failed to report income from sources such as interest, dividends, and state refunds. OCR scanner equipment "reads" the 1099 documents supplied by financial institutions at a rate of over 5,000 per hour, enabling a 100 percent review of the documents. The information is then matched against tax returns.

In one recent year, the IRS detected more than 400,000 instances in which taxpayers did not list income reportedly paid by third parties. The IRS is quietly perfecting the art of processing assorted bits of information into a complex and personal file.

What you tell the IRS about yourself is augmented by one billion annual information reports that third parties are obligated to provide. These include complete wage information that your employer submits on your W-2 form as well as reports from financial institutions and brokerage houses concerning your earnings on savings and investments. These documents account for 90 percent of all income reported by individuals and 40 to 50 percent of the deductions they claim. This is the principal reason that the percentage of returns audited by the IRS dropped from 1.75 percent in 1981 to under 1 percent in 1992.

Banks are also required to report transactions involving $10,000 or more in U.S. currency, foreign transactions involving $5,000 or more, and any other exchanges that management deems unusual. Form W-2G, filed by casinos and racetracks, reports on taxpayers' gambling windfalls. If you are self-employed, any company paying you more than $600 per year must report that fact.

The IRS receives third-party reports on mortgage interest payments and detailed data on IRA deposits. These are all stored in a computer and matched with your tax return via your Social Security number. If you failed to repay the student loan that got you through college, the IRS may know that, too, for it is empowered to withhold your refund money in order to pay those obligations.

Many states now also have the power to withhold state tax refunds to pay for any delinquent child support payments, and the IRS is moving in that direction as well. In fact, information sharing between state tax agencies and the IRS is a busy two-way street. If you owe your state money for any reason, the state can apply for payment out of your federal tax refund. State tax agencies also file reports concerning refunds you received. Conversely, if the IRS audits you and levies additional tax, it will send that information to your state tax agency, which will bill you for its share of the IRS–determined underpayment.

SUMMARY

This chapter presents information that will enable taxpayers to make financial decisions for their best tax advantage and to avoid paying unnecessary taxes. Understanding the structure of the U.S. federal tax system and methods of minimizing its impact is essential to effective financial planning. The structure consists of determining gross and taxable income; recognizing available deductions, exemptions, and tax credits; and learning how to cope with a tax audit.

Records are required by the IRS to substantiate any and all claims. The burden of proof is always on the taxpayer. Records should be kept for separate categories of items such as charitable contributions, work-related expenses, travel on the job, business use of your car, real estate expenses, investments, and medical bills. Successful tax planning requires that you keep adequate and careful records in an organized manner. These records must be kept for at least three years from the date you file.

Tax returns must be filed by April 15 of the year following the tax year. Extensions can easily be obtained, but the taxpayer will be liable for interest on any taxes due and not paid as of April 15. The nature and complexity of the taxpayer's return will help determine which tax form to file. The three choices are 1040, 1040A, and 1040EZ. The IRS provides tax information as well as assistance in the preparation of tax returns.

Taxpayers must also decide whether to file themselves, have an IRS official assist them, or hire a tax preparer, CPA, accountant, or enrolled agent. The decision should be based upon the complexity of the individual return. Many people need only the assistance of a tax guidebook to prepare their own tax returns. For complicated tax problems, it is best to consult a professional tax preparer, a CPA, a tax attorney, or all three.

The IRS provides specific guidelines and tests to determine what items can be deducted from income. Taxpayers should be familiar with all the deductions, credits, and exemptions legally available and should utilize them to the maximum. Wise taxpayers keep up with the ever-changing rules of the IRS and take the fullest possible advantage of them to avoid taxes legally. Finding ways to legally minimize or to avoid income taxes is an important part of successful financial planning.

Taxes are calculated using the IRS tax tables. The 1986 Tax Reform Act, under a provision popularly termed the "kiddie tax," has eliminated the use of children as tax shelters by their parents. Any passive income in a child's name that is above

$1,200 is now subject to the parents' tax bracket. The IRS checks the accuracy of tax returns through its computer program known as the Discriminant Function System. This program picks out returns that do not conform to normal patterns of income and deduction levels, and then the IRS follows up with an audit. It levies severe penalties on taxpayers who are found guilty of tax evasion.

An IRS audit of an honest taxpayer's return need not be an intimidating and perplexing affair. A taxpayer who understands the audit process, knows his or her rights, and comes prepared and organized to the audit has enhanced the chances for a successful resolution.

KEY TERMS

Abusive shelters

Adjusted gross income (AGI)

Alternative minimum tax (AMT)

Amended return

Capital gains

Certified public accountant (CPA)

Commercial tax preparer

Correspondence audit

Dependents

Discriminant Function (DIF) System

Employees Withholding Allowance Certificate (Form W-4)

Enrolled agents

Exemptions

Field audit

Filing status

Head of household

Home office deduction

Internal Revenue Code of 1986

Internal Revenue Service (IRS)

Itemized deductions

Joint return

"Kiddie tax"

Marginal tax rate

Married filing separate return

Office audit

Optical character recognition (OCR)

Other incomes

Passive investment

Personal interest

Private letter ruling

Problem Resolution Program

Standard deduction

Taxable income

Tax brackets

Tax credits

Tax-filing extension

Tax guidebooks

Tax Reform Act of 1986

Tax shelters

Tax Table

Tax withholding

Tele-Tax

1040 form

1040EZ form

W-2 form

W-4 form

REVIEW QUESTIONS AND PROBLEMS

1. Fred tells you that he has too much tax deducted from his paycheck and thus obtains a sizable tax refund at the end of each tax year. What can you tell Fred about the inefficiency of having too much tax withheld from a paycheck? Discuss your answer using the concept of "opportunity cost."
2. Why are tax records important? Explain.
3. Explain the difference between gross income and adjusted gross income.
4. Explain the difference between the following tax forms:
   A. Form 1040
   B. Form 1040A
   C. Form 1040EZ
5. Discuss the various kinds of tax preparation services available and the disadvantages and advantages of each.
6. Who must file a federal income tax return?
7. How can a taxpayer best minimize the chances of getting audited?
8. If your friend receives an audit notification, what advice can you offer to best cope with the situation?
9. List several sources of income that are excluded from gross income for tax purposes.
10. List all sources of income that taxpayers must include in the calculation of gross income.
11. Joan Simpson is a systems analyst earning $50,000 a year. She is engaged to be married to a full-time graduate student during intersession. The couple is considering two possible wedding dates, either on Christmas day or on New Year's day. What tax considerations may influence the couple's ultimate decision? Explain.
12. What filing extension options are available for taxpayers who cannot meet the April 15 deadline? How and until when are these obtained? Explain why the filing extension does not affect the fact that any money you owe is still due as of April 15.
13. Give examples of some tax credits.
14. Under what circumstances might your tuition and other related expenses for this course be tax deductible?
15. Explain the significance of "private letter rulings."
16. Why would the alternative minimum tax (AMT) possibly discourage someone who can legally take numerous deductions from doing so?
17. Explain how the "kiddie tax" has eliminated the use of children as a tax shelter by their parents.
18. How does the IRS detect unreported or underreported income?

19. (MARGINAL) If an increase in your weekly pay of $75 causes you to take home an extra $40 per week, what is your marginal tax rate?
20. (PENALTY) Your friend has been penalized $1,000 by the IRS for late filing. He owed taxes of $7,230. The late filing penalty (per month) was 5 percent. Late payment penalty (per month) was 0.50 percent. Annual interest was 8 percent. How many months was he late?

SUGGESTED PROJECTS

Visit a local IRS office and find out what free services it offers the taxpayer. Make a list of the services available and indicate the types of individuals who would benefit most from these services.

INFORMATION RESOURCES

"The Alternative Tax's Wider Reach." *The New York Times,* November 17, 1991, F-5.

The Arthur Andersen Tax Guide and Planner. New York: Perigee, annual.

The Arthur Young Tax Guide. New York: Ballantine Books, annual.

"Avoiding the Tax Squeeze." *Changing Times,* August 1989, 57–61.

The Complete Book of Tax Deductions. New York: Harper and Row, 1990.

Guide to Income Tax Preparation. Consumer Reports Books.

Dingle, Derekt. "Digging Out from the Worst Tax Storm." *Money,* January 1992.

Ellis, James. "H&R Block Expands Its Tax Base." *Business Week,* April 22, 1991, 55.

Gottschalk, Earl Jr,. "Fighting Uncle Sam." *The Wall Street Journal,* March 8, 1991, R-24.

H&R Block Income Tax Guide. New York: Collier Books, annual.

"How You Can Still Cut Your Taxes." *Money,* September 1989, 84–103.

Internal Revenue Service. To order forms, call 800/TAX-FORMS.

Jasen, Georgette. "If You're Confused by the Tax Forms." *The Wall Street Journal,* February 27, 1992, C-9.

J.K. Lasser's Your 1993 Income Tax. New York: J.K. Lasser Institute, annual.

P-H 1040 Handbook. Englewood Cliffs, NJ: Prentice-Hall, annual.

"Lower Taxes." *Kiplinger's Personal Finance Magazine,* October 1991, 36–40.

McCormally, Kevin. "Taking the Pain Out of Taxes." *Kiplinger's Personal Finance Magazine,* February 1992, 54–58.

McCormally, Kevin. "Your Tax Return." *Kiplinger's Personal Finance Magazine,* March 1992, 97–100.

Sawyer, Tom. "The Fine Art of Coping with Taxes." *The New York Times,* March 3, 1991, F-11.

Sprouse, Mary. *Sprouse's Income Tax Handbook.* New York: Penguin, 1990.

Sylvia Porter's Income Tax Book. New York: Avon, annual.

"Through the Form 1040 Step by Step." *The New York Times,* March 3, 1991, F-14.

Worth, Gretchen. "How to Avoid a Tax Audit." *Working Woman,* March 1989, 86–88.

CHAPTER SIX

Buying and Financing Your Home

- To examine the factors to consider in deciding whether to rent or to purchase a home

- To explore ways to determine how much housing one can afford

- To consider the steps involved in purchasing and selling a home

- To discuss the various aspects of financing a home, including how to obtain a mortgage

- To discern between the many different mortgage options and features available

- To study the application, procedures, closing costs, and various related costs associated with mortgage loans

The financial aspects of home buying are highlighted in this chapter, which outlines the basic investment forms available and the procedures followed in this arena. The many issues, problems, opportunities, and risks of home buying are also explored.

This chapter is by no means a definitive home buyer's guide. Special real estate courses and books are available for that purpose. The suggested reading list at the end of this chapter also can help you to obtain more extensive knowledge in this field. Investing in real estate may also require familiarity with topography, architecture, engineering, construction, aesthetics, and law, but this chapter focuses on the financial issues.

Home Buying

The biggest single investment most people ever make is buying a home. For many young adults, this is one of the first goals in financial planning. Although buying a home is more difficult for young people today, it is still a possible dream. But this dream requires careful preparation, planning, saving, and familiarity with the real estate market and the financial intricacies involved. In the course of their lifetime, a typical couple will own three houses. This involves a lot of buying and selling.

Buying a home is not a scheme for getting rich quick. It is more a means of providing shelter and family security and comfort, with long-term asset building as a possible bonus. The decline of both mortgage rates and real estate prices during the early 1990s brought home ownership within easier reach in most parts of the country. Yet many Americans felt too uneasy financially to venture into the housing market.

The Power of Leverage

LEVERAGE

A major allure of home ownership as a personal investment arises from the wonders of **financial leverage.** Leverage means buying something with a small amount of your own cash and borrowing the rest. If, for example, homeowners put down $20,000 and borrow $80,000 to purchase a $100,000 home, they get the use of the $100,000 home and the power of appreciation on all of it as well. They have leverage of 4 to 1; for every $1 put down, they borrow $4. Suppose that after five years they sell the property for $150,000. They repay the lender the amount still owed, about $78,000,

Motivations for Home Buying

1. **Shelter**   A roof over one's head
2. **Tax benefits**   The deductions for mortgage interest and property taxes
3. **Creation of a future asset**   Frequently the largest asset a family ever accumulates
4. **Home ownership**   Also considered a protective hedge against inflation
5. **The psychological motive**   The home as the family castle is a strong incentive for ownership
6. **The tangibility of property**   One of the main appeals to first-time homeowners
7. **Familiarity**   Since most investors have previously bought or rented a home

and use the remaining $72,000 as a down payment on a new larger property. They have more than tripled their initial investment, from $20,000 to $72,000.

Leverage works both ways, of course. A 20 percent drop in a property's value, from $100,000 to $80,000, would entirely erode a homeowner's equity, leaving him or her with only a large unpaid mortgage. Leverage is therefore the concept of making or losing magnified amounts of money with the use of other people's money.

Property can often be bought with a down payment of 10 to 25 percent and a mortgage taken on the balance. The higher the leverage (that is, the smaller the down payment), the higher a buyer's potential return.

For example, suppose you bought that property priced at $100,000. You put 20 percent ($20,000) down and covered the $80,000 balance with a mortgage loan. You made an astute decision, and in a year you sell your property for $110,000. You repay the bank the $80,000 owed and are left with $30,000 (minus fees and commissions)—a 50 percent return on your $20,000 investment. However, if you had persuaded the bank to lend you $90,000 and made a down payment of only 10 percent ($10,000), you would be left with $20,000 (minus fees and commissions) on your $10,000 investment—a return of 100 percent.

Another important advantage of leveraged home purchases is the tax savings gained by deducting interest payments from one's gross income. Since most mortgage payments are composed almost entirely of interest in the first years, the deduction can be nearly the full amount of a buyer's monthly payment.

The Other Side of the Coin

However, there is another side to this shiny coin. Home buying, like any other investment, has no guarantee of profitability. In the early 1980s, for instance, high mortgage interest rates nearly halted appreciation on real estate. Real estate also appreciates more slowly whenever the inflation rate slows down, as happened during the late 1980s and early 1990s.

Keep in mind, therefore, that real estate is a cyclical business. Though a house is still one of the sturdiest long-term investments individuals or families can make, the anticipated appreciation could easily be delayed for years by high interest rates, low inflation, or declining demand. But remember, too, that home ownership provides a lot more than a chance to earn sizable profits. It gives many people a feeling of security and freedom and plays a vital part in most Americans' dreams. And, if bought judiciously, a family home can still offer good chances of long-term profits. It also provides an investment for later years. Paying off a mortgage during their younger years provides people an opportunity to live mortgage free in later years.

The Down Payment Dilemma

Many would-be home buyers have the income for monthly home payments but not enough cash for a down payment. A typical house in 1993 cost about $98,000. With a standard 20 percent down payment and about $3,000 in closing costs (explained later in this chapter), buyers need at least $22,600 cash up front, an amount that is out of the question for many couples or individuals.

Most young people find this to be the greatest obstacle to buying a home and will consequently postpone a home purchase. Saving up enough money for the down payment may entail taking on an extra job or overtime, and curtailing or postponing other expenditures. This can best be achieved by resorting to a budget (discussed in Chapter 1). In many cases, parents, if they can afford to, can give the money as a gift, provide a loan, or share in the ownership in exchange for cash up front.

The Condo or Co-op Option

Other housing options are condominiums and cooperatives. **Condominiums** and **cooperatives** are usually multifamily units (apartment buildings), although many condos are garden apartments, townhouses, and detached housing units within a real estate development. Form of ownership is the key difference between a condo and a co-op.

In a condominium, each person individually and directly owns his or her apartment unit. The common areas or shared amenities—such as the land surrounding the building, the elevator, the swimming pool, corridors, and central heating—are jointly owned. In a cooperative, an occupant's ownership is indirect. The actual owner is a corporation, which issues shares of stock to the people who live in the building. The occupants own the shares of stock, not the apartment units. Each shareholder is given a "proprietary lease," which legally entitles him or her to occupy the unit. The occupant is legally a shareholder in the owning corporation as well a tenant.

The corporation, which owns the property, finances it with a single mortgage covering or blanketing the entire building, called a **blanket mortgage.** If a co-op's blanket is $4 million on a 100-unit building, then each homeowner has to assume a share of the obligation, which is $40,000 per owner-tenant. This price is paid to buy the shares of the co-op. If homeowners do not have $40,000 in cash, they may obtain a **share loan** to finance the purchase of the shares that entitle them to occupy a specific apartment.

The market in cooperatives and condominiums is highly segmented and difficult for buyers to assess. Would-be buyers can find the going hard when it comes to measuring the positive and negative potential of the units that they are considering buying. Little compiled information is available on the market in specific localities or regions. Co-op owners generally can sell their shares (or apartment) subject to the corporation's approval. The prices are determined by market forces as in any other real estate.

Renting versus Buying Your Home

Another option, of course, is not to buy your home but to rent instead. About one-third of the nation are renters. Even if you can afford to buy a home, a strong case can be made for renting. Besides holding out the promise of easy gains that are actually highly speculative, homes have further drawbacks as investments. They require large down payments. They do not pay cash dividends. In fact, they consume money for their maintenance. They are also nonliquid assets, subject to volatility in property values and much harder to cash in than most other types of investment. People involved in or considering a career that requires frequent moves may find that renting is a better approach.

Some Guidelines for Renters

Many people, especially during their younger years, resort to renting while others find this an acceptable form of housing throughout their lifetime. The following points may be useful for tenants to consider prior to entering into a rental commitment.

Does Buying Make Dollars and Sense?

Let's weigh the choice between renting a $700-a-month apartment and buying that $100,000 house to be sold after five years (about the average amount of time that Americans keep homes). You would need, on average, $28,000 for your down payment and closing costs and could expect to pay $800 a month on a 30-year 12.5 percent mortgage. Over five years, you would pay more than $48,000 on the mortgage, $15,000 for property taxes, $750 for insurance, and more than $2,000 for maintenance—almost $66,000 in total expenses before the tax break, about $47,000 after it.

Assuming annual appreciation of 3.5 percent for the house, it would sell for $118,750 after five years. Your profit, after closing costs and commissions, would be about $8,500. Your net cost of ownership for this five-year period would be $38,500 ($47,000 − $8,500). A renter, meanwhile, would pay about $42,000 ($700 × 60 months), which is $5,000 less than your net expenses. If the renter invested the monthly savings in a tax-free bond mutual fund, and the original $28,000 down payment in a municipal bond, he or she would have more than $45,000 after five years. The gain {$45,000 − ($28,000 + $5,000)} would be $12,000. Subtracting this $12,000 gain from the $42,000 cost of renting, we derive the net cost of renting as ($42,000 − $12,000) equal to $30,000. This is $8,500 less than the cost of buying this home. The above holds true if home prices increase by only 3.5 percent each year. If home prices increase 5.5 percent annually, the homeowner would break even with the renter.

1. When you rent an apartment or house, you are normally required to sign a lease agreement or contract. A tenancy is created when an owner of a property grants to another the right of occupancy of the property. The agreement is called a *lease,* and the parties are referred to as *lessor* and *lessee,* or as *landlord* and *tenant.*

2. It is of utmost importance for tenants to know the terms of their **lease.** The contract (lease) specifies the amount of the monthly payments, the payment date, penalties for late payments, the length of the lease agreements, any deposit requirements, renewal options, restrictions (such as no pets, children, etc.). Married couples moving into a rental apartment should get both their names on the lease. Some state laws provide that a landlord is not required to offer a renewal lease to anyone other than the tenant who had signed the expiring lease.

3. The tenant or tenants who sign on a lease are known as **tenants of record.** If this tenant of record (for married couples, usually the husband) dies or moves out, his family may be subjected to eviction. Unmarried people sharing a rental apartment should try to get the landlord to agree to put both names on a renewal lease. Family members who are threatened with eviction after the lease holder dies or moves out should consult an attorney. Only a court can order an eviction, and a lawyer can check to see whether the landlord has complied with the strict notice and procedural requirements that the law imposes prior to any eviction.

4. Many states require landlords to provide premises that are fit for habitation and free of conditions harmful to health and safety. Therefore, if the noise a neighbor subjects you to is so excessive that it seems health threatening, or there is illegal activity going on in a neighboring apartment, you usually have a right to complain to the landlord and, if necessary, to sue in housing court.

5. The **Fair Housing Amendments Act of 1988** provides legal rights for handicapped renters. Under this law, landlords may not ask prospective tenants whether they have handicaps or illnesses, including AIDS. Neither may landlords request to look at medical records. Landlords, however, may turn away applicants with a recent history of disruptive, abusive, or dangerous behavior. Building owners must make "reasonable accommodations" for the handicapped. For instance, if a tenant has difficulty walking, a landlord must reserve a parking space near the tenant's unit when the apartment complex has a "first come, first served" lot.

6. Tenants with disabilities have the right to modify their quarters at their own expense in order to have "full enjoyment" of the premises. This right extends to common areas such as lobbies. A handicapped person can pay to have an apartment building entrance door widened to accommodate a wheelchair. A person with limited hand strength must also be allowed to install lever doorknobs.

7. Rental laws are set by state or municipal governments and therefore vary from state to state. It is important for tenants to consult an attorney familiar with the local laws governing tenancy prior to signing a lease. Some items to clarify with an attorney are:
   a. Security
   b. Down payment
   c. Liability for damage to premises
   d. Penalties for breaking a lease
   e. Rent control legislation
   f. Landlords' obligation such as repairs, maintenance, and painting
   g. Tenants' rights as well as obligations

If your main criterion is financial, you can quickly calculate whether it's better to buy or rent (see the box "Does Buying Make Dollars and Sense?"). To start, figure all the costs of owning a home for a given period, say, five years. That includes mortgage payments, property taxes, insurance, utilities, and repairs. From that, subtract anticipated tax benefits. Then estimate how much you could earn on the house if you sold it in five years. Assuming that you have made a profit and are not buying another house right away, capital gains taxes, closing costs, and broker fees must also be figured in. Then calculate the cost of renting a similar house. Include rent and utilities, making allowances for annual rent increases and the forgone interest on any security deposit.

Renters do not have to make a down payment. Therefore, you should estimate what kind of after tax-return could be earned by investing that money. Subtract that income from your rental costs to determine the overall cost of renting. Of course, you could take into account also the psychic advantage of owning a house and not having to deal with landlords or having to move if the landlord decides to sell. But you should ask yourself how much this peace of mind is worth in extra monthly or annual expenses.

From a strict investment point of view, owning a home may at times be a relatively poor investment unless price inflation picks up or unless a given home appreciates at a rate well above the national average. Not surprisingly, some people who can afford to buy homes choose not to.

Buying Your Home: Selecting a Location

Let us now assume that you have taken all the previously discussed factors into consideration and have decided to buy a home of your own. What do you do now? By far the most important factor affecting a home's future market value is location. Before choosing a specific size or type of house, home buyers confront a question that is even more essential to the success of their investment: Where to buy? Houses appreciate more rapidly in some sections of the country than in others, and the trends are constantly shifting. Some factors to consider are the state of the local economy and the ratio between typical family income and the price of an average house. If the local economy is robust and there is plenty of disposable income to pay for houses, then it is likely that home prices will appreciate.

Other features to search for in a community are high-quality schools, easy access to a major business district, and such amenities as recreational facilities, shopping centers, and cultural attractions. Another gauge is the variation between asking and selling prices. In choice neighborhoods, the difference is small, often 3 to 5 percent. Another measure is how quickly houses have been selling. If the average time on the market is less than three months, the area is in demand.

How to Handle a Hungry Broker

When looking to buy a home, home buyers generally resort to the services of a **real estate broker**. Real estate has traditionally been sold through brokers who bring together sellers and buyers. Good brokers can be found everywhere, in small offices and in nationally franchised firms. Prospective home buyers should ask around the neighborhood to learn which brokers have been most successful in the area they are looking at.

Brokers Represent Sellers   It is all too easy for first-time home purchasers to believe that sellers' agents are working for them, especially when a buyer and broker spend a lot of time together looking at houses and discussing the buyer's wants and needs. A survey conducted in 1990 by the Consumer Federation of America revealed that just 33 percent of respondents knew that real estate brokers usually represent only sellers.

Buyers often mistakenly believe that the broker or agent is negotiating on the purchaser's behalf, but it is the seller who usually pays the broker. The higher the price of the home, the bigger the broker's commission. Therefore, the broker's interest dictates a high settlement price, which is not in the buyer's interest. Brokers' commissions normally average about 6 to 7 percent of the selling price, although some brokers charge as low as 4 percent, while others charge as high as 10 percent.

Although brokers chauffeur buyers around and give them the royal treatment, it is in the broker's interest to avoid disclosing critical information to house hunters. Buyers frequently share information with agents that they never should. For instance, they may admit that they can afford to pay $90,000 but are going to offer only $85,000.

In recent years 44 states have passed disclosure laws. These laws require agents to disclose to potential house buyers just whom it is that they are representing in any deal.

Buyers' Brokers   During the past decade a new phenomenon has appeared that reverses the situation. Some brokers offer to represent just the buyer, who hires them for a flat fee or an hourly rate. A flat fee removes any temptation for the broker to steer the client to more expensive houses. Most or all of the fee is due only if the client purchases a house. **Buyers' brokers** use their expertise in sifting through house lists with agency and private offerings to locate suitable houses for their clients. They are expected to examine houses for flaws or problems and to drive hard bargains for their clients.

During the 1990s, competition in the real estate brokerage field has become much more fierce. As national companies such as Merrill Lynch and others move into the market, many smaller traditional brokers have felt compelled to join nationwide franchises such as Century 21 and Electronic Realty Associates (ERA). This has resulted in offers of more services and lower commissions.

The Real Estate Contract

Every real estate transaction is unique, and a good strategy in one sale may not be appropriate in another. But in every deal, buyers must pay special attention to the terms of the contract. Buying or selling a home presents a host of potential problems and hazards for the unwary. Structural defects, encumbrances, title claims, boundary disputes, financing hassles, and broken appliances are just some of the things that buyers commonly encounter. The contract, therefore, provides the key to both the buyer's and seller's protection. Whether buying or selling, keep these basic points in mind:

1. The sale or purchase of real estate is a business deal. Always view it as an adversary process in which you are competing for the best terms and conditions.

2. Beware of suggestions that you can sign an agreement today and change it by yourself later. Once a contract has been signed, it can be changed only by mutual agreement between both parties. But no matter how lengthy or official-looking they are, all real estate contracts can be modified by the people negotiating them. Basic preprinted contract terms can be modified simply by crossing out unacceptable language and inserting changes. Such revisions must then be initialed by all parties to the agreement. There is no limit to the conditions that can be specified or the ways in which they can be written into the contract. If the parties agree to add new material, it may be written on separate pieces of paper and attached to the basic contract. Such "addenda" must be signed by both buyer and seller to be valid. The basic contract should indicate the existence of addenda so that accidental detachment will not undermine their work.

3. The written word is most important. A friendly verbal promise—such as "Yes, you can have the washing machine, outdoor furniture, or lawn mower"—is no substitute for a written understanding. Good contract forms spell out what comes with the property and what the sellers can take with them.

4. Contract forms spell out the financing terms in great detail with spaces for principal, interest rates, and other loan terms. A buyer must make a good faith effort to find the financing described in the contract. But what happens if interest rates change and the buyer no longer qualifies for a loan or does not want to pay such high rates? Some forms obligate the buyer to pay either a specified level of interest or, if that cannot be obtained, "the best available rate." Such language may force the purchaser to pay higher interest costs than originally expected if rates suddenly rise. Buyers can protect themselves by making the entire transaction contingent upon their ability to get the financing outlined in the contract. A buyer should limit interest costs by setting a maximum rate and stipulating that if the agreed-upon rate is not available, the deal is void and the deposit must be refunded in full. This is known as a **break or "contingency release clause"** and is a key provision. Buyers who cannot get such a clause should not sign.

5. Because realty transactions have become more complex, it is essential for buyers and sellers to have their respective attorneys inspect or review any document before either party signs it. A sufficient period of time should be specified in the contract for a legal review. Such reviews can often be completed within one week.

6. Because there is usually a period of one to six months between the signing of a purchase contract and the closing of the transaction, the seller is at risk of holding the home off the market. Sellers usually demand that a buyer put up enough "earnest" money, often 10 percent of the purchase price, to show that they are sincere. Buyers, however, should refuse to make a payment to sellers before receiving possession of the home. This problem is commonly overcome through the means of an **escrow**. Escrow is an important concept. *Webster's New Collegiate Dictionary* defines it as "a written agreement or something of value put in the care of a third party and not delivered until certain conditions are fulfilled." Escrow applies to situations other than home purchases but it is during negotiations for a home that most people first come up against the concept. In most cases, the escrow is deposited by the buyer when the contract is signed. A separate agreement is drawn to specify the terms and conditions of the escrow. The escrow money is deposited with a person mutually agreed upon by both sides, known as the **escrow agent**. The escrow agent can be the lawyer for the seller or buyer, real estate agent, or any other individual with no financial connection to either party. The amount of the escrow can range from as much as the down payment to a much smaller fee negotiated between buyer and seller.

Sell Before You Buy

It is much safer, when deciding to move, to sell your present house before buying a new one. Otherwise, you may find yourself owning and making monthly payments on two houses and desperate to sell the old one. Homeowners could easily find themselves in such a predicament if they are offered a truly irresistible deal on a house or are suddenly relocated by their employer.

If you have to buy first, make the purchase contract on the new home contingent upon the sale of your present house. The contract should stipulate that if you are unable to sell your present house within a specified period, the deal is void. Naturally, sellers may not agree to such provisions. A buyer can offer the seller a higher price to make the offer more attractive or pay a deposit of a few hundred dollars to the seller, which is nonrefundable if the buyer does not buy the house in a certain time period, such as two months. In this manner, the seller is compensated for waiting two months and the buyer has this time to sell the old house before having to buy the new one.

Some real estate brokers, as inducement to buy the new home, will promise to buy a buyer's old home if it fails to sell in a specified period, typically seven months. Brokers will not offer full market value on the house because they want to earn a profit on it. Therefore, a buyer should obtain a written agreement from the broker specifying under what conditions, when, and for how much the broker will buy the house.

Another possibility that an astute agent may suggest to satisfy both buyer and seller is a **break** or **contingency release clause**. This provision allows the seller, after the contract is signed, to continue to offer the house for sale. If another buyer is found, then the original buyer typically has up to 72 hours in which to sell his or her old home or otherwise release the contingency and free the seller to accept the other buyer's offer.

Inspection

Housing inspections by professional inspectors for both new and old homes are becoming increasingly common. A thorough examination of the property determines whether repair or new equipment is needed and helps estimate future costs for maintenance and replacement. Sellers permit such inspections before going to contract because they reassure the purchaser and can limit future claims.

The Closing

After a person selects a home, co-op, or condominium and enters into a contract or sale, a date is set for the **closing**, at which time the title or ownership is legally transferred from seller to purchaser. In this mysterious and often intimidating ritual, a flurry of legal documents is properly inscribed and duly notarized, with a good deal of money beyond the agreed-upon price of the home exchanging hands. In some parts of the country the closing is called **the settlement** or **closing of escrow**.

A hodgepodge of local customs dictates how closings are conducted, such as who may or may not attend, where each party sits, the role of the escrow agent, and so on. It's best to consult a local real estate agent, lender, or attorney about procedures in your area. Buyers may want to read a book on real estate law before they start wading through the dizzying number of legal papers at closing. Buyers will, no doubt, find themselves signing their name over and over again, sometimes on multiple copies of the same document. They should make certain that their lawyer sits next to them. Here's a rundown of the "paper chase" at a closing:

1. *Warranty deed*   This document officially transfers title to the buyer. The seller, not the purchaser, signs it and thereby warrants that the title is free and clear. After the closing, the closing agent will have this deed recorded at the local courthouse and will send the buyer a copy.

2. *Quit claim deed*   This is a device often used to clear up problems with the title. The seller, or anyone else with a potential claim against the property, signs it, thereby releasing any rights he or she might have.

3. *Mortgage,* or *deed of trust*   These documents secure the loan. When a debt is secured by a mortgage, the borrower signs a document that gives the lender a lien, or legal claim, on the property. When the mortgage is secured by a deed of trust, the buyer conveys title to a third party, who holds it until the note is paid in full. The lender does not receive title but only the right to request that the property be sold if the borrower defaults.

4. *Promissory (mortgage) note*   This establishes the borrower's obligation to the lender to repay the loan. It sets forth the terms under which the money is to be repaid.

5. *Owner's affidavit*   The seller affirms in this document that there are no unpaid liens, assessments, or other encumbrances against the house. This protects the purchaser, lender, and title company.

"So why do I have to sign it if it's called a deed of trust?"

Additional papers that buyers may also encounter during the closing include a termite inspection report, survey, title policy, truth-in-lending statement, and various liability releases.

Closing Costs

Once a buyer actually applies for a mortgage loan, he or she is generally entitled under the **Real Estate Settlement Procedures Act (RESPA)** to receive specific information about the **closing costs**. Within three days of receiving the loan application, the lender must mail a good faith estimate of the buyer's closing costs.

Closing costs can amount to several thousand dollars, generally 4 to 6 percent of the loan amount, and must usually be paid at the time of settlement. Buyers will be expected to appear at the closing with a certified check made out for the amount of the estimated settlement costs. There may be last-minute expenses that buyers will have to cover with a personal check, such as the value of fuel oil left in the tank and measured just prior to closing. At the closing, the settlement agent will hand the buyer a breakdown of the amounts due. It will usually contain the following:

1. *Real estate brokers' commission*   This is divided between the real estate agent who listed the home and the agent who consummated the sale. The seller usually pays this expense.

2. *Lender's charges*   This includes the lender's administrative costs of processing the loan (or origination fee), loan discount points (discussed later in this chapter), the appraisal fee, and the fee for the borrower's credit report.

3. *Mortgage recording tax*   The buyer must pay this tax, which is required by some local authorities.

4. *Prepaids*   Estimated mortgage interest, annual property taxes, and annual mortgage and homeowners insurance premiums are frequently paid in advance at closing. The amount of mortgage interest owed usually covers the period between closing and the end of the month. These amounts are held in an escrow account.

5. *Reserves*   The borrower is usually required by the mortgage lender to pay an initial amount into a reserve fund, which will be added to each month to ensure a sufficient sum to pay future taxes.

6. *Government charges*   This covers transfer taxes as well as the recording of the mortgage and property documents at the county courthouse as required by law.

7. *Lawyers' fees*   Buyers generally pay both their own lawyer's and the bank's lawyer's fees. Their own lawyer can charge as much as 1 percent of the house price.

8. *Title charges*   This pays for the title search, title insurance, document preparation, notary fees, and lender's attorneys' fees.

9. *Other charges*   These can cover the property survey, termite inspection, reports concerning termites and structural and internal defects, and such.

The Title Search

Among the most baffling aspects of the transaction is the role of the title search and title insurance. Often it is perceived as an unnecessary expense. But both the home buyer and the mortgage lender want to make sure the buyer gets clear title to the home he or she is purchasing. A **title search** is therefore conducted to determine whether there is any obstacle to the buyer's full ownership of the property.

Several problems can adversely affect the title to the property that you are buying:

1. A lien may be riding against the property because of an unpaid debt.

2. Easements may give others access to your land.

3. There may be restrictions on the use of the property.

Those are the kinds of things a title search should discover. When they do turn up, a buyer has several choices: (1) insist that the seller rectify the problems, (2) renegotiate the deal, or (3) cancel the transaction.

Title insurance normally combines two separate services: a careful search of public land records to ensure buyers and lenders that the property is being described correctly by the seller, and a written guarantee protecting the buyer against any claims not discovered in the search. The policy protects against liens left unpaid by a previous owner that do not show up in the records, prior boundary line disputes, or even a fraudulent sale.

Almost all buyers of single-family homes or condominiums are compelled to buy title insurance. Mortgage lenders insist on it because they may want to sell their mortgages later in the capital markets, and investors in those markets want this safeguard from loss. The title company normally makes its searches between the signing of a contract to buy and the closing. A buyer of title insurance pays only once, when the policy is taken out. The payment on a $100,000 home typically varies (from state to state) from $400 to $650.

Co-op buyers may request a title company to make what is called an **attorney's search**. This determines whether there are any liens on the building or against the seller, factors that could affect the soundness of the sale.

Homeowners Warranty

Homeowners warranties are a relatively new consumer protection feature for those who buy a new home from a builder. These are provided by Home Owners Warranty Corporation (HOW), a consortium of builders that provides home warranties. They were introduced in 1974 by the National Association of Home Builders (NAHB). HOW provides 10 years of protection against faulty construction. If a builder refuses to fix the mistake, insurance covers the repairs. It also provides a dispute-settling process to determine the outcome when buyer and seller cannot agree.

HOW policies cannot be purchased on the open market and must be obtained through an active HOW member-builder. The builder pays a one-time fee and usually passes it along to the buyer in the home's selling price. Premium costs range from $2.20 to $5.00 per $1,000 of a home's selling price, depending upon the house's location. Thus, a buyer of a $100,000 home could expect to have $220 to $500 added to the price of the home to cover the HOW policy. This is also usually paid at the closing. HOW is the only nationwide service of its type and operates in every state except Alaska.

The Limitations of "HOWs" Many home buyers who depend on new home warranties from HOW and other local companies are unaware of the limits of such coverage. Typical problems, such as foundation wall cracks, basement leaks, bad wiring, or faulty plumbing are covered only during the first year. After that, coverage is usually limited to major structural defects in load-bearing components that make the home unsafe, unsanitary, or otherwise unlivable. Only the most extraordinary situations are covered after the first year. Warranties, therefore, are intended more to shield builders from open-ended liability than to protect consumers.

There are warranties on old homes as well, if you buy an old home through a real estate agent with a warranty program. For instance, the one offered by ERA Realty in every state protects buyers against unexpected major repair bills for a year after the purchase. The premiums cover built-in appliances as well as electrical, plumbing, heating, and cooling systems.

The Mortgage Maze

Finding a house and negotiating for it brings you halfway home. Financing it completes the journey. Since buying a home and obtaining a **mortgage** to finance it will most likely be among the most important and largest financial decisions of your lifetime, they need to be done with care, deliberation, preparation, and knowledge of the mortgage and real estate markets.

Today's home buyer faces a seemingly endless variety of mortgage choices and must also cope with constant changes in the cornucopia of offerings that go far beyond any fluctuations in interest rates. The evolution and rising popularity of many new residential mortgages in the last few years have made it imperative for the informed potential home buyer to vigorously comparison shop and have a clear idea of the various mortgage options before deciding which mortgage is most suitable. It is best therefore to shop for a mortgage even before starting to look at houses, in order to know how much house you can afford.

Let us then examine the various mortgage instruments on the market, to learn the various strengths and drawbacks of each as well as the methods and terminology common to the mortgage market. By the time you finish reading this chapter, mortgage-related terms such as "negative amortization," "points," "ARMs," "caps," "buy-down," "balloons," "GEMs," and "GPMs" should no longer frighten you. Understanding these concepts can save time and money and can save buyers from obtaining a mortgage ill suited to their needs.

Broker-Provided Mortgages

People who buy a home through a broker are likely to be offered the added convenience of direct access to mortgage financing through the broker's real estate agency. Mortgage brokers have grown in importance in recent years with the demise of hundreds of savings and loans and the increasing complexity of mortgage loan products. The broker will be able to obtain a mortgage commitment, and in some cases, even deliver the loan papers at the closing without the hassle of dealing separately with a lender. However, broker-provided financing must be approached with caution. In some instances, brokers earn an extra commission if they persuade the buyers to use their in-house mortgage service. This, of course, could impair the broker's objectivity. The terms or rates may not be the best available. They should be compared with those of outside lenders.

Computerized Database Services

Home buyers struggle to locate the best deal in a maze of more than 500 different mortgage plans can eliminate much legwork by consulting a computerized mortgage listing service, which serves as a clearinghouse for lenders. Computerized **mortgage database services** can conduct a regional or national search for lending institutions that offer the lowest rates and best terms. They generally maintain an inventory of hundreds of mortgages. This service is available at a growing number of real estate and financial firms.

These computerized mortgage database services can also perform an initial evaluation of how much a buyer can afford to buy. They can search their data bank and match a buyer with the institution extending the most favorable mortgage terms given the buyer's income, available cash, and debt load. Buyers can lock in a specified loan amount and interest rate, provided the home appraisal and their loan application prove satisfactory. Then the lender will take the loan application, verify the credit and property information, and either grant approval or deny the application.

Use of these database services generally costs little or nothing. Their costs are often borne by subscribing lenders and real estate agents. Such services can be a useful resource, a kind of one-stop shopping arcade for mortgages. However, such services may not list every loan in your community.

There are quite a few mortgage database services throughout the country, and more are on the way. But only three currently resemble a national or regional mortgage department store. They are Compufund (714/960-8421), Loan Express (703/556-2918), and Shelternet (800/822-5587).

How Much House Can You Afford?

Before mortgage shopping, buyers should catalog their spending priorities as well as their income prospects. First, they need to find the kind of financing that is appropriate for their specific situation. Buyers should ask themselves the following questions as they embark upon their mortgage hunt:

1. How large a monthly mortgage payment can I afford?

2. How much cash can I safely afford to put down?

3. How long do I expect to live in the house?

4. What are the chances of my annual income increasing by about 5 percent over these years?

5. Can my income accommodate expenses for medical problems and payments for child care or the care of an elderly parent?

6. What kind of mortgage programs are available in my community?

Mortgage Payment Calculation

The monthly cost of a mortgage can be calculated by using the information in Table 6–1. It shows what a buyer will pay monthly in mortgage principal and interest per $1,000 borrowed on either a 15-year or a 30-year fixed loan. For example, payment on a 30-year, $100,000 loan at 9 percent is $805 ($8.05 × 100) per month. The monthly payment on a 15-year, $100,000 loan at 9 percent is $1,014 or $10.14 × 100. This can also be seen in Table 6–2, which shows the monthly payments for various mortgage amounts and mortgage terms.

Current studies suggest that only a minority of home buyers bother to check with more than a few lenders before signing up for a mortgage. That can be expensive. Renting money, which is what home buyers do when they get a mortgage, costs money; and the longer they rent it, the more they pay. Even a fraction of a percentage point more on a loan means that a lot more dollars have to be paid. For example, by referring to Table 6–1, we derive that a 30-year 9.75 percent $1,000 mortgage would cost $8.59 per month. A 30-year mortgage for $100,000 at 9.75 percent would therefore cost $859 per month. At 10 percent, monthly payments on a $100,000 mortgage grow to $878. A mere $19 difference? Hardly. Multiply the $19 by 12 months per year and then by 30 years, and the difference becomes $6,840. That is the extra amount a home buyer will pay for the same $100,000 borrowed at a quarter percentage point higher.

Once buyers determine their monthly mortgage payments, they must decide whether they will be able to afford them. If not, they should settle for a less costly home. The National Association of Realtors claims that home buyers need an annual household income of $30,000 for a mortgage on a $95,000 house, $40,000 for a $126,000 house, $50,000 for a $158,000 house, and $60,000 for a $190,000 house. As a rough rule of thumb, the price of a house should not exceed three times a buyer's total family income. But of course much depends on the mortgage interest rates that determine the monthly payments.

Borrowers should consider the size of their savings, the amount of current monthly installment payments (such as for a car and furniture), and reserves for emergency expenses. They also need to factor in the cost of obtaining a mortgage, as well as the closing costs. The cash-flow sheet in Chapter 3 can be used to work out the figures.

When taking out a variable-rate mortgage (which will be discussed later), you should understand how much risk you are taking. Can you handle the "worst case" scenario of a maximum rate rise? It is very difficult to make that determination if the mortgage has no limit on rate increases. It is tempting to hope that a rising

TABLE 6–1	Mortgage Payment Table	

Interest Rate	Monthly Payments per $1,000 Borrowed	
	15 Years	30 Years
7.00%	$ 8.99	$ 6.65
7.25	9.13	6.82
7.50	9.27	6.99
7.75	9.41	7.16
8.00	9.56	7.34
8.25	9.70	7.51
8.50	9.85	7.69
8.75	9.99	7.87
9.00	10.14	8.05
9.25	10.29	8.23
9.50	10.44	8.41
9.75	10.59	8.59
10.00	10.75	8.775
10.25	10.90	8.97
10.50	11.06	9.15
10.75	11.21	9.34
11.00	11.37	9.53
11.25	11.53	9.72
11.50	11.69	9.91
11.75	11.85	10.10
12.00	12.01	10.29
12.25	12.17	10.48
12.50	12.33	10.68
12.75	12.49	10.87
13.00	12.65	11.07
13.25	12.82	11.26
13.50	12.99	11.46
13.75	13.15	11.66
14.00	13.32	11.85
14.25	13.48	12.05
14.50	13.64	12.24
14.75	13.80	12.44
15.00	13.97	12.64

income will enable you in the future to afford higher payments than you can now. But predicting the future is a highly uncertain business.

Home buyers who purchase their dream house by overextending themselves and ignoring the above considerations are likely to be living in a dreamland.

Meeting Banks' Mortgage Eligibility Requirements: PITI

The state of the economy may influence people's home-buying decisions, but it is the lender who decides whether or not you can afford to buy a given house. Lenders take many elements of a buyer's financial profile into account, but until recently they

TABLE 6–2	Monthly Payments Needed to Amortize (Pay Off) a Loan at 9 Percent Interest			
Amount	**Term**			
	15 years	**20 years**	**25 years**	**30 years**
$ 10,000	$ 101.40	$ 90.00	$ 83.90	$ 80.S0
20,000	202.80	180.00	167.80	161.00
30,000	304.20	270.00	251.70	241.50
40,000	405.60	360.00	335.60	322.00
50,000	507.00	450.00	419.50	402.50
60,000	608.40	540.00	503.40	483.00
70,000	709.80	630.00	587.30	563.50
80,000	811.20	720.00	671.20	644.00
90,000	912.60	810.00	755.10	724.50
100,000	1,014.00	900.00	833.90	805.00

used a formula referred to as **PITI**. This rule held that the monthly payments for loan principal (P), loan interest (I), property taxes (T), and homeowners insurance (I) should not exceed 28 percent of gross monthly income, and total long-term obligations—including car loans, tuition, student loans, credit card balances, alimony, and child support—should not exceed 36 percent of gross income. Gross income is what borrowers earn in before-tax wages. It must be earnings for work that they have been doing for a year or longer, not the extra job they took a few weeks ago.

These guidelines are often modified for buyers who make bigger down payments, say, a third or more of the cost of the house. Lenders know that the bigger the borrower's stake in a house, the less likely he or she is to default on the mortgage. A family with a gross income of $50,000 could qualify if monthly costs did not exceed $1,167 ($50,000 ÷ 12 months × 0.28).

Although many people are spending much more than 28 percent for housing costs, this benchmark is used by conservative lenders. It is not a hard and fast rule. Some lenders will issue mortgage loans if total housing outlay does not exceed 33 percent of monthly income. But most lenders will not exceed the 28 percent guideline. By applying these rules, bankers seem to be protecting borrowers from getting into more debt than they can handle. But they are actually more interested in protecting the bank from having to foreclose.

The Mortgage Terms

When home buyers finance the purchase, they become debtors and the lender has a claim (hence, the term "mortgage") against most of the property if the buyer defaults.

The home's value is of great importance to lenders. Mortgage lenders want to be sure there is enough market value left in the home to recover the loan principal if a borrower defaults. The lender will appraise the property that a home buyer plans to buy and seldom will lend more than 80 percent of its appraised value. Its appraised value may differ from the sale price. But it is the appraised value that determines the mortgage amount.

The major terms of the mortgage that buyers negotiate with a bank pertain to:

1. Equity (the down payment)

2. Principal

3. The interest rate

4. Amortization (the amount of each installment payment)

5. The maturity date

6. Points

7. Prepayment rights

8. Assumption of the mortgage (assumable mortgages)

Payments on mortgages are made in equal periodic installments that include both interest and repayments of principal. The amount of each installment payment does not change, but the proportion of interest and principal contained in each installment changes every time a payment is made. The portion going toward repayment of principal grows slightly while the interest portion declines slightly. Gradually, as homeowners pay off principal, they build up equity, or ownership, in their home.

Equity   Equity (ownership) is the amount of the house's worth that is the home buyer's, over and above the mortgage. The down payment is the buyers' initial equity in their home. But as they pay the principal and especially if real estate values rise, the equity should increase steadily.

Principal and Interest   The amount of interest you owe a lender is the product of the monthly interest rate on the loan and the loan's outstanding balance. The monthly interest rate is simply the annual interest rate divided by 12. If the annual rate is 12 percent, the monthly rate is 1 percent.

EQUITY

Calculating Your Equity in a Home

If you bought a home for $80,000, took a $60,000 mortgage, and made a down payment of $20,000, the latter was your equity, or initial investment in the home. If you resold the home right away for $80,000, you would get back your $20,000 (minus brokerage commission and legal fees). After, say 15 years, you have paid off about $15,000 principal of the $60,000 mortgage. Your outstanding mortgage is $45,000. If you can sell the house for $125,000, then your equity is the home's value minus the mortgage, or $80,000 ($125,000 − $45,000) .

Suppose you take a 30-year fixed-rate mortgage of $85,000 at 10 percent interest. Table 6–1 shows that the monthly payment per $1,000 at 10 percent for 30 years is $8.775. If we multiply that by 85, we get $745.94. The $745.94 monthly payment will stay the same for 30 years, but because the balance is reduced with every mortgage payment, the portions of each payment going for principal and interest are constantly changing. During the first years your payments are largely interest. In time, more of each payment is credited to the loan itself, or the principal. This is shown in the box "Amortization."

For your first (12 monthly) payments, the interest you owe the lender is nearly 10 percent of $85,000, or $8,478.73. The extra $472.50 goes toward reducing your principal, leaving a balance of $84,527.50. For your second year's payment, you owe the lender 10 percent of $84,527.50, and so the interest amounts to only $8,429.26 with $521.97 going to retire your debt. The shift from interest to principal (equity) accelerates each year as more of the mortgate is repaid. This process continues until the end of your mortgage term. Most of the payments for the initial years are composed of interest. Your fixed monthly payment is calculated (projected) to be able to pay off the remaining balance and any interest still due by the end of the mortgage term. By making equal monthly payments for the length of the loan to the lender, the borrower will just pay off the loan and provide the lender with the agreed-upon rate of return.

Amortization   This process of gradually reducing debt through the payment of principal and interest is called **amortization**. Amortization is one of those ominous-sounding words capable of triggering math anxiety in many homeowners. But it is actually a simple concept, and once understood, it can help homeowners keep tabs on how much of their monthly mortgage is going for interest and how much is added to their equity. Nearly all mortgage loans are self-amortizing. Lenders use loan amortization tables to determine monthly payments. These tables are used to find the equal monthly payments necessary to amortize or pay off the loan at a specified interest rate over a 20- to 30-year period.

Maturity Date   The **maturity date** of a mortgage is the final date by which it has to be repaid in full. Most borrowers prefer 30-year mortgages. But if they want to build up equity faster in their home and can afford the larger monthly payments, borrowers might be better off with a 15-year fixed-rate mortgage. These rates are usually about a percentage point lower than those for 30-year loans. But monthly payments are moderately higher (see Table 6–2) because borrowers pay off the principal faster. Another option may be to take a 30-year mortgage and, if your income allows, to pay back more than the required monthly payment or to make a 13th payment each year. This will result in the mortgage being paid off faster. Your extra payments will be used in their entirety to pay off principal rather than interest.

Points   Banks also levy other fees to cover their cost of making a loan. Most mortgage lenders charge **points** (sometimes called an **origination fee**) in addition to the stated interest rate on a loan. Points are prepaid interest charges imposed by a lender. They are calculated as a percentage of the loan. Each point equals 1 percent of the loan amount. For instance, if the bank charges three points to get a $50,000 loan, borrowers must pay $1,500 cash "up front." This is a one-time expense traditionally

Amoritization

The following amortization table shows the interest cost, principal reduction, and loan balance for a 30-year, $85,000 mortgage at 10 percent (APR) interest. Monthly payments are $745.94 throughout the term of the loan.

At the End of Year	1 Interest Payment	2 Principal Payment	3 Balance Due
1	$ 8,478.73	$ 472.50	$ 84,527.50
2	8,429.26	521.97	84,005.53
3	8,374.60	576.63	83,428.90
4	8,314.22	637.01	82,791.89
5	8,247.51	703.72	82,088.17
6	8,173.83	777.40	81,310.77
7	8,092.42	858.81	80,451.96
8	8,002.49	948.74	79,503.23
9	7,903.15	1,048.08	78,455.14
10	7,793.40	1,157.83	77,297.32
11	7,672.16	1,279.07	76,018.25
12	7,538.23	1,413.00	74,605.24
13	7,390.27	1,560.96	73,044.28
14	7,226.81	1,724.42	71,319.86
15	7,046.24	1,904.99	69,414.88
16	6,846.77	2,104.46	67,310.42
17	6,626.40	2,324.83	64,985.59
18	6,382.96	2,568.27	62,417.32
19	6,114.03	2,837.20	59,580.12
20	5,816.94	3,134.29	56,445.83
21	5,488.74	3,462.49	52,983.34
22	5,126.17	3,825.06	49,158.28
23	4,725.64	4,225.59	44,932.69
24	4,283.16	4,668.07	40,264.62
25	3,794.35	5,156.88	35,107.75
26	3,254.36	5,696.87	29,410.88
27	2,657.83	6,293.40	23,117.48
28	1,998.82	6,952.41	16,165.07
29	1,270.82	7,680.41	8,484.66
30	466.58	8,484.65	0.01

Total Interest Payments 183,536.00   **Total Principal Payments** 85,000.00

Examine the table. What relationship do you find between columns 1 and 2 throughout the 30 years? If you add (column 1) interest payments and (column 2) principal payments for any given year, you will find that they total $8,951.23 each year. This total is the sum of the 12 equal monthly payments of $745.94. What changes each year is the percentage of the mortgage payment that goes toward paying interest and the percentage that goes toward paying off principal. Since the loan balance due is declining, then less interest is charged and more of the payment is used to pay off principal. Therefore, the interest payments decline and the principal payments increase each year.

The Principal of Equity

Equity in your home can increase in two ways:

1. As the principal on the mortgage is paid down
2. As the home appreciates in value

Bob Houseman bought a house in 1984 for $100,000. He paid $20,000 in cash and took an $80,000, 30-year mortgage. By 1994 Bob has paid off $25,000 on his $80,000 mortgage. His mortgage balance is thus $55,000. The market value of Bob's home is currently $175,000. How much equity does Bob have in his house?

Answer:

$175,000	=	Current market value of home
− 55,000	=	Mortgage balance
$120,000	=	Current home equity

Bob's equity is rising due to rising real estate prices and due to amortization of his mortgage.

paid by check at the mortgage closing. In essence, borrowers are obtaining a net loan of only $48,500 but must pay interest on, and repay, $50,000.

Home buyers sometimes do not fully understand how points affect their overall costs. Points are a device for increasing the bank's effective return on the mortgage without having to change its publicly stated interest rate. The bank may want to charge some borrowers more than the stated rate, either because it considers them a higher credit risk or because it expects interest rates to rise shortly. But for reasons of competition or public relations, it may prefer to keep a publicly advertised lower rate.

Lenders often offer a menu of rates with one, two, or three points. Some lenders offer mortgages with no points, or low points, in return for slightly higher interest rates, which can be an attractive option for borrowers with limited cash savings. Conversely, loans with lower rates may require payment of more points. Borrowers may therefore be able to trade more points for a more comfortable interest rate, and lower monthly payments.

On a 30-year, fixed-rate mortgage, each point equals about one-sixth of a percentage point of the rate. On a 12 percent fixed-rate $60,000 mortgage, borrowers can reduce the rate to 11 percent by paying six points, which is $3,600. Borrowers are paying this lump-sum amount to reduce their monthly payments by approximately $50 per month. Is this a worthwhile investment? Like everything else, it is a gamble. If borrowers did not do it, their monthly interest payments (leaving out principal) would be ($60,000 × 12 percent = $7,200 ÷ 12 months =) $600 per month. If they pay the $3,600 in points, their monthly payments are now ($60,000 × 11 percent = $6,600 ÷ 12 months =) $550 per month. They would be saving

$50 in interest payments each month, which over 30 years comes to a savings of ($50 × 12 months × 30 years) $18,000.

However, the borrowers' $3,600, if invested in a money market fund or CD at 6 percent, could earn them $216 a year (÷ 12 months = $18 per month). Interest rates could go higher, and they could conceivably earn more than $18 a month. They would have to decide whether it pays to give up the liquidity or potential use of $3,600 for a net gain of $32 a month, which over 30 years is a net savings of ($20 × 12 months × 30 years) $11,520.

The appropriate answer to such questions depends on a buyer's particular needs, outlook, and style of investing. How long the buyer plans to stay in a house is a major factor. For a buyer who expects to be in a house for more than a few years, paying more points to get a lower rate can be cheaper. In effect, the buyer is pre-paying part of the cost to use the money for 30 years. Spread over that long, the points have little impact on the effective annual mortgage rate. But the less time the buyer plans to keep a house, the more the points add to the effective annual rate.

The rule of thumb for the first few years is to equate each point with about 0.25 percent on the interest rate. Thus, a 9.75 percent loan with two points is equivalent to roughly a 10 percent mortgage with one point.

Another consideration is the effect of taxes. Points are fully deductible on income tax returns for the year in which they are paid—under certain conditions. When shopping for a mortgage, buyers should ask each lender whether points are considered prepaid interest (which is tax deductible) or a service charge (which is not). Mortgage buyers should be especially careful of origination fees, which are similar to points but often fail to qualify as tax-deductible interest.

Mortgage Prepayment   If borrowers can afford to pay off all or part of their mortgage, should they do it? The rate they are paying on the mortgage is the primary factor in determining whether paying ahead is worthwhile. Different rates call for different strategies. Suppose you have an old 7 percent mortgage with 10 years to go. If secure investments—such as bank certificates of deposit, money market funds, Treasury bills, and U.S. savings bonds—pay more than 7 percent after taxes, you would be better off investing your money. Your interest earnings will be greater than the interest payments saved by prepaying your mortgage. Remember, your mortgage interest payments are tax deductible. Therefore, your investment

When It Doesn't Pay to Prepay

Assume that you have a 12 percent, 30-year loan for $50,000. Monthly payments are $514.50. Also assume that money market funds, Treasury bills, certificates of deposit, and U.S. savings bonds offer around 10 percent. In this case, prepaying the mortgage is only marginally advantageous. The deciding factors would probably be liquidity and taxes. Keeping money in liquid form may be worth the 1 or 2 percent difference in rates. Also, the higher your tax bracket, the more valuable the mortgage interest payment is to you. If you are in the 28 percent tax bracket, a $514.50 monthly interest payment costs you only $370.44 after taxes.

DISCOUNT

should provide an after-tax yield of 7 percent in order for it to be worthwhile not to prepay the mortgage.

An alternative strategy for a holder of a low-rate mortgage is to buy it back from the lender at a discount. Many lenders will offer to forgive part of the principal just to get rid of such loans. To decide whether it would be worth the investment, compare what your money could earn elsewhere with the return represented by the discount offered by the lender. Suppose you owe $40,000 and the annual interest at 7 percent is $2,800. Calculate the outlay you would need to earn that much at current market rates. If current rates are 10 percent, you would have to make an investment of $28,000. That's the "discounted" value of the $40,000 you owe on your mortgage. If the lender will sell you that mortgage note for $28,000 or less, it is worth considering.

Prepayment Penalties As in the case of refinancing, homeowners may face **prepayment penalties** on their existing loans. These penalties, which typically apply to mortgages paid off in five years or less, are usually restricted to 2 percent of the outstanding loan balance. This reduces any anticipated gains by 2 percent and may change the picture entirely.

Accelerated Repayment Program One approach with a moderate-rate mortgage is to consider an accelerated repayment program. If a loan can be repaid in whole or in part without penalty, borrowers can shorten their own repayment schedule by paying more than the monthly amounts due to the lender.

What is gained by doing this? Suppose that instead of paying $514.50 each month on a 30-year, $70,000 mortgage at 8 percent interest, a borrower elects to pay $600. The result is that the entire loan would be repaid in 15 years instead of 30. Eliminating 15 years of $514.50 monthly payments eliminates a total of $92,520 in mortgage interest payments. But this is not a "something for nothing" deal. Remember that interest on a home mortgage remains fully tax deductible, which means that Uncle Sam really pays part of it. The borrower is in effect investing $85.50 per month for 15 years. That amount compounded at, say, 12 percent annual interest would be equal to over $50,000 if invested in a money market fund. The extra money paid each month on a 15-year mortgage could therefore be considered as a forced savings plan.

Assumable Mortgages An **assumable mortgage** is a mortgage that can be passed on to a new owner at the previous owner's interest rate. For example, suppose a buyer is interested in a $100,000 home. He or she makes a down payment of $25,000 and owes $75,000. The previous owner (or seller) of the home has paid off $20,000 out of an 8 percent $60,000 mortgage. The buyer assumes (or takes over) the present owner's mortgage, which has $40,000 outstanding. The buyer also makes additional financing arrangements for the remaining $35,000 by borrowing that amount from a lender at current rates. The buyer's overall interest rate is lower than the market rate because part of the money he or she owes is being repaid at the low rate of 8 percent.

Most lenders no longer issue assumable mortgages. Before "assuming" someone else's mortgage, buyers should read the contract carefully and have their attorney check to determine if there is a **due-on-sale clause** in it. A due-on-sale clause gives the lender the right to require immediate repayment of the balance owed if the property changes hands. Such clauses have been included in many mortgage contracts for years. They are being enforced increasingly by lenders when buyers try to assume sellers' existing low-rate mortgages.

Types of Mortgages: Creative Financing

There is an endless variety of mortgage designs. The arrangements, stipulations, and conditions are as unlimited as human imagination and creativity, hence the name "creative financing."

The remainder of this chapter describes some of the more common mortgages now available. However, new types of mortgages with new names are constantly being created.

Fixed-Rate Mortgages

Until recently, most home loans were **fixed-rate mortgages**, with a fixed interest rate and identical monthly payments over the life of the loan, and full amortization over a period of 20 to 30 years. This set a maximum on the total amount of principal and interest paid during the loan. These features worked in the buyer's favor. Although the payments seemed hard to meet at first, over time as the buyer's income usually rose, they became easier. Inflation made the monthly payments easier to afford as a result of rising incomes, while property values rose substantially. Inflation appeared to be the homeowner's friend but a foe to banks.

The demise of many savings institutions, as discussed in Chapter 2, can be attributed directly to fixed-rate mortgages. A typical savings bank in 1975 accepted savings deposits at 4 percent, issued 30-year 6 percent mortgages, and expected to earn a 2 percent gross profit on the $1 billion of its outstanding mortgages. However, interest rates had risen by 1979. The bank then had to offer 10 percent on saving certificates, but were still earning only 6 percent on the old 30-year mortgages. Thus, the bank was losing 4 percent on its investment—a $40 million annual loss on the $1 billion of its outstanding mortgages. Moreover, the bank was stuck with this problem for decades because the mortgages had 25- to 30-year maturities. In desperation, many banks switched to adjustable- or flexible-rate mortgages (discussed later in the chapter).

Many thrift institutions, fearful of having profits squeezed or erased should interest rates rise again, restrict their issue of fixed-rate mortgages. Fixed-rate mortgages generally carry an interest rate at least 2 percentage points higher than the initial rate on the same bank's adjustable-rate loan. By issuing an adjustable rate mortgage, the bank transfers to borrowers some or all of the risk of being harmed by rising interest rates. It is therefore willing to give borrowers a lower rate to start with if they will accept that risk.

Additionally, many banks that offer fixed-rate mortgages no longer keep them until maturity. They sell them quickly to Fannie Mae, Ginnie Mae, Freddie Mac, or other federal **pass-through agencies** (see Chapter 13). Commercial mortgages are often sold directly to pension funds, insurance companies, and other investors. Therefore, the predicted and much-touted demise of the fixed-rate mortgage has never really happened. With signs of inflation slowing, the fixed-rate mortgage actually made a comeback in the mid-1980s.

To consumers, the obvious advantage of a fixed-rate loan is predictability. Many consumers prefer the certainty of knowing that their monthly payments on principal and interest cannot change for the next 30 years. This feature reassures many borrowers, especially those whose income is likely to remain steady in the foreseeable future. They are willing to pay a price for this predictability, in the form of rates that run higher than the starting rate on an adjustable loan. If interest rates decline substantially, they can refinance by paying off the mortgage and taking out a new one at a lower rate. However, this switch may involve several thousand dollars of points and other costs, which will be discussed later on.

Many mortgage shoppers will lock in a fixed-rate loan if they think interest rates are headed up over the next several years. If they think rates will go down or stay about the same, they will opt for an adjustable-rate loan. Either way, if they guess right, they gain. If they guess wrong, they lose. The mortgage market, like every other investment, involves an element of risk, decision making, and proper timing. In short, it can be considered a gamble.

One possible drawback of fixed-rate mortgages is that very few of those being written in recent years are "assumable," which, as stated, permits the loan to be assumed by another buyer.

"Locking In" a Mortgage Rate   If interest rates seem to be headed up, lenders will tend to be wary of committing themselves to a rate too early in the application process, which can take 60 days or more before the loan is closed. But there are ways that borrowers can protect their interests, too, while waiting to close on a fixed-rate deal. The expensive way is to pay a fee to lock in the going rate at the time of the loan application. That could cost one-half of 1 percent or more of the amount borrowed. But lenders' practices vary on this matter. Some lenders regularly commit to a rate at application time for no extra fee, while others will do it at the time the loan is approved, which is generally two to four weeks later.

Refinancing a Fixed-Rate Mortgage   When home buyers take a 30-year conventional fixed-rate loan, they may appear wedded to it for 30 years or as long as they live in that home. But there is a way out, a divorce of sorts. They can refinance. **Refinancing** simply means obtaining a new loan to pay off the old one. This is quite a common practice when interest rates decline. To determine if mortgage refinancing makes economic sense, six key factors must be considered:

1. How much the interest rate has declined

2. The number of points being charged (remember, one point equals 1 percent of the loan) to obtain a new lower-rate loan

3. The individual's tax bracket

4. How long the new mortgage is to be held

5. All other charges that need to be paid to get a new loan

6. Whether there is a prepayment penalty provision in the old loan

There is more to refinancing than simply substituting one loan for another. To get an accurate picture of the cost of refinancing, borrowers have to take into account the interplay among these six factors. This should help determine the feasibility of refinancing as well as the rate of return.

Refinancing Costs   Refinancing costs often exceed those for an original first mortgage. Borrowers may have to pay most of the closing costs all over again, including an origination or processing fee; a commitment fee; the costs of such services as a title search, an appraisal, a credit report, and the recording of documents; title insurance; policy document preparation; and attorney's fees. These typically total between $750 and $1,000. The biggest cost is likely to be points. On the average, lenders charge two to four points, which must be paid immediately when a mortgage is issued or refinanced.

Prepayment Penalty   If it is stipulated in their original loan, borrowers also may have a hefty prepayment penalty. Many conventional fixed-rate loans require the borrower to pay 1 to 2 percent of the outstanding mortgage principal if the mortgage is paid off early. What borrowers need to know is whether they would save enough to justify the up-front costs. Many homeowners shy away from refinancing because of the added costs, particularly the points charged by the lender for the new mortgage. But if the refinancing cost is looked at as a long-term investment, the benefits usually far outweigh the drawbacks.

As a rule, when borrowers have a three- to five-point spread between their existing mortgage and new mortgage rates available and they are dealing with a term of 20 to 30 years, a new mortgage will be cheaper. The longer they plan to live in the house, the smaller the spread necessary to recoup their closing costs. Because the primary purpose of refinancing a home loan is to reduce monthly payments, total savings on interest payments must be greater than the closing fees involved in refinancing. Therefore, before they start negotiating a new loan, borrowers need to do a preliminary cost-benefit analysis.

How Long It Takes to Recoup Refinancing Costs   With a mortgage payment table (see Table 6–1), it is easy to compute how long it would take to recoup the refinancing costs. Simply divide the total refinancing costs by the monthly payment savings at any given interest rate.

For example, assume that refinancing a 12.75 percent, $100,000 mortgage involves closing fees of $4,000. If the current rate is 9.75 percent, a monthly payment on a

---

The Refinancing Calculation

You can gain a clearer perspective on refinancing by considering the potential savings over the life of the mortgage. Assume that you were able to refinance a 30-year, $100,000, 16 percent mortgage by replacing it with a 30-year, $100,000, 13 percent mortgage. The total interest cost over 30 years for the 16 percent mortgage would be $384,128, while the total interest cost on a 13 percent mortgage is $298,232. The long-term savings are $85,896. These long-term savings obviously dwarf the possible $2,000 to 4,000 closing costs.

30-year loan would be $859. That is a savings of $228 from the monthly payment of $1,087 required on a 12.75 percent loan. Dividing the total refinancing cost of $4,000 by $228 gives a recovery period of 17.5 months. The result shows how many months it will take to recoup your up-front investment in a lower interest mortgage. If it is more than the number of years you plan to live in the home, then refinancing will be a losing proposition.

Homeowners should not forget to calculate the effect of refinancing on their income taxes. A home mortgage is the best tax shelter most people have, and lower interest payments reduce the tax benefits. The savings from lower interest payments resulting from refinancing depend on your marginal tax bracket. For example, $100 a month saved on a refinanced mortgage would be worth only $72 a month for someone in the 28 percent bracket.

If the homeowner in the our example is in the 28 percent tax bracket, then a savings of $228 from the monthly mortgage interest payments would be a net after-tax savings of $164. Therefore, the recovery period after taxes would be 24 months. This 24-month wait to recoup expenses is most likely still worthwhile.

But it is not quite that simple. A sophisticated analysis of the deal would take into account the opportunity cost of the transaction, that is, the income the homeowner would lose by tying up the closing costs in the deal when that money could be earning income somewhere else. Homeowners should factor in the (opportunity cost) loss of income from their $4,000 up-front costs over the same period. In a money market fund paying 10 percent, it would earn $400 annually, or $33 a month.

But we also cannot ignore taxes here. A homeowner who earns $33 extra a month and is in the 28 percent tax bracket has a net after-tax income of only $24. Consequently, the net savings, by prepaying, would be $164 minus $24, which equals $140. Dividing the total refinancing cost of $4,000 by the $140 monthly net savings (after taxes and after taking into account opportunity costs) results in a recovery period of 28.5 months, or 2.33 years. Refinancing for an owner in the 28 percent tax bracket, in this case, is attractive only if he or she plans to reside in the house that long.

These calculations assumed that there is no prepayment penalty in the mortgage contract. Many states prohibit or restrict prepayment penalties, although they still exist elsewhere. Such penalties, which frequently amount to six months' interest, can be the biggest cost of refinancing. If there were a prepayment penalty, then the loss of income (opportunity cost) would be much greater and the recovery period would be much longer. An $8,000 prepayment penalty, for instance, would bring the recovery in our example to 130 months, or almost 11 years; not an attractive proposition. The average family lives in the same house for seven years, but homeowners should generally hope to recover the cost of refinancing in under five years, or less if there is not any prepayment penalty. The work sheet in Figure 6–1 will guide you through the calculation required to help you consider the real costs of refinancing.

The Element of Timing If the numbers look good, homeowners then face another decision: act now and refinance, or wait in hope that the rates will decline further. That is always an agonizing decision. If they wait, market mortgage rates may rise and they may have missed a lucrative opportunity. During 1993 mortgage rates reached their lowest levels since 1973. Millions of homeowners were faced with the decision to refinance or to wait for even lower rates.

| FIGURE 6–1 | **Work Sheet to Calculate Savings or Losses of Refinancing** |

This work sheet can help you roughly estimate the savings (or loss) of refinancing an existing home mortgage. In this work sheet the assumption is that the new mortgage would be similar in length to the old mortgage.

How many months do you plan to stay in your present house? (If it is easier to think in terms of years, multiply the number of years by 12 to come up with this answer.) _____

Multiply by the amount you will save each month with the new loan.

$\times$ _____

= _____

Subtract the higher amount you would pay in income taxes with a lower-rate mortgage. (You can estimate this figure by multiplying the amount on the line above by your combined federal and state tax rate.)

− _____

= _____

Subtract approximate closing costs you pay on the new loan.

−

= _____

Does your current mortgage impose a penalty for early payment? If so, subtract the amount of the payment.

− _____

= _____

HERE IS YOUR ESTIMATE: This is roughly how much you would save (or lose) by the time you sell your home if you refinance.

= _____

Adjustable-Rate Mortgages (ARMs)

Adjustable-rate mortgages, a phenomenon of the late 1970s and early 1980s, represented a radical change in home finance. Mortgages with fluctuating interest rates were first offered in California in 1970, but by the early 1980s they had spread across the country. By 1988, an estimated 63 percent of new housing loans were ARMs.

For a period of 50 years, beginning in the 1930s, homes in the United States were financed by what we now call **conventional mortgages**—20 percent down and the balance paid over 20 years at a fixed rate of interest. In the 1970s, 25-year loans became common and in the 1980s, 30-year loans became predominant. Because of fear of rising inflation and interest rates, lenders in the 1980s moved increasingly toward adjustable rates. ARMs shift the risk of inflation and a spurt in rates from

Mortgage Refinancing Calculator

Whe does it pay to refinance? Find the amount on the left that is closest to what it would cost to refinance your mortgage. Follow that row to the right until the column is over the amount that is closest to what you would save each month by refinancing. Where the cost row and the savings column intersect shows the approximate number of months it will take for refinancing to begin paying off. Actual payback periods will be affected by tax considerations.

Costs of Refinancing

$7,000	140	94	70	56	47	40	35	32	28
6,000	120	80	60	48	40	35	30	27	24
5,000	100	67	50	40	34	29	25	23	20
4,000	80	54	40	32	27	23	20	18	16
3,000	60	40	30	24	20	18	15	14	12
2,000	40	27	20	16	14	12	10	9	8
1,000	20	14	10	8	7	6	5	5	4
Monthly savings ($)	50	75	100	125	150	175	200	225	250

lenders to consumers, by allowing the mortgage rate to rise within a specified range in step with the financial markets.

The profusion of adjustable-rate mortgages has further complicated the experience of mortgage shopping. Prospective home buyers need to examine the many options available within the adjustable spectrum as well as compare them with fixed-rate mortgages.

A typical family owns three dwellings over the course of a lifetime. A young couple begins with a modest starter home. Then they have children and move up to a bigger place. When the kids are grown, the parents buy a smaller house. The fixed-rate mortgage is most appropriate for people in the second and third stages, who most likely will stay in their house for a long time.

But for many people in the first stage, ARMs offer distinct advantages. ARMs enable homeowners to take advantage of declining interest rates without incurring the expense of refinancing. And mortgage rates tend to be quite volatile. If interest rates drop, monthly payments may come down. Once limited almost exclusively to first-time home buyers who could not qualify for fixed-rate loans, ARMs are becoming popular even among people who are trading up to second and third houses and who anticipate a steadily rising income.

Lenders price ARMs to compensate borrowers for taking part in the interest rate risk; thus, their initial rate is usually three percentage points lower than a fixed rate. Buyers who are scaling the income ladder or plan to move in three to five years are looking beyond the predictability of fixed-rate mortgages to the short-term cash flow benefit of ARMs. Their strategy is to capitalize on discounted loan payments in the early years of an ARM and then refinance their house or convert to a fixed-rate loan later if the ARM proves too expensive.

The Drawback of ARMs

The virtue of ARMs is that they enable more home buyers to meet the criterion that housing expenses consume no more than 28 percent of gross monthly income. But ARMs have drawbacks as well. A major drawback is uncertainty. It is difficult to plan for monthly mortgage payments that can change as often as every three to six months. What one gives up with an ARM is peace of mind. Homeowners do not relish being in constant suspense about the size of their mortgage payments.

ARMs make it more difficult for a family to plan its financial future because it can never be sure what its mortgage payments are going to be. People working within the confines of a tight budget find that ARMs can play havoc with their financial plans. Mortgage insurers recognize that ARMs pose a higher risk of default than fixed-rate mortgages. When a homeowner struggling to make initial ARM mortgage payments has to pay substantially more as a result of an upward adjustment, the risk of default increases. Consequently, mortgage insurance premiums are higher for ARMs than for fixed-rate mortgages.

Lenders, recognizing the higher ARM default rate, have tightened eligibility qualifications. ARMs are often limited to those with high income levels. The concern is that if lenders qualify borrowers based on their ability to afford the first year of payments, borrowers may go into "payment shock" when monthly payments jump to market levels.

ARMs can cost substantially more in up-front fees and points than a fixed-rate or conventional mortgage. More employees and computers have to be used by the financial institutions to track all the adjustments and to inform borrowers of those changes. The cost of all this office work is passed on to the borrowers.

The Variety of ARMs

There is no such thing as a standard ARM. ARMs vary in the safeguards they offer, and their terms and requirements vary among lenders. Many ARMs allow borrowers to switch to a fixed-rate mortgage some time between the first and fifth year of the loan for a modest fee. To get the best deal, borrowers should know how adjustable-rate loans are structured. Let's therefore examine the specifics of ARMs in more detail. You should keep at least three things in mind when shopping for an ARM: the index tie-in, the margin of profit, and the cap.

The Index Tie-In

With an ARM, the interest rate paid is subject to periodic adjustments based upon movements of a selected index of the lender's choosing. Lending institutions may tie the interest rate to almost any index they want. The government's main requirement is that the index be out of the lender's control.

In practice, the vast majority of ARMs are indexed to the one-year Treasury securities yield, which can be volatile. The Federal Home Loan Bank Board's national "average mortgage contract rate," which tends to change more slowly, is also popular. Three- and five-year U.S. Treasury securities are also common. The use of Treasury security rates makes loan agreements easy to monitor since the information is widely available. These rates are also representative of interest rates in the general economy.

Some lenders use an index that measures the "cost of funds" to banking institutions nationwide, that is, what the banks must pay to attract deposits. This index could be preferable from the borrower's point of view since it tends to move slowly, an advantage specifically at a time when interest rates are more likely to rise than fall. In 1988, several U.S. lenders began issuing ARMs linked to the London Interbank Offered Rate. That interest rate, known as LIBOR, is what big commercial banks pay to borrow dollars in the short term from one another in the huge London market.

Some states require lenders to give borrowers a disclosure of important ARM information before they apply. This information package includes a 10-year history of the index used. It gives borrowers an idea of how often and to what extent the interest rates have been changed in the past.

The Adjustment Schedule   The interest rate (or payment) adjustment schedule is stated in the mortgage contract: every six months, once a year, once every three years, or once every five years, depending upon the type of ARM. To see if that new payment was calculated correctly, borrowers need to find out what their ARM index has been doing lately and then apply the adjustment formula themselves. This information can be obtained from the financial section of newspapers or by contacting the Federal Home Loan Bank Board in Washington (1700 G Street NW, Washington, DC 20552, 800/424-5405), which reports on the most popular indexes. Buried somewhere in the papers that borrowers signed at settlement is a description of how the lender selects the index date that pinpoints the index rate on which the new payment will be based.

How Lenders Twist Your "ARM"   Under federal regulations, lenders are required to notify borrowers of a payment change between 30 and 120 days before the new amount goes into effect. The announcement states the new interest rate, the date it goes into effect, and the new monthly payment. It may also state the original interest rate and monthly payment, the index used to determine adjustments, and the lender's profit margin added on top of the index figure. It is not uncommon for lenders to calculate adjustments using the wrong index, the wrong index date, the wrong interest rate equation, or the wrong payment amount at the right rate. Since ARMs are relatively new, some banks and other lenders have not fully gotten the hang of them yet. If borrowers suspect an error, they can ask the lender to work through the numbers with them when the rate is adjusted. If borrowers are still not satisfied, they can complain to the Federal Reserve Board (202/452-3946).

Margin of Profit   Knowing the index does not tell borrowers what their loan rate will be. This is because lenders impose a margin of profit above the index. A loan agreement may call for borrowers to pay the Treasury security rate plus two percentage points. If a loan, for instance, is tied to the one-year Treasury index that is currently at 6.7 percent and includes a typical lender's profit margin of 2 percent, borrowers would be required to make payments at an 8.7 percent rate after their loan is adjusted.

Put a "Cap" on Your ARM   What has helped sell ARMs in recent years are irresistibly low initial rates, typically 2 to 3 percent lower than fixed-rate loans. But enticing loss-leader low rates are often a trap, luring home buyers into adjustable-rate mortgages with no limits on future interest rates. If interest rates rise significantly, many of those people could be headed for a financial crisis, including the loss of their house.

Homeowners often do not realize that their initial rate is the least important feature of the loan. The catch is that the single-digit teaser rates normally vanish within a year or two, plunging the borrower back into the real world of market rates, the index plus the lender's profit margin. The result can be monthly payments that nearly double at the first adjustment. These teaser mortgages are quite common nationwide. In locations marked by overbuilding and a slow rate of sale of the new inventory, builders may offer such below-market rates as a purchase incentive.

When adjustable-rate mortgages were first introduced in the early 1980s, the potential for rising payments was so great that wary borrowers soon dubbed them "the neutron mortgage." Like the neutron bomb, which would kill people but preserve property, the mortgage would quickly eliminate those who are unable to keep up with the payments while leaving the house intact.

After a few years, to make ARMs more palatable to consumers, lenders placed tight **caps** on how much the interest rates can fluctuate. Borrowers knew that if interest rates started to climb, their liability was limited to 2 percentage points on yearly interest rate changes (up or down) and a lifetime limit of 5 or 6 percentage points above the original rate. For many, the loans became well worth considering as an alternative to the traditional fixed-rate mortgage.

Caps limit the extent of the borrower's risk. A 1985 study by the United States League of Savings Institutions showed that more than 95 percent of all adjustable-rate mortgages had a payment cap or maximum interest rate built into the agreement. There are, however, different kinds of caps. Borrowers need to make sure that their caps fit their needs. Caps come in five basic varieties: periodic, aggregate, bottom-end, cumulative, and payment caps.

Periodic Cap   A **periodic top-end cap** limits the amount the rate can increase at any one time. For example, a mortgage could provide that even if the index increases 3 percent in one year, the rate can go up only 1 percent.

Aggregate Caps   An **aggregate top-end cap** limits the amount the rate can increase over the entire life of the loan. This means that even if the index increases 2 percent each year, the rate cannot increase more than 5 percent over the entire loan. For example, a 7 percent loan might be capped at 12 percent, meaning that borrowers will never have to pay more than the latter rate.

Fannie Mae (Federal National Mortgage Association; see Chapter 13), for instance, will not purchase a mortgage in the secondary market unless the buyer is given the option of a two percentage point periodic cap on the rate rise during the first year and a 5 percent aggregate cap over the life of the loan. That is a good rule of thumb for consumers, too. It means, for example, that the rate on a 9 percent 30-year ARM cannot rise to more than 11 percent in the first year or above a maximum of 14 percent over the full term of the loan.

The aggregate is obviously more important than the periodic cap. But caution is essential here because periodic and aggregate caps may have catches to them.

Bottom-End Caps   Borrowers who do not read the loan contract carefully may be in for a surprise if interest rates start to fall. Some loans have top-end and **bottom-end caps.**

This means that some lenders establish a floor as well as a ceiling for changes in interest rates. An 11 percent loan might have a 16 percent top-end cap but also carry a 9 percent bottom-end cap, meaning that the rates cannot fall below 9 percent.

Cumulative Caps

Cumulative Caps A cap may also be **cumulative**, meaning that if borrowers hit the cap in one year, any interest points they do not have to pay as a result can be carried forward to a year in which they do not hit the cap. For example, if the rate rises 3 percent in a year and the cap is 2 percent, that extra 1 percent will be stored away for a later adjustment.

Payment Caps

Payment Caps Payment caps, another form of capping, apply to the payments themselves. When rates increase, the monthly payment is capped but the difference is added to the principal. This may lead to a false sense of security. For example, suppose the mortgage provides for unlimited changes in the interest rate but the loan has a $50 per year cap on payment increases. You start with a 13 percent rate on your $60,000 mortgage and a monthly payment of $663.72, but your index increases by two percentage points in the first year of your loan. Consequently, your rate increases to 15 percent and your payments in the second year should rise to $758.67. Because of the payment cap, you will pay only $713.72 per month in the second year. But this does not mean that the difference will not have to be paid. There is a catch to payment caps, and it's called *negative amortization.*

When you were paying $663.72 on your 13 percent mortgage, $500 went toward interest and $163.72 went toward amortizing the principal. Then the rate increased to 15 percent, but because of the cap, your monthly payment increased to only $713.72. Since this change in interest rate increases your debt, the lender may now apply a larger portion of your payment to interest: ($758.67 − $713.72 =) $44.95. If rates get very high, even the full amount of your monthly payment may conceivably not be enough to cover the interest owed. Then the additional amount of interest you owe is added to the principal.

When this happens, you have experienced negative amortization. **Negative amortization** occurs when a borrower's payments do not cover all the interest due on your loan and the unpaid interest is added to the loan balance. In other words, your debt rises even though you are making regular payments. This can stretch the term of the loan well beyond the 30-year contract term or increase the loan balance. You end up paying interest on top of interest and may wind up owing more in principal than you originally borrowed.

Negative Amortization Cap

Negative Amortization Cap Borrowers can get protection against such rate increases by insisting that their payment cap put a limit on the negative amortization they must absorb if their payment cannot be raised fast enough to keep up with their debt. A typical limit is 125 percent, meaning that they cannot be forced to pay back more than what they paid plus 25 percent.

Borrowers may find little comfort in this and even less in the fine print. When they reach that negative amortization cap, the lender may do one of three things:

1. Declare the loan due in full, meaning that you would have to refinance at going rates or sell

Declining Mortgage Rates

Mortgage interest rates have steadily declined since the early 1980s, with zigs and zags along the way, as shown below. They peaked in October 1981 at 18.2 percent for fixed rate loans and 17.54 percent for ARMs.

This pattern is part of an overall trend of declining interest rates throughout the economy. The result has been a refinancing boom. Homeowners with fixed-rate loans have been taking advantage of these unprecedented low rates by refinancing their mortgages.

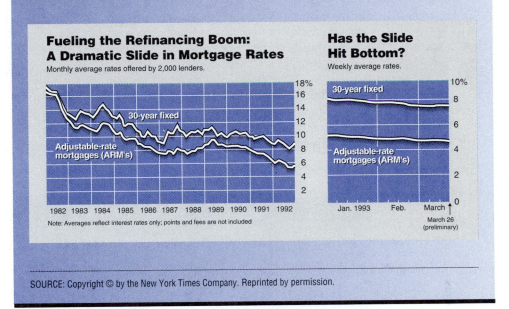

**Fueling the Refinancing Boom:
A Dramatic Slide in Mortgage Rates**
Monthly average rates offered by 2,000 lenders.

30-year fixed

Adjustable-rate mortgages (ARM's)

1982 1983 1984 1985 1986 1987 1988 1989 1990 1991 1992

Note: Averages reflect interest rates only; points and fees are not included

**Has the Slide
Hit Bottom?**
Weekly average rates.

30-year fixed

Adjustable-rate mortgages (ARM's)

Jan. 1993   Feb.   March
                              March 26
                              (preliminary)

2. Renegotiate the loan as a fixed-rate mortgage to be paid off by the end of the original loan term

3. Extend the term of the loan so that it will be paid in full even though the monthly payments cannot be increased

Negative amortization means that you are merely postponing the day of reckoning, not escaping it. It may be a road to perpetual debt and should be avoided. Borrowers therefore need to be sure they are getting interest rate caps, not payment caps.

Under disclosure rules required by the Federal Reserve Board (as of October 1, 1988), all details about the frequency of rate adjustments and the limits or caps on rate boosts must be disclosed at the time of application. Lenders also must give applicants an educational packet and explain the mechanics of available ARMs before accepting an application. The rules call for lenders to explain the index to which the ARM is tied, the points added to the index to set the mortgage rate, and how often the rate can change.

Growing-Equity Mortgages (GEMs)

A **growing-equity mortgage (GEM)** is a variation of a fixed-rate loan that calls for gradually rising payments as the years go by. It combines an interest rate fixed for the life of the loan with an increasing monthly payment. The increase each year goes to reduce the principal, which permits an accelerated repayment of the loan and more rapid acquisition of equity.

Monthly payment changes are based on an agreed-upon schedule of increases. The interest rate is usually a few percentage points below market rate. Although the mortgage term may run for 30 years, a GEM loan is paid off more rapidly than other fixed-rate mortgages, usually within 15 years, because prescribed annual increases in the monthly payment go directly into reducing the principal of the loan. This means a faster paydown. Actually, any mortgage loan can be converted to a GEM simply by paying ahead on the principal.

Graduated-Payment Mortgages (GPMS)

The **graduated-payment mortgage (GPM)**, a variation of the GEM, is designed for homeowners who expect to be able to make larger monthly payments in the near future. They can be applied to both fixed and adjustable mortgages. During the early

---

An ARM Checklist

In shopping for any type of flexible-rate loan, use the following checklist to find the best terms available:

1. How long is the discount in effect, and when will payments start at full market rates?
2. What is the monthly difference in dollars between the discounted rate and the full rate?
3. What is the initial interest rate?
4. How often may the rate change (periodic cap)?
5. How much may the rate change (aggregate cap)? (What is the highest rate that may ever have to be paid on this loan?)
6. How much may payments change (payment cap)?
7. How often may payments change?
8. What are the initial monthly payments?
9. What is the mortgage's term (maturity date)?
10. How much may the term change (prepayment penalty)?
11. What are the limits, if any, on negative amortization?
12. What is the bank's margin of profit?
13. How many points does the lender charge?
14. How much are processing fees?
15. To which index is the loan tied?
16. What are the conversion rights to a fixed-rate mortgage, and what fees and points are involved?

years of the loan, payments are set low; then they are increased according to a fixed schedule, usually over a 5- to 10-year period, until finally the payments are higher than they would have been for a loan without the graduated payment feature. They then remain constant for the duration of the loan.

During the early years, payments are lower than the amount dictated by the interest rate. The difference between what should be paid in the early years and what the borrower actually pays shows up as negative amortization. During the later years, the difference is made up by higher payments. This reflects the assumption that in later years a borrower's earnings will be higher and it will therefore be easier to pay off the mortgage. It essentially is a partial mortgage payment deferment plan. But what is not paid back now will have to be paid back later with interest. Even though the payments change, the interest rate is usually fixed. At maturity, the entire debt will have been paid off.

Balloon Mortgages

Yet another variation of GEMs and GPMs is the balloon mortgage. **Balloon mortgages** have a series of equal monthly payments and a large final payment. Typically, there is a fixed interest rate, but the equal payments cover interest only; they do not amortize

Some Guidelines for ARM Shopping

1. Accept only an adjustable-rate mortgage with a cap.
2. Shop around extensively to find the most favorable terms available. It is often necessary to contact 20 lenders in order to find the best deal.
3. When applying for an ARM, look for a cap of no more than five percentage points over the initial rate during the entire life of the mortgage, and no more than two percentage points in any given year.
4. Seek a clarification by the bank, if necessary, on how to convert the index to which the rate is tied into a dollar amount.
5. Look for an index pegged to the one-year Treasury security rate, which fluctuates up and down. This is the most desirable.
6. Seek a low lender's margin, preferably no more than 2 percent.
7. Request an annual adjustment of the interest rate and the monthly payments.
8. Shop for an initial interest rate that is several percentage points below the price of fixed-rate loans.
9. Agree to no more than two points in loan fees; each point is 1 percent of your mortgage principal.
10. Request the option to convert an ARM to a fixed-rate loan in two to five years at the then prevailing interest rate.
11. Do not accept an ARM with prepayment penalties for repaying ahead of schedule.
12. Do not accept a cap on monthly payments. If interest rates rise and the monthly payment is capped, the unpaid interest is added to the mortgage principal and you get deeper in debt (negative amortization).

SOURCE: "Your Money Matters," *The Wall Street Journal,* October 9, 1992, C-1. Reprinted by permission of Giora Carmi.

the loan. The unpaid balance, usually the principal or the original amount borrowed, comes due in three to five years.

For example, suppose you borrow $25,000 for five years. The interest rate is 12 percent, and the monthly payments are $250. The payments cover interest only; you gain no equity, and the entire $25,000 principal is due at maturity. This means that you will have to make 60 equal monthly payments of $250 and a final balloon payment of $25,000 in the 60th month. The risks are substantial. If you cannot make that payment, you will have to refinance, if refinancing is available, or sell the property to pay it off.

Some lenders guarantee refinancing when the balloon payment is due, although they do not guarantee a certain interest rate. But balloon mortgages offer certain advantages. If a borrower plans to move and sell well before the balloon comes due, this type of mortgage may be right if proceeds from the sale are used to pay off the loan. It offers lower monthly payments and relatively lower interest rates than conventional mortgages.

Buy-Down Mortgages

A **buy-down** is a mortgage interest rate subsidy that helps the buyer meet the payments during the first few years of the loan. Real estate developers, eager to make a sale, pay a lender a lump-sum in exchange for the lender's pledge to make below-market-rate loans to buyers of the developer's property. Buy-downs typically reduce interest rates by two to three points. This makes the monthly payments much more affordable. The buy-down feature enables some buyers to qualify for this loan who otherwise would not be eligible for financing. For the seller it is a sales promotion, a loss leader that frees up capital for new investment.

Before accepting a buy-down mortgage, buyers should calculate what their payments will be after the first few years. Some buy-down plans provide interest rate reductions for the first few years only, while others last the life of the loan. Also, the cost of a buy-down often finds its way into the price of the house. The home's sale price may have been increased to cover the builder's interest subsidy. Buyers should check comparable home prices that do not offer buy-downs. It pays to comparison shop.

Insured Mortgages

Most banks require a 20 percent down payment when financing a home. Buyers who do not have the down payment can apply for a mortgage insured by the **Veteran's Administration (VA)**, the **Federal Housing Administration (FHA)**, or private mortgage insurance companies. These mortgages are obtained from banks or other lenders. The VA, FHA, and private mortgage insurance companies do not actually issue mortgages or lend money to a home buyer or a bank. They only insure the bank against loss if buyers do not repay their loans. These are designed primarily for people who cannot afford the required down payment. The mortgages generally cover between 85 and 95 percent of the cost of the home, which means they require as little as a 5 percent down payment.

VA and FHA Mortgages

VA mortgages, available to eligible veterans, can cover 100 percent of the cost of a home, subject to certain price limits. The VA also sets a maximum interest rate and limits the buyer's loan origination costs to one point, or 1 percent of the loan. To be eligible, a veteran must have served 180 days in peacetime or 90 days in wartime, including the recent Gulf War.

FHA insurance against any loss arising out of default enables the bank to accept a down payment that is usually 5 to 10 percent. This mortgage, known as a "section 203(b)" mortgage, is available to anyone who can meet the ordinary credit requirements of the bank. It is not just for low-income families. The only drawback is the low ceiling on FHA mortgages. The local FHA office or brokerage can tell you which ceilings apply in your area.

As with a VA mortgage, the stated interest rate will usually be below market rates. However, FHA insurance is not free. The FHA charges an annual insurance premium of 0.5 percent of the outstanding installment payments.

Private industry has come up with an alternative to the VA and FHA mortgage: the privately insured mortgage. This is a conventional mortgage with one added feature—insurance. The bank will accept a smaller down payment as a result. Buyers have to pay for the insurance premium, which is added to the mortgage installment payments.

Condo and Co-op Mortgages

Condominiums have become a significant part of the nation's housing inventory. Like the purchaser of any single-family house, a condominium buyer has to decide among various mortgage products, fixed-rate loans, or adjustable rates. The cooperative buyer will probably have less choice among lenders and among types of loans, although this may change over time becasue the secondary mortgage market makes it as easy for lenders to resell co-op loans as condominium loans.

In recent years, the acceptability of condominium loans for purchase by the main secondary market institutions, Fannie Mae and Freddie Mac, has made possible the surge in condominiums. In 1984, Fannie Mae began purchasing cooperative loans as well.

The cost of a condominium mortgage is identical or nearly identical with the cost of a single-family home loan. The cooperative loan, which is secured by shares in a co-op corporation rather than by the property itself, is normally marginally higher and available mainly from the larger institutions that keep the loans in their portfolios.

However, condo buyers must clear one extra hurdle in lender requirements. In deciding the size of the loan for which the borrower qualifies, the condominium's monthly maintenance charge is added to the borrower's annual budget requirements. This reduces the size of the loan that the condominium borrower, as opposed to the single-family home buyer, can get.

Conclusion: Home Free

There is no limit to the variations of mortgages that lenders can and do concoct. Each one must be examined to discover the advantages and disadvantages contained within. Comparing different mortgages is like comparing different cars. The objective should be to find a mortgage loan that best suits a home buyer's specific needs, requirements, and financial situation. It is not necessarily an easy task; a calculator, some mortgage and interest tables, and a session with an accountant or financial planner will be helpful. But the effort can be well worthwhile because this is the largest loan most consumers will ever negotiate.

SUMMARY

Choosing a house should be based on a rational evaluation of your family's housing needs, where you want to live, and how much you can afford to pay monthly for housing costs. The largest element of personal finance for most people is the ownership of a home. Home ownership is not necessarily suitable or desirable for everyone. Evaluate the renting-versus-buying decision carefully.

The housing decision includes not only considering several housing alternatives but also investigating various financial arrangements and choices. The major financial aspects of the decision to buy a home are the down payment, mortgage payments, taxes, insurance, and operating expenses. Monthly payment capacity is the prime consideration.

Real estate brokers offer valuable services to buyers and sellers in the housing market. When buying a home, the real estate contract is the key to the protection of both the buyers' and the sellers' interests. Buyers and sellers must understand all aspects of the contract, as well as conventions and contract procedures, before entering into contract negotiations. Legal advice is essential for this transaction.

A major part of buying a house is negotiating a mortgage. A mortgage is usually a 15- to 30-year contract between the buyer and a lender. Buyers need to know how to look for and buy the best mortgage terms, rates, and provisions available.

Home buyers should shop for a mortgage before they start looking at houses so that they know how much house they can afford. The common types of mortgages are conventional fixed-rate loans and adjustable-rate mortgages. There are many variations of these two types. The down payment, annual percent rate of interest, and point charges differ with the type of mortgage as well as the mortgage lender. The proliferation of different types of mortgages in recent years has made comparison shopping imperative. A portion of the monthly payment is amortized over the life of the loan, which is generally in the range of 15 to 30 years.

KEY TERMS

Adjustable-rate mortgage (ARM)

Aggregate top-end cap

Amortization

Assumable mortgage

Attorney's search

Balloon mortgage

Blanket mortgage

Break or contingency release clause

Buy-down mortgage

Buyers' brokers

Caps

Closing

Closing costs

Condominium

Cooperatives

Cumulative cap

Due-on-sale clause

Equity

Escrow

Escrow agent

Fair Housing Amendments Act of 1968

Federal Housing Administration (FHA) mortgage

Financial leverage

Fixed-rate mortgage

Graduated-payment mortgage (GPM)

Growing-equity mortgage (GEM)

Homeowners warranty (HOW)

Housing inspection

Lease

Maturity date

Mortgage

Mortgage database services

Negative amortization

Origination fee

Pass-through agencies

Payment caps

Periodic top-end caps

PITI

Points

Prepayment penalty

Real estate brokers

Real Estate Settlement Procedures Act (RESPA)

Refinancing

Settlement or closing of escrow

Share loan

Tenant of record

Title insurance

Title search

Top-end cap

Veteran's Administration (VA) mortgage

REVIEW QUESTIONS AND PROBLEMS

1. Discuss the relative advantages and disadvantages of owning a home.
2. List the major costs of purchasing and financing a home.
3. What tax advantage does owning a home have over renting? Do the tax advantages benefit everyone equally?
4. Differentiate between a *cooperative* and a *condominium*.
5. Discuss the function and role of real estate agents in the housing market.
6. Your friend is about to go to contract on her first house purchase. How can you advise her as to the real estate sales contract clauses, procedures, and associated costs that she can expect to encounter?
7. What are mortgage loans? How many types of mortgage arrangements can you identify? What are the financial implications of each?
8. Briefly define the following terms: (a) equity, (b) down payment, (c) multiple listing services, (d) quit claim deed, (e) closing costs, (f) prepayment penalty, (g) balloon payment.
9. Describe why points exist and how they affect the cost of mortgage credit.
10. What is the purpose of title insurance?
11. How do you build up equity in a house?
12. Would you consider owning a house as an investment, a consumer durable expenditure, or both? Explain.
13. Suppose you are applying for a 30-year, $100,000 mortgage loan. How much would an increase in interest rates from 12 to 13 percent change the monthly payment on your loan? (See Table 6–1.)
14. Define the term *mortgage amortization*. Explain what happens to principal and interest amounts with each subsequent payment.
15. Sally and Greg Michaels want to buy a home. They applied for a $150,000, 9 percent, 30-year mortgage that carries a monthly payment of $1,207.50. Property taxes would cost them $300 monthly and insurance $75 a month. Sally and Greg have a combined gross monthly income of $4,500. Their other long-term loan obligations amount to $300 a month. What are this couple's chances of getting their mortgage application approved by a lending institution?

16. (LEVERAGE) Suppose you bought property priced at $120,000 with a 5 percent down payment. When you sell, you notice that you have doubled your investment, the amount you used for a down payment. For how much did you sell your property?

17. (EQUITY) You paid $215,000 for your home. Your down payment was 20 percent. You have paid off 10 percent of the principal. The bank says that the equity in your home is $42,000. What is the current market value of your home?

18. (DISCOUNT) Suppose you owe $160,000 on your mortgage at an annual interest rate of 9 percent. You learn that the discounted value of the mortgage is $140,000. What is the current interest rate?

SUGGESTED PROJECT

Interview three different housing lenders in your community (preferably an S&L, a commercial bank, a credit union, or a mortgage finance company). What types of mortgages are they offering? What rates are being charged? What down payments are required? Compare and contrast the offerings of these different institutions as to points, and closing costs. If you were to buy a home today, which mortgage offer would you consider the best deal? Explain.

INFORMATION RESOURCES

Brooks, Andree. "Warranty on New Houses." *The New York Times,* September 19, 1993, LIR-5.

Compufund. A computerized mortgage database service (714/960-8421).

Consumer Handbook on Adjustable Rate Mortgages. Board of Governors of the Federal Reserve System (20th and C Streets NW, Washington, DC 20551).

Federal Home Loan Bank Board. 1700 G Street NW, Washington, DC 20552 (800/424-5405).

"Fixed-Rate Mortgages May Be No Bargain." *The Wall Street Journal*, September 9, 1991, C-1.

Gottschalk, Earl C., Jr. "How to Find a Good Mortgage Broker." *Wall Street Journal*, March 26, 1992, C-1.

Horowitz, Sherry. "The Right Way to Refinance." *Kiplinger's Personal Finance Magazine*, March 1992, 63–64.

"How to Buy Your First House." *Money*, April 1989, 137–144.

"How to Shop for a Mortgage." Mortgage Bankers Association of America, Consumer Affairs, 1125 15th Street NW, Washington, DC 20005, free brochure.

Irwin, Robert. *Tips and Traps when Mortgage Hunting*. New York: McGraw-Hill, 1992.

Liscio, John. "Gimme Shelter (Economic Advantages of Buying or Renting Housing)." *Barrons*, May 21, 1990, 16–19.

Loan Express. A computerized mortgage database service (703/556-2918).

McCarty, James A. *Home Buyers Guide: Financing and Evaluating Prospective Homes.* Northeast Regional Agricultural Engineering Service. 152 Riley-Robb Hall, Cooperative Extension, Ithaca, NY 14853.

Miller, Peter. *The Common Sense Mortgage*. New York: Harper and Row, 1987.

Nessen, Robert L. *The Real Estate Book*. Boston: Little Brown, 1981.

Pollan, Stephen. *The Field Guide to Home Buying in America*. St. Louis: Fireside Books, 1988.

Rothstein, Mervyn. "When the Broker Works for the Buyer." *New York Times,* September 19, 1993, LIR-7.

Shelternet. A computerized mortgage database service (800/822-5587).

"Shopping for a Mortgage." *Consumer Reports,* January 1992, 26.

"To Buy or Rent Is a Question for the 90's." *U.S. News and World Report*, April 17, 1989, 68–75.

"What Mortgages Cost." *Changing Times*, June 1991, 20–22.

A Foreword to Insurance

The following three chapters deal with various types of insurance. Before discussing the specifics and details of insurance, we should explore the terms and concepts of insurance in general that are common to all three chapters.

About 3,000 companies nationwide offer insurance against casualties such as automobile accidents, fire, theft, personal negligence, malpractice, hailstorms, and floods. Insurance can be classified according to the type of loss it covers, The five main types of insurance are **property**, **liability**, **health**, **life**, and **income**.

Insurance does not provide protection from these perils but rather from financial losses that result from their occurrence. Consumers protect themselves from financial risk by joining with other people who face similar risks. In this manner, they insure themselves against large losses that are sustained by a very small percentage of those who buy a given coverage.

An **insurance company**, or insurer, is a risk-sharing firm that agrees to assume financial responsibility for losses that may result from an insured risk. A person joins the risk-sharing group by purchasing a **contract** or **policy**. Insurance contracts, or policies, are written agreements that specify under what set of conditions the person being insured will be paid, as well as the dollar amount.

Each insured policyholder pays what is termed a **premium** to the insurance company in exchange for the promise that he or she will be indemnified (or reimbursed) for losses incurred. When an individual pays a certain insurance premium, he or she is thereby freed from the possibility of a large financial loss. The premium represents the cost of the risk transfer. In exchange for protection, insurance companies receive carefully calculated premiums from policyholders that enable the companies to pay for their losses and administer the plan. The person (or persons) named to receive the proceeds of, or benefits accruing under, an insurance policy is known as the **beneficiary**.

Risk

Market insurance involves the pooling of risk. For each of us individually, it is difficult to forecast with any certainty whether we will be a victim of burglary or an auto accident this year. However, it is possible to predict how many burglaries and auto accidents will take place nationally this year. The ability to accurately predict the probability of events for large numbers of people allows us to join

"You're home now, dear. You can stop smiling."

SOURCE: "Pepper…and Salt," *The Wall Street Journal*, December 7, 1992, A-15. Reprinted by permission of Cartoon Features Syndicate.

together and pool our risks. The insured individual benefits from the ability to transfer risk to the insurer.

Insurance **underwriters** determine whether or not, and on what basis, the company will accept an application for insurance. Underwriters use the probability calculations devised by an **actuary**. Actuaries are highly specialized insurance company mathematicians trained in the risk aspects of insurance. The underwriters design rate classification schemes to ensure that policyholders will pay a premium commensurate with their chance of loss. Actuarial work may be done by an underwriter.

Insurance rates are set partly according to the magnitude of risk. The greater the risk, the higher the premium that must be paid to obtain coverage for that risk. Conversely, the smaller the risk, the lower the premium. If the insurer accurately predicts actual loss experience, it gains from the profit that has been built into the premiums charged the insured.

The insurance industry is regulated and supervised almost exclusively by the states in which it operates. There is little federal involvement. State insurance commissions set ranges for rates, enforce operating standards, and exercise supervision over company policies.

Before insurance companies assume the risk of insuring people, they insist that specified requirements be met.

Heterogeneous and Diversified Policyholders

Market insurance cannot protect us all from risks that simultaneously affect the entire group at one time. There must be a fairly large and diversified pool of premiums. If everyone in the group suffered a loss at the same time, the insurance company's reserves would be insolvent. We therefore cannot insure ourselves against risks that affect the group as a whole. This explains why private insurance companies do not cover losses resulting from wars, floods, mass rioting, or nuclear accidents.

Law of Large Numbers

An insurable risk must be common to a large number of people. Insurers base their rate calculations on what may be loosely called "the law of averages" of large numbers. The **Law of Large Numbers** helps us understand why something that is not predictable for the individual *is* predictable for the group. It is a statistical concept that says that the larger the number of exposures, the greater the accuracy in predicting the future outcome. As the number of objects exposed to loss increases, the variations in losses decline. Hence, the risk declines. Seemingly haphazard events will follow a predictable pattern if enough events are observed. For example, the probability of predicting with accuracy the death of any particular 34-year-old male is very risky. However, if in a given state with 2 million people, actuarial mortality studies show that the probability of death for 34-year-old males is 2 per 100, or .02 percent; such increased accuracy decreases uncertainty and therefore risk. The insurance companies need this accuracy to estimate losses and establish reasonable premiums, dividends, and reserves.

Fortuitous

The loss should be **fortuitous** (accidental). It cannot be expected or deliberately brought about by the insured. The loss should be beyond the control of the insured. An insured will not collect insurance by deliberately setting his or her own house on fire. Similarly, a beneficiary will not collect if the insured commits suicide because the death was not accidental or fortuitous.

Insurable Interest

An **insurable interest** in the person or property insured must be present. A policyholder has an insurable interest in a property if he or she can show that the destruction of the property in question will result in personal financial loss. An insurable interest is present in the case of an automobile insurance policy purchased on one's car. However, an individual cannot collect on a life insurance policy written on the life of Michael Jackson or President Bill Clinton, for example. The law requires an insurable interest so that insurance policies are neither gambling devices nor tools for those who would profit deliberately by destroying the property of others.

Measurable

The insured loss should also be **measurable**. That is, the loss must be definite in regard to time and place.

Indemnity

Insurers generally apply the principle of **indemnity** when paying property losses. This principle states that an insured should not benefit from his or her loss. This means that an insured should be paid up to the amount of the loss and no more. This principle is not applied to life insurance since it is hard to place a value on human life. Indemnity is a large doctrine that limits recovery under an insurance policy to the lesser of the actual cash value of a loss or the amount that will restore the insured to his or her financial position prior to the loss.

Insurance Agents and Salespeople

In the 1969 comedy *Take the Money and Run*, jailed bank robber Woody Allen endures what he considers the ultimate punishment—confinement with a life insurance salesman. But for many people, an insurance agent is a necessity. There are roughly 400,000 of them in the United States, eager to sell us one sort of policy or another. Before selecting an agent, we should know something about agents.

Life and property insurance agents come in essentially two varieties—those who represent just one company, often called **captive agents** or **direct writers,** and **independent agents,** who work for a number of different insurers. The adage that "life insurance isn't bought, it's sold" carries a cautionary corollary: insurance agents are primarily salespeople, not unbiased advisers. Each type is likely to try to sell on the alleged merits of his or her particular companies.

Agents who belong to a local Life Underwriters Association are generally the more experienced agents in their communities. An agent who is a graduate of the two-year course on insurance-related subjects offered by the Life Underwriting Training Council is entitled to use the designation of **Chartered Life Underwriter** (CLU) after his or her name. This certification is awarded by the American College of Life Underwriters.

Consumers can comparison shop for life insurance, just as they do for a mortgage or car loan. Before purchasing, they also need to examine several alternative insurance policies. Price quotes for the amount and kind of coverage needed should be obtained from four or five agents recommended by friends. Consumers can readily purchase insurance without the medium of an agent. Several low-cost companies sell policies by telephone and mail.

Credit Rating the Insurer

Any investment, even one as conservative as insurance, is a risk. It pays to minimize the risk by researching the company. There are hundreds of insurance companies to choose from. Many are strong and solvent, while others are of questionable standing.

The insurance industry is not as sound as it used to be. During the 1980s, insurance companies, both large and small, invested in junk bonds, real estate, and other high-risk investments. Between 1975 and 1982, the number of insurance company insolvencies stayed relatively low, roughly five per year. Since 1982, the number has risen, averaging 16 per year, and soared to 37 in 1989. In 1988, roughly 21 percent of the companies that report to the National Association of Insurance Commissioners (NAIC) appeared on its special "Watch List" of insurers with financial troubles. By 1990, the financial health of many insurers was in jeopardy. In 1991, the financial problems of First Executive Corp., the troubled California-based life insurance company, made many people anxious about the health of other insurers too. Between 1991 and 1992, 5 major life insurers and 36 smaller ones collapsed, leaving as many as one million policyholders dependent upon a state-by-state patchwork of guarantee funds.

Unlike savings and loan depositors, consumers cannot count on the federal government to bail them out should their insurance company fail. In 1945, the insurance industry mobilized congressional support to pass the McCarran-Ferguson Act, under which insurers are exempt from federal supervision. Insurance regulation takes place at the state level. Since there is no national oversight, there is no obligation for the U.S. government to bail out insolvent insurers. That responsibility has fallen to the industry itself in the form of the aforementioned system of state guarantee funds—pools underwritten by assessments on insurers—to pay claims. These funds typically reimburse up to $100,000.

In all 50 states there is an industry-financed property/casualty guarantee fund to step in if an insurer fails. All states (except for Louisiana and the District of Columbia) also offer guarantee funds for health and life insurance. In practice, a state-supervised guarantee fund compensates policyholders when an insurer cannot pay a claim. But insolvency may subject policyholders to the delay of applying to a fund administrator or insurance company liquidator for payment. They might have to wait as long as two years for compensation. The majority of state guarantee funds are insufficient to handle a large number of failures. Many states also limit the amount policyholders may collect, regardless of their loss. Therefore, depending on location of residency and the kind of insurance bought, consumers may be partly or totally unprotected. Consumers can protect themselves, however, by learning as much about their insurance companies as possible and by keeping a continuous close watch on their financial situation.

Consumers can receive a report of the financial condition of their insurers by requesting a copy of NAIC's "Watch List" of companies whose financial condition has recently deteriorated. (This list costs $5 and is available from Belth's Publication, The Insurance Forum, P.O. Box 245, Elletsville, IN 47429.) Also, both A.M. Best and Co.'s *Flitcraft Compend* and *Standard and Poors Insurance Solvency Review* (800/765-8362), available in most public libraries, rate 4,000 life, health, property, and casualty insurance companies based on their financial strength, claims-paying ability, and reliability. Best announced a revised rating system in June 1992. Insurers judged to be healthiest qualify for the top rating, A++ (superior). The second best category is A+. Consumers should not purchase insurance from any company rated lower than A+. They should also check to see whether an insurer is on Best's "Watch List" of insurers whose ratings may soon be downgraded. The "Watch List" is published periodically in the monthly magazine *Best's Review*. Additionally, A.M. Best Co.'s phone line sells Best ratings to the public (900/420-0400) at $2.50 per minute. Policyholders can request their insurance agent or broker to check regularly on any insurer he or she represents and, if there is a problem, to transfer the coverage.

Rating services vary in their interpretations of the financial data supplied by insurers. An *A–* from one service may not mean the same as an *A–* from another. Consumers should be aware that the school grading system does not apply to an insurance company's financial situation. A *B* rating is not at all considered as good a rating as it may be in a college course.

A consumer's best protection is to rely on as many sources as possible and to be on the lookout for news articles about the insurance company. Most bad news about an insurer surfaces well in advance of a failure. It is advisable also to find out if your insurance company is licensed to sell insurance in New York State. New York has the most rigorous standards and requires all companies that sell insurance in that state to maintain those standards wherever they issue policies.

Now that we have introduced the basics of insurance, let us turn to the next three chapters, which discuss the entire gamut of insurance that every individual and household needs as part of their personal financial management package.

KEY TERMS

Actuary	Insurable interest
Beneficiary	Insurance company
Captive agents	Law of Large Numbers
Chartered Life Underwriters (CLU)	Liability insurance
Contract	Life insurance
Direct writers	Measurable
Fortuitous	Policy
Health insurance	Premium
Income insurance	Property insurance
Indemnity	Underwriters
Independent agents	

Health and Disability Insurance

- To appreciate the need for adequate health and disability insurance
- To identify and to describe the various types of health and disability policies available
- To determine how much disability insurance one needs
- To delineate the key factors and provisions that need to be considered when purchasing health and disability insurance
- To understand policy provisions, exclusions, and features, and learn how to evaluate the benefits and disadvantages of each

Although health and disability insurances are vital to our financial security, few people delve into the fine points of such insurance before buying these essential items. Many select these insurance policies on the basis of the charm of the salesperson or choose a plan because their coworkers selected it.

Medical and disability coverages are too important to be left to casual decisions or whim. This chapter therefore examines the importance of these insurances and familiarizes you with their terminologies and features. It also helps you learn to differentiate between the various options available and select appropriate and adequate coverage for your needs and circumstances.

Ever-Rising Health Costs

The United States spends far more than any other country for health care. From 1969 to 1993, the overall annual cost of health care in the United States skyrocketed from about $50 billion to more than $912 billion. In 1992 the United States devoted 14 percent of its gross domestic product, the total spending for goods and services in the country, to health care, up from 5.9 percent in 1965. Canada spends less than 9 percent, Japan less than 7 percent. The average for industrial nations is a little above 7 percent. A single day in an American hospital averaged $1,160 in 1992, not counting doctor bills. With ever-increasing costs of medical care (see Figure 7-1), it is easy for Americans to incur astronomical expenses for an extended hospital stay.

Despite touted remedies and precautions, health care inflation strikes every year and no cure is in sight. For the federal government, medical costs have become the fastest-growing major item, increasing at more than 8 percent annually during the early 1990s

| FIGURE 7–1 | Health Costs Outpace Inflation |

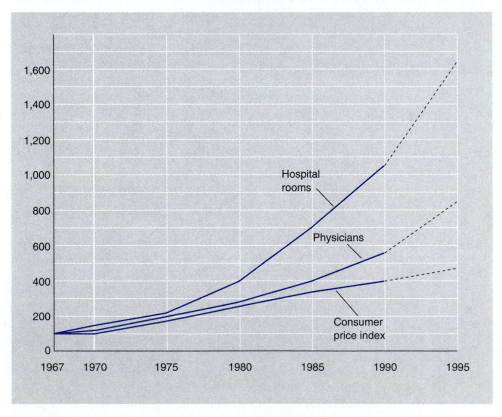

Since 1967, when all components of the Consumer Price Index are pegged at 100, the cost of hospital care and physicians' services have far outpaced overall consumer prices.

SOURCE: U.S. Bureau of Labor Statistics for 1967 to 1990; 1991 to 1995 data are estimates.

Health Care Inflation

Health care inflation has proven to be as stubborn as the common cold. A survey conducted by A. Foster Higgins and Co., a benefits consulting firm, reported that health care cost an average of $3,217 for each worker in 1990, an increase of 17.1 percent from 1989. The 1990 costs are almost double those for each worker in 1985.

The Department of Commerce reports that spending on medical care and health insurance accounted for more than 14 percent of after-tax income in 1990. In 1960, these costs were only 6 percent of after-tax income.

when inflation was less than 5 percent. Between 1965 and 1992, health costs (mainly for Medicare and Medicaid) rose from 2.6 to 16 percent of federal outlays. Some of the reasons for rising health care costs are beyond anyone's control. In 1992, 12.5 percent of the American population was over age 65, up from 9.8 percent in 1970 and up from less than 5 percent in 1900. The U.S. Census Bureau projects more than 20 percent of the population will be over the age of 65 by the year 2040.

The aging U.S. population is pushing up the demand for medical care. As Americans live longer, they are consuming more and more medical services. The effects of

FIGURE 7–2   **Effects of Demographic Change on Spending for Health Care: 1965 to 2040**

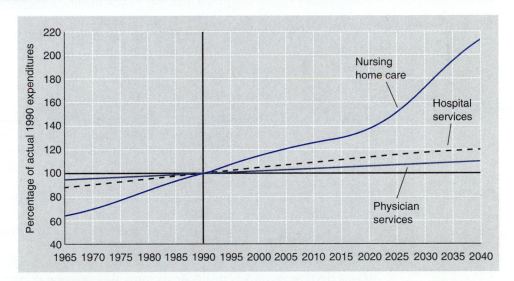

Using 1990 expenditures as a reference point, the Office of National Health Statistics plotted expenditures back to 1965 levels and estimated costs ahead to the year 2040. (The apparently sharper increases shown in Figure 7–1 result from the use of 1967 expenditures as a basis.)

SOURCE: Health Care Financing Administration, Office of the Actuary; Data from the Office of National Health Statistics; as shown in *Health Care Financing Review* (Fall 1992), 6.

the aging population compound the effects of increasing health care inflation. The federal Health Care Financing Administration estimates of this result are in Figure 7–2.

Across all demographic groups, demand has increased for quality health care and state-of-the-art treatment. Increases in the treatment of mental health problems, including drug and alcohol abuse, have also sharply added to medical costs. So have increases in the number of visits to doctors and the costs of prescriptions.

In most industries, technological advances result in lower costs. But in medicine, advances have traditionally been directed more at improving care than reducing expenses. Thus, new methods for treating patients often add significantly to the expense. Lifesaving but enormously expensive medical equipment—such as computerized tomographic scanners and magnetic resonance imaging, which give physicians detailed pictures of the body's interior—cost as much as $2 million each. Another problem is what economists call the "intensification of services." The heightened use of new diagnostic and life-prolonging technologies accounts for as much as 25 percent of annual cost inflation. Technological advances have enabled doctors to treat more patients with so-called catastrophic illnesses or injuries, which can cost hundreds of thousands of dollars per patient. These patients were given up as hopeless just a few years ago. Now transplants, implants, microsurgery, and bypasses are restoring life and health to many of them.

Doctors' expenses have continued to rise. Increased malpractice suits have caused insurance premiums to soar, and physicians pass along those added costs in higher fees. And because more patients are treated in doctors' offices instead of in hospitals, physicians say that their costs have gone up as they have added more technology, staff, and space to handle new in-office tests and procedures.

President Clinton presented a health-care reform plan before a Joint Session of Congress on September 22, 1993. As of this writing the bill is being discussed in Congress. The highlights of the Clinton plan are at the end of this chapter. This chapter discusses insurance as it existed in 1993. Passage of the Clinton health reform plan by Congress will necessitate an updated version.

Don't Risk Financial Disaster

The principle of **health insurance** is to protect individuals and their families against catastrophic medical bills. That means comprehensive, basic protection, which pays for hospitalization and certain other costs and protects individuals financially against a long bout with a complicated and expensive illness. About 37 million people, 13 percent of the nation, have no health insurance at all. Many of those who have health insurance have policies that offer only very limited coverage. After that coverage is depleted, a patient's assets—such as a home, savings, and pensions—may have to be liquidated to meet medical expenses.

A study released in January 1993 revealed that even more than finding a job or paying the rent, most Americans worry most about paying doctors and hospital bills.

One of the new responsibilities students face as they move from the campus to the workday world is making sure they are protected against health care costs. Students may be covered for a while if their parents have a family health insurance policy. The typical insurance program covers grown children who remain in the household up to a specified age, generally between 19 and 25, if they are full-time students. Students in this category should check their parents' policy to see if they are still covered.

SOURCE: "Pepper...and Salt," *The Wall Street Journal,* October 23, 1992, A-13. Reprinted by permission of Cartoon Features Syndicate.

A recent graduate who has no family coverage should consider a temporary short-term policy. Temporary insurance is designed specifically for people who are leaving school, looking for work, or between jobs. The policies run for 3, 6, 9, or 12 months. Rates are reasonably low because the policies are generally nonrenewable or renewable only once. This limits the risks to insurers.

Employer-Provided Health Care Benefits

For about two-thirds of Americans, protection against the high cost of routine health care and major illness is provided through employer-sponsored **group coverage** medical insurance plans. Not only are these plans paid for or subsidized by employers, but also the coverage is often superior to any that individuals could obtain from private insurers at a cost of $1,500 to $4,000 a year for a family. Most group plans are comprehensive so that individuals need not augment their coverage. But there can be gaps. It is therefore important to examine a group policy to determine what it does and does not cover before the need for medical services arises.

When you consider a job offer, get full details about the company's health care program. Examine the coverage being offered by the employer, and then add to it as your needs demand. Employer-sponsored group plans often present a bewildering array of health insurance options, and employees need to select the one that is best for them.

Surveys have shown that most people do not understand their benefits very well, even when employers carefully explain the details. These details have become part of the problem. Economic and social forces have led to the creation of ever more complex health, retirement, and disability benefits, with far more choices and options than anyone imagined even a decade ago. With the diverse array of new insurance options, many aimed at reducing employers' rising health costs, sorting out the choices is no simple matter. Choosing the wrong coverage could cost employees dearly in uncovered medical expenses that they will have to pay for themselves.

As your family grows, insurance needs and the way you use health care change. For example, if you have dental coverage, paying a higher premium for orthodontic treatment makes no sense when your children are out of braces. The changing needs of the adults in a family should also be considered. Every health insurance plan should be given a periodic checkup.

Individual Coverage

People who are self-employed, unemployed, or otherwise ineligible for group health insurance can still get individual or family protection. Individual health insurance policies cost more and generally cover less than group plans. Individuals may become eligible for group coverage through professional and fraternal organizations, which offer health insurance at group rates to their members. It may pay to join such an organization just for its group insurance coverage.

When shopping for **individual coverage,** the first policies to examine should be Blue Cross and Blue Shield plans. They are the largest and most established plans and generally set the standards for the industry. For most people, the indispensable coverage is a hospital policy plus a major medical or medical catastrophic policy, available from Blue Cross and Blue Shield as well as large commercial companies. Because Blue Cross and Blue Shield are nonprofit organizations, their rates are generally among the lowest and they may have a broader range of policies than other insurers. However, their products and plans vary from one area to the next, and so one cannot automatically assume that they always offer the best plan.

The Ingredients of Health Insurance Policies

To select a health plan, consumers must weigh the options available to them. They should also decide which plan they are comfortable with, both in terms of services available and physicians who will provide those services. Consumers need to

COBRA

The Consolidated Omnibus Reconciliation Act (COBRA) of 1986 is a federal law that lets people keep their policy at the same rates for at least 18 months after they lose their job, or if they leave voluntarily. (Those fired for cause are not entitled to continuation of insurance.) But COBRA exacts a price: the former employee must pay 100 percent of the premium plus 2 percent for administrative expenses. COBRA also guarantees coverage for a covered dependent who gets divorced or whose spouse dies.

determine their exact needs and also their budget constraints, not only for coverage but also for the portion of medical costs that will not be paid by insurance.

Before we can describe and compare various policy options, it is necessary to know some elementary health insurance terminology as well as the components of a policy. The following terms appear in many health plan policies and plan descriptions.

Basic Coverage

Basic coverage provides for hospitalization and many medical and surgical services. It is generally based on a set fee schedule for each type of service and often pays less than the total cost of the service.

Major Medical

Major medical is the backup coverage that is the keystone of a good insurance plan. It picks up when basic coverage runs out and pays the bulk of most hospital and medical costs and services in case of a long illness or serious injury, when costs can reach hundreds of thousands of dollars. It usually is offered in conjunction with a basic health insurance policy.

Comprehensive Major Medical

Comprehensive major medical is a policy that combines basic and major coverage into one plan. It usually has a very low deductible and is offered without any separate basic plan. Most company group plans have both basic and major medical coverage.

Deductibles

A **deductible** is the first dollar amount of coverage that a policyholder pays out of his or her own pocket each year before coverage begins. Naturally, the higher the deductible, the lower the premiums. A healthy person willing to risk a $500 or $1,000 deductible can dramatically reduce premiums. Some health insurance policies require more than one family member to meet the deductible before coverage for the whole family becomes effective. Often policyholders will have to pay a $100 deductible or more for each family member before the policy will start paying any claims.

Copayment

COPAYMENTS

Copayment or **coinsurance** is charged after the deductible is met each time a policyholder uses a health care service. For example, under an 80 percent coinsurance clause, after the policyholder pays the deductible, the health insurance plans generally pay up to 80 percent of the insurer's approved payment amount, leaving the policyholder to pay the other 20 percent as a copayment. A person in good health is generally better off with a policy that has a high copayment. For a person in poor health, accepting a higher deductible probably makes more sense if it means lower copayments for more frequent visits.

Henry's Financially Painful Surgery

Henry Wilson is scheduled to undergo minor surgery which costs $2,000, but his basic insurance policy's set fee for this particular procedure is $1,100. His policy additionally provides for a $300 deductible. Without major medical, the insurance company will pay 80 percent of $800 ($1,100 minus $300 deductible), which is $640. Henry must pay the difference between $2,000 and $640, which is $1,360. If Henry also has major medical, this will usually pay about 80 percent of the excess, minus the deductible, which is:

$$
\begin{array}{rl}
\$2,000 & \\
-\quad 300 & \text{deductible} \\
-\quad 640 & \text{basic coverage} \\
\hline
\$1,060 & \text{excess expenses} \\
\times\quad .80 & \\
\hline
\$848 & \text{major medical reimbursement}
\end{array}
$$

If Henry does not have major medical, he is inadequately covered. Notice that even with basic and major medical coverage, he receives only ($848 + $640) $1,488 reimbursement for a $2,000 surgery. Therefore, he will have to pay out of pocket $512 of expenses despite having both coverages.

Excess Major Medical

If a group health insurance plan pays most of the medical bills, an **excess major medical** policy is needed to take over where the group major medical insurance stops. The deductible amount of this policy should equal the maximum benefits paid under the group major medical plan. If your group major medical plan pays up to $30,000, for example, you could buy a $2,000,000 excess major medical policy with a $30,000 deductible. Such policies are relatively inexpensive but will provide that reassuring feeling that in the event of a major health crisis, there will be $2,000,000 backing you up.

Stop-Loss Provision

This is an important feature to look for with coinsurance. **Stop-loss privision** limits a policyholder's liability to a predetermined maximum, usually around $2,000 each calendar year. Once an insured pays $2,000 in copayments during a given year, the insurer will pay 100 percent of his or her medical expenses for the rest of that year, up to the limit of the insurance.

Preexisting Condition

Most companies limit coverage for **preexisting conditions**: those illnesses or diseases a buyer has when the policy is issued. The preexisting conditions clause acts as a gatekeeper, turning away those who want to buy the coverage because they know they need it.

Most policies define a preexisting condition as any health problem experienced by the policyholder in the six months prior to buying the policy. But some policies count back up to three years. If the insurance company sells a policy to a person with a preexisting condition, it sets a waiting period before coverage for that condition can begin. These periods range from six months to two years. Look carefully at preexisting condition clauses. Some policies make you wait two years for coverage, even if you had no knowledge of the problem.

Waivers

Many companies offer coverage to people with less-than-perfect health by applying **waivers,** which exclude coverage for any costs related to that condition or procedure. But buying a policy with a waiver for an illness that's likely to land you in a hospital is a waste of money. Waivers are characteristic of individual policies and are not usually found in group contracts.

Substandard Risk

Instead of waivers, some companies offer coverage at higher rates to people who have health problems. Depending on the severity of the illness or condition, a person who is considered a **substandard risk** could pay as much as 100 percent more than someone whose health qualified him or her for the company's standard rate. This is also generally found in individual policies but not in group policies.

Exclusions

Many policies do not cover (or place low limits on) certain medical conditions or treatments such as mental health costs, private nursing or nursing home costs, dental or optical services, hearing aids, cosmetic surgery, abortions, regular checkups, or preexisting conditions (see Figure 7–3). These exclusions can be very expensive items if patients have to pay for them themselves. Many policies have severe restrictions on stays in mental hospitals or at alcoholic and drug rehabilitation centers.

Supplemental insurance is available for such excluded services, but most policies are very expensive and so limited that they are not worth their costs.

Single Disease Coverage

Some health policies insure against a single disease only, such as cancer, or are otherwise highly restrictive. Such **single disease coverage** is a poor type of insurance. Policyholders should have comprehensive coverage for any kind of disease or injury.

Renewal Coverage

Renewal coverage is one of the most important health insurance considerations. Most health insurance policies are **guaranteed renewable,** a most desirable feature that insurance companies like to highlight in their sales literature. The company must renew coverage each time the policyholder pays the premium irrespective of the policyholder's current state of health. This guarantees a lifetime of renewability.

| FIGURE 7–3 | Survey of Health Plans on Selected Medical Treatments |

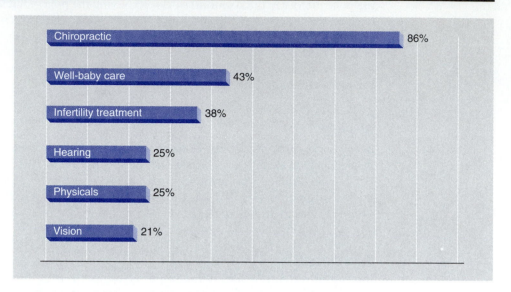

Shown are the percentages of employers' fee-for-service health care plans that offer coverage for several types of medical coverage.

SOURCE: Foster Higgins Health Care Benefits Survey, 1991.

The next best thing is a policy that is **conditionally renewable.** The insurer cannot cancel the policy unless all policies of that classification in the state are canceled. That could happen if an insurance company discovers it is losing money on this type of coverage. A policy that makes renewal contingent upon periodic physical examinations or that can be dropped at the company's option is likely to leave a person without insurance just when he or she needs it most.

Maximum Benefit Limit

The policy's dollar limit, or **maximum benefit limit,** on claims per year or per illness is a main indicator of its true value. Typical limits range from as low as $25,000 for basic coverage policies to as high as $2,000,000 for excess major medical policies. This is far more important than the clause stating a policy will pay $20 or $30 for every visit to the doctor.

The Main Types of Health Plans

Workers are often offered a health plan by their employer that will give them either broad coverage but few choices as to their doctor, hospital, and level of care—known as **managed care health plans**—or more choices but narrower coverage—known as **traditional fee-for-service health plans.** Here are the typical options.

Traditional Fee-for-Service Plan (Indemnity Insurance)

There are two key parts to a policyholder's protection in traditional fee-for-service plans. The first is basic coverage and the second is major medical coverage. Increasingly, basic and major medical coverage are packaged and offered as a single comprehensive policy.

These plans pay a set amount of money per doctor's office visit and per day an insured is hospitalized and lump sums based on a fixed schedule for surgical fees, regardless of the actual cost. If surgery costs $4,000 and the indemnity schedules pay only $2,500 for the operation, the insured has to pay the $1,500 difference plus the deductible and copayment, as explained previously. If the policyholder also has major medical, it will take over where the indemnity left off and pay the extra $1,500.

Many services are readily reimbursed, but cost-conscious insurers and employers (who pay most of the bills) are demanding more and more justification before certain procedures or a hospital stay is authorized. Requiring second opinions for surgery is now commonplace.

In a fee-for-service plan, the patient generally pays the doctor directly and the insurer reimburses or indemnifies the patient. The patient accepts the chore of dealing with insurance forms in exchange for the freedom of being able to select his or her own doctor and being treated in the doctor's own office. Some physicians accept direct payment from the insurance company and also handle the paperwork involved in submitting the claim forms. Policyholders who contract a serious, rare disease or condition, for example, can search the country for the best specialists, and the plan will cover and reimburse them according to a predetermined fee schedule. At a growing number of companies, employees can select from a variety of fee-for-service plans. They might, for example, be able to choose a lower deductible and lower premium and have to spend more out of their own pocket only if they accumulate thousands of dollars in health bills. That may sound like a good deal for healthy people, but in the long run policyholders are better off protecting themselves and their family against high out-of-pocket costs.

Managed Care Health Plans

Insurance companies have been trying for some time to move American workers out of traditional fee-for-service health plans. Businesses are becoming increasingly concerned that skyrocketing employee health benefits may hurt their ability to compete at home and abroad. As a result, many companies are searching for ways to save money on their employee health insurance packages and to transfer a portion of expenses to employees.

The rising costs of health care have brought intense pressures on the health care industry to provide less expensive services. For many people, a less expensive alternative to traditional insurance is a managed care health plan. Employers, worried about exploding health care costs, have been leaning more and more toward managed care health plans options and away from the traditional free-choice or fee-for-service plans that let patients choose their own doctor.

Many insurers—including Cigna, Metropolitan Life, and Prudential—have stepped up pressure on companies to shed the traditional free-choice indemnity plans. Insurers are shocking clients with rate increases of 25 percent or more or are even refusing to renew the plans at any price. These efforts will likely continue the trend away from free-choice plans. For many families, the traditional free-choice plan means contributing a bigger share of the premiums, receiving more limited coverage, and being charged higher deductibles. As a result, many families have been persuaded to switch to a managed care plan.

Health Maintenance Organizations (HMOs)   The most common form of managed health plan is the **health maintenance organization**. An **HMO** provides a wide range of comprehensive health care services to a voluntarily enrolled population. Covered individuals receive care from specified providers who receive a fixed prepaid fee per member, rather than on a fee-for-service basis. HMOs may serve both as health care insurers and as providers of health services to subscribers. Traditional insurers concentrate only on financing health care, while insured individuals seek out their own providers.

HMOs either have a group of hired physicians at a particular site or have a group of self-employed physicians in an area who are part of the plan and who typically receive a fixed price for a visit from patients. The HMO group of doctors provides all of an insured's health care. Depending on the group, everything from medical and dental services to vision care and medications is provided for one annual fee with some minor copayment charges, generally no more than about $2 to $7 per visit.

HMOs, which provide comprehensive medical coverage for a fixed prepaid monthly fee, grew at a snail's pace for decades after the opening of the first one in Los Angeles in 1929. During the 1980s and 1990s, as the emphasis on containment of health costs has grown rapidly, so has the enrollment in HMOs (see Figure 7–4).

Today, the number of people participating in health care delivery systems outside of traditional insurance plans continues to grow dramatically. Between 1984 and 1987, for instance, free-choice plans dropped from 96 to 40 percent of insurers' group business, according to the Health Insurance Association of America, a trade group of health insurers. Faced with traditional insurance rate increases averaging 20 percent a year, employees have been switching to HMOs. Currently, HMOs are generally offered alongside the fee-for-service plans so that employees can choose. In the future, fee-for-service plans choice may cease to be an option, as we will see later in this chapter.

Blue Cross and Blue Shield, the nation's largest provider of health insurance with more than 80 million subscribers, has become a leading sponsor of HMOs. Federal legislation mandates that an employer of 25 or more workers that offers conventional health insurance must offer HMO coverage as an option, if a federally qualified HMO is located nearby and if at least one representative approaches the employer.

However, the recent surge in the number and size of HMOs has caused some problems. Since the late 1970s, dozens of federally qualified HMOs around the country have suffered losses, become insolvent, or collapsed from financial mismanagement. The industry is currently undergoing restructuring, which may lead to an industry consisting of fewer but larger, better managed, and more cost-efficient firms.

Types of HMOs   There are two basic types of HMOs: the group-staff model and the independent practice association (IPA).

The original HMOs, and those that still tend to be the most successful, are groups of physicians and other health care professionals hired and paid on a salaried or contractual basis who deliver comprehensive services at one or more centralized

FIGURE 7–4	The Rising Enrollment in HMOs

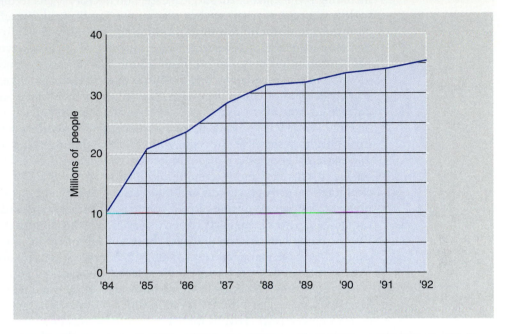

SOURCE: Industry estimates, for 1984 to 1985; *Statistical Abstract of the United States: 1992,* Table No. 156, for 1986 to 1991; editorial estimate for 1992.

facilities. This type of HMO is called the **group-staff model**. A premium paid monthly or quarterly covers most care, which is provided by a **primary care physician** who will usually hear patients' medical problems, examine them, and then treat them or decide whether they should see a specialist or be hospitalized.

More than half of all HMOs are **independent practice associations (IPA)**, in which the insured prepays the premium. A network of doctors in private practice, affiliated with the plan, is paid by the HMO on an agreed fee-for-service schedule. The doctors, in turn, agree to provide care to HMO subscribers in their own offices as well as to their regular fee-paying patients.

The chief advantages are a wider choice of physicians and the possibility of retaining one's regular doctor, since some doctors in private practice also participate in IPAs. Both types of HMOs generally preserve the traditional arrangement of one patient, one physician. When policyholders enroll, they either must select a primary care doctor from a list or have one assigned to them (a "gatekeeper"), and they may not see any other doctor until they see him or her. If policyholders choose another doctor, they get no coverage. If they are not satisfied, they can choose again or request to be reassigned.

HMOs: Pros and Cons The main reason for joining an HMO is the simple prospect of saving money at no threat to the quality of health care. While monthly premiums for HMOs are about the same as for standard insurance, the difference is that HMOs cover virtually all costs after that. As a rule, they provide unlimited hospital care, including room and board, surgical care, and doctors' visits to the hospital—with no or low charges over subscriber premiums. Traditional free-choice plans almost always have deductibles or coinsurance provisions and require patients to pay a percentage, generally 20 percent of most bills. Most also have ceilings on dollar payments and limits on the maximum number of days of hospitalization coverage.

Another potential saving with HMOs is time. Patients do not encounter the paperwork and reimbursement delay that come when they visit their fee-for-service doctor and file a claim with a traditional health insurance company.

How can HMOs provide more comprehensive coverage for less cost than traditional health insurance? To begin with, offices, laboratories, diagnostic equipment, and patients' records are often under one roof. Health care delivered in a clinical setting is inherently more economical. In addition, an HMO can minimize costs by avoiding overuse of hospitals and unnecessary treatments, stressing outpatient and home health care, requiring second opinions on surgery, and ordering fewer laboratory tests. Doctors in an HMO receive salaries, which means that they have no incentive to run up bills. Although HMOs have not succeeded in containing rising health costs, they have managed to provide health care at significantly lower rates per worker than traditional fee-for-service plans, as shown in Figure 7–5.

An important feature of HMOs is indicated in their name: health maintenance. Since consumers pay a flat fee for all health care, it is in the interest of the HMO to detect illnesses early. HMOs therefore keep expenses down by emphasizing preventive care and surpass conventional insurance in covering checkups, routine child care examinations, and other early detection medical exams. Traditional insurances usually do not cover routine periodic physicals, well-baby care, or immunizations. HMOs provide such services and even sponsor free health education classes and exercise clinics.

The better HMOs offer more than cost savings; they also have a built-in quality control mechanism. Because patients' medical records are in one place, every doctor the patient sees can refer to them. Doctors are thereby subject to a healthy kind of peer review. In addition, the staff of general practice physicians and specialists can consult one another. Patients do not have to search for a specialist on the outside.

However, HMOs do have potential drawbacks. Some people shun HMOs because they would rather select their own doctors. A patient can visit a doctor outside the HMO's framework only if the group cannot provide what he or she needs and one of the HMO's own doctors gives a referral. This provision could create serious problems if a family member has a major medical problem. Sometimes it may take weeks to get a referral letter from an HMO physician. (In an emergency, of course, patients may get care wherever they find it.) Also, at many HMOs, patient-physician relationships are impersonal. Patients see different physicians from visit to visit, even for the same ailment. Some HMO members complain of long waits for routine appointments.

To trim costs, HMOs emphasize a team approach to medicine. Doctors work closely with physician assistants and nurse practitioners, who perform many of the routine tests and exams done by physicians in traditional settings. If you prefer to have a physician handle all of your medical concerns or if you require a great deal of attention and reassuring from a physician, you may be dissatisfied with HMO care.

Critics of HMOs charge that top-quality care cannot be possible in organizations that are striving to keep costs low. HMOs often do not cover substance abuse

| FIGURE 7–5 | Costs of Fee-for-Service Plans Outpace Costs of HMOs |

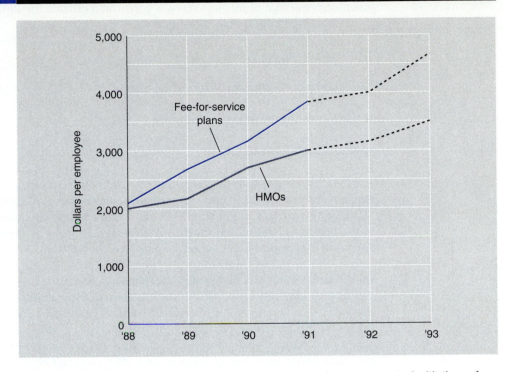

The costs of health benefits for fee-for-service plans are shown contrasted with those for HMOs. Costs shown are the average cost per U.S. employee.

SOURCE: Foster Higgins Health Care Benefits Survey, 1991; industry estimates. 1992 to 1993 are estimates.

services or psychiatric care. They may have restrictions on out-of-town coverage and may only partially cover prescription drugs. Critics also claim that they may put more emphasis on costs than on care by sending patients home from the hospital earlier than is medically advisable.

Studies by the American Medical Association and Johns Hopkins University, however, concluded that the quality of medical care in HMOs is generally as good as that of traditional fee-for-service medicine or even better. But HMOs, like doctors and hospitals, range from superlative to poor. Individuals without group health insurance may also find HMOs an attractive alternative to health insurance, although the majority of HMOs accept only group membership.

Preferred Provider Organizations (PPOs) **Preferred provider organizations** give employees the option of using a network of "preferred" doctors and hospitals, often for a small copayment per visit. PPOs are a cross between the HMO and traditional fee-for-service insurance. They provide a full range of HMO services but follow the IPA model. In exchange for being included on the PPO's list, cooperating doctors and hospitals agree to accept discounted fees for treating those who have PPO coverage.

If the employee wishes to visit a doctor not on the list, the PPO provides limited insurance coverage of medical services performed outside the PPO network.

PPOs offer the following enticements:

1. No or low deductibles

2. Flat $10 or $15 payment for office visits

3. Coverage for preventive health care

4. Low monthly premiums

PPOs have been growing rapidly over the past few years because they allow employees to save money but still preserve some freedom of choice.

When the growth in PPOs, HMOs, and other managed care plans is compared to the decline in traditional indemnity coverage, it looks as though the traditional approach may soon be a thing of the past (see Figure 7–6).

Traditional Fee-for-Service Managed Health Programs Some traditional health insurance delivery systems are now also practicing **managed care health plans**. Patients still choose their physicians, but the system requires stringent cost-containment measures—such as hospital preadmission authorization, where a panel of physicians agrees on a patient's proposed hospitalization and treatment—and second opinions are mandated before elective surgery, and often required before any surgery.

General Motors (in 1985) took the lead in offering its employees a "triple option," where workers can choose either HMOs, PPOs, or traditional insurance with managed care cost-containment procedures. Other companies have followed the GM lead. No one form of prepaid insurance coverage is inherently superior, but personal preference may make you more comfortable with one type than with another.

When companies present employees with a choice of health plans, the employees must decide which plan is best for their individual needs. Figure 7–7 presents a comparison of four health plans offered annually to employees of the County of Nassau in New York. Employees have the option of switching from one plan to another once a year.

The Cafeteria Plan

The fastest-growing trend in employee benefits is the **cafeteria plan**. Instead of plunging workers with diverse needs into one big pot of fixed benefits, companies are giving them a menu of various benefits and letting them pick and choose, thus the term "cafeteria."

Many companies give their employees "credits," or a budget to buy the benefits they want, across a wide range of choices and prices. The employees pay, with paycheck deductions, for the expense of all coverage that exceeds the total of their credits. A worker might choose, for example, to forgo dental coverage that would cost $250 a year and use the money instead to buy lower-deductible medical coverage or extra life insurance protection. The cafeteria style plan is likely to become widespread in the coming years.

FIGURE 7–6   **Changing Sources of Health Care**

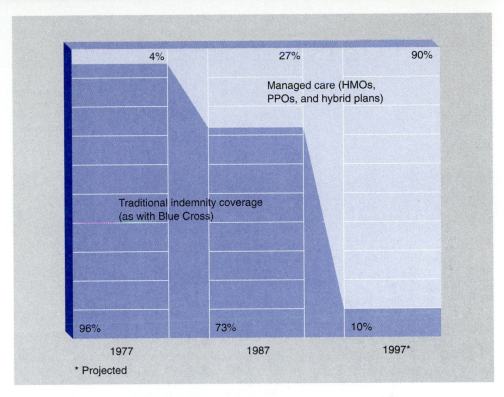

According to industry estimates, the ratio of coverage between managed care and the traditional indemnity approach will have flip-flopped in less than 20 years.

SOURCE: Hewitt Associates, 1990.

Table 7–1 provides a price comparison among the four types of plans in 1991.

Medicare

The federal government provides health insurance for 34 million people who qualify. The **Medicare** program is a federal health insurance program created in 1965 to ease the financial burden of health care for Americans 65 years and older and for other qualifying Social Security recipients.

Medicare pays only a part of health care bills. (See Table 7–2) The Catastrophic Care Act passed by Congress in 1988 filled most major gaps in Medicare coverage for extended hospital stays. The program was dubbed "catastrophic coverage" because it was designed to reduce the odds of a beneficiary being driven into bankruptcy by hospital costs. However, this act imposed a surtax on retired people to

FIGURE 7–7	Sample Comparison of Four Health Plans

This fictional comparison, simplified to save space, shows how some employers may organize descriptions of the employees' options among different health care providers. The full comparison would also likely cover physical therapy, X rays, lab tests, maternity care, ambulance use, chiropractic care, psychiatric care, treatment for substance abuse, hearing aids, and other topics.

Services	Emerald Plan	Ruby Plan	Sapphire Plan	Zircon Plan
	Core plan with enhancements.	Must use services of HMO physicians and facilities except in cases of emergencies.	Must use services provided or authorized by a Medical Group Physician.	All services must be medically necessary and authorized by the Primary Care Physician.
Hospitalization (semiprivate room, board, etc.)	Paid in full 365 days per spell of illness for medical or surgical care; 120 days per spell of illness for pulmonary tuberculosis or psychiatric care in a general or public hospital.	Unlimited days. Psychiatric care, 30 days per calendar year.	Covered in full 365 days each year.	Fully covered, unlimited days; private room when medically necessary.
Hospital Outpatient Care— Accident & Emergency Illness	Paid in full within 72 hours of an accident or within 24 hours of the onset of a medical emergency.	Paid in full within 72 hours of an accident or within 12 hours of an emergency illness.	Paid in full within 72 hours of an injury or within 12 hours of an emergency illness.	Fully covered after $25 copayment (fee waived if admitted into hospital).
Medical/ Surgical	Paid-in-full benefits through Emerald Plan participating providers. Major medical coverage for nonparticipating providers: Annual deductible—$300 individual, $900 family maximum. Maximum enrollee copayment of $1,500 per family per year. Annual lifetime maximums of $1,00,000.	Covered in full when arranged and provided by medical group physicians.	Covered in full.	Fully covered when services rendered on an in-patient basis. Doctor's office visits fully covered after $10 copayment.
Prescription Drugs	$5 copayment at participating pharmacies. At nonparticipating pharmacies, the lesser of the actual charge minus $5, or average cost plus dispensing fee minus $5.	Covered in full when arranged and provided by medical group physicians.	Covered in full.	Fully covered when services rendered on an in-patient basis. Doctor's office visits fully covered after $10 copayment.
Ambulance	Provided by admitting hospital: paid in full. Professional: $50 plus major medical coverage. Voluntary: $75 over 50 miles, $50 under 50 miles.	Covered in full when ordered by Plan physician or in a covered emergency.	Covered in full when ordered by a Medical Group Physician.	Fully covered.

TABLE 7–1	The Costs of Care

Shown is the average cost per employee for each of four types of plans. This data comes from an industry survey conducted in 1991.

Plan	Cost
Fee-for-service	$3,573
Preferred provider	3,355
Point-of-service	3,291
HMO	3,046

Source: Foster Higgins Health Care Benefits Survey, 1991.

help finance its cost. This surtax aroused such a storm of protest from senior citizen groups that Congress repealed the act in November 1989.

Medicare Exclusions

Medicare does not provide total protection from potentially crushing medical bills. Neither does it ease the financial burden of long-term nursing home patients. It covers only short-term nursing home care that consists of actual medical attention prescribed by a physician.

Medicare additionally pays nothing for (1) eyeglasses, (2) hearing aids, (3) private duty nurses, (4) most immunizations, (5) routine physical exams, (6) dental care, (7) foot care, (8) eye examinations, (9) hearing exams, and (10) medical care outside of the United States.

Medicare recipients consequently need to supplement their medical coverage with private health insurance. This is available in policies specifically designed for Medicare recipients, known as Medigap policies.

Medicare Tax

Since January 1, 1991, employed persons have had to pay 1.45 percent of their income up to $125,000 for a new Medicare tax. Before 1991, the Medicare tax was part of the larger Social Security tax and was levied on only the first $51,300 of a wage earner's income. This Medicare tax is matched by a worker's employer. Self-employed individuals pay their own 1.45 percent as well as the employer's half, or 2.9 percent.

Medigap: Medicare Supplement Insurance

A **Medigap policy** is a private health insurance policy for Medicare recipients, designed to supplement Medicare. Such policies typically pay an amount equal to Medicare's basic hospitalization deductible, plus much of the difference between what Medicare allows for medical bills and what doctors actually charge. Group

TABLE 7–2	Medicare Benefits

Effective January 1, 1991, Medicare covers the following medical expenses:

Service	Medicare Benefits
Medicare: Part A	
Hospital care in the United States per benefit period (pays for semi-private room, plus lab work, operating room, X rays, rehabilitation, and other services)	
1 to 60 days	All charges except the deductible of $652
61 to 90 days	All charges except coinsurance of $157 per day
90 days and beyond	No coverage except for "Medicare Lifetime Reserve Days." Medicare pays nothing for any stay longer than 90 days unless patients choose to use some of their Medicare Lifetime Reserve Days. Medicare provides 60 Lifetime Reserve Days for inpatients that eligible patients can use at their option when no other benefits are available. Once used, they are never available again.
Medicare lifetime reserve days	All charges except coinsurance of $296 per day during 60 nonrenewable Lifetime Reserve Days. No coverage is given after the 60 Medicare Lifetime Reserve Days have been used.
Skilled nursing care	Covers 100 days of skilled nursing care for each spell of illness, but only after the patient has been in a hospital for 3 days. Copayments are required for each day of care between 21 and 100 days.
Blood	The cost of all blood in a hospital or skilled nursing facility, except the first 3 pints
Medicare: Part B	
All Part B services are subject to a $100 calendar-year deductible. Thereafter coverage includes:	
Physician services and supplies	80 percent of "Medicare-approved charges"
Blood	The cost of all blood except the first 3 pints

policies (such as those offered to members of the American Association of Retired Persons) are often less expensive than individual coverage. Medigap premiums range from $300 to $1,200 per year.

The problem of adequate health insurance coverage plagues many older Americans. For most, the switch from a company group health plan to Medicare comes with retirement. Unfortunately, the change often brings a barrage of high-pressure salespeople and "Medi-scare" mail, trying to frighten senior citizens into hastily purchasing coverage that may be both expensive and unnecessary. All too many people give in to these tactics. In 1978 the Federal Trade Commission estimated that older Americans waste as much as $1 billion per year buying unneeded health insurance to supplement Medicare.

Medicare recipients should research, compare, and inspect Medigap policies as they would any other insurance policy. Most Medigap policies cover the $652 hospitalization deductibles and extended hospital stays, as well as doctors' bills in excess of Medicare's maximums for particular services.

To help simplify the hunt for Medigap insurance, the National Association of Insurance Commissions (NAIC) in 1990 established new minimum benefit standards upgrading those of former years. The following are among the benefits that all Medigap policies must now deliver:

1. A choice between covering all of Medicare's $652 hospital deductible or none of it. (Insurers used to offer a whole range of deductibles.)

2. The $157 per day copayments that Medicare does not cover for semiprivate rooms during days 61 through 90 of a hospital stay.

3. The $296 per day copayments that Medicare does not cover for hospital services and supplies, such as drugs, X rays, and lab tests, during a person's lifetime reserve days.

4. The 90 percent of Medicare-approved expenses for 365 days of hospitalization once Medicare's lifetime reserve coverage has been used up.

5. The 20 percent of Medicare-approved fees for doctors and related services and supplies, after a $100 annual deductible. Medicare, as stated, pays only 80 percent of allowed charges.

In 1990, Congress passed tough legislation to protect the 24 million older Americans who buy Medigap policies. As of August 1992, newly offered policies must conform to the following standards:

1. All insurers must offer a standard package of different insurance policies to be established by NAIC. The standard packages will make it easier to compare and choose packages.

2. Agents or mail order companies who knowingly sell Medigap policies to people who already have one and intend to keep it will face penalties.

Give Your Health Plan a Thorough Checkup

Questions to Ask Before Enrolling in a Health Plan

Your choice of health care plans will be made easier if you ask your company's benefit planner for help in answering the following questions:

1. When does coverage start?
2. Does the plan have payment limits? (Reimbursements are often set at daily, yearly, or lifetime amounts, which may apply to specific illnesses or services or across the board. After such limits are met, you begin paying out of your own pocket. This is most likely to happen if there is a chronic condition in your family.)
3. How much are the copayments and deductibles? (These clauses require you to share in the costs. Even HMOs may have such clauses.)
4. How many family members must meet the deductible before benefits begin?
5. What happens in an emergency or if patients need after-hours care? (Is prompt help available at the plan's offices or over the phone? Can patients use any other facilities during an emergency?)
6. How much choice do you have in selecting a doctor or hospital? (Generally, HMOs limit the choices more than traditional plans do, but the amount of flexibility varies greatly.)
7. Do the hospitals you favor, or does your family doctor, participate in the plans you are considering? Will they accept a plan's rates as full payment?
8. How many days of hospital care does the policy cover per illness or per year? (Top policies will pay for a 365-day stay.)
9. Is there dental coverage?
10. Is there mental health coverage?
11. What are the plan's preventive care programs? (Even if you do not want a program in nutrition or stopping to smoke, the availability of such programs is often a sign of the quality of medical service offered.)
12. Is coverage updated to keep up with inflation?
13. If a policyholder leaves the company, can he or she convert the group policy into an individual one?
14. How many patients are on a doctor's roster? (The larger the number, the less time the doctor will have for each individual.)
15. How many specialists are in the group, and what are their qualifications? (Are they board certified, with advanced training and testing, or merely general practitioners who concentrate in one area?)
16. Must visits to specialists (such as gynecologists or ophthalmologists) within the group be authorized by the primary care physician?
17. Does the plan cover corrective lenses, eyeglasses, contact lenses, and corrective eye surgery?
18. How soon can I get an appointment? (Patients should normally be able to see a doctor within 24 hours for an urgent problem and within two weeks for a routine visit.)

"Do you have any 'Get-Well-if-You-Can-Afford-It' cards?"

SOURCE: "Pepper...and Salt," *The Wall Street Journal,* March 4, 1992, A-13. Reprinted by permission of Cartoon Features Syndicate.

3. Insurers cannot cancel or refuse to renew a policy because of a policyholder's health or for any reason other than unpaid premiums or misrepresentations.

4. Strict limits were placed on agents' first-year commissions. This is aimed at discouraging attempts to sell retirees new policies each new year.

5. Insurance companies are required to pay out at least 65 cents of every premium dollar in benefits to policyholders.

Long-Term Care Insurance

A major fear of growing old is the cost of long-term care for people too feeble or crippled by illness to look after themselves, an ongoing expense that can quickly deplete resources built up over a lifetime. The fear of going broke in a nursing home and having to turn to public assistance haunts many independent elderly people.

This fear may be realistic. The biggest catastrophic health expense for which many older Americans have no insurance is the long-term care required when age, illness, or disability renders them dependent. Most Americans have done little or nothing to prepare for the high risk of needing long-term care, or its catastrophic cost. A Brookings Institution study showed that in 1986, about 2.3 million of the 31.2 million Americans 65 years of age and older spent at least part of a year in a nursing home. The study estimated that 35 to 50 percent of all the elderly would spend some time in a nursing home.

In 1987 a congressional subcommittee on aging found that 70 to 80 percent of nursing-home residents used up all of their capital in a year or so and were forced onto welfare. The cost can be crushing. At average rates, nursing homes charge $30,000 a year, and the fees are escalating and outpacing inflation.

Medicare pays for skilled nursing home care in Medicare-approved facilities for only 100 days. After that, Medicare pays nothing. And Medicare does not cover stays in nursing homes where medical care is not the principal service.

Almost half the cost of long-term care is borne by **Medicaid**, the medical assistance program for the indigent financed jointly by the federal and state governments. But before a person can become eligible, assets, including life savings, must be pared down to a minimum level which amounts to virtual impoverishment.

Growing numbers of insurance companies are offering long-term policies that are more comprehensive and affordable than earlier versions. They are designed to cover a large chunk of the costs of long-term care. Before discussing long-term care insurance, let us examine the long-term care facilities that are provided under these policies.

Types of Long-Term Care Facilities

Most insurers divide long-term care facilities into three main categories: **skilled**, **intermediate**, and **custodial**, defined as follows:

1. *Skilled Care Nursing* This is medically necessary care provided by licensed, skilled medical professionals, such as nurses and therapists, working under a doctor's supervision. Such care must be prescribed by a doctor and be available 24 hours a day. These facilities are licensed by the state, and daily medical records are kept on each patient. Restoring the patient to a condition approximating his or her state of health before the illness or accident is the goal.

2. *Intermediate Care* These facilities provide supervision by a physician and skilled nursing care to keep the patient stabilized. The care is provided intermittently, rather than continuously, over a prescribed period. The level of care is somewhat less than that given in a skilled care facility. For example, a nurse may be on hand only to give patients injections and medications or to change bandages.

3. *Custodial Care* Even without any disabling illness or injury, many elderly people reach a stage when such routine activities as getting out of bed, walking, eating, bathing, and dressing become difficult or impossible for them. Supervised custodial care may become necessary. It may be performed by people without professional skills or training, but some insurance policies require that the facility be licensed. Benefits cover mainly room and board plus payments for assistance with daily living.

The Long-Term Care Policy

Private insurance policies can in theory meet the increasingly urgent need for **long-term care coverage** at a moderate cost. But in reality many of these insurance policies are very expensive, severely limited in their coverage, or both. Like any competing products, long-term policies have contingencies and options that fit the needs of one person but are inappropriate for another. Whether you want to consider such coverage for yourself or for an aging family member, it is essential to have the facts.

Nursing home coverage can be for as little as two years or as long as a "lifetime," with a cap that can range from $12,000 to $200,000. Long-term care insurance pays a set amount each day for a specified period of time, provided that a policyholder stays in what is called a "covered nursing facility." Unlike other kinds of health insurance, these policies usually do not reimburse the policyholder for fees actually charged. Coverage is essentially an indemnity type. That is, insurers pay a fixed sum (typically, $50 to $100) per day rather than a percentage of the fees customary in the community.

Inflation Rider   The fixed benefit is one major drawback of nearly all such policies. An indemnity policy tends to become outdated almost as soon as it is bought. If you buy a policy today and enter a nursing home 10 years from now, you may find that the benefit pays a much smaller part of the actual cost than you thought it would when you bought the policy. Therefore, look for a policy with a rider that adjusts the benefit annually for inflation. If a policy has no index for inflation, the policyholder must try to guess how much protection will be enough many years in the future.

Nonforfeiture Clause   This clause provides for the insurer to return some of the premiums paid over the years in the event the insured stops paying premiums. As an alternative, the clause can provide that in the event the insured stops paying premiums, the insurer will guarantee prorated benefits based on the amount that was paid in. This clause guarantees that your premiums paid will not be wasted if for whatever reason you stop paying further premiums.

Confinement Must Be Medically Required   Long-term care policies do not provide blanket coverage for an extended nursing home stay simply because the family believes that a frail elderly person would be better off in such surroundings. Before any level of care is covered, it must be defined as medically necessary or be preceded by a medical event. Then, depending on the beneficiary's condition and the terms of the policy, care proceeds through applicable stages: skilled, intermediate, or custodial.

Very few people need skilled care for long periods. Much of the care in nursing homes is intermediate or custodial. Stroke victims, in particular, often require a long period of custodial care while recovering. Most policies provide three or four consecutive years' coverage for skilled and intermediate care facilities. This should be adequate for most people. Custodial care costs are paid for as few as 60 days and as long as five years. The longer the coverage, the more attractive the policy.

Prior Hospitalization Prerequisite for Eligibility   A policy may or may not cover all three types of care, and different policies may define the three types of facilities differently. Entry to one level is sometimes contingent upon a period of confinement in another. Some policies require that nursing home care be preceded by a hospital stay of at least three days. Furthermore, the person must check into the nursing home within a certain period after checking out of the hospital. However, policies differ in the maximum number of days that may elapse between hospital discharge and nursing home admittance. That period is usually 30 days, but it can be as short as 14 days or as long as 90 days. As of 1988, the above provision that requires prior hospitalization before benefits are paid for long-term care was declared illegal in 32 states for new policies. Old policies (issued prior to 1988) may still contain such a provision, but most new policies no longer require it.

Premiums Premiums are determined by the benefits available, by an applicant's age, and sometimes by his or her health. Once a policy is issued, most companies guarantee that the premium will remain the same for life regardless of a policy-holder's health or advancing age. In 1991 a 65-year-old in good health on average paid $1,015 a year for basic policies that covered skilled and custodial care. Figure 7–8 shows premiums for long-term care policies with inflation protection and non-forfeiture clauses.

FIGURE 7–8	Advancing Years and Rising Premiums

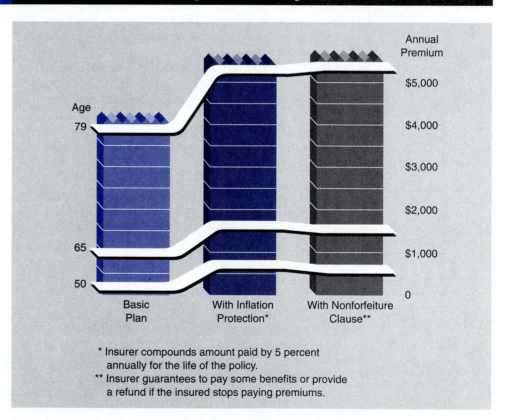

* Insurer compounds amount paid by 5 percent annually for the life of the policy.
** Insurer guarantees to pay some benefits or provide a refund if the insured stops paying premiums.

Premiums for policies with inflation protection and nonforfeiture clauses are significantly more expensive than for a basic policy.

SOURCE: Health Insurance Association of America, 1991.

Asking the Right Questions

If you are considering a policy for yourself or an aging parent, ask insurance agents the following questions:

1. Is the whole spectrum of nursing care covered?
2. What does coverage cost?
3. When do benefits begin?
4. Are benefits adjusted for inflation?
5. How long do benefits last?

More than 100 life insurance companies specializing in universal life insurance (discussed in Chapter 9) offer a rider that allows the policy's death benefit to be "prepaid" to a living policyholder to help cover nursing home expenses. First developed by National Travelers Life in 1987, these long-term health care riders are being sold at an additional cost of between 5 and 15 percent of the base policy premiums and stipulate that the company will pay out a percentage of the death benefit in monthly installments directly to a policyholder in a nursing home. These riders represent only a redistribution of benefits, not an increase in total coverage. Every dollar policyholders receive to defray nursing home expenses is subtracted from the money that will come to their beneficiaries. Some insurance companies are disturbed by the idea of a husband inadvertently pauperizing his widow-to-be during a long nursing home stay and therefore will not prepay more than half the death benefit in this fashion.

Whether nursing home insurance is suitable for you depends mostly on your age, health, and financial condition. In general, such coverage is not such a good deal for people in their fifties and early sixties, despite the low premiums at those ages, because the risk of having to check into a nursing home is small. But the chances of needing nursing home care increase dramatically with age. People approaching old age, or their children, should consider preparing and planning for this contingency.

Table 7–3 can be used as a guide to evaluate long-term care insurance policies.

Disability Income Insurance

Disability insurance provides for regular periodic payments to a person who is unable to work as a result of long-term illness, injury, or permanent disability. This may well be the most neglected area of insurance.

Most Americans do not have a long-term disability policy. Either they have not thought about it or they think that their employer and Social Security offer enough coverage. Many people are hard pressed to describe exactly what kind of disability coverage they have. Only about 30 percent of all working Americans have private long-term disability insurance to protect their earnings in the event of illness or injury. The 70 percent majority is taking much more risk than it may realize.

TABLE 7–3	A Quick Guide to Policy Quality

Policy Feature	Good	Fair	Poor
Daily Benefits What a policy pays for each day of care in a nursing home.	$60–$120	$60–$100.	$60 or less
Cost-of-care adjustment A policy rider that raises benefits each year by a set percentage, not tied to the rate of inflation, to adjust for rising nursing home costs.	Yes, 5% or more a year over 15 years or longer	Yes, 5% or more for a maximum of 10 years	None
Level premium A premium that remains constant over time.	Yes	Yes	No, can rise with age
Guaranteed renewable for life A clause that guarantees to renew coverage as long as the premium is paid.	Yes	Yes	No, insurer has right to terminate policy
Maximum benefit period The maximum number of days the policy will cover nursing home stays or home-care benefits.	Unlimited	1,825 days (5 years) to 2,555 days (7 years)	730 days (2 years) to 1,095 days (3 years)
Waiting period The number of days a policyholder must be in a facility before benefits begin.	0–20 days	20–60 days	Over 60 days
Type of institutional care covered Defines the kinds of nursing homes that a policy covers: skilled-care facility, intermediate-care facility, or custodial-care facility.	All types, same policy terms and daily benefit	All types, but reduced benefits for custodial care	Skilled nursing-home care only
Prior-hospitalization rule Whether a hospital stay, usually a minimum of three days, is required before long-term care costs will be covered.	No	No	Yes; must move to nursing home within 30 days
Prior skilled-nursing rule Whether time in a skilled nursing-care facility is required before custodial care is covered.	No	No	Yes
Home-care benefit Coverage for the cost of nursing or custodial care at home.	Yes, $50–$100 a day; unlimited benefit period	Yes, $50 or less a day; 5–7-year benefit period	None
Preexisting condition rules Whether a policy will cover care rendered for a medical condition that existed when the policy was purchased.	Covers 6 months before coverage starts	Covers 6 months before coverage starts	Unlimited exclusion for previous illness
Alzheimer's rules Whether a package excludes coverage of care that results from Alzheimer's disease or other mental illness.	No	No	Yes

SOURCE: Adapted from *U.S. News & World Report*, January, 23, 1989, 56–57. Updates by author.

Statistics show that disability is far more probable than death. People die only once but can be disabled several times. A person's chance of being unable to work for 90 days or more because of a disabling injury or illness is far greater than the chance of dying, as Figure 7–9 shows. Therefore, disability insurance is not a luxury but a necessity which every wage earner should consider.

For many families, disability insurance may be more important than life insurance. Long-term disability insurance can be a family's most vital defense against financial ruin. While employer-sponsored health insurance generally covers most medical expenses, it will not pay the rent or grocery bills. Lost income from prolonged disability can be substantial. While the likelihood of becoming totally disabled for 30 years may seem remote, the potential for loss is not to be belittled. A permanently disabled 35-year-old earning $36,000 a year stands to lose nearly $2 million in income by age 65 if opportunity loss of future salary increases is factored in. Long-term disability is one of the major causes of mortgage foreclosures in the United States. Nevertheless, disability is one of the neglected insurances by many homeowners. The lack of a policy to replace income lost because of long-term illness or accident is the most common weakness in people's insurance protection. Therefore, disability insurance ought to be given the same priority as life insurance.

Even a short-term disability can similarly wipe out savings and have a devastating effect on a family's or individual's life. Think for a moment what six months of no income will mean to you or your family. If you will be one of the unlucky 3 out of 10, will you be prepared financially, or will you face a financial crisis? In order

FIGURE 7–9	The Odds of Disability

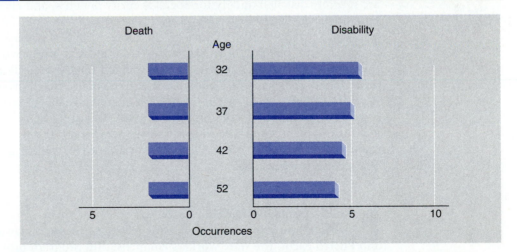

Before the age of 65, a person's odds of suffering a major disability (90 days or longer) are substantially greater than the odds of dying. See the ratios above for four age groups.

SOURCE: National Association of Life Underwriters, 1986 data.

to buy disability insurance, you must have good health and an income. If you wait until you need it, you may not qualify.

People who cannot work because of sickness or injury must have income from somewhere, preferably enough to replace most of their normal earnings as long as the need exists, which could be for life or to age 65. Unless you have large financial resources, this "somewhere" will have to be some sort of disability insurance. It can come from four disability insurance sources:

1. Social Security disability insurance

2. A state workers' compensation program

3. Employer-sponsored disability coverage

4. Individual coverage bought privately

Social Security Disability Insurance

One source of disability income insurance which almost everyone with sufficient work experience has is Social Security. If you are unable to work at all for more than six months, Social Security will begin paying you a monthly benefit. This is not likely to meet your family's needs and may most likely be less than half of your former income, with a top monthly benefit in 1992 of $1,700.

Social Security Disability Insurance (SSDI) has rigid eligibility requirements which prevent 70 percent of those applying from collecting anything. Only applicants who are severely disabled qualify for Social Security benefits, and even then it takes six months for the first check to arrive.

Social Security does not consider you disabled unless you are totally unable to do any substantial gainful work, not just your current job or work that suits your training. Social Security does not cover a person for a partial disability, an impairment that affects the performance of one or more major functions of a particular job. Also, the disability must be expected to last at least a year. The payments cease when you can do any kind of work, not necessarily your regular work. To receive benefits you must have worked 5 of the past 10 years or, if under age 31, at least one and one-half of the past 3 years. Clearly, one cannot rely on Social Security for adequate disability coverage.

The State Workers Compensation Program

In some states (notably New York, New Jersey, California, Hawaii, Rhode Island, and Puerto Rico), the **state workers compensation** program provides limited term benefits for those who become disabled on the job. This coverage is only for diseases or injuries related to or incurred on the job. In other states, more than 75 percent of all wage earners have some sort of workers compensation required by state law. It is generally available for only 26 weeks. Benefits vary widely from state to state but are generally less than the coverage offered by private insurers.

Employer-Sponsored and Private Disability Coverages

Since government-sponsored disability insurances have strict qualification rules as well as relatively low maximum amounts of compensation, most people need some form of supplementary disability insurance to help maintain their lifestyles in the event of illness or injury. There are two options: group policies, which are provided by many employers, and individual policies, which can be purchased privately.

Before considering individual disability insurance, workers should look into their company's coverage. If a good policy is available, then they may decide to buy a policy that will only supplement that of their employer. If long-term disability insurance is a fringe benefit of the job, you may be adequately protected without private coverage. But a group policy plus any government benefits should ideally replace a maximum of 80 percent of your *net* salary.

The gap between what is available and what you normally need to live adequately should be bridged by private disability insurance. Suppose you take home $3,000 a month after taxes. You should have a disability benefit totaling 80 percent of that, or $2,400. If your group plan would pay $1,000 a month, you need to buy extra coverage only for the difference: $1,400.

DISABILITY

How Much Do You Need?   To determine how much disability coverage you need, figure out how much your household would need to live on if a breadwinner were permanently disabled and where this amount would come from. To achieve this, refer to your family's budget statement again (shown in Chapter 1). This illustrates your annual living expenses. From this total, subtract all income you will receive while disabled, including Social Security, your spouse's income (if any), and dividends, interest, and net earnings from any rental properties. The difference is the amount of coverage needed to maintain your standard of living while disabled.

The 80 Percent Rule   Most policies replace at least 60 percent of the net monthly salary, and some replace 80 percent of net (after-tax) income. No individual disability plan will replace 100 percent of the previously earned income, because disability payments are tax free, and insurance companies do not want to make it more desirable to be disabled than to work. By limiting the amount they will replace, insurers provide a financial incentive to recover from disabilities.

For the same reason, the higher your salary, the smaller the portion you can protect. If you earn $50,000, you can probably insure around two-thirds of your gross income. But if your salary exceeds $300,000, it's unlikely you will be able to protect more than a third of it. The **80 percent rule**, therefore, applies to low- and middle-income earners but cannot be obtained for very high incomes.

Like other forms of insurance, disability coverage needs to be reexamined regularly to make sure it reflects your current and future financial needs and conditions. As income rises, you may wish to increase the coverage to protect your new living style. Conversely, as you grow older, your savings may increase and financial obligations decline; consequently, insurance might be reduced.

Shopping for Disability Coverage   As with any kind of insurance, selecting a disability policy requires some comparison shopping. Consumers have to sort through a number of options that control premium amounts. Premiums can vary greatly, depending on such things as:

1. The policy's definition of disability

2. How much the insured will receive if he or she becomes disabled

3. How soon benefits begin after a disability removes the insured from the job payroll

4. Whether benefits are linked to inflation

5. The insured's age, occupation, and sex

6. The insured's state of health

Insurance companies take an applicant's health and occupation into consideration when calculating premiums and amounts of coverage. They have rating methods that place each individual into an insured class based on risk of disability.

TABLE 7–4	Yearly Disability Insurance Premiums by Profession

Assumptions: Policies are noncancelable, providing annually renewable individual disability coverage for a 40-year-old who earns $60,000 a year and wants to be able to replace 60 percent of lost income to age 65. Premiums include "own-occupation" coverage (policy pays benefits if the insured is unable to engage in the insured's own profession).

Profession	Benefits Start After...			Partial Disability	Cost-of-Living Adjustment
	90 Days	180 Days	180 Days		
Executive	$ 1,092	$ 973	$ 862	Add $171–$231	Add $252
Computer programmer	1,281	1,141	1,010	Add $205–$272	Add $321
Carpenter*	1,429	1,265	1,129	NA	Add $399
Part-time editor**	NA	NA	NA	NA	NA

* Can buy coverage for only five years, and then only for $2,400 a month in benefits.

** No coverage generally available for people working fewer than 26 to 30 hours a week.

NA = No coverage available

SOURCE: Reed & Reed Insurance Agency, Plainville, Massachusetts., 1993.

White-collar workers in service organizations are in the low-cost class. Laborers who operate machines belong to the high-cost class. Women pay more than men, because despite a longer life expectancy, they have a higher incidence of disability. High blood pressure or heart disease can cause premiums to skyrocket. And naturally, the higher the age, the higher the cost. Table 7–4 shows some typical annual premiums for different professions and coverage amounts.

Unfortunately, disability is one of the least standardized forms of insurance. Even when written in plain English, policies can be hard to understand. Applicants should be prepared with a list of the important features they want when meeting with an insurer to discuss a disability policy. Comparison shopping and careful reading of the contracts are the best guarantee of getting the most suitable policy. As with most insurance, in purchasing disability coverage, applicants may have to choose between the level and definition of protection they want and their ability to pay.

Features of Disability Insurance   The following list of disability insurance features should enable you to comparison shop and select the best individual policy and the one most suitable for your needs.

1. *The Definition of Disability ("Your Own Occupation" Clause)*   The most important feature to consider is the policy's definition of disability. Defining disability is not a simple matter. The Health Insurance Association of America (HIAA) defines disability as the "inability to perform substantially all important duties of one's own occupation for 6 months with the subsequent inability to perform substantially in any gainful occupation to which one is reasonably-fitted by reason of education, training and experience." This is known as a **"your own occupation" clause**.

   Most private insurance policies contain such a clause. It means that if the insured person cannot actively participate in his or her regular occupation because of a disability, the company will replace the lost income regardless of other types of work performed. In selecting an individual policy, you should think about whether your primary concern is protecting yourself against being unable to perform your regular line of work or simply not being able to work at any acceptable job. An **"any occupation clause"** restricts benefits if you are capable of working at a job that is a reasonable alternative to your original occupation. This is naturally open to interpretation.

   Many insurance companies adhere to the HIAA definition of disability for the first one to five years of a disability and then cease coverage if the insured can perform any occupation thereafter. While insurance companies do not expect an insured to sell shoelaces in the street, they would expect you to work in a modified form of your old job. A surgeon who cannot practice because of a hand injury cannot collect full disability benefits if he or she can work as a physician in a clinic or as a medical consultant. Some insurance companies may even claim that if a gym teacher or engineer can no longer perform their normal job functions, coverage would cease or be reduced if they can work as cashiers at the local lunch counter. A policy with an "any occupation clause" would be considerably cheaper but obviously offers more restrictive coverage.

2. *Proportionate or Residual Benefits*   "Residual" refers to payment of a partial-benefit. Some policies pay benefits only if the insured is totally disabled. Others pay partial benefits for partial disability. If you are well enough to work one day a week or to earn 20 percent of your former income by doing less-demanding tasks, a policy offering residual benefits will pay you 80 percent of the full benefit. A policy that provides partial benefits on a prorated basis if you are partially disabled is obviously preferable.

   Benefits are prorated according to the amount of income loss due to the disability. If you can work only half time, you should get half of the policy's monthly payout. Private insurers usually require only a 25 percent minimum loss of prior function. A good policy will make up losses even if you work in a lower-paying occupation. If you are self-employed, find a policy that will pay the overhead for your business and keep the office open in your absence.

3. *The Elimination (or Waiting) Period*   This is the deductible in disability insurance. It is the amount of time that must elapse between the onset of a disability and the start of benefit payments. The longer the elimination or waiting period before benefit payments start, the lower the premium. Buying a policy whose benefits begin after 90 days, 180 days, or even a year after the disability will result in significant premium payment discounts.

   In estimating how long your family can live without policy benefits, consider your savings, accumulated sick leave, vacation time, and any state or employer-provided benefits which could be used to fill in (including a good relationship, if any, with your in-laws). Most people have some of these benefits and therefore do not need to collect disability from the first day or week they become disabled. They can get along for six months, especially with short-term protection from their employer. People who can wait even longer, say a year or two before drawing benefits, can save even more on premiums.

4. *Exemptions*   **Exemptions** are types of disability that do not qualify for benefits. A policy should be read closely for all exemptions from coverage. Some common ones are normal pregnancy or childbirth, miscarriage or abortion, war or an act of war, unsuccessful suicide, or disability due to participation in a riot, insurrection, or rebellion. Some newer companies offer policies which regard pregnancy as a temporary disability.

5. *Incontestable Clause*   This important provision forbids an insurance company from contesting the validity of a contract once it has been in effect for a certain period, usually two years.

6. *Benefit Period*   Policies can be purchased that will pay benefits for one, two, or five years, until age 65, or for a lifetime. The most important coverage

needed is for permanent work disabilities. While about 80 percent of the labor force has some disability coverage (separate from Social Security disability benefits), such as accumulated sick days on the job, only about 20 percent have policies that pay benefits for more than two years. A significant number of small- and medium-sized firms have no coverage at all.

Select a policy that, in the event of permanent disability, will continue paying and offering benefits for a lifetime, or at least until age 65. Remember, a prolonged disability could wreck your family's standard of living, and some plans barely meet the five-year minimum for being considered long term. Most disability coverage ceases at the insured's retirement or upon the insured reaching the normal retirement age.

7. *"Cost of Living" Rider*   This option in some policies provides for increasing benefits based on inflation. This is especially important for long-term disability. If an insurance company will pay 80 percent of an insured's wages upon disability, the payment's buying power will diminish substantially over the years, unless it is increased annually to keep up with the inflation rate.

8. *Guaranteed Renewable Noncancelable*   The best type of policy is **noncancelable** and **guaranteed renewable**. This is not double-talk. Most people should buy a policy that is both. This means that the insurance company cannot cancel the policy before a specified age, usually 65, as long as premiums are paid, even after the insured has an accident and has collected previously on the policy. Nor can the insurance company raise the premiums even if the insured changes occupations or contracts an illness that could result in a long-term disability. This policy costs a little more, but it gives a lot more quality protection.

9. *Waiver of Premium Clause*   This clause stipulates that if the policyholder is disabled, he or she is exempted from paying future premiums during the duration of the disability. This is a significant money-saving provision that will keep the policy paid up and in force, enabling the policyholder to keep it after he or she recovers.

10. *Top-Rated Company*   The policy is only as good as the insurance company issuing it. An insurance policy should not be considered unless the issuing company has the top A++ from A.M. Best and Co., a major insurance rating firm, and a Triple A (AAA) from at least one of the other major rating firms, Moody's, Standard and Poor's, Duff and Phelps, or Weiss. The leading companies in the disability insurance field include Paul Revere, Provident Life & Accident Insurance Co., Northwestern Mutual Life Insurance Co., and UNUM Life Insurance Co.

11. *Accidents and Mental Illness*   Be sure to select a policy that covers disability due to accidents and mental illness.

President Clinton's Health Reform Plan

On September 22, 1993 President Bill Clinton presented his health care reform plan before a joint session of Congress. The Clinton plan aims to contain spiraling costs and provide medical insurance for all Americans.

Plan Features

1. *Universal Insurance*   The plan provides for universal medical coverage. Many Americans are concerned that they will lose their coverage because of layoffs or cut-backs in employer-provided insurance. The Clinton plan aims to make it impossible for anyone to lose their coverage, a deep and consuming American fear. The Clinton plan would ensure that workers would be able to get insurance at any new employer at comparable prices. No one would pay higher insurance premiums or be denied coverage altogether because of pre-existing medical conditions. Those with severe disabilities would get long-term care, regardless of age or income. No one would be excluded because of inability to pay.

2. *The Poor and Unemployed*   Families and individuals with incomes less than 150 percent of the poverty level, and the unemployed, would pay subsidized rates and reduced premiums. Premiums for the unemployed and poor would be subsidized or paid entirely by the government through Medicaid and Medicare. Self-employed workers would be able to deduct 100 percent of the premiums from their taxes.

   The White House estimates that in 1994 such policies would cost $1,800 for an individual and $4,200 for a two-parent family.

3. *Uninsured*   The 37 million people who now lack health insurance would be covered either through their employer or through expanded welfare schemes (government subsidies).

4. *Premiums*   The new health insurance system would be employment-based, just as it is now. It would require all employers to contribute to the cost of their workers' health care. Employers would pay 80 percent of whatever an average health insurance plan costs with workers paying the remaining 20 percent. It would dramatically cut health care costs for many large, high-wage companies, such as auto makers. But, those costs would increase for many small businesses that now pay nothing toward their workers' health insurance and would be required to pay at least 5 percent of payroll under Clinton's proposal. However, the employer contribution to workers' health insurance would be capped at 7.9 percent of payroll.

5. Health Alliances   The health care industry has historically avoided competition on the price and value of its products because there has been no real bargaining between consumers and medical providers (doctors and hospitals), since third parties (employers or the government) actually pay the bills. This has allowed both patients and doctors to ignore the cost.

continued

President Clinton's Health Reform Plan (continued)

The plan's effort to cut medical inflation is built upon managed competition, an attempt to create price competition among health care providers. The plan calls for the creation of wholly new institutions known as health alliances. The health alliances could be quasi-governmental bodies created by the states, large organizations that would represent consumers in a given region. Health insurance buyers would band together in large regional purchaser cartels, or "alliances," to bargain with competing networks of doctors, hospitals, and other health care providers for the best service at the best price. They would collect premiums paid by employers, individuals, and the federal government, and use those premiums to purchase health insurance group coverage for all enrollees. Doctors, hospitals, and insurance companies would likewise reorganize in "provider networks." Provider networks would be forced to compete for patients on the basis of price and value in order to sign contracts with health alliances. The alliances would use the leverage of their large membership to negotiate the best deals with provider networks.

The theory is that such bargaining will encourage lower costs and greater efficiency, such as fewer unnecessary tests. Insurers would no longer be able to pass along rising health costs in the form of higher premiums. They would be compelled by market pressure to resist price increases by doctors and hospitals. Under the Clinton proposal, each health alliance would mail a directory to all local residents once a year, listing the certified health plans offered by approved providers. A person would select a plan for the year and receive all medical care exclusively through that provide.

The most expensive option would be traditional fee-for-service. Less expensive would be the PPOs. An even cheaper option would be the HMOs. The Clinton plan includes strong price incentives for patients to switch to more economical HMOs and PPOs. The health alliances would collect premiums from employers and consumers and use them to pay the provider networks for the health care they deliver.

States could begin setting up alliances as early as 1995 and would be required to do so no later than January 1997.

6. Medical Cost Controls   Additionally, doctors, hospitals, and insurance companies will most likely face caps on service fees and premiums. The Clinton plan would enforce limits on health care spending through a new National Health Board that would set national standards, oversee implementation of the program by the states, and decide when health care providers were charging too much.

SUMMARY

Medical care expenditures have been rising for a number of reasons: the U.S. population is aging, Americans are consuming more health services, newer medical technologies and more sophisticated treatments are extremely costly, and increased malpractice suits have caused physicians' insurance premiums to soar. The soaring cost of health care has made adequate coverage essential. A variety of types of health coverage is available for meeting this need.

Major kinds of health insurance include policies covering physicians' expenses, hospital expenses, surgical costs, major medical protection, dental coverage, and disability income loss. Health insurance can be obtained on both individual and group plans. Group policies generally offer greater coverage at reduced premiums. Employees should know how much they need to pay out of their own pocket before the policy starts to reimburse them. It is a rare policy that will cover 100 percent of the costs starting with the first dollar spent on medical care.

Important limitations include the deductible, the coinsurance requirement, and the limitations on the types of losses covered. Many health insurance plans have a coinsurance or copayment provision which requires the insured to pay a certain percentage of all expenses over the deductible, such as 20 percent, while the insurer pays 80 percent.

A newer type of health coverage provider is the Health Maintenance Organization (HMO). HMOs stress "managed care," which attempts to offer good health services while maintaining cost control. HMOs are not for everybody. In sizing up a plan, consumers should get an explanation of its policy on outside care and not enroll unless they feel comfortable with the rules. Medicare is government-provided health insurance for most Social Security recipients. Medigap covers any gaps in Medicare coverage.

The largest gap in the health insurance program of most people is inadequate long-term care protection. Consumers should know the difference between the three types of *long-term care* facilities: skilled care nursing, intermediate care, and custodial care. It is important to check which facility will be covered under the policy and under what circumstances. The maximum length of stay, the amount paid per day, the medical requirements for eligibility, as well as exclusions and limitations also need be carefully examined.

Disability income insurance replaces income lost when an insured is unable to work due to an injury or illness. It is a crucial part of one's insurance protection package. These days only the very poor, the very wealthy, or the foolhardy would be likely to go without life or medical insurance. But too often people fail to protect one of their most valuable assets: their ability to earn income. An income earner should make certain that the employer-provided disability coverage, plus private savings and Social Security disability, will be sufficient to provide 80 percent of after-tax income in the event of a prolonged disability.

On September 22, 1993, President Clinton introduced a health care reform plan that, if passed, is likely to revolutionize health care in the United States.

KEY TERMS

"Any occupation" clause	Copayment
Basic coverage	Custodial care facility
Cafeteria plan	Deductibles
COBRA	Disability income insurance
Coinsurance	80 percent rule
Comprehensive major medical	Excess major medical
Conditionally renewable	Exclusions

Exemptions

Group coverage

Group-staff model

Guaranteed renewable

Health insurance

Health maintenance organizations (HMOs)

Independent practice associations (IPAs)

Individual coverage

Intermediate care facility

Long-term care coverage

Major medical

Managed care health plans

Maximum benefit limit

Medicaid

Medicare

Medigap policy

Noncancelable policy

Preexisting condition

Preferred provider organizations (PPOs)

Primary care physician

Renewal clause

Single disease coverage

Skilled care nursing facility

Social Security Disability Insurance (SSDI)

State workers compensation

Stop-loss provision

Substandard risk

Traditional fee-for-service (indemnity) health plans

Waiver

"Your own occupation" clause

REVIEW QUESTIONS AND PROBLEMS

1. List the key factors to consider when evaluating a health insurance plan.
2. Discuss the most important features to look for when purchasing a disability income policy.
3. What major risks are covered by health insurance?
4. What are the major types of health insurance?
5. Discuss several reasons why health care costs have increased dramatically in recent years.
6. Discuss the pros and cons of enrolling in an HMO–type health plan.
7. Gary has a major medical policy with a $250 deductible and an 80 percent coinsurance feature. Gary was hospitalized for infectious mononucleosis and incurred the following medical expenses: $400 for physicians' fees, $1,800 for hospital room and board, $500 for blood tests and X rays, and $130 for medications. How much of these expenses will Gary have to pay out of pocket?
8. What is major medical coverage? Discuss the basic features of a major medical policy.
9. Describe and discuss (a) the cafeteria plan, (b) single disease coverage, (c) stop-loss provision, (d) Medigap, (e) PPO, and (f) IPA.
10. Marie is single and earns $35,000 a year. Her take-home pay is about $21,000 a year. How much disability coverage would be sufficient for Marie's needs? Explain your answer in light of the 80 percent rule.
11. What is Medicare? What benefits does it provide?

12. What factors should one consider in determining the length of the waiting period when purchasing a disability income policy?

13. (COPAYMENTS) Linda is considering buying health insurance. She is concerned about a medical procedure she thinks is likely. The cost of this procedure is $12,000. The health insurance will pay 80 percent. She wishes to limit her maximum out-of-pocket expenses to $1,500. What deductible should she select?

14. (DISABILITY) Caring Corp. would like to reduce to zero the additional disability coverage required by its engineers, over and above the company's group plan. The engineers' take-home pay per month after taxes is $4,000. The disability benefit is 80 percent. The current amount paid by group plan is $1,000. How much should the firm increase the amount paid by the group plan?

SUGGESTED PROJECTS

1. Bring a health insurance policy to class. Read the provisions, and have the class explain and discuss them. Make a list of those provisions that are unclear or confusing. Check with your instructor or insurance agent to determine their meaning. Have the class discuss the strengths and weaknesses of this policy.

2. Talk to at least two people who have used an HMO "managed care" health provider and at least two people who have used a fee-for-service health plan. Obtain their views as to quality of service, cost, and convenience. Present your findings to the class.

3. Your father (who is helping to pay your tuition) has just turned 65 and knows you are taking a Personal Finance course. He phones you at your dorm and asks you to help him put together a comprehensive health insurance plan. He wants to integrate Medicare into his plan and have overlapping coverage, including long-term health care. Draft a letter responding to his requests, providing him with the guidelines for a comprehensive health package.

INFORMATION RESOURCES

Asinof, Lynn. "Buying Individual Disability Coverage Is Best." *The Wall Street Journal,* April 20, 1993, C-1.

Bailard, Thomas, David Bieh, and Ronald Kaiser. *How to Buy the Right Insurance at the Right Price.* Dow Jones-Irwin, 1989.

"A Blow to Your Benefits." *U.S. News and World Report,* October 21, 1991, 96–100.

"Can You Afford to Get Sick?" *Newsweek,* January 30, 1989, 44–52.

"Catching Up with Medigap." *Changing Times,* November 1990, 81–83.

Clark, Jane. "Health Insurance 101: Filling the Gaps at College." *Kiplinger's Personal Finance Magazine,* September 1993, 36.

————. "What to Do If You Lose Your Group Coverage." *Kiplinger's Personal Finance Magazine,* July 1992, 74–77.

"Condition: Critical." *Time,* November 25, 1991, 32–42.

The Consumer's Guide to Medicare Supplemental Insurance. Available free from the Health Insurance Association of America, P.O. Box 41455, Washington, DC 20018.

"Disability Insurance." *Money*, February 1989, 77–79.

"Finding Care for Your Aging Parents." *Changing Times*, March 1991, 57–60.

"Getting What You Need in Disability Insurance," *Kiplinger's Personal Finance Magazine,* February 1993, 98.

"Health Plans That Cut Costs Gaining Favor." *The New York Times,* November 11, 1991, LB-1.

Henderson, Nancy. "Questions to Ask Before You Switch to an HMO." *Kiplinger's Personal Finance Magazine*, May 1992, 110–113.

Horowitz, Lawrence, M.D. *Taking Charge of Your Medical Fate*. New York: Random House, 1988.

"How Healthy Is Your Health Insurer?" *Kiplinger's Personal Finance Magazine,* July 1991, 78–79.

Kuttner, Robert. "Health Care: Why Corporate America Is Paralyzed." *Business Week*, April 8, 1991, 8.

Long-Term Care: A Dollar and Sense Guide. Write to United Seniors Health Cooperative, 1334 G Street, NW, Suite 500, Washington, DC 20005, $6.95.

"Medical Insurance for the College Grad." *The New York Times,* May 21, 1989, F-13.

"Medicare's Sickbed." *U.S. News & World Report,* February 6, 1989, 20–21.

"Medigap: Costs More, Covers Less." *Changing Times*, April 1989, 57–62.

Merline, John. "Who Pays for Our Health Care?" *Investors Business Daily,* September 7, 1993, 1.

National Association of Life Underwriters. Write them at 1922 F Street NW, Washington DC 20005, or call at 202/331-6032 for free pamphlets on disability income protection, medigap insurance, and other topics in their "Shaping Your Financial Fitness" series.

National Consumers League. *A Consumer's Guide to Health Maintenance Organizations.* National Consumers League, 815 15th Street, NW, Suite 928, Washington, DC 20005. 202/639-8140.

Quinn, Jane Bryant. "Lost: Another Health Benefit." *Newsweek*, June 17, 1991, 49.

———. "When Health Plans Fail." *Newsweek,* February 24, 1992, 45.

"Removing Hurdles to Buying Health Insurance." *The New York Times,* December 8, 1991, 12-1.

Rowland, Mary. "Saving on Disability Insurance." *The New York Times,* May 24, 1992, F-13.

"Running for Coverage in Anxious Times." *Business Week*, May 18, 1992, 156–57.

Schultz, Ellen E. "What You Can Do When Your Insurer Slams the Door." *The Wall Street Journal,* May 4, 1992, C-1.

Stout, Hilary. "Ten Standard Medigap Plans Devised." *The Wall Street Journal,* May 7, 1991, B-1.

"When Your Health Insurance Makes You Sick." *Kiplinger's Personal Finance Magazine,* October 1991, 64.

"When Your Parents Need Your Help." *Changing Times,* May 1989, 81–84.

"Who Can Afford a Nursing Home?" *Consumer Reports,* May 1988, 300–311.

Wilcox, Melynda D. "Long-Term Care Insurance: Your Choices." *Kiplinger's Personal Finance Magazine,* March 1992, 77–81.

———. "Getting Your Share from Managed Care." *Kiplinger's Personal Finance Magazine,* February 1993, 63–67.

CHAPTER EIGHT

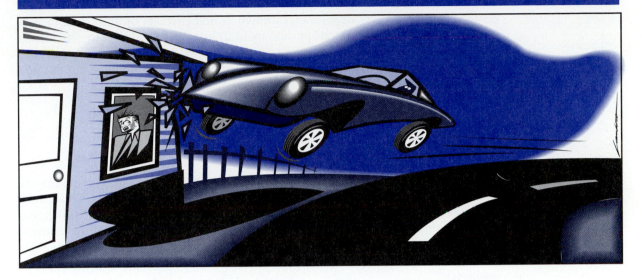

Homeowners and Automobile Property & Liability Insurance

- To assess the need for adequate homeowners and automobile insurance

- To examine how home and automobile owners can protect themselves through insurance

- To find out how consumers can evaluate their auto and home insurance needs

- To identify the major components and features of home and automobile owners insurance policies

- To analyze the standard sections and special provisions, riders, and floaters of homeowners and automobile insurance policies

- To appraise the coverage exclusions and limitations of homeowners insurance coverage

- To illustrate how to fill any gaps in home and automobile policies

- To explore ways to reduce and to control the cost of insurance premiums through the use of deductibles, discounts, and other cost-cutting methods

- To evaluate the importance of comparison shopping for insurance and the key factors to consider

- To investigate the no-fault auto insurance laws

This chapter discusses how to insure your home against damage, yourself against lawsuits, and your car against a variety of risks. It describes the various components of the "packages" of insurance known as homeowners or auto insurance. It also explains how to determine appropriate insurance needs and how to avoid being overinsured or underinsured. Insurance is not a commodity that is simply bought and held. It must be researched, analyzed, evaluated, and periodically updated as one's circumstances and needs change.

Homeowners Insurance

Be it humble or extravagant, condo or mansion, your home and its contents are probably your most valuable possessions, and therefore homeowners insurance becomes one of your most important purchases. You cannot insure your home against slumping real estate prices. But you can protect your biggest investment from uncovered losses resulting from disasters such as fire, floods, hurricanes, and earthquakes, as well as theft and vandalism, by buying the right **homeowners insurance**.

The need for homeowners insurance extends to renters and homeowners alike. The policies insure both the house and the personal property. Homeowners need it to cover damage and losses to the structure and contents in the event of fire, theft, vandalism, or other perils and to protect against liability claims in case a passerby slips on your front sidewalk and sues for negligence. Renters need specially tailored policies to cover their personal possessions in case of fire or burglary and to protect against liability claims if a guest sustains injury inside their home.

Nearly all homeowners have some insurance on their belongings because banks, when issuing mortgages, insist that the home buyer take out a standard homeowners policy. However, about 75 percent of apartment dwellers have no insurance for their belongings and a similar percentage of homeowners fails to insure their personal property adequately.

Because homeowners policies combine different types of insurance covering the house, its contents, liability claims, and certain associated costs such as medical expenses, different homeowners policies do not offer equal protection.

Read Your Policy

Your insurance policy is a contract between you and the insurance company. Insurers have spent the last several years simplifying language in all property and casualty policies. Despite the simplified language, not all insurance buyers understand what they are purchasing, what their policy covers, and what they can expect to recover after a loss. The result can be too little insurance for their most valuable assets or too much for too high a price. It is therefore expedient to examine this package carefully, to make sure you do not find yourself uninsured or underinsured when trouble strikes. When a loss occurs, it is painfully easy to find out too late that a small extra premium could have saved you a large sum of money and eased the financial pain. (See Figure 8-1, which shows some potential homeowner liabilities.)

FIGURE 8–1   An Ordinary Day around the House

This rather alarming drawing shows some of the potential hazards covered by homeowners insurance.

1. Fire	*3. Water damage*	*5. Additional living expenses*	*7. Property damage liability*
2. Theft	*4. Storm damage*	*6. Bodily injury liability*	*8. No-fault medical payments*

SOURCE: "Some Coverages Provided by Homeowners Insurance," Copyright 1980 by Consumers Union. Reprinted by permission of Consumer Reports, August 1980, 485.

Updating

Our own situations as well as the policy terms are constantly changing. Home values change, we acquire new possessions and make renovations, and insurance companies are constantly revising their policies, offering new features and making special offers. Therefore, homeowners policy should be reviewed annually to make sure the coverage is sufficient for today's circumstances.

The Coverage

Here is a rundown of what is usually covered by a homeowners policy:

1. *Damage to the house* The exterior and interior structure of the house is covered. This includes any built-in or installed fixtures. It does not cover furnishings or house contents. Insurance for the house itself is based upon replacement cost (which is discussed further on).

2. *Damage to other structures*   This applies to garages, tool sheds, and such. The coverage is usually equal to 10 percent of the coverage of the house. If a house is insured for $100,000, the coverage for other structures is an additional $10,000.

3. *Damage to trees, shrubs, and lawns*   Greenery and landscaping around the house will be covered for 5 percent of the amount of coverage on the house, typically up to $500 per item.

4. *Losses in personal property*   The contents of the house and other buildings, excluding cars, are covered for an amount equal to half the coverage of the house. Although the amount of personal property coverage is linked to the amount of coverage on the house, they are actually separate units of insurance. If a house is covered for its replacement cost of $100,000 and the entire house and its contents are totally destroyed, a policyholder may be able to collect as much as $150,000. The personal property is also covered for losses incurred away from home, anywhere in the world. However, the maximum coverage for away from home losses is $1,000 or 10 percent of the personal property coverage, whichever is larger.

5. *Additional living expenses*   If a house is damaged and the insured has to move elsewhere temporarily, the insurance company will cover these extra expenses up to 20 percent of the coverage on the house. This is in addition to the real property or personal property coverage.

6. *Liability*   All homeowners policies contain personal **liability coverage** in case a negligence suit is brought against the homeowner or tenant. It provides protection against claims for damages, including lawsuits arising from injury to visitors on your property or from accidents caused by you, your family, or your petaway from home as well. Suppose a visitor falls down a flight of stairs in your house (your kids left those marbles scattered all over the floor again) and is seriously injured. Since you are responsible for this injury, you could be sued for medical expenses and for any other losses incurred because of the injury, including that elusive loss known in liability cases as "pain and suffering." Standard coverage is $100,000 per occurrence.

7. *No-fault medical payments*   Homeowners policies separately provide $500 per person to cover medical expenses for minor injuries occurring on the insured's property, regardless of who was at fault. People who employ household cleaning help, babysitters, or maids should augment the liability policy to ensure coverage for their injuries. This coverage also applies to injuries occurring elsewhere. For example, if your dog bit a stranger's leg on the beach, you could submit a claim to pay the victim's medical expenses.

8. *Credit card losses*   Most new homeowners policies include $500 coverage for losses due to forgeries, counterfeit money, or unauthorized use of your credit cards.

Types of Policies

Although the details vary from company to company, there are five standard policies that cover owner-occupants of one- and two-family homes. There is also a policy for renters and one for condo or co-op owners. They differ in the number of perils they cover against and the degree of protection they provide, as shown in Table 8–1.

HO-1 Policy   The most common basic form, policy **HO-1,** insures a house and its contents, shrubs and trees, and outside structures, such as tool shed or garage, against 11 major perils. Perils are persons, things, or conditions that can cause damage or destruction. They include damage from fire, lightning, windstorms and explosions, vandalism and theft, as well as that caused by planes or cars. It offers basic protection with many restrictions.

HO-2 Policy   The broad form **HO-2** policy, which costs 5 to 10 percent more, adds another six perils that are common enough to warrant consideration. Among them are leaks from hot water systems, plumbing, heating or air conditioning, such as burst pipes or exploding furnaces, as well as injury from falling objects; weight of ice, snow, or sleet; faulty electrical wiring; and collapse of the building.

HO-3 Policy   With an HO-1 or HO-2 policy, homeowners are covered only for losses from perils that are specifically named in the policy. An **HO-3 "all-risk"** policy covers everything not specifically excluded. The items that are usually specifically excluded in all policies are floods, earthquakes, war, and nuclear accidents. HO-3 coverage, which can cost up to 30 percent more than HO-1, may also protect fixtures that are not part of the structure, like wall-to-wall carpeting and dishwashers.

"No, it doesn't say whose hill it was, or if they were liable...it just says Jack fell down it and broke his crown and that Jill came tumbling after."

SOURCE: "Pepper...and Salt," *The Wall Street Journal,* March 3, A-15. Reprinted by permission of Cartoon Features Syndicate.

TABLE 8–1	Guide to Homeowners Policies

These are the principal features of standard homeowners policies. The policies of some companies differ in a few respects from the standard ones. Policy conditions may also vary according to state requirements.

You can usually increase coverage for some items by paying an additional premium. The special limits of liability refer to the maximum amounts the policy will pay for the types of property listed. Usually, jewelry, furs, boats, and other items subject to special limits have to be insured separately if you want greater coverage.

	HO-1 (basic form)	HO-2 (broad form)	HO-3 (special form)	HO-4 (renters' contents broad form)	HO-6 (units or condominiums)	HO-8 (older homes)
PERILS COVERED (see key)	1 to 11	1 to 17	1 to 17 on personal property except glass breakage; all risks, except those specifically excluded, on buildings	1 to 17	1 to 17	1 to 11
STANDARD AMOUNT OF INSURANCE ON House and attached structures	based on structure's replacement value	based on structure's replacement value	based on structure's replacement value	10% of personal insurance on additions and alterations to unit	$1,000 on owner's additions and alterations to unit	based on structure's market value
Detached structures	10% of insurance on house	10% of insurance on house	10% of insurance on house	no coverage	no coverage	10% of insurance on house
Trees, shrubs, plants	5% of insurance on house; $500 maximum per item	5% of insurance on house; $500 maximum per item	5% of insurance on house; $500 maximum per item	10% of personal property insurance; $500 maximum per item	10% of personal property insurance; $500 maximum per item	5% of insurance on house; $250 maximum per item
Personal property	50% of insurance on house; 5% for property normally kept at another residence or $1,000, whichever is greater	50% of insurance on house; 5% for property normally kept at another residence or $1,000 whichever is greater	50% of insurance on house; 5% for property normally kept at another residence or $1,000, whichever is greater	based on value of property; 10% of that amount for property normally kept at another residence or $1,000, whichever is greater	based on value of property; 10% of that amount for property normally kept at another residence or $1,000, whichever is greater	50% of insurance on house; 5% for property normally kept at another residence or $1,000, whichever is greater
Loss of use, additional living expenses; loss of rent if rental unit uninhabitable	10% of insurance on house	20$ of insurance on house	20% of insurance on house	20% of personal property insurance	40% of personal property insurance	10% of insurance on house
SPECIAL LIMITS OF LIABILITY	Money, bank notes, bullion, gold other than goldware, silver other than silverware, platinum, coins and medals—$200. Securities, accounts, deeds, manuscripts, passports, ticket stamps, etc.—$1,000. Watercraft, including their trailers, furnishings, equipment and outboard motors—$1,000. Trailer not used with watercraft—$1,000. Grave markers—$1,000. Theft of jewelry, watches, furs, precious and semiprecious stones—$1,000. Theft of silverware, silver-plated ware, goldware, gold-plated ware and pewterware—$2,500. Theft of guns—$2,000.					Theft on premises limited to $1,000. No coverage for theft of items named at left off premises.
CREDIT CARD, FORGERY COUNTERFEIT MONEY, ELECTRONIC FUND TRANSFER	$500	$500	$500	$500	$500	$500
COMPREHENSIVE PERSONAL LIABILITY	$100,000	$100,000	$100,000	$100,000	$100,000	$100,000
DAMAGE TO PROPERTY OF OTHERS	$500	$500	$500	$500	$500	$500
MEDICAL PAYMENTS	$1,000 per person	$1,000 per person	$1,000 per person	$1,000 per person	$1,000 per person	$1,000 per person

KEY TO PERILS COVERED

1. fire, lightning
2. windstorm, hail
3. explosion
4. riots or civil commotion
5. damage by aircraft
6. damage by vehicles not owned or operated by people covered by policy
7. damage from smoke
8. vandalism, malicious mischief
9. theft
10. glass breakage
11. volcanic eruption
12. falling objects
13. weight of ice, snow, sleet
14. leakage or overflow of water or steam from a plumbing, heating or air-conditioning system
15. bursting, cracking, burning or bulging of a steam- or hot-water heating system or of appliances for heating water
16. freezing of plumbing, heating and air-conditioning systems and domestic appliances
17. injury to electrical appliances, devices, fixtures and wiring (excluding tubes, transistors and similar electronic components) from short circuits or other accidentally generated currents

SOURCE: Reprinted by permission from the June 1988 issue of *Changing Times Magazine.* Copyright © 1988 The Kiplinger Washington Editors, Inc.

HO-4 Policy   This policy is especially designed for tenants. **HO-4** policy insures the tenants' property, not the structure.

HO-5 Policy   For maximum coverage, homeowners can choose **HO-5** (not shown in Table 8–1), the all-risk policy covering both house and personal property against all perils except those specifically excluded in all policies.

HO-6 Policy   **HO-6**, designed for condominium unit owners, is a scaled-down version of a homeowners policy. It covers the contents of a house, apartment, or cooperative unit but not the structure and grounds.

HO-8 Policy   **HO-8** is more limited insurance for very old homes that are considered high-risk homes as well as very expensive to replace if damaged.

Not all companies use the above names and numbers. Policyholders may have to ask their agent to clarify which policy they already have or should buy.

How Much Coverage Do You Need?

Now that we have clarified what a policy covers, the next step is to figure out how much coverage we actually need on the house and its contents and liability.

Property insurers encourage homeowners to purchase coverage that will protect them in worst-case situations, such as a total loss. It is important for policyholders to have sufficient property insurance coverage from the onset and keep coverage up to date as the cost to rebuild a home increases. Without adequate coverage, a total loss means borrowing, using up savings, or reducing the family's standard of living with a replacement home of less quality.

Gross *underinsurance,* leaving a family exposed and vulnerable, is quite common, but it is no justification for **overinsurance**, which results in wasted premiums and imposes an unnecessary financial burden. Both should be avoided.

The first point a homeowner buying insurance needs to understand is the differences between market value, mortgage value, and replacement cost of a home.

Market Value   The price policyholders could sell their home for today, taking into account the location and the cost of land, is its **market value**. This is also affected by many factors beyond construction costs, such as taxes, school system, and so on. It may be higher or lower than replacement cost, depending upon supply and demand. For a new house, market value might be close to replacement cost. For an old house with a distinctive style, replacement cost might substantially exceed market value.

Mortgage Value   The total amount of the mortgage loan is the **mortgage value**. If a homeowner buys only enough insurance to cover mortgage value, the lender (usually a bank) is protected and satisfied, but the homeowner could lose personal equity if the house has increased in value beyond the amount of the mortgage and down payment.

Replacement Cost   **Replacement cost** is the amount required to rebuild the house in the same location, with the same amount of floor area and comparable quality materials, at current local construction prices and without figuring in depreciation.

Homeowners insurance should just cover the replacement cost of the structure and its contents, but normally not the value of the land. Replacement cost excludes the value of the land and the cost of the foundation, since these are rarely damaged.

Deriving Replacement Cost   Before deciding how much coverage to buy for a house, homeowners need a fairly accurate estimate of its replacement cost. The replacement cost of a home, not its market or mortgage values, is used to determine how much coverage is needed. Determining replacement cost may be essential, but it is also complex. A professional appraiser may be able to provide an accurate estimate. However, most appraisers are in the business of appraising property for market value, not replacement cost, so homeowners need to make sure their appraiser is familiar with current costs of construction in their area.

Most insurance companies provide forms and formulas for homeowners who want to calculate replacement cost on their own. Homeowners who provide their insurance company with some basic information about the house, such as the exterior construction material, the kind of heating, and the total ground floor area, can receive the insurance company's estimate of the approximate replacement cost. Another method is for homeowners to measure the square footage of usable floor space in the house and ask their county builders' association to give an estimate of the current cost per square foot for constructing a similar house.

The 80 Percent Rule   Homeowners often do not insure for the full replacement cost. Even homes that catch fire or are struck by a hurricane usually escape total destruction so one may be tempted to buy less than full coverage. However, being underinsured is courting trouble. Most homeowners policies include a replacement cost provision for the dwelling and other structures covered. This is available only if the policyholders carry insurance equal to at least 80 percent of the replacement cost of the structures. Insurers have set 80 percent as the minimum level needed for the policy to pay replacement cost for any loss up to the policy limits.

For complete replacement cost in case of total loss, homeowners need to insure their home for 100 percent of its replacement cost. However, anyone insured for less than 80 percent receives reimbursement based upon a **prorated share** of the actual cash value. **Actual cash value** is equal to the replacement cost new minus the amount the property depreciated since it was built. Buildings are considered to depreciate physically even if their market values increase.

This means that not only will depreciation be subtracted but that the insurance company considers the homeowner a coinsurer. As far as most insurance companies are concerned, a house that is covered for at least 80 percent of its replacement cost is adequately insured and a house with less coverage is underinsured and thereby coinsured by the owner.

When a home is insured for less than 80 percent of the current replacement cost, the insurance company will pay one of two amounts, depending upon which is greater:

1. The "actual" cash value, which is replacement cost minus depreciation.

2. A percentage of the replacement cost based upon the ratio of coverage purchased compared to 80 percent of the replacement cost. The amount can be computed by the following formula:

$$\frac{\text{Actual Insurance Carried}}{80\% \text{ of house Replacement Cost}} \times \text{Actual Cost to Repair}$$

An example of this calculation is provided in the box below.

It is therefore important to keep your coverage up to date, increasing the face value to at least 80 percent of appraised value periodically.

Inflation Guard Your Policy   Most homeowners obtain homeowners coverage and then forget about it. They fail to realize that if the inflation rate is 8 percent, the replacement cost of a property doubles every nine years. To make certain that coverage automatically equals at least 80 percent of a home's replacement value, **inflation guard endorsements** to a policy should be purchased. This rider to a policy automatically updates coverage, using multipliers devised from national indexes. A multiplier is a factor which approximates how much the replacement cost of a dwelling has increased over a period of time. For a small additional premium, homeowners can be certain that their insurance is adequate from one year to the next.

It is naturally safer to insure for 100 percent of a home's replacement cost and keep that coverage current. Eighty percent coverage is generally adequate for partial losses such as a small fire in the kitchen. The vast majority of homeowners insurance claims are for partial loss claims. However, the difference in cost between the premium for 80 percent coverage and that for 100 percent coverage is insignificant when compared to 20 percent of the cost of the home's full replacement. It is important also to review coverage after making major improvements to a house. Improvements most likely increase its value and could put the owner below 80 percent of the home's new higher appraised value.

REPLACEMENT

Calculating Replacement Cost

Suppose the replacement cost of your home is $100,000 and you have a fire in the kitchen that costs $7,000 to restore. If your house is insured for at least $80,000, the insurer will pay the kitchen's replacement cost of $7,000. If your house has less than $80,000 coverage, however, the insurance company will be much tougher about calculating your payment. It will make two separate damage estimates and pay you whichever is larger. If the replacement cost comes to $7,000 and the company figures the kitchen and its destroyed equipment have depreciated $6,000, the actual cash value is $1,000.

The second estimate is based on your actual coverage compared with adequate coverage (80 percent). If your house's replacement cost is $100,000, then adequate coverage would be $80,000. If your actual coverage is $40,000, you only have half as much coverage as you should have, according to the insurance company. Consequently, the company will pay you only $3,500 on your $7,000 claim. They consider you a 50 percent insurance partner in the house, according to the formula:

$$\frac{\$40,000}{\$80,000} \times \$7,000 = \$3,500$$

Some companies offer a **guaranteed replacement cost coverage** endorsement to homeowners policies. This arrangement provides the homeowner who purchases less than 100 percent coverage but more than 80 percent with full replacement in the event of a total loss, regardless of policy limits.

Personal Property Coverage: The Contents of Your Home

Even if a homeowner's coverage equals the home's full replacement cost, the home's contents may be underinsured. Most homeowners policies include personal property coverage for 50 percent of the amount of insurance on the structure. This means that if a $100,000 home is insured against fire for $80,000, the contents automatically are insured up to a maximum of $40,000. That may not be enough for your personal possessions.

ACTUAL

Moreover standard policies generally insure personal property only on an "actual cash value" basis, which, as mentioned, is the cash amount an object is worth at the time of the loss. Such coverage leaves the owner vulnerable to both depreciation and inflation. This has caused many homeowners to be unpleasantly surprised. You may be convinced that your VCR or compact disc player were as good as new and in perfect working condition, but the insurance adjuster's depreciation tables will mainly consider their age. You may get what you could have sold them for at a garage sale.

Replacement Cost   Homeowners can obtain much better protection by upgrading their policies to "replacement cost" coverage for an extra 10 to 15 percent basic premium. This reimburses claimants for the cost of replacing property without adjusting for depreciation. But there is one catch. A replacement cost endorsement is often limited to 400 percent of an item's actual cash value at the time of the loss. For example, it might cost $300 to replace an old suit with an actual cash value of $10. You would collect only $40 in reimbursement. Nevertheless, the current trend is toward replacement cost coverage.

Coverage Limitations and Exclusions   Standard homeowners and tenants property insurance policies are packaged to provide comprehensive damage and liability protection. But there are gaps. No insurance policy covers everything. Although a standard homeowners policy usually provides personal property coverage adequate to cover most things people own, many people own more than the basic stuff of life. Some people collect stamps, coins, antiques, jewelry, books, or guns. Others are hobbyists with costly tools, cameras, or instruments.

When it comes to protecting such valuables, the standard homeowners policy is full of holes and may leave policyholders with a false sense of security if they do not carefully examine it. These policies are hedged with all sorts of exemptions, exclusions, and dollar limits. That applies even to policies sold as "all-risk" or "special" contracts.

Although reading an insurance policy, even a simplified one, is not the easiest nor most pleasant task, policyholders should make the effort to go over the whole policy with particular attention to **coverage exclusions** and **coverage limitations** sections. These sections may cause dangerous gaps in insurance coverage. It is important to understand policy limits—what the insurer has agreed to cover and what the policyholder's responsibilities are in the event of a loss.

After analyzing the coverage and its limitations and exclusions, you may find that the basic policy must be adjusted in order to fully protect you. Otherwise, after a burglary or fire, you may find, to your rage, that the premiums you paid for years did not cover what you thought they covered. You end up feeling that you have also been robbed or burned by the insurance company.

Personal property coverage does not insure all contents equally. Regardless of whether one has "actual cash value" or "replacement value" coverage, there are actual dollar limits on certain items such as jewelry, furs, silverware, cash, stamp, and coin collections. These limitations generally are quite low. The usual aggregate limit for the loss of all these items may be no more than $3,000. Probably the most important limitation is the coverage ceiling for each specific category or property. This is where many people experience a rude shock after a loss. Personal property, including collectibles, remains an area for which most people are excessively underinsured.

Simply because policyholders have a high amount of personal property coverage does not mean they are fully covered. Even if the losses in one category, such as jewelry, were less than the face value of their total personal property coverage, they would be covered for only that category's specific limit.

Student Coverage Students sometimes learn the hard way that valuables can walk off from dormitories, fraternity and sorority houses, and off-campus student housing. Their parents' homeowners insurance often covers the damage, but there are limits and exceptions. Some companies (such as GEICO and Aetna) cover students' possessions up to the parents' full personal property limit. Most limit coverage of a student's property stored away from home at 10 percent of the parents' personal property coverage. For example, if your house is insured for $100,000 and personal property for $50,000, your scholar gets $5,000 worth of protection. Some companies differentiate between students living on campus and those living off-campus.

Adding Insult to Burglary

Suppose you have $100,000 personal property insurance. You are burglarized and $6,000 of jewelry, $3,000 of rare coins, $4,000 of silver and antiques, and $3,000 of furs as well as $1,500 in cash, are stolen. You rush to your insurance policy, read the fine print and are surprised to discover that while you are covered for $100,000 of total damages, you will not be reimbursed the full $17,500 damages you incurred. Why? Your policy states that you are covered only up to $1,000 for jewelry and furs, $2,000 for rare coin or stamp collections, $1,500 for silver or antique items, and $200 for cash. Note that these are total limits for each loss occurrence. Although the burglar stole jewelry worth $6,000 and furs worth $3,000, you do not get back $1,000 for each item but a total of $1,000 since both are in the same category. You therefore qualify for only ($1,000 + 2,000 + 1,500 + 200) $4,700 of compensation for the $17,500 loss suffered.

Students living off-campus are considered to be independent and therefore ineligible for coverage under their parents' policy.

Supplemental Coverage There are several kinds of supplementary coverage to fill in any such gaps in a policy.

Floaters The way to increase the coverage on items of high intrinsic value which are subject to exclusions and limits is to buy a **personal articles floater** (named for the fact that the coverage "floats" or travels with the insured property wherever it may be taken). This will provide additional coverage for specified items, usually at reasonable cost. If you have many fine art, jewelry, furs, rare collections, or expensive functional items, such as computer equipment, cameras, musical instruments, silverware, or guns, the standard homeowners policy may not be enough.

A personal floater is usually sold as an extension to a basic homeowner's policy. Each item is **scheduled**—described in terms of quantity, quality, style, manufacturer, value, and so on. These items can be insured for higher amounts by special endorsement and protection against all risks, rather than just specified perils.

Riders As noted previously, most homeowners policies provide contents coverage based on 50 percent of the value of the insurance on the house. Policyholders who need or want extra coverage have the option of requesting more than the standard minimum. This is often done by adding an **endorsement** or **rider**, a paragraph amending the original insurance policy, and by paying an additional premium.

There are two other kinds of supplementary coverage of which policyholders should be aware.

Earthquakes Earthquakes are among several sources of damage that are specifically excluded in standard homeowners policies. However, supplemental earthquake

Professional Appraisal

If you experience a loss, you will have to be able to prove ownership and value to collect an item's current worth. Unless the value of the item is easily determined, it must be supported by a professional appraiser's report to support value. A bill of sale is generally required to document ownership. Objects that cannot be easily replaced, paintings or antiques, require an insurance evaluation.

The **appraisal report** should include a complete description of each article, with such details as size, cut, weight, color, and quality. Appraised values have to be updated periodically to keep pace with market values.

An accurate appraisal is obviously important. If an item is undervalued, the money collected in a claim may not be enough to replace the item. If it is overvalued, the inflated appraisal could bring you a windfall from the insurance company if you have a loss, but the odds are you will not have a loss. In the meanwhile, you pay for more insurance than you need and rates are not cheap. Floater premiums vary with the incidence of crime in your area and may generally range from $ .10 up to $2 per $100.

coverage can be added to a policy by a rider or endorsement. By law, companies in California must at least offer it as an add-on. Earthquake coverage on the west coast costs between $2 to $4 extra per $1,000 of coverage on a $100,000 home, which means $200 to $400 a year. Rates, however, vary widely. In regions considered low-risk earthquake areas, the rates are as low as 20 cents per $1,000 of coverage. The San Francisco earthquake of 1989 showed the importance of this rider. Although Californians are by far the largest buyers of earthquake insurance, only about 20 percent of those affected by the 1989 quake were covered.

Flood Insurance   The most important risk universally excluded from homeowners policies is flood insurance. It can be obtained through the National Flood Insurance Program, administered by the Federal Emergency Management Agency (FEMA), or through private insurers. It is available only for those who live in a community that participates in the program by complying with the government's guidelines for flood prevention (mostly in California, Florida, Louisiana, and Texas). Under the program, a home can be insured for up to $185,000 in structural damage and for $60,000 in losses to the contents. Premiums vary according to FEMA's assessment of the risk of flooding for a particular home, with more risk-prone areas costing more. The national average is about $300 per year for $80,000 in coverage. Nearly 80 percent of the $16 billion of damage caused by Hurricane Andrew in 1992 was insured in part by the National Flood Insurance Program.

Loss of Use Rider   Loss of use coverage pays living expenses if a home becomes unusable. Traditionally, this part of a policy has been limited to 20 percent of the amount of coverage bought for the contents. However, for a modest increase in premiums, policyholders can buy loss of use coverage with no dollar limit. This additional coverage should enable policyholders to maintain their standard of living for up to a year or more.

Deductibles   The first step is, as stated, discerning how much insurance you need. When buying a policy, you are paying the insurer to assume the risk that disaster will strike. If you can afford to cover at least part of the risk on your own, you do not need as much insurance. The standard deductible has long been $100, but there is a trend toward increasing that amount.

Insurance **deductibles** were introduced to avoid the costs of processing small claims. A deductible forces the policyholder to absorb relatively minor losses. This saves insurers the cost of the claim and the expense of processing it. Since people tend to have small losses much more often than larger ones, the savings for insurers in paperwork alone can be considerable. Insurers pass a portion of these savings on to policyholders in the form of lower rates. When an insurance company offers a deductible, it says, in effect: "If you spare us the cost of processing trivial claims, we'll give you a discount. We'll give you a small discount if you draw the line at $250, and we'll give you a larger discount if you draw the line at $500 or $1,000."

Deductibles are therefore one way to reduce insurance expenses. Policyholders should consider accepting the largest deductible they can afford. This form of self-insurance is nearly always worth the risk since premiums can be lowered by up to 35 percent. If you opt for a $250 deductible, you can save about 10 percent on premiums compared to identical coverage with the standard deductible.

DEDUCTIBLES

Higher deductibles can be traded for higher coverage. Raising the deductible on a $50,000 HO-3 policy from $100 to $250, homeowners choosing this option could save enough to raise their coverage from $50,000 to $60,000. Most people can handle a deductible approximately equal to one week's net salary. Thus, if one's income is $40,000, a $600 deductible should be manageable. Moreover, half of all homeowners insurance claims are for less than $500; two-thirds are for less than $1,000. Someone with a $250 deductible who suffers a $500 loss often decides not to file the claim because the action might force up future premiums. Over the years, the premium savings from the larger deductible should more than outweigh the cost of paying for a minor accident yourself.

Fire Insurance

Fire insurance is included in every standard homeowners or tenants insurance. Fire damage is one of the most common causes of property damage. Each year more than half a million American families suffer the trauma of a serious fire in their homes and the annual bill for damages is close to $3 billion. But, as people discover every day, the fire is only the beginning of the trauma. Assessing the damage, negotiating a fair reimbursement with the insurance company, and arranging for adequate repair and rebuilding can be a major headache. The process can last for months. Let us therefore discuss how to cope with the possibility of a fire in your home.

Establishing Proof of Ownership and Value of Personal Possessions   If you have $50,000 personal possessions coverage, that does not necessarily mean you will be reimbursed this full amount after a serious fire or other loss. Being adequately insured is not always enough. When catastrophe strikes, your insurance company will normally request proofs of purchase and of the value of damaged or lost items. How much insurance money you get depends on your ability to prove values and a certain amount of negotiation, too. But a little organization and advanced planning may save a lot of grief in case of a disaster.

Taking Inventory   Losing money because of a house fire may be unavoidable, but there are a few steps that can be taken to reduce the misery considerably. The first step is probably the hardest to follow because it involves a good deal of boring legwork. As soon as you buy a homeowners insurance policy, start making a record of everything you own. You might simply expand the Net Worth Statement (discussed in Chapter 1) and develop it in much greater detail, or use a household inventory worksheet. Most insurance companies provide inventory worksheets (The Insurance Information Institute offers an inventory worksheet at no charge; call 800/221-4954). Your inventory list should be brought up to date each year.

Describe each object as graphically as possible—including its age, brand name, size, model number or serial number, date of purchase, and price paid. If an appraiser's estimate is available, record the figure and the date. Write down everything you own, from coffee mugs to candelabras. Although such items as coffee mugs may not seem valuable enough to record, the total loss of all such household goods is major. In some categories of property, such as clothing, you can lump together a number of articles and attach a single estimate of value, such as 20 shirts ($200), 12 pairs of shoes ($300).

Proving a loss can be exasperating, especially if an item is several years old. Receipts, canceled checks, credit card vouchers, certificates of ownership, and warranties for purchases of everything from suits to videotapes should be systematically filed into file folders. The file folders should be stored in a fireproof cabinet. If you

Filing a Claim

Suppose your house just burned down. You stand in a pile of rubble where just yesterday you were curled up on the couch with your family, nibbling potato chips and watching television. Within 24 hours a fire has completely shattered the security on which you based your life. Almost all your material possessions have disappeared or been damaged beyond repair.

What do you do now? First, keep calm. Before you get to the point of filing a claim, you must get through the first few hours that follow a bad fire. The following are recommended steps to take after the fire trucks pull away:

1. *Call Your Insurance Agent*   Your agent will get the claims process started. The agent should also advance cash for immediate expenses until you can find your credit cards and reconstruct your checking account records. The advance will eventually be deducted from the settlement.
2. *Call Your Lawyer*   Your lawyer will keep you from making potentially damaging mistakes. For one thing, make no statements and sign no papers offered you by the insurance company unless your lawyer approves. The lawyer will find and engage a public adjuster to handle negotiations and will advise you on any settlement.
3. *Tour the House*   Tour your house with a pad, recording whatever remains and is salvageable and whatever details you recall on furnishings destroyed.
4. *Secure the House*   You are expected to use "reasonable means" to preserve the property, meaning that you should act as though you do not have any insurance. If the home is unfit to be lived in, board up the windows, lock all doors, shut off the gas, electricity, and water and do whatever else is necessary to prevent further damage. You can do this yourself, or hire a "board-up" service that within hours will nail up wood panels and patches to keep looters out. Often this is a local municipality requirement. Your insurance agent should be able to recommend a "board-up" service.
5. *Visit Your Safe Deposit Box*   Assemble your home furnishings inventory, photograph negatives, movie film or video cassette tape, insurance policy, and house deed. Your lawyer and insurance agent will need these papers to process the loss claim so you should always store them in a safe place outside your home.
6. *Sign No Papers*   This includes release forms, settlements, or retainer agreements from public adjusters, unless your lawyer approves them first.
7. *Open a New and Seperate Checking Account*   Do this both to handle any advances received from the insurance company and to pay the bills related to the loss.

own an audio tape recorder, you could walk through your house, room by room, and describe all the furniture, the rugs, carpets, the art hung on the walls, even the bric-a-brac on the piano. Many homeowners methodically photograph the contents of each room and store the negatives, together with the tapes, in a safe deposit box.

Videotaping possessions is currently in vogue. Increasingly, homeowners are hiring professional photographers to make a detailed inventory of their homes, both inside and out. But this is no substitute for an itemized inventory worksheet. Rather, it may be used as supportive evidence to back up an inventory list. Photographs should include close-ups of expensive objects, such as silverware and jewelry. Insurers are less likely to question claims based on such inventories, especially when they are submitted along with photos, videotape, receipts, or appraisers' statements for particularly valuable items. The last step is absolutely vital: Leave a copy of your inventory with your insurance agent, in your safe deposit box, or somewhere else

Adjusters

Adequate records are only the beginning of the claim settlement process. From the moment of the first flame, the insured and the insurer become adversaries. With documentation to substantiate their claim and a good lawyer and public adjuster, policyholders stand a good chance of being fairly and fully compensated for their losses.

Many victims discover that the insurer wants to settle as fast and as cheaply as possible. Perseverance on the victim's part may sometimes yield more results because the insurance company may find it easier to compromise than continue to argue. Disputes typically start when the insurance company's adjuster and the insured disagree on the value of what you lost. An **adjuster** is the insurance company's specialist on loss, who will decide how much a policyholder should receive in settlement. In such a situation, policyholders may want to hire a **public adjuster** to represent them in negotiations with the insurance company.

When hiring a public adjuster, policyholders should ensure that he or she is a member of the National Association of Public Insurance Adjusters or is licensed by the state. The adjuster gets an agreed-upon percentage of the settlement, usually between 3 to 10 percent, depending on the size of the claim. They can be well worth their fee when they find things that the insured and the insurance company may have overlooked.

Having an experienced professional act as your representative in negotiating with the insurance company has many advantages. Adjusters know how to read an insurance policy, which is often very technical and uses symbols to designate types of policies, such as the previously mentioned HO-2 and HO-3. They can make a claim settlement easier by completing inventory and other insurance company forms.

The adjuster generally is also a great help in taking inventory of the charred remains after a fire. An adjuster will walk through the house and ask questions: What was hanging on that wall? Was this a couch or a chair? What was the material? How many suits or jackets do you think were in that closet? An adjuster is usually trained to recognize structural aspects of a burned house. He or she can tell by looking at the rubble whether you had a plaster wall. If so, he or she will not let the insurance company offer to replace the walls with sheetrock (drywall), which costs only one-fifth as much as plaster walls.

The adjuster also mediates between the company's designated contractor and your own renovator if you have engaged one. When he or she has brought them together on costs and both you and the company representative have approved the final figure, his or her job is done.

Condominium Insurance

As dwelling styles change, so does dwelling insurance. Style, economics, and advanced technology have moved many people out of traditional frame and brick single-family homes into condominiums and rental units. The insurance industry has responded with policies to fit each need. Because a condominium can represent as large an investment as a home, it requires similar protection. However, since each condo owner purchases a **unit** that is attached to others and to common areas, insurance has to be somewhat different from a basic homeowner policy. Each condo owner, before buying, should make sure that the condominium association has adequate coverage on common areas. Otherwise, in the event of a loss, each unit owner could be assessed for damages to common areas.

Single Entity or Barewall Condo Coverage   Condo association insurance is written according to one of two concepts: **single entity** or **barewall**. Under the single entity concept, the unit owner is responsible for insuring only personal property inside the unit and any additions or alterations made to the original structure. It is the responsibility of the association to insure the unit as it was built. The common areas of a building or development, such as the roof, elevator, boiler, and walkways, are insured in a commercial policy bought by the condo or co-op association. The contents of the apartments are insured through personal policies purchased by the individual owners.

Under the barewall concept, the condo association has no responsibility to insure the unit inside except for the unfinished surfaces of the perimeter walls, floors, and ceilings. The condo owner is therefore responsible for insuring such property as kitchen cabinets, built-in fixtures and appliances, interior partitions, plumbing, wiring, wallpaper, carpeting, and any other permanent additions known as improvements and betterments. Most condominiums choose the barewall concept, which makes each unit owner responsible for repair and maintenance of everything within his or her dwelling space.

Laws differ from state to state, but generally a condo owner should be sure that whatever the association has not insured is covered under a separate condo ownership policy. The association's policy and the unit owner's policy should combine to cover the entire scope of loss exposure. As with homeowners insurance, it is important to know the exclusions in a condo owner's policy. Excluded perils and coverage are generally the same as those listed in homeowners policies. Exactly who is responsible for insuring what can vary from building to building, so owners must read the association's bylaws and proprietary lease. If a condo owner finds the association's coverage inadequate, or if the association carries a high deductible, the owner may want to purchase supplemental coverage.

Loss Assessment Endorsement   A unique aspect of condo owners insurance is a **loss assessment endorsement** available from most companies. This coverage protects the unit owner from inadequacies in the association's coverage. It reimburses the unit owner for special assessments when a large liability claim exceeds the association's policy limits, when property not covered by the association is lost or damaged, or when property loss is not covered by the association because of a high deductible.

Renters or Tenants Insurance

Insurance industry researchers estimate that 75 percent of U.S. renters have no dwelling insurance. **Renters insurance** is inexpensive, but the lack of it can be tragic. Renters insurance covers household contents and most personal belongings against many of the same perils listed in a homeowners policy, as well as the same liability coverages. Covering the structure itself is the responsibility of the owner.

The key to renters insurance is to make certain coverage is adequate. Most renters do not see the need for insuring their property. They often feel that the structure is the landlord's responsibility and that their belongings do not amount to much. Renters have a tendency to underestimate the value of their property because the investment does not seem large when it is purchased piece by piece. However, if they take a household inventory, most renters, like homeowners, would be surprised at the total value of their belongings.

Not only would an inventory of these possessions likely reflect a substantial value but also a potential negligence suit by a guest who trips and falls could create an enormous liability. Renters insurance can help cover both of these contingencies.

Insurance Discounts

Many insurance companies will offer discounts to homeowners and renters if they improve the safety in their home, lowering the probability of a loss. The following discounts are commonly available and could reduce a homeowners insurance costs:

1. *Nonsmokers*   Because smoking is considered a leading cause of home fires, insurers are experimenting with a special nonsmoke discount for homeowners insurance. To be eligible, all residents of the household must be nonsmokers for at least a year prior to the policy application.

2. *Renovation*   Complete renovation of an older home, which usually includes revamping the electrical, heating, cooling, and plumbing system, as well as repairing the roof, will qualify a homeowner for a sizable rate discount with some insurers.

3. *Safe Homeowner*   Some insurers offer discounts for homeowners who do not file a claim for one to two years. Higher discounts are available for two to three years of loss-free experience. When a loss is incurred, the homeowner loses this discount.

4. *Security System*   Most companies offer a 2 to 10 percent premium credit for security systems, depending upon the type installed, such as deadbolt locks and burglar alarms. The largest is given for homes in which fire and burglary detection devices report automatically to a UL-approved central alarm monitoring station, where trained operators promptly notify police or fire departments. If these alarms sound only at the house, the usual savings is 2 percent.

5. *Smoke Detectors/Sprinklers*   Insurance companies regularly give a 2 percent premium credit for homes equipped with a UL-approved smoke detector, which has proved effective in preventing fire deaths and injuries as well as reducing property damage. Insurers also offer a 2 to 5 percent rate credit for home sprinkler systems, which also are effective in minimizing fire damage.

6. *Marking of Valuables*   Policyholders who mark their easily stolen valuables receive rate discounts on their property insurance from many insurance companies.

7. *New Home*   Newly built homes often receive rate discounts on property insurance ranging from 15 percent for homes under two years old to 5 percent for a five-year-old home.

8. *Direct Writers*   There are companies known as **"direct writers"** that either do not use agents or employ their own agents, sometimes passing on commissions savings to customers in the form of lower rates.

9. *Other Factors*   Rates and discounts allowed can vary greatly from state to state because each state has its own regulatory commission. And the 3,500 individual companies may have differing structures, depending upon their own claims experience in the area. Factors that influence cost include the:
   a. Type of structure being insured
   b. Incidence of crime in the area
   c. Proximity and availability of fire protection
   d. Proximity to fire hydrants
   e. Age of the home
   f. Home structure—brick or frame
   g. Number and size of the rooms
   h. Term of the policy (one or three years)

It is therefore difficult for policyholders to judge the fairness of their homeowners premium by comparing it with the premiums of their neighbors or friends. So many factors go into calculating insurance rates that two houses across the street from each other may differ substantially.

Excess Liability Insurance: Umbrella Policy

Accidents often happen and when they do, the law requires those who were to blame to pay the victim's financial losses. The standard homeowners policy, as discussed earlier, includes only property damage and bodily injury to people on or off your property. But a widely available high-limit coverage called **extended personal liability, or umbrella insurance**, extends beyond liability assessed for physical injury.

Umbrellas are called that because they rise above the basic protection and shield policyholders against damages that could be assessed for any number of reasons. Umbrellas typically cover policyholders and their family members living in the house against lawsuits for such things as false arrest, wrongful conviction, libel, slander, defamation of character, invasion of privacy, mental anguish, shock, malicious prosecution,

Negligence

You can be sued for liability if you can be proved negligent. **Negligence** is the failure to exercise the necessary degree of care to protect others from harm. It refers to conduct which falls below the standard established by law for the protection of others against unreasonable risk of harm. For example, failure to clear snow or ice from a sidewalk or path in front of your home may lead to a liability lawsuit if someone slips as a result. The courts generally require property owners to exercise reasonable care and to act in a reasonable manner.

A person is said to have been negligent when he or she fails to exercise the care expected of a prudent person or does what a prudent person would not have done. Negligence may be caused by acts of omission, commission, or both. A negligent party is responsible for any injuries or property damage that results from a specific incident, even if the incident was unintentional.

Naturally, the definition of negligence is open to interpretation by the various courts throughout the country. However, if you are accused of negligence, it often must be proved that you had a responsibility to be more careful than the person accusing you.

Contributory Negligence

It is not uncommon for defendants or their lawyers in a liability suit to try to prove **contributory negligence.** This common law principle states that one negligent individual cannot be held liable by another individual who was also negligent in the same accident, regardless of the relative degrees of their negligence.

With a defense of contributory negligence, the defendant maintains that the plaintiff contributed to his or her own loss by also acting in a negligent manner. This defense might be used, for example, in the above case of a slippery sidewalk when the plaintiff was racing down the street during an ice or snow storm, or that the plaintiff was intoxicated when her or she slipped. If it could be shown that the accident would not have occurred had the plaintiff exercised prudent or reasonable care, the plaintiff's claim against the defendant might be defeated.

Comparative Negligence

It used to be that injured persons lost their entire claim if their own negligence contributed to the accident in any way. However, some states have enacted **comparative negligence statutes.** Under this statutory principle, when two or more individuals are negligent in an accident, an attempt is made to apportion the loss to each party in proportion to the degree each was negligent. Therefore, even if an injured person was somewhat at fault, the person should recover at least partial damages through the claim. These same concepts of negligence hold true for auto accidents, which is why liability coverage is one of the most important parts of automobile insurance (discussed next).

disease, and illness. They therefore provide protection that is not available in other policies. If you were sued for libel, for example, the insurance company would pay for your legal defense. If you lost the case, it would pay the amount the court awarded to your opponent, up to the limit of the policy.

You actually could be hauled into court for any number of reasons, including mishaps beyond your control. A neighbor could take offense at a joking remark and sue you for slander. Your lovable fox terrier could bite somebody. Your child could beat up the block bully. A neighborhood child could cut through your yard, trip over the garden hose, and fall into your smoldering barbecue pit. Someone who is injured on your property, whether invited or not, may be able to collect damages if you are shown to be negligent in some way. That could include neighborhood children running through your yard or driveway if you take no action to stop them. Posting "No Trespassing" signs may not be enough. A party guest who gets drunk in your home and has a car accident on the way home could sue you for causing his or her intoxication. The New Jersey Supreme Court ruled in 1984 that a person who directly serves liquor to a guest and lets him or her drive away intoxicated can be held liable for damages if the guest causes an accident in which people are injured.

Most of us just do not have enough assets to defend ourselves against a serious lawsuit, let alone pay for any settlement the court might award. Without excess personal liability insurance, you may not literally lose your shirt, but you could conceivably lose your savings, your home and property, and even a large part of your salary for years to come. An umbrella policy supplements not only the liability coverage in your homeowners policy but also any other policy with liability coverage, such as an auto policy, picking up where these other policies leave off.

Suppose you have one of the standard homeowners policies. Although the basic liability coverage is $100,000, you can increase your coverage to perhaps as much as $300,000. If you have $300,000 coverage and lose a $600,000 injury case, your insurance company will pay $300,000. But if you also have a million-dollar umbrella policy, it will cover the additional $300,000 your homeowners policy did not cover. Without adding much to premiums, this extra coverage protects your assets that otherwise might be seized to pay damage compensation to an accident victim.

Umbrella Policy Limitations   There are some exceptions, however. Umbrella policies do not cover, among other things, bodily injury or property damage which occurs in the course of your business activities, or which are intentionally caused by you or another adult member of your family. If you lose your temper during an argument with your neighbor over the fence he put up between your house and his and slug him with your snow shovel, you will have to pick up the tab and protect yourself in court if he sues.

Occupational liability is excluded in most contracts. Therefore, a personal umbrella liability policy will not cover you for malpractice on the job. Claims against you for bodily injury or property damage that you cause on the job will have to be covered by a separate **malpractice** or **professional liability policy**. Such coverage might be needed if you are self-employed. A doctor who is sued for malpractice cannot look to an umbrella for protection but would have to buy a special malpractice policy for physicians.

Even if you do not have much in terms of money or assets yet, you could benefit from an excess liability policy, because a judgment against you could lay claim to your future income for years to come. The future income of a job is a valuable asset that needs to be protected. To minimize this risk, more and more people are buying personal liability umbrella policies with limits of $1 million or more.

Umbrella policies are comparatively cheap. A million-dollar policy can be bought for $70 to $140 a year, depending upon the company selected and such factors as the number of cars and homes the insured owns.

The cost of such coverage is low because claims are rare. Despite increasing litigation, insurers have not had to pay off very often. Fewer than 1 of every 1,000 policyholders a year invokes their protection. But the need for such protection is growing.

Lawsuits are in style for almost any occasion. In this age of rampant litigation, Americans are suing one another in sharply rising numbers, and some are hitting jackpots. Juries in recent years have tended to side with accident victims and often award them lavish sums of $1 million or more. In 1982, for example, juries awarded a million dollars or more in 251 personal injury cases alone. This does not include numerous out-of-court settlements that were in the six-figure category.

Just about anybody can be sued. The wealthier you are, the greater the threat, and a court battle could be calamitous even if you win. With lawyers charging $100 to $250 or more an hour, defense costs can be extremely expensive.

Don't Flaunt Your Umbrella   One inescapable irony of excess liability insurance is that it not only protects against huge damage suits but also may provoke them. Someone is more likely to sue you if he or she knows that you have a million-dollar excess liability policy. So if you have an umbrella policy, don't flaunt it.

Nevertheless, although the chances of needing excess liability are still remote, the case for buying it is compelling. The more you have to lose, the less you should go without it. The low cost of this coverage for a million dollars of insurance makes it foolish to run the risk of a horrendous judgment against you.

"We're starting first-aid training, Dad. I need $150,000 for malpractice insurance."

SOURCE: "Pepper...and Salt," *The Wall Street Journal*, December 5 1990, A-15. Reprinted by permission of Cartoon Features Syndicate.

Policy Cancellation

Once an initial homeowners policy has been in effect for at least 60 days, the company is prohibited from canceling it for three years, except for specific legal reasons, such as nonpayment of premium, physical changes in the property insured after issuance, or discovery of fraud in obtaining the policy. Nor can it raise just *your* premium. Unlike automobile insurance, the frequency of claims does not affect the premiums for personal property coverage. But if the insurance company can prove excessive loss due to owner negligence, it may decline to renew a policy. Getting canceled is a real possibility for policyholders with a history of claims or with a single large claim that puts them into the company's high-risk categories.

At the end of each three-year period, a company may cancel a homeowners policy or insist on altering the coverage in some way to lower its risk, but it must give written notice between 45 and 60 days before the termination of the policy. If it does not do so, the policyholder is automatically protected for another three years.

Auto Insurance

After their home, many people's second most valuable possession is likely to be their automobile. Shopping for auto insurance can be baffling. Unless insurance consumers take the time to read their policy carefully, they probably are not aware of the numerous provisions that make auto insurance one of the most comprehensive insurance packages they can buy.

All states have financial responsibility laws and many also have compulsory insurance laws. Although financial responsibility laws vary, in general drivers must be able to show that they are financially able to pay a set minimum amount of money after an accident. The minimum is usually high enough to make automobile insurance a necessity. Nevertheless, in some states insurance is not mandatory. (These states are Maine, Mississippi, New Hampshire, Ohio, Rhode Island, Tennessee, Virginia, Washington, and Wisconsin.)

Mandatory or not, it would be extremely foolhardy for anyone to own and drive a car without hefty insurance coverage. Many states with compulsory insurance laws require car owners to carry a minimum amount of liability insurance. Generally, these minimums are far too low to cover all of your potential losses, leaving you vulnerable to be sued for much more than the amount of your liability coverage.

The cost of additional liability coverage is minimal compared to the risks in driving without adequate insurance. In New York State, for example, where most of the legal minimums have not been changed since the 1940s, minimum policies will pay only up to $10,000 for injuries to an individual, even though claims often run far in excess of those limits. Similarly, the minimum liability limits pay up to $5,000 for property damage, about half the average price of a new car.

Beyond what the law in your state specifies as minimum automobile coverage, you need protection against losses that do not concern the state. They include theft as well as damage to your car for which no one else is liable.

The typical auto policy is called *auto insurance,* but in fact it is a package of five major types of coverage, each with its own premium. A car owner should know each part of the package well before shopping for a policy. The following are the five parts.

Bodily Injury and Property Damage Liability Coverage

Bodily injury and **liability coverage** are the most important and most expensive parts of the auto insurance policy. In most states, this is the only type of auto insurance that is mandatory. In its basic form, auto insurance provides liability coverages to pay for injuries and property damage the policyholder becomes legally obligated to pay as a result of accidents involving the insured car. For example, if you are involved in a collision with another vehicle and you are found to be at fault, the auto liability coverages would pay the occupants of the not-at-fault car for their injuries and property damage.

Liability insurance covers injuries an insured causes to pedestrians and occupants of other cars as well as damage to other people's property. Coverage is often quoted in three sets of numbers, known as a **split-limit policy**. An example of a standard split-limit policy would be 100/300/25. This means the company will pay a maximum of $100,000 for bodily injury suffered by any one person in each accident, as much as $300,000 for injuries suffered by all persons in any one accident, and up to $25,000 for related property damage per accident.

Many motorists limit their liability to the modest state minimums, usually 25/50/10. For people with substantial assets or income, that is woefully insufficient. Million-dollar injury judgments have multiplied in recent years, so the threat of a financial disaster is very real. A minimum of $100,000 per person, $300,000 per accident, and $25,000 for property damage is widely recommended. Higher limits do not cost much more. About $50 more in premiums a year increases your liability limit to $500,000 per accident. Most drivers buy as much as they can afford to protect against catastrophic financial loss. Suppose you inadvertently pulled out in front of a loaded tractor-trailer, forcing it off the road. The rig and its contents were totaled. The liability was in excess of $200,000. If you have only minimal property damage coverage, you may be personally liable for the difference.

Your auto liability policies also cover your legal obligations when you are carrying passengers in someone else's car, when you lend your car to someone else, or when using a rented car, small truck, or small trailer. Another little known benefit: When you are driving out of state, the liability coverage automatically expands to meet any special liability limits or situations required by the insurance laws in the state where you are traveling.

One of the most overlooked benefits contained in the auto liability coverage is the insurance company's obligation to investigate claims made against you. If the investigation determines that you or someone using your car was legally responsible for the damage, the insurer will negotiate a settlement and pay what you owe up to the liability limits you purchased. However, if the investigation indicates that you were not at fault, your insurer is obligated to defend you against the liability claim or lawsuit.

Investigation, negotiation, and legal defense costs are not subject to the policy limits—a fact that may turn out to be the most valuable "hidden benefit" in an auto policy. For example, say you are involved in a traffic accident resulting in serious injury to a passenger in the other car. Investigation by the insurer indicates that you were not responsible for the crash. Both you and the other party are paid for damages under the **no-fault** provisions (explained further on). However, the injured party sues you for $500,000 in damages.

The insurance company provides a legal defense for you and due to a lengthy trial, incurs more than $25,000 in legal expenses, even though the limit of liability on your policy is only $20,000. You win the lawsuit and pay no liability damages. However, without auto insurance you could have found yourself $25,000 in debt for legal expenses, even though the accident was not your fault. If you lost the case, and the judge ordered you to pay $50,000 in damages to the plaintiff, then the insurance company would pay only the liability limit on your policy of $20,000 and you would be responsible for the rest. But as mentioned earlier, you can avoid such expenses by buying a high-limit umbrella liability coverage. Remember: Always carry high bodily injury liability coverage to protect against the potentially ruinous costs that can arise from accidents involving serious injury or death.

Medical Payments

Medical payments insurance usually covers medical bills resulting from accidental injury to you, your family members, or any passengers in your car, without regard to who caused the accident. It also covers you and family members injured while riding in another person's car or hit by a car while out walking. Even if your family has full health insurance, other passengers in your car may not, so it pays to take the coverage. You get to choose how much coverage to buy, ranging from $1,000 to $100,000 per person.

Uninsured Motorist Coverage

Uninsured motorist coverage pays medical and related expenses for injuries caused by a hit-and-run driver or a driver who is uninsured and cannot pay a judgment. It covers bodily injuries but also property damage in some states. This coverage is most important in states that do not have a no-fault law (discussed further on). Uninsured motorists are always a potential threat, but low-cost protection is readily available from most insurance companies. Each state determines the minimum mandatory level of such insurance. For a small extra charge it is possible to greatly augment this coverage. For example, in Virginia uninsured motorist insurance typically costs $11 for 25/50/10, but for $20 one can get 100/300/50. The extra $9 a year is well worth the difference.

Collision

Collision insurance covers damage to the insured car as a result of accidents with another vehicle or some stationary object, regardless of who causes the accident or is at fault. You generally share part of the cost via a deductible that makes you pay for the first $50 to $1,000 of repairs (discussed further on). If it is the other driver's fault, your insurance company will likely seek reimbursement from the other driver or the driver's liability policy and should prorate a refund of your deductible if it is able to collect. Under this coverage, if an insured car is totaled, the policyholder generally receives only its current retail value. Collision coverage accounts for as much as 30 percent of the insurance premium on a new car.

Comprehensive (Other Than Collision)

The **comprehensive coverage** of the policy insures against damage to a car caused by mishaps other than a crash, such as fire, theft, vandalism, glass breakage, damage from falling objects, earthquakes, floods, and collisions with animals. It is often referred to in the standard personal auto form as "other than collision." It also compensates policyholders to some extent for what they must spend to rent a car if the insured car is stolen. As with collision insurance, this coverage is usually sold with a deductible.

No-Fault Laws

Auto accidents exact an enormous toll in deaths, injuries, and property damage. For years, state governments and insurance companies struggled to find a fair and efficient way to compensate auto accident victims. **No-fault** auto insurance has proved to be an equitable solution to the problem. In fault, or tort-liability systems, victims attempt to recover losses from negligent drivers or others. When such claims are paid, the money comes from liability insurance carried by the parties at fault. Under no-fault insurance, people who are injured in accidents are compensated by their own insurance companies for the cost of their care plus certain other expenses and lost income. It does not matter who, if anybody, was to blame for the accident.

No-fault systems limit the rights of victims to sue for nonquantifiable costs such as pain, suffering, anguish, emotional trauma, or other noneconomic damages. Since the late 1960s, when no-fault auto insurance laws were first enacted in the United States, the goals of such laws have remained constant. They seek to:

1. Pay more people for their medical costs and lost wages

2. Pay them faster and more equitably regardless of driver negligence

3. Reduce the number of accident cases in the legal system to the most serious ones

4. Cut legal costs and court congestion associated with auto accident injury settlements

5. Contain or to reduce auto insurance premiums

Under no-fault law, the policyholder buys **personal injury protection (PIP)**, which provides first-party reimbursement for medical expenses, lost wages, rehabilitation costs, service replacement costs (such as housekeeping and child care expenses), funeral expenses, and other direct expenses. Thus, no matter who is at fault in an accident, people injured in the policyholder's car will be quickly compensated for their medical expenses and other economic losses, up to the limits the policyholder chose when he or she purchased PIP auto coverage.

No-fault insurance in no way diminishes the need to affect adequate physical damage coverage. In the event that you are involved in a one-car smash-up, such as smashing your car into a tree, you will not be compensated under no-fault unless you have collision coverage. Likewise, if your car is stolen or burned or vandalized, then you will be indemnified only if you have comprehensive coverage.

No-fault insurance guarantees coverage whether policyholders are hit by an uninsured motorist or are themselves at fault in an accident. Only three states—New York, Michigan, and Florida—have relatively strict no-fault insurance. However, most of the 26 states that adopted the no-fault system left the door open to litigation.

Therefore, no-fault laws do not give careless drivers immunity from retribution. Drivers at fault in an accident are still subject to state traffic laws and can be sued if they cause loss in excess of the state's mandated ceiling. The claim amount that is covered by no-fault is called the *threshold*. For example, in a no-fault state with a $5,000 medical threshold, insured drivers agree not to sue for noneconomic damages unless medical expenses exceed $5,000. When medical bills do surpass the threshold, accident victims have the right to initiate tort (damage) action for losses due to pain and suffering.

Premium Surcharges, Penalties, and Cancellations

A driver who has an accident and is deemed negligent can expect to be hit with a surcharge, which amounts to a considerable increase in insurance rates. Surcharges commonly are imposed after the insurer pays a substantial damage claim to the insured or another party. The same thing may happen if the driver is convicted of a serious traffic violation and the insurance company finds out about it.

Under one widely used formula, the first chargeable accident in which a driver is held blameworthy brings a 40 percent boost in total annual premiums for the ensuing three years. A second accident during that period increases the rates by an additional 90 percent of the original base rate. Thus, a driver whose base rate was $400 a year would pay a (40% + 90% =) 130 percent increase in rates after two misadventures. The premium would soar to $920.

Not all penalties are as severe. Some companies are more lenient. State Farm, the biggest auto insurer, raises premiums by only 10 percent for the first accident, 20 percent for the second, 50 percent for the third, and another 50 percent for a fourth accident. A few insurers, such as Penney, have perceived a marketing and advertising opportunity in this area and forgive the first accident.

To avert a rate increase or cancellation, motorists often pay out of their own pocket for minor collision damage. This makes sense if the repair costs are no higher than the cost of a surcharge which the insured will pay for three years. Policyholders might also be able to soften the impact of a surcharge by raising their deductible.

Proposition 103: The Auto Rate Revolution

Auto insurance premiums have risen steadily since 1980 at 9 percent a year. Between 1986 and 1988, rates rose more than 25 percent. The insurance industry attributed the rapid increase to the following factors:

1. Weaknesses in the no-fault laws

2. Deteriorating roads

3. Rising medical costs

4. High car repair costs

5. Increased car thefts

6. Increased numbers of drivers on the road

7. New cars getting more expensive

8. Motorists logging more driving miles

9. More lavish damage awards made by the courts

For a couple with a 17-year-old son and two cars, premiums of as much as $4,000 a year were common in major urban metropolitan centers, such as New Jersey and California. As Table 8–2 shows, rates for a single male aged 19 could have run over $6,000 a year.

There was widespread suspicion among the public that insurance companies were gouging policyholders. Rising auto insurance rates in particular became a political and economic issue in most states. The high and ever-rising cost of automobile insurance in California stirred a public clamor for government action to protect consumers.

Auto rates in California were the third highest in the country, exceeded only by New Jersey and Alaska. A California group known as Voter Revolt to Cut Insurance Rates brought the question to a vote in a public referendum in 1988. **Proposition 103**, which was passed by a majority of voters, mandated a reduction of 20 percent or more in automobile and other property and casualty insurance rates. It also tightened public control over the industry in California and served as a catalyst for change across the nation. Proposition 103 also called for an elected insurance commissioner to replace the commissioner appointed by the governor. The commissioner was given sweeping power to review the financial records of any insurer seeking rate increases. The California Supreme Court, in May 1989, upheld the primary pro-

TABLE 8–2	The High Price of Auto Insurance

Shown are average annual insurance rates as of December 1988 for typical liability, collision, and comprehensive coverage for a 1987 Chevrolet Caprice. These rates were based on a good driving record, a commute of 4 to 9 miles one way, and 8,000 miles driven annually.

City	Married Couple (husband age 45)	Single Male (age 19)
Denver	$ 657	$ 1,933
Houston	790	2,298
Los Angeles	1,840	4,882
Miami	1,663	4,675
Milwaukee	506	1,670
New York (Bronx)	1,946	4,438
Philadelphia	1,893	6,039
Phoenix	1,066	3,417
San Francisco	1,211	3,863
Washington, DC	819	2,637

SOURCE: Insurance Information Institute.

visions of Proposition 103. It has been slowly implemented, however, due to legal challenges. As this book goes to press, only the issue of rebates is still in the courts.

California is not the only state where drivers have been trying to reduce auto insurance premiums. Consumers in other states are promoting California-like referendums, which would force rates downward for years to come. Insurers and drivers are in head-to-head confrontation in Massachusetts, Ohio, New Jersey, and Florida. Activist groups are also on the move in Arizona, Colorado, and Pennsylvania.

Massachusetts officials ordered a rate cut of about 8 percent for 1989 after outraged motorists denounced retroactive 1987 premium bills which arrived in September 1988. The legislature also enacted a law that limits lawsuits and lets drivers choose higher deductibles and refuse certain coverage. Insurers responded by warning that a spread of forced rate reductions would make coverage scarce and expensive even in states where that isn't an issue. In June 1990, the Travelers Corporation, the company that invented car insurance back in 1897, announced that it will stop selling auto and homeowners policies in nine states. Other leading firms such as State Farm, Allstate, Fireman's Fund, Liberty Mutual, Aetna, and Kemper have declared that they would rather curtail policies than continue, as they claim, to be drained by spiraling repair and medical bills.

The insurance companies argue that Proposition 103 ignores the industry's underlying cause for raising rates, that of soaring costs. As long as litigation and medical costs keep increasing at a rapid pace, insurers claim they will be compelled to raise rates. The industry would prefer tougher curbs on the right to sue for damages, controls on medical bills, stiffer penalties for fraudulent claims, and greater competition among repair shops. Where the confrontation will lead is uncertain. But it has highlighted the burdensome costs of auto insurance and the need for basic reforms to remedy the situation.

The Rate Structure: A Crash Course in Lower Rates

The high cost of auto insurance provides a strong incentive for drivers to find ways to trim premium costs. But the search for the right coverage at the lowest price can be aimless unless drivers understand the formula that insurance companies use to determine coverage costs.

Each company has its own formula to figure the risk associated with you and your vehicle. Your total insurance premium combines a base rate with other charges determined by your risk factors. These factors usually include age, sex, marital status, type of car, where you live, how you use the vehicle, your driving record, and the number of claims you have had. For example, young drivers pay much more than most others because as a group, they are far more accident prone. Young single male drivers pay higher rates than young single females because, as a group, they drive more miles and have more accidents. But a young driver's rates will drop several notches when he or she reaches age 25 or gets married.

Mature drivers with a good driving record often receive a 20 percent discount by some companies when they turn 50, and a further 10 percent if they are over 55 and retired. If they stop driving to work and drive less than 7,500 miles a year, they probably are eligible for another 10 percent discount.

Where you live affects insurance rates. If vandalism, theft, and accidents are common in your area, your rates will be higher.

How to Save Money with Insurance Discounts

Regardless of what happens to rates in general, drivers can reduce their premiums by hundreds of dollars annually without assuming substantial additional risk. Policyholders should examine an insurer's rate discounts. A rate discount is a pricing device that insurers use to compete for preferred customers, just as banks give their lowest interest rates on loans to their preferred customers. Rate discounts attract low-risk policyholders by offering them lower rates to reflect their smaller exposure to risk.

Policyholders should also study the following list of the most frequently offered discounts, premium credits, and money-saving ideas for auto insurance. These discounts vary from one company to the next, and one or more of them may substantially cut a policyholder's premium. Before purchasing insurance, policyholders should request the company's list of discounts.

Most Frequently Offered Discounts

Good Students People under age 25 who are enrolled in the 11th grade through college can save substantial amounts if they know what to ask for. Many companies will drop 25 percent or more off liability premiums if the insured student maintains at least a B average or makes the honor roll or dean's list. Good students make safer drivers, perhaps because the time spent studying is time off the roads.

Taking a Higher Deductible Physical damage (collision and comprehensive) insurance should cover losses a policyholder cannot afford, such as several thousand dollars worth of damage to the car or its replacement if it is stolen. Don't try to make it cover every $200 dent in your car. Carry the maximum deductible you can comfortably handle to minimize the cost on this expensive coverage.

On a new car, one-third of the collision premium can be reduced by increasing the deductible from the standard $100 to $500. If you can shoulder a $1,000 repair without having to starve the family, you can save more than 40 percent of the premiums. As with homeowners insurance, a good rule of thumb is to set the deductible equal to your weekly paycheck. At State Farm Insurance, for example, a driver can cut collision premiums in half by opting for a deductible of $500 rather than $50. Similarly, you can save 25 percent on comprehensive premiums by settling for a $100 deductible rather than full coverage.

Antitheft Devices Insurers usually offer a 5 to 15 percent credit on comprehensive (other than collision) coverage if a vehicle is equipped with a hood lock which can be released only from the inside, plus one of two types of disabling devices which make a vehicle's fuel, ignition, or starting system inoperable, and an alarm which can be heard for 300 feet for 30 minutes. The 15 percent discount applies to autos with antitheft devices that automatically go into operation when the car's ignition is turned off.

Good Driver This discount assigns the lowest rate to drivers whose record is free of accidents and moving traffic violations. Drivers get a 5 percent discount from most companies for going five years without an accident. Those who have had recent accidents or violations may be surcharged to reflect the higher likelihood of future accidents and expenses.

Carpool   Motorists who cut their driving sharply by joining a carpool may qualify for insurance savings of as much as 18 percent of the total premium.

Senior Citizens   Some insurers offer a flat 10 percent discount to policyholders 65 or older if their car is rated for pleasure use only and there are no youthful drivers in the household.

Low Mileage   Certain companies provide a 15 percent lower auto insurance premium across the board for cars that are driven less than 7,500 miles a year and are rated for pleasure use only.

Resident Student   Many insurers will drop the family liability premium by 10 to 30 percent if a student moves more than 100 miles from home to attend college and leaves the family car behind.

Driver Training   Teenage drivers in a family can double the family's insurance costs. A driver under the age of 21 can trim that increase by successfully completing an approved course in driver education. The average discount is 10 to 20 percent.

Car Models   Ideally, motorists should consider and investigate auto insurance before deciding which car to buy. Insurance companies generally charge different rates for different car models, with the rate dependent upon the loss and crash experience of the particular models and model years. Insurance companies keep a close watch on a given model's accident claims record, repair costs, and theft losses. Premiums are usually much higher for vehicles that are high priced, accident prone, easily damaged, frequently stolen, or hard to repair. Car models that rate well for safety, durability, and the lowest frequency of claims for collision repairs and theft often cost less to insure. This can save drivers up to 30 percent for collision and comprehensive coverage, which protects the car itself. The Insurance Institute for Highway Safety (IIHS, Watergate 600, Washington, DC 20037), regularly publishes its findings on those cars with the best or lowest loss experience. Upon request, insurance companies also provide consumers with lists of their discounted and surcharged car models.

Generally, subcompacts rate few discounts and many surcharges, while large cars rate many discounts and few surcharges. Compacts and intermediaries fall in between. Two doors are rated as least safe, four doors safer, and station wagons safest. Such information gives car buyers a way to control the cost of their insurance by the choices they make as car buyers, whether the vehicle is used or new.

If you want to reduce your auto insurance premiums, avoid buying an expensive car. The costlier the car, the more expensive the physical damage (collision and comprehensive) coverage. People who drive the least expensive cars pay only about half as much as those who drive the big bucks specials.

Passive Restraints   Many insurers offer premium credits for drivers of cars equipped with air cushions or automatic seat belts. A typical discount calls for a 30 percent reduction in the cost of insurance for injuries to the driver or passengers.

Multicar Discounts   Insurers regularly offer multiple-car discounts if two or more cars are covered by the same company. This discount ranges from 10 to 25 percent.

Overlapping Coverage Policyholders often pay twice for the same coverage. They may find some unnecessary overlap in coverage in their various insurance policies. A homeowners policy, for example, may cover the contents in a car.

Forgoing Car Ownership As mentioned previously, young drivers, particularly single males, are considered accident prone, and therefore pay much higher rates. A young driver can, however, save as much as 30 percent in premiums by forgoing car ownership and sharing the family car with a parent who is the principal driver.

Tune Up Your Collision Coverage After five years, American cars are worth no more than a third of their original value. Minor collision repairs will likely cost little more than the deductible. And the insurance company will pay no more than the car's (book) market value if it is totaled or stolen. They will not pay more to repair a car than it is worth. Each year's depreciation, therefore, shrinks the maximum claim a motorist can make against his or her collision coverage. The law of diminishing returns takes over and you can easily wind up footing an increasing bill for a depreciating car.

Once a car is six years old, or when the collision premium equals 10 percent of the car's market value, it would be wise to drop collision insurance altogether. The premiums saved may well offset the cost of any losses. A policyholder would be better off banking what he or she would spend on the premium. A car's value can be found by consulting the *Blue Book*, which lists average prices of used cars and is available at most public libraries.

Comparison Shop Prices for identical protection can vary tremendously. Car insurance premiums not only vary by state but also can be sharply different in the same locality. In New York City, for example, premiums among the 20 largest-selling companies can vary by more than 100 percent.

Insurers set rates based on their experience in paying out claims, so premiums for identical coverage for drivers with similar backgrounds and safety records can vary drastically from one firm to the next. Consumers therefore should take the time to shop around for the best rates. Indeed, the search should start three to four months before the current policy is up for renewal. Insurance shoppers should contact several insurance companies for quotes and keep thorough notes of the specifics on coverage and prices.

Compare Forgiveness Policies Your survey of insurance companies should establish which are the most forgiving if you have an accident. One insurer may raise your rates 30 percent if you file a claim for more than $400. Another company may increase its premiums 10 percent after the first $200 property damage claim. Some companies will also increase your premium if you get more than one ticket for speeding or another moving violation.

Don't Skimp on Coverage Keeping an eye on one's auto insurance may help a policyholder avoid a head-on collision with his or her checking account. But cutting back on coverage indiscriminately is not the way to economize. This can leave a motorist's financial assets and even future earnings exposed to potentially devastating liability claims.

SUMMARY

Home and automobile ownership both require insurance. Insurance is the principal defense against major risks to one's property from damage and liability. Adequate insurance protection that fully ensures against the hazards that may arise is an essential component of every financial plan. Homeowners and auto insurance are sold in standard formats or packages covering the important needs of most insured.

Homeowners insurance is designed to protect homeowners and renters from property and liability losses. Insurance is available in a single policy that gives broad protection against most losses arising out of home occupancy. There are six different types of homeowners insurance policies, numbered HO-1 through HO-6. HO-1 is called the basic form for homeowners; HO-2 is the broad form; HO-3, the special "all risk" form; HO-4, the broad form for renters, insures only contents; HO-5 is a comprehensive form; and HO-6 is for condominium owners. HO-8 is for high-risk or unusually expensive homes.

Homeowners insurance offers coverage on a full replacement cost basis if the insured carries coverage equal to or exceeding 80 percent of the replacement cost of the home. Homeowners insurance may also be supplemented by endorsements or amendments to the basic policy as well as by floaters or riders designed to protect specific valuables regardless of their location. These can also be used to obtain coverage for a variety of special threats such as earthquakes and floods.

Special policies are available for renters, owners of condominiums, and owners of older, remodeled buildings. One can obtain large increases in liability insurance limits for a modest amount by purchasing a liability umbrella policy. This policy provides liability coverage beyond that offered by homeowners and automobile insurance.

Responsibility for documenting and verifying a loss lies with the insured. The first step in insuring one's personal property is to take a complete inventory, listing all items and date of purchase. It is helpful to take photographs or videotapes of one's household effects, especially of important items. Receipts are important as proof of purchase.

Automobile insurance is designed to protect the insured from property and liability losses arising out of the use of a motor vehicle. There are five basic types of automobile insurance: (1) bodily injury and property damage liability insurance, (2) medical coverage, (3) uninsured motorist coverage, (4) collision, and (5) comprehensive (other than collision) coverage.

Bodily injury and property damage liability coverage is the most important part of the package. It provides liability coverage to pay for injuries or property damage as a result of accidents involving the insured's car. Medical payment insurance covers injury to the driver and passengers without regard to liability. Uninsured motorist coverage protects against accidents caused by people lacking insurance. Collision insurance pays for accident damage to the insured's automobile. Comprehensive (physical damage) insurance covers losses from car thefts, fires, break-ins, vandalism, floods, and such. The need for collision coverage depends upon the value of the insured's car. The lower the value of the car, the less the need for this kind of insurance.

The premium for automobile insurance is based on the characteristics of the insured driver, including the place of residence, age, sex, driving record, marital status, and the type of car owned. The many ways to reduce auto insurance premiums are outlined and discussed in this chapter. One important way is to choose a higher deductible for collision coverage.

KEY TERMS

Actual cash value	HO-5 policy
Appraisal report	HO-6 policy
Barewall condo policy	HO-8 policy
Collision coverage	Homeowners insurance
Comparative negligence	Inflation guard endorsement
Comprehensive (auto) coverage	Insurance discounts
Contributory negligence	Liability coverage
Coverage exclusions	Loss assessment endorsement
Coverage limitations	Negligence
Deductible	No-fault provision
Direct writers	Personal Injury Protection (PIP)
The 80 percent rule	Public adjuster
Floater	Rider
Guaranteed replacement cost coverage	Single entity condo policy
HO-1 policy	Tenants policy
HO-2 policy	Umbrella policy
HO-3 (all risk) policy	Underinsurance
HO-4 policy	Uninsured motorist coverage

REVIEW QUESTIONS AND PROBLEMS

1. Define and explain the following: (a) floaters, (b) riders, (c) 80 percent rule, (d) policy restrictions.
2. What are deductibles? (a) How can they be used to substantially reduce premiums on auto and homeowner insurance policies? (b) What guideline should you follow in deciding how high to set your deductibles?
3. How does an HO-1 homeowners policy differ from an HO-3 policy?
4. Identify some perils that are not generally covered under an HO-3 policy.
5. Explain the difference between replacement cost coverage and actual cash value coverage. Which one offers better protection?
6. Describe the functions performed by a public adjuster in settling an insurance claim.
7. Name the various types of losses covered under an "all-risk" homeowners insurance policy.
8. (a) What is the best way to document all of one's possessions in the home? (b) How can these be used in substantiating a loss claim?
9. Why is it necessary for homeowners and renters to carry an excess liability (umbrella) insurance policy in addition to the homeowners policy?

10. In addition to your normal household possessions, you have a collection of rare antique clocks. What should you do to make certain that your collection is fully insured?

11. George and Diane live in a $100,000 home. The house is worth approximately $80,000 and the land is worth $20,000.
    A. How much should they insure the house for?
    B. What is the minimum they must insure it for in order to be fully compensated in event of a fire (use the 80 percent rule in answering your question)?
    C. George and Diane insured the house for only $60,000 with a $500 deductible and had a fire which caused $20,000 damage to their kitchen and basement. How much compensation can they expect to receive for this casualty?

12. In your view, how has no-fault auto insurance benefited society? What problems did it create?

13. Most auto insurances identify their dollar coverage in the form of a split-limit policy such as 100/300/25. Explain what each of these amounts means.

14. When would it be to a car owner's advantage to drop collision coverage for his or her car?

15. If your car gets damaged in a parking lot by a hit-and-run driver, under what part of your policy would you collect to repair damages? Explain the difference between automobile comprehensive (other than collision) insurance and automobile collision insurance.

16. You have just reached your 20th birthday and received a straight A average in school. Your parents have surprised you with a new Honda for your birthday.
    A. What would you estimate your insurance costs to be if the car is registered and insured under your name?
    B. What other options exist that may substantially reduce your annual insurance premiums?

17. Automobile insurance is described as a package of five coverages. Explain the different coverages that make up the typical automobile insurance policy.

18. List as many ways as possible for you to reduce your automobile insurance premiums without reducing your coverage.

19. What factors are used by insurance companies in determining your automobile insurance premiums?

20. What is California's Proposition 103?
    A. Present arguments for and against it in your state.
    B. Do you believe that forced, government-mandated reductions in insurance rates are possible?
    C. How believable are the threats of the insurance companies to stop selling insurance in states that mandate rate reductions?

21. (DEDUCTIBLES) You have a $100 deductible. The premium you are paying is $1,000 per year. At a $200 deductible, the premium is $900 per year. What is the percent savings with the higher deductible?

SUGGESTED PROJECTS

1. Apply to four or more auto insurance companies for a rate quote for your car.
    A. How much of a discrepancy in rates did you find?

B. Can you find any differences in the policy terms and conditions other than premium rates?

    C. Which company offers you the best insurance for your money? Explain.

    D. Prepare a presentation of your findings for your class.

2. Locate the automobile and homeowners policies owned by your family.

    A. Read them carefully and determine whether they are up to date and provide adequate insurance for your family.

    B. Are there any clauses or terms that are not clear to you? If so, try to look up their meaning in an insurance dictionary or manual, or call your insurance broker or insurance company.

    C. Are there any exclusions or restrictions in the policy that you were not previously aware of?

    D. Discuss with your family whether those gaps should be filled by supplementary riders or floater policies or umbrella policies.

    E. Call a family meeting to discuss your findings and to consider whether the family's insurance needs are being adequately met.

3. What are the financial responsibility laws in your state? Does your state have no-fault laws? If yes, to what extent? Prepare a report evaluating the adequacy of your state's laws and describing how car owners can best protect themselves in your state under existing statutes.

INFORMATION RESOURCES

"Auto Insurance." *Consumer Reports*, October 1988, 622–636.

The Buyer's Guide to Insurance (has valuable advice on home and auto insurance). National Insurance Consumer Organization, 121 North Payne Street, Alexandria, VA 22314 (send $3.00 plus a self-addressed stamped envelope).

"The Compelling Case for No-Fault Insurance." *Changing Times*, July 1989, 49–52.

"The Five-Minute Insurance Checkup." *Changing Times*, June 1991, 31–34.

"Getting What You Deserve on a Homeowners or Auto Claim." *Money*, June 1989, 147–150.

Golonka, Nancy. *How to Protect What's Yours*. Washington, DC: Acropolis Books, 1988.

Harowitz, Sherry. "Home Insurance: Tailored to Fit." *Kiplinger's Personal Finance Magazine*, June 1992, 73–76.

Insurance Institute for Highway Safety. Watergate 600, Washington, DC 20037.

"Insurance Myths You Probably Believe." *Changing Times*, August 1983, 31–33.

"Insurers under Siege." *Business Week*, August 21, 1989, 36–42.

Lubeck, Scott. "The Day the Tree Crushed Our House," *Kiplinger's Personal Finance Magazine*, July 1993, 68–74.

Ten Questions Consumers Most Frequently Ask about Auto and Home Insurance. Insurance Information Institute, 1988, 800/221-4954.

"When the Insurer Totals Your Car." *Changing Times*, January 1991, 69–73.

CHAPTER NINE

The Facts of Life Insurance

- To identify the people who may need life insurance

- To determine the appropriate amounts of life insurance needed

- To differentiate between the major types of life insurance: term, whole life, universal, variable life, and single premium

- To examine the factors to consider in selecting a life insurance agent and company

- To calculate and to compare life insurance costs

Now that we have insured our health, home, property, and cars, it is time to discuss insuring the most valuable asset we have—our life. Although the only two things that are certain in life are death and taxes, **life insurance** is an investment that can help people plan for both. Life insurance is not exactly fun to buy. It forces people to think about circumstances they do not want to confront, such as their own death. As a result, many people choose not to think about it at all. The consequences of such poor planning do not show up until it is too late to do anything about it.

Therefore, as you begin building your living estate, you should give consideration to your death estate. Stocks, bonds, real estate, and other investments build living estates. Life insurance provides an estate at death for the benefit of dependents. It does quickly what a deceased investor hoped to do over a lifetime. It is an indispensable and integral element of any individual's or family's financial program. For most people, financial security cannot be achieved without adequate life insurance coverage.

Life insurance, just like other insurances, comes in a larger variety of packages, styles, and sizes than does toothpaste, with more features and accessories than a stereo unit. Prospective buyers may be bewildered if they do not know what specific coverage they need, how much of it they need, and what choices are available.

This chapter presents a basic explanation of life insurance. It can assist you in purchasing life insurance based on a well-thought-out and planned calculation of your family's actual and realistic needs. It also discusses how to select the most appropriate coverage to meet those needs.

There is a logical, sequential approach to buying life insurance. First, consumers need to estimate how much insurance coverage they need and for how long they need it. Next, it is necessary to learn about the major kinds of policies available. Consumers should determine which type or types of insurance fit them best. Insurance is a dynamic and variable product, not a static one. As people's age, income, goals, and family responsibilities change, so invariably do their insurance needs and preferences.

Who Needs Life Insurance?

Life insurance has two basic purposes: to provide estate liquidity and to provide sufficient assets for a surviving family to live on after the wage earner has passed away. Unless substantial assets have been accumulated, there may not be adequate provision for survivors. Further, if an estate is not sufficiently liquid, it may be necessary to sell other assets at a loss in order to pay estate costs such as estate taxes, final medical expenses, funeral costs, and so on. Such a forced sale of assets may cause considerable hardship to surviving members. For instance, the sale of a home due to inability to meet monthly mortgage payments, or the sale of a car for the same reason, could be distressing indeed.

If substantial assets are accumulated, then survivors may already be adequately provided for. If some of these assets are liquid, then providing additional liquidity through life insurance may not be necessary. The funds used to purchase such insurance could provide a higher return if invested elsewhere.

Not Everyone Needs It

The first question to ask yourself is, Do I need life insurance at all? Probably not, if you are single, have no dependents, or are wealthy or retired. If, however, you are not wealthy and have children under 21 or a dependent spouse or parent, you likely need coverage. The people who most need life insurance in large doses are young couples who have not yet accumulated sizable financial assets to fall back on and who have young children to support. They need a lot of coverage because their children are young, their debts are high, and loss of income could be devastating. For such people, the basic goal is to have enough insurance to maintain the family's standard of living, to provide for the children's education, and to help support a nonworking spouse in retirement. The key consideration is whether it will take insurance money to ensure your dependents some measure of financial security in the event of your death. You may want the money also to pay for your burial expenses, medical bills, debts, and estate settlement costs and taxes.

Although insurance agents offer reasons for insurance coverage at all ages, life insurance is not a critical need unless a person's death would bring financial hardship to someone who depends on his or her salary or services. Like many things in life, the need for life insurance tends to run in cycles. At certain stages in our lives there will be a vital need for a large amount of coverage. But at other times in our lives, despite the sales pitches of insurance agents and company promotions, we may need little or none. Young single persons with no children or elderly parents to support can easily do without life insurance, or with just enough to cover funeral expenses and debts. Childless couples with both spouses having reliable jobs and earning good salaries, can also rationalize buying no more than the modest amounts needed to pay funeral expenses and the portion of any debts, including mortgage payments, that would be too burdensome on the surviving spouse's income alone.

The insurance industry argues that single people and childless couples need to buy insurance in order to get a low premium rate while they are young and to avoid being disqualified later on by serious illness. However, the risk of becoming ill enough not to qualify for insurance is statistically extremely low for people in their 20s and early 30s. It can also be argued that one would probably be better off banking the money saved on insurance premiums and paying the higher rates later when insurance protection is needed. The extra years of savings plus compounded interest should more than compensate for the higher rates to be paid in later years for insurance premiums.

People can likewise get by with less insurance if their children are grown and self-sufficient, their home mortgage is paid, debts are low, net worth is substantial, and their spouse will have adequate income from employment, a pension, or other sources when they die. Elderly or retired people may need little or no insurance if their accumulated savings and assets, pension income, and Social Security are sufficient to take care of the financial needs of the surviving spouse. On the other hand, the tax deferral features of certain (cash value) policies and the forced savings which they require may enhance their appeal for undisciplined or conservative investors.

Not for Men Only

Historically, companies sold life insurance as a man's product. In the traditional family, the husband worked while the wife stayed home with the children. Conventional wisdom had it that women did not need insurance, since they had no incomes to replace. But today most women are wage earners, either as sole breadwinners or as one provider in a two-income family. Their earnings are a vital part of the family's income. Those women need insurance just as much as men do, if not more so.

Families usually insure the life of the working spouse. The intent is to protect the earning power of the wage earner so that survivors will be provided for adequately. But not only the breadwinner's life requires insurance. Unfortunately, the value of a "nonbreadwinning" spouse is often overlooked. There should be adequate life insurance on the nonworking spouse to provide the homemaking activities which would be lost if the nonworking spouse dies. This is particularly crucial when dependent children are involved, because child care can be very expensive. When the costs of hiring cooking, house cleaning, babysitting, errand running, laundry, and shopping help are added up, the "nonbreadwinning" spouse may need as much coverage as the working one. Consequently, an employed spouse who is also a homemaker may need enough insurance to protect both the income loss that would occur in event of her

"I've just figured how much I'm worth as a housewife. The only trouble is that it's more than you earn."

SOURCE: "Pepper...and Salt," *The Wall Street Journal,* March 3, 1992, A-15. Reprinted by permission of Cartoon Features Syndicate.

or his death, plus the extra expenses the family would have to incur to provide for hired homemaking services.

Children's Insurance

Parents often buy life insurance policies on their children's lives. Such policies rarely make economic sense unless the policy pays interest comparable to current market rates. Contrary to the claims of many sales agents, pure life insurance is not an investment. Its purpose is to protect heirs who are dependent upon the insured's earnings for support and to provide liquidity for the estate. Normally, no one is dependent upon a child's earning power. While the loss of a child would be a great emotional trauma, it almost never leads to loss of family income. Instead of buying life insurance, the premium dollars could be better utilized if put in a custodial account to fund expenses in the unlikely event of a child's death, or for the child's future education needs.

How Much Insurance Do You Need?

The next step in choosing life insurance is deciding just how much you need. As stated, life insurance should be bought to make up for the financial contribution that would be lost if the policyholder died. Simply put, the amount needed is found by subtracting the family's monetary needs from its resources. In other words, the shortfall between your other financial resources and your family income objective equals your life insurance needs. This approach is called a "needs analysis" method. Many insurance agents use this approach to determine amounts of coverage needed.

A family has to estimate the income it would need, and for how long, if the bread-winner(s) died. That is not a simple task. Estimating adequate income for a family is highly subjective. Each family or individual can decide only for themselves just what "adequate income" means. That requires taking a hard look at such things as education and housing. The monetary worth of an individual is reflected in part by current earnings and future income-earning ability. Therefore, the amount of insurance protection needed is most difficult to gauge correctly.

One must determine first how much income the family needs to live on each year. The budget worksheet in Chapter 1 can be used to estimate more accurately how much annual income the survivors will need if a family's breadwinner suddenly dies. It is then necessary to calculate the amount of life insurance proceeds the surviving members of the family will require to produce that amount of income, assuming they invest the money in risk-free vehicles, such as insured money funds or bank CDs. Bear in mind that inflation will continue to diminish purchasing power as the years go by and that unforeseen events, such as illness or unemployment, could drain a family's resources.

The total amount of these expenses will not necessarily be the amount of insurance required, because families often have other sources of income to draw upon, such as Social Security survivors' benefits and company-provided life insurance coverage as well as company pensions, plus personal savings and investments.

According to the American Council of Life Insurance, the average insured household owned approximately $100,000 of coverage in 1992. This sounds impressive until you analyze it. Take $100,000 and place it in a money market fund earning 6 percent and it will produce a taxable $6,000. That is not much of an income to leave your family; don't expect to be fondly remembered for it. Even if you add other income your survivors can expect, such as pension checks and Social Security survivors' benefits, the total is likely to be substantially less than your family's current income.

The NICO Rule of Thumb

A number of complex formulas have been devised for deriving life insurance needs. Some of them require computer programs to calculate and many insurance agents are prepared to run the numbers for you. But you would probably do just as well with a rule-of-thumb approach recommended by the **National Insurance Consumer Organization** (**NICO**), a private research and consumer advocacy group. For most one-income families with two young children, the working parent should carry coverage large enough to replace six times present after-tax annual income.

Thus, if a family's after-tax salary is $40,000, it would need $240,000 of life insurance, and if its after-tax salary is $60,000 it would need $360,000. This coverage should be increased or decreased, depending on such variables as family assets, the likelihood of the surviving spouse remarrying or returning to work, the number of children, and their ages. For example, a family should add a year's salary for each additional child. This amount strikes a reasonable balance between the protection such a family needs and the desire to minimize costs.

One consideration to take into account when calculating insurance needs is the likelihood that a non-working surviving spouse would remarry or be able to get a good job. The more income your spouse can anticipate in the years ahead, the less insurance you need. Ideally, the amount of life insurance carried should be designed to maintain a dependents' standard of living, not increase it.

Cost of Living Riders

Some policies help consumers fight inflation by offering a **cost of living rider,** which increases a policy's coverage (and the premium payments) by a percentage equal to the rise in the consumer price index. This is important because inflation can devastate one's insurance coverage—not just life insurance but nearly all kinds, as can be seen in Figure 9–1.

Periodic Insurance Review

What was sufficient a few years ago may be woefully insufficient today. Not only do circumstances and personal philosophy vary widely among individuals, but your own financial circumstances will also change over time. Consequently, insurance

FIGURE 9–1 | **Inflation and the Decline of Purchasing Power**

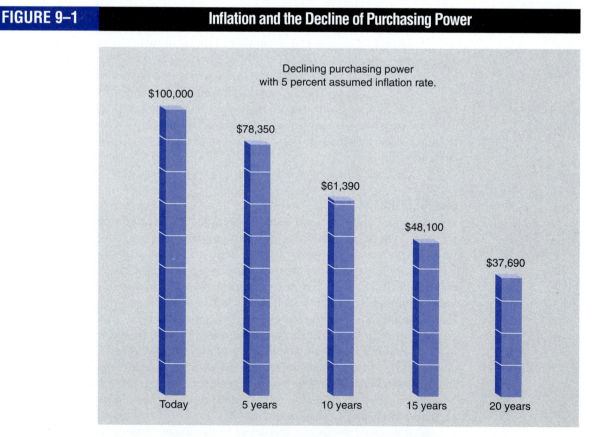

Inflation can devastate the purchasing power of your life insurance. This graph shows the purchasing power of $100,000 over time.

Wanted: Tom Anderson's Income—Dead or Alive

Tom and Betty Anderson and their four kids compose a one-income family. Tom earns $60,000 a year, which comes to $40,000 after tax and is covered with a $120,000 term life insurance policy. If Tom should die, Social Security would pay about $13,200 a year to support the children until they are 18. If the $120,000 death benefit is invested in long-term bonds at 8 percent, that would provide $9,600 a year. If the Andersons want to replace Tom's entire $40,000 income, then Tom is inadequately insured. He needs an additional $215,250 in life insurance, for a total of $335,250. This sum, invested at 8 percent, would yield $26,820 annually. That, together with the $13,200 Social Security benefit, would provide his family with a $40,000 annual income.

If Tom and his family decide to follow the NICO rule of thumb, then Tom would need insurance equal to 6 times his annual after-tax salary plus another 2 times his annual salary for his two additional children, which amounts to 8 times his annual salary, or $320,000. Since he already has $120,000 of insurance from his employer, he needs an additional $200,000 coverage. The $320,000 invested at 8 percent would yield $25,600 annually. Add to this the Social Security benefit of $13,200 and the Andersons would have $38,600 a year, which nearly replaces Tom's income.

needs and coverage should be reviewed every few years as well as whenever a new situation arises, such as the birth of a child, a death, the marriage of a child, or a divorce.

Types of Life Insurance Policies

Term Policies

Once you decide how much insurance to buy, you must choose between a policy that doubles as a savings account—whole, universal, or variable life—and one that provides only a death benefit, which is **term insurance**. For most people, the overriding purpose in buying life insurance is to assure those closest to them of financial resources in the event of premature death. When the first policies were sold, about 250 years ago, that was the only purpose. People calculated how much they wanted or could afford and bought it. There were, however, some shortcomings. Depending on the type of policy, the premiums rose or the amount of coverage decreased as the policyholder got older, and the policies terminated after a specified period of time, or term, hence the name "term" insurance.

Term insurance covers the policyholder for a fixed period, such as one year or five years. It is the most basic and least expensive life insurance because it neither builds savings nor offers other benefits. When a term policy runs out, the insured receives nothing. At the end of the term, the policyholder must either renew or be without

SOURCE: *Assets,* November/December 1990, 71. Reprinted by permission of Michael Witte.

insurance. It is popular because people can buy large amounts of term coverage at affordable rates while they are young and need life insurance the most. Term insurance, which is pure death protection, offers far more protection per premium dollar than any of the other kinds of insurance policies. It is therefore no surprise that it is the most common form of group life insurance offered.

The Varieties of Term   There are several important variations of this basic form of insurance.

1. *Renewable Term Policy*   After buying, say a five-year term, your main objective is to live out the five years and let the insurance company win. This bet—term life insurance—is one form of betting you do not mind losing because you have to die to win. But you would like to be certain of getting a new, five-year policy at the end of the five-year term. Suppose your health deteriorates and you become uninsurable during the five years. Insurers may require you to undergo a complete physical examination to verify that you are in good health. They will not renew your policy since they refuse to take a chance on you, thereby leaving you without insurance at a time when you need it most.

   It is therefore important to purchase term policies that are guaranteed to be renewable regardless of the insured's state of health. Even those who consider themselves in perfect health and top physical shape should not forgo purchasing a term policy with a renewable option. In recent years, features of **renewable term policies** have become almost standard and commonly can be continued until age 70 when all coverage terminates.

2. *Decreasing Term Policy*   The renewable feature ensures that policyholders can keep renewing the term insurance policy. But the guarantee that you can buy it does not guarantee that you can afford it. The cost of basic insurance keeps rising with age. One way of coping with this problem is to decrease coverage as you get older. Many people find that not only their premiums but also their insurance needs change. At 65, policyholders may not need $300,000 of insurance if their children are grown and self-sufficient, the home mortgage is paid off, and their pension is secure. **Decreasing term policies** meet these decreasing insurance needs. The amount of insurance coverage decreases gradually each time the policy is renewed but the premium stays constant. For example, if a woman paid $196 when she was 35 for $100,000, she still could pay $196 when she is 65 but get only $10,000 worth of insurance. This amount may be sufficient for her insurance needs at that time. The benefits usually decrease in intervals of five years, but different varieties exist.

3. *Level Term Policy*   Statistically, our risk of dying increases each day we live, because we are getting older. Theoretically, the insurance company should constantly be raising our premium to offset the increasing mortality risk. Naturally, such a **level term policy** would not be attractive. Insurers therefore write policies that guarantee level premiums over the term. The most popular terms are 1, 5, and 10 years. At the end of the term, policyholders can renew the policy, but at a higher premium.

4. *Convertible Term Policy*   A **convertible term policy** provides an option to switch to a whole or universal life policy (explained further on) without a new medical examination. A term policy can be guaranteed renewable and convertible.

Term Policy Premiums   A major unknown confronting life insurance buyers is what it costs. Insurance prices are often obscure and confusing. A firm that is a low bidder on nonsmoking males may overcharge for women or smokers. Or it may charge below market rates for younger buyers, hoping they will stay as they climb up the age scale into expensive territory. Many insurers cloud comparisons with such extras as double indemnity for accidental death or cost of living increases. Sometimes it is impossible even to discuss costs without agreeing to have an agent visit you at home. The industry's defense is that a life insurance policy is not an easily explained and uniformly priced asset like a share of stock, and its cost cannot be quoted quickly over the phone.

Although all term prices rise as policyholders age, some companies' rate schedules are graded more steeply than others. When buying life insurance, it is easy to compare first-year premium costs. But that figure reveals nothing about what the policy will cost over the long run. A low first-year premium does not guarantee that the policy will be cheap in future years. Some are very low priced for the first year and then increase sharply in the next few years.

Policyholders who plan to keep a term policy for some time, 10 years for example, need to calculate the total premium for the 10 years. Likewise, given a choice between two policies, it is necessary to determine which will be cheaper over the life of the policy or the number of years one expects to keep it. Over a period of years, some policies with similar initial premiums can prove thousands of dollars costlier than others. The Interest-Adjusted Net Cost Index, discussed later, will be helpful in making this calculation.

The measuring stick for term insurance is the annual cost per $1,000 of death benefits. Cost per thousand allows a comparison of rates for any age, sex, or health status and amount of coverage. For example, at age 25, $1,000 in term insurance would cost about $1.50 a year; at 45, $3.00 a year; at 55, more than $7.00 a year.

Term insurance costs increase only a few cents per $1,000 of insurance coverage per year in the 30s age bracket until around age 40. Then the pace of increase accelerates more rapidly and rises dramatically at age 60. By age 60, term can become too expensive unless a policyholder benefits from unusually low group rates at work or from a professional society. The more term insurance bought, the cheaper should be the cost per $1,000. Rates tend to decline at common breakpoints: $50,000, $100,000, $250,000, $500,000, and $1 million. A healthy, nonsmoking 35-year-old can buy $1 million of term insurance for less than $1,000 a year.

Insurance companies do not encourage their agents to sell much term insurance since it does not bring in big profits. Insurance agents earn their smallest commissions (or often none) on term policies. Therefore, many agents discourage clients from buying term coverage and promote the more profitable and higher-priced whole life and universal life plans. They sell term only if all else fails and they cannot convince consumers to buy the more expensive policies. The argument they often use is that term policies get very expensive at age 60 and prohibitively expensive when policyholders reach their 70s and 80s. That is true, but so what? Life insurance is protection against the risk of premature death. Once you reach your 70s and 80s, you most likely will not need life insurance; you can hardly die prematurely.

In summary, term is for anyone under 40 with great financial responsibilities. It enables people to insure themselves for enormous sums with minimum outlays. Most peoples' insurance needs drop after a period, such as when their children finish college. If their insurance coverage is temporary, so too, in all likelihood, is the need for much of it.

Whole Life Policies

Whole life, also known as **straight life, permanent,** or **cash value insurance,** is a combination or hybrid policy consisting of term insurance plus a savings account deposited with the insurance company rather than with a bank. Whole life was developed to answer some of the problems with term insurance, such as increasing premiums and the potential to become uninsurable. With term insurance, the cost of protection increases as policyholders get older, since their chances of dying are greater. In a sense, the same is true for whole life, but the level premium disguises the fact.

Whole life policies average out the cost for insurance over the policyholder's lifetime. In effect, policyholders overpay in the early years so that they can underpay in the later years. Thus, the premium can be kept at a constant dollar amount. The level premiums make it easier to maintain a policy until old age or death. This was the rationale when whole life was developed in the 19th century, and it accounts for the name since payment of premium guarantees coverage throughout the insured's life.

Overpaying for whole life coverage is not necessarily bad, because only part of the premium goes for insurance coverage. The balance goes into a company-managed, interest-earning savings account set up in the policyholder's name. All earnings in the cash value account accumulate tax free.

A whole life policy has three essential elements:

1. The premium	This is the amount policyholders pay each year to keep the policy in force.
2. Cash surrender value	This is the amount policyholders would receive if they "cashed in" or surrendered their policy.
3. The death benefit	This is the amount guaranteed to beneficiaries should policyholders die.

PREMIUM

Premiums Premiums on whole life policies often start off about five to six times higher than for term, but typically remain fixed for life. The annual premium on a good $100,000 whole life policy at age 35 is about $1,300 for a nonsmoking man, $200 or so less for a woman. A whole life policy usually becomes cheaper than an existing term policy once the owner's age reaches the upper 50s.

Most whole life policies are sold through agents or brokers whose commissions are incorporated into the premium payments. The bulk of a first-year premium on a whole life policy may go toward paying an agent's or broker's commission and other expenses of initiating the contract. After the first year, the agent's commission is 5 to 10 percent of the annual premium paid by the policyholder. Each premium paid is divided into four categories: sales commissions, company overhead and profit, insurance payment, and cash value accumulation.

Cash Value The higher early premiums, which accumulate interest, form the basis for a growing equity called the **cash value** of the policy. This precludes the need for future premium increases as the policyholder grows older. The cash value increases through the interest earned on previous cash accumulations. During the later years, more and more of the premium payment will go toward paying for the life insurance coverage and less and less toward new cash accumulation. This is because actuarially the risk of dying is greater. During earlier years, the reverse is true. Whole life is attractive to those wanting to combine income protection and forced savings. Policyholders pay a fixed premium based on the age at which they enroll. Part pays for death protection and some goes to the company for commissions, expenses, and profit. What is left goes to a policyholder's savings fund, which provides him or her with a liquid source of funds.

Borrowing Privileges   One of the attractions of a whole life policy is the ability to borrow against the cash value. These loans generally carry lower interest rates than loans available elsewhere. If the premiums are paid, the policy stays in force even if the insured borrows against the policy. When you take out a policy loan, the death benefit is automatically reduced by the amount you have borrowed. If you have a whole life policy with a face value of $40,000 and borrow $10,000 of the $20,000 cash value that has accrued, your survivors will receive $30,000 when you die, the $40,000 death benefit minus the $10,000 borrowed. Your benefit rises again as you repay the loan.

Cash Surrender Value   Borrowing is not the only way to extract the cash value of whole life policies. Generally, the holder can voluntarily terminate or "cash in" the policy. Cashing in means you stop paying your premiums, fill out some simple forms, and the company will send you a check for the cash value of your policy. The **cash surrender value** is roughly the excess premiums plus interest accumulated against the policy. Cashing in a policy will, however, leave you without life insurance protection since the company will cancel the entire policy if you withdraw its cash value. At retirement age this might be a viable option. Many individuals purchase such policies to accumulate supplemental retirement funds.

Rate of Return on Cash Value   Cash value accumulation could be an attractive feature of a whole life policy if the assumed investment returns are competitive with other market rates. A policy's rate of return, or yield, depends upon the insurer's financial performance and the product design. The better companies offer yields comparable to those paid on bonds and other fixed-income investments.

Besides the interest rate, policyholders need to be concerned with the rate of accumulation of the principal. How much of the premium each year goes toward the cash value? Cash values are usually low or nonexistent in the first year, build up slowly in the early years, and accelerate only in later years. Before purchasing a policy, policyholders should ask the agent or carrier for a ledger statement which shows the policy's premiums, cash, and face values year by year, based on an assumed rate of return. The policy may have an advertised 10 percent return, but your money may grow at a 3 percent rate when your family is young and 25 percent when you are a senior citizen.

In buying cash value insurance, it is essential to understand two key words: *current* and *guaranteed*. The company's current interest rate or dividends paid to policyholders should be higher than the guaranteed contractual minimums, which are generally around 4 percent. Guaranteed values are worst-case outcomes, the lowest cash values the company is allowed to credit according to terms of the policy. Cur-

The AIDS Epidemic and Insurance Rates

A decades-long decline in the basic cost of life insurance may be coming to an end because of the AIDS epidemic. In the past, lengthening life expectancies have allowed insurers to make repeated cuts in so-called mortality charges (the death insurance part of the policy). This meant faster growth in the cash value of whole life policies and reduced premiums for term insurance. During recent years, citing the spread of AIDS, several major insurance companies, such as Prudential, Northwestern, and Executive, have raised mortality charges.

rent values are based on the optimistic assumption that rates currently being earned will continue to be stable long into the future.

The cash values of policies sold in the 1950s and 1960s earned less than a passbook savings account. This brought the insurance companies a lot of much-deserved criticism and competition from other forms of savings and investments. The insurance companies upgraded their offerings in response. In recent years, it has become possible for a cash value policy usually to earn a rate of return that is at least equal to what banks pay account holders. To determine if a policy pays a good current rate of return, it should be compared with the prevailing rates on CDs, Treasury bills, and bonds. A key point to bear in mind is that the interest earnings are accumulated on a tax-deferred basis, which enhances attractiveness of the return.

FACE

Face Value (The Death Benefit)   Life insurance policies are written for a specific **face value,** which is the amount of money that will be paid upon death of the insured party. Agents often encourage policyholders to switch from a term policy to a whole life or a universal life policy on the claim that it builds a cash value. The first question policyholders should ask themselves is whether the new policy meets their insurance needs. Policyholders need to make sure the new policy provides the same amount of (face value) coverage at a price they can afford. The cash values will not help a policyholder's family much if he or she dies suddenly and is severely underinsured.

It is essential for policyholders to ask themselves whether they can afford to cover their insurance needs adequately with whole life insurance. For young people, the answer may likely be no. The premiums are simply too high. A 35-year-old man, for instance, would pay between $2,000 and $3,000 for $200,000 of coverage from most companies. That is a good chunk of the budget for most families. Term insurance is more affordable. A healthy nonsmoker under 40 can buy annual renewable term coverage for 80 cents to $1.50 per $1,000 of insurance per year, about one-tenth of the premiums for whole life. Thus, $200,000 of coverage in a term policy would cost only between $160 and $300 a year. Young people may decide instead to carry $400,000 or $500,000 worth of term coverage, which would cost less than $500 a year, rather than burden themselves with $2,000 to $3,000 annual whole life premiums for $200,000 in coverage.

Cash value policies rarely provide buyers with adequate **death benefits,** though they bring in big profits for insurance companies. Those who want to invest money as well as buy insurance coverage could buy term insurance and invest the premium dollars they save in the early years when term premiums are relatively low. However, the interest earned will be subject to taxes on current income. Policyholders who invest the difference, for instance, in a money market account should be able, over the years, to amass more money than the cash value that would have built up in a whole life insurance policy. The difference lies in the fact that they are investing their own money and do not have to pay any fees to insurance companies to do it. They also have the flexibility of moving their money to higher-yielding investments as quickly as rates change.

Whole Life Policies—An Evaluation   If whole life policies are used correctly, they shelter earnings throughout one's lifetime. They let policyholders' money grow income tax free and let them borrow it at a low interest rate, and at death, the money passes to their beneficiaries income tax free. Whole life policies offer insurance protection for the whole of one's life. This can be a big advantage to people who want to continue coverage into old age.

Whole life policies can be considered as a form of a forced savings incentive to help with retirement expenses for people who have great difficulty in saving money systematically. Insurance agents often tout the "forced savings" argument in promoting permanent policies. People who have the discipline and the free cash to invest steadily need not automatically assume that an insurer can invest money on their behalf better than they could themselves.

Moreover, there are many other investment opportunities which can yield a respectable interest rate together with a tax deferment until age 59 and a half. Some of these investments (such as IRAs, Keoghs, 401 Ks, municipal bonds, and zero coupon bonds) are discussed in following chapters of this book. There are likewise better ways to force oneself to save, including payroll deduction savings plans. But for those who find it hard to put money away or manage investments, then the discipline of a whole life policy to build a nest egg may be appropriate. But they will pay for it with lower returns, front-loading fees, and agents' commissions.

A key point to remember about all cash value insurance is that the policy with the lowest premiums is not necessarily the best choice. Premiums are just one factor in building cash value. The others are investment results, interest rate guarantees, fees and charges for mortality risk, commissions, and favorable borrowing rules.

Whole life policies are very poor investments if held only a short time since many insurers charge higher fees in the early years of the policy and only a small portion of the premium is allocated to the cash value. Unless policyholders are sure they will keep up the premium payments for 15 to 20 years, they should avoid a cash value policy entirely. Too much money can be lost by surrendering a cash value policy in the first 10 years or so. Those who drop such a policy in the first few years will have actually paid very dearly for term protection. Despite the appealing features of cash value policies, if all you really want is pure life insurance, a guaranteed death benefit paid to your survivors, there is no reason to buy anything but term.

Universal Life Policies

During the 1970s, the life insurance industry's best-selling and most profitable product, whole life, was widely assailed as costly, complex, and inflexible. Critics charged that consumers could not learn the true cost of such policies because insurers refused to disclose rates of return on the savings component in any meaningful way. In

| FIGURE 9–2 | How the Insurance Company Spends Its Money |

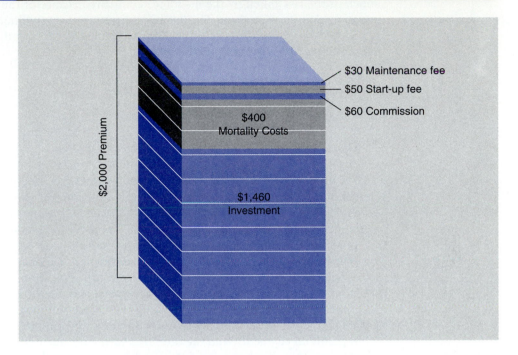

The insured, a 40-year-old male nonsmoker, has just paid a $2,000 premium on $250,000 low-commission universal life policy. Here is how the company will spend the money.

SOURCE: USAA Life.

1979 a Federal Trade Commission study concluded that rates of return averaged a paltry below-market interest rate of 1.3 percent in 1977. After that report, sales of whole life fell precipitously.

Deregulation of interest rates in the 1980s also pressured insurance companies to give their buyers more competitive policy cash values. The life insurance industry responded to these pressures and drastically changed its ways. To recapture funds which were flowing elsewhere, it came up with new products such as **universal life** and **variable life.** These were designed to match the returns of other high-yielding investments such as money market funds and bank money market accounts. For example, some new types of policies combine term life insurance with investment in a money market fund or something similar, such as a stock market mutual fund.

Although sold under a bewildering variety of brand names, all universal life policies operate on the same basic pattern. As shown in Figure 9–2, part of each universal life premium payment is used to pay for (mortality cost) term insurance protection on a policyholder's life. The company also deducts sales commissions, load charges (startup fees), administrative costs, and profits (maintenance fees). The remainder, the cash value reserve, is invested in low-risk financial instruments, such as bonds and mortgages, and earns returns at or near market rates.

In older whole life policies, all parts were merged in a monolithic instrument, with much of the risk taken by the insurance company because of the guaranteed minimum yield and cash values. The insurers, therefore, were willing to commit themselves only to a low rate of return. In recent years, the trend has been toward "unbundling" or separating the three parts:

1. The death benefit, or "pure" term, insurance

2. The savings or cash values

3. The administrative costs, including sales commissions

By "unbundling" the funds, insurance companies give the owner wider latitude in making the payment than is the case with whole life contracts. Policyholders, for example, may vary premiums, sending extra money when rates are high or skipping premiums when they are short of cash. If no payments are made for the death benefit, most policies allow the company to apply money from accumulated savings to maintain the insurance. Policyholders must make sure their accumulated cash value is enough to cover the monthly deductions for death protection. If they pay too little, the monthly charges can exhaust their cash value, making the policy worthless. Policyholders receive annual reports showing the amount of insurance protection, the cash value, costs of the insurance, company fees, the amounts credited to savings from premium payments, and the rates of return from savings.

Many universal policies come close to buying term and investing the difference, except that the insurer is a sort of broker or mutual fund or money market manager with the policyholder taking the risk.

The projections used to market these plans typically show how the policy will perform at a current or assumed interest rate as well as in a worst-case scenario involving a minimum guarantee rate of, say 4 percent and maximum insurance charges. Both sellers and buyers tend to focus on the higher interest rates. But a high interest rate may be an overly optimistic projection to lure prospective buyers into a costly policy. Because of big initial fees and charges, your withdrawable savings will not amount to much unless the policy is kept for at least 10 years. What has been saved on paper may be impressive but a policyholder should always look at the policy's surrender value rather than its account value (the prepenalty or paper amount that's presently accumulating interest).

It is also important to bear in mind that the advertised rates are paid on the money that goes into savings *after* load charges and the cost of insurance are deducted. When agents talk about rates of return, consumers should make sure they distinguish between "gross" and "net" rates. Often in advertising their universal life policies, companies will offer a high rate, say 9 percent. But that is what is earned on remaining money after all the fees and charges are deducted, not on the total contribution. A 9 percent gross rate can turn out to be a 6.5 percent net.

Another reason that universal life quickly became a popular alternative after its introduction in 1979 was that it offered policyholders the flexibility, within limits, of increasing or decreasing premium, payment, and coverage as age and income vary. For example, a 30-year-old male could buy a universal life policy with a death benefit of $300,000 for an annual premium of $2,400. If at age 50 the policyholder decides to drop his insurance coverage to $150,000, he may be able to reduce his premium by $600 or put that much more in the savings portion of the plan.

Universal life comes in two forms, called Option A and Option B. Under Option A, a policyholder's survivors receive only the face amount of the policy, just as they do with term or whole life policies. Under Option B, they will receive both the face amount and the accumulated cash value. Option B obviously costs more because the company stands to pay out a larger amount in the end.

Variable Policies

Variable insurance has set premiums of which a portion is put aside for investment purposes. With variable insurance, a policyholder stands to earn a greater return than with universal because the premiums are often invested in more risky vehicles, such as stocks or real estate. The insured is given a choice of investment options to choose from. The name "variable" refers to variable income (e.g., stock alternatives). The policy offers a fixed-minimum death benefit. Above that level, both the death benefit and the cash value are determined by the performance of the investment portfolio. There is no minimum cash value. The cash value of the policy can go down if the investment portfolio declines. Because this policy transfers investment risk from the insurance company to the policyholder, potential risks and rewards are greater.

Variable life insurance may be inappropriate as primary life insurance because so much of its value hinges on investment performance. Not just the cash value but also the death benefit can fall as well as rise. As stated earlier, life insurance should be viewed as a means to insulate survivors from the financial consequences of a policyholder's death, not as a way to invest speculatively.

Another variation of variable insurance is variable universal insurance.

Variable Universal Policies

Variable universal life is the newest offspring of universal life. It behaves exactly like its parent, variable life, with one major exception. The insurance company offers policyholders a group of mutual funds to choose from. If you buy a variable universal policy, you choose your investment vehicles and your money earns whatever rate the underlying investments earn. You can usually invest in stocks, bonds, money market funds, or a combination of the three, to spread your risk and to pick a comfortable level of risk.

Limited Payment Policies

The **limited payment life** policy is a variation of straight life. This policy, also known as **paid up life insurance,** is whole life insurance that allows premium payments to cease after a certain number of years. Two common examples are "20 pay life" policies, which provide for premium payments to cease after 20 years, and "paid at 65" policies, which require payment of premiums only until the insured turns age 65.

The insurance is called *limited* because payments are limited to 10, 20, 25, or 30 years. Limited payment life policy provides insurance protection throughout the lifetime of the insured by the payment of a fixed premium for a predetermined period of years. If a policyholder purchases a 30-payment life, for example, no further premiums are due after 30 years, but the full face amount of the policy remains in force

Paying All at Once: Single Premium Life Insurance

Most people never consider life insurance as a potential tax shelter. Some types of policies, however, are such appealing shelters that cash-rich investors pump their money into them instead of other attractive investment forms such as municipal bonds or mutual funds (which will be discussed in future chapters).

In recent years, companies have designed a set of policies, known as **single premium life insurance (SPLI),** designed to make the most of tax-free compounding. Single premium policies have been marketed as one of the few tax shelters left by the 1986 tax act. As the name implies, policyholders pay the premium only once, not gradually over the years. For their lump-sum payment, usually $5,000 or more but typically $25,000, policyholders get a much larger paid-up permanent insurance policy.

The size of the guaranteed death benefit policyholders get for their money depends on their age when they buy the policy. A $10,000 payment at age 30 provides a face-value death benefit, before earnings, of perhaps $40,000 to $50,000. For men under age 40, the payout is at least 250 percent of the premium. A woman of 40 will typically receive a death benefit of four to six times the amount of her premium.

With most policies, the entire premium immediately starts earning interest and building cash value, so policyholders or their beneficiaries can get even more. None of the premium is skimmed off to cover an up-front load or pay for the insurance. Policies generally quote the "net" interest rate earned by the cash value—the yield after subtracting costs of the insurance and administrative expenses. Each year, policyholders "pay" for the insurance by letting the company keep part of the money earned on the cash value of their policy.

The insurance company takes out its expenses and makes its profit on the difference between what it earns on premiums and the interest it pays policyholders on single premium whole life. Usually, the insurance or maturity cost, administrative charges, and other expenses come to between 2 and 3 percent annually. But as long as the reduced rate of interest earned inside the policy remains competitive with other investments, such as bonds and CDs, policyholders can consider the insurance protection as really not costing them anything.

The insurance is not necessarily the main attraction of these policies. The tax benefit is often the real selling point. Because this is a life insurance policy, the earnings are permitted to compound with taxes deferred, and with no taxes at all if the policy is in force until death. These policies are promoted as a means of accumulating cash for future needs without paying taxes on the earnings. Tax law even permits policyholders to exchange one policy for another within certain guidelines without triggering the tax bill, much as they may transfer funds from one IRA to another tax free.

SPLI Borrowing Privileges   A special attraction of SPLI is its liquidity. A policyholder may borrow up to 90 percent of the cash value of the policy for as little as 1 percent net cost, the spread between earnings and interest charged. Death benefits are reduced, of course, by the amount of the withdrawal. A loan of $50,000 on a $100,000 policy, for example, leaves your heirs with only $50,000 in the event of your death. Borrowing against the income on your policy, on the other hand, does not disturb the policy itself.

A tax bill passed in 1988 eliminated the previous ability to take tax-free loans from single premium life policies. Money taken out before age 59 and a half now is subject to a 10 percent penalty as well as ordinary income tax on gains. This tax bill has sharply reduced the appeal of single premium policies, although their other tax benefits remain in force.

until the policyholder's death or until he or she surrenders the contract for its cash value. This policy provides for level premium payments up to a certain age or for a number of years. The insurance protection remains effective over the entire life span if the insured does not withdraw the cash value of the policy.

A limited payment whole life policy offers coverage for the entire life of the policyholder but schedules premium payments to end after a limited period. Regular whole life premiums, on the other hand, are paid until the policyholder dies or reaches age 100. This type of policy enables the policyholder to meet the cost of the insurance during his or her income-producing years. It offers the insured the advantage of having paid off his or her life insurance before retirement. The limited payment life policy is attractive to those who, for one reason or another, want to cut short the burden of paying premiums. The drawback of such plans is that they offer young people with family responsibilities less protection for their premium dollars than they would if they bought ordinary life term insurance.

Paid up policies will continue to accumulate cash values because the insurer continues to pay interest on the funds. Upon retirement, the policyholder can choose to surrender the policy and withdraw the money. However, by doing so, he or she gives up the additional insurance protection that could have been purchased had a continuous premium policy been chosen.

Needless to say, the annual premiums for paid-up life insurance policies are higher than ordinary policies with continuous premiums because the insurance company has fewer years to collect premiums. Of course, the shorter the period of time over which premiums are payable, the larger the amount of the annual premium.

An extreme version of limited payment life insurance is the "single premium" life insurance.

Single Premium Whole Life and Single Premium Variable Life   There are two major types of single premium insurance policies. One, **single premium whole life,** comes with an insurance company guarantee against erosion of principal. Like a certificate of deposit, it pays a fixed return for a fixed duration, usually one to five years. Then rates readjust to reflect the prevailing market. The other major type of policy is **single premium variable life,** a riskier investment, for the cash value varies with investment results, although the insurance portion is guaranteed.

Individuals can direct how they want their premiums to be invested. The choices range among mutual funds that invest in stocks, bonds, foreign currencies, and so on. They are, in effect, buying professional management as they would with a mutual fund.

Surrender Charges   Single premium policies should be considered only as a long-term investment since there are surrender charges. Surrender charges, or what policyholders will pay to give up the policy, are usually between 7 and 8 percent of the account value after the first year and gradually decrease to zero after 8 to 10 years.

The attraction of single premium whole life is that policyholders can build up assets, tax free, while providing insurance protection for their families. Single premium life, however, is designed more for tax shelter than for family protection. The death benefit, like the back seat of a sporty two-door, is usually too small for comfort. If, for example, you are 30 years old and have $10,000, putting it into a single premium policy would probably bring you a $50,000 or $60,000 death benefit. You may be better off, if you have small children and other dependents, spending a few hundred dollars a year for $500,000 worth of term insurance and investing your $10,000 elsewhere.

With all these policies, the key element to remember is that the main point is the insurance and the investment aspect is secondary. Single premium whole life plans may represent a prudent way of making your money work for you tax sheltered. But if the death benefit is not sufficient to protect your family, then SPLI should be supplemented with a low-cost term policy.

Endowment Policies

An **endowment policy** is one that is written for a given period of time and for a stated face value. It offers life insurance protection for some specified age or a specified number of years. Endowment at age 65 and 20-year endowments are the most common types.

Endowment life insurance provides for payment of the policy's face value either at the policyholder's death or at a previously agreed upon date, whichever comes first. The special feature of the endowment policy is that if the policyholder lives to the end of the period, the policy may be redeemed for its face value. The cash value of the policy is equal to its face value at the end of the endowment period. If the policyholder dies before the stated period is up, the beneficiary receives the full face value. If the policyholder lives to the end of the endowment date, he or she receives the full face value. However, once the policyholder receives the full face value on maturity, he or she is no longer insured. The company has paid off under the contract and the policy terminates.

A person buying an endowment is paying for a combination of temporary insurance and a savings account. Endowment policies are for persons who need not only life insurance protection for dependents but also a definite sum of money or income at some future date. Endowment insurance can provide a given sum of money at a specific time for a specific need such as college costs or retirement. Many endowment policies are established by parents upon the birth of a child and name the child as beneficiary of the endowment for payment at the age of 18 when he or she is about to enter college. They can also be purchased to provide for retirement needs beginning at a predetermined age, such as 65.

Since the cash value must build up to the face value by the time the contract period is up, an endowment policy entails very costly annual premiums. It also offers less insurance protection per premium dollar than other policies. With recent changes in the tax law, the cash value buildup on most traditional endowment policies no longer qualifies for tax deferral. Because of its high cost, persons interested in maximum life insurance protection against premature death are advised not to buy an endowment policy. Such policies are intended primarily for the savings element. Because of their drawbacks, endowment policies are purchased by very few people. Many insurers have in recent years voluntarily withdrawn from writing endowment insurance.

Both endowment and limited payment policies place the emphasis on savings rather than on protection. There is a great difference between a limited payment life and an endowment policy. When policyholders finish paying on a limited payment life policy, they are insured for life but collect nothing although they have cash value. In the case of endowment, once policyholders have finished paying, they are no longer insured. They collect the face amount of the policy and the policy terminates.

"Of course, if your policy includes a double indemnity clause, I can arrange for you to die in an accident instead of by natural causes."

Double Indemnity Clauses: Accidental Death Policies

Double indemnity, or accidental death benefit, pays survivors double or triple the face amount of the policy if the policyholder dies in an accident rather than of natural causes. It may increase the cost of a $100,000 policy by $100 a year. However, this may make little sense. Policyholders need enough insurance to protect their dependents if they die tomorrow, not to gamble on how they may die.

Dividend-Yielding Policies: Participating and Nonparticipating Policies

Some insurance companies, in addition to paying interest on a policy's cash value, also pay a dividend. Policies that pay dividends are called **participating policies.** They are the favorite product of **mutual insurance companies.** Policyholders are nominally the legal owners of a mutual insurance company and thereby participate in the company's profits. A dividend on a participating policy can be viewed as a partial refund of a premium that subsequent experience shows was too high. Mutual insurance companies protect themselves against the worst by "overcharging" and then refund the excess if things were not so bad. Dividends are the keystone of participating whole life policies.

Nonparticipating policies are issued mainly by **stock insurance companies,** which are organized to make a profit for stockholders. Premiums for participating cash value policies are generally higher than those for nonparticipating policies. But when you buy a participating policy, you are hoping that the dividends eventually will reduce your net cost below what it would have been with a nonparticipating policy. For the past nearly 50 years, that hope has generally come true. Participating cash value policies usually have been better buys in the long run than nonparticipating ones.

Comparing Insurance Costs: Interest-Adjusted Net Cost Index

How can a consumer compare the costs of different insurance policies? We previously discussed comparing costs of $1,000 of coverage when it comes to term insurance. However, the insurance industry has an additional tool known as the **interest-adjusted net cost index.** The index is an industry-accepted yardstick for measuring and comparing the costs of similar insurance policies among different companies. It is used for both whole and term life policies. Devised in the 1970s, the interest-adjusted net cost index is an improvement on the previous techniques for measuring a policy's cost over a period of years.

·The index is not hard to understand, though the actual calculation is complex. By way of explaining how this index is computed, let us first look at the traditional method of comparing the cost of life insurance policies. Under the traditional method, you simply add up all the premiums you would pay over the life of the policy, subtract the cash value and any dividends received, and consider the result the actual total cost of the death insurance. The problem with this calculation is that it does not consider a third element—the "time value" of your money (discussed in Chapter 2). It gives as much value to a premium paid 20 years from today as a premium paid one year from today. It ignores the interest you could have earned on the money if you had not used it to pay life insurance premiums for 20 years. It also ignores the fact that the purchasing power of the dollar is likely to be far less in the future.

Suppose two policies have equal total premium payments over 20 years. One policy has higher payments in the early years and relatively lower payments in the later years. The other policy is the opposite. It has lower payments in the early years and higher payments in later years. The one with lower payments in the early years is a better deal because you can bank or invest the money saved through the initially lower premium.

Many policies start out cheap but end up expensive. Buyers of these policies pay very low first-year premiums but dramatically higher premiums later on. The net cost index unmasks that kind of pricing strategy, since the ultimately higher premiums are reflected in a higher index number.

The interest-adjusted net cost index corrects for this deficiency by adjusting each future premium and dividend for interest and inflation. The index takes the timing into account and gives a more accurate picture of a policy's projected true costs. The index is often expressed as a cost per $1,000 of insurance. Thus, a John Hancock policy (see Table 9–3) with a 10-year net cost index of 1.44, for example, is estimated to cost $1.44 per $1,000 of coverage per year, or about $360 annually for a $250,000 policy.

What matters is not the index number as such but how it compares with the index numbers for competing policies. The lower the index number, the better the buy. The index can be used only to compare similar policies with each other. It cannot be used to compare a term policy with a cash value policy.

Frequently, the indexes for low-cost cash value policies will be negative. The more negative the number, the cheaper the policy. A negative cost index means that the accumulated dividends plus the cash values exceed the accumulated premiums you have paid. The word "accumulated" means that the yearly figures are not simply added but rather grow at compound interest.

A whole life policy should not be judged solely by its premium. A low or high premium is neither good nor bad. The index will usually provide comparisons for periods of 10 and 20 years. The best available method of comparing costs of similar

TABLE 9–3	Interest-Adjusted Net Cost Index

Index numbers depend on a person's age, sex, insurance amount, and policy type. Shown below are index numbers for an annual renewable term life insurance policy of $250,000 for a 35-year-old male nonsmoker, held for 10 years. The 10 largest U.S. companies are compared in this example for 1993.

TIAA	1.30
Northwestern Mutual	1.32
Equitable	1.40
Metropolitan	1.42
John Hancock	1.44
New York Life	1.46
Travelers	1.49
Aetna Life	2.13
Prudential	2.64
Connecticut General	2.76

Source: Bests' Review. Reprinted from The Participant, April 1993, quarterly news for TIAA-CREF participants.

types of policies is to ask the insurance company or the agent for the interest-adjusted net cost index for the policy you are considering. In many states, an agent is required to furnish it to customers on request. If an agent refuses to provide these indexes, it is best to shop elsewhere. The net payment cost index for various policies is available in the *Flitcraft Compend* published by A.M. Best Company.

This chapter presents the basic techniques for determining which type and how much life insurance a person needs. However, the life insurance industry is constantly changing. Consumers must keep informed of new developments, new tax laws, and current rates of return and periodically update their insurance in line with these changes. Moreover, since insurance needs change as people enter different stages of their life, periodic additions, deletions, and amendments in one's insurance coverage will inevitably be necessary.

SUMMARY

Life insurance is a basic financial necessity for most, although not all, households. It is designed to protect potential dependent survivors from the financial losses that result from a premature death. The best method for estimating the amount of life insurance a family should have is the loss replacement approach. A family should calculate how much income it will need after the loss of a provider. Next, it must estimate all of the resources and income available upon the death of a provider. Once the amount of resources is determined, it is compared to the total resources needed to maintain the family in its current lifestyle. Any gap in income indicates the amount of life insurance necessary. The death benefit must be sufficient to provide adequate income if invested in interest-bearing investments.

Life insurance companies have developed many types of policies to fit a variety of individual circumstances. Life insurance can consist of either cash value insurance or term insurance. Each category has a unique variation in premium payment, death protection, or cash value buildup. Variations of term life insurance include decreasing term insurance, level term insurance, guaranteed renewable term insurance, and convertible term.

Term insurance is written for a stated number of years, generally for a five-year term, and terminates at the end of that period. It can usually be renewed at a higher premium rate. This happens because as the insured becomes older, the probability of death increases. Term insurance offers a large amount of death protection at a relatively low rate for a person under age 40. With decreasing term insurance, premiums remain level while coverage decreases. Many people choose the less expensive term insurance because they believe they can avoid fees and charges and invest the difference between the premiums more effectively than can the life insurance company.

Variations of cash value insurance include whole life insurance, universal life insurance, variable life insurance, and single premium life insurance. Cash value policies combine death insurance with a savings plan, whereby part of the premiums are invested and earn interest or dividends for the policyholder. This serves as a form of savings for the policyholder, who can withdraw or borrow against these savings readily.

Premiums on a whole life policy remain the same throughout the policy. However, policyholders pay more than is necessary to cover the cost of pure death insurance in the early years and less than would be necessary in the later years. Consequently, policyholders build up a surplus or cash value fund which is available to the policyholder as a form of saving.

An informed consumer must be knowledgeable enough to open a life insurance policy, analyze its individual components, and determine whether the package meets his or her specific needs. Second, a cost analysis should determine the basic dollar cost of the insurance coverage as well as the return on any cash value investments.

Life insurance should be purchased only after the actual dollar amount and type of policy needed is determined and comparative premiums are analyzed. The interest-adjusted net cost index provides a means of comparing similar policies. Prior to buying insurance, one should also check on a company's rating and financial strength in Best's Insurance Reports.

KEY TERMS

Cash surrender value

Cash value

Cash value insurance

Convertible term policy

Cost of living rider

Death benefits

Decreasing term policy

Endowment policies

Face value

Interest-adjusted net cost index

Level term policy

Life insurance

Limited payment life policy

Mutual insurance company

National Insurance Consumer Organization (NICO)

Nonparticipating policies

Paid up life insurance

Participating policies

Permanent insurance

Premiums

Renewable term policy

Single premium life insurance (SPLI)

Single premium variable life

Single premium whole life

Straight life insurance

Stock insurance companies

Term insurance

Universal life policy

Variable life policy

Variable universal life

Whole life insurance

REVIEW QUESTIONS AND PROBLEMS

1. What is the difference between term insurance and whole life insurance?
2. List types of people who do not need life insurance. Explain why.
3. Why do life insurance agents try to encourage you to buy whole life policies rather than term policies? What is the rule of thumb used to determine the amount of life insurance needed?
4. What are the advantages and disadvantages of term insurance?
5. Why would some policyholders want to buy a decreasing term policy?
6. What is the interest-adjusted net cost index and how is it used in shopping for the lowest insurance rates?
7. Should children be insured? Explain.
8. What is single premium life insurance and what advantages does it offer over other cash value policies?
9. Explain the difference between a stock life insurance company and a mutual life insurance company.
10. What is the major attraction of term insurance?
11. Discuss how a person's insurance needs may change during different stages of life. Which types of insurance would be most suitable at each stage?
12. Present arguments for and against the phrase "Buy term insurance and invest the difference yourself."
13. What is universal life insurance? What benefits as well as potential risks does it offer a policyholder?
14. Jack Henderson has a net annual income of $50,000 from his job. If he died, Social Security would pay his widow and children $10,000 a year. How much life insurance does Jack need in order to make sure his family will not suffer any income loss in the event he dies? (Assume that bond yields are 10 percent.) Jack's wife, Pat, also works and earns $35,000 net income a year. She estimates that if she were to die, her family, in addition to losing her income, would also have to spend an additional $15,000 a year to pay for the homemaking services that she currently provides to her family. For how much should Pat insure her life?
15. Explain why the following categories of people may or may not need life insurance:
    A. A 16-year-old high school student who lives with and is supported byhis parents.
    B. A retired widow with grown children and self-sufficient parents.
    C. A young single mother with two children ages 3 and 6 and one-half years.

D. A divorced man paying alimony and child support.

E. A wealthy individual with assets of $50 million.

F. A single schoolteacher who supports her elderly and infirm parents.

G. A single lawyer with no dependents.

16. (PREMIUM) Your friend owns $40,000 of permanent life insurance at a cost per thousand of $1.20. (Use $1.20 for both high and low premium values.) She would like to keep her premium the same but get more coverage. You have found term insurance at $0.17 per thousand. How much insurance can she buy for the same premium?

17. (FACE) Your friend is considering the purchase of life insurance. She wants $250,000 of coverage. Cost per $1,000 of whole life is $12. The cost per $1,000 of term is $0.83. What is the whole life premium and what is the term premium?

SUGGESTED PROJECTS

1. Get estimates of the price of a five-year term renewable policy for yourself, worth $100,000, from five insurance companies. Compare the costs and conditions of each. Which would you select? Explain why.

2. Phone or write an insurance company and request information on a cash value insurance policy.

A. Analyze how much it costs for the pure death benefit.

B. Compare the death benefit cost to pure term insurance (get costs on a term policy from the insurance company).

C. Find out how much of your monthly premiums goes for fees, charges, and other costs.

D. How much of your monthly premium is invested for you?

E. How much does the invested premium (cash value) earn annually?

F. Compare the earnings to other investments, such as bank certificates of deposit, money market funds, or mutual funds.

G. Do you consider this insurance a good investment?

H. If you bought term insurance and invested the difference, would you be better or worse off?

I. Present your finding to your class. Use facts and figures in making your presentation.

INFORMATION RESOURCES

Baldwin, Ben. *The Complete Book of Life Insurance.* Chicago: Probus, 1991.

Daily, Glen. *The Individual Investors Guide to Low-Load Insurance Products.* Chicago: International Publishing Company, 1990.

Davis, K., and M.D. Wilcox. "Life Insurance—What to Do Now?" *Kiplinger's Personal Finance Magazine,* November 1991, 45–51.

Davis, Kristin. "Making Life Insurance Easier to Swallow." *Kiplinger's Personal Finance Magazine,* August, 1993, 42–48.

"The Facts of Life Insurance." *Changing Times,* March 1988, 27–36.

"The Facts of Life Insurance." *Consumer Reports,* March 1986, July 1986, August 1986 (three-part series).

"How Healthy Is Your Own Life Insurer?" *The Wall Street Journal,* April 11, 1991, C-1.

Kosnett, Jeff. "When Cash-Value Life Insurance Makes Sense." *Kiplinger's Personal Finance Magazine,* April 1993, 63–67.

———. "Good Reasons to Drop Your Life Insurance." *Kiplinger's Personal Finance Magazine,* June 1993, 69–71.

"Life Insurance after 40." *Changing Times,* May 1989, 65–70.

"Life Insurance—Choices That Can Save You Money." *Changing Times,* February 1991, 45–48.

"Life Insurance—The New Math of Cash Values." *Changing Times,* April 1991, 63–66.

National Association of Life Underwriters. Write them at 1922 F Street NW, Washington DC, 20006-4387, or call at 202/331-6032 for free pamphlets on life insurance and other topics in their "Shaping Your Financial Fitness" series.

National Insurance Consumer Organization. *Taking the Bite Out of Life Insurance.* NICO, 121 Payne Street, Alexandria, VA 22314 (703/549-8050).

Rowland, Mary. "A Little Caution in Life Insurance." *The New York Times,* December 15, 1991, F-5.

———. "Life Insurance in the Low-Rate Era." *The New York Times,* August 15, 1993, F-17.

Schultz, Ellen E. "Variable Life Insurance Offers Flexible Option." *The Wall Street Journal,* August 12, 1993, C-1.

Sloane, Leonard. "Life Insurance Isn't Just for the Healthy." *The New York Times,* February 1, 1992, F-14.

CHAPTER TEN

The Computer as a Personal Finance Tool

LEARNING OBJECTIVES

- To examine how computers can be used in personal finance

- To illustrate how computers can help organize our budgeting, checkbook balancing, record keeping, and planning activities

- To explain the use of personal computers for investing and banking

- To evaluate the use of computerized programs for tax preparation and electronic tax filing

The computer age has arrived. It has permeated all facets of our economy and society. Computers are standard equipment in practically every office, factory, school, and government agency. A course or book on personal finance would not be complete without giving the computer its due recognition and rightful place in our financial life. Therefore, this chapter explores the possible role of computers in our personal finances.

This chapter obviously will not teach you how to use, operate, or program a computer. For that you need to take courses designed specifically for computers. This chapter will discuss how the computer is applied by individuals to enhance and improve their personal finance affairs and may help you decide whether or not and how to incorporate the mighty microchip into your financial life.

A personal computer (PC) can be an invaluable tool in budgeting, tax preparation, and investment. Although most people can still manage and survive without a PC, more and more people who want to improve the management of their personal finances are tempted to use it.

Keeping a budget, managing investments, and preparing taxes can be tedious and time-consuming chores. A personal computer and several floppy disks can liberate one from bulky file drawers full of financial records. The computer's attributes are manifold, ranging from an awesome memory capacity to an ability to calculate data and to follow instructions from various software packages in order to perform different tasks.

Like much in good management, the idea is to delegate. By harnessing the computer's speed and number-crunching prowess, some of money management's most tedious tasks can be made easier and more efficient. Computers are, for example, great filers, researchers, and analysts. They can manage a person's day-to-day spending by helping to set a budget; write, print out, and record checks; and index and file every expenditure in the proper tax category, as well as assist in tax filing. Or they can assist in a thorough investment analysis, giving investors access to the latest research on stocks, bonds, commodities, and mutual funds, helping make timely buying and selling decisions and track all the elements of an investor's portfolio.

Before you get swept away by visions of fingertip control over your financial affairs, however, you should candidly assess your needs and habits. The personal situation for many people may not be worth the substantial investment of time and money that computers require. If your monthly financial duties are confined to meeting a few bills, making a mortgage payment, and occasionally reviewing a handful of blue-chip stocks, all that is really needed is a pocket calculator and a notebook.

Organizing and Acquiring the Proper Equipment

Let us assume you are burdened with time-consuming budgets, investments, portfolio management, and tax preparation. You have decided to computerize your financial life. How do you start?

Getting Some Hardware: Grabbing a Byte

Granted, the computer is a wizardly machine. The real question is, which one will do the best job of organizing your finances at a reasonable rate. Virtually any computer can be used to manage money, but a system that meets the following criteria will make the job easier:

1. IBM compatible—most high-powered financial software is designed for the IBM line (although a Macintosh is quite adequate, it will not be compatible with IBM software)

2. A minimum of 640K RAM memory—that's enough to run most financial software, though you may eventually want to add more memory

3. Two disk drives—one to run the software and one to store the financial data.*

4. A monitor capable of displaying graphics, since many finance programs can convert numbers into charts and graphs

5. A printer capable of printing graphics

6. A modem which enables your computer to interface with other computers and databases via the telephone. The modem should support a minimum speed of 2400 baud; a 9600 baud is preferable. In addition, a phone line for the modem, and, optionally, a switching device to route calls to modem or phone may be required.

Many IBM–compatible computers come with Microsoft Windows installed. This product has two benefits:

1. It allows you to organize and run the programs on your computer under a graphical menu system. You use a special device (called a mouse) to point to pictures of the things you want to do, push one button, and the program begins to run. It is not necessary to remember long, complicated commands.

2. Programs written specifically for Microsoft Windows have the same "look and feel" about them. This means that a given activity, such as reading information, is always accomplished the same way and in the same sequence, whether you are dealing with words or numbers, business or games. This makes the job of learning to use such programs much simpler.

If you decide to use Microsoft Windows (currently at version 3.1), you will need a machine with at least 4 Mb (megabytes) of RAM (actually, the minimum is 2 Mb, but that's rarely enough for productive work) and more RAM is better. You *must* have a hard drive, the larger and faster the better. You will also need a mouse to "point" to the functions you want to perform.

Software (To Do the Hard Jobs)

To get a computer to do anything helpful, you must make or buy some software programs. They usually come on floppy disks, which are delicate, flexible plates of plastic sheathed in protective paper-like sleeves. The disks are "played" in a slot in the computer called the disk drive. Diskettes come in either 5¼ inch or 3 inch form factors. The former stores 360,000 to 1,200,000 characters (for double density—high density versions) while the latter stores 720,000 to 1,440,000 characters. The 3½ inch disks are rapidly replacing the 5¼ inch disks.

All programs cannot be all things to all people. Choices have to be made based on which tasks the user would like the computer to perform. The magic words on

---

*Although the dual floppy disk drives may be sufficient, they are rather inconvenient and time consuming to use. A "hard disk drive" is far more convenient and more expensive. It is well worth the extra expense for those willing and able to spend more.

any computer program are "user friendly," which generally means that clear and easy to follow instructions will appear on the screen to tell users how to get the results they expect. But often users have no way of knowing whether a program will do what they want until they buy it and try it on their computer.

Therefore, it is recommended that before making a choice, users should try to take home a copy of any program they are considering. Consumers need to find out the following about each program before they purchase it:

1. How hard is it to learn? Software with so-called tutorials, which lead users through one or several sample procedures, make mastering a program much easier. Ease of understanding and of use, speed of entering and of working with data, and a program's overall ability to explain its key features well should be the main criteria.

2. How do users get help when stumped? The documentation, or instructions, that comes with most software is a user's lifeline. It should be able to be followed easily. Check by flipping the manual open at random and reading what you see. One invaluable aid is an 800 telephone number to call with questions.

3. How quickly can corrections be made? It's easy to type "589" for "598." Fixing this error should be just as fast, whether on the spot or a month later.

4. What happens if you make a big mistake? How easily can errors be corrected? Some programs flash useless explanations such as "syntax error." The best will give on screen help or refer users to a specific page in the manual.

5. How quickly does the package work? For instance, after logging in data for one check, can you begin typing the next right away or must you wait?

6. What hardware is needed? Be sure the program will work on your brand of machine and that you have the memory and type of disk drives (single or double sides) needed to make it run. Some programs require a minimum DOS version in order to run. Typically, DOS 3.1 and above will suffice. DOS releases currently go to version 6.0.

7. What do other objective users say about this and other software? Question other people about what they are using and how they like it. But because people tend to become wedded to the programs they have and are often unaware of later developments, check for yourself about new programs. Look for an independent review of the package. Computer and financial publications frequently publish reviews on investment software.

8. Is a demo disk available? For a nominal amount ($10 to $35), many software vendors offer a demonstration package containing a disk and written material that illustrate in some detail the features of their software package. Often the cost of the demonstration material is deducted from the cost of the complete package if you decide to purchase it.

"I can carry my own software, thank you."

SOURCE: "Pepper...and Salt," *The Wall Street Journal*, September 11, 1990, A-23. Reprinted by permission of Cartoon Features Syndicate.

Upon purchasing a computerized personal finance program, some serious reading and studying are required to become familiar with it. A program package typically contains one or more floppy disks holding recorded instructions for the computer, along with a database, but users often receive a manual that may run up to 300 pages. Consumers should count on spending several hours of hard work learning how to use any money management program and another chunk of time each month logging in data.

The tasks that software packages can perform range from the trivial to the complex. At the low end of the scale, there are simple checkbook register programs that do nothing more than help balance a checkbook. At the other extreme are programs that can project a user's tax situation five years ahead and help make decisions now that will pay off then. For the active investor, computers can collect daily stock market data over the telephone, graph the price performance of an investor's favorite stocks automatically on the screen, and compute an up-to-the-minute valuation of a portfolio.

Spreadsheets and Databases

It is important for computer users to understand that most financial software is modeled on one or the other of two basic kinds of programs: the spreadsheet or the database.

Spreadsheets

Spreadsheets are software programs often used to perform financial calculations. The spreadsheet is an electronic replacement for the traditional modeling tools: the accountant's columnar pad, pencil, and calculator. In some ways spreadsheet programs are to those tools what word processors are to typewriters. Spreadsheets divide a computer's display into a series of rectangles, called *cells,* arranged in rows and columns. The cells may be thought of as boxes where numbers or text entered in the machine appear. The text usually serves to label the numbers, which are related. They might, for example, be the share prices, numbers of shares, and total value of individual stocks in a portfolio.

Users work with these numbers by entering mathematical formulas, usually supplied with the spreadsheet, into the computerized memory. A simple formula might instruct the program to add up the worth of all the portfolio's stocks. One can change the value of a number on the spreadsheet and the program will calculate the effect, if any, on all the other numbers. A set of stocks can be extracted from their spreadsheet listings and arranged by number of shares of each issue owned or by their dollar value.

The spreadsheet assists investors in tracking gains and losses. Brokerage costs are quickly determined by plugging in fee tables. Spreadsheets are particularly good at storing target prices. Enter predetermined buy and sell levels and the program will flag each stock requiring action.

The most remarkable feature of a spreadsheet is its ability to do "what if" computations. Electronic spreadsheets allow users to speculate about the effect of different circumstances by specifying the relationships among such variables as price, earnings, dividends, and so forth, and then playing "what if?" by changing each of the variables in turn. After a set of mathematical relationships has been built into the worksheet, the worksheet can be recalculated with amazing speed, using different sets of assumptions. If only paper, a pencil, and a calculator are used to build models, every change to the model will require recalculating every relationship in the model. If the model has 100 formulas and you change the first one, you must make 100 calculations by hand so that the change flows through the entire model. If, on the other hand, a spreadsheet is used, the same change requires the press of only a few keys. The program does the rest.

By plugging in hypothetical data, users can ask the computer what financial decisions they made today might mean to them tomorrow. They could see, for instance, what the net effect on their monthly cash flow would be if they took on a new mortgage payment from an investment property that produces a given amount of rental income. As they change one, the spreadsheet program automatically changes all the others so that the relationships specified remain constant.

The first breakthrough for home investment came in 1978 with the introduction of the spreadsheet accounting program, *Visicalc.* In mid-1983 Lotus Development Corporation announced *Lotus 1-2-3.* The product is built around an enhanced spreadsheet. *Lotus 1-2-3* is in many ways similar to *Visicalc* and other electronic spreadsheet programs. But *Lotus 1-2-3* also combines business graphics and data management (database) functions with its spreadsheets.

Now spreadsheet packages are offered by most of the major suppliers. By means of a spreadsheet, the investor can place numbers and formulas in a video grid. After attaching labels, the result looks similar to paper entries, but myriad calculations are performed instantaneously. The various figures and formulas may be linked. This allows investors to test more strategies than they ever had time to try with manual methods. You can link not only figures and formulas but entire spreadsheets. For example, spreadsheet 1 can refer to data in spreadsheet 2. Change the values in spreadsheet 1 and the software updates the other.

Lotus, in 1984, introduced *Symphony,* a so-called integrated software package that combines the spreadsheet with a database, business graphics, a simple word processor, and communications functions, which permits users to write and store notes to themselves. However, the introduction of this integrated program has not reduced *Lotus 1-2-3's* popularity. *Lotus 1-2-3* remains one of the most popular and powerful spreadsheet, graphics, and database programs on the market. It continued to outsell all of the integrated packages combined throughout the 1980s. But software giant Microsoft Inc., and the smaller Borland International, have both been vigorously promoting their own spreadsheets in recent years and have been making inroads into the market.

Extremely popular with professionals and small businesses, electronic spreadsheets are also widely used by individuals. If set up to follow the steps in a tax return, taxable income can be determined as fast as income and expense items are entered, and changes can be accomplished instantaneously. Similarly, users can compare the effects of different assumptions for budget, investment, or tax purposes in the blinking of an eye.

Database

After spreadsheets, the second most important kind of computer program for personal finance is the **database.** These programs can perform many of the same tasks as spreadsheets, but they work quite differently. A spreadsheet appears on a screen as a grid of interconnected information. Users see only a small part of it at any one time but can move around the grid in any direction they choose. A database, by contrast, is more like a card file. The cards appear on the screen one by one, each containing a discrete block of information. Some of the most popular databases are *dBASE III Plus, dBASE IV, Paradox, FoxPro* and *Access.* Databases are useful for handling and organizing large volumes of data and are probably less suitable for average individuals and more oriented to business applications.

The Financial Software Menu

Those who decide to buy dedicated software have hundreds of financial programs to choose from. Basically, they break down into four categories: budgeting and planning, investments, electronic banking, and taxes. In each of those areas, there are plenty of trustworthy products. To help you select the most appropriate programs for you, let us examine the features available in each genre.

Budgeting and Planning

At their most elementary level, financial budgeting and planning programs are electronic bookkeepers. Most finance programs allow users to prepare budgets, to record transactions, and to issue reports on their financial position, and many show users how their budget figures compare with their actual expenses. If you do not already own a computer and have relatively simple finances, you probably will not get your money's worth if you buy one for the purpose of budgeting alone. As previously mentioned, a ledger book, pocket calculator, and shoe box may do just fine for you.

The Virtues of a Computerized Budget

If you already own a computer, a good software package can certainly make your budgeting and financial record keeping more pleasant and life considerably easier at tax time. The best of this software makes relatively short work of budgets, expense reports, long-range financial planning, and management of specific financial assets, particularly securities, providing, of course, that you keep your spending and investing accounts up to date. If you have not been in the habit of maintaining such records, merely collecting the information these programs call for will be an achievement.

Not for the Lazy and Sloppy

There is much argument about the virtue of using a personal computer for budgeting. People who are for it claim that a computerized record of expenses is clearer and easier to work with than a paper and pencil budget. Those against it point out that to create those records, users still have to enter the same information into a computer that they would on their budget sheet and that they are less likely to keep their records up to date with a computer because of the steps involved just to get the program running. Those who despair of ever balancing their checkbooks may find the exacting demands of computerized record keeping more frustrating than friendly. Some functions, such as maintaining household inventory, take a great deal of work. They may be in for a disappointment by assuming that switching from pencil and paper to floppy disks or tapes is going to transform them from a sloppy reluctant record keeper into some sort of space age droit.

Both points of view are fair, but the balance can be tipped in favor of the computer when we add in special features found in some budget programs, such as the ability to create graphs of your own spending patterns or to call up a list of all the expenses that you have marked as tax deductible. Particularly useful is the capacity actually to write checks on a computer and print them onto special check forms fed into a printer. Your financial data are entered automatically into your budgeting program the instant you write the check. A good budgeting software program also lets you store all your financial records, including several bank and credit card accounts, on floppy disks. These records can later be retrieved and displayed either chronologically or by type of transaction. And once having mastered the basics of the software, monitoring your finances should not take more than a half hour or so each week. Personal finance programs enable setting up a home accounting system that, in addition to keeping tax records neat and close at hand, will help you plan and achieve your financial goals.

What's Available?

Thousands of people in recent years have sought financial refuge in dozens of personal accounting programs, sporting such names as *Quicken, CheckWrite Plus, MacMoney, Wealth Builder, Dollars and Sense, Money Counts, Andrew Tobias's*

Managing Your Money, and *Microsoft Money.* These packages are designed to help consumers use a balance sheet, maintain a household budget, and discover how they spend money. More than 50 financial planning programs are on the market, priced from about $30 to $200, and handling such chores as checkbook balancing, budgeting, and tax planning.

Quicken is one of the most popular personal finance programs. People use *Quicken* to keep track of checking accounts, expense categories, and investments, as well as to pay bills, either electronically or by creating and printing checks on the computer's printer. Typing a mortgage payment, for instance, into a program called *Money Counts* records it in a checking account file, enters it in a home-budget file, and flags the interest and property tax deductible items. Any time of the year, a user can have a list of how much he or she spent on his or her home and how much has accumulated in tax deductions. These programs will not make users fiscally responsible but will make it harder to kid themselves about where the money is going. Users can view or print out analysis of such things as net worth and cash flow, as well as comparisons of budget projections with actual income and spending in various categories.

To reduce the bother of entering information into a computer, the publishers of a home finance program called *Dollars and Sense* (by Softsel Computer Products) have developed a service with Bank of America and Citibank that enables bank customers to electronically transfer checkbook and credit card information into *Dollars and Sense.* More will be discussed later about this and line investing via modems.

How Does It Work?

Suppose that your program is in place. You sit down at the computer and review your monthly expenses. Most budgeting and home accounting programs revolve around the user's checkbook. The computer can be used instead of a checkbook to record deposits and checks. You enter each transaction—deposit, check, —on the computer as it occurs or in batches every week or so. If you enter all your checks, deposits, and other bank transactions into the computer and then enter those that your bank statement indicates have cleared, the computer can reconcile your account. When the bank statement arrives, you flag the checks that have cleared, then sit back while the computer works to reconcile the balance. The software can thereby check your accounts to ensure that you and the financial institutions you deal with correctly record your financial transactions.

In addition, users can code checks, assign each deposit and check to an income or expenditure category, designated by them or by the software program. By coding checks by type of expense or other category, users need merely press a key to find out whether their spending for entertainment is greater or less than budgeted or to summon a list of tax deductible payments.

One of the more important functions is **automatic double-entry bookkeeping,** which means if users pay their monthly gas bill, their checking balance is decreased and their gas expense account is increased. What they are doing with any of these programs is creating their own financial database. And that makes it a lot easier to keep track of where their money comes from and where it is going. If users need to know whether they have already paid a bill or made a charitable contribution, they can search the computer's memory instead of their check stubs. Some programs can handle more than one checkbook or other financial accounts and maintain separate credit card accounts. It can also provide users with reports such as balance sheets, plus income and cash flow statements.

Balance sheets show a user's assets, liabilities and net worth as of a given date. **Income statements** show, for a specified period, users' income, expenses, and net gain or loss. In addition, they compare their actual versus their budgeted amounts and provide the variance between the two. Together with a budget, which indicates how much cash you actually have on hand to pay bills or save, they can help you point out areas where you can reduce your spending.

Users can set up a monthly budget for each expenditure category and record their spending as it occurs. The computer will keep running totals and compare them with their budget. Some programs will provide a tabular comparison, indicating the difference between budget and actuals; others will also graph the comparison, generally using bar graphs. The most flexible systems will let a user create dozens of expense categories and follow several checking accounts. Better information means that the opportunities for sophisticated financial tax planning are much greater.

Investing Via Computer

There is an elemental notion about investing. The more investors know, the better their chances of success. To that end, the personal computer is proving itself the most important new tool for small investors since the telephone. Investing is no longer a leisurely gentleman's business conducted over a martini at private clubs. Nor is it merely a matter of reading Wall Street research reports of cash cows and rising stars. Technology has become the dominant force in the investment climate of the 1990s. It has redefined how stocks are traded and tied the world together into a global market.

There are an estimated 500,000 plus small investors who utilize data banks, computer information services, and on-line systems. A good investment software package can make a personal computer a valuable tool for practically every step in the investment process, identifying securities to buy and sell, placing orders on line, or monitoring securities after investors buy them. Investors can search through databases containing thousands of stocks for those that meet their own criteria, generate scores of market indicators, and perform complex technical analysis on individual securities. They give small investors access to reams of data that used to be the private preserve of investment professionals. There is software to help investors make decisions about stocks, bonds, commodities, options, real estate, and even mutual funds.

Is It for You?

Whether using a computer to manage your investments would actually help you make more money depends on the size of your holdings, how actively you manage them, the extent to which you are interested in managing them more closely and the capability of your computer and the software you select. Generally speaking, the less active an investor is, the less it makes sense to go electronic. But for those who devote a fair amount of time to stock trading and who enjoy the game, a computer can put a lot of information at their fingertips. Whether that information will be helpful will depend more on how they use it than on how powerful their computer may be.

Theoretically at least, investors equipped with computers should have lots of advantages over their pencil and paper counterparts. Their main advantage is access to information. The investment markets are built on information, some of it sound, some of it chimerical, all of it potentially powerful. Investors can update the value of their portfolios in the blink of an eye, compare their performance with the market averages by punching a couple of keys, collect up-to-the-minute price quotes and news about their holdings, and perform analysis in a matter of minutes that would take hours or even days to do without a computer. What a computer can do best is make vast and complicated calculations quickly, organize and reorganize data efficiently for reporting and analyzing, and, when connected to a data bank, provide a variety of past and current economic and financial news and dates that can be used for making investment decisions.

To take best advantage of all that, and to justify the often considerable cost, you should be at least a moderately active trader (investor) more interested in improving your investment performance than in playing with a sophisticated toy or gadget.

It Won't Think for You

Most of the investment software available assumes that investors already have a good working knowledge of the investment approach they intend to use. It is not designed to teach investment analysis but to do it faster. If investors know what they are doing, the time they save should enable them to make more informed investment decisions.

But if investors do not know what to do with the information and analysis a computer can generate, the most expensive investment software package will not do much good. A computer can help pick winners, but it is not a substitute for thinking. Ultimately, the computer's owner, not the machine, has to make the decisions.

Investment software can perform basically four specific investment tasks: **portfolio management, technical analysis, fundamental analysis,** and **on-line trading.** Each package can usually handle only one or two of those tasks.

Let us now examine each of these investment tasks and see how, if at all, they can be of use to investors.

Portfolio Management

The first order of business for most users is to keep a computerized record of the securities they buy and sell. **Portfolio management** does just that. It tracks an individual's holdings of stocks, bonds, or commodities.

The most common kind of report simply shows the portfolio's current status. A good portfolio package, properly used, can instantly update the price and values of all holdings electronically. With each update, the software computes the new value of an investor's portfolio. As an investor buys and sells shares, it calculates his or her profit or loss, factoring in interest, dividends, and commissions. Some sophisticated programs let investors compare changes in the value of their portfolio with changes in the broad stock indexes, such as the Dow Jones Averages or Standard & Poor's Indexes.

Most portfolio management programs permit investors to track the performance of a portfolio of stocks, bonds, options, mutual funds, Treasury bills, and other investments. Each security an investor owns is displayed along with information about its type, dates, number of shares or units bought or sold, whether it was purchased for cash or on margin, purchase price, current price, and the unrealized gain or loss.

Other common reports reflect dividend and interest income automatically. In addition, reports often provide advance notice of dividend payments coming due and options expiring. By inserting the current unit price of each security, investors can determine the current value of their portfolio instantly. If an investor has access to a data bank, many programs will automatically pick up current prices, then calculate the total value of each holding and of the portfolio as a whole. Another kind of report conveys vital income tax information. For each security you sell during the tax year, you get the name, number of shares, purchase date, sale date, total cost, total proceeds, and gain or loss. All the information needed to complete one's federal income tax return is included in this report.

Some popular portfolio management software include the following:

1. *Dow Jones Market Manager Plus* (Dow Jones & Co., 609/520-4641)

2. *The Equalizer* (Charles Schwab & Co., 800/334-4455)

3. *PFROI* (Techserve, 800/826-8082)

4. *Metastock Professional* (EQUIS, Inc.)

5. *Pulse* (EQUIS, International)

Fundamental Analysis

No investor task better demonstrates the computer's time saving graces than **fundamental analysis** screening. This information can be obtained through a modem and a phone line to an on-line data bank, discussed further on, instead of a floppy disk.

Many investors do not want to go to the expense of on-line systems. They get their current stock quotes from the newspapers. But they still want access to fundamental data in order to do their own stock analysis. There are a number of data services to which they can subscribe. They are known as **off-line databases** since they are not connected via the phone lines. Instead, on a periodic basis, normally monthly, subscribers receive a database floppy disk containing up-to-date financial information on a group of stocks.

The amount and type of information available for screening varies with the software package. For example, with *Value Line's Value/Screen Plus,* one database disk is available containing information on the more than 1,600 stocks that account for about 95 percent of the trading activity on all U.S. stock exchanges. The disk contains 37 separate pieces of information for each stock, including historical growth rates, measures of current performance and volatility, and key projections. Another popular data system, *Vestor,* provides investors with each stock's percentage of price change and net-on-balance money flow for the previous 10 weeks, profit-earnings ratio, last dividend yield, plus a variety of complex signals, indicators, and projections. Other similar software packages include *Disclose* and *Investext*.

Essentially, fundamental analysis software sorts through a huge database and finds, ranks, and highlights stocks and other securities that meet certain criteria which an investor has specified. The criteria may be price earnings ratios, rate of growth in earnings, ratio of debt to equity, or other data. For example, if you are looking for stocks, say, with a price earnings ratio of less than 10 which are selling for less than $20 a share, you punch those requirements into your computer. It will sift through data obtained from an information bank or other source and display a list of all Big Board issues which fall into your specified category. The right software can convert your computer into a lightning-fast securities analyst.

Such investment packages seem to conjure up images of the executive going home, analyzing his or her portfolio, studying various market trends, running a number of charts, and discovering 10 stocks that are bargains. The executive gets rich fast, with profits that easily pay for the price of a computer. In reality, it is far from that simple. The package arms investors with the means to make a much more informed and sophisticated selection of investment. But no one, human or computer, can provide a fool-proof guarantee of success, profits, and wealth.

Technical Analysis

CHARTS

Technical analysis is the study of charts that convey price movements and other market indicators. The mathematical calculators and endless charting by which technical analysts track statistical trends and look for buy and sell signals make the job a natural for computers. Technical analysis software is essentially for investors interested in charting fluctuations in the stock market. It allows investors to plot standard high-low-close-volume bar charts along with various other technical market indicators and studies.

Before buying technical analysis software, investors should decide what they need it to do. Three features form the core of the technical analysis packages now available: retrieving data from an on-line database, drawing price charts with moving averages and resistance lines, and printing copies of the charts and data. With the proper screen and printer, the computer can completely take over the tedious job of plotting graphs. Technical analysis software sets up routines for calculating and charting such indicators as moving averages, volume, relative strength, and momentum. Some programs emphasize broad market trends; others deal only with individual stocks. Although the investment software can make the computer do technical analysis, it cannot turn you into a technical analyst. Unless you already understand the approach or have a desire to learn it, these programs will not help you despite their sometimes excellent documentation and data.

Programs that perform technical analysis include the following:

1. *Telescan Analyzer* (Telescan, 800/727-4636)

2. *Wall Street Investor* (Pro Plus Software, 800/227-5728)

(The above programs handle fundamental analysis as well.)

On-Line Investment: Get On Line

The stuff of yesterday's futurist fantasies is now commonplace fact for tens of thousands of active investors with a personal computer, a modem, and a telephone. An investor with this equipment may access a varied "menu" of database services: quotations and profiles of stocks, bonds, and options; market and research briefs; tax tips; personal account information; and electronic mail to the brokerage firm.

To be used via telephone lines, a computer must be equipped with a **modem,** a device that lets you transmit and receive computerized information via phone lines and the appropriate communications software, some of which comes with modems. The two most popular modem choices are the Hayes Smartmodem 9600 and U S Robotics.

Just about every evening you can head for your den, sit down at your IBM or Macintosh computer, and run a one-person brokerage house whose only client is you. With the touch of a few buttons on the computer, you automatically fetch stock quotations for about a dozen securities, some in your portfolio and some you are contemplating buying.

If you are thinking of buying a stock, bond, or other security, you can tap into a commercial database and get displayed on your screen recent news about the company, estimates of its future earnings, and financial statements it filed with the Securities and Exchange Commission, as well as current and past stock, bond, commodities and option, price, and volume data. These data can be up to the minute or go back several years.

The so-called "Big Four" databases are *Dow Jones News/Retrieval, Compuserve, The Source,* and *Prodigy.* These services offer up-to-the minute stock quotes, corporate earnings figures, historical pricing, company statistics, and the latest financial news. Dow Jones News/Retrieval, for example, pools several different information banks to provide subscribers with news reports, current and historical stock quotes, fundamental data on over 4,000 companies, information from public filings, news of tender offers, extracts from proxy statements on 9,400 public companies, and highlights of weekly analyst investment research.

On-Line Trading—How Does It Work? **On-line** systems, the basic service connecting investors to the brokerage firms, typically also allow users to place their orders and check their portfolios through programs that automatically update the value of their holdings. Let's say you get a tip on a stock from your used car dealer, Howie Cheetum, who tells you to invest in Citicorp (NYSE). In the past, you called your broker and asked for an annual report, a prospectus, and perhaps a Standard and Poor's (S&P) credit rating sheet on the company. Now your personal computer can tell you a lot more than your used car dealer, barber, mother-in-law, or broker, at relatively little cost and almost instantly.

Do you want to take information from the on-line data service and analyze it at your leisure? With your *Dow Jones Market Analyzer,* for instance, you can tap into the Dow Jones News/Retrieval Service and download (store on your own disk) price and volume information on Citicorp for the last year. Such downloading greatly expands the power of your personal computer. It is like taping a television program for later viewing.

Most services make it easy to download information and sell all sorts of software to help investors interpret and analyze the data. Some investment programs will not only collect these data automatically, but once stored in the computer's memory, they can also feed them to one of the stock analysis programs. Many programs can convert the raw data into charts. *Dow Jones Market Analyzer* may draw a graph showing that Citicorp is trading at a low of 47⅝. As a bargain hunter, this depressed stock may intrigue you. You may also find the five-year sales growth figure to be 42 percent and price/earnings ratio of 3. You then check the corporate earnings estimate, which is $16.30. You decide to buy.

Before buying, you need to review your cash position and general investment portfolio. You decide to access your personal account to get current information. You call up a display of account information that is automatically updated to reflect trading activity and also shows your cash and margin account balances.

Some data sources (such as *Trade Plus, Knight-Ridder, Telerate, Telemet America, PC Quote,* and *Marketview Software*) even permit investors to trade stocks, bonds, and options, directly via their computer without the need to talk to a broker. Investors call, via computer (to Trade Plus), check the price of the security, place an order to buy (or sell) through a cooperating discount broker, and are advised that the order has been executed, normally within about 10 minutes.

As more investors buy personal computers and software and information services become widely available at lower cost, we may very likely see more investors tinkering with portfolios at the strangest places at the oddest hours. It's already happening.

An Insomniac's Dream

You're an insomniac on an overnight business trip in a motel in Burbank. At 4 AM you can power up your Macintosh to monitor your investments. Or perhaps you're thinking of buying stock in GM? You can get news on GM that came across the Dow Jones News Service as recently as 90 seconds before, and as far back as three months. For example, when employment is high, more people have the money to buy cars. Before making the decision to invest in GM, however, an investor would compare the financial performance of GM, Ford, and Chrysler during boom years. A personal computer can be used to obtain financial data about the Big Three automakers as well as employment and unemployment statistics. But you should not stop there. You then can poll Data Stream for information on Sweden's Volvo, Germany's Daimler-Benz and Japan's Honda.

If you still cannot decide whether to buy or not, there is even periodic literature on the subject available through the computer. In addition to numbers, data banks such as Dow Jones News/Retrieval, Warner Computer Corp., or Compuserve offer information in text form. From the Dow Jones service, for instance, you get articles from back issues of *Barron's* and *The Wall Street Journal,* or summon up a corporation's annual report. You can again download pages of information onto a floppy disk in a matter of minutes and then read it at your convenience after you have disconnected your computer from the data bank. You will encounter virtually every publicly-known fact about a company's fundamental and technical performance, management, and ownership. This enables you to compare thousands of stocks by criteria you choose, read analysts' reports, and find current and historical prices for the stocks and bonds in question.

On-Line Trading: An Evaluation

Hundreds of thousands of investors use an electronic investment-information service. For most individual investors, an on-line quotation system is alluring because it weans them from dependence on brokers for buy and sell decisions. Increasingly, their buy and sell orders are executed via computer, not by traders shouting on the floor of an exchange in New York, London, or Tokyo. Many professional "on-line" investors no longer deal with another human being when they invest. Over the past few years, completely electronic markets, such as **Instinet,** have emerged. Hundreds of Wall Street firms can have their clients buy and sell securities now with just a few strokes on a computer.

Almost all **on-line data base systems** are accessible 24 hours a day, seven days a week. Most data banks charge by the hour. Rates range from about $5 per hour in the evening to $75 per hour during peak business hours.

The largest computer broker is Bank America's Schwab. Clients who own the firm's Equalizer Package can obtain price quotes and up-to-the-minute news, place orders, manage their portfolios, read research reports on stocks of interest, and even program stock "alerts" that signal when selected issues encounter specified price targets. Investors who subscribe to on-line services are committed and professional investors who typically own some $150,000 worth of stocks or bonds and on average, trade about once a week.

Can all of these data and state-of-the-art software and hardware really give investors an edge in the market? The answer is certainly no. Stock selecting is an art. As in any art, performance improves if the artist has good tools. But good tools alone do not make for a good artist.

On-line trading will not insulate investors from losses or even guarantee that their long-term returns from the market will improve. But they facilitate certain styles of investing. Some investors who have taken this step like to trade directly because they believe it is quick and convenient. But whether on-line trading is just another gimmick or an indispensable service that really aids investors remains to be seen.

On-Line May Be Off-Base The benefits to investors are far from clear. Often the services simply are not what they are cracked up to be. Despite sponsors' claims that orders placed through home computers are executed almost immediately, there are still delays. Most people seem to prefer dealing with a live broker rather than an instrument.

Access to an on-line trading system can lead to overtrading or impulse trading. Having instant access to market information can tempt investors to trade stocks too quickly and too frequently. Investors can also incur considerable costs if they overuse the system. There is a per minute usage fee, and almost all of the best sources of investment analysis also tack on surcharges.

Computerized investing has scarcely captivated masses of investors. Despite the hoopla about personal computers becoming self-sufficient investment centers, brokerage firms that market trade-at-home services say they have attracted only a tiny fraction of the nation's investors. A few discount brokerage firms encourage clients to enter orders by computer, though the public seems reluctant. Those who practice the art are alone on the cutting edge. Despite wildly optimistic market forecasts, their numbers are meager. Only 20,000 users subscribe to computerized investing.

"We've decided to offer full partnership to your computer instead."

SOURCE: "Pepper...and Salt," *The Wall Street Journal,* October 30, 1991. Reprinted by permission of Cartoon Features Syndicate.

But the major discount brokers, and now the banks, are still rushing into the business, convinced that within a few years the phone call to the broker will be on the way out.

Many community education courses, college classes, and vendors offer inexpensive training courses for the novice in some of the more popular software investment and money management packages. Additionally, many large public libraries and college libraries offer access (sometimes for free) to some of the popular on-line investment services.

Electronic (Home) Banking

Electronic banking enables individuals to conduct most of their banking and central asset management without having to leave the comforts of their home or office. Basically, a home banking setup lets account holders instruct the bank to pay bills by taking money from their account and electronically transmitting it to the electric company, credit card concern, mortgage holder, phone company, or any other payee. It enables, likewise, an individual's employer, stockbroker, and anyone else to electronically pay by transferring money into his account.

The basic hardware requirements are simple—personal computer, a video display monitor, a modem, and preferably a printer. Software requirements vary. Banks that have proprietary systems provide customers with special software to run their home banking programs. A popular software package, *Checkfree* (available for as little as $17 at discount stores or by mail), contains a simple program to keep track of all transactions in your checking account.

By far the most popular feature is **electronic bill paying,** a system that offers several advantages over check writing. The bank provides customers with a list of hundreds of merchants, banks, insurance companies, and the like that it will pay. Instead of writing checks and licking envelopes, all customers have to do is select a payee's code number and the dollar amount and press a button on their home computer to pay the bill instantly. Users can pay bills 24 hours a day. They can also postdate payments up to 90 days in advance with some systems, which is convenient for people on vacation. Recurring payments can be made automatically.

Like so many computer programs, home banking is usually menu driven. This means that once you have entered your passwords, the PC screen displays a list of choices. Flitting your fingers around the keyboard, you can, at any time, call up a current "statement" on the computer screen. It will show your balance and recent transactions, including any checks that you wrote the traditional way. You can also confirm that your employer has deposited your paycheck as well as pay bills, keep records, issue stop payment orders, track and reconcile your checkbook, and even send complaints to the bank. All of this can be done 24 hours a day, seven days a week.

Most systems let users instruct the bank to make automatic payments on a regular basis so they no longer need to remember to send off the monthly mortgage payment or the quarterly insurance premium. They also let users transfer funds from one of their accounts to another, apply for a loan, inquire about balances, send a question to a bank officer, and order checks. Most banks send a monthly statement summarizing all the transactions in a customer's accounts. Users can also get hard copies of transactions on their own printer or request them from the bank.

You can spare the effort of monthly instructions to the bank by supplying your bank with a list of payees: the mortgage holder on your home, your insurance companies for your various insurance policies, college bursar's office, doctor, newspaper delivery service, credit card companies, landlord, stockbroker, phone company, and cable TV company. The bank arranges with these payees to receive periodic payments, either by electronic funds transferred directly to their bank accounts or, if they wish, by check which the bank prints and mails. Some large banks are turning to the home computer as an alternative to the checkbook and the mailed out monthly statement. You can also specify additional personal payees into whose accounts you might need to transfer money occasionally, perhaps your dentist or student at college.

There is little likelihood that an unscrupulous computer hacker will be able to take money out of a user's account. Home banking customers devise a secret password that must be used, just as they use a confidential code with their automatic

"On second thought, don't hand over the loot. I'd like it transferred electronically to a Swiss bank account."

SOURCE: "Pepper...and Salt," *The Wall Street Journal,* January 21, 1993, A-15. Reprinted by permission of Cartoon Features Syndicate.

teller machine card. Funds can be moved only to the accounts of people or companies that the customer specified with the bank at least three days in advance.

The Drawbacks

Home banking does not transform a computer into a cash dispenser. Account holders still have to physically put in an appearance at their bank or automatic teller machine (ATM) to make cash withdrawals and deposits. But they can do the rest of their banking at home, in their den, living room, or office.

Some banks charge a monthly fee plus a phone line surcharge. If the communications software is slow, the cost can mount up. For most people, writing and mailing a few checks each month is not an onerous chore. But users who are electronically minded take to the idea, particularly if they operate any sort of small business.

Home banking is a slowly growing system. When Chemical Bank unveiled the idea of home banking in 1983, it projected that 10 percent of its customers would eventually pay bills and make banking transactions from their home computers. Other optimistic experts even predicted that between 8 to 12 million households would use it by 1990. But this optimism thus far has been misplaced. As of 1991, only about 100,000 people out of 28 million households that have personal computers have availed themselves of this new technology. Although some banks, including Chemical Bank, have pulled out of home banking, others are nevertheless actively promoting it. Only some 36 banks out of 14,000 in the country offer the service. Among them are such giants as Citibank, Bank of America, Chase Manhattan, Manufacturers Hanover, and Wells Fargo & Co.

Tax Preparation Software

The following were some leading tax programs in 1993:

For IBM and Compatibles

Andrew Tobias's Taxcut 1040
(MECA Software $49.95)
800/288-MECA

TURBOTAX (Chipsoft) $49-personal
tax planner
619/453-8722
(*TURBOTAX* has companion
programs for every state that
has an income tax.)

*J.K. Lasser's Your 1993 Income Tax
Software*
(Simon & Schuster Software, $74.95)

For Macintosh

MACINTAX
(Softview $99)

TURBOTAX (Chipsoft) $89

Computerized Tax Preparation: The Tax Byte—(Kid Video versus Uncle Sam)

Filing a tax return is nobody's idea of fun, but tax software can bring a degree of speed and organization to the process. A bewildering and growing array of tax planning and tax-form preparation software packages is available. A *Journal of Taxation* review in 1988 listed 74, ranging in price from less than $100 for most programs aimed at individuals to more than $2,500 for those geared to professional tax preparers. The professional models can crank out hundreds of returns and complete every form. They also include modules for each state.

Some tax programs are only for planning; they help organize data but do not actually complete a return. For as little as $50, a tax program can help assemble a return faster and do it more accurately than can be done by hand. Tax programs for personal computers have been around for nearly a decade. They have kept up with the changing tax laws year by year. Most manufacturers issue annual updates to keep their software synchronized with changes in IRS laws and statutes. Many packages also include modules for state and local tax changes. Most have become better and also have gotten cheaper.

Computers are great organizers and calculators, two indispensable factors in tax planning. But none of these programs can do all the work automatically. With all of them, the value and accuracy of the result depends upon the quality and consistency of the data that are fed into the computer.

GIGO—garbage in, garbage out—applies as much to tax return programs as anything else. The hardest part of using software is entering the data accurately. In the case of tax preparation programs, this means typing in all one's financial transactions for the entire year. To streamline the process, a few tax programs work in tandem with the previously mentioned budgeting and check-writing packages so the data can be transferred between them automatically, saving hours of data entry. Some programs review completed returns and flag areas where data are missing or obviously wrong. There is no magic involved. Taxpayers still gather all the information about their income, deductions, credits, and so forth.

Thus, despite the hi-tech marvels, tax payers cannot escape entirely from the perennial agonies of tax filing and tax paying. The program is a labor-saving computational tool rather than a brain substitute. Even so, what a tax program can do is impressive.

Computerized Tax Preparation Most of the tax software on the market will automate the actual preparation of the return, as long as you tell it what numbers to grind and where to put them. You provide the expertise; it acts as the clerk. Once you enter the right figures, the programs will speed you on. To speed your way through the return, tax software offers various levels of on-line help, available at the touch of a key to steer you to the forms needed to file and let you know what's supposed to be entered on them. If you need answers and advice, you can thumb through a tax reference book and look it up or call an accountant.

Tax programs do not stop at doing the arithmetic and transferring data to appropriate forms. They enable taxpayers to enter items in different categories, such as medical expenses in one column and business expenses in another and then add them up and plug them in when they sit down to do their returns. They also allow a user to move between related parts of various IRS forms by just pressing a button; for example, data can be moved from the line on Form 1040, referring to a taxpayer's capital gain or loss for the year, to Schedule D, where specific gains and losses are listed.

This reporting feature can save hours of compilation time. Taxpayers who use accountants or financial consultants can reduce their billing time by giving them reports to review rather than to prepare. Some software lets taxpayers plan for the following year or even beyond. Most useful are the programs that make automatic adjustments for upcoming changes, such as indexing. A computer can be more useful for tax planning than for the actual preparation of a return. Any tax program lets taxpayers plan the way they report their taxes by comparing the results of different "what if" situations to come up with the lowest tax liability. Programs that use a spreadsheet format let taxpayers compare several scenarios side by side. Taxpayers also can test different strategies, such as how much to contribute to an individual retirement account, and see for themselves the bottom-line result.

Correcting an Oops One of the great virtues of these programs is the ease with which they let users correct a mistake. Upon completing a return, you may discover a receipt that earns you a tax deduction. If you computed by pencil, you may decide to forgo the tax savings rather than redo the arithmetic and start from scratch on the affected forms. With a tax program, you enter the new deduction and almost instantly get the new result.

After working your way through a tax program, it is no longer necessary to pencil the numbers onto the IRS schedules. Most tax preparation programs complete the return by printing totals directly onto a 1040 and generating computer-printed versions of other forms and schedules. The IRS will accept all of these, including the 1040 and its variant. As of 1991, the IRS has allowed taxpayers who bought IRS-approved software to file tax returns on forms printed by their computers instead of using regulation IRS forms.

Electronic Tax Filing For those who prepare their tax return by computer, the logical next step would be to electronically file their returns with the IRS on a disk. Since 1986 the IRS has accepted the realities of the electronic age and approved filing by disk or (modem) phone lines. Taxpayers cannot, however, simply electronically transmit their returns from their home computers by using a modem. The IRS accepts electronically filed computer returns only from IRS-authorized professional tax preparers. The IRS claims that its computer system cannot handle large volumes of transmissions from individual taxpayers. Additionally, it is concerned about security. Tax preparer firms generally charge between $25 to $40 to file a return via computer. The charges can make it relatively costly to file electronically just to speed a small refund. But the fee may be worth it for people awaiting large rebates. Electronic filers should get their refund check within two to three weeks, compared with five to eight weeks when filing via mail.

Electronic filing is available to taxpayers nationwide. For example, H&R Block offers its *Rapid Refund* electronic filing program at most of its offices. Many independent accountant firms also offer similar services. Form 1040 and many of its schedules can be filed electronically. In 1992 the basic tax instructions mailed to most taxpayers with Form 1040 included a special pitch for a new form, 1040PC, which is done on a personal computer. *Rapid Refund* customers can receive a loan equal to the amount of their tax refund from one of four affiliate banks a few days after electronically filing their returns. If no problems arise concerning the return, the IRS sends the actual refund directly to the bank, paying off the loan in about two weeks. Meanwhile, Block collects a bank fee of about $29 to process the early

| FIGURE 10–1 | The Increase in Electronic Filing |

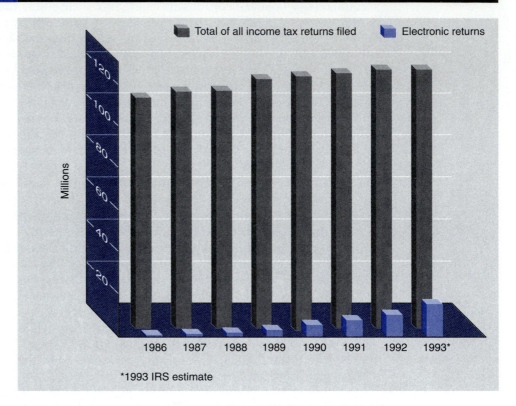

*1993 IRS estimate

In seven years the number of electronic fillings grew from 25,000 in 1986 to 10 million in 1992.

SOURCE: Internal Revenue Service.

refund, plus up to $25 for electronic filing, in addition to its regular tax-preparation fee of about $50 per return. But that does not eliminate all paper work. The IRS still wants the taxpayer's signature and W-2 wage withholding statement. Taxpayers satisfy those requirements with Form 8453, which they mail in the old fashioned way. The number of returns filed electronically surged from 25,000 in 1986 to 11 million in 1992 (see Figure 10–1). The IRS expects to see 35 million returns, or about one-third of the annual total, filed electronically by the mid-1990s. The IRS is encouraging this new service and provides a list of authorized transmitters nationwide. (This can be obtained by phoning 800/424-1040.)

Telefile In 1992 the IRS introduced a new pilot program in Ohio called *TeleFile*. That enables taxpayers who use Form 1040EZ to file using a touch-tone telephone. The system uses an interactive voice response technology and is planned to be expanded nationally. In the future it will be geared to include more complex forms. There is no charge to taxpayers for this service.

Is a Tax Program for You?   All this does not mean that if you have a computer you should buy a program to do your taxes. If you file the 1040A, 1040EZ, or use the 1040 but have only a few deductions, you probably need only a pencil, scratch

How Tax Returns Are Processed

By Mail

1. Taxpayers mail returns to IRS.
2. IRS personnel open returns and sort them.
3. Checks (if present) are compared with returns, credited to the taxpayers' accounts, and sent to the U.S Treasury.
4. IRS workers code returns and edit data for computer input.
5. IRS workers key data into computer; data stored on magnetic tape.
6. IRS mainframe computers read data and check math and the accuracy of information.
7. Tapes are sent to IRS Computing Center in West Virginia, where the information is recorded.
8. Refund tapes are sent to the Treasury Department's regional financial centers; there refund checks are issued and mailed.

By Modem

1. Using computers and modem, authorized electronic filers send tax return information to IRS over telephone lines.
2. If information is correctly formatted, IRS computer accepts returns and stores them on tape.
3. Refund payments are electronically transmitted to the Treasury Department's regional financial centers.
4. Refunds are directly deposited in the taxpayer's financial institution, or check is sent to the taxpayer.

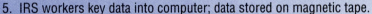

By Telefile

1. A 1040-EZ filer calls TeleFile to input information from the W-2 form.
2. Caller signs 1040-TEL and mails it to the IRS.
3. TeleFile computer calculates tax due or refund for the filers and sends data to IRS mainframe computers.
4. The IRS refunds within two weeks.

SOURCE: Internal Revenue Service.

paper, pocket calculator, and bottle of aspirin to do your taxes. If your tax situation is more complex, though, you may find that computerized tax programs make your life somewhat easier. On the other hand, tax software is not for people with the kind of complex returns that call for a tax attorney's or tax accountant's attention. The utility of most tax programs lies somewhere between that of a tax book and a low-budget tax preparer. Therefore, before rushing out with cash in hand, consider what tax software will not do.

Computer programs will not give you tax advice. In a questionable area, you are the one who will have to be familiar with the tax rules and decide whether to challenge the IRS or play it safe. An accountant is usually necessary because the tax laws change frequently and are quite complicated.

The computer provides mechanical assistance in the mathematics and printing of returns, not legal advice. The computer cannot go with the taxpayer to an IRS audit. Although some tax programs provide on-line tax advisers, on-line IRS instructions, and an audit detector, no program can replace a good accountant. A computer cannot make sure you have claimed each deduction you are entitled to or tell you the odds on taking a questionable one. While these programs can provide superb mathematical assistance and lots of tax information, they are unequipped to deal with gray areas, such as interpretation of the tax code, and remembering which expenses, deductions, and credits are applicable. Keep in mind that tax preparation software needs to be updated annually as tax laws change.

As software gets more complex, the various functions of budgeting, tax planning or preparation, and investing become easier to interconnect. It seems likely that we are all destined eventually to entrust the stewardship of our finances to its humming memory banks.

SUMMARY

If your finances are simple and under control, then you probably do not need a computer. But a computer can be a valuable aid and enhancement for those who need help with their record keeping, check balancing, budgeting, planning, banking, investing, or tax preparation. Financial software enables people to achieve a control over their finances that, before the advent of the home computer, could not have been achieved without either a significant investment of time or the help of a financial consultant. Computers can transform a not-so-organized money manager into a streamlined one. Computers can also serve as windows to a universe of investor information, tapping into numerous commercial databases.

The realities of computerized investing include considerable expense and investment of learning time. Both may often be wasted unless the electronic player is willing to use the system regularly. Additionally, no matter how sophisticated the technology which is available, no one has figured out a way of taking the risk out of investing.

Although the computer was heralded a decade ago as the future basic tool of every household, its growth in the personal financial sphere has been sluggish. Most people choose to use a calculator, pad, and pencil and shy away from computerized investing and electronic banking. Whether the personal computer will remain a convenient gadget or an indispensable household financial tool remains to be determined in the future.

KEY TERMS

Automatic double-entry bookkeeping

Balance sheets

Computerized budgets

Computerized tax preparation

Database

Electronic banking

Electronic bill paying

Electronic tax filing

Fundamental analysis

GIGO income statement

Modem

Off-line database

On-line database systems

On-line trading

Portfolio management

Spreadsheets

Technical analysis

REVIEW QUESTIONS AND PROBLEMS

1. What considerations should factor in to your choice of appropriate software?
2. What is a spreadsheet? How does it differ from a database?
3. What are the advantages and disadvantages of a computerized budget?
4. What advantages does an investor who uses an investment software package have over other investors?
5. What is the difference between on-line and off-line databases?
6. Explain each of the following tasks performed by investment software: (a) Portfolio management, (b) Fundamental analysis, (c) Technical analysis, (d) On-line trading
7. What are the advantages and disadvantages of on-line trading?
8. List the banking functions that electronic home banking enables you to do from the comfort of your home. Why do you think this system has experienced sluggish growth?
9. In which ways can a tax preparation software package make your tax filing easier? In which ways can it not help you? Explain why you would or would not consider buying it.
10. How can you file your taxes electronically directly to the IRS? What are the advantages of doing so?
11. (CHARTS) Experiment with the template and its charting capability as follows:
    A. Enter data that would show a U-shaped graph.
    B. Enter data that would show an increasing graph.
    C. Enter data that would show a decreasing graph.
    D What conclusions would you draw about the stocks whose prices are being charted? Which one would you want to by? Why?

SUGGESTED PROJECTS

Give some serious thought to whether you or your family can use a computer software program to assist you in the following areas:
1. Budgeting and planning
2. Check balancing
3. Investing
4. Banking

 5. Tax preparation
   A. Select one area that you or your family need assistance in the most.
   B. Do some research by reading periodicals, visiting software stores, and talking to friends.
   C. Prepare a list of the five leading programs in the area you choose.
   D. Try to get the stores or your library to give you demo disks wherever possible.
   E. List the strong points as well as shortcomings of each program.
   F. Decide which program will best suit your needs and explain why.
   G. Present your findings to your class and get their reaction to your choice.

INFORMATION RESOURCES

"Best of the Almost-Free Software." *Changing Times,* May 1989, 41–44.

"Computerized Investment Systems Thrive." *The Wall Street Journal,* September 27, 1988, C-1.

Davis, Kristin. "Money Management Made Easy." *Kiplinger's Personal Finance Magazine,* January 1992, 65–70.

———. "The Line-Up of On-Line Services." *Kiplinger's Personal Finance Magazine,* May 1993, 57–62.

"Electronic Banking May Have to Log Off." *Business Week,* April 10, 1989, 75.

Feinstein, Selwyn. "Get with the Program (Popular Tax Packages for the Personal Computer)." *The Wall Street Journal,* March 8, 1991, R-13.

"Home Banking Gets Another Chance." *The Wall Street Journal,* December 7, 1989, B-1.

"Investing: Hangups with On-Line Data." *Changing Times,* February 1988, 89–105.

"Let Your Computer Help You Out." *U.S. News & World Report,* March 14, 1988, 74.

"Let Your PC Do the Talking to the IRS." *Business Week,* March 21, 1988, 164–165.

Lewis, Peter H. "For Finances Past the Checkbook, a Small-Business Helper." *The New York Times,* May 3, 1992, F-12.

Rosen, Jan M. "Speedier Refunds But for a Price." *The New York Times,* March 1, 1992, F-27.

Rothfeder, Jeffrey. "Turn Your Den into a Trading Room." *Forbes,* June 24, 1991, 177–180.

"Taxes: Software to the Rescue." *Changing Times,* February 1991, 56–58.

"Taxpayer-Friendly Software That Almost Does It All." *Business Week,* March 20, 1989, 170–171.

"Taxpayers: Start Your Computers." *Kiplinger's Personal Finance Magazine,* February 1992, 56.

Wald, Matthew. "The Latest Pitch: 1040PC and the Promise of a Speedy Refund." *The New York Times,* February 28, 1993, F-17.

White, J. D. "Individual Investors Stay on Their Toes with Financial Software." *Black Enterprise,* October 1988, 39–41.

"Your Tax Return: Software That Does the Hard Part." *Changing Times,* March 1988, 51–56.

CHAPTER ELEVEN

Reading Economic Indicators

- To consider the economy's and the business cycle's impacts on our personal finances

- To analyze the business cycle and its phases

- To learn how to monitor and to use basic business indicators as a guide to financial decision making

- To learn the fundamentals of monetary and fiscal policy

- To learn how to formulate an intelligent view of economic events and to sense the probable range of future developments

The U.S. economy is the habitat in which we work, spend, invest, save, and plan. We are inseparably bound to this system. Our prosperity and that of our family, our business, and even our government depend upon the workings of this economic system. To survive and prosper, therefore, we must learn to read and interpret the immense profusion of signals sent out by the economic system.

The collection and processing of these signals is an industry unto itself. The federal government grinds out economic statistics and data on output, employment, prices, profits, income, and a host of other economic indicators almost every day. Most major banks have an economics department whose job is predicting interest rates and other key economic variables. Some firms, such as Chase Econometrics and Data Resources, Inc., make the forecasting of economic variables their main business.

Economic forecasting has become a favorite sport of journalists, commentators, public officials, university professors, and folks on park benches. There is never a shortage of professionals to venture opinions of what the figures mean, while ordinary consumers and investors often remain confused. They find it hard to incorporate the abundance of information into their personal financial strategy. It seems that the more one studies, the more overwhelming the job becomes.

It takes several courses in economics to get a thorough understanding of the workings of the economy. This chapter is designed to give students with little or no economic background some basic understanding of how the economy affects their lives. It can enable students to become economic observers, to follow economic events, and to keep their fingers on the economic pulse.

We all live and work in the economy. We cannot make any intelligent economic decisions about investing or saving without some basic understanding of the economy. A reasonable, careful study of the economic data could improve your ability to understand current economic events and to sense the probable range of future developments. For instance, if you were a businessperson, would you expand your business without knowing something about economic trends in your industry or in the economy? As a consumer, would you delay purchasing a house or car if you thought the price was going to drop in the near future? If you were an investor, would you buy or sell stocks or commodities if you did not expect to make a profit? Would you try to change jobs if you did not expect a favorable job market? Each of these questions involves a prediction of the future course of the economy.

Throughout your life you will be required to make such financial decisions. There is no getting away from it; even no decision is a decision.

What Is Forecasting?

A major task of economic forecasting is to anticipate turning points in economic activity—times when a business expansion will reach its peak or a business contraction will reach its trough. Forecasting also is a means of reducing the uncertainty that surrounds the making of business and economic decisions. As you become a more seasoned and sophisticated investor and money manager, you may come to prefer certain economic indicators over others. But virtually all of these economic statistics are produced on a regular basis and are freely available. They can be used to develop a better sense of what is happening and where the economy is headed. Although our financial decisions will still be based on guesswork, an educated guess based on hard statistical facts is far more reliable than a crystal ball or a rabbit's foot.

Our decision may not always be right, but we should make sure it is the best decision we could make at the time, based on the facts and figures available to us. So far, nobody has discovered a foolproof way of foretelling the future. Economists do not have clairvoyance. All they do is make educated guesses based on as much evidence as they can muster. But most businesses prefer to rely on the guesses of economists. They consider the economic statistical indicators and forecasts as solid clues, if not predictors, of changes in overall economic activity.

Sophisticated computer programs enable such firms as Data Resources, Inc., and Chase Econometrics to factor in hundreds of different components of the economy.

Using complex statistical models, they make forecasts for the total economy and for individual segments. But a reliable method for forecasting turning points in the economy has continued to elude forecasters despite advances in mathematical and statistical techniques. The optimistic claims made for statistical models when they first came into widespread use in the early 60s have not been justified. The world's economies are growing far too complex and interrelated and are subject to too many sudden changes. Nevertheless, techniques are improving and the forecasts do help in understanding the economy and in policy making.

Forecasting Is an Inaccurate Necessity

Although economic forecasts are not perfectly accurate, they are still useful. Since most businesses, governments, policy planners, researchers, consumers, and investors must continually make decisions that hinge on what they expect will happen, there is no way that they can avoid making forecasts. As with weather forecasts, people prefer to have imperfect information from economic forecasts rather than no information at all. The only question is how best to make them.

Millions of small businesses, small investors, and individual consumers, who cannot afford to hire economists, make their financial decisions quite informally. They have many diverse information sources available to them. However, resource and time constraints restrict the amount of information they can employ. Consequently, they learn to sample financial and investment information efficiently. This chapter therefore presents a selection of basic information sources that will enable you to be an informed personal financial manager.

To make sense of economic statistics, we must first understand the framework that gives them shape, known as the *business cycle*.

The Business Cycle

The economy is subject to various types of disturbances, but the most pronounced is the business cycle. **Business cycles** are recurrent but irregular fluctuations in general business and economic activity that take place over a period of years. The business cycle may be defined as a process of cumulative change over a time span longer than a year. During the cycle, all parts of the economy display marked changes in activity as they move through different phases.

The Four Phases of the Cycle

Economists have identified four phases in a business cycle: peak, contraction, trough, and expansion.

The First Phase—Peak The first phase of a cycle is called the **peak** or **prosperity phase**. During this phase, most economic indicators move upward sharply. As the peak of prosperity is reached, business output is at a maximum, new plant capacity is added, and inventories are squeezed, which prompts the increase in productive capacity. Most managers are paying less attention to operating economies than to productive

FIGURE 11–1   **The Four Phases of the Business Cycle**

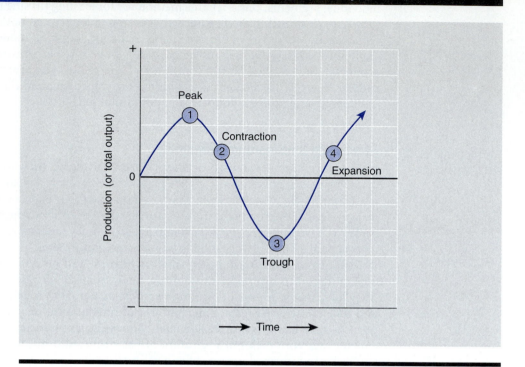

output. The use of credit expands and profits are high. Employment is at a peak, as are consumer demand and retail sales. This prosperity period eventually sows the seeds of its own correction. Plant expansion tends to provide overcapacity, inventories pile up, commodity prices climb too high, stock prices rise to a level not justified by prospective earnings, and interest rates increase.

The Second Phase—Contraction   The second phase of the cycle, the **contraction** or **recession,** is a time when business activity slows down. It is marked by a decline in production and an increase in unemployment. Inventories pile up higher and new orders for raw materials decrease. Outstanding credit contracts, profits recede, demand for consumer goods declines, and business failures increase. If the decline persists, it is called a *recession.* Economists differ about when a decline becomes a recession. One widely accepted definition is that when the output of goods and services declines for two consecutive quarters, the economy is in a recession.

The Third Phase—Trough (or Decline)   A recession will continue into the **trough,** the low point of the cycle. Stock prices reach depressed levels, interest rates decline, and credit becomes easier to obtain. A severe and prolonged trough is known as a **depression.** But since our economy has not experienced a depression in more than 50 years, it is no longer considered part of the normal business cycle.

At some point in the trough phase, inventories become thoroughly liquidated and consumer demand begins to increase slowly because prices drop faster than income. The abundant availability of credit and consequent low interest rates spur purchasing.

"Do you have a card that will wish clients a 'Happy Recession'?"

SOURCE: "Pepper...and Salt," *The Wall Street Journal,* March 28, 1991. Reprinted by permission of Cartoon Features Syndicate.

The Fourth Phase—Expansion (or Recovery)   Conditions slowly begin to improve and thus we enter the fourth phase, called the **expansion** or **recovery**. More people are rehired, orders increase for raw materials, and production expands. This phase brings increases in demand, which are reflected in increases in production, employment, and prices. All measurements of business activity will not rise at the same time. However, most indicators will be moving upward. When most indicators reach a high or a near high, we are in the peak or prosperity phase again.

The four phases of the cycle are by no means equal in scope or intensity. The transition from one phase into the next is often imperceptible. Although the phases of business cycles repeat themselves, each one differs in length, intensity, or size (rate of change), in the combination of forces responsible for the upswing or downswing, and in the severity of the relapse or recovery. In short, each business cycle is unique. Each involves a combination of circumstances which will never recur in just the same form (see Figure 11-2). Nevertheless, each individual cycle fits into a common framework whose essential characteristics can be outlined.

Measuring the Duration of the Cycle   The period of a business cycle is measured either from peak to peak or trough to trough. Studies reveal that the average length of a full cycle is slightly less than four years, and that more time is spent in economic expansion than in contraction and in prosperity than in troughs. However, the variations in time and severity of cycles are so great that these statistics are not useful for analyzing any one cycle.

There have been 31 upturns since 1854, the first year for which such business-cycle data are available (see Table 11-1). They lasted an average of 33 months. Inflation usually accelerates in the third year of an expansion.* Interest rates also tend to move up as an expansion lengthens. In nearly every postwar expansion that lasted so long, interest rates generally rose briskly in the third year.

Not every fluctuation in the economy is considered a cycle. The U.S. Department of Commerce qualifies a cycle as having a duration of at least 15 months, with any

---

Inflation is defined as an above average rise in the overall level of prices.

FIGURE 11–2 | **Comparing Recoveries**

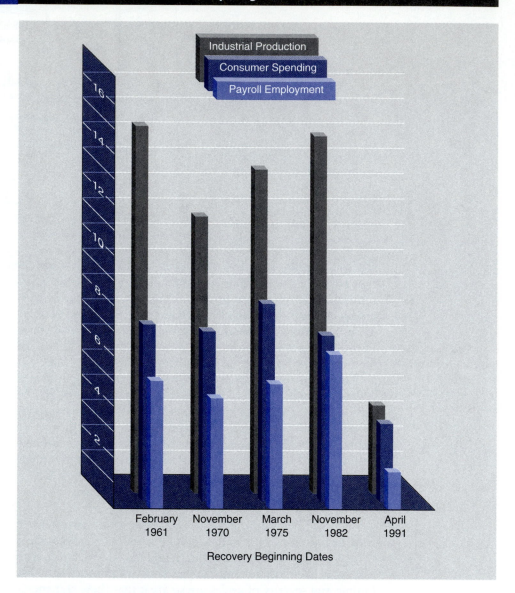

Shown are the percentages of growth during the first 15 months after the start of a recovery.

SOURCE: Adapted from "Comparing Recoveries," *The Wall Street Journal*, September 8, 1992, A-8.

significant upward or downward phase of the cycle lasting for at least five months. Deviations shorter than this, or too mild in their change of direction, are screened out as temporary aberrations.

TABLE 11–1	U.S. Business Cycles

| Business Cycle Reference Dates | | Duration in Months | |
Trough	Peak	Contraction (trough from previous peak)	Expansion (trough to peak)
December 1854	June 1857	—	30
December 1858	October 1860	18	22
June 1861	**April 1865**	8	**46**
December 1867	June 1869	**32**	18
December 1870	October 1873	18	34
March 1879	March 1882	65	36
May 1885	March 1887	38	22
April 1888	July 1890	13	27
May 1891	January 1893	10	20
June 1894	December 1895	17	18
June 1897	June 1899	18	24
December 1900	September 1902	18	21
August 1904	May 1907	23	33
June 1908	January 1910	13	19
January 1912	January 1913	24	12
December 1914	**August 1918**	23	**44**
March 1919	January 1920	**7**	10
July 1921	May 1923	18	22
July 1924	October 1926	14	27
November 1927	August 1929	13	21
March 1933	May 1937	43	50
June 1938	**February 1945**	13	**80**
October 1945	November 1948	**8**	37
October 1949	**July 1953**	11	**45**
May 1954	August 1957	**10**	39
April 1958	April 1960	8	24
February 1961	**December 1969**	10	**106**
November 1970	November 1973	**11**	36
March 1975	January 1980	16	58
July 1980	July 1981	6	12
November 1982	July 1990	16	92

Numbers in **boldface** identify periods of wartime expansion or contraction.

SOURCE: National Bureau of Economic Research, "Survey of Current Business," October 1991, C-45.

Seasonal Variations Cycles should not be confused with **seasonal variations**. Heavy spending during the Christmas season and the subsequent decline in activity in January and February are not considered a business cycle. The same holds true for high sales of air conditioners, swimwear, and soft drinks during the summer months. These seasonal fluctuations are not business cycles because they are short, periodic,

---

Decisions, Decisions

Your six-month bank CD is about to mature; you receive a notice from the bank to renew. You must decide whether to move your money into a variable-rate money market account or purchase a three-month, six-month, one-year, three-year, or five-year CD. Decisions, decisions. If you expect a recession, then you should lock in a three- or five-year CD today, because during a recession interest rates generally decline. If the economy is in the midst of a recovery, you are better off keeping your money in a money market account. Normally, interest rates rise during a prosperity phase and money market rates rise along with them. You can purchase higher rate CDs later on, when the business cycle peaks and the high rates start to decline.

---

and predictable. The statisticians who study cycles smooth out these seasonal variations and describe the resulting statistics as seasonally adjusted.

Gauging the Business Cycle Although the study of business cycles is relatively new, a product of the past 50 years, it has produced numerous theories about the causes of business fluctuations. But so far, no one theory completely and satisfactorily explains them. Therefore, instead of looking for causes of business cycles, let us explore how to gauge where we are in the business cycle and where we are heading.

The importance of this exploration is obvious from today's headlines. Suppose that just released government figures show that the economy is turning sluggish. What should you as a consumer do? Drop your newspaper and race to the phone to liquidate all your investments? Or yawn and turn to the sports page?

Mortgage and loan interest rates and availability fluctuate with the business cycle. The stock market is highly influenced by (and influences) the business cycle. Therefore, a person trying to function in the financial world without a good handle on the business cycle is like a sailor at sea, trying to navigate without knowing where land is. By following the business cycle indicators closely, individuals should be able to capture the general mood of the economy and thus anticipate pending changes in the level of business activity which may affect their financial plans.

Economic Stabilization Policies

No discussion of the business cycle and economic indicators can ignore the government's economic stabilization policies or its countercyclical efforts. The government is always expected to seek and maintain a prosperous economic environment. To accomplish this objective, there are two powerful sets of economic instruments, known as *fiscal policy* and *monetary policy*.

Fiscal Policy

The federal government establishes **fiscal policy** by setting tax and spending levels. By taxation, the federal government withdraws money from the economy. During an inflationary, overheated peak phase, fiscal policy would call for both a tax increase and spending cuts to reduce overall demand.

Large tax increases tend to depress financial markets because money must be used to pay taxes rather than on spending or investments. Government spending cuts decrease the overall demand for goods and services and therefore tend to have a recessionary impact on the economy. In times of recession, a logical fiscal policy calls for a tax reduction as well as an increase in government spending. These moves would serve to stimulate the economy and bring about a recovery, but if overdone may stimulate inflationary pressures. Such fiscal measures tend to create or augment the government's budgetary deficit. Public pressure to balance the budget or at least minimize the deficit may restrain stimulative fiscal policy.

The Federal Reserve and Monetary Policy

The **Federal Reserve System (Fed)**, which is the central bank of the United States, is an independent government agency responsible for the U.S. money supply. The Fed performs a wide variety of functions:

1. The Federal Reserve Banks hold deposits called *reserves,* which are made by banks and thrifts.

2. The Federal Reserve serves as fiscal agent of the federal government. The government collects money through taxation, spends money, and sells and redeems bonds. The government avails itself of the Fed's facilities in carrying out these activities.

3. The Fed provides the mechanism for the collection of checks. (For instance, if Pat writes a check on his Richmond, Virginia, bank in favor of Sally, who deposits it in her Memphis, Tennessee, bank, the Fed enables the Memphis bank to collect the check against the Richmond bank by adjusting the reserves of the two banks.)

4. The Fed supervises the operations of member banks.

5. The most important of all the Fed's functions is to regulate and manage the supply of money in accordance with the needs of the economy as a whole.

This instrument of economic stabilization is known as **monetary policy**. Monetary policy describes the activities directed at effective changes in the quantities of money and bank credit on the premise that control of these quantities is the prime way of maintaining a stable price level and modifying the business cycle. Since the Federal Reserve is the chief instrument of monetary policy, it is the single most powerful force at work in the economy. In carrying out its policy of maintaining a stable, fully employed, and growing economy, the Federal Reserve uses three instruments together to affect the cost, supply, and availability of credit to banking institutions. These three instruments are:

1. Changing banks' reserve requirements

2. Raising or lowering the discount rate

3. Buying and selling government securities in the open market

RESERVE

Reserve Requirements   A change in **reserve requirements** is the most powerful tool the Fed has in its arsenal, but it is the one used least. Banks must maintain a percentage of reserves in their vaults to back up their deposits. For example, if the Fed sets reserve requirements at 10 percent, then a bank with a $100 million in deposits can lend out only $90,000,000 because it must keep 10 percent or) $10,000,000 in reserves. If that percentage is raised, banks have fewer excess reserves that they can lend out and thereby create deposits, and therefore interest rates rise. If the Fed lowers reserve requirements, it enables banks to lend out more of their deposits, which should increase economic activity. Most of the money that people spend is checkbook money or payments by check, which entails transferring deposits from one bank to another. Thus, if the Fed enables banks to lend out more reserves, this money will be spent and redeposited in a bank creating new deposits. The increased supply of loanable funds generally results in lower interest rates. Altering the reserve requirement is administratively awkward and is seldom done.

The Discount Rate   The **discount rate** is the rate of interest the Federal Reserve charges deposit-taking institutions when they borrow from the Fed. It can be changed at the Fed's will. Raising or lowering the discount rate influences all money market rates, which, in turn, affect long-term rates and virtually every other interest rate. Changes in the discount rate are strong statements by the Fed about the way it is leaning, whether toward easing or tightening. A rise in the discount rate is therefore likely to generate expectations regarding future interest rates. A high discount rate tends to discourage borrowing and thus slows the economy down; a low rate tends to encourage borrowing. When the Fed adjusts the discount rate, banks usually follow by adjusting their **prime rate.** This is the rate of interest that commercial banks generally charge their most creditworthy commercial customers. Interest rates on other types of bank loans are often pegged to the prime rate.

The Federal Reserve changes its discount rate at most only a few times each year. These changes always make the headlines. The discount rate is reported daily in *The Wall Street Journal* and other major newspapers (see Figure 11–3, the third item down).

Open Market Operations   While far subtler, **open market operations,** the Fed's purchases and sales of government securities, are the most important, most useful, and most frequently used monetary policy tools of the Federal Reserve Board. The Fed's main policy-making body is its Federal Open Market Committee, made up of the seven board members and presidents of 5 of the 12 regional Federal Reserve Banks. Eight times a year it reviews the economy and decides whether to tighten or loosen credit.

The mechanism for transmitting the Federal Reserve's policy action to the commercial banks in general and money market conditions in particular is complicated. In simple terms, here's how it works: When the Fed buys a Treasury bill, it writes a check to the government securities dealer who sold it. The dealer deposits the check in his or her bank account. Unlike you or me, the Fed can write the check with nothing behind it, literally out of thin air. This process creates reserves for the banking

FIGURE 11–3	The Money Rates

Monday, November 22, 1993
The key U.S. and foreign annual interest rates below are a guide to general levels but don't always represent actual transactions.

PRIME RATE: 6%. The base rate on corporate loans posted by at least 75% of the nation's 30 largest banks.

FEDERAL FUNDS: 3 1/16% high, 3% low, 3% near closing bid, 3% offered. Reserves traded among commercial banks for overnight use in amounts of $1 million or more. Source: Prebon Yamane (U.S.A.) Inc.

Discount Rate: 3%. The charge on loans to depository institutions by the Federal Reserve Banks.

CALL MONEY: 5%. The charge on loans to brokers on stock exchange collateral. Source: Telerate Systems Inc.

COMMERCIAL PAPER placed directly by General Electric Capital Corp.: 3.06% 30 to 59 days; 3.35% 60 to 179 days; 3.37% 180 to 239 days; 3.45% 240 to 270 days.

COMMERCIAL PAPER: High-grade unsecured notes sold through dealers by major corporations: 3.14% 30 days; 3.44% 60 days; 3.42% 90 days.

CERTIFICATES OF DEPOSIT: 2.56% one month; 2.71% two months; 2.74% three months; 2.87% six months; 3.03% one year. Average of top rates paid by major New York banks on primary new issues of negotiable C.D.s, usually on amounts of one million and more. The minimum unit is $100,000. Typical rates in the secondary market: 3.10% one month; 3.37% three months; 3.40% six months.

BANKERS ACCEPTANCES: 3.05% 30 days; 3.30% 60 days; 3.27% 90 days; 3.27% 120 days; 3.28% 150 days; 3.29% 180 days. Offered rates of negotiable, bank-backed business credit instruments typically financing an import order.

LONDON LATE EURODOLLARS: 3 3/16%-3 1/16% one month; 3 1/2%-3 3/8% two months; 3 1/2%-3 3/8% three months; 3 1/2%-3 3/8% four months;3 1/2%-3 3/8% five months;3 9/16%-3 7/16% six months.

LONDON INTERBANK OFFERED RATES (LIBOR): 3 3/16% one month; 3 1/2% three months;3 9/16% six months;3 13/16% one year. The average of interbank offered rates for dollar deposits in the London market based on quotations at five major banks. Effective rate for contracts entered into two days from date appearing at top of this column.

FOREIGN PRIME RATES: Canada 5.50%; Germany 6.14%; Japan 3.375%; Switzerland 7.50%; Britian 6%. These rate indications aren't directly comparable; lending practices vary widely by location.

TREASURY BILLS: Results of the Monday, November 22, 1993, aution of short-term U.S. government bills, sold at a discount from face value in units of $10,000 to $1 million: 3.14%, 13 weeks; 3.30%, 26 weeks.

FEDERAL HOME LOAN MORTGAGE CORP. (Freddie Mac): Posted yields on 30-year mortgage commitments. Delivery within 30-days 7.22%, 60 days 7.29%, standard conventional fixed-rate mortgages; 3.625%, 2% rate capped one-year adjustable rate mortgages. Source: Telerate Systems, Inc.

FEDERAL NATIONAL MORTGAGE ASSOCIATION (Fannie Mae): Posted yields on thirty-year mortgage commitments (priced at par) for delivery within 30 days 7.23%, 60 days 7.33%, standard convonventional fixed rate-mortgages; 5.05%, 6/2 rate capped one-year adjustable rate mortgages. Source: Telerate Systems, Inc.

MERRILL LYNCH READY ASSETS TRUST: 2.69%. Annualized average rate of return after expenses for the past 30 days; not a forecast of future returns.

SOURCE: Reprinted by permission of *The Wall Street Journal*, June 22, 1993, C-26. All Rights Reserved Worldwide.

system, which lends them out and thereby creates deposits (which are real money).

Thus, when the Open Market Committee buys securities in the open market, new money comes into the financial marketplace. This increase in the total supply of money eventually filters into every corner of the financial markets and the economy. The result is to increase demand, production, and jobs. If the economy is at full employment and at capacity output, this policy can be inflationary.

Conversely, when the Fed sells a Treasury bill (T-bill), the dealer who buys it has to pay for it with real money from his or her checking account. That money comes out of the banking system and into the Fed's coffers, where it cannot be spent until the Fed buys another T-bill and puts it back into the economy. By selling government securities, the Fed reduces the supply of money that financial institutions have for making loans. This withdraws money from the general economy. This in theory should cause total demand or purchases to decline. When businesses experience a decline in overall demand, they normally reduce prices, thereby helping to reduce the price level. Thus, by affecting the ability of the commercial banking system to advance credit to borrowers, the Federal Reserve System can accelerate or decelerate the spending and investment in the economy. This same process allows the Fed to determine the level of interest rates. Why? Because if people spend less, they will borrow less to finance these spendings. When banks experience a decline in demand for borrowing, they respond by lowering interest rates. The growth of the money supply is reported weekly by the Fed and appears in the financial section of most newspapers.

The Federal Reserve has the power, in the words of former Fed chairman William McChesney Martin, "to take away the punchbowl when the party gets good," that is, to tighten credit and money when the economy booms. When the party gets too dull, the Fed can liven things up by bringing back the punchbowl, spiked with money and credit.

Too much money chasing too few goods yields inflation. Too little money available to buy too many available goods yields not only disinflation but also recession. The nation's past six recessions came about when the Fed fought the inflation dragon and ended up slaying the economy as well. Therefore, a careful monitoring of Federal Reserve activity is always prudent.

Interest Rates Analyzed

Interest rates are the price of credit. Like other prices, they are affected by the fundamentals of supply and demand. Fluctuations in interest rates are closely related to the business cycle. Falling interest rates lower the cost of credit purchases and reduce the incentive to save. Lower rates encourage consumption and boost stock and bond prices.

Conversely, sharp rises in interest rates deter buyers and increase the reward for saving. They are thus a major constricting force on business conditions. A sustained advance in interest rates usually puts an end to stock market rises. Because interest rate changes precede movements in the investment markets, they are vital guides to the planning of investors, as well as borrowers and lenders.

Many types of interest (or money) rates are published. Figure 11–3 shows various interest rates on short- and long-term debt instruments. The first one listed in Figure 11–3 is the aforementioned so-called **prime rate**, described as the loan rate that banks charge their most creditworthy customers.

The next one on the list is the **Federal funds rate**, the rate of interest charged for overnight loans between commercial banks. Federal funds arise when banks hold reserves in excess of the minimum amount that the Federal Reserve requires all banks to hold. A bank with more reserves than it needs can lend some to a bank that's temporarily short of reserves to enable it to meet Federal Reserve Board liquidity requirements. Borrowing to boost their reserves also allows banks to satisfy more of their customer's cravings for credit. While the Federal Funds rate is determined by the supply of and demand for reserves, it is also influenced by the Federal Reserve Board, which can raise or lower the rate through the purchase or sale of these funds and setting the discount rate.

The Federal funds rate, more commonly called **Fed funds rate**, is therefore considered a good early short-term indicator of Fed credit tightening or easing in the U.S. money market. When the Fed funds rate is high, credit may be tight in the banking system and loans may be hard to obtain.

In summary, anything the Federal Reserve does is considered a significant economic indicator. Changes in the discount rate or the Federal funds rate are reflected quickly in the prime rate, the Treasury bill rates, car loan rates, and indexes that govern adjustable rate mortgages and home equity loans. For example, the Fed may keep interest rates high in an effort to reduce demand and relieve pressure on prices. The high rates are likely to slow the economy by making it expensive to finance the purchase of cars, factory equipment, and other costly items. A savvy investor will keep tuned to the doings of the Fed. Any changes in discount rates, reserve requirements, open market operations, or Fed funds rates need to be watched and analyzed.

Averages and Indexes

Many key aggregate financial variables are expressed as index numbers. Although the terms *average* and index tend to be used interchangeably when discussing market behavior, technically they are different types of measures. **Averages** reflect the arithmetic average price of a representative group of variables at a given point in time. **Indexes** measure the current price or other behavior of a representative group of variables in relation to a base value set at an earlier point in time, usually referred to as a *base year*.

The **base year** is the point in time when the index begins. It is usually assigned a value of 100. If an index rose to 110, then clearly a 10 percent increase took place. A price index, for example, compares the average of a group of prices in one period of time with the average of the prices of the same group of commodities or services in another period. Prices are determined for a base period and the prices in all subsequent periods are measured in relation to the base period prices.

Index numbers are statistical measures that are used to give summary answers. They point to overall tendencies or general drifts. They are convenient means of tracking percentage changes that have occurred in some broad average over a particular time span. Many of the economic indicators are indexes.

Economic Indicators

Economic indicators are key variables that signal changes in economic activity. Changes in the value of such variables often indicate forthcoming changes in the value of other important economic variables. In making forecasts, the Federal government and others use the economic indicators.

The set of indicators published by the Department of Commerce contains graphs, charts, and tables for more than 100 National Bureau of Economic Research (NBER) business cycle indicator series. The Commerce department plots 34 NBER leading indicators, 25 NBER roughly coincident indicators, 11 NBER lagging indicators, and numerous other U.S. Series with business cycle significance. These series are presented in convenient form for analysis and interpretation. The Department of Commerce, however, makes no attempt to interpret them or to make business forecasts.

Current and recent values of the key indicators are quoted in the financial news. Most local newspapers and many radio and television news programs also quote the latest indicators as soon as they are released. You can follow overall trends with published numbers.

Government Economic Indicators

Most investors consider the data produced by the U.S. government by far the best in terms of their accuracy, comprehensiveness, and timeliness. However, there are several problems with government data. First, the amount of data available is so overwhelming that most investors find it difficult to handle. Second, the government often revises the data on key variables such as **gross domestic products (GDP)**, money supply, and unemployment, thereby undermining previous predictions based on them. Third, not all indicators move in the same direction, making the task of forecasting difficult. Many reports will tend to contradict one another, over the short run at least. Because not all indicators move simultaneously in the same direction, a careful analysis is needed to develop an informed opinion of the direction in which the economy is likely to move. Even the best numbers require watching over time to spot trends.

Economic indicators do not provide any passkey to profits and the achievement of financial goals. All indicators are just that. They indicate, rather than predict, an important distinction that is sometimes forgotten even by so-called experts. At times the indicators have clearly signaled turning points in the economy as well as peaks and troughs in the business cycle before the turn of the cycle. At other times, the indicators have not preceded the actual cycle change.

There is no single index or average or indicator which faithfully represents the state of the economy. Because each indicator is limited, you cannot rely on any of them too much. Imperfect though they may be, they can be of considerable help in managing your finances. They are readily available clues that you can use to improve substantially your chances for making successful financial decisions. In time, you may come to rely on certain favorite indicators. That will be fine as long as you monitor the overall situation and look for patterns that will help you make intelligent (and hopefully correct) forecasts of the business cycle.

Composite Indicators

Business cycle analysts have tried to give the indicators more "clout" by combining different indicators measuring several economic activities into a composite picture of the economy. Such a general indicator is known as a **composite index**. Economists have also organized indicators that supposedly give us hindsight, foresight, or a current picture. Those that give us an idea of the future are known as **leading indicators**. Those that reveal only the past are **lagging indicators,** and those that tell us about the current situation are called **coincident indicators**.

Composite Index of Coincident Indicators

Coincident indicators are series whose peaks and troughs roughly coincide with those of general business conditions. These include GDP, industrial production, wholesale prices, and retail sales. They decline at the peak and rise at the time of the trough. Coincident indicators are designed to show the current path of business conditions and to verify that a turn is taking place.

The composite index of coincident indicators comprises eight roughly coincident indicators:

1. Gross domestic product (GDP) in current dollars

2. GDP in constant dollars*

3. Industrial production

4. Unemployment rate

---

*Constant dollars means inflation is subtracted out of this years GDP to get real rate of economic growth.

5. Personal income

6. Retail (store) sales

7. Employee payrolls

8. Manufacturing and foreign trade sales

Composite Index of Lagging Indicators Lagging indicators are economic variables whose values typically rise or fall after corresponding increases or decreases in GDP. They tend to confirm that a turn has taken place. They decline after the peak and rise after the trough. The composite index of lagging indicators includes activities that respond only slowly to changing business conditions or that reflect the pressures created during the immediately preceding expansion or contraction. This index has six components:

1. Labor cost per unit of output in manufacturing

2. Average prime rate charged by banks

3. Commercial and industrial loans outstanding, weekly reports from large commercial banks

4. Ratio of consumer installment debt to personal income

5. Average duration of unemployment

6. Manufacturing and trade inventories

The Leading Indicators Investors can ignore the lagging indicators because by the time they move, "the horse is already out of the barn." Even the coincident indicators can only confirm a turning point two or three months after it has occurred. The only predictive guide is the **leading indicators**, which normally move ahead of the business cycle.

By their nature, a number of statistical series foreshadow future business activity and are therefore useful measures of cyclical tendency. Ideally, investors should anticipate impending changes in the nation's economy months ahead of the turning points in industrial activity. The composite indicator that combines the 11 most-watched leading indicators is known as the **index of leading economic indicators** (see Figure 11–4). This widely followed composite index is put out monthly by the U.S. Department of Commerce. It measures monthly changes in 11 different indicators that have been found to be the most reliable predictors of movements in the business cycle.

The composite index of leading indicators includes the following series:

1. Average work week of production workers in manufacturing

2. Average weekly claims for state unemployment insurance

3. New orders for consumer goods and materials, adjusted for inflation

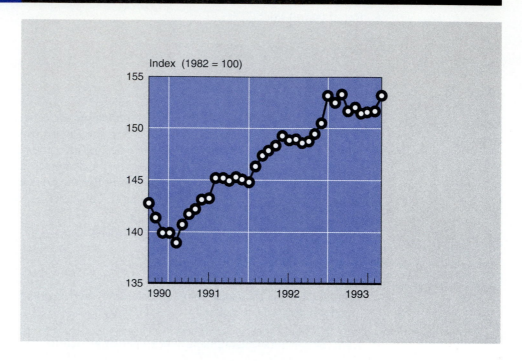

4. Vendor performance (companies receiving slower deliveries from suppliers)

5. Contracts and orders for plant and equipment, adjusted for inflation

6. New building permits issued

7. Change in manufacturer's unfilled orders, durable goods

8. Change in sensitive materials prices

9. Index of stock prices (Standard & Poor's Composite 500 Index)

10. Money supply: M-2, adjusted for inflation (M-2 is the total amount of money in circulation. This includes currency in circulation and checking account deposits as well as savings accounts.)

11. Index of consumer expectations

The Department of Commerce revises the list of components of the composite index from time to time as the usefulness of some series wanes and new or improved series become available. The index was last revised in January 1989.

Gross Domestic Product

In reading reports of the nation's economic condition in a newspaper or magazine, we will often encounter the term **gross domestic product** (see Figure 11–5). The

Everyman's Indicators

If such esoteric indicators as capacity utilization and M2 leave you befuddled, there are alternatives. Simply by observing the world around you, it's possible to get a reading on how the economy is doing. According to economists, the following garden-variety indicators really work. Add or subtract the points indicated in parentheses. If your total is on the plus side, be of good cheer. At the very least, it's safe to serve butter instead of the low-priced spread.

- At a giant shopping mall, you drive around for 20 minutes before finding a parking spot. (Add 10 points. Everybody is spending money, so the economy must be healthy.)
- It takes four hours to get to the head of the line at the passport office. (Add 4 points. When the dollar is strong and Americans have lots of money—signs of a booming economy—people tend to travel.)
- Your broker calls you once a week to ask about the family. (Subtract 5 points. You merit such attention only when the stock market is comatose, and that means a gloomy prognosis for the economy.)
- Local department stores start running sales to celebrate American Dental Week. (Subtract 8 points. When the public's purchasing power appears weak, retailers unload whatever they can.)
- You call your Social Security office to ask a question, and a clerk puts you on hold for 35 minutes. (Add 3 points. Arrogant civil servants indicate high levels of government spending, which stimulates the economy.)
- Aunt Hilda, who has every dime she earned since the first Eisenhower administration, pays for a family dinner at Hamburger Hamlet with her MasterCard. (Subtract 2 points. Everyone is buying on credit, so inflation must be on the rise.)
- You are repeatedly overtaken on the highway by BMWs and Mercedes that don't have M.D. plates. (Add 6 points. The economy is booming when people who aren't doctors buy luxury cars.)
- Your boss calls you in and tells you that you have been laid off. (Unless you were fired for incompetence, subtract 30 points. A decrease in jobs means hard times are ahead.)
- Monthly payments on your variable-rate mortgage threaten to equal your original down payment. (Subtract 4 points. Borrowing costs are so high that recession is in the wind.)
- Aunt Hilda dies, leaving you $14 million. (Add 20 points. For you, the state of the economy is now irrelevant.)

SOURCE: *Money*, October 1984, 14.

FIGURE 11–5	Real Gross Domestic Product

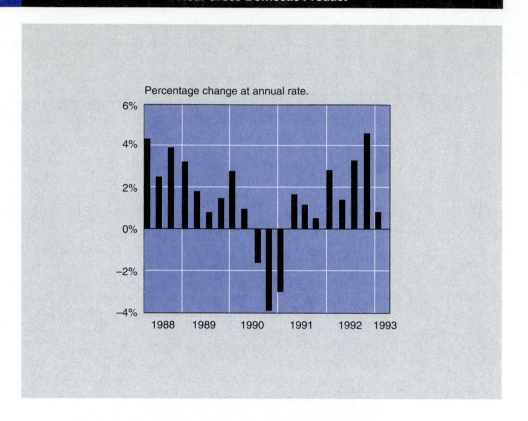

Percentage change at annual rate.

U.S. national accounting system, often referred to simply as the **GDP**, is a summary of economic activity in the United States. It is defined as the total market value of all final goods and services produced in a country in one year.

Because the GDP covers all facets of production in the economy, it is the best and broadest indicator of the general level of business activity. Government and business alike use it to determine their future policies and plans. To keep businesspeople, public officials, and others informed and to have current figures available to guide national economic policies, the Department of Commerce publishes quarterly reports on the GDP and related figures.

The rate at which GDP grows is of interest to everyone. Government officials, from the president down, are interested because these figures indicate how prosperous we are, and because they are useful in forecasting the future health of the economy, the price level, employment, and total output. Politicians use the GDP in their campaign speeches, economists use it as their basic tools, and investors react—and often overreact—to changes in it.

GDP in constant dollars is GDP adjusted for inflation. This gives us the real output this year (or real GDP), and is a more meaningful statistic than GDP in current dollars.

GNP versus GDP

The Commerce Department has published the gross national product (GNP) since 1941. At the start of 1992, the GNP was deemphasized and GDP was placed into the primary spot. The difference between the GDP and GNP is small but significant. The GNP measures all the goods and services produced by workers and capital supplied by U.S. residents or corporations, regardless of location. The GDP measures all the goods and services produced by workers and capital located in the United States.

Thus, profits a U.S. company receives from its overseas operations are included in the GNP, while profits foreign-owed businesses made in the United States are excluded. The profits on the overseas operations of U.S. companies are excluded from the GDP, while the earnings of foreign companies in the United States are included. GDP thus is a better measure of how the U.S. economy is producing inside its own borders than what it is producing all around the world. The Commerce Department still publishes the GNP figures monthly, but the primary focus remains on GDP.

Unemployment Rate

Early every month, the Bureau of Labor Statistics produces the results of a massive sample survey of the employed and unemployed. Unemployment is expressed as a percentage of the civilian labor force that is unemployed but actively seeking employment.

Looking at the employment statistics shown in Figure 11–6, we can see how the unemployment rate is derived. The civilian labor force was given as 128,100,000 for the month of May. This is derived by adding (lines 2 and 3) civilian employment and unemployment. The number of people working (119,300,000) plus the number of workers unemployed (8,900,000) constitute the labor force. (The numbers are rounded off). Therefore, the jobless or unemployment rate was equal to the unemployed civilian labor force members divided by the total labor force, or 8,900,000 divided by 128,100,000, which is equal to (line 4) the unemployment rate of 6.9 percent for all civilian workers.

Types of Unemployment

Economists distinguish between frictional and structural unemployment.

Frictional Unemployment
Frictional unemployment means, for example, that ABC, Inc., goes bankrupt, through bad management or for any other reason, and its workers are thrown onto the job market. After a period of unemployment, they find new jobs. Nationwide, this kind of upheaval occurs all the time.

Structural Unemployment
Structural unemployment means that ABC, Inc., goes bankrupt, but so do DEF, Inc., and XYZ, Inc., and lots of other firms in the same sector or in several sectors.

FIGURE 11–6	Unemployment Statistics

EMPLOYMENT

Here are excerpts from the Labor Department's employment report. The figures are seasonally adjusted.

	May 1993	April 1993
	(millions of persons)	
Civilian labor force........................	**128.1**	**127.3**
Civilian employment	119.3	118.4
Unemployment	8.9	8.9
Payroll employment......................	**110.0**	**109.8**
Unemployment:	(percent of labor force)	
All civilian workers	6.9	7.0
Adult men	6.4	6.4
Adult women..................................	5.9	6.0
Teen-agers.....................................	19.7	20.7
White...	6.0	6.0
Black..	12.9	13.8
Black teen-agers...........................	40.3	46.8
Hispanic..	9.7	10.4
Average weekly hours:	(hours of work)	
Total private nonfarm..........................	34.8	34.4
Manufacturing................................	41.5	41.5
Factory overtime............................	4.2	4.2

This happens because the structure of the national, or world, economy has changed so that the whole industry is now troubled or even dead. In the long run, workers from these defunct industries can be reabsorbed in others, especially if there is general growth in the economy. The classic example is the millions of people who were engaged in carriage making, horse breeding, and horseshoeing when the automobile drove their special skills and jobs into the trash can.

Structural unemployment is caused by such phenomena as technological innovation; automation; demographic changes; new trends, patterns, or lifestyles; or new political developments. All of these are inevitable, and therefore some structural unemployment, just like frictional unemployment, is unavoidable. This is calculated into the definition of the term *full employment*.

Full Employment

Since some frictional and structural unemployment is an inevitable fact of life that will occur even in the best of times, economists consider an unemployment rate of about 5 percent as the lowest realistically achievable, and thus consider an economy at 5 percent unemployment to be at **full employment**. The paradoxical definition of full employment, therefore, is either 95 percent employment rate or 5 percent unemployment rate.

Cyclical Unemployment

Any unemployment above the 5 percent rate is generally attributed to a weakness in the business cycle or a recessionary trend. This is therefore known as **cyclical unemployment**. If the **unemployment rate** rises to 7 percent, economists would argue that we have 2 percent cyclical unemployment. This is another indicator of the business cycle, signaling whether we are in a peak or recession and how severe a recession may be.

Measuring Unemployment

The Labor Department's widely reported monthly unemployment statistic (see Figure 11–7) is an imprecise figure because the way it defines unemployment makes it very nearly a state of mind. It defines an unemployed person as someone who is not working but is actively seeking full-time employment. Someone who is out of work and has not been job hunting during the previous four weeks is not counted.

Many economists claim that the unemployment rate understates the problem because it does not include the so-called **discouraged workers**, who have given up looking for a job. Nevertheless, a low unemployment rate (usually below 7 percent) supports the feeling that we have a strong economy, while a higher or rising

| FIGURE 11–7 | Unemployment Rate |

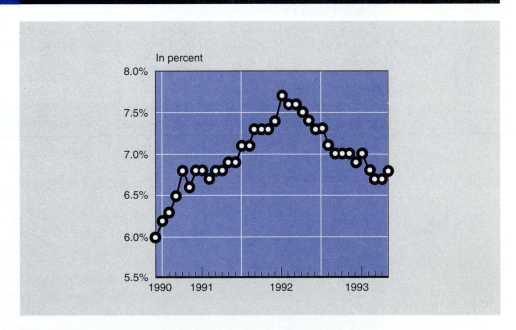

Unemployment in October rose to a seasonally adjust 6.8 percent of the civilian labor force from 6.7 percent the preceding month, the Labor Departmentreports.

unemployment rate causes concern and uncertainty in the economy. Perceptions, whether accurate or not, can sway the entire investment market. Therefore, the unemployment rate must be considered a major coincident indicator.

Price Indexes: Indicators of Inflation

Prices constantly move up or down, depending on business conditions. Sometimes almost all prices are moving in the same direction, while at other times some may be rising while others are declining and still others remain unchanged. It is impossible to remember all these individual movements. It may be interesting to know that Fritos are rising and frisbees are declining and pogo sticks are stable. But such details can cause us to lose sight of what is happening to prices generally in the economy. It is important, therefore, to have some device which tracks the overall or average movement of all prices in the economy. That is why we construct **price indexes**.

A *price index* is defined as the ratio of the value of a set of goods and services in current dollars to the value of the same set of goods and services in constant (base year) dollars. It is worthwhile to know something about the makeup of such an index. Economists measure the rate of inflation by using one of several price level indexes that they construct.

The CPI and PPI

The two principal monthly price indexes, which are tabulated by the U.S. government's **Bureau of Labor Statistics**, are the **Consumer Price Index (CPI)** (see Figure 11–8), which measures the average change in the retail price of a fixed basket of goods

---

Practical Applications of the Price Indexes

An important function of a price index is to convert values expressed in current dollars into values expressed in constant dollars. This conversion, known as *deflating,* can be achieved simply by dividing values expressed in current dollars by the price index. For example, you invested $10,000 in a stock mutual fund three years ago. Today your mutual fund shares are worth $12,500—an increase of 25 percent. But what is your real gain after subtracting inflation? If three years ago the CPI was 160 and today it's 184, how do you convert your investment into constant dollars?

To determine the rate of inflation over this period, divide your base of 160 into the increase of 24, or 24/160. This results in a 15 percent inflation over the three years. If your investment increased by 25 percent but the value of your money decreased by 15 percent, then you have a real gain of 10 percent over the past three years. This investment gain no longer looks so glamorous when the inflation is factored in; your mutual fund averaged approximately 3.33 percent real growth annually. The same calculations can be used to determine any other deflated price change over time.

FIGURE 11–8 | The Consumer Price Index

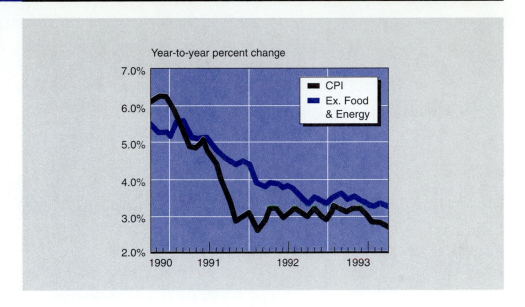

Year-to-year percent change

Legend:
- CPI
- Ex. Food & Energy

Consumer prices rose 2.7 percent in the 12 months ending in September. Excluding the food and energy sectors, the change was 3.2 percent.

and services, and the **Producer Price Index (PPI)** (see Figure 11–9). The PPI measures wholesale prices—everything from raw materials used by domestic producers to finished goods sold by wholesalers. The CPI is the most common and widely used index. It is an effort to represent in one number the rate of inflation confronting consumers. It covers prices of products and services commonly bought by households.

Changes in the value of the CPI are meant to measure changes in the typical household's "cost of living." Bureau of Labor Statistics employees go to different parts of the country at regular intervals to buy (or price) a "market basket" of the goods and services that consumers buy in urban areas of the United States. The basket includes about 400 basic commodities and services out of the more than 1400 required by an average family of four in a moderate-sized industrial community. It is made up of such categories as durable goods, nondurable goods, foods, apparel, transportation, education, rent, housing, recreation, and health.

These items are weighted according to the percent of total spending applied to each of the categories. The price of this hypothetical basket changes from month to month. The amount of that change is stated as a percentage of the CPI for the previous month, and this figure is the rate of inflation.

The CPI does not try to duplicate the spending patterns of any actual consumer. For example, it includes the cost of both owning and renting a home and the price of both new and used cars. The statistically average consumer does not really exist,

INDEX

FIGURE 11–9 **The Producer Price Index**

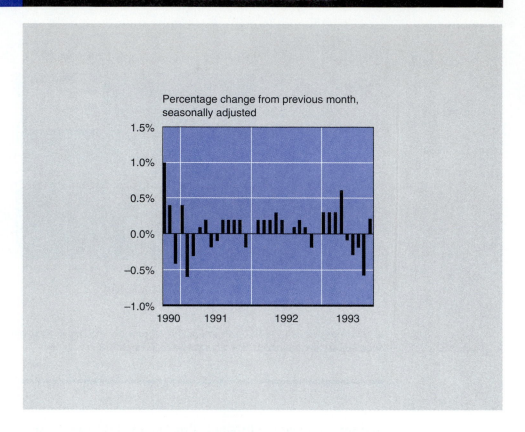

but the index lets us see how well we are doing versus the average and how prices are changing over time. More than half of the CPI is based on services, such as college tuition and movie admissions. The CPI also includes import prices.

Both the CPI and PPI break down their data into dozens of different product indexes. A separate index is calculated for each of the categories as well as a composite for all of them.

Indexation

Because it represents the price level confronting consumers, the CPI is frequently used to adjust personal incomes, converting them into their real purchasing power equivalents, by removing the impact of inflation. It is widely used in labor negotiations as an indication of the rate of inflation to which wage earners have been subjected. Many unions bargain for wage adjustments, known as **COLAs (Cost of Living Adjustments),** based on the CPI. In such agreements, any change in the index calls for an adjustment in income flows. The income thus is said to be subject to **indexation.** Social Security benefits are also subject to annual indexation based on the CPI.

The CPI is simple enough as a measure of inflation, but it is best at telling us what has already happened rather than what is going to happen. It's therefore a lagging indicator.

Stock Market Indicators

The Dow Jones Averages

Perhaps the best-known and most widely quoted stock market indicators are the Dow Jones averages. The **Dow Jones Industrial Average (DJIA)** of 30 stocks, also known as the **Dow** or **the industrials,** is one of four so-called stock "averages" compiled and published by *The Wall Street Journal* and its sister publication *Barron's*. They are designed to serve as indicators of broad movements in the securities markets. There are three other Dow Jones Averages: the **transportations,** composed of 20 transportation issues; the 15 **utilities;** and a **composite** of all 65 stocks in the other averages.

Figure 11–10 shows the first three averages over a period of six months as well as a list of the stocks contained in each average.

DJIA

The best known of the four Dow Jones Averages is the Dow Jones Industrial Average (DJIA). This average covers only 30 **New York Stock Exchange (NYSE)** stocks—less than 2 percent of the approximately 1,500 common stocks listed on the NYSE and less than 1 percent of all actively traded U.S. stocks. However, the DJIA companies are among the largest in the United States; all are well-established companies and leaders in their industries. The 30 DJIA stocks account for approximately 25 percent of the total market value of all NYSE stocks and 20 percent of all U.S. stock values. Their stocks are widely held by individuals and institutional investors. The 30 Dow Industrials are chosen to represent the broad market and American industry.

The value of the DJIA is meaningful only when compared to earlier values. For example, the DJIA for June 22, 1993, closed at 3510.82 points (as shown on the first line of Figure 11–11), but this value becomes meaningful only when we note on the first line under "Net Change" that it closed +16.05 points higher than the previous day. Note that one DJIA "point" does not equal one dollar in the value of an average share, but in the total value of the 30 DJIA stocks. If the sum total value of one share of each of the 30 corporations in the group was worth 3494.77 points yesterday and today is worth 16.05 points more, or 3510.82 points ($3,510.82), does this mean the average share went up $16.05? Certainly not. If all 30 companies together rose 16.05 points, then if we divide 16.05 by 30, we find that the average stock in the DJIA rose only an average of 0.53 points, or $0.53. Figure 11–11 further shows that the percentage increase in the 30 shares came to approximately .46 percent. It also indicates that the average was 230.02 points higher than its high during the past 365 days or 12 months.

The Dow is a good comparative index of the major industrial companies in the country, but it is not an accurate barometer of what the whole market is doing since

FIGURE 11–10	The Dow Jones Industrial, Transportation, and Utilities Averages

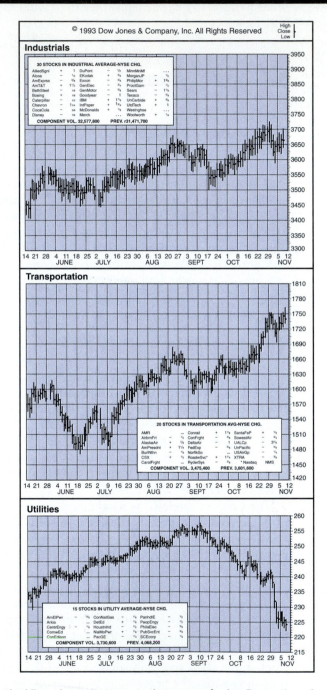

Each short vertical line above represents the range of price fluctuations for the index during a given day. The dot in each line represents the indexes value at close of trading (4 p.m.) that day.

SOURCE: Reprinted by permission of *The Wall Street Journal*, June 22, 1993, C-3. All Rights Reserved Worldwide.

FIGURE 11–11	Stock Market Data Bank

Major Indexes

HIGH	LOW	365 DAY)		CLOSE	NET CHG	%CHG	365 DAY CHG	%CHG	FROM 12/31	%CHG
DOW JONES AVERAGES										
3710.77	3223.04	**30 Industrials**		3670.25	− 23.76	− 0.64	+ 447.21	+13.88	+369.14	+11.18
1759.98	1365.40	**20 Transportation**		1711.26	− 16.03	− 0.93	+ 345.86	+25.33	+262.05	+18.08
256.46	216.45	**15 Utilities**		223.97	+ 0.33	+ 0.15	+ 5.33	+ 2.44	+ 2.95	+ 1.33
1373.66	1165.54	**65 Composite**		1346.99	− 8.51	− 0.63	+ 181.45	+15.57	+142.44	+11.83
445.26	402.72	**Equity Mlt. Index**		433.96	− 3.52	− 0.80	+ 31.24	+ 7.76	+ 20.67	+ 5.00
NEW YORK STOCK EXCHANGE										
260.48	234.11	**Composite**		253.25	− 2.28	− 0.89	+ 19.14	+ 8.18	+ 13.04	+ 5.43
313.74	287.65	**Industrials**		309.40	− 2.74	− 0.88	+ 20.67	+ 7.16	+ 15.01	+ 5.10
246.95	203.00	**Utilities**		225.13	− 1.40	− 0.62	+ 21.07	+10.33	+ 15.47	+ 7.38
267.34	204.56	**Transportation**		260.87	− 1.66	− 0.63	+ 56.31	+27.53	+ 46.15	+21.49
233.33	190.25	**Finance**		208.27	− 2.59	− 1.23	+ 17.98	+ 9.45	+ 7.44	+ 3.70
STANDARD & POOR'S INDEXES										
469.50	425.12	**500 Index**		459.13	− 3.47	− 0.75	+ 34.01	+ 8.00	+ 23.42	+ 5.38
540.25	496.48	**Industrials**		533.12	− 3.94	− 0.73	+ 34.62	+ 6.94	+ 25.66	+ 5.06
425.62	350.92	**Transportation**		417.13	− 1.68	− 0.40	+ 66.21	+18.87	+ 53.38	+14.67
189.49	152.68	**Utilities**		171.11	− 1.01	− 0.59	+ 17.43	+11.34	+ 12.65	+ 7.98
48.40	38.23	**Financials**		42.49	− 0.47	− 1.09	+ 4.26	+11.14	+ 1.60	+ 3.91
177.84	152.73	**400 MidCap**		169.03	− 2.92	− 1.70	+ 16.30	+10.67	+ 8.47	+ 5.28
NASDAQ										
787.42	638.84	**Composite**		738.13	− 13.43	− 1.79	+ 99.29	+15.54	+ 61.18	+ 9.04
809.72	660.17	**Industrials**		762.41	− 15.13	− 1.95	+ 73.66	+10.69	+ 37.47	+ 5.17
956.91	738.91	**Insurance**		872.38	− 7.72	− 0.88	+ 133.47	+18.06	+ 68.47	+ 8.52
725.65	491.90	**Banks**		678.11	− 3.61	− 0.53	+ 186.21	+37.86	+145.18	+27.24
348.22	283.52	**Nat. Mkt. Comp.**		325.54	− 6.10	− 1.84	+ 42.02	+14.82	+ 24.98	+ 8.31
323.59	263.79	**Nat. Mkt. Indus.**		304.17	− 6.24	− 2.01	+ 27.47	+ 9.93	+ 12.77	+ 4.38
OTHERS										
484.28	389.30	**Amex**		460.88	− 7.10	− 1.52	+ 70.14	+17.95	+ 61.65	+15.44
293.73	255.18	**Value-Line**(geom.)		284.11	− 3.64	− 1.26	+ 28.93	+11.34	+ 17.43	+ 6.54
260.17	209.73	**Russell 2000**		246.85	− 4.14	− 1.65	+ 37.12	+17.70	+ 25.84	+11.69
4701.68	4158.07	**Wilshire 5000**		4539.02	− 48.63	− 1.06	+ 380.95	+ 9.16	+249.28	+ 5.81

†-Based on comparable trading day in preceding year.

it does not reflect pricing trends for smaller firms or for most service-oriented firms. Nevertheless, the Dow Jones retains its popularity because most people are familiar with it and can detect immediately from it whether stock prices are moving higher or lower. It is even monitored on a minute-by-minute basis, as Figure 11–12 shows.

NYSE Composite Index

If you look again at Figure 11–11, you will notice another set of indexes under the heading of New York Stock Exchange. For many years the Board of Governors of the New York Stock Exchange was dissatisfied with the DJIA. In 1966 it began to publish

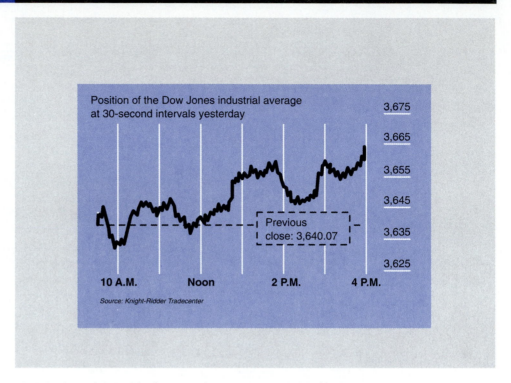

FIGURE 11–12   **The Dow: Minute by Minute**

Position of the Dow Jones industrial average at 30-second intervals yesterday

3,675
3,665
3,655
3,645
3,635
3,625

Previous close: 3,640.07

10 A.M.   Noon   2 P.M.   4 P.M.

Source: Knight-Ridder Tradecenter

SOURCE: Copyright © 1993 by the New York Times Company. Reprinted by Permission.

a new, more comprehensive price index of common stocks listed on the exchange. The **NYSE Composite Index** covers all the common stocks listed on the Big Board. In addition, there are four separate NYSE indexes for the industrial, transportation, utility, and financial company stocks included in the composite. The NYSE Composite Index is much broader and encompassing than the Dow Jones Average and more accurately reflects what is happening in the entire market. But the Dow Jones averages have been in existence longer and appear to be more popular.

Standard and Poor's (S&P) Indexes

The next listing on Figure 11–11 shows the **Standard and Poor's Indexes**. Standard and Poor's corporation, another large financial publisher, publishes five common stock indexes:

1. *Industrials*   The industrial index is made up of the common stock of 400 industrial firms.

2. *Transportation*   The transportation index includes the stock of 20 transportation companies.

3. *Public utilities*   The public utility index is made up of 40 public utility stocks.

4. *Financials*   The financial index contains 40 financial stocks.

5. *Composite 500 Index*   The composite index contains all 500 stocks included in the other four indexes.

Unlike the Dow Jones averages, Standard and Poor's indexes are true indexes. They relate the current price of a group of stocks to a base established for the period 1941 to 1943, which has an index value of 10. Thus, if the S&P 500 index is at 410.06, the average share price of stock in the index has increased by a factor of 41 (410.06/10) since the period 1941 to 1943.

The **Standard & Poor's Composite 500 Index** is the second most followed index next to the Dow. It is a more accurate guide than the Dow Jones Industrial Average because it includes the indexed value of 500 stocks from three exchanges and is therefore a far broader measure. Its broad industry coverage makes it a good substitute for the average common stock portfolio. It is reported daily in the financial section of most newspapers (see Figure 11–13 below) and is considered a major leading indicator of the strength or weakness of the economy.

FIGURE 11–13 **Standard & Poor's Composite 500 Index**

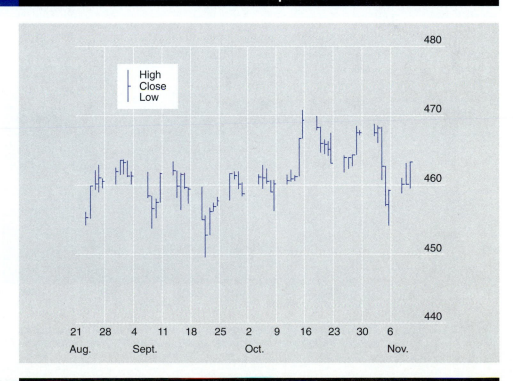

You may notice on Figure 11–11 that there are also two other exchange-based indexes—the National Association of Securities Dealers Automated Quotations (NASDAQ) for over-the-counter stocks and the AMEX for the American Stock Exchange. The NYSE, AMEX, and NASDAQ indexes, like Standard & Poor's 500 Index, cover a much broader cross-section of stocks than do the Dow Jones averages.

An old Wall Street joke says the stock market has predicted nine out of the last five recessions. The market may be nervous to a fault, but it is the one indicator that many economists credit with being the most prophetic. This is borne out when the ups and downs of the stock market over many decades are placed alongside the ups and downs of the economy as a whole. In the post–World War II era, there have been eight economic downturns and well before each, the stock market entered a long decline (except for the market crash of October 1987, which seems to have been unrelated to the business cycle). This pattern helps explain why business forecasters rate the market as one of the best leading indicators of overall economic activity.

The Wilshire Index

A lesser-known index is the **Wilshire Index** (Figure 11–14), which covers some 5,000 stocks, including a good cross-section of the over-the-counter market, and thus gives a clearer reflection of what the smaller companies are doing. It can be followed daily in *The Wall Street Journal* (see Figure 11–11, bottom line).

FIGURE 11–14	The Wilshire Index

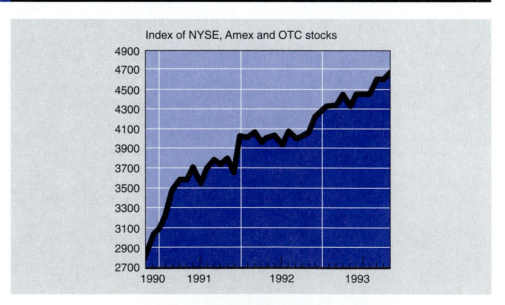

The Wilshire 5000 Index representing New York and American stock exchange issues and actively traded over-the-counter stocks was 4672.77 on October 29. This was up from 4601.84 on the last trading day in September.

In addition to the major indexes, a number of others are available. *Barron's* publishes a 50-stock average. *The New York Times* publishes its own average, which is similar to the Dow Jones averages. Moody's Investors Service prepares market indicators for a variety of groupings of common stock. Value Line publishes an index that contains 1,700 stocks traded on a broad cross-section of exchanges, as well as in the over-the-counter market. Each of these averages or indexes reflects the general behavior of all the securities markets or a specific segment of them.

CURVE

The Yield Curve

A reliable indicator of overall economic growth and inflation, some believe, is the **yield curve**. A yield curve is a line that charts the relationship between bond yields and bond maturities for bonds of a similar risk class. Thus, it shows the relationship between short-term interest rates and long-term rates. It calculates, for example, how much more or less 10-year Treasury bonds are yielding than three-month Treasury bills. The yield curve for U.S. Treasury issues is the most commonly used, because that market is relatively free of factors that might muddy the crystal ball, such as risk of default. It is used by many bond investors as a basis for predicting interest rate shifts and restructuring their portfolios.

The normal shape of the yield curve is a rising curve (see Figure 11–15A). Lenders expect to be compensated for tying up their money for a longer period of time. Thus, a three-month bill will generally yield less than a one-year bill, which usually yields less than a three-year note, and so on. And so what? Since investors in Treasuries need not worry about losses from a default, they must be demanding a higher yield for longer issues to compensate for something else: the possibility of higher interest rates, which would depress the price of a bond, or higher inflation, which would reduce its real value.

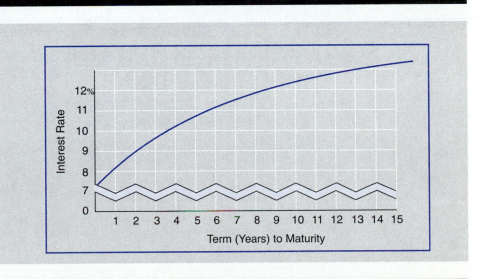

FIGURE 11–15A	The Normal Yield Curve

FIGURE 11–15B   **Yield Curve When the Market Expects Rates to Rise**

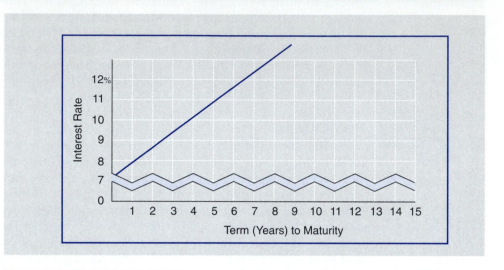

Thus, a yield curve that ascends steeply (see Figure 11–15B), indicates that the markets expect that interest rates and inflation are headed higher. Investors will settle for relatively stingy short-term rates and shun substantially higher long-term yields to protect their capital if they think rates will be rising. A steep yield curve could be a signal that higher interest rates and inflation lie ahead.

An inverted yield curve (see Figure 11–15C) appears when short-term interest rates are higher than long-term rates. Yield curves normally do not look like this. Thus, an inverted curve often signals economic sluggishness or recession. Yield

FIGURE 11–15C   **An Inverted Yield Curve**

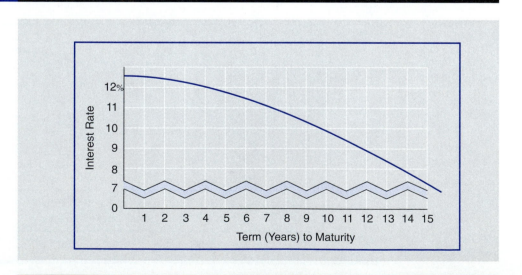

curves generally become inverted when the Federal Reserve pushes up short-term rates to slow an overheated economy and cool inflationary pressures. Meanwhile, long-term rates remain stationary because investors do not see inflation as a long-term threat. If the Fed overreacts and raises short-term rates too high, it risks pushing the economy into a recession. Consumer and business spending declines, unsold inventory begins to build up, factories slow down, and workers are laid off.

The yield curve thus is merely a chart of the interest rates on debt instruments as they increase in maturity from a few months to a generation or more. But that simple line actually embodies the sum of the financial markets' expectations about the future. The differential in available returns and the shape of the curve indicate whether short-term investments (Treasury bills, short-term certificates of deposit, or money market funds) or longer-term investments (Treasury, municipal, or corporate bonds) are more appropriate.

By carefully watching the changing shape of the yield curve, investors can avoid getting stuck in a bond portfolio when prices are sinking by moving into shorter-term investments. Conversely, if the yield curve starts signaling a sustained drop in rates, that could be the best time to buy bonds. The objective is to lock in a high yield that soon may no longer be available.

The yield curve which is published daily in *The Wall Street Journal,* however, is far from infallible. If it were perfect, professional portfolio managers would not make wrong decisions so often. There are many pitfalls, misconceptions, and structural changes in the market that have increased the risk of using the yield curve as an investment guide.

SUMMARY

Just as the physician measures the health of a patient by checking all of the vital signs, so an investor must examine all the vital economic signs to judge when the economy is working properly. The first step is to understand the business cycle and its four cycles: peak, contraction, trough, and expansion.

An understanding of monetary and fiscal policy is also essential. Monetary policy involves the Federal Reserve's manipulation of the nation's money supply and banking system to promote full employment and price stability. Fiscal policy entails the federal government's use of its taxing and spending powers to promote the same goals as the Federal Reserve.

The gross domestic product, which measures the total output of the nation annually, as well as the unemployment rate, which measures how many of the nation's labor force members are jobless, are key indicators of economic events. Several other economic indicators, including price indexes, stock market indicators, and the yield curve, also were discussed in this chapter.

These indicators make up the regular diet of business-cycle analysis and forecasting. Professional forecasters examine each new number for its cyclical significance. But there is no rule regarding which indicators you must follow in order to be on top of business conditions, the economy, or the business cycle. With time, you can select a menu of indicators that work for you. The financial section of your newspaper lists many representative indicators.

Although you may not follow economic indicators as closely as you follow the sports scores or your TV guide, your financial health will not permit you to ignore them either. Therefore, it would be wise to get to know them well enough so that they will benefit you.

KEY TERMS

Average

Base year

Bureau of Labor Statistics

Business cycle

Coincident indicators

Composite index

Consumer Price Index (CPI)

Contraction

Cost of living adjustments

Cyclical unemployment

Depression

Discount rate

Discouraged workers

Dow Jones Industrial Average (DJIA)

Economic forecasting

Economic indicators

Expansion

Federal funds rate (Fed funds rate)

Federal Reserve System

Fiscal policy

Frictional unemployment

Full employment

Gross domestic product (GDP)

Index

Indexation

Index of leading economic indicators

Industrials

Lagging indicators

Leading indicators

Monetary policy

New York Stock Exchange (NYSE)

NYSE Composite Index

Open market operations

Peak phase

Price indexes

Prime rate

Producer price index (PPI)

Prosperity phase

Recession

Recovery

Reserve requirements

Seasonal variations

Standard & Poor's Composite 500 Index

Standard & Poor's Indexes

Structural unemployment

Transportations

Trough

Unemployment rate

Utilities

Wilshire Index

Yield Curve

REVIEW QUESTIONS AND PROBLEMS

1. What is the business cycle? Describe its various phases.
2. Distinguish between fiscal and monetary policy.
3. Describe an economic indicator and give three examples of indicators.
4. Define the gross domestic product. What does it tell us about the economy?
5. What are some shortcomings of the unemployment rate?

6. Five percent unemployment is considered by economists to be "full employment." Explain this apparent contradiction of terms.

7. Explain what is meant by the Dow Jones Averages. What are the four Dow averages and what information do they provide?

8. Discuss a major shortcoming of the Dow Jones Industrial Average (DJIA).

9. What is a price index? How is it compiled?

10. How can an investor use the yield curve? Explain its basic structure and what it reveals.

11. Define and explain each: (a) Index of leading economic indicators, (b) Index of coincident economic indicators, (c) Index of lagging economic indicators.

12. (RESERVE) You own a bank. You have deposits of $200 million. You have the minimum amount on deposit, given a reserve requirement of 5 percent. The Federal Reserve raises reserve requirements to 6 percent. By what amount must you reduce the maximum amount of loans you can have outstanding to comply with the new reserve requirement?

13. (INDEX) Your grandmother set aside $10,000 for you 20 years ago when the CPI was 20. Now you have inherited the money, which through careful investment has grown to $60,000. Meanwhile, the CPI has risen to 120. How much real gain has the money enjoyed over the period?

14. (CURVE)

A. Generate or modify data to create separate yield curves to demonstrate each of the following characteristics:
1. The same interest rate at all maturities
2. Increasing interest rates
3. Decreasing interest rates

B. What would account for yield curves with these shapes?

SUGGESTED PROJECTS

Look through the financial sections of several newspapers and magazines from two months ago. Find as many economic indicators as possible. Try to put together a composite of these indicators and see if it suggests some trend in the economy. Then look in today's newspaper and see whether this trend actually has developed. How would your information have helped you in any investment decisions? Which indicators seem most useful and which would you rely upon most in any of your future financial decisions? Explain why. Present your findings to your class and elicit your classmates' reaction.

INFORMATION RESOURCES

Anderson, Gerald M., and John J. Erceg. "Forecasting Turning Points with Leading Indicators." *Economic Commentary*, Federal Reserve Bank of Cleveland, October 1, 1989.

"The Dow Mystique." *Personal Investor*, January 1986, 20–28.

"How Low Can Rates Go?" *Business Week*, August 23, 1993, 14–15.

"How to Tell When a Recession Is Coming." *Changing Times*, March 1989, 18.

"A Mess of Misleading Indicators." *Time*, June 13, 1988, 37.

Penmar, Karen. "The Business Cycle Isn't Dead, Just Resting." *Business Week,* October 4, 1993, 68–69.

Stevens, E. J. "Is There a Message in the Yield Curve?" *Economic Commentary,* Federal Reserve Bank of Cleveland, March 15, 1989.

"To Keep Profits on a Roll, Stay Tuned to the Business Cycle." *Money,* May 1989, 169–172.

Tregarthen, Timothy. "The Economy Recovers but It Takes It's own Sweet Time." *The Margin,* Spring 1993, 18–19.

Willoughby, Jack. "Dangerous Shapes." *Forbes,* January 23, 1989, 40.

CHAPTER TWELVE

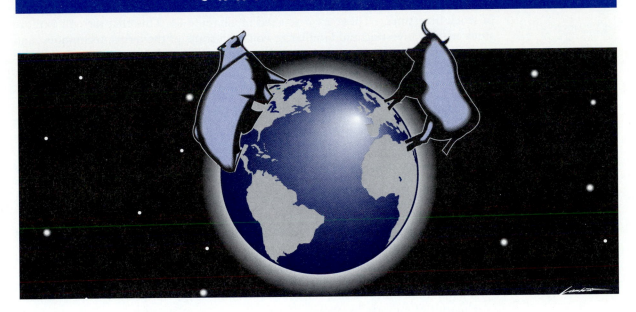

The World of Stocks

- To analyze why people invest in stocks and the inherent risks of doing so
- To explore the securities markets and how they operate
- To discuss the factors that should be considered in an investment decision
- To examine buying on margin, selling short, and stop-loss orders for stocks
- To identify and explain the major features and types of stocks
- To clarify the services that can be expected from full service and discount brokerage firms
- To illustrate the main sources of investor information
- To consider guidelines to assist potential investors in developing a defensive investment strategy

If you are thinking about investing in stocks, you have lots of company. By and large, the more than 40 million Americans who invest in stocks have found this a sound method of investing. You need not necessarily ever buy stocks, although the chances are you will at some point in your life. People can live a full, happy, and prosperous life and never own stocks, but the fact still remains that the stock market is a major source of investment opportunity, risk not withstanding.

423

For those not able or willing to tolerate the tension and risk inherent in stock investing, there are stock mutual funds which are another somewhat less risky form of stock investment. These are discussed in Chapter 14. This chapter will explore stock market investing and familiarize you with some of the terms, techniques, and methods of investing, as well as provide some basic guidelines on how to minimize risk and maximize the chances of having your money grow in the stock market.

The Elements of Advantage and Risk

Stocks represent shares in the ownership of corporations. Companies issue them to raise money for their activities. Investors buy stocks in the hope that their price will rise as the company prospers (a type of investment return which is known as *capital gains*) and that some of the company's profits will be paid to the investors as dividends.

Whether one invests in individual shares or in mutual funds, the stock market offers key investment advantages:

1. Stocks are highly marketable. Investors do not have to advertise if they wish to sell nor sit around waiting for a buyer to call. Stocks can be sold and bought in a matter of minutes by phone.

2. Stocks can provide income through dividends payments. If the company prospers, stockholders may receive a share of its earnings in the form of additional stock or cash dividends.

3. More alluring to most investors, stocks offer a greater chance at capital gains. Stocks offer the possibility that they will appreciate in value.

4. There exists the opportunity to start with a modest amount of investment capital— less than $5,000 buys an average 100 share (which is known as a *round lot*) order.

Therefore, many financial advisers still view common shares as a recommended long-term investment form for most individuals.

But investors always need to be aware that the stock market can also be a turbulent arena because it reflects the economy with its constant ups and downs. The uncertainty and risks inherent in stock market investments were most profoundly highlighted by the sudden and brutal stock market crash of October 19, 1987. In that single day the Dow Jones index dropped an astounding 508 points, wiping out $500 billion of paper stock value.

However, a puzzling thing happened when the market crashed on October 19, 1987: nothing else did. In the aftermath, economists glumly predicted an imminent recession or worse, pointing out similarities to the chart lines of 1929. The 1929 stock crash was followed by the Great Depression of the 1930s. Most Americans simply shrugged off the 1987 crash. Consumers went on spending for new cars, refrigerators, and the like. Inflation remained modest. Corporate earnings kept rising. Indeed, a year after the crash, the economy performed so robustly that fears of accelerating inflation caused the Federal Reserve to tighten credit.

What did it all mean? The fact is, of course, that no one has been able to precisely figure it out. The events of that day can be seen as a financial panic rather than an economic disaster. Nevertheless, many investors are still haunted by the memory of having their portfolio decline by an average of 25 percent in a single day. For those who did not sell their shares, this proved to be only a temporary loss since the market recovered within several weeks thereafter. Equally disquieting were the crash of Friday, October 13, 1989—which witnessed a 190-point plunge in the Dow Jones Industrial average—and the bear market of 1990.

Investors, therefore, should never lose sight of the fact that stocks involve risk taking. From 1960 to 1990, the stock market delivered compounded total returns of 10.2 percent a year (according to Ibbotson Associates, a Chicago research firm).

An advertisement by the Chicago Mercantile Exchange recently proclaimed that "risk" is not a four-letter word. Today, risk is a fact of life. You may find the stock market a worthwhile place in which to keep part of your assets. Many investment theorists regard the stock market as a rational arena in which risk and reward go together. **Risk** is usually viewed in terms of the stock's fluctuations. The more volatile the stock, however, the greater the potential for profit or loss.

Beginning investors often hope to find a magic formula that will consistently beat the market and lead them unfailingly to winning stocks. Such formulas do not exist. The secret to successful investing is that there are no magic secrets, no foolproof formulas or methods. Everyone who does well does it in his or her own way. There are losers (who are usually very quiet) and winners (who are usually boisterous and boasting), but no certainty or guarantee of profiting.

"Buy low and sell high" is a hackneyed Wall Street maxim. It sounds great, but it is difficult to follow. People are exuberant after a big market rise, depressed after a decline, and tend to buy at the top and sell at the bottom. There is another adage on Wall Street: "The broker made money, the company made money—and two out of three ain't bad."

It would be wonderful indeed to have a secret formula that would guide you to sell at the highs and buy at the lows. Technicians and investment analysts have devised various formulas in an attempt to make this dream come true. None of these formulas is foolproof. If there were a method that guaranteed success, everyone would use it. Following a given formula can be helpful as a guide or indicator to assist investors in making decisions, but no philosophy, formula, method, or theory is guaranteed to bring success in the stock market. Rather, a number of intelligent approaches can increase the chances for small investors with common sense and self-discipline to realize big profits.

Risk is everywhere. It is an inseparable part of the stock market. The key is to risk intelligently. Those who are unwilling to risk their funds should not be in the market. However, controlling and limiting risk is possible by following certain prescribed guidelines and policies. These, as well as an explanation of the workings of the securities markets, will be discussed in this chapter .

Once you have learned to live with risk—and have shed the illusion that the price of your stocks can only go up—you still have another valuable lesson to learn: The market is not always a reliable indicator of business conditions, as the crashes of '87 and '89 clearly demonstrated. Emotion probably is as large a factor as logic in governing the price movements of common stocks. Therefore, one can never really be certain of anything in the stock market.

How to Get Started

Stock investing is appropriate only for those who have already provided for their basic needs—food, clothing, and shelter—and who have established an emergency fund consisting of three to six months of net income in liquid assets for that proverbial rainy day. Before investing, you should have a firm fix on your financial goals. Your particular objectives should reflect your age, family status, income level, net worth, and earning prospectus. Such considerations influence how much risk you want and can afford to take. Once having identified your goals, you should begin to seek the appropriate stocks that match your needs. Successful investing depends as much upon correctly matching your personality to your stock-selecting strategy as it does on diligently applying the rules of that strategy. Whether you are daring, moderate, or cautious, some of the strategies that follow can help steer you toward profits. It should be noted that stocks are not necessarily for every investor. Many financial goals may often more appropriately be met through other types of securities discussed in future chapters.

Investing Time

Intelligent investing requires an investment of time as well as money. Investors should first learn as much as possible about the securities market, its institutions, rules, regulations, techniques, strategies, and so on. Then they should learn as much as they can about the companies and industries that they are investing in. Reading this chapter may be a good start making intelligent investment decisions, but it will also be necessary to continue to read financial publications and possibly subscribe to an advisory service.

Investors who cannot afford even one evening a week of serious concentration on their investment might consider mutual funds or turning over their portfolio to professional management. Those who have only several hours a week for their portfolio may find it advantageous to limit themselves to a few stocks, no more than 10. Sticking to this pruning principle should also prevent the kind of helter-skelter accumulation that makes a portfolio unwieldy, although, on the other hand, the benefits of diversification will be significantly reduced.

The 10-stock maximum, with the stocks from several different industries, allows enough diversification to spread risk but also contains enough concentration of holdings to enable you to adequately monitor them. However, these stocks must be carefully selected to ensure that correlation of returns is such that the risk will be reduced at this small a level of holdings. If you feel strongly about a new stock you have discovered, you can still buy it by casting out the weakest of the 10 you already own.

Conducting Your Own Research

Investors who want to pick stocks themselves must, as mentioned, consult more in-depth and specialized sources of information. They need at least the past 10-year history of each firm, in-depth reports of its activities, trends and the outlook for the company in the industry. They should assemble as much additional information as they can about each of their companies. Investors can write or call the company's investor relations department to get the annual reports, quarterly reports, and proxy statements (see appendix).

Those who use a full-service brokerage may ask for up-to-date reports from its research department. Much of this material is available in local libraries. Nationwide, there are better research facilities in any medium-size or large city library than in many brokerage firms. Of course, investors have to be willing to spend the time and effort to obtain it, but the information to make one an informed investor is readily available.

Beginning investors can also get an impression of what professional investors think will happen in the market by reading their local newspaper if it has a good stock market column. Such opinion may not always be accurate, but it is important to know what pattern of thinking is forming.

Serious investors should regularly review such financial periodicals as *The Wall Street Journal, Barron's, Business Week* and *Forbes Magazine.* Publications such as *Barron's,* issued every Monday, follow and analyze the past week's events on Wall Street. *The Wall Street Journal* is considered the leading financial daily that reports and interprets news as it affects the business and financial communities.

Sources of Information

Many people are unfamiliar with the other basic sources of investment information. These publications provide the basic statistics and other information investors need to research and evaluate companies on their own.

1. *Standard and Poor's Corporation Records*   Its seven volumes contain detailed descriptions of operations, financial structures, and securities on more than 10,000 publicly held firms, plus the latest news on recent developments.

2. *Standard and Poor's Stock Guide*   It provides recent pricing information (monthly), including P/E ratios, dividends, yields, and so on.

3. *S&P's Stock Reports*   Good for analysis; this 12-volume source of information contains periodically revised two-page profiles of more than 3,700 companies. Included are company descriptions, sales, earnings and debt levels, and the business outlook for the firms.

4. *F&S Index*   This is essentially a reader's guide to everything in print about a company or industry. In minutes investors can track down years of magazine and newspaper articles on a stock and dig deeper than most investors ever take time for.

5. *Predicasts F&S Index of Corporate Change*   This index guides investors through years of organizational changes, such as joint ventures, bankruptcies, liquidations, reorganization, name changes, takeovers, and so on.

6. *Wall Street Journal Index*   It covers everything *The Wall Street Journal* has written about by company, industry, or topic. Investors can quickly check out anything it has printed about a specific company or subject.

7. *The Wall Street Journal Transcript*   This is a good source of the latest thinking on Wall Street. It covers brokerages and firm reports, publishes text from

newsletters, and conducts interviews with security analysts and money managers. All mentions of stocks from previous issues are indexed.

8. *Wards Directory* This list by Zip Code has almost all corporations, and investors can check them out regionally.

9. *The SEC's Official Summary of Insider Transactions* This summary gives a monthly breakdown on officers and directors who have been buying and selling their own stock.

10. *The Business Periodicals Index* This index provides a quick scan on recent articles about a business, person, or subject. It covers articles from over 800 publications.

11. *Standard and Poor's Daily Stock Price Record* This record provides prices for each stock in decades past.

12. *Value Line Investment Survey* This is a regularly updated compilation of facts, figures, and analysis on some 1,700 companies. It suggests stocks to buy or avoid and ranks them by such characteristics as safety or income yield.

In addition to the above, many investors use *Moody's Handbook of Common Stock* which is similar to *S&P's Stock Reports*.

Investment Clubs

A popular way to start investing in stocks and learn about the stock market is to join an **investment club.** Nearly half a million do-it-yourself investors around the country have formed an estimated 20,000 clubs to invest in stocks. Investment clubs date back to 1900, and over the years their popularity has waxed and waned with the stock market.

An estimated 7,000 of the 20,000 clubs belong to the **National Association of Investment Clubs (NAIC),** a nonprofit volunteer organization operated by and for the benefit of member clubs. NAIC offers information ranging from the basics of starting a club to stock analysis and investment philosophy. Investment clubs are an ideal way for new investors to learn the basics of stock market investing. No prior investment experience is necessary to join or start a club.

Clubs generally meet once a month on a rotating basis in the homes of the members. They operate as partnerships and share profits and losses on their combined holdings. The typical monthly contribution per member ranges from $20 to $30. Investment clubs function much like mini mutual funds in that members pool their money to invest in a diversified portfolio of stocks.

Clubs also keep their books like a mutual fund (which are discussed in Chapter 14). Shares start at $10 and rise and fall in value with the performance of stocks. At each meeting, the club's treasurer calculates what a share is worth at that time. Each member knows how many shares he or she has, so getting out of a club is as simple as getting in. Members who leave can convert their shares to cash or transfer the stock.

Instead of hiring a fund manager, each member actively participates in making the investment decisions. At meetings, members present reviews of specific stocks they have been asked to research, talk about market prospects, and make buy and sell decisions. All members are responsible for coming up with companies that are investment possibilities, doing the research on those stocks, and making reports and recommendations to the membership. The typical investment club is about nine years old and consists of 10 to 20 persons.

You and the Stockbroker

Investors need the services of a **stockbroker** to execute their buy and sell orders. Stockbrokers are formally called **account executives** or **registered representatives** at a brokerage firm and they are usually the closest contact an individual has with the stock market. In the purest sense of the word, they act only as investors' agents in executing investors' orders to buy and sell securities. In most cases, they do not directly sell investors anything nor buy anything from them. They charge a commission for filling an order at the best price. They have a fiduciary obligation to get investors the best price.

In order for a broker to buy or sell stocks for you over the phone, you will be required first to open a brokerage account. This means you deposit a sum of money with the broker, which is then used to execute your purchase orders. If you buy stocks by phone, you will have five business days to send in a check or have your brokerage account debited.

There are two choices when it comes to buying stocks: pay extra for the advice of a **full-service broker** or get a **discount broker** who provides no research or advice but just executes trade orders at reduced commissions. Merrill Lynch, Smith Barney, Dean Witter, and Prudential-Bache are a few well-known full-service houses. Charles Schwab, Fidelity Brokerage, and Quick & Reilly are among the prominent discounters.

Full-Service Brokers

A full-service firm assigns investors a broker who is expected to be more than a simple order taker. With access to investment research and current financial products, the full service broker can supply investors with research material on specific stocks and industries as well as investment advice and portfolio recommendations.

If the broker is familiar with an investor's investment needs and objectives, he or she may phone the investor to recommend a possibly good opportunity or talk the investor out of a bad move. An individual does not have to depend upon such professional advice to make money, although it could be helpful, particularly for a beginner. The higher fees that the full-service brokers collect go in part toward supplying these services to the investor.

Stockbrokers are in business to earn money. They do so primarily on the commissions investors pay when they trade. The more active an account and the more commission it yields, the more attention it will get. While an average broker in a major investment house may have as many as 300 clients, most brokers generally earn some 80 percent of their commissions from just 20 percent of their accounts. When they apportion their time, it is only natural that they turn first to their best clients.

Brokers stand to profit whether their advice makes money for clients or not and whether their clients follow the broker's suggestions or pick their own stocks. The broker is paid commissions on every trade, whether a client buys or sells, so frequent trades always benefit the broker, although they may not be in the client's best financial interest. This practice is known as *churning*. Recognizing that inherent conflict of interest, and the potential for churning, is the beginning of a realistic brokerage relationship.

If your full-service broker calls with suggestions, review them closely, just as you would any other major purchase. You should not invest without a clear understanding of why a stock should be bought. Questions to pose to a broker on a recommendation are these:

1. What is the general outlook for this industry?

2. What is the company's position within the industry?

3. How volatile is the stock?

4. How much risk is involved?

5. How much does the broker expect it to rise in price and how quickly?

6. How much might it drop in value?

Ask enough questions to be sure the investment is in line with your expectations for the market as well as your financial goals.

Discount Brokers

The distinguishing feature of no-frills or discount brokers is that they offer only one basic service. Acting on a client's orders, they buy or sell shares and charge a set fee for each transaction—perhaps $25 to $55—for trading up to 100 shares at any price and about $25 to $107 for trading as many as 300 shares at $30 each. Full-service brokers, on the other hand, charge a percentage—1 percent to 2 percent—of the dollar amount of each transaction, usually taking a smaller percentage as the size of the trade increases. In Table 12–1, based on a survey of Mercer, Inc., the same 300 shares that can be traded for $25 in discount brokerage fees would cost $207 at a typical full-commission broker.

Experienced investors who make their own decisions and feel they do not need a broker-adviser consider solicitations from brokers a nuisance and are usually delighted with the silence of discount firms. These investors like the fact that discounters do not steer them into trading just to get some action and earn brokerage commissions. A discount broker will phone only to confirm that an order has been filled.

Discount brokers are probably not the best choice for beginning investors because novices often need help and advice from a broker, at least until they gain

TABLE 12–1	How Brokerage Commissions Compare

Typical charges for buying or selling a $30-a-share stock.

	Number of Shares Traded			
Brokerage Firm	**100**	**300**	**500**	**1,000**
Pacific Brokerage Services	$25	$25	$42	$70
Scottsdale Securities	29	47	55	75
Quick & Reilly	49	82	97	128
Charles Schwab	55	107	127	166
Full-commission broker*	84	207	310	507

Note: Charges are based on standard New York Stock Exchange trades; some firms offer discounts for active investors, for trades placed by computer, or for over-the-counter trades.

*Average of two major firms.

SOURCE: Mercer, Inc., as reported in *The Wall Street Journal*, December 13, 1991.

some experience. Furthermore, small investors get little advantage from using discounters. Although discount brokers cut commissions as much as 75 percent below regular brokerage rates on large trades, there is usually no savings at all on trades below $1,000 because of the minimums they charge. Therefore, inexperienced investors requiring expert advice, market research, or access to bond markets, tax shelters, and other investment vehicles may be better served using full-service brokers.

Many active investors maintain both types of accounts. They use a full-service broker to provide some recommendations and to execute orders based upon those recommendations and a discounter for the rest of their trades.

Competition for clients has resulted in some no-frills discount brokers routinely offering services that traditionally only full service-brokers provided. These services might include safe keeping of securities, collection of dividends and interest, money market accounts for clients' idle cash, and margin accounts (explained further on).

Selecting a Broker

Finding a broker suited to one's style of investing and financial goals is not easy, although there are plenty to choose from. Between 1981 and 1987, the number of securities representatives registered with the **National Association of Securities Dealers (NASD)** more than doubled to 459,000.

When investors contact a broker, they should be prepared to ask a lot of questions. Investors should inquire about the broker's background, length of time in the business, and which firms he or she has worked for, as well as the types of investments the broker understands best. It is also important to ask whether the broker comes up with his or her own investment decisions or simply follows the suggestions of the firm's research department. Investors should additionally inquire about the broker's fees and compare them with those of other brokers.

It is also important for brokers to know their clients' financial goals, as well as the amount of risk clients are willing to assume to achieve them.

Securities Investor Protection Corporation (SIPC)   When brokers sell stocks for investors, the proceeds are usually transferred into the investor's brokerage account until further orders are received. In order to make future trading easier, most brokers, when they buy stocks for investors, keep the stocks in the broker's name, known as **street name.** The stocks are registered in the brokerage house's name and the broker sends investors a

Characteristics of a Good Broker

Here are some characteristics of a good broker that investors should look for:
1. *Accessibility*   When an investor calls with buy and sell orders, the broker will act on them quickly.
2. *Follow up*   A good broker confirms quickly. Investors have a right to expect timely notice that shares were sold, quick responses to any request for background information, and speedy collection and forwarding of the proceeds from their transactions.
3. *Affiliation*   A broker affiliated with a large firm has extensive support services, such as a research department and investment and tax specialists.
4. *Familiarity with client*   A good broker must have a thorough understanding of a client's needs and objectives before making a recommendation. A broker's commitment should be ongoing, not just an initial commitment. After a transaction is completed, the broker should monitor its status every few months to make sure the investment still meets the client's objectives. A good broker will help keep an eye on a client's investment, but the responsibility is never the broker's alone.
5. *Specialist*   Like most professionals, stockbrokers tend to specialize. There are those who concentrate on tax shelters, undervalued stocks and bonds, options, financial planning, or other financial products. Investors should choose a broker whose expertise most closely matches their own needs.
6. *Performance*   Investors should request a list of the broker's clients that can be called for references to check his or her performance record. After having selected a broker and followed his or her suggestions, investors' gains at least should match those posted by the Standard & Poor's Stock Index (S & P 500, discussed in Chapter 11), a broad-based measure of stock performance.

The bottom line is simple: If a broker is not making money for you, then change brokers. Clients as a rule should never give a broker more than 20 percent of the money they plan to invest until they have worked together for as long as it takes to feel comfortable with the broker's recommendations.

statement crediting their account with the amount of shares of a particular stock bought. The only risk with this is if the brokerage house should declare bankruptcy. Clients have a claim against the broker but do not legally own the specific stocks which were bought for them. The stocks are part of the broker's general assets, which investors can claim. Investors can of course specify that the stock be purchased in their own name, request to receive the stock certificate, or both.

Because of several brokerage house bankruptcies, a form of brokerage insurance was created by Congress. **The Securities Investor Protection Corporation (SIPC)** (202/371-8300) is a private nonprofit corporation created to protect customers against insolvencies at brokerage firms. Almost all broker-dealers registered with the **Securities and Exchange Commission (SEC)** are SIPC members and are assessed a fee to finance the organization. SIPC has a $200 million fund plus a $7 billion line of credit from the Treasury. It can be used to pay customers of brokerage firms that go bankrupt for the value of securities held in the name of the firm and for cash deposits.

If a stock brokerage firm fails, SIPC may arrange to have the investors' accounts transferred to another brokerage firm or it may elect to pay off clients of the failed firm. In the latter case, SIPC will pay the claims of each account up to a maximum of $500,000, including up to $100,000 on claims for cash.

National Association of Securities Dealers (NASD) The vast majority of broker-dealers in the United State belong to the **National Association of Securities Dealers (NASD)** (301/590-6500), the self-regulatory agency of the securities industry. NASD has the power to censure, fine, suspend, or even bar an individual broker or brokerage firm for violation of NASD professional and ethical guidelines.

The SEC also sets rules which govern a broker's behavior. Investors who want to investigate whether a broker has been accused, acquitted, or convicted of SEC violations can write to the SEC (Public Reference Branch, SEC, 450 Fifth Street NW, Washington, DC 20549. Investors must give the name of the broker in question and indicate that they will pay the 10 cents per copy fee. Those who desire quicker results can phone the SEC library in Washington, DC, at 202/272-2618 and ask for assistance.

The Stock Markets

Companies often issue new shares of stock in order to raise money. This process of selling securities to the investing public takes place in what is called the **primary market.** Investment bankers assist companies in primary markets by selling and distributing new stocks and bonds as an intermediary between issuing corporations and the original purchasers. Investment banks perform a function known as **underwriting,** or guaranteeing to the issuer that it will receive at least a specified minimum price for the stock issue. This involves actually purchasing the securities from the issuer and then reselling them to the investing public. After that, investors can easily resell the stocks or bonds when they wish, time and again, in **secondary markets,** which include stock exchanges and the over-the-counter market.

Secondary markets involve the subsequent trading of those securities once they are already outstanding. Here buyers and sellers exchange money for shares but none of the proceeds goes to the companies that issued the shares.

The New York and American Stock Exchanges

The New York Stock Exchange is an example of a secondary market. Popularly known as the Big Board, the **NYSE** is one of the largest stock exchanges in the world. Only the largest and soundest corporations qualify for listing on it. Reputable and large companies whose stocks, for one reason or another, are not quoted on the NYSE may be traded on America's second largest stock exchange, also located on Wall Street—the **American Stock Exchange** or **AMEX**. In addition to these two national stock exchanges, there are seven smaller regional exchanges: Boston, Cincinnati, Midwest, Pacific, Philadelphia, Intermountain, and Spokane. Each exchange has its own listings, which it trades primarily, but not exclusively.

The Over-the-Counter Market—OTC

Not all stocks are listed on the registered exchanges, but a thriving market in them exists nonetheless. Several thousand smaller companies are traded in the **over-the-counter (OTC) market**. This market involves essentially private transactions between dealers and investors. These stocks are not really traded over any counter. The OTC is not an actual place with a large trading floor like the NYSE and AMEX. The term "over the counter" came into use more than 150 years ago when securities were sold in stores and banks (over counters) to distinguish from trading done at exchanges.

Today these issues are traded electronically through a highly sophisticated, far-flung national network of dealers connected by telephone and computer lines and 11,500 interlocking computer terminals that make up the **National Association of Securities Dealers Automated Quotations (NASDAQ)** system. NASDAQ (pronounced nazdak) sounds like a kind of computer—which it is, on a grand scale.

NASDAQ is the third largest stock market in the world in terms of dollar volume of equity trading, trailing only the NYSE and the Tokyo Exchange. The NASDAQ computer quotes daily prices for 4,723 stocks, with most of the buying and selling done over the telephone. The over-the-counter securities are usually smaller than exchange listed stocks, with less trading interest. But by no means are all OTC stocks those of little or obscure firms. Well-known names such as Apple Computer, Intel, MCI, and Anheuser-Busch are listed here.

Nearly 5,000 member broker-dealer firms are able to call up on their terminal screens the up-to-the-minute quotes, last sale, and daily volume of all NASDAQ stocks in the National Market System, and the quotes and daily volume for all the other NASDAQ issues.

Members must report the price and number of shares of each of their NASDAQ trades within 90 seconds of the transaction for all National Market System companies and by the end of the day for all other NASDAQ firms. Stocks traded in this market may be found in the OTC listing.

The Pink Sheets

Finally, there are about 20,000 OTC issues not plugged into NASDAQ's computers. These are companies whose market capitalization does not usually exceed $15 million, that are too small to even be listed in the NASDAQ system or traded on the OTC market, and that inhabit what might be termed the under-the-counter market. The under-the-counter market is a loose network of local stockbrokers who deal in the shares, usually closely held and thinly traded, of companies that are regionally based. These stocks do not appear in local newspaper stock quotations either. The only record of market trading of these shares appears in the daily **pink sheet listing,** a directory of bids and offers (not trades) toward the end of the day. These printed lists, updated just once daily, are generally available only to brokers.

Pink sheet listings are published by a privately owned listing service based in New Jersey, The National Quotation Bureau. Most brokerage offices subscribe to this 300-page daily publication. Investors who want to buy or sell shares of one of those small firms would have to contact a brokerage house that receives the pink sheets in order to obtain a price quote. A disadvantage of shares that trade in the under-the-counter market is lack of market liquidity. There may not be any buyer or seller for a particular stock which an investor wants to trade.

Reading Stock Quotes

Investors who own stock or who are considering stock purchases must be able to obtain basic data from daily newspapers and other specialized sources. There is a wealth of information in the daily newspaper stock tables alone, such as the last price, the high, the low, trading volume, dividend, yield, and price earnings ratio. With these figures, investors can determine the current market value of the shares they own or are following. Investors can also determine their profits or losses, basic trends, and so on.

Most large metropolitan newspapers cover the stock market in varying degrees of detail. Major dailies, such as *The New York Times* and *The Wall Street Journal,* publish an entire business section each day. These include price listings of the seven regional U.S. stock exchanges (selected quotes), the two national stock exchanges, over-the-counter securities, and Canadian and popular foreign equities.

The regional exchanges and the NYSE are closely integrated. Trading results for stocks listed both on the NYSE and regional exchanges are combined on the NYSE page. This is called **composite trading.** They are linked together by electronic communications. Shares of large NYSE–listed companies are frequently traded on regional exchanges. AMEX listings are also composite and have a page of their own (see Figures 12–1 and 12–2). In effect, we have a national market system.

You can easily become proficient in translating financial quotations, otherwise known as "stock prices." Here is how to read a typical newspaper stock page.

Sample Stock Quotation of General Motors (GM):

Columns

1	2	3	4	5	6	7	8	9	10	11
High	Low	Stock	Div	Yld %	P/E Ratio	Sales 100s	High	Low	Close	Net Chg
75	49	GM	3.87	6	16.5	8362	64¾	63	64	+⅜

Stock quotes are read from left to right. Stock price movements of $1 or more are quoted in **points** (+1 for example, means the stock is up $1.00 per share). Fractions of a dollar are reported in eighths. *Columns 1 and 2,* the "High" and "Low" columns at the far left, show the trading range, the stock's highest and lowest values, for the past 52 weeks. These figures show where the stock's price today stands relative to its

FIGURE 12–1 New York Stock Exchange Composite Transactions (Sample)

Quotations as of 5 p.m. Eastern Time
Friday, June♣ 199♥

	52 Weeks Hi	Lo	Stock	Sym	Div	Yld %	PE	Vol 100s	Hi	Lo	Close	Net Chg
			–A–A–A–									
	14 5/8	10 3/4	AAR	AIR	.48	3.5	...	515	14	13 3/4	13 7/8	–1/8
	11 3/4	10 3/4	ACM Gvt Fd	ACG	.96e	8.2	...	371	11 3/4	11 5/8	11 3/4	..
	10	9	ACM OppFd	AOF	.80	8.2	...	300	10	9 3/4	9 3/4	–1/8
	11 7/8	9 7/8	ACM SecFd	GSF	.96	8.7	...	410	11 1/8	11	11	..
	9 3/4	8 5/8	ACM SpctmFd	SI	.80	8.4	...	377	9 5/8	9 3/8	9 1/2	+1/8
	11	9 1/4	ACM MgdIncFd	AMF	1.08	9.9	...	234	10 7/8	10 3/4	10 7/8	+1/8
	11 3/4	8 5/8	ACM MgdMultFd	MMF	.85e	9.4	...	240	9 1/8	9	9	..
n	15 1/8	14 5/8	ACM MuniSec	AMU		...	...	423	14 3/4	14 5/8	14 5/8	..
	9 7/8	6 3/8	ADT	ADT		...	...	1965	9 3/4	9 3/8	9 5/8	+1/8
	2 1/2	7/8	ADT wt			...	...	155	1 3/4	1 5/8	1 5/8	..
	40 1/4	27 1/8	AFLAC	AFL	.50f	1.3	16	960	38 7/8	38 1/2	38 5/8	–1/8
	29 3/8	18	AL Labs A	BMD	.18	.7	34	397	28 1/4	27 1/2	27 1/2	–1/2
	65 7/8	52 5/8	AMP	AMP	1.60	2.6	22	978	61 3/8	60 3/4	61 3/4	+1/4
	72 7/8	54 3/8	AMR	AMR		...	dd	2732	71 7/8	70 5/8	70 3/4	–5/8
	47 1/4	39 1/4	ARCO Chm	RCM	2.50	5.5	23	162	45 5/8	45	45 3/8	–1/2
	2 1/4	**1 3/8**	**ARX**	**ARX**		**...**	**13**	**42**	**2 1/8**	**2**	**2**	**–1/8**
	51 1/2	29 3/4	ASA	ASA	2.00	4.1	...	476	49 5/8	49	49 1/4	+1/4
	33	22 5/8	AbbotLab	ABT	.68f	2.6	17	16925	26 7/8	25 1/2	25 7/8	–1 1/8
			• • • • • •									
			–B–B–B–									
	39 7/8	32	BCE Inc g	BCE	2.64	...	...	3382	35 3/4	35 1/2	35 5/8	..
	11 7/8	5 1/8	BET	BEP	.41e	5.9	...	35	7 1/8	7	7	..
	31 5/8	12 5/8	BJ Svc	BJS		...	36	948	31 1/8	30 1/2	30 5/8	–1/2
	13 3/8	6 1/2	BMC	BMC		...	10	35	13 1/8	13	13	..
	32 1/4	29 3/8	BP Prudhoe	BPT	2.82e	9.5	...	129	29 7/8	29 3/4	29 3/4	–1/8
	39 7/8	29 3/8	BRE Prop	BRE	2.40	6.9	11	111	35	34 3/4	34 7/8	..
	4 1/4	1 7/8	BRT RltyTr	BRT		...	dd	17	3 3/8	3 1/4	3 1/4	..
	8 1/2	4 3/4	Baimco	BZ	.20	3.4	9	414	6 1/8	5 7/8	5 7/8	–1/8
	29 5/8	17 3/4	BakrHughs	BHI	.46	1.6	dd	2373	29 3/8	29 1/8	29 1/8	–3/8
	19 1/8	16 5/8	BakrFentrs	BKF	1.81e	9.9	...	83	18 1/2	18 1/4	18 3/8	–1/8
s	24 1/8	16 1/4	BaldorElec	BEZ	.40f	1.7	21	57	23 1/8	22 7/8	23	+1/8
s	33 7/8	24 3/8	Ball Cp	BLL	1.24	3.8	13	292	32 5/8	31 7/8	32 3/8	+1/4
			• • • • • •									
			–C–C–C–									
	34 1/2	21 3/4	CBI Ind	CBH	.48	1.9	16	1457	24 7/8	24 3/4	24 7/8	–1/8
	250 1/2	176	CBS	CBS	1.00	.4	dd	186	249 1/2	247 1/2	248 1/2	–2
n	30 1/2	12 3/8	CCP Insur	CCP	.06e	.3	...	138	23 7/8	23 1/4	23 3/4	+1/2
	1 1/8	1/2	CCX	CCX		...	...	8	5/8	9/16	5/8	..
	10 3/8	6	CDI	CDI		...	23	35	7 5/8	7 1/2	7 5/8	..
	3/8	3/32	CF IncoPtnr	CFI	.12j	...	dd	952	1/4	15/64	15/64	...
	68	47 1/8	CIGNA	CI	3.04	5.1	15	372	59 3/4	59	59 1/2	–1/4
	8 3/4	7	CIGNA High	HIS	.90a	10.6	...	374	8 1/2	8 3/8	8 1/2	..
	33 5/8	27 1/2	CIPSCO	CIP	1.96f	6.1	14	303	31 7/8	31 3/4	31 7/8	+1/8
n	33 1/8	18 1/4	CMAC	CMT	.20	.8	...	215	25 1/4	24 7/8	25	–1/2
			• • • • • •									

NYSE EXTENDED TRADING

June♣ 199♥

	Total Volume	Market Value
First crossing session	188,600	b-$6,794,162
Second session (baskets)	2,012,200	$79,241,332

MOST ACTIVE ISSUES

(First session)

Issue	Sym.	a-Volume 100s	Close	NYSE Comp. Close
BankBost	BKB	250	22 1/4	22 1/4
Asarco	AR	250	20 3/8	20 3/8
SciAtlanta	SFA	200	33 3/4	33 3/4
Kellwood	KWD	200	29 7/8	29 7/8
BearStearns	BSC	200	22	22
BankTrst	BT	152	71 5/8	71 5/8
Gillette	G	150	49 3/4	49 3/4
BrisMyrsSqb	BMY	120	59 1/4	59 1/4
CMS Engy	CMS	100	24 1/2	24 1/2
Albertsons	ABS	67	52 7/8	52 7/8

a-From 4:15 p.m. to 5:00 p.m. Eastern time, NYSE only. b-WSJ calculation, estimate.

price in recent months and whether the stock is approaching a new annual high or low. Our same share of GM ranged from a low of $49 a share to a high of $75 a share. This information can be useful in examining the stability or volatility of the stock by comparing how the stock's price range compares with that of other stocks. *Column 3* lists the exchange code or name for each listed company. General Motors Corp. is listed as GM.

Column 4, the **dividend** column, indicates the annualized payment per share designated by a company for distribution to the stockholders. On common shares, the dividends vary and are issued at the **board of directors'** discretion. Sometimes dividends reflect the corporation's degree of prosperity, but growth companies generally pay little or no dividends because profits are reinvested in the business. Dividend rates are quoted in dollars, not percentages, and represent expected annual dividends, based upon those of the last quarter.

A lower case *x* in front of sales volume *(Column 7)* indicates the stock is trading **ex-dividend,** meaning that those buying the stock on that day will not be entitled to receive the next dividend since the company has already tabulated which stock holders will receive payment. Selling ex-dividend may temporarily weaken a stock's price, but it has no effect on its underlying value. Extra or stock dividends are indicated by footnotes following the cash amount.

| FIGURE 12–2 | American Stock Exchange Composite Transactions (Sample) |

Quotations as of 5 p.m. Eastern Time
Friday, June♦ 199▲

52 Weeks Hi	Lo	Stock	Sym	Div	Yld %	PE	Vol 100s	Hi	Lo	Close	Net Chg
						–A–A–A–					
9 1/2	8 1/2	AIM StratFd	AST	.75e	8.2	...	334	9 1/8	9	9 1/8	+1/8
19	4 1/8	ALCComm	ALC			24	546	17 3/4	17 5/8	17 3/4	—
8 3/4	4 1/8	AMC Entn	AEN	1.14e	13.0	24	38	8 3/4	8 1/4	8 3/4	+3/8
9/16	3/32	AOI Coal	AOI			dd	142	5/32	1/8	1/8	—
1 3/4	5/8	ARC Int	ATV			dd	302	1 5/8	1 9/16	1 5/8	+1/8
6 1/2	1 1/2	ASR Inv	ASR	.20j		dd	136	1 11/16	1 5/8	1 11/16	—
4 3/4	1 1/4	**AcklyComm**	**AK**			15	1415	5	4 3/8	4 13/16	+7/16
6 3/8	3 7/8	AcmeUtd	ACU	.15j		dd	10	4 3/8	4 1/4	4 3/8	—
5 5/8	2 1/4	ActionInd	ACX			dd	5	2 5/8	2 5/8	2 5/8	—
6 1/2	3 1/4	AdamsRes	AE			10	52	5 1/4	5	5	—1/4
5	3	AdvancFncl	AVF			11	86	3 15/16	3 7/8	3 7/8	—1/8
16 1/8	10 5/8	AdvMagnet	AVM			cc	101	14	13 5/8	14	—
11 3/8	3 3/4	AdvMed	AMA			dd	40	5 1/4	5	5 1/8	—
7	3 1/4	**AdvPhotonix**	**API**			...	2730	4 3/4	4	4 3/4	+5/8
3 7/8	1 3/4	Aerosonic	AIM			7	50	3	3	3	+1/16
17	7 3/4	AirWaterTech	AVT			dd	245	13 3/8	13 1/4	13 1/4	—1/4
s 29 1/2	17 3/8	AirExprss	AEX	.14	.7	12	251	19 1/2	19 1/8	19 1/4	—3/8
1 1/2	3/4	AircoaHotel	AHT			dd	5	1 5/16	1 5/16	1 5/16	—
10 5/8	6 1/4	AlbaWalden	AWS			13	5	10 1/4	10 1/4	10 1/4	+1/8
1 7/8	11/16	Alfin	AFN			dd	131	1 1/2	1 7/16	1 1/2	—

52 Weeks Hi	Lo	Stock	Sym	Div	Yld %	PE	Vol 100s	Hi	Lo	Close	Net Chg
						–B–B–B–					
5 3/4	1 7/8	B&H Ocean	BHO			dd	11	3 1/16	3 1/16	3 1/16	—1/16
s 7 7/8	6 3/8	BAT Ind	BTI				376	6 11/16	6 1/2	6 5/8	—1/16
72	56 3/4	BHC Comm	BHC		2.8	11	86	71 7/8	71 3/8	71 1/2	—1/4
3 3/8	7/8	BSD Bsp	BSD	2.00p		dd	52	1	15/16	15/16	—1/8
s 15	8 3/8	**BakerMichael**	**BKR**			15	108	9 1/2	9	9 1/2	+1/2
5 3/4	3 3/8	Baldwin Tech	BLD			dd	31	4 1/2	4 3/16	4 1/4	—1/8
s 19 1/4	12 5/8	Bancfirst	BNF	.64f	3.9	&	24	16 3/4	16 1/2	16 1/2	—3/8
21 3/4	18 3/4	BancroftFd	BCV	1.82e	8.4	...	47	21 5/8	21 1/2	21 5/8	+1/4
12 1/4	5 5/8	Banister g	BAN				28	12 1/8	12	12 1/8	—1/8
3/8	3/32	BanyanHtl	VHT			dd	1365	1/2	3/8	13/32	+1/32
2 5/8	1 1/8	BanyanIncoTr	VST			dd	1	2 1/16	2 1/16	2 1/16	...
27	9 3/4	Barnwell	BRN	.30	1.4	9	1	20 7/8	20 7/8	20 7/8	—1/4
19 3/4	5 7/8	BarrLabs	BRL			cc	161	18 1/4	17 3/8	17 7/8	+1/2
1 3/8	1/2	BarristerInfo	BIS			dd	65	15/16	7/8	15/16	+1/16
9	5 5/8	BarryRG	RGB			9	165	8 1/8	7 3/4	7 7/8	+1/4
14 3/4	9 7/8	BayMeadws	CJ	.30m	2.8	42	80	10 7/8	10 5/8	10 7/8	+3/8
6	2	BayouStl	BYX			dd	5	4 3/4	4 3/4	4 3/4	...
1 1/8	1/2	BeardOil	BOC			dd	27	1 1/16	1 1/16	1 1/16	+1/16
13 1/2	1 5/8	**Belmac**	**BLM**				221	2 3/4	2 5/8	2 5/8	—3/16
19 1/4	12	BenchmkElec	BHE			19	15	16 3/4	16 5/8	16 5/8	...

P/E

Column 5, the **yield** column, refers to the current yield on the investment. It is calculated by dividing the annual dividend ($3.87) by the closing share price ($64), which in the above example results in a 6 percent yield. Yields vary in size and measure the current income return offered by the stock, but not its capital gains potential. If there is no dividend, the yield is 0 percent. This yield can be compared with other stocks and with the interest paid on debt instruments such as bonds.

Column 6, the **price/earnings ratio (P/E)** column, shows what investors are willing to pay for a stock at any given time. The P/E ratio formula is the stock's current price ($64) divided by the latest available annual earnings per share ($3.87). The P/E ratio is used as an indicator of stock performance. It is probably the single most important number an investor can know about a stock. In essence, it indicates how much investors are willing to pay for each dollar per share a company earns. A P/E can be underinflated or overinflated in relation to a stock's real value. A low P/E ratio of less than 7 or 8 may signify an undervalued bargain, a struggling company, or an uncertain economy. You would need additional information on the stock to make a valid judgment. A stock's P/E should be measured against the P/E ratio of companies within the same industry and its own P/E record over the last 10 years.

The higher the P/E ratio, the higher priced the stock, relative to its earning power. But some industries traditionally have higher P/E ratios than others. These differences may reflect growth prospects, accounting policies, or risks, as well as the stability of earnings.

Column 7, the day's **sales volume,** is expressed in hundreds with trades in lesser amounts preceded by a lower case *z.* Thus, 8362 means that 836,200 shares were traded. Transactions generally take place in units of 100 shares known as **round lots.**

Columns 8 to 10 show the price fluctuations during the day. The **high** (64¾) reflects the highest price paid for the stock during that day's session ($64.75); the **low** (63) is the lowest price paid; and the **close** (64) is the day's final sale of that stock.

Column 11 represents the **net change,** the difference between a stock's closing price on a given day and its close in the preceding session. The direction of that change is shown with a plus or minus for each point or fraction of a point. In the GM illustration, +⅜ indicates that today's closing price of $64 was three-eighths of a dollar (or 37.5 cents) higher than yesterday's closing price. This means that yesterday's closing price was 63⅝ (or $63.62).

Unless followed by a symbol indicating a special stock issue, listed stocks are **common stocks,** shares without any fixed rate of return on investment. A *PF* designation indicates a **preferred stock** (discussed further on). Stock names are abbreviated alphabetically under the exchanges on which they are traded—NYSE, AMEX, or OTC. An *S* after the stock name indicates a **stock split.** A split occurs when a company issues additional shares to its stockholders. It is simply a proportionate increase in the number of shares outstanding without a similar increase in assets. In a two-for-one split, for instance, the 100 shares you own in a given company would be doubled, giving you 200 shares, although it does not change your stake in the company. You still own the same percentage of shares outstanding as you did before. It is like swapping a $20 bill for two $10s. The value of each share should normally be approximately half of what it was before the split. What is the purpose of a stock split? Many firms split shares to move the price into a more favorable trading range. It may serve to make a company's stock more accessible to the public and thereby create more demand, thus driving the price of the stock upward, although in most cases this has largely been discounted.

It is important to realize that there is no clear-cut way to analyze a particular stock from the quotation pages. They just give you some basic data, past and present, about the stock, but no in-depth analysis. The information is comparable to the sports scores reported in your daily newspapers.

Over-the-Counter (OTC) Quotes

Although all over-the-counter stocks are essentially traded the same way, investors may have to hunt in different places for prices. NASDAQ lists in its **national market issues** about 3,000 of the most actively traded stocks.

Figure 12–3 (NASDAQ National Market Issues) lists the more heavily traded OTC stocks. It shows actual transaction prices, such as those quoted for exchange-listed stocks. The format is similar to that for the NYSE.

Another 3,000 NASDAQ–listed securities are quoted under NASDAQ Small-Cap Issues (see Figure 12–4). These are securities that, primarily because of smaller size (capitalization) or very thin trading volume, are not on the national market issues list. The smallest firms, as mentioned previously, are listed on the pink sheets.

The pink sheets contain two prices for each stock, known as a *bid* and *ask price.* The **bid price** (the lower figure) is the price offered by the market maker or broker if you wish to sell. The **ask price** (the higher figure) is what you must pay to buy—the

FIGURE 12–3 NASDAQ National Market Issues (Sample)

52 Weeks Hi	52 Weeks Lo	Stock	Sym	Div	Yld %	PE	Vol 100s	Hi	Lo	Close	Net Chg
				–A–A–A–							
s 39	12 1/4	AtlanSEAir	ASAI	.28	.7	37	3320	38 3/4	38	38 1/2	+1/8
25 3/4	10 1/4	AtlTeleNtwk	ATNI	.40	2.5	15	378	16 1/4	15 3/4	16	+1/4
24 3/8	7 5/8	Atmel	ATML		...	27	762	24 1/4	23 5/8	24 1/8	+1/8
10 1/2	**6 1/4**	**AtrixLabs**	**ATRX**		**...**	**...**	**316**	**8 1/2**	**7 3/8**	**8 1/4**	**+5/8**
12 1/4	8 1/2	AtwoodOcn	ATWD		...	dd	11	11 1/8	10 5/8	10 5/8	–1/8
29	13 1/2	AiBonPain A	ABPCA		...	52	475	24 3/4	24	24 3/4	+1/4
6 3/8	2 1/2	AuraSystems	AURA		...	dd	1966	5 5/8	5 1/4	5 5/8	+1/8
n 15 1/2	12 1/2	AusoexSys	ASPX		...	...	723	13 1/2	12 3/4	13 1/2	+1/2
12 3/8	8 1/4	Autocam	ACAM	.52t	5.3	12	28	10	9 1/2	9 3/4	–1/4
8 3/4	6	AutoclvEngr	ACLV	.24	3.2	cc	51	7 1/2	7 3/8	7 1/2	–1/8
56 1/2	32 3/4	Autodesk	ACAD	.48	1.0	25	9875	50 1/2	49 3/4	50 1/4	+1/2
10 5/8	3 5/8	AutoFinGp	AUFN		...	...	368	10	9 1/2	9 3/4	–1/4
n 15	**6 1/2**	**AutoImmune**	**AIMM**		**...**	**...**	**169**	**12 1/2**	**11 1/4**	**12 1/4**	**+7/8**
5	3	AutoInfo	AUTO		...	17	58	4	3 5/8	3 7/8	–1/8
27 3/4	13	AutoIndus A	AIHI		...	26	1075	27 1/2	26 7/8	26 7/8	–5/8
50 1/2	8 3/4	Autotoe A	TOTE		...	63	1693	45 1/4	44 1/4	44 1/4	–5/8
38 3/4	24 1/2	Avatar	AVTR		...	dd	213	36 1/4	35 1/2	36 1/4	+1/4
n 27 1/2	19	AvidTch	AVID		...	...	230	22 1/4	21 1/2	22 1/4	+3/4
3 1/4	**7/8**	**Avondale**	**AVDL**		**...**	**dd**	**32**	**2 7/8**	**2 5/8**	**2 5/8**	**–3/16**
9 1/8	**4 5/8**	**AztarCp**	**AZTR**		**...**	**21**	**13607**	**9 1/8**	**8 5/8**	**9 1/8**	**+1/2**
4 1/2	2 1/16	AztecMfg	AZTC	.10	2.6	19	26	3 7/8	3 5/8	3 7/8	–1/8

52 Weeks Hi	52 Weeks Lo	Stock	Sym	Div	Yld %	PE	Vol 100s	Hi	Lo	Close	Net Chg
				–B–B–B–							
36	26 1/2	BB&TFnl	BBTF	1.00	3.1	11	210	32 3/8	31 7/8	32	–1/4
14 3/4	8 3/4	BE Aerospace	BEAV		...	16	341	13 3/4	13 1/4	13 3/4	..
9 1/2	**6 1/4**	**BEI Elec**	**BEII**	**.08**	**1.1**	**7**	**61**	**7**	**6 1/4**	**7**	**+3/4**
5 1/2	2 3/8	BEI Hldg	BEIH		...	10	44	5 1/8	5 1/8	5 1/8	–1/8
12 1/2	2 3/4	BFS Bank	BFSI		...	7	65	12 1/8	11 3/4	12 1/8	–1/8
43	32	BGS Sys	BGSS	.60a	1.8	16	77	33 1/2	33	33	–1/4
19 3/4	**14**	**BHA GpA**	**BHAG**	**.05p**	**.3**	**24**	**1014**	**18**	**14 3/4**	**15 1/4**	**–1 3/4**
n 21 1/4	17 1/4	BHC Finl	BHCF		...	...	10	19	18 3/4	18 3/4	–1/4
12 1/8	6 3/4	BI Inc	BIAC		...	30	81	8	7 1/2	7 1/2	–3/8
21 7/8	11	BISYS Gp	BSYS		...	dd	612	20	19 5/8	19 5/8	+1/8
n 7 1/4	4 1/2	BKC Semi	BKCS		...	...	2	5 3/4	5 3/4	5 3/4	..
84 1/8	**37 1/4**	**BMC Softwr**	**BMCS**		**...**	**20**	**10701**	**52 1/4**	**47 1/2**	**50 7/8**	**+3 1/8**
14 3/4	8	BMC Wst	BMCW		...	12	17	14	13 3/4	13 3/4	+1/4
3 7/8	**7/16**	**BNH Bcshr**	**BNHB**		**...**	**dd**	**20**	**2**	**2**	**2**	**–1/2**
7 3/4	4 1/4	BPI Pack	BPIE		...	dd	353	6 5/8	6 1/8	6 3/8	–1/4
n 3 1/8	**1 5/8**	**BPI Pack wtA**			**...**	**...**	**310**	**2 1/8**	**2**	**2**	**–1/4**
n 2 1/2	**1**	**BPI Pack wtB**			**...**	**...**	**733**	**2 3/8**	**2 1/8**	**2 1/8**	**–1/4**
35	20 3/4	BSB Bcp	BSBN	1.00f	3.1	8	9	32 1/4	30 3/4	32	+1/8
▲ 32 3/4	20 7/8	BT Fnl	BTFC	1.08f	3.3	12	128	33	32	32 1/4	+1/4
3 1/4	**1 1/2**	**BTR Rlty**	**BTRIC**		**...**	**...**	**84**	**3 1/8**	**2 7/8**	**2 7/8**	**–3/16**
4 5/8	1 1/8	BT Ship	BTBTY		...	...	84	3 1/8	3	3	+1/8

• • • • • •

price sellers are asking for. On most actively traded stocks, bid and ask are only pennies apart. The gap between bid and ask is known as the **spread.** This represents the OTC broker's costs and commissions. In general, the less frequently a stock is traded, the wider the spread.

When an investor places a buy order in the OTC market, the broker may fill it from a personal inventory if he or she has a client who has put in a sell order. If it is not available in inventory, the broker may tap into NASDAQ's electronic network to locate other brokers and buy from whoever offers the lowest price.

In December 1984, NASDAQ started the new Small Order Automated Execution Service. Traders with on-line computer terminals who want to buy or sell up to 500 shares of any NASDAQ stock simply enter their request onto a terminal and have the NASDAQ computer complete the transaction for them. The computer automatically selects the best price in the nation. Investing via on-line computers is discussed in Chapter 10.

Common Stock and Preferred Stocks

There are two basic types of stock known as **common stock** and **preferred stock.** Both are perpetual securities. This means they have no expiration date and are valid as long as the company exists. Common stockholders, as part owners of a corporation, receive dividends only if the company earns a profit and decides to issue some

FIGURE 12–4			NASDAQ Small-Cap Issues (Sample)			

Issue Div	Vol 100s	Last	Chg	Issue Div	Vol 100s	Last	Chg	Issue Div	Vol 100s	Last	Chg
A&A Fd g	154	1	...	Caprck	549	7/16	+ 1/16	FnData	65	3 1/8	+ 1/16
AAON	6304	1 3/16	+ 5/32	Capucin	100	1 1/32	− 1/32	FnDt wtA	60	15/16	...
ACR	20	1/2	− 3/32	CarMrt	170	4 7/8	...	FnDt wtB	120	15/16	+ 1/16
ACS Ent	392	14 1/2	− 3/4	CarMt wt	77	1 3/4	...	Finlind	3	45	...
ACTV	578	6 7/8	+ 3/8	CareCon	204	3	...	Fd SVP	4	1 7/16	...
AFP	70	13/16	+ 1/8	viCreEn	20	4 1/4	+ 1/4	Firetct s	105	1 3/8	+ 1/8
AGBag	186	1 1/4	...	Caretnd	116	1 21/32	− 3/32	FAmHlt	662	4 5/8	+ 1/8
AGP & Co	161	2 3/4	− 1/4	CaroFt pf2.08	3	31 1/2	...	FCmcBsh1.00	4	70	− 3 1/2
APA	40	2 3/4	− 1/4	CaroF pf2.40	4	27 1/2	...	FtFdBcp.14e	17	20 3/4	− 3/4
ASA Int	139	2 1/4	− 1/8	CarolB	59	6 3/8	+ 1/8	FFnBcp.30e	30	14 3/4	+ 1/4
ATC Env	71	4 7/16	+ 3/16	CascS Bk	11		...	FtFCrb pf1.05	11	23	− 1
ATC wtB	8	3/8	− 1/4	CecoEn s	43	3 3/4	+ 1/2	FtLbty pf.24e	22	29 1/4	− 1/4
ATC	264	11/32	+ 1/32	CellCm	144	4 1/2	...	FtNtFlm	4667	7 5/16	− 11/16
Abatix	175	4 3/4	− 1/8	CelrPr	1	11/32	...	FStMn	20	17/32	+ 5/32
AberRs	178	3 1/8	− 1/8	CellrTc	85	6 3/4	− 1/8	FUtBG pf2.12	13	43 3/4	+ 2 1/2
Abraxas	430	8	...	CellTc wt	30	2 1/2	− 1/8	FFFnpfA1.75	34	34	− 2
AcrnVn	14	1 3/4	...	CelTel	40	2 5/16	...	Fstmark	14	4	...
ActnPr	80	2 1/2	− 1/4	Celox	165	2 7/32	− 1/32	FschWt	40	17/32	
Actrade	80	2	...	CtrlVA	4	14 1/2	...	Fonar	3784	1 5/8	+ 3/16
Admar	259	2 5/8	− 3/16	CntMne	2242	15/16	+ 1/32	Fonic s	6530	7 1/2	+ 5/8
AcvEnv	471	1 9/16	+ 1/8	Cerprbe	110	4 1/8	+ 1/8	Fonic wt	237	12	+ 1 5/8
AdvFn pf .42	1	4 3/4	...	Certron	4	1 1/4	− 3/16	Foreind	89	4 9/16	+ 1/8
AdvMam	254	8	...	Challnt	12	2 1/8	− 1/8	Forld wtA	50	2 7/16	+ 1/8
AMam wt	358	2 7/8	− 7/16	ChmpSpt	322	15/16	+ 1/16	Forld wtB	30	1 3/8	− 1/8

• • • • • •   • • • • • •   • • • • • •

or all of it as dividends. The corporation has no responsibility to grant common shareholders any set amount of dividends. Therefore, the common shareholder takes on greatest risk for a company's success or failure. Preferred stock is a hybrid investment, containing some characteristics of stocks and some of bonds. Preferred shares typically pay more dependable, generally much higher dividends than a company's common share but normally yield less than its ordinary bond. The dividend is usually fixed, like the interest on bonds, so investors do not share in higher profits if the company prospers. With preferred shares, investors are generally primarily interested in getting income from their investment.

Preferred stocks, however, should not be confused with bonds. They are legally stocks. Like shares of common stock, preferred shares represent ownership interest in a corporation. A company risks bankruptcy when it halts or even interrupts payments on its bonds. But it runs no such risk when it skips a dividend on its common or preferred stock. That might occur if, for example, earnings are insufficient to meet dividend payments or to support the company's plans for future growth.

Preferred stock gets its name because holders get preferential treatment in certain areas. Preferred stockholders must receive their full dividend before common shareholders can get any dividends. In the event of bankruptcy, preferred stockholders are first in line after creditors (bond holders, accounts payable, notes, etc.). If the company is dissolved, its assets sold off, and there are not enough assets to go around, preferred stockholders have a prior claim and must be paid off in full before any money goes to owners of common stock. If a company is liquidated, the money due to preferred shareholders for their equity equals the "par" value of the stock, the price at which the preferred stock originally was issued.

Preferred stocks generally do not behave like stocks. (To test this rule, turn to your paper's financial pages the day after a dip in stock prices. Find the list of the big gainers—stocks that bucked the trend. Chances are that some of them are preferred issues.) This happens because the price of a preferred stock is determined much like that of a bond. When investors purchase a share of preferred, they are buying a stream of income, a stable dividend, similar to the interest on a bond. When prevailing interest rates move up, the preferred's price tends to move down along with bond prices. When rates fall, the preferred's price rises (this inverse relationship is explained in greater detail in Chapter 13, The Bond Market).

The extra degree of safety of preferred stock also provides an additional convenience. While the yield on a share of common stock may fluctuate from year to year, the payments on most varieties of preferred stock usually remain constant. Firms rarely eliminate the dividend on their preferred stock, so investors can count on a steady flow of income and plan their investments accordingly.

Most preferred stock issues are **cumulative.** That means that any preferred dividend that is skipped must be paid at a later date before common shareholders receive any dividends at all. For example, if a firm skips preferred stock dividends of $12 per share for two consecutive years, preferred stockholders must receive the $24 in arrears the following year along with the current dividend due before common stockholders can receive any payments.

There are several shortcomings in owning preferred stocks. While investors get greater security from preferred stock than from common, they usually miss out on the chance to share in common's growth. Consequently, the price of a preferred stock will not rise with the improved prospects of a firm, as common stock will. This is partly offset by the fact that the value of preferred is insulated from the effects of a downturn in the common stock. Another drawback is that owners of preferred stock do not participate in year-to-year corporate decision making since they usually do not vote for corporate directors.

Moreover, most preferred stocks are sold with a "call provision" similar to those on many bonds. That gives the issuing corporation the right to retire the outstanding issues after a certain date. It can buy them from investors at a specified price, usually higher than par. The difference between the call price and par is the **call premium.**

Dividends and Ex-Dividend

The return on common stock investment comes from either of two sources: the periodic receipt of **dividends,** which are payments made by the firm to its shareholders, or capital gains, which result from selling the stock at a price above that originally paid. The board of directors of a corporation meets and declares a dividend of a stated amount to its stockholders. These stockholders are often referred to as **holders of record.** The holders of record are the persons recorded by the corporation as owning its stock.

When a corporation's board of directors specifies the date of record, it means that all investors who are official stockholders of the firm as of the close of business on that date will receive the dividend that has just been declared. The directors indicate the payment times and other important dates associated with the dividend.

Categories of Stocks

When evaluating a stock investment, it is useful to classify stocks in a variety of categories. The following are five commonly used stock groupings:

1. Blue Chip
The name "blue chip" is a traced to the game of poker in which there are three colors: blue—the highest value, red—next in rank, and white—the lowest value. These high-grade, relatively low-risk stocks, usually refer to very large companies with many millions of shares outstanding. Being a Blue Chip stock is no guarantee of safety. IBM, the classic blue chip stock, declined by nearly 50 percent in 1992 to 1993. Blue chip companies generally have a long history of good earnings performance in recessions as well as in booms, and a long and consistent history of cash dividend payments. General Motors, Exxon, Kodak, and Dow Chemical are some examples of blue chip companies.

2. Growth
Growth stocks are those of companies that usually pay relatively low current dividends because earnings are being plowed back. They are considered attractive because of future prospects. A growth company typically suffers less of a setback than the average company during a recession, recovers more quickly, and moves forward more rapidly.

3. Income
These stocks pay higher than average dividends in relation to their market price. In order to pay these dividends, such companies must have a steady and reliable source of revenue. Investors purchase these stocks more for their price appreciation potential. Electric, gas, telephone companies, and other utilities are good examples of income stocks.

4. Cyclical
These are stocks that often furnish impressive earnings when economic conditions are improving rapidly but which suffer most when business conditions begin to weaken. Automobile, steel, cement, and construction equipment companies are examples of cyclical stocks. As a result, their stock prices tend to be more volatile.

5. Defensive
Defensive stocks are likely to do better than average, from an earnings and dividend point of view, in a period of declining business. When a recession is feared, a growing interest tends to develop in such recession-resistant and highly stable stocks. Many utility stocks are regarded as defensive issue since their slow but steady growth rate tends to hold up in recession as well as in boom years.

Three dates are particularly important to the stockholder: date of record, ex-dividend date, and payment date. The **date of record** is the date on which the investor must be a registered shareholder of the firm to be entitled to receive a dividend. Because of the time needed to make bookkeeping entries when a stock is traded, dividends remain with the stock until four business days before the date of record. On the fourth day preceding the date of record, the stock begins selling **ex-dividend.** This means that the dividend will be received by persons owning the stock on the fifth business day preceding the dividend record date.

Shareholders who sell a stock after the ex-dividend date will receive the dividend. If they sell before, the new shareholder will receive the recently declared dividend. Thus, the ex-dividend date for all practical purposes determines whether or not you were an official shareholder, eligible to receive the declared dividend. The **payment date** is the actual date on which the company will mail dividend checks to holders of record.

Double Taxation

Unlike the proprietorships or partnerships, which are both considered to be extensions of their owners, corporations are treated legally as separate entities. This results in the income earned by corporations to be taxed twice. First, corporations pay corporate income taxes on every dollar of earnings. Second, the people who own the corporation's shares must pay federal income taxes on the earnings they receive from the corporation in the form of dividends (as well as on capital gains) their shares yield. This **double taxation** weakens the incentive to make corporate investments.

Trade Orders

The most common order used on the exchange is the **trade** (or market) **order.** This order requires the broker to buy or sell at the best price available at the time the order is placed. It is usually the quickest way to have orders filled since market orders are usually executed as soon as they reach the exchange floor or are received by the broker.

Investors wishing to buy or sell at a particular price can use a **limit order.** This is an order to buy at or below a specified price, or to sell at or above a specified price. This order can be placed to remain in effect until a certain date or until canceled. It is called a **GTC** or **good till canceled** order. For example, if ABC shares were selling at $40, a limit order might be placed to buy at $38. If the quote fell to that level or below, the order would be executed. Limit sell orders are also possible. A seller might give a limit sell order at $43, which would be filled if and when the price rose to at least this level.

Losing money is inevitable. No investor buys only winners. But investors can make mistakes and still do just fine if they cut their losses short. Selling quickly prevents a stock from inflicting real damage to a portfolio. One effective way to limit losses or to preserve profits is a special type of limit sell order known as a **stop-loss order.** This is a standing order placed with a broker to automatically and immediately sell a stock if the price falls to a specific level.

Stop-loss orders can remove the investor from an unexpected, deteriorating environment before losses get out of control. They predetermine risk and prevent serious loss. Stop-loss orders thus eliminate emotional decisions and enforce a certain discipline. They are most valuable for people not disciplined enough to take small losses. They are also useful for those who are too busy to constantly monitor stock market prices and developments.

It is important to be systematic in deciding when to sell a particular stock. A prudent investor should have a predetermined stop-loss price in mind the moment he or she buys a stock. This is a figure indicating the amount the investor is willing to lose on any given issue. That keeps investors from taking too heavy a loss while they wait, perhaps forever, for the stock to turn around. The stop-loss figure might be 5, 10, or 20 percent lower than the original purchase price, and it need not be the same for every stock. Investors may want to give their speculative stocks extra latitude.

Stop-loss orders are easily placed. An investor can ask his or her stockbroker to enter an **open** or **good till canceled order,** known in the brokerage trade as *GTC orders*. Such orders remain in effect indefinitely until canceled by the customer. Placing the order costs nothing. When it is exercised, the investor pays the brokerage commission for the stock sale.

A trader should be careful not to place a stop-loss order too near the market price because there is the danger that it could cause avoidable expenses. A temporary price reversal will touch off the sale, resulting in brokerage sales commission costs.

Stop-loss orders are also used by highly disciplined investors who do not need enforced loss limits. Many will set stop-loss orders when they go on vacation so that their stocks will be monitored while they are away.

It is important to note that stop-loss orders cannot always guarantee the exact level at which a stock will be sold. Although a stop-loss order becomes effective when the stock price hits a stipulated level, the stock is sold on the next trade, which could be a great deal lower. Investors do not have any definite assurance a trade will actually be executed. Orders are generally executed in the sequence they are received. There may not be enough shares at a certain price to fill all of them. Therefore, stop-loss orders alone are not guarantees against excessive losses. This is where **stop-limit orders** come in. An investor may want to sell if his stock drops to $20 but not if it plunges any further. A stop-limit tells the broker that the price specified for the stop-loss order is the lowest his or her client will accept. If the market price takes a sudden dive, the stock will not be sold until it comes back up to $20.

During the stock market crash of October 1987, for example, the market tumbled so quickly that the stop-loss orders could not be executed at the requested price. As a result, many stocks without stop-limit orders were sold for far below the stop-loss sell price.

Standing orders can also be used to lock in profits. Suppose an investor bought 100 shares of Apple for 50 and set a stop-loss order at 10 percent, or 45. As the stock rises, the best strategy would be to move the stop-loss order along behind it. When the stock climbs to 62, the stock loss might be set at 57½, locking in a profit of 15 percent or 7½ points.

Investors may also set a **stop-profit** price, a point at which they will take their profits, for instance, when their stock has gone up by 40 percent. This is essentially analogous to a limit sell order. Such discipline will keep investors from succumbing to greed, a sin often punished by a sudden price drop.

The Magic of Margin

Margin—the very word implies risk. To be on the margin, the dictionary says, is to be on the edge, or the brink. For some investors, **margin buying,** which means buying with money borrowed from a broker, often represents being on the brink of disaster. But when used successfully, margin can multiply an experienced investor's profits.

Margin is buying and selling securities, options, or commodities on credit. Actually, buying on margin is the same as borrowing money to buy more of anything. Borrowing can vastly multiply a speculator's gains and losses because margin allows speculators to make a larger investment than they could if they had to pay entirely in cash. This is known as *leverage* (discussed in Chapter 6). The box below is an illustration of the magic of margin.

The Federal Reserve sets the percentage of cash an investor must put up to trade on margin. Since 1974, this initial requirement for common stocks has been 50 percent. That means depositing $20,000 into a margin account will get an investor a maximum $20,000 loan so he or she can buy $40,000 worth of stock. After that, stock exchanges and brokerage houses require investors to keep a maintenance margin, which is usually equal to 30 percent of the value of the position at all times. In other words, he or she must have 30 percent equity in the position at all times. Any decline comes out of the buyer's equity, not the margin debit.

Hy Roller's Hair-Raising Saga

Mr. Hy Roller, a stock speculator, overhears a hot tip in a steaming Jacuzzi at the local health spa about a biogenetic company called New Genes. The stock is selling for $5 and Hy purchases 8,000 shares. Instead of putting up $40,000 in cash, he buys on 50 percent margin, paying 50 percent, or $20,000, in cash and borrowing the other 50 percent, or $20,000, from his broker. His broker holds the shares as collateral. Mr. Roller retains ownership, but not title, to the shares.

Now the fun begins. New Genes announces a new genetic breakthrough that can restore hair growth to bald heads. The stock jumps 60 percent to $8 and Hy's holdings are worth $64,000. He sells to take his profit. After repaying his margin debt of $20,000 he has $44,000 left (minus interest charged on his loan and broker's commission). Hy started with $20,000 and now has more than doubled his money. Had he bought the stock for all cash, his gain would have been 60 percent, not the 120 percent profit which he actually earned. By buying twice as much as he could afford, he doubled his profits.

The other side of margin buying is that it can just as easily backfire. Margin buying can prove to be only a fair-weather friend to investors. It is when the stock declines that the fun is over and the trouble begins.

Suppose Mr. Roller's Jacuzzi dip was ill-fated and the hot tip had turned out to be wrong and the New Genes stock plunged from $5 to $2.50. His holdings would be worth $20,000, or just enough to cover his margin debt, leaving him wiped out of his $20,000 investment. Had Hy bought the stock for cash, he would have lost one-half of his original investment, instead of all of it. By buying twice as much as he could afford, he risks doubling his losses as well.

If the value of the position were to drop so that his or her equity were less than the maintenance margin requirement, the investor would get a margin call, requiring a deposit of some more money to bring his or her stake back to the 30 percent mark. If the investor cannot produce the extra money, the loan gets called and the broker sells out the investor's position to pay back the margin debt. The investor would get whatever remains.

Margin accounts costs should not be overlooked. Brokers do not put up margin money out of altruism but charge interest based upon the broker's loan rate. This rate is usually reasonable and generally below the rate banks charge for loans. Nevertheless, these interest charges can take a hefty chunk out of investors' profits, particularly if they hold a steady or slow-moving stock for a long time. For the investor to come out ahead, the price has to increase enough to more than offset commissions and interest rates. Any dividends earned on the stocks could also partially offset the interest charges. For that reason, investors will probably get the highest return if they move fairly quickly in and out of stocks bought on margin.

Margin leverage allows an investor to buy twice as many shares of stock for the same dollar outlay. But, as illustrated above, leverage is a double-edged sword. If the stock price drops, investors lose on the shares they bought with borrowed funds as well as on those they purchased with their own stake. Since the risks involved in trading on margin are inherently greater than investing with cash, it is by no means a suitable strategy for every investor. Certainly those who lack the temperament or the financial resources to absorb a significant loss if their investment does not materialize should not buy with borrowed funds. Similarly, those whose portfolio consists mainly of income-producing stocks should stay with a cash account. The interest on a margin loan could devour investors' dividends.

The Art of Selling Short: Catch a Falling Stock

SHORT

Though not for the novice, investors can even make money when stocks slump by selling shares short. **Selling short** reverses the market's usual prescription to "buy low and sell high." The idea is to sell high and buy low—that is, borrow stock from a broker and sell it at the current price. Your hope is that later you can buy the shares at a lower price to replace the borrowed ones. But if prices go up, you will suffer a loss when you buy the replacement shares for more than what you sold them for. *Shorting* is therefore the upside-down process of selling first and then buying.

All that individual investors need to play the short-selling game is a **margin account** with any broker. Investors use their regular portfolio or brokerage account as collateral to borrow the shares they want to sell, worth up to twice the value of their portfolio, and then sell the stock.

The key difference between just selling a stock and selling one short is that in a short sale, you are selling something you do not own. Brokers often prefer short sellers, since the money in the short account earns interest for the broker. But short selling can be very costly and risky. If you buy a stock, your potential losses are limited to the price paid. If you short a stock, your losses are limited to the price of the stock. In practice, stocks rarely lose 100 percent of their value. But losing all your margin (collateral) on a short sale is relatively easy. If the Pizza Hut stock

---

Gary Gambler Downs a Pizza

Gary Gambler becomes convinced that Pizza Hut stock will decline sharply in two weeks. He asks his broker to borrow from someone else 1,000 shares of Pizza Hut, currently selling at $42 each, and lend them to him. Gary promises to return to the broker 1,000 shares of Pizza Hut in two weeks. At the same time, he requests his broker to sell these 1,000 shares for him and credit his account ($42,000 – $250 commission =) $41,750. Within 10 days, sure enough, the stock declines to $35. Gary can collect his profit by covering his position. That is, he purchases 1,000 shares in the market for $35,000, plus $250 commission, and returns the stock to his broker. The broker debits his account $35,250, leaving ($41,750 – $35,250 =) $6,500 profit for Gary. Actually, Gary also will have to pay the broker interest for the stock loan for two weeks. If interest rates were 10 percent per annum, he would owe the broker approximately $161. Thus, Gary's net profit is ($6,500 – $161 =) $6,339. Not bad for a two week investment.

---

mentioned in the accompanying box defied Gary's expectations and rose to $62, Gary would lose over $20,000.

Given the high risk, selling short is probably a speculative activity best left to the pros. Most amateur investors do not have the time, patience, nerves, nor contacts to develop short positions and monitor them.

Another form of stock investing is through stock options known as *puts* and *calls*. This topic is discussed in Chapter 16.

The widely acclaimed stock market indexes and averages are carefully selected "representative stocks" that act as barometers of overall market conditions, trends, and day-to-day fluctuations. The major stock market indicators are the Dow Jones averages and the Standard & Poor's indexes discussed in Chapter 11.

Do Penny Stocks Make Good Cents?

Penny stocks, a designation once limited to shares trading at less than $1 but now inclusive of stocks up to $5, are another form of investment popular with many novice small investors. Because a small amount of money will buy hundreds of shares, many first-timers erroneously conclude that they are risking less. The belief that it is easier for a stock to go from 20 cents a share to $1 than from $20 to $100 keeps interest high in penny stocks. In fact, because penny stocks require enormous amounts of research to select and are difficult to track, they can fluctuate up and down 100 percent in a single day and are among the most volatile and risky investments available.

These securities, which are issued at $1 a share or less, sometimes double, triple, or quadruple in price within days after they are first sold, as speculators bid them up. Some penny stocks have even been known to increase tenfold in a short time. More often than not, buying and holding these stocks over the long run will leave the investor a loser. Other securities fluctuate but rarely become virtually worthless. When a penny bubble bursts, there is usually nothing left of the investment.

Between 1985 and 1987, nearly one-third of the companies for which penny stocks were sold went out of business, leaving their investors with nothing to show but a pained grin and empty pockets. About the only consolation investors have is that they usually invest small sums of cash to own a huge number of shares.

A typical penny stock company is often a shaky firm whose assets may be nil or limited to a small amount of capital invested by the founders. The companies are unable to borrow money from banks or raise money anywhere but in the penny stock market. Their underwritings average between $1 million and $4 million. The company therefore prices its stock at rock bottom to attract the kind of investor who naively assumes that having 10,000 shares at 10 cents each is a better deal than buying 100 shares at $10 each.

The corporate names and industries sound impressive. Still, why should a company issue 100 million shares at a dime a piece instead of say, one million at $10 each? Because the stock is a pure gamble. Some prospectuses even warn that the stock "should not be purchased by anyone who cannot afford a loss of the entire investment."

The risk of manipulation with penny stocks is great because most companies that issue them are insubstantial. The stock prices depend more upon hype and rumors or outright fictions circulated by unethical brokers than on such measurable values as earnings or assets. In addition to the steep up-and-down swings of individual stocks, the penny market was in the past subject to periodic boom followed by busts and scandals as hoodwinked investors complained about broker practices to which they turned a blind eye while the market soared. After a decade of abuses by con artists who permeated this market, the SEC stepped in. Since the crackdown, which started in 1988, the number of companies selling penny stocks had declined by about 25 percent by 1990.

New penny issues are frequently underwritten by one of a group of small investment firms located in either Denver or Boca Raton, Florida, but also found in Spokane and Salt Lake City. They often do not trade on any exchange but in markets made by these firms who also serve as brokerage houses. They are thinly traded and often can be bought from or sold back to only one or two market-making brokerage firms.

The problem of judging companies is exacerbated by hard sells from underwriting firms and by a shortage of independent analytical research due to a lack of institutional interest. Once investors have found a hot prospect, they are on their own. Once a new penny stock, known as an **IPO (initial public offering)**, hits the market, the shares are traded over the counter along with hundreds of high-priced OTC issues. Some low-priced stocks make the supplemental OTC charts of *The Wall Street Journal,* but most do not and are found only on the pink sheets, the daily listing of the most obscure publicly traded stocks. These are hard to find unless investors call a broker or read a specialized publication. An estimated two-thirds or more of so-called IPO stocks trade below their offering price within the first year.

Pink-sheet penny stocks are especially ripe for abuse because investors cannot get up-to-the-moment price quotes easily and because the companies do not have to issue regular financial reports as do NASDAQ and exchange-listed companies. To deal with high-pressure sales tactics involving pink-sheet stocks, the SEC adopted its **cold-calling** rule in 1990. The rule mandates that before a broker unfamiliar to a client can sell him or her penny stocks over the phone, the client must sign a suitability statement and a purchase agreement the first three times he or she buys shares covered by the rule. (For a copy of the rule, write to Securities and Exchange Commission, Publications, Mail Stop C-11, Washington, DC 20549.) Under another SEC rule, effective January 1993, brokers are barred from selling penny stocks without first disclosing to investors current bid and ask prices and the broker's commission. The broker must also provide a monthly update on the value of investors' holdings.

Despite these safeguards, penny stock abuse and fraud still continue. The best safeguards are still investor caution and vigilance.

Investors can usually buy and sell OTC penny stocks through any broker. It is important to make sure to trade through a firm that figures its commission on the dollar value of an order, not on the number of shares. After all, it takes only $100 to buy 1,000 shares of a 10-cent stock.

Hot Tips (Insider Information)

Information is the most precious commodity on Wall Street. Any advance, or secret, or **insider information** offers a shortcut to riches that is proving irresistible. It is a rare investor who has not been burned on a "hot tip." Hot tips offer an image of immediate wealth for little or no work. The typical tip predicts an imminent but unannounced corporate merger, a new invention, or an unexpected rise in corporate earnings. Those who hear and act on the "tip" assume they are especially knowledgeable and shrewd, being privy to privileged information.

The stock that is the focus of the "hot tip" usually experiences a price run-up because of buying pressures created by those in on the tip, each of whom almost always enthusiastically buys more shares than he or she can afford or had planned to buy. Eventually, the tip may be proven either to be false or else a partial truth embellished by wishful thinking. Reality is soon reestablished, sellers soon outnumber buyers, and the inflated stock's price collapses. The stock wizards are left angry and impoverished.

"I got this great inside tip. Buy me 5,000 shares of the Acme Prison Uniform Co."

SOURCE: "Pepper...and Salt," *The Wall Street Journal,* April 16, 1991, A-21. Reprinted by permission of Cartoon Features Syndicate.

Moreover any trading based on inside or privileged information, known as *insider trading* is illegal.

Guidelines for Evaluating Insider Information (Tips)

Investors should discipline themselves to invest with confidence and patience and to regard all rumors, hot tips, and the latest Wall Street rages and enthusiasms as mere entertainment. Life will be much safer although probably less exciting. If you know the risks but are still unable to resist the lure of a sizzling hot tip, at least learn how to evaluate one.

The following guidelines could be helpful in "managing" tips:

1. Beware of people who claim to have special information not generally available.

2. Begin by considering the source. "What is in it for him?" Perhaps your source owns the stock and wants you and others to buy it to help his or her investment along.

3. Never act on a tip that urges you to buy or sell a stock but does not explain why. You cannot readily judge what effect the information will have on the stock if you are kept in the dark.

4. If you do buy on a hot tip, place a stop-loss order at the same time. Then, if the stock's price falls, your broker will sell it when it drops to an agreed-upon level.

Hot Tips Could Get You into Hot Water

Even if your red-hot, first-hand, genuine stock tip pays off, the SEC may be waiting for you at home. It is a Federal crime for corporate officials to profit from nonpublic information about their firms. Criminal penalties are up to five years in prison and a $10,000 fine. Although criminal prosecution is rare, courts often impose civil penalties, forcing the accused to give up his gains.

Under current law, a broker caught trading on information that is not public may lose his license. Contrary to what you might expect, catching illegal inside traders is not very difficult. The NYSE, the American Stock Exchange and OTC markets all have computerized systems that can readily identify the first evidence of suspicious activity in a stock price movement. A price movement of 10 percent in a stock during the course of the trading day will flag the computer as will unusually heavy volume in an issue. It is consequently possible to retrace the rumor's path, particularly if it leads to a specific broker's office. A computer will show whether a large percentage of a stock's trades were handled by one brokerage firm. The exchange can then require brokers to produce clients' names and account records which would be passed on to the SEC.

5. Do not invest immediately after hearing a "hot tip." First conduct the necessary research, often arduous and boring, on the company and its industry to verify whether your "tip" was hot or ice cold.

Stock Market Investment Strategies

For small investors to maximize their natural edge, they may need to do what does not come naturally: shrug off what most people are saying and doing, overcome their own doubts, and rein in their enthusiasm. Discipline is one of the secrets of successful investing.

If investors were ranked according to their performance, the results would resemble a bell-shaped curve. At one end would be a very small number of individuals who do extremely well, and at the other end a very small number who do extremely poorly. The overwhelming majority's performance would be average, falling in the middle of the curve. Investors who find themselves in this middle territory frequently end up with investment results that underperform the market averages. After they pay fees and commission to brokers and investment managers, their average returns are not very impressive.

Investors who develop successful strategies share certain traits. They are willing to do enough homework to be well informed about the market. They follow guidelines to limit their risk, such as buying only stocks that have relatively low price earnings ratios, stocks whose prices have recently fallen to new 12-month lows, and others which will be discussed further on.

When to Buy, Hold, or Sell

The leading question investors often face is when to get in and out of the market. For starters, beware of trying to time the market, which involves predicting reversals in price trends in order to sell at the top and buy at the bottom of market cycles. Professionals and academicians point to statistical studies that show that picking market peaks and bottoms, a tempting mistake, is almost impossible. Trying to second-guess the immediate direction of the stock market is a very rough indoor sport. Investors should try to catch only the market's major moves, not its short-term twitches. A consistent disciplined trading plan may not be as spectacular as picking the turning points but is far more likely to be profitable over the long run.

Investors who handle their own investments should have objective data to help them decide whether to hold or sell. They need a clear picture of what is in their portfolio, what it costs, the current valuation, and most important, the prospects for further gains or losses. The critical information about an investor's portfolio should fit on one sheet of paper, no matter how many backup documents are kept stored in the investor's file cabinet.

Once an investor has all the data at hand, each stock should be evaluated as though the investor were going to buy it for the first time. Bear in mind that brokerage houses generally dislike publishing clear-cut "sell" signals because too much negative advice is bad for business. Investors can therefore view many of their **hold** recommendations as euphemistic warnings to unload. A good rule of thumb: If you would not buy a stock with today's dollars, you should not own it with yesterday's. The best strategy may be to sell.

Dollar Cost Averaging

Investors who want to avoid market timing altogether can follow a strategy called **dollar cost averaging.** This is a mechanical technique in which investors pick one or more securities and invest a fixed dollar amount each month in the same investments, over a long period of time. The idea is that the investors buy more shares with their fixed dollar amount in months when the price is low and fewer shares in months when the price is high. This method lessens investors' profits in bull markets but buffers the loss in bear markets. The seemingly magic result is that investors' average cost per share in the long run will be lower than the stock's average price.

For example, suppose a stock starts at $10, rises to $13 the next month, then falls to $7 a month later, and finally rebounds to $10 the following month. An investor who simply bought $4,000 worth at the outset would have the same $4,000 at the end, disregarding commissions. But a person who invested $1,000 a month through dollar cost averaging would end up with approximately $4,200 because of the extra shares bought when the price was down. This is illustrated in the accompanying box. Thus, dollar cost averaging helps investors follow one of investing's soundest rules: buy low.

Dollar Cost Averaging and Nondollar Cost Averaging

Dollar Cost Averaging

Date	Share Price	Shares Purchased	Amount Invested
January 1	$10	100	$1,000
February 1	13	77	$1,000
March 1	7	143	$1,000
April 1	10	100	$1,000
		Total share 420	Total invested $4,000

Current total value of 420 shares at $10 each equals $4,200.

Nondollar Cost Averaging

Date	Share Price	Shares Purchased	Amount Invested
January 1	$10	400	$4,000
February 1	13	0	0
March 1	7	0	0
April 1	10	0	0
		Total shares 400	Total invested $4,000

Current total value of 400 shares at $10 each equals $4,000.

Ratio Plans

Another popular formula plan entails maintaining a specified ratio among the different types of securities in your portfolio. For example, say you split the dollar value of your holdings 50-50 between growth stocks and highest grade (AAA) bonds. If your stocks rise while the bonds hold steady or fall, the formula tells you to sell some stocks and buy bonds in order to maintain a 50-50 ratio. The aim is to smooth out

Extrinsic/Intrinsic News and the Rise and Fall of Stock Prices

EXTRINSIC NEWS

Prices Usually Move Up	**Prices Usually Move Down**
Before a presidential election	After a presidential election
Before New Year's Day	After New Year's Day
When oil prices decline	When oil prices increase
When rate of inflation (CPI) declines	When the rate of inflation increases
When interest rates decrease	When interest rates rise
When GNP reports show growth	When GNP reports show sluggishness
When raw materials prices decline	When raw materials prices increase
	With international tensions or war
	With a sudden illness or death of a U.S. president

INTRINSIC NEWS

Prices Usually Move Up	**Prices Usually Move Down**
When companies announce dividend increases	When a company issues new shares to finance a takeover, dilutes per share value
When projections of future earnings increase	When dividends are skipped or reduced
With restructuring to reduce current debt	When acquisition rumors are disproved
When earnings increases exceed expectations	When an acquisition plan fails
With rumor of a takeover attempt	When an earnings decrease is projected or rumored
When a lengthy strike is settled	When earnings decline
When a company succeeds in increasing prices	With unexpected losses
When a company is awarded a large contract	When a company is involved in price cutting or a price war
When a company elects a new chief executive officer (CEO)	With labor unrest orwhen a major strike begins
When cash flow improves	When a company loses a big contract
When a company buys back its own shares	When a popular CEO dies or resigns.
When a company announces a new invention; files for patent	When raw materials prices increase
	With international tensions or war
	With the sudden illness or death of a U.S. president

The 21 Commandments of the Stock Market

1. **Never put more than a small fraction of assets into any investment, no matter how safe it seems.** The most important commandment is that an investor must never overcommit available risk capital.
2. **Invest only as much as you are willing and able to lose.**
3. **Do not expect to make a killing.** Over the long run, the typical stock pays a return, counting capital gains and dividends, of less than 10 percent a year. Keeping this in mind, many solid companies with a record of steadily-rising profits will look good, even if they do not promise a fortune overnight. Investors who preserve and increase their capital and earn more than that 10 percent average should consider this a satisfactory return on the investment.
4. **To evaluate your own stocks, watch several vital signs.** Easiest to monitor is the stock's P/E ratio. A sharply rising P/E can signify wild enthusiasm among investors. The stock may have reached its high for the moment. It may be time to be wary. If it goes up more than 50 percent in the time since you bought the stock, you probably should consider selling. Such a signal frequently tells you first that the bargain you found has been discovered by others and second that the price being paid may be based upon unrealistic expectations of future earnings.
5. **Know something about the industry in which the firm operates.** If you invest in high-tech issues, familiarize yourself with the scientific thinking, complex equipment, and rapidly changing markets and technologies in this field.
6. **Do not buy fad stocks.** Buying fad stocks is a common temptation for individual investors. Often these individual investors come in just when the smart money is moving out. The stock may continue to increase in price for a short time, but inevitably the pyramid collapses after many investors are drawn in.
7. **Do not overreact to the day-to-day news in making investment decisions.** When investing for long term, be reconciled to the fact that market values will fluctuate. The real question is not whether the stock price is going up or down, but whether the company is going up and down.
8. **Do not fall in love with your stocks by confusing your emotional feelings about a company with its stock.** Too often investors let their emotions interfere with their reasoning. If their stock drops, they do not want to admit that they made a mistake. Do not start defending a declining stock.
9. **Remember why you bought.** Sell if the investment premise that attracted you to a stock in the first place changes.
10. **Do not rush to sell winning stocks while hanging on to losers.** A mistake investors often make is to hold a poorly performing stock rather than sell out. Losses should be taken to conserve capital. Many traders will not admit they were wrong and are slow to cut losses and quick to take small profits. Suppose an investor has a portfolio of five stocks and there are two that

continued

The 21 Commandments of the Stock Market (continued)

are up and showing a profit, one that is unchanged, and two that are down.She will hold the two that are down and maybe the unchanged one and sell the ones that are up. But there is likely to be a good reason for the ones that are being up. So what people tend to do is sell their better stocks and retain their weaker ones, ending up with a portfolio full of losers, instead of winners. That is exactly the opposite of what should be done. Investors should be quick to cut losses and let profits run.

11. **Do not buy stocks without any overall objective and without any thought about when to sell.** However investors approach the downside evaluation, they should not make the "I'll sell when I break even" mistake. That kind of mentality is unsuitable for investment. Countless gamblers have sat in casinos mumbling to themselves "I'll quit when I break even" as they were losing it all.

    The upside evaluation may be even more difficult since contending with a rising stock is a lot tougher than selling a loser. Investors need disciplined self-control since they may have to sell when their stock is surging. Investors who lack discipline tend to ride a stock up and then back down again, finding they have made a "round trip," wiping out their unrealized gains. Few investors ever decide an objective price for a stock before they buy and sell when it reaches that price.

12. **Diversify!** A basic mistake is having too little diversification. Too often, stock portions are too concentrated in a few industries or sectors. By owning several stocks, investors boost the odds that at least some picks will be right. There is no magic number of stocks that ensures proper diversity.

    Many experts suggest that the minimum number of stocks in a diversified portfolio is five. Successful investors select stocks that respond to different economic conditions. They also do not confine themselves just to the stock market. They often have some of their money in real estate, bonds, or a money market fund. That way they can stay calm when share prices plunge and thus stick with the strategy they have laid out for themselves.

13. **Keep in mind that no one can foretell the future.** Sophisticated analysts go wide off the mark in attempts to forecast what companies will earn a year, or even a few months, in advance.

14. **Do not buy a stock just because a broker or a friend says it is sure to go up.** A do-it-yourself investor must be personally willing to check the facts about any prospective investment. What does the company do? What new products or services is it developing? What does it earn and pay per share? How healthy is the balance sheet?

15. **Never make an investment decision based upon a single telephone call.**

16. **Do not make speedy commitments.**

17. **Make sure to get in writing any unusual claims about an investment.**

18. **Do not be impressed by glossy pamphlets or fancy-sounding names.**

19. **Get proof of the broker's registration with regulatory authorities.**

20. **Make sure to ask what the risks are in an investment.**

21. **Beware of exceptional returns on very short-term investments.**

results by locking in gains and minimizing losses over the course of market cycles. Ratio plans require orderly buying and selling and periodic adjustments to maintain the ratio. Theoretically, if your portfolio is managed properly, you enhance your chances of buying low and selling high.

Dividend Reinvestment Plans

More than 1,000 companies let investors purchase additional shares without paying stockbroker commissions. This is done by reinvesting dividends directly in new shares. These plans provide an opportunity at forced savings, since investors receive increased stock holdings rather than a check which could readily be spent. It also provides the investor with dollar cost averaging on the reinvested dividends, since the dividends are reinvested in bull or bear markets on a regular basis and thus the costs average out. Dividend reinvestment plans have been popular with small investors in recent years.

Self Defense Investment Guidelines

Over the years, a number of trading rules have been accepted as guidelines on how to participate in potentially profitable but risky stock investment while conserving risk capital. To improve their chances of greater returns, investors need to be aware of common investment pitfalls and steer clear of them. The "21 Commandments" on pages 454 and 455 are some defensive guidelines that may not help investors "make a killing" in the market but may protect them from becoming like those disgruntled investors cursing and mumbling into their beer mug at the local bar.

SUMMARY

Stock ownership is evidenced by shares of stock. A share of stock reflects part ownership in a corporation. Stock ownership offers the possibility of earning dividends and price appreciation while it also presents the risk of financial losses. In the stock market, shares of American and foreign businesses are bought and sold by the general public and institutions. Of all the organized stock exchanges, the most well known are the New York and the American Stock Exchanges.

The over-the-counter market does not have a specific location as do the organized exchanges. Rather, it is composed of a computerized network of brokers who place customers' buy and sell orders into the terminal or sell out of their own stock. The most risky stock market and the one often most attractive to young and small investors is the penny stock market.

Preferred stocks are a cross between stocks and bonds. There are many types of preferred stocks, including cumulative, participating, and callable.

Investors need to decide whether they want the advice offered by a full-service broker or a low-commission, no-frills discount broker. The investor is charged a commission on both buying and selling transactions handled by the broker.

Investment in stocks offers high liquidity for the person whose financial situation is solid enough to permit some risk taking. For the experienced investor who can afford higher risk, there are some more sophisticated methods of stock investing, such as selling short and buying on margin. An intelligent investor must know how to handle and be wary of hot tips. Additionally, an investor needs to develop an overall investment strategy and follow certain guidelines in order to reduce risk and maximize gains. Securities should be bought only after acquiring a proper background and understanding of the techniques and workings of the market. Selected books and periodicals will provide investors with useful information.

KEY TERMS

Account executives

American Stock Exchange (AMEX)

Ask price

Bid price

Board of directors

Call premium

Close

Cold-Calling rule

Common stock

Composite trading

Cumulative stock issues

Date of record

Discount brokers

Dividend

Dividend reinvestment plans

Dollar cost averaging

Double taxation

Ex-dividend

Full service brokers

Good till canceled order (GTC)

Holders of record

Initial public offering (IPO)

Inside information

Investment clubs

Limit order

Margin

Margin account

Margin buying

Market order

National Association of Investment Clubs (NAIC)

National Association of Securities Dealers (NASD)

National Association of Securities Dealers Automated Quotations (NASDAQ)

National Market Issues

Net change

New York Stock Exchange (NYSE)

Over-the-counter markets (OTC)

Payment date

Penny stocks

Pink sheet

Points

Preferred stock

Price/Earnings (P/E) ratio

Primary markets

Registered representatives

Risk

Round lots

Sales volume

Secondary markets

Securities and Exchange Commission (SEC)

Securities Investor Protection Corporation (SIPC)

Selling short   Stop-loss order

Spread   Stop-profit price

Stock split   Street name

Stockbroker   Trade order

Stocks   Underwriting

Stop-limit orders   Yield

REVIEW QUESTIONS AND PROBLEMS

1. What is a share of stock? Describe the differences between common and preferred stocks.
2. Explain, using an example, how dollar cost averaging works.
3. List the different types of preferred stock and explain the features of each.
4. Discuss the practice of buying on margin and how it affects an investor's risks and potential chances of earning or losing money.
5. Define and briefly discuss each of the following institutions:
    A. SIPC
    B. SEC
    C. NASDAQ
    D. AMEX
    E. NYSE
    F. OTC
6. Give reasons why an investor would (and would not) buy a preferred stock of a company rather than its shares of common stock.
7. Where can an investor find information on over-the-counter securities?
8. What was unusual about the stock market crash of October 1987?
9. Explain how, why, and when an investor could sell a stock short.
10. How should a defensive investor handle a "hot tip"?
11. Explain how the price/earnings ratio is calculated and explain what it tells you about a particular stock.
12. Why do people invest in stocks despite the risks of doing so? Discuss.
13. If you were to buy stocks, would you use a full service or discount broker? Explain. Discuss the advantages and disadvantages of each.
14. When would you use a stop-loss order? How does it work? What problems are associated with it?
15. What sources of information are available to an investor?

16. (SHORT) You would like to sell short 500 shares of Shakey Earnings, Inc., at a market price of $50. All commissions are 2 percent, plus $32. You think the market price of Shakey will fall to $45. The annual interest rate charges by your broker is 14 percent. How many days can you leave your short position open and still make a profit?

17. (P/E)
    A. You want to purchase stocks with a P/E ratio of 6 or lower. Rave-Up Chemicals is selling at $80 per share with $1 per share of earnings. How much must earnings rise before you buy?

B. Rave-Up's earnings have risen to the target level. But its competitor's price is now $85 with earnings of $13. Which stock has the lower P/E ratio?

18. (QUICK)

A. Your firm wants to maintain a quick ratio of 2 to 1. You have current liabilities of $12,000. What quick assets must you build up to reach the desired ratio?

B. You have reached the desired ratio. Then your current liabilities triple due to an expansion of the business. By what dollar amount must you now increase quick assets to maintain the desired 2 to 1 ratio?

SUGGESTED PROJECTS

1. You have just won $100,000 in a state lottery. Explain why you would (or would not) invest the money in the stock market. How would you go about investing in stocks? What types of stocks would you pick and why? What would be your overall investment objectives? What strategies would you use to achieve your objectives?

2. Look at the financial page of your local newspaper. Find out what all of the various financial quotations mean. Make a list of all the quotations and symbols that you cannot figure out and bring it to class. Ask your instructor to explain these to you.

3. (MANAGE) Your parents hire you as their money manager and give you $10,000 to invest for them in the stock market. Look through the financial pages of the newspapers and invest this money over the next two months. Keep track of your investments and after two months calculate the percentage gains or losses of your portfolio. Evaluate and analyze your investment record over the past two months and explain what conclusions you can draw from this exercise. Keep a record of your investments on a chart similar to the one below.

1	2	3	4	5	6	7	8	9	10
Name of stock	Date of purchase	Quantity purchased	Purchase price	Total value	Date sold	Quantity sold	Selling Price	Total amount received	Percentage gain or loss

INFORMATION RESOURCES

Angrist, Stanley. "What's Your Order?" *The Wall Street Journal,* October 20, 1989, R-22.

Boyd, Brendan, and Louis Engel. *How to Buy Stocks.* New York: Bantam Books, 1990.

"Buy High, Buy Low, Sit Pretty (Dollar Cost Averaging)." *Changing Times,* November 1990, 77–78.

"Cheap Thrills from Cheap Stocks (Penny Stocks)." *Changing Times,* April 1991, 49–52.

Churbuck, David. "Free Advice." *Forbes,* June 24, 1991, 176.

Dunham, Nancy. *Dunn & Bradstreet's Guide to Your Investments.* New York: Harper and Row, 1988.

"Futures Shock." *Time,* June 29, 1992, 69.

Giese, William. "Awesome Stock Picks from Your Kids." *Kiplinger's Personal Finance Magazine,* March 1992, 67–70.

———. "Cutting Out the Broker." *Kiplinger's Personal Finance Magazine,* April 1993, 85–86.

Gitman, L. and M. Joehnk. *Investment Fundamentals.* New York: Harper and Row, 1988.

Graham, Benjamin. *The Intelligent Investor.* 4th ed. New York: Harper and Row, 1986.

Graham & Dodd. *Security Analysis.* 5th ed. New York: McGraw-Hill, 1987.

Herman, Tom. "Preferreds' Rich Yields Blind Some Investors to Risks." *The Wall Street Journal,* March 24, 1992, C-1.

"How to Launch an Investment Club." *Money,* May 1989, 117–125.

"Investment Clubs Beat the Pros." *The Wall Street Journal,* March 27, 1992, C-1.

Jasen, Georgette. "Cheap Margin Loans Are Tempting, But Beware." *The Wall Street Journal,* April 21, 1993, C-1.

Lynch, Peter. *One Up on Wall Street.* New York: Simon and Schuster, 1989.

———. *Beating the Street.* New York: Simon and Schuster, 1993.

Malkiel, Burton. *A Random Walk Down Wall Street.* New York: Norton Books, 1985.

National Association of Investors Corporation (NAIC). Write the association at 1515 East Eleven Mile Road, Royal Oak, MI 48067.

National Association of Securities Dealers (NASD). Call the association at 301/590-6500.

"The Penny Stock Boys Are Back." *Business Week,* July 20, 1992, 42–44.

"The Penny Stock Scandal." *Business Week,* January 23, 1989, 74–82.

Pring, Martin. *Technical Analysis Explained.* New York: McGraw-Hill, 1985.

Rosenberg, Claude N., Jr. *Stock Market Primer.* Warner Books, 1987.

Rothchild, John. *A Fool and His Money.* New York: Penguin Books, 1990.

Schiffres, Manuel. "Best Brokers for Small Investors." *Kiplinger's Personal Finance Magazine,* November 1991, 54–58.

———. "The Discount Connection." *Kiplinger's Personal Finance Magazine,* July 1993, 63–67.

———. "Getting Started in Stocks." *Kiplinger's Personal Finance Magazine,* July 1992, 51–55.

Securities and Exchange Commission (SEC). To check whether a broker has been accused, acquitted, or convicted of SEC violations, investors can call or write the SEC, Public Reference Branch, 450 Fifth Street NW, Washington, DC 20549. 202/272-2618. (For a copy of the cold-calling rule, write to the SEC, Publications, Mail Stop C-11, Washington, DC 20549.)

The Securities Investor Protection Corporation (SIPC). Congress created this private nonprofit corporation to protect investors in cases of brokerage house bankruptcy. (202) 731-8300.

"Trading on the Inside Edge." *Time,* June 15, 1992, 47–49.

"Victims of Brokers Have a Powerful Ally." *The Wall Street Journal,* April 16, 1992, C-1.

The Wall Street Journal Guide to Understanding Money and Markets. Access Press, 1988.

"You, Too, Can Own Stock." *The Wall Street Journal,* October 17, 1989, C-1.

The World of Stocks

How to Read a Corporate Annual Report

In order to reduce the chance that any one stock becomes a severe disappointment, investors need to acquire some basic accounting knowledge and take the time to use it. The challenge to small investors is to know how to decipher and digest often arcane information and to dig out the important data from annual reports. Most nonprofessional investors do not know how to read a balance sheet and miss a significant portion of the investment information contained in an annual report.

If you are already a shareholder or are considering investing in a company, the annual report is a valuable storehouse of information and should be "must reading." It may not be as exciting as a mystery novel, but it is full of clues that can help you become a sleuth in ferreting out the lowdown on each company. It will provide you with the relevant financial and operating facts about a company and a chance to evaluate the "quality" of is earnings.

Shareholders' reports can de daunting. For the most part, they have been getting slicker and fatter. Some weigh in like a fashion magazine or sales catalogue. They are crammed with esoterica and many look as if they were written not just by but also for accountants. But an investor need not be a CPA or MBA to glean the important information. What is needed most is a little perseverance.

The annual report is a ritual of corporate America. It is a company's number one public relations tool and is meant to impress not only actual and potential shareholders but also Wall Street analysts, bankers, and customers.

Unfortunately, most shareholders look at the colorful layout, the flashy photographs, and some of the topical items but do not read the financial statements and the footnotes. Few shareholders spend much time studying the financial tables and detailed footnotes that contain the real vital information needed to evaluate the condition of a company, mainly because they do not know what to look for.

Professional investors, however, focus their attention upon the back of the report, where the numbers are. The main function of a report is financial disclosure.

Companies do not put out annual reports voluntarily. They are required be the Securities and Exchange Commission to inform shareholders of the past year's audited financial results and disclose any relevant information that can materially affect the way investors evaluate a company and its stock.

Balance Sheets and Income Statements: Barrels of Facts

When reading an annual report, most shareholders have a tendency to focus only upon a company's **earnings per share.** Based on that figure and its change from the previous year, many shareholders feel they can predict the future direction of a company. The tendency to go for the bottom line may be natural and tempting, but the figure is virtually meaningless unless the numbers behind it are also investigated. A company's earnings per share may be inflated or reduced by some special item, such as the sale of a subsidiary or other assets. While an income statement immediately reveals rising or declining revenues and earnings even to the most naive investor, a **balance sheet** is more subtle.

A balance sheet can tell an investor how deeply a company is in debt, how well it will be able to meet its short-term financial commitments, and how much asset value lurks behind its stock. The balance sheet gives a picture of the financial condition of a company on the last day if its fiscal year, which for most firms is December 31. It presents assets, liabilities, and share equity for the company as that date. The income statement, on the other hand, reflects a company's operating results during the entire year covered by the reports. It depicts revenues, expenses, and income or losses for the year.

Chief Executive's Message

This message, which contains a synopsis of the firm's annual earnings and sales figures, should not be dismissed as mere corporate window dressing. Investors can learn a lot about the trustworthiness of management and how it intends to move the company ahead by evaluating the chief executive's comments.

Investors should look for comments on how the company plans to meet its goals for the year. Are new products, marketing programs, or major capital projects in the works? Look for an honest, forthright discussion of factors, both good and bad, that have affected the company's performance. It may be a good idea to examine a few years' worth of reports to check the chief executive's track record for prediction. Investors can request the company's shareholder relations department to send them annual reports for the three previous years to review along with the current one.

Auditor's Report

After analyzing the stirring message from the chief executive and poring over the vital statistics, an investor would do well to peruse the auditor's opinion. It is not enough just to note that a reputable accounting firm has reviewed the company's annual statements. It is imperative to know what the auditor had to say about it. The auditor's report will indicate whether the auditor had any problems or quibbles with the company's figures and if there are any contingencies worth knowing about. A long auditor's statement usually spells trouble.

But no mater what the auditor's report says, an investor must carefully analyze and review an annual report because there are certain things the auditor's report definitely does not do. Because it is just an opinion as to whether material misstatements exist in the financial statements, the auditor's report does not evaluate the financial quality of a company. The reader must interpret those financial statements and make his or her own assessment of what condition the company is in. Neither does the auditor pass judgment on the wisdom of management decisions. These decisions are reflected in the financial statement to a certain extent, helping the investor assess the wisdom of management's decisions for themselves.

Ratio Analysis

If you really want to do some digging, use a procedure called **ratio analysis,** which involves comparing various financial statement figures, such as current assets to current liabilities. The numbers you get should be checked against industry averages. *Dunn and Bradstreet's Industry Norms and Key Business Ratios,* which can be found in many libraries, gives average ratios for a broad range of businesses.

The following are some key ratios that you can examine:

Current Ratio

For an important indicator of a company's financial soundness, divide the company's total current assets by its total current liabilities. Total current assets consist of cash, marketable securities, accounts receivable, and inventories. Total current liabilities are all items due or payable within 12 months. The result is called the **current ratio.** Generally a ratio of 2 to 1 indicates that the company has sufficient assets on hand to meet its immediate debt. If it is less, the company could be overburdened with debt. In this kind of bind, a firm will have no funds left to invest in itself after paying off its debts. The trend in the current ratio should be looked at over the past several years. Some annual reports provide the current ratio for the past 10 years in a financial summary.

$$\text{Current Ratio} = \frac{\text{Total Current Assets}}{\text{Total Current Liabilities}}$$

Long-Term Ratios

The next thing to calculate is a company's long-term debt relative to its total capitalization. Total capitalization refers to the assets a company has to work with and is calculated by subtracting intangible assets and current liabilities from total assets. When a company is burdened with much long-term debt, it has substantial debt service to sustain. The risk of having profits threatened by a rise in interest rates makes a company's stock less attractive. If long-term debt exceeds two-thirds of a company's capitalization, the stock should be avoided.

Of course, taking on long-term debt in itself is not an indictable offense. It is only the magnitude of debt and the burden it will impose on the company that need to be considered. It is also important to compare a company's long-term debt to its equity. Debt that is growing much faster than, or is already close to or greater than, the stockholder's equity is cause for concern.

Short-Term Debt Ratio

Investors should also study short-term assets as a proportion of total assets. This gives some sense of a firm's liquidity. For example, a company might have total assets of $80 million and current assets of just $8, which would leave the firm with $72 million in fixed assets (such as land, building, equipment). This company could not easily liquidate or dissolve if it had to.

Therefore, investors also should study so-called **liquidity measures.** Look for increasing current (or short-term) assets. These are assets earmarked for use within 12 months. They include cash, marketable securities, accounts receivables, and inventories. They can protect a company in an unexpected financial crisis.

So-called **quick assets** are perhaps even more significant as a liquidity measure than current assets. These are defined as current assets minus inventories. Inventories are subtracted because they are relatively illiquid and usually cannot be sold for cash on short notice. Quick assets are what a company has immediately available to meet financial emergencies.

$$\text{Quick Assets} = \text{Current Assets} - \text{Libilities}$$

Quick (Asset) Ratio

The quick (asset) ratio (quick assets divided by current liabilities) can be even more useful than the current ratio. With inventories set aside, the investor gets an even better idea of how much a company has immediately available to match each dollar of current liabilities. A ratio of 1 is considered a standard rule of thumb.

$$\text{Quck Asset Ratio} = \frac{\text{Quick Assets}}{\text{Current Liabilities}}$$

Total Assets

Total assets also serve as a simple gauge of a company's ability to carry long-term debt, which is usually listed on a balance sheet just below total current liabilities. Look for a safe margin of at least twice as many total assets as debt outstanding.

All these measures are very important in determining investment attractiveness. If liquidity ratios are deteriorating, they are warning signals which can be ignored only at your own peril. Investors are better off with a firm that has little or no debt because from a safety standpoint, there will be fewer problems if something goes wrong.

Net Asset Value

The investor should turn to the equity section of the balance sheet and calculate **net asset value (NAV)** per common share. This is the total equity divided by the number of shares outstanding. Ideally, investors should find a rising trend over the past five years. Investors may also want to compare NAV per common share to the per share market price. If the stock sells for less than the NAV, it could be undervalued.

$$NAV = \frac{\text{Total Equity}}{\text{Number of Shares Outstanding}}$$

Often the net asset value per common share, also known as the **book value per common share,** is calculated in the annual report. Investors can also look up a company's book value in Standard & Poor's Stock Guide or the Value Line Investment Survey. These two terms are used interchangeably and are essentially what the company would be worth from an accounting standpoint after paying all of its debts. Subtract total debt from total assets; what remains is shareholder's equity.

Earnings per Share

Usually earnings per share has the greatest impact on a stock's price and is the most closely watched figure. It is a key measure of a company's profitability. Earnings per share is equal to a company's net earnings after taxes less preferred stock dividends divided by the number of common shares outstanding. For example, if net earnings is $2,000 and number of shares outstanding is 5,000,000, the earnings per share is $.40 ($2,000,000 ÷ 5,000,000 shares = $.40/share).

What a company earned in its past fiscal year, its net income per share, could be overstated to hide problems that invariably come back to haunt investors. For example, you should be suspicious if a firm's net income has continued to rise in recent years despite a dip in sales. Many companies feel compelled to report increased earnings, however small, to satisfy shareholders. The earnings could come from selling off assets to compensate for operating losses.

This can be determined by checking the income statement for an item called **extraordinary** or **nonrecurring gains.** To discourage such subterfuge, the SEC requires that extraordinary gains be listed separately from other earnings-related entries on the income statement. Investors are thus assured by looking at its income statement that a firm did or did not have real profits. For example, a firm reports that profits were up 50 percent, but this could be because it sold its headquarters building and lumped the profits from that sale in with recurring earnings. Take out that sale and profits were down 20 percent. A steady improvement in earnings over the years is a very healthy sign.

Price Equity Ratio or Price to Book Value

Price equity ratio is the price of the stock divided by equity per share. It can be calculated either by dividing the price per share by the net asset value per share, or by dividing the market capitalization by the shareholder's equity. For example, if the price equity was $4/$1 or 4, then in Wall Street terminology, the company would be said to be selling at four times book.

Price Earnings Ratio

Price/earnings (P/E) ratio is the share price of a company divided by its net income per share. For example, if the share is selling for a price of $4 and the company's net income per share is $.40, the P/E ratio is $4/.40, or 10.

A P/E ratio is often proxy for a stock's popularity. For the most part, low multiples reflect doubts about a company's or industry's prospects. Stocks sporting high P/E ratios, on the other hand, often belong to companies with seemingly nothing but blue skies in their future. But such companies are very vulnerable to changes in technology, consumer tastes, and investor perceptions.

However, many investors are convinced that the only stock market strategy that consistently produces good results in both up and down markets and fluctuating business cycles has been to buy the stock of well-capitalized, well-established businesses at a low P/E ratio. Stocks with low price/earnings ratios typically produce better long-term results than high P/E stocks do. Just as investors overpay for the earnings potential of high P/E stocks, so do they underestimate the prospects of low ones.

$$\text{P/E Ratio} = \frac{\text{Share Price}}{\text{Net Income per Share}}$$

Intangible Assets

The balance sheet entry on the asset side that is allocated to so-called **intangibles** is referred to by some as the "fun and games" section of the balance sheet. These entries should raise investors' eyebrows, especially if considerable cash values are assigned to such items. Intangibles are best described as nonphysical assets that may nevertheless be of substantial value to a corporation or may have no value at all. They include goodwill, patents, franchisees, and trademarks. Less is always better

What to Look for in an Annual Report

1. Has the company's accounting firm certified the financial results without qualifications or are there some reservations that spell potential trouble?
2. Are there any extraordinary items or special factors that have boosted or depressed the previous year's earnings?
3. How do operating earnings compare with net income?
4. Are earnings growing faster or slower than sales? In other words, is a company's profit margin or profit per unit of sales rising or declining?
5. Are last year's profits dependent on any special or controversial practices?
6. What is the company's debt structure? How much is long term and how much is short term? How much goes to make interest payments?
7. How much money is the company spending on research and development?
8. How much is the company spending on capital investment?
9. How much business does the company do abroad? Are its earnings affected by foreign exchange fluctuations? Does it have a large investment in a country that is politically unstable or having economic troubles?

when it comes to tangibles. Goodwill, like beauty, is really in the eyes of the beholder. If goodwill is a very big item or a large percentage of assets, this should make the balance sheet reader immediately suspicious and be a signal to stay away.

Inventory Turnover Ratio

Inventories should also be closely examined. The **inventory turnover ratio** is derived by dividing annual sales by inventory. The resulting number provides a measure of how many times a year goods are bought and sold. To determine the significance of this number for a particular company, you must compare it to the inventory turnover rates of its competitors. Causes for concern are declining or seesawing inventory ratios, especially among fledgling growth companies. For instance, some high-tech companies are overstated because their inventory is obsolete.

CHAPTER THIRTEEN

The Bond Markets

- To discuss why people invest in bonds and the benefits as well as risks of doing so

- To outline the positive and negative features of bonds and distinguish between the major categories

- To identify the major characteristics of bonds and the factors that affect bond prices

- To recognize the risk factors inherent in bond investing, such as inflation, interest rate fluctuations, and defaults

- To list the factors that should be considered before investing in bonds

- To illustrate how to calculate the current yield and the yield to maturity on bonds

This chapter examines another basic investment form which is part of many peoples' investment portfolio. As with stocks, there are benefits as well as risks to bond investing. This chapter will explore the bond market and how to calculate bond yields. Moreover, the techniques of assessing the safety of a bond and the risks inherent in bond investing will be examined.

There is a wide variety of bonds and other debt instruments available, and the choice is ever expanding. This chapter will explore the choices currently available and the advantages and drawbacks of each, as well as how they work and how to select the bond most appropriate for one's financial needs.

What Is a Bond?

A **bond** is, in essence, simply an IOU, a debt or a written promise by a company or a government to repay the money it borrowed no later than a specified date and at a specified interest or "coupon" rate, which is usually a percentage of the amount loaned. Bonds are issued in order to raise capital by institutions ranging from local school districts and corporations to the federal government. When you buy a $1,000 bond, you are in effect lending $1,000 to the company or government body that issued it. The borrower agrees to repay the original $1,000 **principal**, also known as the **face value** or **par** at a specified time, known as the **maturity date**, usually from 10 to 30 years in the future. Meanwhile, the bond issuer promises to pay a specified, usually fixed, rate of interest on the principal for the duration of the bond. If the bond purchased pays 10 percent a year, you can expect to earn $100 annually, usually in semiannual installments over the life of the bond.

Let us look at how stocks and bonds differ. Bondholders are not part owners of a company, as are stockholders. Bondholders are creditors and as such do not share in earnings through dividend payments, nor do they have voting rights on company matters. The return of their investment is not dependent upon how successful the company is. The value of stocks' price fluctuations is often tied to the issuing company's performance. However, the price of a corporate bond does not usually rise and fall based on the company's earnings since the face value is returned to the investor at maturity and the interest income is fixed. Furthermore, in the event of bankruptcy, the bondholders stand ahead of the stockholders to collect any of the remaining assets of the company. Other similarities and differences between stocks and bonds are noted further in this chapter.

Bonds, Notes, and Bills

Debt instruments come in long, intermediate, and short-term maturities. If the agreed-upon repayment period (or maturity date) is more than 10 years, it is called a **bond**. An instrument with a maturity date of 1 to 10 years is referred to as a **note**. If the maturity is less than one year, then it is known as a **bill**. The only difference between bonds, notes, and bills is their length of time to maturity. Bonds, notes, and bills are issued from four sources:

1. The U.S. government

2. Federal agencies

3. States and municipalities

4. Corporations

The Market for Bonds

There are two markets for bonds, the new issue (primary) market and the secondary market, where previously issued bonds are traded. The largest organized secondary bond market in the world is the New York Stock Exchange Bond Trading Division, located in the same building as the New York Stock Exchange on Wall Street. Many bonds also trade on the OTC market. If everyone who bought bonds just held them until they matured, there would not be a secondary bond market. But bonds are bought and sold daily, and their value changes when interest rates rise or fall. When issued, a bond is priced at the current market level interest rate. But when changes in the economy cause a change in interest rates or in inflationary expectations, the bond's resale market price may either increase or decline, even though its face value remains the same.

Why do bond values change when interest rates rise or fall? Because when a bond is issued, the interest rate it promises to pay until it matures reflects the prevailing interest rates in effect at the time. Let us assume that the currently prevailing interest rate for 30-year bonds is 7 percent. If a company wants to issue bonds today, a $1,000 bond must promise to pay 7 percent (or $70 each year) to attract buyers. But suppose that a year later interest rates jump to 8 percent. The same company must now promise to pay 8 percent on each new $1,000 bond it issues.

But what happens to the market value of the 7 percent bond? Clearly, no one would pay $1,000 for a bond that pays only $70 per year when he or she can obtain a bond that pays $80 a year. Accordingly, the owners of the 7 percent bond would have to accept a lower price (than its face value) if they want to sell the bond. In this way, the market value falls in response to a rise in interest rate.

In the preceding example, a price of approximately $875 (or 87.5 percent of face value) would attract investors because $70 a year of interest on an $875 investment would produce a current yield of 8 percent, the same return available on newly issued bonds. Actually, the bond would not fall quite that far in value. Its redemption value of $1,000 at maturity would buoy it somewhat, depending on how close the maturity date is. The closer the maturity date, the more buoying power it has.

Any increase in market rates will cause the price of a longer-term bond to fall more sharply than that of an intermediate or short-term security. For instance, the price of a 10 percent bond due in 30 years generally falls 8.7 percent in value if interest rates rise one percentage point. But a 10 percent bond due in three years should decline just 2.5 percent with a similar 1 percent rise in interest rates. The price would drop further on a 30-year bond to compensate the buyer for earning a lower coupon for a longer time.

The rule of thumb is as follows: There is an inverse relationship between bond prices and interest rates. Bond prices generally go down when interest rates rise, and bond prices go up when interest rates fall.

Discounts, Premiums, and Yields

Bonds are usually sold in multiples of $1,000, so $1,000 is the par or face value of a bond. In bond market shorthand, bond prices are quoted without the last zero, so $1,000 becomes 100. Bonds traded with prices above par (100) are sold at a **premium,** and those traded with prices below par (100) are sold at a **discount.** For example, assume that an investor buys a bond due in 10 years with a 7 percent coupon. When the bond trades at 102 (two points above par), the investor pays $1,020 for the $1,000 bond, therefore paying a $20 premium. If the same bond trades at 98 (two points below par), the investor pays $980 for the $1,000 bond and buys it at a $20 discount.

When an investor receives $70 a year interest on a $1,000 bond, his or her return of 7 percent is the same as the stated interest rate on the bond. However, suppose the bond is held for only one year and then resold to someone else at a $20 discount for $980. The new purchaser will receive $70 a year on an investment of $980. Clearly, he or she has received a return of more than 7 percent.

Yield is the rate of return earned on a bond. It is determined by the price paid for the bond. If you pay less than par for the bond, the yield will be more than the coupon rate. If you pay more than par, the yield will be less than the coupon rate. In other words, the yield varies inversely with price.

Calculating a Bond's Return

Current Yield

CURRENT

An integral part of any bond investment decision concerns calculating yield. **Current yield** (or **coupon yield**) shows how much one can expect to receive from a bond investment each year. It is the dollar amount of interest received each year divided by the market price of the bond. It tells in percentage terms the yearly return on the purchase, given the price paid for the security.

Assume a bond with a $1,000 face value paying a 7 percent coupon interest rate, having a 10-year maturity, is currently selling for $890. The current yield is derived by the following formula:

$$\text{Current Yield} = \frac{\text{Annual (\$) Interest Payment}}{\text{Current Market Price of Bond}} = \frac{\$70}{\$890} = 7.86\%$$

The current yield would be 7.86 percent.

Current yield is much like dividend yield on stocks and should not be confused with the rate of return, a broader performance measure that includes any capital gains or losses.

Yield to Maturity (YTM)

MATURITY

When comparing alternative bond investments, a more useful yield measurement is the **yield to maturity**. The yield to maturity is the most popular measurement of a bond's rate of return and the true annual yield that an investor would receive on a bond if it were held to maturity. It calculates the relationship between the maturity value, the time to maturity, the current price, and the coupon yield of a bond. This yield calculation allocates the bond premium or discount over the life of the security.

The yield to maturity, using the same example bond as in current yield, is derived by using the formula:

$$Y = \frac{C + [P - M]/N}{[P + M]/2}$$

Y = Yield to maturity
C = Coupon yield in dollars annually
P = Par value of bond
M = Market value of bond
N = Number of years to maturity

Plugging in the figures from our above example we get:

$$Y = \frac{\$70 + [1{,}000 - 890]/10}{[1{,}000 + 890]/2} = \frac{81}{945} = 8.57\%$$

The yield to maturity would be approximately 8.57 percent. This formula provides an approximate yield figure only. A more accurate and far quicker method to calculate yield to maturity is to use a book of bond value tables.

YTM, however, assumes that the bond owner will invest the bond's periodic coupon (interest) payments at the same rate over the term of the bond. But if this interest income is spent or invested at a lower rate, the real return will be much lower than that indicated by YTM. The assumption that reinvestment rates will remain constant is a key weakness of YTM. But since no one can predict the future, we have no choice but to assume the current interest yield for the duration of the bond.

How Safe Are Bonds?

The traditional assumption was that buying bonds brings stability to an investor's portfolio. Unless the issuer runs into severe financial trouble, investors are guaranteed regular income and interest, usually paid twice annually. And if the bond is held to maturity, the investor gets back his or her original investment. Bond buyers were therefore motivated by a desire to invest their money in a safe haven with fixed returns and certain income. These qualities could cushion their losses when more volatile investments declined in value.

Bonds, therefore, used to be the financial market's haven for frightened and nervous investors. But since the mid-1970s, bonds have undergone somewhat of a transformation and behave much like stocks. This was due to two factors, both of which are related—inflation and volatile interest rates. Moreover, recent bankruptcies and defaults by corporations and public agencies are another reminder that bonds are losing a lot of their worry-free appeal.

Inflation and Volatile Interest Rates

Fears of renewed inflation, higher interest rates, or both, naturally give the bond market an acute case of price jitters. Bond investors are forever haunted by the uncertainty of interest rates, which move in ways unpredictable even by self-proclaimed experts. Interest rates can fluctuate as sharply in a day as the Dow Jones industrial average, playing havoc with bond prices. If one invests $1,000 in a bond today, there's an equal chance that in a few weeks or months the bond will be worth $850 or $1,200.

Interest rates actually have two principle components: the return that investors demand for the use of their money and the return they demand to compensate for the erosion of their money's value by the expected rate of inflation during the life of the bond. While stocks can tend to keep up with moderate inflation through rising earnings which lead to higher dividends and share prices, bonds cannot because they are fixed dollar investments. If inflation consistently runs higher than the rate an investor locked in, the interest and principal received will be worth less in purchasing power than what was paid for the bond.

Inflation is the enemy of bondholders for two reasons: it erodes the purchasing power of the bondholder's fixed investment, and it pushes interest rates higher. This means that during an inflationary period new bond issues will pay more interest than does the old bond already held by the investor, which, as mentioned, reduces the value of the old bond in the market place.

Interest Rates and Economic Conditions

But even a strong noninflationary economy could sharpen demand for credit and cause interest rates to rise, which causes bond prices to fall. Conversely, fluctuating bond prices also create an opportunity for growth of capital. A less robust economy puts a brake on inflation. There is less borrowing and less demand for goods. Interest rates tend to decline. If interest rates decline, bond prices rise because outstanding bond yields will appear very attractive. Bondholders would then be able to sell their bonds at a premium (i.e., for more than 100 points). Sluggish economic growth or recession, the nemesis to the stock market, is therefore good news for bondholders.

Investing in bonds rather than stocks requires different analytical tools and a different frame of mind. Stock prices are affected by profit expectations, bond prices by the interest rate outlook. Stocks do best in a rising economy. High-quality bonds thrive in a recession. The bond market is a safer place for investors than is the stock market, only if inflation is controlled and interest rates are stabilized. More aggressive investors trade bonds for capital gains. They buy when they think interest rates will soon decline. Then when rates fall, they sell at a profit. Beginning investors generally lack both the skill and the cash to trade bonds. Proportionately large commissions (as high as 5 percent) on small transactions make frequent buying and selling impractical.

While investors cannot avoid the risk that interest rates might rise higher than when the bonds were bought, they can hedge against it by buying shorter-term securities. As a rule of thumb, the shorter the maturity of a debt security, the less volatile will be the price fluctuations in the secondary market. Bonds with longer maturities generally pay higher yields, but, as previously mentioned, are subject to greater price fluctuations than those of shorter-term issues. The longer the maturity, the greater the risk. The extra yield has to be measured against the risk. As long as inflation is subdued, bonds remain a highly attractive investment vehicle.

Interest rates for both corporate and Treasury bonds have been declining in recent years as indicated in Figure 13–1.

The Rating Game

A bond is only as good as its issuer's creditworthiness. Because bonds represent a company's or governmental agency's ability to pay interest and repay principal many years in the future, each bond carries a rating as to its creditworthiness.

FIGURE 13–1 | **The Trend toward Lower Rates**

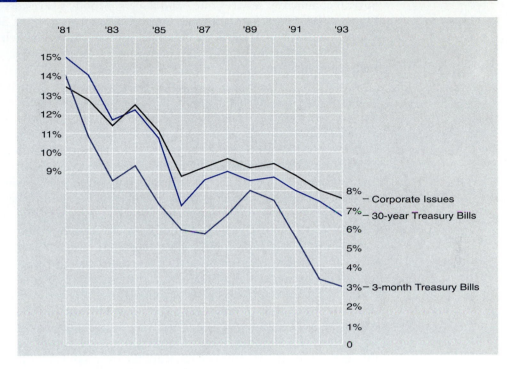

SOURCE: Industry reports for average rates of corporate issues; the Federal Reserve for Treasury bonds.

Before purchasing any corporate or municipal bonds that promise a tempting yield, the investor's first consideration should be to know about the **credit rating** of these securities. Unlike a Treasury bond or one from a blue chip company, most bonds come from borrowers whom investors may never have heard of previously—a small town in Iowa, a school district in Arkansas, an airport authority in Wyoming, or a corporation unknown to most people.

There are thousands of cities, towns, villages, counties, special districts, and private corporations all across the country issuing bonds. There are also, fortunately, a few centralized sources of information. Rating agencies make it their business to gather all the information they can about creditworthiness and to sum up their findings in just a single letter grade, very much like your performance in a college course is summed up at the end of a semester.

Essentially, ratings are assessments made by independent firms of a private corporation's or government's ability to pay interest and return principal when due. While ratings will not protect a bond from falling in value as interest rates rise, they do provide an indication of how likely an issuer is to default. They are well worth considering carefully because investors often buy bonds with the intention of holding them for a long time, quite possibly until they retire or their kids are ready for college. At that time, they expect to get their principal back and have been paid uninterrupted interest on time throughout.

Credit-Rating Agencies

Several commercial services rate bond issuers. **Moody's Investors Services**, a unit of Dun and Bradstreet Corp., lists about 11,000 issuing agencies. **Standard & Poor's Corp.**, a subsidiary of McGraw Hill, Inc., lists 8,000, while **Fitch Investors Service, Inc.**, limits itself to about 200. Another major bond-rating agency is **Duff & Phelps, Inc.**, based in Chicago.

Whatever system the credit-rating agencies use, the key distinction is between bonds considered investment grade and those below investment grade. For Moody's, the lowest investment grade is Baa; on the Standard & Poor's scale it's BBB. Anything below investment grade is popularly referred to as *junk* bonds, discussed later.

Investment grade bonds are the lowest risk investments, second only to U.S. Treasury bonds. Many institutional investors, such as pension funds, insurance companies, and mutual funds, are restricted to buying only investment grade securities for their portfolios. This policy would be a reasonable rule for an individual investor as well.

The rating process differs somewhat at each rating agency, but it follows a general pattern. The decisions are made by ratings committees of experts who investigate the creditworthiness of each bond issuer and carefully review the offering terms of each issue. They cross-examine bond analysts on their recommendations. The rating committees study statistics and usually visit the issuer as well as the investment banker handling the underwriting before recommending any rating revisions. Evaluations deal with long-term quality, not interim operations or short-term conditions. Although the ratings are not infallible, very few A-rated borrowers default on their debts. But a good grade is not an iron-clad guarantee of safety. As careful as the rating agencies are, their procedures are far from fail safe. The ratings cannot, for example, forecast market trends. Nevertheless, many investors place a great deal of reliance on the ratings provided by the major rating agencies.

WPPSS or Whoops!

S & P and Moody's both rated WPPSS (the Washington Public Power Supply System, known as "whoops") A+ early in 1981. Mismanagement, an overly optimistic view of future energy demands, and public disillusionment with nuclear power caused cancellations of all but one of the plants. The rating of the bonds tumbled all the way down to CCC by February 1983 and then the utility defaulted on $2.25 billion worth of debt. Although the downgrading gave investors time to bail out, many suffered huge losses. The bond's value dropped as low as 12, which means 12 cents on the dollar, and resulted in the biggest default in municipal bond history.

While defaults like "whoops" are rare, downgrading goes on all the time. They result from any weakened state and local government tax revenues, cutbacks in grant programs, problems of utilities financing nuclear construction programs, or corporate financial problems. In the era of merger mania, the term "high grade" or AAA-rated corporations has lost some of its allure. The mountain of debt heaped onto a company to finance a takeover can turn an investment grade bond into a junk bond practically overnight. Low-rated bonds, however, offer buyers a special incentive. They usually pay higher yields than issuers with a sounder payback record.

There is normally an inverse relationship between the rating of a bond and its (interest rate or) yield to maturity. Investors can generally depend on the ratings to run true to form, with BBB averaging higher yields than issues rated A, and A-rated

Credit-Rating Agency Classifications

Credit Risk	Moody's	Standard & Poor's
Prime	Aaa	AAA
Excellent	Aa	AA
Upper medium	A-1, A	A
Lower medium	Baa-1, Baa	BBB
Speculative	Ba	BB
Very speculative	B, Caa	B, CCC, CC
Default	Ca, C	D

Description of Moody's Four Highest Bond Ratings

"Aaa" Rating—Bonds rated Aaa are judged to be of the best quality. They carry the smallest degree of investment risk and are generally referred to as "gilt-edged." Interest payments are protected by a large or by an exceptionally stable margin and principal is secure.

"Aa" Rating—Bonds rated Aa are judged to be of high quality by all standards. Together with the Aaa group, they compose what are generally known as high-grade bonds. They are rated lower than the best bonds because margins of protection may not be as large as in Aaa securities, or fluctuation of protective elements may be of greater amplitude, or there may be other elements present which make the long-term risks appear somewhat larger than the Aaa securities.

"A" Rating—Bonds rated A possess many favorable investment attributes and are considered as upper-medium grade obligations. Factors giving security to principal and interest are considered adequate, but elements may be present which suggest a susceptibility to impairment sometime in the future.

"Baa" Rating—Bonds rated Baa are considered as medium-grade obligations. This means that they are neither highly protected nor poorly secured. Interest payments and principal security appear adequate for the present but certain protective elements may be lacking or may be characteristically unreliable over any great length of time. Such bonds lack outstanding investment characteristics and in fact have speculative characteristics as well.

The hyphenated ratings A-1 and Baa-1 indicate those credits that are considered to be better quality in the respective categories.

Within each category, Moody's has assigned the numerical modifiers 1, 2, and 3: 1 indicates that a security ranks in the high end of that rating category, 2 in the mid range of a category, and 3 nearer the low end of a category.

Description of S & P's Two Highest Bond Ratings

"AAA" Rating—Bonds rated AAA have the highest rating assigned by S & P to a debt obligation. Capacity to pay interest and repay principal is extremely strong.

"AA" Rating—Bonds rated AA have a very strong capacity to pay interest and repay principal and differ from AAA issues only in a small degree.

Plus (+) or Minus (−): The rating AA may be modified by the addition of a plus or minus sign to show relative standing within the major rating categories.

S & P's two highest ratings are followed by A, BBB, BB, B, CCC, CC, and C. It also has a D rating for bonds in default.

bonds yielding more than AA. This reflects a type of risk-return trade-off for the lender. The search for higher returns may lure the investor to the debt paper of smaller, more obscure, or troubled companies. Sacrificing safety for higher returns, of course, can be costly down the road if the company you invest in cannot meet its interest or principal payments.

The Bond Smorgasbord: The Variety of Bond Issues

The choice of bonds is enormous and ever-growing. There are several basic categories of bonds, each featuring special benefits and advantages and each offering its own risks and security. Let's explore these main bond categories.

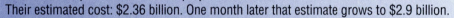

The Saga of WPPSS

February 1957   Seventeen Washington State utilities form the Washington Public Power Supply System, a construction consortium.

October 1968   The Bonneville Power Administration, a federal agency, announces plans to build 20 nuclear plants by 1990.

July 1976   Eighty-eight Northwest utilities agree to back tax-exempt bonds to finance projects 4 and 5. Their estimated cost: $2.36 billion. One month later that estimate grows to $2.9 billion.

February 1977   WPPSS issues the first of its long-term bonds for projects 4 and 5.

July 1979   The cost to complete projects 4 and 5 now is estimated at $5 billion.

March 1981   WPPSS issues the last of its project 4 and 5 bonds. Two months later it estimates that 4 and 5 will cost $12 billion. Construction is halted.

January 1982   WPPSS cancels projects 4 and 5.

June 1983   The Washington State Supreme Court bars WPPSS participants from paying their share of the project 4 and 5 debt, ruling that they lacked authority to enter into the power purchase contracts. Investors file suit, alleging securities fraud.

July 1983   WPPSS acknowledges it cannot repay the project 4 and 5 debt and defaults on $2.25 billion in bonds.

September 1987   The bonds' underwriters settle, agreeing to pay $92 million.

September 1988   WPPSS settles with investors, though it will pay them no money. The case against 20 participating utilities, WPPSS's financial adviser, and others continues.

SOURCE: "How It Happened," *Business Week,* October 3, 1988, 27.

U.S. Treasury Bonds

Government-backed bonds are specifically suitable for investors to whom guaranteed safety of principal is a paramount consideration. Because they are issued and backed by the federal government, they are virtually risk-free investments as far as reliability of repayment of principal plus interest is concerned. Treasury issues are also easy to sell in a hurry because of the enormous size of the government bond market.

But reliability of repayment should not be an investor's only concern. There are other risks involved in buying bonds, no matter who is backing them. These risks stem from tying up money in a fixed investment for a long period of time. Many people, confusing credit risk that results from changing interest rates with default risk, are surprised to discover that Treasury bonds—especially long-term ones, which they had assumed were the safest investments possible—could turn out to be more volatile than high-yielding junk bonds.

Volatile market interest rates, inflation rates, and economic uncertainty will cause fluctuations in the resale price of all bonds, including Treasury issues. Like any other type of bond, government bonds already in circulation decline in value on the secondary markets when interest rates rise. Since newly issued bonds offer higher rates, prices of older, lower interest rate bonds decline. When interest rates fall, holders of higher interest bonds see their investment rise on the secondary bond markets.

The Biggest Borrower on Earth—Uncle Sam The most widely held bond issues are those of the Treasury and other federal agencies. In fact, the U.S. government is the biggest borrower on earth, with a total national debt of over $3 trillion. The Treasury issues a variety of IOUs or debt securities, collectively known as **Treasuries**. The main ones are Treasury bills, notes, and bonds shown in the accompanying box. Interest rates on these securities usually rise as the maturities lengthen.

The U.S. Treasury sells billions of dollars of these securities each and every week to cover the federal government's huge budget deficit and to pay off maturing issues. The bulk of these bills, notes, and bonds is sold to dealers, financial institutions, and even other federal agencies. But a significant portion is bought directly by individual investors, attracted by respectable yields, unbeatable safety, and because, unlike corporate bonds, the interest from Treasuries is exempt from state and local taxes. They may be an attractive choice for residents of states with high local income tax levies. They are, however, subject to federal income taxes. Moreover, Treasuries can readily be sold early if investors need to get their money back before maturity since there is a huge and active secondary market in Treasuries.

The Treasury Auction New bills, notes, and bonds are sold in an auction at which dealers put in competitive tenders expressed in terms of the securities yield. Individuals may submit noncompetitive bids. Naturally, buyers want the highest yield, while Uncle Sam wants to pay the lowest interest rate. The Treasury accepts all the bids at the lowest yields until it gets the amount it wants. Noncompetitive bidders all get the average price and yield, while competitive bidders (the big dealers and institutions) may end up paying a higher price and getting a lower yield or may bid too low a price and get shut out. Most small investors who buy less than $1 million of Treasury issues enter noncompetitive bids.

T-bills are short-term securities. They come in three-month, six-month and one-year maturities. Minimum purchase at auction is $10,000, but buyers may purchase

Buying U.S. Treasury Bills, Notes, and Bonds

Ⓝew Treasury securities can be purchased directly from the Federal Reserve through the Treasury direct system, or through banks and brokerage houses.

Type	Maturity	Minimum Purchase	Issued
Treasury bills	3, 6, and 12 months	$10,000 (sold in multiples of $5,000 above the minimum)	3- and 6-month bills issued weekly, usually on Monday; one- year sold monthly
Treasury notes	2 or 3 years	$5,000 (sold in multiples of $5,000)	2-year notes issued monthly; 3-year notes sold quarterly
	4–10 years	$1,000 (sold in multiples of $1,000)	Semiannually
Treasury bonds	Over 10 years	$1,000 (sold in multiples of $1,000)	Semiannually

SOURCE: Federal Reserve Bank of New York.

additional $5,000 increments. The minimum denomination for two- to three-year notes is $5,000 and $1,000 thereafter. Longer notes and bonds come in units of $1,000. T-bills are quoted differently from notes and bonds because they do not pay a stated rate of interest. They are sold at a discount and are redeemed at face value. Buyers pay less than the full face value of the bill. Rather than paying interest, the government redeems them at full value when they mature. An investor's return on a T-bill is the difference between the purchase price and the face value of the bill paid by the Treasury at maturity. See the box "Figuring the Real Annualized Yield" for more detail on how this works.

How to Buy Treasuries The simplest way to buy a Treasury at auction is to pay a broker or bank to do it. Brokers sell Treasuries just like stocks, and banks offer them alongside their CDs. Buyers are charged a handling fee of $25 to $50 or more per transaction regardless of the amount. The Treasury and local Federal Reserve district banks sell new offerings of government securities directly to the public without any fees. Buyers simply need to phone the Bureau of the Public Debt at 202/287-4113 or any one of the 12 Federal Reserve banks (see the box "The Federal Reserve Banks") or their 23 branch offices to obtain a "noncompetitive tender" order form which the buyer mails in together with a certified check for the amount of securities requested.

Figuring the Real Annualized Yield

T-bills are quoted at a discount from face value, with the discount expressed as an annual rate based on 360 days. This means the yield on bills is more than their stated discount rates. Say you buy a six-month $10,000 bill paying 8 percent. A week or so later the government will deposit $400, which is the amount of the discount, directly to your bank account and then pay you $10,000 at the end of six months. You have invested only $9,600 in the bill since you have received the $400 discount. Your real annualized yield is higher than 8 percent. To figure out the yield, you need a formula. For Treasury bills maturing in three or six months, the following formula gives the approximate yield:

$$\text{Investment Yield} = \frac{\text{Face Value} - \text{Purchase Price}}{\text{Purchase Price}} \times \frac{360}{\text{Number of Days to Maturity}}$$

For instance, in the above example a six-month (180-day) bill was auctioned at an average price of $9,600 per $10,000 face value.

$$\text{Step 1:} \quad \frac{10,000 - 9,600}{9,600} \times \frac{360}{180}$$

$$\text{Step 2:} \quad \frac{400}{9,600} \times 2$$

$$\text{Step 3:} \quad .04166 \times 2 = .0833$$

To change the result into a percentage, move the decimal two places to the right. The result is 8.33 percent. So your real annualized yield is not 8 percent but 8.33 percent.

Question

If you received the $400 and paid only $9,600 for the $10,000 T-bill, the quoted price for your T-bill would be 96. If, for example, you read that last Monday's three-month or 90-day auction resulted in T-bill prices of $97.46, do you know what that means? Simply, that a $10,000 bill sold for $9,746 or 97.46 percent of face value and that buyers will receive $254. Each investor who mailed in $10,000 would receive a refund check for ($10,000 − $9,746 =) $254 in the mail. How much of an annual yield is that? Following the formula above should quickly give you the answer:

$$\frac{254}{9,746} \times \frac{360}{90} = .0260 \times 4 = .1042, \text{ or } 10.42\%$$

T-bills, notes, and bonds are sold only in book-entry form. Buyers get a computer receipt, which is not marketable. Previously issued notes and bonds are still available as engraved securities.

Buyers who do not have a "tender" order form can still buy 13-week or 26-week T-bills by writing a letter to the Fed. Your letter should state: "This is my tender and non-competitive bid for the Treasury bill auction on (date)." Specify whether you are bidding for 13-week or 26-week bills, the face amount, and whether you want the funds automatically reinvested when the bill matures. Include your Social Security number, bank and bank account number, mailing address, phone number during business hours, and your signature. Enclose a certified personal check or official bank check for the face amount of the issues, payable to the specific Federal Reserve Bank you contact. Address your request to the Treasury Department, Bureau of the Public Debt, Washington, DC 20239; or to the Fiscal Agency Department of your nearest Federal Reserve Bank.

You can also bring your forms and checks in person to the local federal branch of the Treasury anytime before 1 PM on the day of the auction. If you buy the securities by mail, your envelope must be postmarked before midnight of the day before that Monday's auction.

The Federal Reserve Banks

FRB Boston 600 Atlantic Avenue Boston, MA 02106 617/973-3810	FRB New York 33 Liberty Street New York, NY 10045 212/720-6619
FRB Philadelphia 10 Independence Mall Philadelphia, PA 19105 215/574-6680	FRB Cleveland 1455 East Sixth Street Cleveland, OH 44101 216/579-2490
FRB Richmond 701 E. Byrd Street Richmond, VA 23219 804/697-8000	FRB Atlanta 104 Marietta Street, NW Atlanta, GA 30303 404/521-6653
FRB Chicago 230 South La Salle Street Chicago, IL 60690 312/322-5369	FRB St. Louis 411 Locust Street St. Louis, MO 63166 314/444-8665
FRB Minneapolis 250 Marquette Avenue Minneapolis, MN 55480 612/340-2075	FRB Kansas City 925 Grand Avenue Kansas City, MO 64198 816/881-2409
FRB Dallas 400 South Akard Street Dallas, TX 75222 214/651-6362	FRB San Francisco 101 Market Street San Francisco, CA 94105 415/974-2330

Treasury Direct   As of January 1988, the Treasury started selling Treasury securities electronically. When they enter a bid for Treasury issues under the new **Treasury direct system,** buyers now have to specify a bank where they have an account and provide their account number. All sums for purchase discounts, interest payments, and returns of principal get fed electronically into the buyers' bank accounts. All they will get in the mail is a quarterly statement showing the status of their securities. The Treasury Direct System provides investors immediate access to their money, eliminates standing in line at banks, and removes the worry about lost or stolen checks. (For information from the Treasury on buying bills directly, free of bank or broker's fees, call 202/287-4113.)

The Secondary Treasuries Market   After having bought Treasury bonds, notes, or bills, investors may want to sell them before their maturity date. For this they will need the secondary market. The secondary market for government securities is the focus of worldwide attention and is the biggest such market in the world. Daily average trading volume exceeds $100 billion, or more than 10 times the value of transactions on the New York Stock Exchange.

Brokers cannot be avoided in this market and brokerage fees can be considerably expensive for sums under $100,000. But investors have much more flexibility regarding maturity dates. They could sell or buy a government security maturing in one day or two weeks or 20 years.

The bulk of these secondary market transactions in government securities is among banks, dealers, and brokers which buy and sell securities after original issuance for their accounts or for customers. A complete list of Treasury bill, note, and bond prices in the secondary market is published daily in the financial pages of most newspapers.

U.S. Savings Bonds

In addition to Treasury bills, notes, and bonds, which are auctioned to the public, the Treasury sells another bond in small denominations on a nonauction basis. These instruments, known as **savings bonds,** are geared to give the "small guy" a chance to lend money to the government and thereby save as well. Many employers offer workers the opportunity of saving regularly by offering an automatic monthly payroll deduction plan for the purchase of U.S. savings bonds. This plan is known as the **payroll savings plan.**

Savings bonds, unlike municipal, Treasury, or corporate bonds, will never be worth less than their purchase price, nor do they vary inversely with interest rates. This happens because after six months they are redeemable at any bank or post office for the amount paid plus accrued interest.

The main features of savings bonds are the following:

1. They are sold in small denominations.

2. They are guaranteed by the federal government.

3. They are sold without brokerage fees.

4. Their interest is exempt from state and local income taxes.

5. No federal tax has to be paid until bonds mature or are cashed.

6. They require no sales or redemption fees.

7. No management charges are assessed.

8. They are readily available for purchase over the counter at most financial institutions throughout the country.

9. They do not pay out interest periodically but let it accrue.

10. There is a limit on annual investments of $30,000 per person.

There are three different classifications of savings bonds.

Series EE Bonds   **Series EE,** which succeeded **Series E** bonds in 1980, are at the core of the savings bond program. They are accrual securities. Interest is credited (accrued) periodically, increasing the bond's total redemption value. Interest is paid only when a bond is redeemed. EE bonds start at $50 face amounts and can be bought at a 50 percent discount. It takes $25 to buy a $50 EE bond.

They are sold in face amounts of $50, $75, $100, $200, $500, $1,000, $5,000, and $10,000. No individual can buy more than $30,000 face amount in a calendar year. Those who wish to buy more than that in a year can have their spouse and each child buy $30,000 each.

In November 1982, the U.S. Treasury broke with long-standing tradition by converting savings bonds from fixed-yield to variable-rate securities. The Treasury sets a new savings bond rate twice a year, on May 1 and November 1, so that it equals 85 percent of the average yield on marketable five-year Treasury securities during the holding period. The rules state that the bond must be held at least five years from date of issue to receive the variable rate. They are guaranteed to earn at least 4 percent annually if held for the full five years.

The variable rate makes it actually impossible for the Treasury or anyone else to establish how long it will take for $25 to grow to $50. If the rates were to average 11 percent, $25 would hit $50 in six-and-a-half years. Individuals can hold EE bonds beyond the time it takes to accumulate enough interest to bring the bond to face value. The bonds continue to accumulate interest if held beyond this time. For example, over 30 years, a $25 EE bond earning an average of 11 percent would grow to around $650. However, after a final maturity date, usually 30 years, the bond will cease to accumulate interest.

Obtaining Savings Bond Information

General information and simplified tables for the redemption value of Series E and EE are available free from the Office of Public Affairs, U.S. Savings Bond Division, Department of the Treasury, Washington, DC 20226, 202/634-5389.

Education Savings Bonds Effective 1990, Congress created a totally tax-free education savings bond. This bond is just like any other Series EE bond except that the interest is tax exempt if the bond is redeemed to pay college tuition and fees. This tuition shelter does have some stipulations, however. The bond must be purchased and owned only by the parents. The bonds lose their tax free nature as family income rises from $68,250 to $98,250 for parents who file a joint return and from $45,500 to $60,500 for single taxpayers, as of 1993. Those amounts are adjusted for inflation each year. This tax shelter may be a worthwhile means of saving for children's college education for the families in the appropriate income levels.

HH Bonds What if you want some cash flow from your holding of E and EE bonds but do not want to redeem them and pay taxes? Say you have $600 redemption value in EE bonds. You can exchange them for one $500 HH bond and take the other $100 in cash. Series HH bonds pay semiannual interest income. The only way to acquire HH bonds is to trade a minimum of $500 worth of E or EE bonds. **Series HH bonds** cannot be purchased outright. The lure of HH bonds is that you can continue to defer the taxes on your E and EE interest. The interest on previously held series EE bonds becomes taxable income only when the HH bonds are cashed in. However, interest income on series HH bonds must be reported annually for federal income tax purposes. Most banks that issue EE bonds have the forms needed to fill out to exchange Es and EEs for HH bonds.

The Suitability of Savings Bonds for Your Portfolio Although the variable rates and the tax-free education feature have greatly improved the appeal of savings bonds, they remain a vehicle best-suited for long-term saving. Unless these bonds are held for at least five years, they offer little advantage over even the simplest alternatives, such as a savings account at a bank, CDs, T-bills, or money market accounts.

Despite the sweetened rate, the only reason for individuals to buy savings bonds other than saving for their children's college education is if they cannot afford anything bigger, or if they accumulated them in a payroll deduction plan because they do not have the self-discipline to save. Additionally, for patriotic reasons, people may feel an obligation to lend money to their government. But if your motivations are purely economical, then you may likely look elsewhere to invest your money.

Municipal (MUNIS) Tax-Exempt Bonds At the state and city level, investors can choose from among thousands of municipal bond issues or, as they are popularly called, **munis.** In general, munis offer yields similar to those of federal government agency issues and the risk is relatively slight. State bonds are considered a notch above city issues because of the states' greater size and more diversified economies. Also, cities may need state approval to raise taxes, which gives the cities less flexibility in a budget squeeze. The real attractive feature of munis is their tax status. Although the Supreme Court in 1988 ruled that Congress has a right to tax interest on bonds issued by states and municipalities, interest earned from these bonds has so far not been subject to federal income tax.*

Municipal bonds are generally also free from state and local taxes in the states where issued. That makes a big difference in places like New York City, where the

---

* The tax exemption is only for public issue municipals. Private purpose bonds issued by municipal governments are not tax exempt.

combined state and city income tax can total 18.3 percent. A New York City resident, for example, can get what is called a triple-tax exemption (from federal, state, and city taxes) by purchasing a bond issued by a New York City authority. The same is true for Los Angeles or any other city which imposes a city income tax. Munis are especially profitable to investors in the upper income tax brackets, because the yields can exceed the after-tax return on a taxable issue.

Before buying a muni, some tax considerations and calculations are necessary. Investors need to figure whether the tax-free yield is better than the after-tax return on taxable investments. The higher an investor's bracket, the lower a municipal bond's stated return can be to still compete with a comparable taxable investment. The taxable equivalent yield is determined by dividing the tax-free rate by the difference of 1 minus your federal tax bracket. For example, if a muni bond yields 6 percent and your tax rate is 28 percent, then the bond's taxable equivalent yield is 8.3 percent 6 divided by 0.72; see the following box). Even investors in lower tax brackets can often do better owning tax-exempt municipals than they can with regular government or corporate bonds.

Tax Anticipation Notes Municipal bonds generally mature in 30 years. However, states and municipalities also sell notes which mature in six months to one year. These are used for short-term borrowing to bridge short falls in revenue and are backed by the municipality's expectation of income from taxes. They are also known as **tax anticipation** notes and are generally sold in blocks of $5,000.

General Obligation and Revenue Bonds The vast number of municipal securities available ranges from high-quality state highway bonds to unrated obligations of local school districts. There are two main broad categories of municipals.

General obligation bonds (GOs) are backed by the taxing power of the issuing government unit, such as a state or city. They are generally viewed as the safest overall. **Revenue bonds** are backed only by the earnings of the particular facility that offers them, such as a toll bridge authority, airport, or a local water system. They are used to fund public works projects such as a highway or bridge. Although their yield is a little higher, they are not as safe as general obligation bonds because the money used to repay bondholders is limited to the cash flowing in from those specific projects—the revenue from a toll bridge or sports stadium, for instance.

Despite this limitation, revenue bonds generally have a good safety record, and many are considered as safe or safer than those backed by taxes. But some are vulnerable to the risk that hospitals, electric power systems, or toll roads may not generate as much revenue as expected and could default.

The previously defaulted "whoops" bonds, for example, were revenue bonds for construction of nuclear power plants and were guaranteed by contracts from 88 northwestern utilities which won a Washington State court order allowing them not to pay.

How Safe Are Munis? Although munis overall have had an exemplary record for safety, they are by no means a riskless investment. During the past decade, the ability of many state and municipal borrowers to pay their debts has deteriorated. In 1987, 123 issues valued at $1.1 billion defaulted, more than the total number of failures for the entire period between 1972 and 1983. In 1991, the municipal default rate

Calculating Taxable Equivalent Yield

To calculate your own taxable equivalent yield, use the following formula:

$$\text{Taxable Yield} = \frac{\text{Tax-Free Yield}}{1 - \text{Federal Tax Bracket}}$$

Subtract your tax bracket from 1 and divide that number, in decimal form, into the tax-free yield. In the case of the investor in the 28 percent bracket, subtract 28 from 1 to get 72 percent, or .72. Next divide the tax-free return by .72 to arrive at your taxable equivalent yield. Suppose the bond's interest rate was 8.5; 8.5 divided by .72 is equal to 11.81 percent.

The table below shows the taxable equivalent yields for various interest rates in tax brackets.

TAX EXEMPT—TAXABLE YIELD EQUIVALENT

	Tax Bracket		
	15%	28%	33%
Tax-Exempt Yields (%)	Taxable Yield Equivalents (%)		
4.0%	4.71%	5.56%	5.97%
4.5	5.29	6.25	6.72
5.0	5.88	6.94	7.46
5.5	6.47	7.64	8.21
6.0	7.06	8.33	8.96
6.5	7.65	9.03	9.70
7.0	8.24	9.72	10.45
7.5	8.82	10.42	11.19
8.0	9.41	11.11	11.94
8.5	10.00	11.81	12.69
9.0	10.59	12.50	13.43
9.5	11.18	13.19	14.18
10.0	11.76	13.89	14.93
10.5	12.35	14.58	15.67
11.0	12.94	15.28	16.42
11.5	13.53	15.97	17.16
12.0	14.12	16.67	17.91

reached $4 billion, which was eight times the figure for 1982. Although this $4 billion is only a tiny fraction of municipal bonds outstanding, the rising tide of defaults is chilling for investors who view munis as an ideal combination of tax breaks and safety. Therefore, all munis should be approached with caution.

It is not difficult to understand why some investors are hesitant about purchasing long-term municipal bonds. The near default of New York City bonds in 1975 and the widely publicized actual default in 1983 of the Washington Public Power Supply System (WPPSS) on $2.5 billion in debt, were enough to give the municipal bond market a case of the jitters whose repercussions will last for years to come.

Bond Insurance   Many investors want to have some assurance that they will get their money back if an issuer defaults. To overcome investors' fears, many state and local governments have obtained private insurance for their bond issues since 1983.

About 30 percent of the munis issued in 1991 carried some sort of insurance arrangement, compared with just 3 percent in 1980, according to the Municipal Bond Insurance Association. Insured municipal bonds have become popular and have even spread into the corporate bond market.

The insurance guarantees to continue paying interest and return face value at maturity no matter what financial problems a municipality happens to run into. But bear in mind that once a bond is insured, it automatically gets a higher rating, usually AAA, even if the bond has a BBB rating based on its own creditworthiness. It is important to remember that a broker selling an AAA-insured bond may actually be selling a BBB security with insurance.

Peace of mind does not come free. The cost of insurance can reduce some interest from the muni's yield. The insurance cost is paid for by the bond issuer. This enables the bond to sell at a lower yield. The net effect is to reduce bondholders' yield, usually up to half a percentage point lower than a comparably rated uninsured bond. This means that bondholders will receive up to $50 less interest on a $10,000 bond, a trade-off many investors find worthwhile. Bond insurance can be useful if an investor wants to sell a bond before maturity. The investor is more likely to get more bids from buyers on an insured bond than on an uninsured one. Lower interest costs and increased marketability of insured bonds are two reasons that issuers are willing to pay the one-time insurance premium.

Although insured municipal bonds provide protection at a relatively low cost, they do not eliminate risk. Bond insurance is not an iron-clad guarantee. Municipal bond insurance is only as strong as the insurance company backing it. Investors should therefore think of it as an extra "layer of protection." The companies that now insure municipal bonds (such as Municipal Bond Investors Assurance Corp., a unit of MBIA, Inc.; AMBAC Indemnity Corp., a unit of Citicorp; and financial Guaranty Insurance Co., a unit of General Electric Company) are considered high-quality AAA credit risks. But who can foretell what could happen over the life of a 30-year bond? The risk is therefore transferred, not eliminated.

Brokerage Fees—Watch Out   Buying and selling bonds on the secondary market can be expensive even if the dealer is perfectly honest. Since most municipal bonds are thinly traded, it is not unusual to have a two- to three-point difference between what a broker pays for a bond (bid price) and the price at which it sells (asking price). In a market dominated by institutional buyers, anyone who wants to sell less than $25,000 worth of a single issue lacks bargaining power. He almost always pays extra to buy and receives less than big investors when he sells. Therefore, investors should not buy individual bonds if they do not plan on holding them.

Unlike the stock prices listed in many newspapers, the vast majority of muni bonds are not published, and it is difficult to compare prices. Currently, brokerage houses and bond-trading specialist firms set the spreads on munis, a system that makes it practically impossible for small investors to know whether their broker is quoting the best available price.

If investors want to buy tax-exempt bonds, their best bet may be a no-load municipal bond mutual fund. These funds are the most convenient and least risky way for the small investor to invest in munis. The income is reasonably steady, and there are no commissions when they buy and sell. The funds are also actively traded. This will be discussed further in Chapter 14, which deals with mutual funds.

Corporate Issues

A **corporate bond** is a certificate stating that a corporation has borrowed a certain amount of money and promises to repay it at a future date. A **bond indenture** is a legal document specifying the conditions under which the bond has been issued. It states the rights of the bondholders and the obligations of the issuing corporation, as well as specifying the interest, principal payments, and dates. An indenture is normally a quite complex and lengthy legal document. The issuing corporation agrees to pay bondholders a stated amount of interest at specified time intervals, usually semi-annually. Most corporate bonds are issued with maturities of 10 to 30 years and in denominations of $1,000.

The key attraction of corporate bonds is that they usually pay higher interest than U.S. Treasury or municipal bonds. The pledge of a corporation is considered less safe than the "full faith and credit" of the U.S. Treasury. Therefore, corporations must pay more interest to compete for investors' money. They also must offer higher interest rates than municipals because they do not have the federal tax exemption on interest which municipals offer.

Corporate bonds are bought and sold like stocks and their prices change from day to day and in the course of each day. In the secondary market, most corporate bonds are traded on either the New York Bond Exchange or the American Bond Exchange. Because bondholders do not participate in the growth of the company, bond price fluctuations reflect only interest rate trends and the general ability of the company to meet its obligations. Therefore, like preferred stock, bond prices usually do not fluctuate as much as common stock prices. Many older corporate bonds are available at well below face value because interest rates are higher currently than they were when the bonds were issued many years ago. These are known as **deep discount corporate bonds.** Corporate bonds are sold as either unsecured or secured obligations known as *debentures* and *mortgage bonds*.

Debentures   **Debentures** are unsecured bonds protected only by the general credit of the borrowing corporation. Bonds of very large and creditworthy companies are often issued without the pledge of collateral. A debenture bond does not have a claim on any specific asset of the firm but rather on its general assets. A debenture holder is therefore a general creditor. In case of default, debenture holders have a claim on any assets remaining once the claims of all secured creditors have been satisfied. All direct domestic obligations of federal, state, and most municipal governments in the United States are debentures.

It is impossible to judge whether a bond is good or bad solely because it is a debenture. The value of a debenture is obviously based upon the credit and particularly upon the earning capacity of the corporation or government issuing it.

Another type of unsecured debt is known as a **subordinated debenture.** This is a debenture made specifically subordinate to other types of debt. Since subordinated debt holders rank below all other long-term creditors with respect to both liquidation and interest payment, these instruments usually offer a higher interest yield.

Mortgage Bonds If unsecured bonds are not for your nerves or insomnia, then a variety of secured bonds is available. The basic types are **mortgage bonds.** A mortgage bond is a debt instrument accrued with a lien on specific real property, such as land or buildings of the issuer. Mortgage bonds provide a prime, clear, and indisputable claim on a company's specific fixed assets. Normally, the market value of this property is greater than the amount of the bond issue. If the company defaults, the bondholders may obtain a court order to foreclose on the mortgage and take possession of the pledged property.

A **first mortgage bond** gives the holder the first claim on these secured assets. A **second mortgage bond** gives the holder a secondary or residual claim on assets already secured by the first mortgage. Therefore, a number of mortgages can be issued against the same collateral. The first mortgage bond is obviously the safest since the holder has the first claim on the pledged assets. The mortgage claim, however, must be fully satisfied prior to distribution of proceeds to second mortgage holders.

Convertible Securities A **convertible** is a hybrid bond or preferred stock that pays a fixed rate of interest or dividend and can be exchanged for the issuer's common shares at a fixed price or rate of exchange. The conversion privilege lasts until the maturity date of the bond. The conversion option can be exercised by simply mailing the bond back to the company or to a designated bank and receiving common stock certificates in exchange within a few days.

The interest paid on a convertible is usually two to three percentage points below bonds of the same issuer that lack the conversion feature. Convertibles can be viewed as a kind of coin toss gamble whereby the odds are heads you win, tails you do not lose much. They may be a suitable investment for people who are willing to accept a stable (although slightly lower) rate of return in exchange for an opportunity to share in any equity gains if the firm's stock ever appreciates. Convertible bonds or stocks are the fence sitter's delight. They are therefore described as defensive investments for investors who want to share in stock market gains while cushioning themselves against losses.

Convertible bonds' interest yields are almost always significantly higher than the dividend yields of the underlying stock. For this reason convertibles are considered safer and less likely to decline in value than the common. Nevertheless, since the convertibles carry fixed rates, they may slide in price when interest rates rise, as is the pattern with regular bonds.

How can you determine if a convertible is for you? A number of factors must be taken into account, such as:

1. The price and yield of the convertible security

2. The price and yield of the common stock

3. The conversion ratio or rate at which the security can be changed into common and any premium added to that by the convertible's interest or dividend payout

As a rule, investors should not buy a convertible unless they would be willing to own the common. Convertibles often are issued by companies with problems in their capital structure. Companies frequently issue convertibles when they cannot afford to borrow at market interest rates. To obtain the maximum advantage of the conversion feature, it is best to buy when the convertible's price is close to the conversion price.

Convertible owners suffer the worst of both worlds if the common stock goes down in price and interest rates go up, depressing bond prices. Investors may find that their convertible's value both as a bond and as a stock has declined.

Price quotations for convertible bonds are listed in the financial tables of newspapers, along with the prices of ordinary bonds. Convertibles trade on both the New York and American Stock Exchanges. They are identified by the letters CV in the yield column of the bond tables.

Sinking Funds   A provision that is normally included in a corporate bond indenture is a **sinking fund** requirement. This provides for the systematic, gradual retirement of the outstanding bonds prior to maturity. It is akin to the monthly payments a homeowner makes to amortize a mortgage. The idea is to protect the lender. The firm may be required to make periodic payments to provide funds for the retirement of the debt.

A sinking fund is normally established in such a way that the deposits accumulate to the maturity value of the debt. The bond indenture demands that the company retire a certain percentage of the issue each year, either by buying the bonds in the open market or by selecting them by lot for redemption at par.

Baby Bonds (The Baby Boom)   Corporate bonds are usually bought in $1,000 denominations by large investors. In 1983, in a move to bring corporate bonds to small investors, Merrill Lynch introduced the **baby bond**, a corporate bond cut into $25 denominations. These babies were successful and sold well.

Although U.S. savings bonds are also available in $25 denominations, the corporate babies offer distinct advantages. They are relatively high yielding and are convertible. Investors therefore can trade their baby in for common stock when the market turns bullish.

Should You Ride a Convertible?

You have read about a company called XYZ Corp. and want to invest in it. A $1,000 bond of XYZ Corp. features an option to convert every $1,000 into 25 shares of common stock of XYZ, which means if you exercise the conversion option, each share of stock would cost you $40. The current market price of a common share of XYZ Corp. is $33. Additionally, current five-year bond interest rates offer 8 percent interest while XYZ Corp.'s convertible offers a below-market rate of 5 percent. You may be reluctant to purchase the stock outright for fear that it may decline sharply, causing you heavy losses. Which are you better off buying, a $1,000 XYZ convertible bond or 25 shares of common stock at $40 each?

You reason that if the shares go beyond 40 each, you can reap profits. If they fall sharply, say to 20, you stick with your bond until maturity. All you have lost then is the interest differential between a regular bond and your convertible, which in this case is 3 percent, or $30 per year per $1,000 of investment.

For example, suppose you bought a convertible baby bond during the initial offering, when the underlying stock sold for $10 per share. The bond has a conversion premium of 40 percent, which means you can trade the bonds in for common stock at 40 percent higher than the market price of the stock at the time of the initial offering. Two years later, the stock price zooms to $40. You can trade in one of your bonds worth $10 plus pay $4 more to buy a share of stock at $14 and then turn around and sell the stock at $40 for a quick $26 profit.

Commercial Paper

Commercial paper is the term used to describe a short-term unsecured promissory note, sold by a financial or nonfinancial organization as an alternative to borrowing from a bank or other institution. For example, if General Motors Acceptance Corp. (GMAC) needs to borrow money which it uses to lend to car buyers to pay the GM car dealers, it may borrow the money by issuing commercial paper. (GMAC happens to be the largest corporate issuer of commercial paper.)

The paper is usually sold to other institutions (such as pension funds, insurance companies, and money market funds), which invest in short-term money market instruments. But individuals also buy these issues. However, since the face values are typically $10,000 per sheet, most small investors do not directly participate in these offerings. Currently, more than 800 companies in the United States regularly issue commercial paper.

Interest rates on commercial paper often are lower than bank lending rates and the differential, when large enough, provides an advantage, which makes issuing commercial paper an attractive alternative to bank credit. Daily interest rates, on a discount basis on commercial paper with maturities of 30 days to 120 days, are published weekly by the Federal Reserve Bank of New York and listed daily in the financial section of most leading newspapers.

Commercial paper has maturities ranging from 3 to 270 days, but most commonly is issued for 30 days to 90 days. Commercial paper is generally considered a quite safe investment since the issuers are the most creditworthy of the nation's corporations.

Both Moody's and Standard and Poor's rate commercial paper according to the credit standing of the issuing corporation. Moody's top two grades are Prime-1 and Prime-2, usually abbreviated to P-1 and P-2. The comparable S & P designations are A-1 and A-2.

Mortgage-Backed Securities

A strategy for maximizing yields while lowering the risk of owning long-term bonds is to buy **mortgage-backed securities.** Mortgage-backed securities have in recent years become the fastest growing market on the fixed income scene. They have helped make the American dream of owning a house a reality.

Traditionally, banks and thrifts took in money from deposits and lent the funds out as mortgages and other loans. Then they sat on those loans until maturity. That meant that while depositors could come back for their cash at any time, the mortgage loans tied up the bank's money for as long as 30 years.

As interest rates rose over the years, banks were stuck with old-low interest mortgages, while paying out higher and higher rates to depositors. If the banks needed liquidity, they could sell these mortgages only at great discounts or losses. Consequently, if banks experienced heavy withdrawals, they could raise cash only by selling old mortgages at huge losses (as discussed in Chapter 2) which resulted in their becoming insolvent. This devastated many thrifts, the traditional providers of long-term, fixed-rate mortgages.

The banks and the federal government responded to this problem by packaging and selling securities collateralized by pools of mortgages. Mortgage packaging turned residential mortgages, which are primarily local, illiquid assets, into highly liquid securities. By issuing securities collateralized by those mortgages, the lenders were in effect selling or passing on the mortgages to the general public and receiving back cash, which allowed them to issue more loans and remain liquid. It was a way of tapping the capital markets for money that would not ordinarily find its way to mortgage lending. Mortgage securities pass the interest rate risk on to investors who could buy and sell the instruments as though they were bonds and relieve lenders from having to hold mortgages until maturity.

The federal government took the lead in creating investment securities from mortgages. The idea was for the government to buy mortgages from financial institutions that had actually made the loans. If these financial institutions sold old mortgages to the government, they would have additional money to issue new mortgage loans. But where does the federal government get the billions of dollars to purchase these mortgages from the financial institutions?

Pass Throughs   The government sells bonds backed by these mortgages with a return that reflects the interest rates that individual homeowners are paying. How are these bonds repaid? By the homeowners who pay off their mortgage interest and principal in monthly payments. The banks pass the monthly interest, principal payment, and occasional prepayments minus certain fees directly through to the bond owners, just as though they were the direct mortgage holders. Therefore, the government is serving as a guarantor, enabling banks and other financial institutions to have their old mortgages **pass through** them to the investors who buy shares in the pool. In this manner, the amount of money available to banks for mortgage loans is practically unlimited.

If a bank issues a home buyer a $100,000 mortgage and then shortly after sells the mortgage and gets its $100,000 back, it can issue a new mortgage with the same money. Each year hundreds of billions of dollars of mortgages are bundled together in this fashion and resold as securities.

Mortgage interest is one of the biggest monthly cash flows in the U.S. economy and has attracted many new investors in recent years. The following are some of the federal government agencies that engage in mortgage packaging and pass throughs.

Meet the Mae Family: Ginnie, Fannie, Freddie, Sallie, Nellie, and Sonny

Ginnie Maes   This sophisticated investment instrument was created by the **Government National Mortgage Association**, a federal corporation, whose initials, **GNMA**, give the bonds their nickname—**Ginnie Maes.** GNMA is a branch of the Department of Housing and Urban Development (HUD). Ginnie Maes are a mortgage-backed security created in the 1960s to help moderate income borrowers buy homes by making real estate mortgage investments appealing to institutions and individual

How One Mortgage Crisscrossed the United States

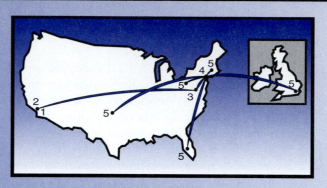

Step 1   *September 1987*   Jim and Erica Vogel buy a four-bedroom home in San Dimas, California. They get a $120,000 mortgage from First Federal S&L of San Gabriel.

Step 2   *December 1987*   First Federal sells the Vogel's mortgage to the Federal Home Loan Mortgage Corp., known as Freddie Mac.

Step 3   *December 1987*   In Preston, Virginia, Freddie Mac puts the Vogle's mortgage into a giant pool with more than 6,000 other mortgages.

Step 4   *May 1988*   Part of that pool is bought by First Boston Corp. in New York. The pool goes into a $550 million offering of mortgage-backed securities.

Step 5   *May/June 1988*   In Hartford, Connecticut, Cigna Investments, Inc., buys $10 million of the Real Estate Mortgage Investment Conduit (Remic) for its pension accounts.
May/June 1988   In El Reno, Oklahoma, Globe Savings Bank buys $66 million of the Remic to expand its loan portfolio.
May/June 1988   In Florida, an S&L buys $40 million of the Remic as an interest rate hedge.
May/June 1988   Other buyers of the Remic range from a Pittsburgh S&L to a London commercial bank to a Florida S&L.

SOURCE: *The Wall Street Journal,* August 17, 1988, 12.

investors. To attract such investors, GNMA works with housing leaders and investment bankers who pool current mortgages and package them, in smaller $25,000 certificates, as collateral for securities, which are sold as Ginnie Maes.

Each GNMA certificate gives an investor a share in a specific mortgage pool, which usually totals at least $1 million. By investing in a Ginnie Mae, private investors are essentially lending mortgage money to homeowners. The bank serves as an intermediary and GNMA insures the investment.

The mortgage bankers run the pools, which are made up of Federal Housing Administration (FHA) and Veterans Administration (VA) guaranteed mortgages. They collect the monthly payments and pass the interest and principal through

A Mortgage Odyssey

Let us see how a mortgage-backed security is born. Suppose you or your parents bought a home and received a mortgage through a local bank, the Tweedum National Bank. Each month you or your parents diligently make the interest and principal payments to Tweedum. Little do you or they know, or even suspect, that Tweedum placed your mortgage in a package or pool and sold it to a federal government agency, which bought it with money it raised through the sale of mortgage-backed bonds. How does the federal agency get money to repay the bonds? You guessed it! It uses your monthly mortgage payments to pay off interest and principal on the bonds. The banks have fresh money to lend out while your mortgage is being passed through to John Q. Public, who indirectly now owns it or has a claim to it and is receiving your monthly mortgage payments.

directly to the GNMA holder. That is why Ginnie Maes are called "pass through" securities. From 1970 to 1985 alone, more than $227 billion in Ginnie Maes were marketed to institutional and individual investors.

Mutual funds, pension funds, and insurance companies, who usually shun investing directly in residential mortgages, have welcomed the mortgage-backed securities which offer high coupons and government guarantees, but do not require the investor to shoulder the responsibility of servicing the loans involved.

The Ginnie Mae certificate has become the most popular form of mortgaged-backed security for the individual. Its chief advantage is that it offers the highest interest rate of any government-backed security.

Regular payments to investors are guaranteed by the GNMA, whether or not payments have been received by the lending institution servicing the loan. More important, the certificates are also backed by the full faith and credit of the U.S. government. This makes Ginnie Maes as risk free as Treasury bonds. But like any bond, Ginnie Maes are subject to interest rate fluctuations. If bond interest rates are to go up, the market resale value of the Ginnie Mae certificate goes down and vice versa. In that respect, Ginnies act like bonds.

Ginnie Maes are generally sold in minimum denominations of $25,000 and in 30-year maturities. However, they mature when all the mortgages in the pool are paid off—which can take as long as 30 years—or they may be repaid in a much shorter time period. Investors can buy older pass throughs which have been partly repaid for less than $25,000 on the secondary markets.

Fannie Mae and Freddie Mac To encourage investment in the housing market, other federal agencies issue securities backed by mortgages. The bonds are known familiarly as **Fannie Mae (FNMA Federal National Mortgage Association)** and **Freddie Mac (Federal Home Loan Mortgage Corporation)**. Each of these quasi-government agencies puts together a pool of mortgages purchased from banks and other lenders. The two companies were created by the government to make the purchase of homes more affordable. These publicly traded corporations accomplish their mission by raising money relatively cheaply in debt markets, using the cash to buy mortgages from commercial banks and thrifts, and

FIGURE 13–2 How Ginnie Maes Are Born

Borrower gets mortgage backed by FHA or VA

Lender pools at least $1 million of these mortgages

Investment banker creates $25,000 certificates backed by the pool, with full federal guarantee from Ginnie Mae

SOURCE: *Business Week*, October 25, 1985, 69.

then either holding the mortgages or repackaging them into securities that are sold to investors. The process provides banks and thrifts with fresh funds to issue more mortgages.

Fannie Mae and Freddie Mac alone bought $1 trillion of mortgages from S&Ls, banks, and other lenders from 1986 to 1991. They operate as intermediaries, charging lenders a quarter percentage point fee for processing a mortgage. The purchase is financed by money from investors who buy either mortgage pass through securities or mortgage-backed bonds. These two companies are the nation's largest issuers of corporate debt. As the accompanying advertisement and Figure 13–3 show, Freddie Mac flaunts its achievements and encourages investors to buy its bond issues.

Ginnie Mae purchases only government-insured mortgages, adding another layer of protection for investors in Ginnie Mae securities. Fannie Mae and Freddie Mac buy conventional mortgages, which do not carry such insurance.

FIGURE 13–D

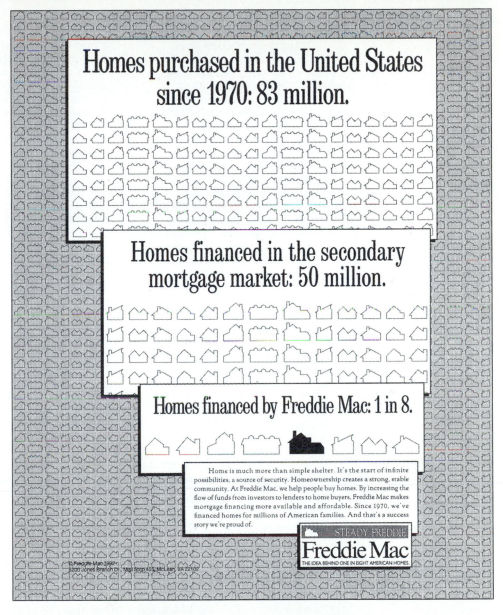

Homes purchased in the United States since 1970: 83 million.

Homes financed in the secondary mortgage market: 50 million.

Homes financed by Freddie Mac: 1 in 8.

Home is much more than simple shelter. It's the start of infinite possibilities, a source of security. Homeownership creates a strong, stable community. At Freddie Mac, we help people buy homes. By increasing the flow of funds from investors to lenders to home buyers, Freddie Mac makes mortgage financing more available and affordable. Since 1970, we've financed homes for millions of American families. And that's a success story we're proud of.

STEADY FREDDIE
Freddie Mac
THE IDEA BEHIND ONE IN EIGHT AMERICAN HOMES.

© Freddie Mac 1992
8200 Jones Branch Dr., Mail Stop 403, McLean, VA 22102

SOURCE: Federal Home Loan Mortgage Association, 1992. Reprinted by permission.

Although they are congressionally chartered corporations, neither Freddie Mac nor Fannie Mae is an official government agency and thus has no explicit government backing. While their securities lack the unconditional guarantee that Ginnie Mae carries, it is highly unlikely that the federal government would refuse

FIGURE 13–3	**Freddie Mac Advertises**

It's no wonder Freddie Mac is first in mortgage securities. After all, investment quaility mortgages and Freddie's sound financial management back the guarantee.

Freddie has issued over $250 billion in mortgage-backed securities to date. And for some very good reasons: high yield, security, liquidity, and flexibility.

It began in 1970, with the Mortgage Participation Certificate, the PC, backed by 30-Year Fixed-Rate Mortgages on single family properties. Since then, Freddie has added the 15-Year, Multi-Family, and ARM PCs, giving investors new product characteristics to choose form with the same security of our standard PC.

Freddie was the first to design and introduce Collateralized Mortgage Obligations (CMOs) to the market in 1983. With CMOs, the duration of the security is sliced in short-term, intermediate, and long-term pieces. This allows investors to select the term that best suits their needs.

Then Freddie issued a new security: the Mortage cash Flow Obligation (MCF) . The MCF, which is an unsecured general obligation of Freddie Mac, is similar in many respects to a CMO, but differs in that it has more streamlined issuance procedure. Now Freddie has Giant PLs (since 1988) it allow investors to consolidate and more easly manage their portfolios. And in 1992 Freddie started offering GNMA-backed Real Estate Mortage Investment Conduits (REMICs) that carry the Freddie Mac Guarantee. So if you're looking for a good investment, check into Freddie. We've got the securities that will give your numbers a boost. Backed by years of experience— every one of them profitable.

Freddie Mac

SOURCE: Federal Home Loan Mortgage Association, 1992.

to bail out Freddy or Fannie should they run into financial difficulties. There are simply too many investors and too much money involved to let them go bankrupt. Although their securities are rated AAA, they generally yield from a fourth to a half percentage point more than Ginnie Maes to compensate investors for the marginally higher risk.

Like Ginnie Maes, Freddie Macs and Fannie Maes pass along to investors on a monthly basis the interest and principal payments made by homeowners on mortgages in the pools. Fannie Mae guarantees that its bond holders will receive their fair share of interest and principal every month even if homeowners do not meet their obligations, just as Ginnie Mae does. Freddy Mac, however, guarantees only timely payment of interest and the ultimate payment of principal. If homeowners do not make their mortgage payments on time, bondholders will still receive their interest payments every month, but they might have to wait as long as a year to receive their rightful share of principal.

Sallie Mae: The Most Popular Co-Ed on Campus   Lending money to needy college students may not sound like an easy way to make big profits, but **Sallie Mae,** known formally as the **Student Loan Marketing Association,** has prospered at it. Sallie Mae does for student loans what Ginnie Mae does for mortgages. She was born in 1972 under authorization from the Higher Education Act of 1965. Her purpose in life is to provide liquidity to the student loan market at time when few banks would touch student loans. With Sallie Mae on the scene, local banks could make guaranteed student loans and then sell them to Sallie Mae while the students were still in college, before the risky repayment cycle begins.

Sallie does not issue any student loans herself. She just buys them from those who do—commercial banks, savings and loan associations, state or private nonprofit student loan agencies. Where does she get all the money to do this? She issues bonds, just like her sisters Ginnie and Fannie do. Her bonds are considered virtually as safe as Treasuries, due to their government guarantee. This takes student loans off lenders' hands and replenishes their supply of funds so they can make more loans to students.

Sallie Mae is actually the world's largest educational financier, holding roughly a third of all guaranteed student loans. Her main strength is her ability to borrow cheap money (thanks to her federal agency status) and lend it out again (buy old student loan notes) at consistently higher rates to cover her administrative expenses.

Nellie Mae   Nellie Mae, formerly known as New England Education Loan Marketing Corp., is a nonprofit corporation created by the Commonwealth of Massachusetts to provide a secondary market for federally guaranteed student loans issued in Massachusetts and New Hampshire. Nellie Mae's AAA bonds mature in three years and are sold in minimum denominations of $5,000. Nellie Mae bonds are also exempt from all federal taxes and from Massachusetts state and local taxes.

Sonny Mae   Sonny Mae, another member of this generous family, is officially known as the State of New York Mortgage Agency or SONYMA. Sonny Mae–issued bonds are backed by fixed-rate single-family home mortgages and use the proceeds to subsidize below-market rate mortgages for first-time home buyers. These are ordinary bonds that pay only interest until they mature. They are likewise exempt from federal taxes for all investors and from New York State and local taxes.

Some Shortcomings of Mortgage-Backed Securities

What the daily ads from brokerage houses in most major newspapers often do not make clear while touting Ginnie Maes, and so on, is that mortgage-backed securities are also highly complex instruments not necessarily suited to everyone.

1. Self-Liquidating (Wasting) Investment   While appropriate for some investment situations, mortgage-backed securities can behave erratically and even be damaging to some investors who do not understand them. The main reason for their complexity is that they combine features of both bonds and mortgages. Like bonds, they bear interest, carry maturity dates, and move up and down in market value as interest rates fluctuate. But unlike bondholders, the owner of a Ginnie Mae receives a monthly check, which includes both interest and repayment of part of the principal, just like a monthly mortgage. When a Ginnie Mae certificate matures, there is no final payment, since the entire principal has already come back to the owner of the certificate. Ginnie Maes are therefore known as **self-liquidating** investments, also referred to as a **wasting asset.**

Getting a share of your principal back at monthly intervals can be either a benefit or a disadvantage, depending upon your needs and the direction in which interest rates are moving. If you require a sizable monthly cash flow to meet living expenses, the larger amount you receive from a Ginnie Mae can be convenient.

But if you do not understand that part of the monthly check is principal, you could be spending what you believe to be income only to find out later that your nest egg had been diminished. Even those who know about this repayment feature must decide what to do with that returned principal every month. Such a monthly investment decision can be a nuisance. However, investors who want high cash flow combined with maximum security can get both from pass throughs.

2. Prepayment Risk   Another catch is called **prepayment risk.** Not everyone with a 30-year mortgage takes 30 years to pay it off. If the property is sold or destroyed by fire or other disaster, the mortgage may be paid off early. If interest rates decline, the homeowner may decide to refinance at a lower rate, prepaying the original mortgage in the process.

Prepayment risk varies with the interest rate on the mortgages, among other factors. The higher the coupon on a mortgage-backed security stands above current mortgage rates, the greater the odds of prepayment. Generally speaking, when interest rates drop sharply, people often refinance their loans and the rate of prepayments speeds up. When interest rates rise, prepayments slow down. This leaves the investor struggling to reinvest cash flows received at now lower interest rates.

Since mortgage prepayments are a common occurrence, Ginnie Maes backed by 30-year mortgages actually have an average life of 12 years, and those backed by 15-year mortgages have an average life of about 7 years.

Investors often do not know what their payment will be until they receive their monthly check because people pay off their mortgage at unpredictable rates. The risk of being surprised with unexpected chunks and often inconveniently high income is ever present. Finally, income from Ginnie Maes is fully taxable in a few states. To compensate investors for the uncertainty surrounding Ginnie Maes, these securities offer a higher interest rate than Treasury issues of comparable maturities.

Collateralized Mortgage Obligations   To appeal to investors who are put off by the imprecise maturities and uneven flow of income from pass through securities, Wall Street has started offering bonds in 1983 called **collateralized mortgage obligations** or **CMOs.** CMOs are securities that are derived or created from traditional mortgage-backed bonds, primarily those issued by the Federal National Mortgage Association and the Federal Home Loan Mortgage Corp. With interest rates down at banks during the early 1990s, more and more individual investors have turned to CMOs in an effort to maintain a higher yield on their investment. Instead of buying mortgage securities directly, investors buy bonds issued by corporate borrowers. Like pass throughs, CMOs are backed by pools of mortgages such as Ginnie Maes or Freddie Macs but the mortgages are grouped into a series of bonds that mature in 5, 10, 20, and 30 years.

If you held the shortest maturity, prepayments on all mortgages would be funneled to you until you were paid off. If you held the longest maturity, you would receive semiannual interest payments but you would not get back any principal until all the shorter-term issues had been paid off. This gives you some protection against early prepayment. It is designed to combine the best of two worlds—the safety and high yields of mortgage-backed securities and the scheduled maturities and semiannual interest payments of bonds.

While they carry the same AAA credit ratings and implicit U.S. government backing as the mortgage-backed bonds underlying them, CMOs represent a quantum leap in complexity. The Federal Reserve, FDIC, and the Comptroller of the Currency decided in 1991 that CMOs are unsafe and unsound investments for banks because of their volatility and complexity. This is a loud and clear indication of the unsuitability of this investment form for the average investor.

Zero Coupon Bonds

Legend has it that Dutch settlers bought Manhattan Island from the Indians for $24. Had the Indians had been able to put the money in a bank account earning 5 percent, by 1994 they would have $1,775,032,242 through the magic of compound interest. This demonstrates the power of zero coupon bonds as well. Unlike virtually any other investment, zeros permit a return to be locked in, not for 300 years but for as much as 30 years.

A **zero coupon bond** is one that is bought at a deep discount from its face value and increases in value at a compound rate so that at maturity it is worth several times the initial investment. When issued, zero coupon bonds get "stripped" of the interest coupons they would carry if they were ordinary bonds. Investors forgo collecting any interest in effect until it matures. Everything rolls in at the end. When it does, the face value will reflect a true compounded yield to maturity, as if interest payments had been received every six months and reinvested at the stated rate. Interest is imputed to the bond.

TABLE 13–1	The Compounded Growth of a $1,000 Zero Bond

Initial price $356, invested at 10.6 percent interest

At the End of Year	Amount Accrued (Principal + Accrued Interest Compounded x 1.106)
0	$ 356.00
1	394.74
2	437.68
3	485.31
4	538.12
5	596.67
6	661.59
7	733.58
8	813.40
9	901.90
10	1000.39

For example, let us assume that you buy a 10.6 percent, $1,000 10-year zero for $356. When the bond matures in 10 years, you will receive $1,000, which includes your original $356 and a single payment of $644 interest earnings. But in the interim, you are not paid any interest income. Your income ($644) is the difference between the selling price ($356) and the maturity value of the bond ($1,000).

Here is one way to look at it. The ultimate payment you get on your zero is equal to what you would receive if it did pay regular semiannual interest and you were compelled to and able to reinvest it at the bond's original coupon rate. For instance, if you had invested $356 in a bank certificate of deposit at 10.6 percent for 10 years, you would also have $1,000 at the end of the 10-year period.

Although zero coupon bonds have been available only since 1982, an estimated $20 billion of the bonds were sold in the first three years and an active resale market has developed for the most popular zeros. Investors often prefer some portion of their portfolio to be in zero coupon issues because it allows them to "lock in" a specified yield on their principal and accrued interest without having to worry about reinvesting interest income over time. Moreover, zero coupon bonds can be purchased at a small fraction of their face value or value at maturity. A zero lets an investor lay out a relatively small amount of money now in exchange for a much larger amount of cash at a specific date in the future. Zeros' charm is simplicity itself.

Zeros enable investors to know precisely the amount of money they must invest today to produce a given amount on a specific date in the future. For example, in saving for a child's education, an investor estimates the annual cost and then buys zeros maturing in each of the four college years, putting them in the child's name to minimize the income taxes (see Chapter 4).

Suppose a new mother and father estimate that the cost of a college education in 20 years' time will run $25,000 a year or $100,000 total over four years. If the current interest rate of zeros was yielding 10.6 percent, the present value of $25,000 in each of these years works out to $3,000 to $4,000. If four $25,000 zeros were bought to mature on consecutive Septembers, the overall cost would be about $14,000.

ZEROS

For a retirement plan, an investor could buy a zero annually, with each due to mature yearly in consecutive years following his or her retirement year, paying out like an annuity at age 65, 66, 67, and so on.

Eliminating the Reinvestment Risk   Zeros also eliminate the worry about the income reinvestment risk. The risk is that rates may decline and that the income from one's high coupon bonds will have to be put to work at progressively lower yields. A zero coupon bond is the antidote to that situation because there is nothing to reinvest along the way. The rate of return is the movement of the price toward par. If the bond has a 10 percent return, the selling price is established so that 10 percent a year compounded semiannually will bring it to full face value at maturity. The compounding rate is not affected by changes in interest rates. The end result of the investments is known. By contrast, the ordinary bond pays interest in cash every six months, which has to be reinvested at prevailing rates. If yields rise, that is fine. But if they drop, the investor loses out.

For example, a $1,000 conventional bond paying 8 percent today will return $2,440 in principal and interest in 18 years. In contrast, $1,000 invested in a zero will pay back approximately $4,000 in the same period. The return on the conventional bond could be much higher also if the $1,440 in interest payments were reinvested as they were received throughout the 18 years. But many individuals are negligent about reinvesting. And even if they did reinvest, they cannot be sure of constantly getting 8 percent interest.

The Zero Jungle: Tigers, Lyons, Cats, etc.

Zeros were first introduced as corporation-backed securities. Brokers created zeros by "stripping" interest-bearing coupons from the "corpus"—the part of the bond that matures at face value—and selling each part separately. But the demand for zero coupon securities has been enormous since Merrill Lynch created the first stripped Treasury receipts in 1982. This introduced the benefit of zeros plus the guarantees of ultimate repayments.

Merrill Lynch, in August 1982, sliced up a half billion dollars' worth of 14 percent Treasury bonds like a crate of melons. It separated the principal of the bonds from the coupons and deposited the lot in a bank. It offered investors the chance to buy one part or the other at a low dollar price. At maturity, investors receive the full face amount of the portion they bought, coupons or principal. The units were called **TIGRs** (Treasury investment growth receipts).

Zero coupon bonds were also given cute animal nicknames. After Merrill Lynch's TIGRs, came **CATS** from Salomon Brothers (certificates of accrual on Treasury securities) and then Merrill Lynch introduced its **LYONs** (liquid yield option notes). There were also **ETRs** (easy growth Treasury receipts) from Dean Witter and TBRs (Treasury bond receipts) from E. F. Hutton.

The Treasury zeros were actually an artificial product created by Wall Street in 1982. Since then bond dealers each year strip billions of dollars in Treasury bonds, most of them with 20- to 30-year maturities. The underlying Treasury bonds themselves are deposited by the sponsoring broker in a trust institution such as a bank for safekeeping. The sponsoring broker sells (zero) certificates that evidence ownership in a particular Treasury maturity, albeit indirect ownership of Treasury obligations. Investors do not directly own the Treasury but have a written promise from the broker and bank serving as trustee that at maturity the money collected from the Treasury bond or coupon will be remitted to the zero buyer.

How a Zero Is Created

To make a zero, brokers buy up huge lots of Treasury bonds, strip the future interest payments from them, package the interest into $1,000 units and sell them as bonds. A 20-year bond with a face value of $20,000 and a 10 percent interest rate, for example, is "stripped" into its 41 component parts, 40 twice-yearly interest payments, and the main body or principal repayment at maturity. The 40 coupons are turned into separate zeros, each worth $1,000 or one-half the annual interest of $2,000 on the specified payment date, with maturities of from six months to 20 years. The body, of course, would be worth the $20,000 face value upon maturity. Each of the 41 zero coupon instruments could be traded until its due date. The price an investor pays for the bond varies with the maturity. The further away the maturity date, the less the present value of the bond.

The World's Greatest Stripper: Uncle Sam

Dealers in government securities have made handsome profits in recent years by taking government bonds and converting them to zero coupon bonds. Treasury officials began to wonder why the intermediaries should make the profits. If the Treasury issued its own zero coupons, it could reap the benefit for itself.

In 1985, in response to the success of the Wall Street felines, the government permitted banks to turn in whole securities such as Treasury bonds and notes and receive separate obligations for each interest payment and for the principal (or corpus). In effect, the Treasury was stripping its own bonds and notes and issuing zero coupon securities.

This could be done easily because the Treasury was adding these securities to its book entry system of record keeping. Uncle Sam merely recorded the ownership of each piece on its books, just as a savings bank records passbook savings. The Treasury's new zero program was called **STRIPS**, or separate trading of registered interest and principal of securities.

STRIPS are the safest zeros of all. **TIGRs** and **CATS** are actually certificates issued by custodian banks which hold in an irrevocable trust the federal government bonds that brokers have stripped. STRIPS, on the other hand, have no certificates. They are bonds the government itself has already stripped and delivered directly to brokers and banks that in turn sell them to the public. STRIPS, therefore, are a direct obligation of the U.S. government to the individual bondholder.

Beware of the Animals   CATS, TIGRs, LYONs, and other financial felines including STRIPS may be attractive and cute animals, but they can also be dangerous. Although zeros do not carry a coupon, they increase in value daily as they steadily move closer to maturity. However, if you wish to sell that value, also gets adjusted by the prevailing level of interest rates.

The odd nature of zeros makes them highly volatile. Because the bonds are discounted so deeply, a relatively small yield change translates into a disproportionately large price move. The real power of the zero is the interest on interest at a high rate on a long-term bond.

However, locking in a "high" interest rate is advantageous only if interest rates later go down. If interest rates later go higher, it can be detrimental. Zero coupon bond prices plummet further when rates rise and soar higher when rates drop. That happens because holders of conventional bonds that throw off cash interest payments can reinvest it in higher yielding paper as rates go up, but must settle for reinvesting for less when rates are sliding.

For these reasons, the prices of zeros fluctuate with every change in interest rates much more than do those of conventional bonds. A 10-year zero is nearly twice as volatile in price as a 10-year conventional bond. A 20-year zero is about three times as risky as a 20-year conventional bond and a 30-year zero is about four times as volatile as a 30-year bond.

Hardly any of the brochures on zeros put out by major brokerage firms mentions this greater fluctuation. In fact, the brochures stress the "safety" of the investment because most of the zeros are based on bonds issued by the government. By stressing credit safety without discussing price volatility, the major brokerage firms are only telling half the story.

When you buy a 25-year zero, you are taking a significant risk because it is impossible to know what interest rates are going to be. If your circumstances change and you are compelled to raise quick cash, you may find that you have jeopardized the liquidity of your assets. You may have to take very severe losses if you sell your zeros to raise cash; or if you are lucky and rates have declined since you bought your zeros, you can make a handsome profit. Zeros, therefore, are best-suited for long-term tax-free IRA accounts or in custodial accounts to pay for children's education. They are not meant to be sold before maturity.

The IRS Skins the Cats   Another disadvantage of zeros is that the Internal Revenue Service considers the "imputed" interest in the zero to be taxable each year. Buyers must pay annual income tax on the "imputed" interest as it accrues—just as though it were mailed to them like interest on a regular bond. This means that investors must pay taxes in today's dollars on theoretical interest, income they will not see for years.

To justify this policy, the IRS argues that the buyer of a zero coupon bond is in fact receiving an annual return, like the owner of a regular bond. It is just that the income is in effect automatically reinvested at the imputed yield, instead of being paid out to a bond holder who can reinvest the money as he or she chooses.

Since investment income in tax-sheltered retirement accounts (such as IRAs) goes untaxed until withdrawn, zeros are well suited to those accounts. Another way around this tax disadvantage is to buy zero coupon bonds consisting of municipal issues.

Brokers' Commission   Some disgruntled investors claim that brokers are charging excessive commissions on zeros by basing the commissions on the face value of the bonds rather than their purchase price. For example, say a $1,000 zero is issued at $275 and a broker charges a $40 commission. That commission is only 4 percent of the zero's face value, but it is a shocking 14.5 percent of the original $275 investment.

If you decide to buy a zero, the most important shopping consideration is to make sure you are getting the best price. To make comparisons, ask several brokers to supply you with three figures:

1. The total amount of money you have to invest now (including all fees and commissions

2. The total amount of money you will receive when the bond matures

The LYON's Cage

Merrill Lynch's liquid yield option note, or LYON, is a variant on an old-style convertible that promises the guaranteed return of a zero coupon bond and the potential capital appreciation of a common stock. Investors buy the zero coupon bonds at a large discount from face value. They get zero interest payments until the bonds mature, typically in 15 to 20 years, when the bonds are redeemed at face value.

The attraction for investors is that a LYON is convertible into stock at any time. If the stock should appreciate considerably, the LYON suddenly becomes a lot more valuable.

Because they are convertible into stock, LYONs accrue interest at a lower than market rate.

3. The effective yield to maturity this growth represents

In general, the longer you commit your money, the higher the yield.

Junk Bonds

The term **junk bonds** (euphemistically known on Wall Street as "high-yield bonds") conjures up an image of useless certificates sitting in a pile in someone's attic. Many investors have latched on to higher yields by buying riskier low-rated bonds, often dubbed "junk bonds." Junk bonds are bonds rated below Baa-3 by Moody's Investors Service Inc. or below BBB minus by Standard and Poor's Corp.

Is it safe to buy a bond with a B rating for creditworthiness? While B might be a decent grade in school, there are actually 14 better gradings available if you use all the pluses and minuses. A rating of B is in fact below an investment-grade rating. Specifically, a B means that "adverse business, financial, or economic conditions would likely impair capacity or willingness to pay interest and repay principal."

These bonds, whose volume quadrupled from 1979 to 1988, earned respectability by outperforming investment-grade debt. In 1988 they accounted for about a fourth of all outstanding corporate bonds. The $180 billion junk bond market included more than 1,000 companies and was a growing sector of Wall Street.

However, due to the collapse in 1990 of Drexel Burnham Lambert, Inc.—the junk bond giant that virtually created and then dominated the market—and the conviction of its leading junk bond broker, Michael J. Milken, the junk bond market has undergone turmoil and confusion. In 1990, the market was shrinking and highly unstable. It is likely that a reorganized but smaller junk bond market will reemerge but this remains to be seen. In 1993 the junk bond market showed signs of robust growth.

The difficulties of making a good decision.

Junk bonds obviously require a more thorough analysis of creditworthiness than investment-grade bonds. Investors cannot rely solely on the credit ratings given by Moody's or Standard & Poor's. One should distinguish between young medium-sized companies with a promising future that are rated low because they are untested and have little credit history, and firms that are graded low because of financial troubles. Unless investors are betting on a financial recovery, they should avoid the latter.

The higher default rate of junk bonds in the early 1990s invariably scared many investors away. Many junk investors did not consider the extra yield as enough to justify the added risk inherent in junk bond investing. But for others, the prospects of higher yields outweighed the greater potential for loss.

Call Provisions

A **call provision** in the bond indenture entitles the bond issuers to redeem the bond at their discretion prior to the maturity date . Unfortunately, a long-term corporate or municipal bond does not always let investors lock in a high interest rate. Many such bonds prove to be short-lived. Unlike Treasuries, most corporate and municipal borrowers issue their bonds with call provisions that allow them to redeem their debt before it is due, after a stated period such as 5 to 10 years if interest rates decline. As a rule of thumb, if an older bond has a coupon one and one-half percentage points above the coupon on newly issued bonds of the same type and maturity, there is a strong likelihood that it will be called. When bonds are called, the issuer generally pays the bondholder a bit more than the bond's face value, something in the nature of a modest bonus. The call price usually starts off at a high premium, decreasing over discrete predefined points in time.

Even the federal government, trying to take advantage of declines in interest rates during the early 1990s, called $1.8 billion of Treasury bonds for early repayment in February of 1992. It was the first time since 1962 that the Treasury called a bond issue. Most Treasury bonds, however, are not subject to be called.

The call price is set above the bond's face value in order to soften the blow by compensating the bond holder for premature redemption. In most cases, the call price premium (which is the term for the amount by which the call price exceeds the bond's face value) paid by the issuer is equal to one year's interest. For example, a $1,000 10-percent bond would be callable for $1,100 ($1,000 principal + $100 call penalty).

The effect is to cap the amount the investor can earn from a bond by both limiting the potential price gain and depriving him or her of high-interest income. Early redemptions frequently mean that investors get back their principal when there isn't any equally attractive place to put it, forcing them to reinvest returned dollars at a time when interest rates have declined. Why should borrowers do such a thing? Because they want to be free to refinance their debt at a lower rate.

The call feature is bad news for investors who thought they were guaranteed a steady stream of interest payments for long periods of time. If you are counting on income from bonds you hold or might purchase, the first priority is to determine what kind of call protection you have. **Noncallable** long-term bonds that cannot be "called" or redeemed before maturity are a preferable choice. Many of these

The Call Feature

The **call feature** is usually advantageous to the issuer since it permits the replacement of current high-interest outstanding debt with lower-interest debt. Suppose company XYZ issued $100,000,000 worth of 20-year, 12 percent bonds with a 10 percent call penalty or premium. This costs the firm $12 million in interest annually. If after one year the bond market interest rates fall to 7 percent, the firm will find it advantageous to pay off the bond holders ($100 million + $10 million premium = $110 million) by selling $110 million worth of new bonds at 7 percent to repay old bonds. True, the firm lost $10 million in call premiums. However, the corporation will from now on have an interest obligation of only $7.7 million instead of $12 million. This is a savings of $4.3 million a year. When multiplied by the 19 years that it would have had to pay the extra $4.3 million, it comes to a total savings of $81.7 million. Bond issuers can be expected to redeem bonds early if interest rates are only a percentage point or two below the level when they sold their securities, making it possible for them to refinance with cheaper debt.

bonds have refunding restrictions which prohibit the issuer from retiring bonds at an interest rate below the coupon of the outstanding issue. This restriction is usually limited to five years from the date of issue. When that protection runs out, they are likely to be redeemed.

Another method is to buy a deeply discounted issue with more than 10 years left to run, such as a bond due in 2005 with a 5 percent coupon. They may be selling for 65 ($650), producing a yield of 10 percent if held to maturity. If, in the unlikely event that rates should decline enough to make the issuer redeem those bonds before they mature, investors will receive full ($1,000) face value and have made such a big profit that they will not object. An additional way to avoid the worry about an early call is to buy Treasury securities. All new Treasury notes and bonds cannot be redeemed prior to their stated maturity dates.

SUMMARY

A bond is basically a debt security representing a loan between an issuer and an investor. The bondholder receives periodic interest payments and return of the face value of the bond (principal) at a specified date in the future, known as the maturity date. On the maturity date and upon repayment of principal and interest, the bond terminates. Bonds offer a fixed return in the sense that interest payments are fixed over the bond's term. The three general types of bonds are corporate bonds, U.S. government issues, and municipal bonds.

Corporate bonds may be classified as debentures or mortgage bonds. The U.S. Treasury issues bills, notes, and bonds, all of which have different maturity dates, from three months to 30 years. U.S. government securities are free from default risk but are subject to the risks of changing interest rates. Municipal bonds are the debt obligations of a state, city, town, village, or U.S. territory. Another form of bond investing is in mortgage-backed securities and pass throughs. These are issued by Ginnie Mae, Fanny Mae, Freddie Mac, and Sallie Mae, among others. They carry an advantage of government guarantees.

Two credit-rating firms, Moody's and Standard & Poor's, analyze and rate corporate and municipal bonds. Their ratings give a good indication of the likelihood of a bond issuer repaying principal and interest when due during the term of the bond.

The values of all bonds, federal, municipal, or corporate, can be affected by changes in market interest rates, a bond's credit rating, and inflationary expectations. A recent development is the zero coupon bond, which pays no interest but is purchased at a deep discount, and junk bonds, which are rated below investment grade.

Bond investing can be as intricate and risky as stocks and other investment forms. It could also be just as rewarding. Successful bond investing requires an understanding of the diverse bond market with all of its components and features. Bond investing can be of value to an investor who wants some conservative diversification or who has an important goal to reach within a few years and wants to reduce the risk of loss of capital. As a rule, the higher the quality of the bond and the shorter the time to maturity, the safer the bond investment. Bonds generally deserve a place in most people's investment portfolio.

KEY TERMS

Baby bonds

Bills

Bonds

Bond credit ratings

Bond indenture

Bond stripping

Call feature

Certificates of accrual on Treasury securities (CATS)

Collateralized mortgage obligations (CMOs)

Commercial paper

Convertible securities

Corporate bonds

Credit rating

Current or coupon yield

Debentures

Deep discount corporate bonds

Discount

Duff and Phelps

Easy growth Treasury receipts (ETRs)

Face value

Federal Home Loan Mortgage Corporation (Freddie Mac)

Federal National Mortgage Association (Fannie Mae)

First mortgage bond

General obligation bonds (GOs)

Government National Mortgage Association (Ginnie Mae)

Junk bonds

Liquid yield option notes (LYONs)

Maturity date

Moody's Investors Services

Mortgage-backed securities

Mortgage bonds

Municipal tax-exempt bonds (munis)

Nellie Mae

Noncallable feature

Notes

Par value

Pass throughs

Payroll savings plan

Premium

Prepayment risk

Principal

Revenue bonds

Second mortgage bond

Self-liquidating (wasting) investment

Series E and EE bonds

Series HH bonds

Sinking funds

Sonny Mae

Standard & Poor's Corporation

Student Loan Marketing Association
(Sallie Mae)

Subordinated debenture

Tax anticipation notes

Treasuries

Treasury Direct System

Treasury investment growth receipts
(TIGRs)

Treasury issues

Treasury STRIPS

U.S. savings bonds

Yield

Yield to maturity

Zero coupon bonds

REVIEW QUESTIONS AND PROBLEMS

1. Your tax bracket is 25 percent. You plan on buying a 9 percent municipal tax-free bond. What rate of return would a corporate taxable bond have to yield to be comparable to the 9 percent muni?
2. Briefly define the following terms: (a) yield to maturity, (b) current yield, (c) discount, (d) premium, (e) par value.
3. Identify both the positive and negative features of investing in bonds.
4. Assume you had $10,000 that you do not need for a number of years. Explain which type of bond you would decide to invest in. Explain why the particular type meets your investment needs.
5. Assume that you are in the 25 percent tax bracket. If you bought a tax-exempt municipal bond with a stated 8 percent annual interest rate, what would be its taxable equivalent for you?
6. Your mother-in-law tells you that if you want to be safe and not risk losing your money, then invest in top-grade bonds. Evaluate your mother-in-law's advice. List the arguments for or against her premise.
7. Compare and contrast a debenture and mortgage bond.
8. Explain the advantages and disadvantages of buying U.S. savings bonds.
9. Explain how bond prices are affected by changes in investment rates. Use a numerical example.
10. Explain the special attraction municipal bonds have for high-income earners.
11. Harry and Harriet Cash are in the 33 percent federal income tax bracket. They can buy a $10,000 AAA corporate bond at face value with a 9 percent interest rate or $900 annually. They can instead purchase a $10,000 municipal bond at face value with a 7.5 percent coupon rate that will pay $750 each year. Assuming both bonds are of equal risk, which bond should they buy? Explain.
12. Describe which kind of investors would prefer bonds over stocks.

13. "A 30-year Treasury bond is the safest form of investment with no risk whatsoever to the investor." Discuss the folly (or wisdom) of this statement.

14. "Investing in bonds is nearly as risky as investing in stocks." Make a list of arguments to support this statement. Do you agree with it? Explain why or why not.

15. How do Series EE savings bonds differ from corporate bonds? To what kind of investor do they have most appeal?

16. An investor tells her broker: "I'm looking for capital gains and therefore am not interested in buying bonds." If you were her broker, how would you respond to this statement? Base your response on your knowledge of bond price movements.

17. Why is a call provision an advantage to the bond issuer and a disadvantage to the bond holder?

18. A. Compute the current yield of a 9 percent, 10-year bond that is currently priced in the market at $920.

    B. What is the current yield of a 9 percent, 15-year bond that is currently priced in the market at $1,280?

19. Explain how mortgage-backed securities or pass throughs have enabled banks to issue more mortgage loans to home buyers.

20. What is a collateralized mortgage obligation?

21. Why is it safer to invest in junk bond funds via a bond fund rather than in individual junk bond issues?

22. What is the primary objective of the Mae "family" (Ginnie Mae, Fannie Mae, Sallie Mae, and Freddie Mac?)

23. What two services analyze and rate municipal bond issues?

24. Explain the purpose of a sinking fund and how it adds to a bond's attractiveness.

25. Calculate the yield to maturity of the bonds in the two parts of question 18.

26. (CURRENT) Current market price of a bond is $1,200. The current yield is 4 percent. What is the annual interest payment?

27. (MATURITY) The annual yield of your $1,000 par bond is $50. The yield to maturity is 11 percent. The number of years to maturity is 14. What is the market value of the bond?

28. (ZEROS) The current interest rate on zeros is 7 percent. Your child will attend college in 12 years. The overall cost of a college education is $100,000. What is the implied future cost of a college education per year?

SUGGESTED PROJECTS

Assume your family has $100,000 and has decided to invest it in bonds.

A. Consider your family's goals and its uses for this money. Income? Growth? Speculation? Retirement? Education?

B. Are your goals short term, intermediate term, or long term?

C. Decide whether you want to buy U. S. Treasuries, municipal, corporate, convertibles, zero coupon, junk, or other bonds.

D. Contact several bond brokers and ask for a list of recommended bonds which meet your goals and requirements.

E. Study the brokers' recommendations. Examine the bonds for safety and yield.

F. Construct a portfolio of bonds worth $100,000. Explain and justify to your class how this portfolio is best suited to meet your family's particular needs.

INFORMATION RESOURCES

Asinoff, Lynn. "Bond Insurance Offers Layers of Protection." *The Wall Street Journal*, May 8, 1991, C-1.

Bureau of the Public Debt. 202/287-4113. This agency will send a "noncompetitive tender" order form to investors who wish to purchase treasury bonds by mail. The forms are also available from any of the 12 Federal Reserve banks or their branch offices.

"The Coming Defaults in Junk Bonds." *Fortune*, March 16, 1987, 26–34.

Donnelly, Barbara. "Weighing Muni Bonds vs. Treasuries." *The Wall Street Journal*, January 27, 1992, C-1.

Federal Reserve Banks. See the box in the chapter for addresses and telephone numbers of all 12 banks; these banks will send a "noncompetitive tender" order form to investors who wish to purchase treasury bonds by mail.

Giese, William. "The Treasury's Investment Superstore." *Kiplinger's Personal Finance Magazine*, February 1993, 69–73.

Herman, Tom. "How to Get Best Price in Buying, Selling Municipals." *The Wall Street Journal*, May 8, 1992, C-1.

———. "While Corporate Bonds May Be Bargains, Too." *The Wall Street Journal*, February 25, 1991, C-1.

———. "Bonds vs. Bond Funds: Which Are Better for You?" *The Wall Street Journal*, April 30, 1993, C-1.

Kosnett, Jeff. "Will Muni Bonds Weather the Storm?" *Kiplinger's Personal Finance Magazine*, November 1991, 73–76.

Lipin, Steven and Constance Mitchell. "Wall Street Is Using Junk Bonds." *The Wall Street Journal*, May 18, 1983, C-1.

Liscio, John. "How to Buy a Treasury Bill—It's a Lot Easier Than You Think." *Barron's*, January 16, 1989, 32.

Markese, John. "Buying Treasuries from the Factory." *Money*, December 1988, 137–141.

Norris, Floyd. "A Complex Route to Higher Yields (CMOs)." *The New York Times*, February 6, 1992, B-1.

Office of Public Affairs, U.S. Savings Bond Division, Department of the Treasury, Washington, DC 20226. 202/634-5389. Call or write for more information on Series E and EE Bonds.

Rowland, Mary. "The ABC's of Bonds." *Working Woman*, January 1988, 43–44.

———. "When Bonds Are Called In Early." *The New York Times*, November 10, 1991, F-16.

"Savings Bonds May Pay Off with High Yields For You." *Money*, December 1989, 183.

Series E and EE bonds. For more information, write or call the Office of Public Affairs, U.S. Savings Bonds Division, Department of Treasury, Washington, DC 20226. 202/634-5389.

Slater, Karen. "Timing's the Thing with Savings Bonds." *The Wall Street Journal,* April 23, 1992, C-1.

Sloan, Allan. "The Rape of the Bond Holder." *Forbes,* January 23, 1989, 67–69.

"Time for Another Date with Ginnie Mae?" *U.S. News and World Report,* October 19, 1989, 77.

Treasury Department, Bureau of the Public Debt, Washington, DC 20239. 202/287-4113. Investors can send letters to the bureau for tender and noncompetitive bids for Treasury Bills (13- or 26-week) on specific dates; see the chapter for more details.

Tucker, James F. *Buying Treasury Securities at Federal Reserve Banks.* Available from the Federal Reserve Bank of Richmond, Bank and Public Relations Dept., P.O. Box 27622, Richmond, VA 23219.

Wilcox, Melynda D. "Savings Bonds Are Great: True or False?" *Kiplinger's Personal Finance Magazine,* March 1993, 75–78.

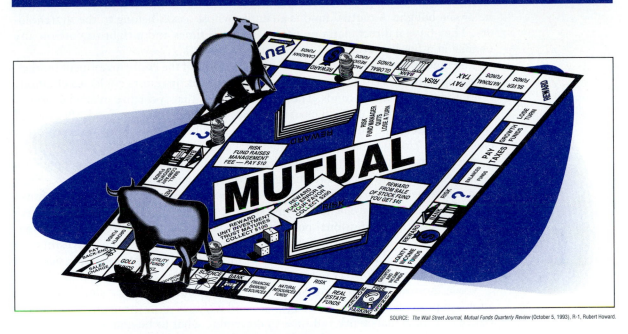

CHAPTER FOURTEEN

SOURCE: *The Wall Street Journal, Mutual Funds Quarterly Review* (October 5, 1993), R-1, Rubert Howard.

Mutual Funds

- To describe the different types of mutual funds

- To examine the benefits and risks that mutual fund investments offer to individual investors

- To discuss the process of selecting a mutual fund

- To explore how a money market fund is structured and its place in an investor's financial life

- To differentiate load from no-load and low-load mutual funds

- To consider the procedures available for analyzing and selecting mutual funds with investment objectives suitable to your needs

- To outline the advantages provided an investor through a family of mutual funds

    This chapter discusses the variety of fund types available and examines the pros and cons of mutual fund investing. It familiarizes the reader with mutual fund terminology and provides information which should be helpful to an investor in intelligently selecting a fund.

    A **mutual fund** is a corporation that allows individuals with similar objectives and a specific predetermined investment philosophy to pool their resources together to buy stocks, bonds, and other securities. Each of the investors' proportional ownership of the **fund's portfolio** is measured by the number of "shares" of the fund he or she bought. A mutual fund is an entity whose assets belong to the shareholders. They have a direct claim on the assets at all times and a right to vote on any change in a fund's status.

The mutual fund industry is actually a microcosm of the entire investment market. Funds specialize in virtually every type of investment. Investors could select among more than nearly 2,300 funds. These include funds that specialize in stocks, bonds, options, commodities, foreign currency, gold, and money market funds. Because of the wide variety and enormous choice, investors who conduct some research often can find one closely tailored to their financial goals.

Are mutual funds a better choice than individual stocks? For many people who lack the time and ability to sift financial news and company reports, to make their own stock investment decisions, and to manage their own portfolio, mutual funds can offer a distinct convenience. Buying shares of mutual fund and leaving the selection of stocks to a professional portfolio manager can be the busy person's alternative to choosing among thousands of stocks and bonds. Many small investors are attracted to mutual funds and consider this method of investment safer, easier, and more convenient than direct securities.

For a modest minimum investment, often $1,000, funds give small investors access to professional money management and a choice of investments. These experienced professionals work full time to determine what to buy, at what price, and when to sell. This generally, though not necessarily, should be preferable to novice investors whose investment moves may be tentative if not haphazard.

Of course, professional money management does not guarantee that investors will strike it rich. Even in a booming stock market, some stock funds manage to lose money. But the fact that the funds sometimes under perform the averages is not very meaningful for the typical investor who owns fewer stocks and thus incurs more risk than do most mutual funds.

Mutual funds have become the centerpiece of the investment strategies of a large and growing number of individuals. They were once thought of as the poor person's approach to money management, but over the past decade, increased participation by wealthier individuals and institutional investors has changed that reputation. Even professional investors often channel at least part of their portfolio into these moderate-risk investment vehicles.

The value of shares in a stock mutual fund rises and falls along with the value of the stocks in the fund's portfolio. Because a mutual fund is diversified, the investor's principal is generally considered more secure than it would be if it were invested in the stock of a single company that fell on hard times. There is a strong possibility that any bad investment by the fund will be offset by several successful ones. The diversification that provides some security against a disastrous loss of principal, of course, also makes it very unlikely that the fund will realize the dramatic gain investors may dream of by lucking out in a directly invested single stock that doubles or triples in value in a short period of time. Additionally, most individual investors either cannot afford or are unprepared to manage a portfolio that has enough stocks to accommodate diversification, so that a single mistake will not spell financial disaster.

How Safe Are Mutual Funds?

Can a mutual fund become insolvent like a mismanaged S&L? There are safeguards provided by the **Investment Company Act of 1940,** the primary federal regulation governing mutual funds. Since 1940, no fund has gone out of business because its managers looted it. In fact, by law funds must give securities to a third party, such as a bank, to hold in trust. Although nothing is absolutely certain, mutual funds thus far have had a good record for integrity. The main risk is the fund's skill in choosing the right stocks and bonds.

Types of Funds

There is a wide variety of fund categories. The most common fund categories in order of declining risk are the following:

1. **Aggressive growth fund**

2. **Growth fund**

3. **Growth of capital and income fund**

4. **Equity income fund**

5. **Balanced (between stock and bonds) fund**

6. **Corporate bond fund**

7. **Municipal bond fund**

8. **Money market fund**

A reliable rule of thumb is that the higher the reward you seek, the higher the risk you must take. Stock mutual funds usually define their objectives to potential investors. By knowing a fund's objectives, you learn something of its risk. The funds objectives are stated in the fund's "prospectus" discussed further on. Funds that emphasize "growth" will typically take higher risks in the hope that the value of their shares will grow faster than the average value of all stocks.

1. *Aggressive Growth Funds* The riskiest funds are clustered in the maximum capital gains, aggressive growth category, also called *capital appreciation, maximum capital gains,* or *small company holding funds.* The most aggressive **maximum capital gains funds** try to maximize capital gains by investing in small and rapidly growing companies whose share prices are more volatile than the norm. They often have a very high portfolio turnover rate and employ speculative techniques of leverage, such as margin buying and short selling. They also invest

TABLE 14–1	Funds in Good Times and Bad

Below are the average cumulative total returns—which reflect share price gains and reinvested dividends—for the past seven bull and bear markets, starting in 1961. Also shown are the annualized returns for the 10, 20, and 30 years ended August 31, 1992.

Performance

Fund Category	Bear Markets	Bull Markets	10 Years	20 Years	30 Years
1. Small company growth funds	–30.7%	158.6%	12.8%	10.8%	11.3%
2. Growth funds	–27.1	131.5	14.2	10.3	10.1
3. Growth and income funds	–23.0	110.8	15.0	11.0	10.4
4. Equity-income funds	–17.0	102.6	14.2	11.8	10.7
5. Balanced funds	–16.4	86.2	14.7	10.9	9.7
6. Capital appreciation funds	–30.1	141.8	13.0	9.7	9.2
7. International stock funds	–23.6	118.3	16.1	8.9	8.3

SOURCE: *The Wall Street Journal*, Mutual Funds Quarterly Review, October 5, 1992, R-28.

in restricted securities, which are shares that have not yet been registered for sale to the general public.

Many of the issues in their portfolio may pay no dividends, since they ignore dividend income and aim for big capital gains. The funds themselves, therefore, ordinarily pay no dividends to their shareholders other than capital gains on securities sale. These funds are not highly speculative by the standards of individual speculative stocks. Even volatile funds do not demand the daily and sometimes hourly attention required to monitor certain individual stocks. A fund changes its share price only once a day and the value of the funds' broad portfolio never fluctuates as quickly as many individual stocks. But in the realm of mutual funds, they usually are the most volatile, leading any market upswing, and are the first to be affected by a down market.

In order to protect their profits, investors in such funds have to stand ready to sell out quickly if the market begins a sharp downturn or need to have a long investment horizon and an above-average risk tolerance. For investors who do not have the time or the interest to monitor their investment that closely or who are unwilling or cannot afford to take steep losses, maximum capital gain funds should be avoided.

2. *Growth Funds* Just below the capital appreciation group are the **growth funds**. These strive for a steady, long-term rise in earnings rather than any immediate gains. There may be some income, but it is considered secondary to appreciation. They generally invest in larger, more established firms whose stock is expected at least to rise faster than the inflation rate and which tend to be less volatile than those owned by aggressive growth funds. Growth is the most popular equity fund category and has the largest number of funds from which to choose.

3. *Growth of Capital and Income Funds* **Growth and income funds,** as their names imply, search for stocks that pay high dividends and have the potential for price appreciation as well. They entail less risk than aggressive and long-term growth funds. Their goal is to provide long-term growth as well as dividend income without much fluctuation in share price, even in declining markets. They generally appeal to more conservative investors.

4. *Equity Income Funds* These funds emphasize income from stock dividends. Their priority is a high level of dividend income. In return, **equity income funds** give up some prospect of price appreciation. They hold varying proportions of common stocks, preferred stocks, and bonds according to changing market conditions.

5. *Balanced Funds* These are among the more conservative funds. They divide their holdings between stocks and bonds according to set ratios. Most **balanced funds** keep 20 to 40 percent of assets in bonds or preferred stocks at all times, with stocks of large established companies making up most of the rest of the portfolio.

6. *Corporate Bonds Funds* **Corporate bond funds** fall into two categories. **Taxable bond funds** invest in corporate bonds, whereas **tax-free bond funds** hold tax-exempt municipal issues. Investors in bond funds usually seek high current income and safety, but in periods of fluctuating inflation, bond funds are subject to price swings because of volatile interest rates.

There are various types of corporate bond funds and government bond funds, such as Ginnie Mae funds, Treasury bond funds, municipal tax-exempt bond funds, high-yield bond funds, and convertible bond funds. Bond mutual funds give small investors the means of buying a piece of a portfolio containing bonds from many issuers. They also offer investors considerable liquidity, the ability to sell when they want to without severe penalties. As with a stock mutual fund, investors can redeem their shares at any time for their portion of the current value of the bonds.

An important factor to look at in a bond fund is the quality of securities a fund buys. At one end of the safety scale are funds that invest only in the highest-rated issues of state and federal agencies or only in AAA-rated corporations. Other funds invest primarily in high-yield bonds termed *junk bonds* (see Chapter 13).

7. *Municipal Bond (Tax-Free) Funds* **Municipal bond funds** exclusively invest in tax-free municipal bonds. This provides investors with tax-free income. Investors need always check to see whether they would be better off in a tax-free fund. Those who live in a high tax state will find it worthwhile to invest in double or triple tax-free funds that are also exempt from state and local income taxes.

8. *Money Market Funds* These are discussed at the end of this chapter.

Each of the preceding standard category of mutual fund, although useful as a broad guideline, encompasses widely different degrees of risk and investment styles. Among funds known as maximizing capital gains, for instance, some may move as much as 80 percent of their assets out of stocks at times to avoid expected market declines, while others will always stay fully invested in stocks.

Selecting a Fund

Mutual funds originally were designed to make investing easy for small investors by offering a diversified portfolio of securities to those who could not afford to diversify by buying individual stocks and bonds. But in recent years there are almost as many mutual funds as there are stocks on the New York Stock Exchange. Selecting a mutual fund is therefore far from simple. However, investors with patience, diligence, and some careful research can select the appropriate funds for their needs. Before setting out to choose a particular fund, an investor should decide which funds are appropriate to his or her investment approach.

The first step should be to clarify your investment goals and risk tolerance. Start by defining your own investment objectives:

1. Do you want your money invested in stocks, bonds, or a combination?

2. Are you looking for long-term appreciation or short-term gains?

3. Do you want income or capital growth?

4. How much risk are you willing to accept?

Investors' long-term plans will depend on their age, family situation, current and expected future income, tax bracket, overall net worth, and temperament. It means sorting through a number of funds to find those whose goals and willingness to take risk match those of the investor. If investors know what they are looking for and how to select it, it should not be difficult to find a fund best suited to their taste, style, goals, and tolerance for risk. For most investors, a mix of different types of funds offers the best solution. A young couple might put 25 percent of their assets in a high-risk aggressive growth stock fund, 50 percent in growth or growth and income funds, and the rest in real estate or money market funds. An older couple might shift its emphasis to conservative income funds that offer some stability to compensate for lower growth.

Once you have decided how to split your assets among different types of funds, you can search for the best funds in each category. The performance of any fund will vary with its investment goals as well as the skill of its management. A few funds consistently outperform the competition, and they are a good place to start one's search. This is discussed further on.

Is Your Fund Loaded?

One critical decision is whether to go with **load** or **no-load** funds. Load funds generally are sold through brokerage houses and bear a substantial fee or commission, which investors pay when they buy. **Front-end loads** or commissions are taken off the top and used by management to pay a sales commission to the broker promoting the fund. A broker, financial planner, or sales representative is much more likely to try to sell an investor a load fund than a no-load fund. Load funds charge an initial sales commission or "load," which ranges from 0.75 percent to 8.5 percent paid to the broker or financial planner who sells the shares. No-load funds offer the advantage of not imposing any initial sales charge or fee when investors buy into the fund.

Investors buy no-load funds directly by mail from the fund management companies. The fund sells directly to investors through newspaper, radio, and TV advertisements. Since they have no sales charges, no-load funds typically have no sales people out beating the doors for customers. Investors have to seek out no-load funds for themselves but it can be worth the effort. (The industry's trade group, The No-Load Mutual Funds Association, 11 Penn Plaza, New York, NY 10001, readily provides information on and lists of no-load funds.)

Despite claims often made by brokers, there is no evidence to suggest that load funds as a group outperform no-loads. The Institute for Econometric Research conducted a study comparing the performance of no-load mutual funds with load funds. The study covered 15 years (1971 to 1985). The results found that no-load mutual funds provided their shareholders with superior returns. Furthermore, that superiority existed before adjusting for the sales charge, which would have made the comparison even more favorable for no-loads. Over the entire 15 years, the no-loads provided an average annual return of 11.2 percent versus just 8.8 percent for the average load fund.

LOAD

Investors who are willing to search for the best funds by themselves would be better served by no-load funds. Moreover, investors who do not intend to stay in a fund for very long will almost always be better off to buy no-load funds rather than load funds. It is not very prudent to give up as much as 8.5 percent of your money to make what might well be a short-term investment. Remember that initially at least, the load sets investors back. After an 8.5 percent load is deducted, a $1,000 investment in a load fund buys $915 worth of shares in the fund. Thus, the fund must appreciate almost 10 percent before investors break even.

If investors intend to stay with a fund for at least five years, a load becomes less significant. When shopping for a fund, focus should first be on performance, not fees. But when choosing between two funds with comparable investment records, a wide difference in annual fees can make the choice clear. While it may seem that all no-load funds offer a better deal than any load fund, that is not necessarily the case. A load fund whose investment gains exceed those of a no-load fund by more than the cost of the commission can be a better investment.

Low-Loads and Fees

In recent years the line between load and no-load funds has become blurred. Some of the best performing no-loads have imposed **low-load** charges of 1 to 3 percent. Mutual fund managers have succeeded in developing new kinds of charges, which reduce shareholders' returns and are often not even obvious to the investor. Fee or no fee, invariably investors end up paying the fund's promotion and administrative costs in one way or another. Usually those charges are buried in the general management expenses, which are paid from operating revenues on a continuing basis, before determining the market price of the shares. This annual management fee of both load and no-load funds often takes 0.5 to 0.75 percent of the average daily assets of the fund.

A new type of fund fee has emerged that is different from fees charged by traditional load funds. A fund resorting to this new type of fee is known as a 12b-1 fund.

"Tough luck, fella! All my money is in the no-load Berger 100 and Berger 101 Funds."

SOURCE: Berger Funds, *Kiplinger's Personal Finance Magazine,* November 1991, 48. Reprinted by permission of Peter Hesse.

12b-1 Funds   True no-load mutual funds are becoming rare enough to deserve a slot on the endangered species list. More and more of these supposedly commission-free funds are dipping into assets to help pay marketing expenses under a SEC provision known as **12b-1**. The 12b-1 fee, named for the section in the SEC regulation that authorized these fees in 1980, has since been invoked by many funds. The SEC permits funds to annually deduct up to 1.25 percent of fund assets for commissions, and advertising and marketing expenses. That is in addition to, and sometimes larger than, the management fee. The average money fund's expense ratio, or annual expenses as a percentage of assets, is about three-quarters of 1 percent (0.75 percent). At that level, a fund earning 10 percent in interest from its securities would deliver a yield to investors of 9.25 percent. More and more supposedly commission-free funds are dipping into assets by imposing what is known as a "12b-1 charge." In addition, many front-end loads have been reduced or eliminated entirely by many funds. The major trend in the industry has been for load funds to reduce the front-end load and add on a 12b-1 fee so that investors pay less up front and have more money working for them but pay a higher annual charge.

Both load and no-load funds use 12b-1, but those costs are particularly irksome to investors who buy no-load funds under the impression that they are not paying any sales charges. These fees must be approved of first by the independent members of the fund's board of directors and then by the shareholders. If you are in a load fund and management proposes a 12b-1 plan, it is asking you to pay a new annual indirect sales load even though you have already paid direct sales charges. If you are a long-term investor, you are better off paying a front-end load, which is a one-time payment. The 1 to 1.25 percent 12-b fees are taken out each year indefinitely and in the long run will cost you more.

Back-End Loads   There is also what is called a **back-end load,** which is a redemption fee that is charged when investors sell or redeem their shares. They are also known as **contingent deferred sales charges.** These are charged on a sliding scale that penalizes short-term investors. A fund, for example, may charge 6 percent if an investor sells within one year. The fees typically decline by a percentage point every year thereafter until they disappear. Ferreting out these deferred charges is simply a matter of reading a funds prospectus. Funds with such charges are also labeled with an *r* in newspaper listings.

Figure 14–1 illustrates that the choice between no-load, load, and 12b-1 funds can result in very significant returns for investors over the long run.

Net Asset Value (NAV)

Net asset value or **NAV** tells investors what each share of their fund is worth. Mutual funds pool the dollars of many investors and buy a portfolio of a variety of securities. In practice, each investor purchases shares in a fund. A mutual fund's gains and

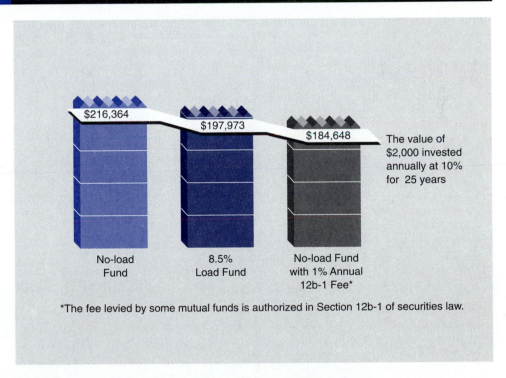

FIGURE 14–1   **How Loads Cut Returns**

$216,364 — No-load Fund

$197,973 — 8.5% Load Fund

$184,648 — No-load Fund with 1% Annual 12b-1 Fee*

The value of $2,000 invested annually at 10% for 25 years

*The fee levied by some mutual funds is authorized in Section 12b-1 of securities law.

The value of an investment varies depending on the load.

SOURCE: T. Row Price, as reported in *The New York Times,* June 9, 1990, 32.

losses are allocated to its investors in direct proportion to the number of shares owned as a percentage of total shares. Stock and bond mutual funds compute how much each share is worth at the end of each trading day.

To calculate NAV, a fund's accountants total the market value of all the stocks, bonds, and cash in the portfolio at the end of each business day. They then add a day's worth of interest and dividends from the securities and subtract a day's worth of fund expenses, including investment management and administrative fees. The accountants then divide the remainder by the number of fund shares outstanding. The result is the market price of one share in the fund known as *NAV*. NAV fluctuates as the prices of the portfolio securities change. The mutual fund tables in the financial section of most major newspapers list the daily NAV for each fund. This is adjusted precisely to reflect the previous day's market fluctuations as they affected a fund's holdings (see Figure 14–2).

Investors can calculate the value of their account by multiplying the NAV by the number of shares they own. If the fund imposes a sales charge, the fee is added to the NAV in another column. A fund with a $10 NAV and an 8.5 percent sales charge would be listed at $10 bid and $10.85 asked or offer price. The higher figure is the

FIGURE 14–2 — **Mutual Fund Quotations (Sample)**

LIPPER INDEXES

Tuesday, June 1994

Prelim: Percentage chg since

Indexes	Close	Prev.	Wk ago	Dec. 31
Capital Appreciation ...	393.60	+ 0.58	+ 0.95	+ 4.99
Growth Fund	715.73	+ 0.83	+ 1.36	+ 6.65
Small Co. Growth.......	395.18	+ 0.53	+ 1.10	+ 4.29
Growth & Income Fd ..	1083.26	+ 0.59	+ 0.98	+ 7.16
Equity Income Fd	698.50	+ 0.61	+ 0.99	+ 7.56
Science & Tech Fd	294.02	+ 1.09	+ 0.82	+ 10.02
International Fund	389.97	− 0.45	+ 1.01	+ 15.92
Gold Fund	179.20	− 3.79	− 2.31	+ 51.96
Balanced Fund..........	820.35	+ 0.55	+ 0.89	+ 6.08

Source: Lipper Analytical Services, Inc.

Tuesday, June 1994

Ranges for investment companies, with daily price data supplied by the National Asssociation of Securities Dealers and performance and cost calculations by Lipper Analytical Services, Inc. The NASD requires a mutual fund to have at least 1,000 shareholders of net assests of $25 million before being listed. Detailed explanatory notes appear elsewhere on this page.

	Inv. Obj.	NAV	Offer Price	NAV Chg.	– Total Return – YTD	13wks	13yrs	R
AAL Mutual:								
Bond	BND	10.57	11.10	+0.03	+5.1	+1.3	+11.6	C
CaGr	GRO	15.15	15.91	+0.09	+3.8	+2.7	+11.5	C
MuBd	GLM	10.99	11.54	...	+4.7	+0.5	+9.9	D

AARP Invst:								
CaGr	GRO	34.18	NL	+0.26	+6.5	+7.1	+10.9	C
GiniM	BND	16.06	NL	+0.03	+4.0	+1.4	+10.8	D
GthInc	G&I	31.48	NL	+0.16	+7.7	+5.7	+14.0	A
HQ Bd	BND	16.53	NL	+0.07	+5.4	+1.2	+11.4	C
TxBd	ISM	18.29	NL	+0.04	+6.0	0.0	+10.8	B
ABT Funds:								
Emrg	CAP	13.45	14.12	+0.10	+5.2	+10.0	+23.8	A
FL HI	MFL	10.40	10.92	+0.02	+6.4k	+1.2k	NS	...
FL TFx	MFL	11.24	11.80	−0.03	+5.8	+0.5	+11.2	...
GthIn	G&I	11.09	11.64	+0.07	+3.8	+1.8	+7.3	E
Utiln	SEC	13.86	14.55	+0.11	+9.5	+2.0	+11.7	C
Acc Mortg	BND	12.26	NL	+0.02	+4.0	+1.2	NS	...
Acc Sht Int	BST	12.36	NL	+0.02	+3.3	+0.9	NS	...
AHA Funds:								
Balan	S&B	12.84	NL	+0.08	+6.4	+4.2	+11.9	C
Full	BND	10.62	NL	+0.04	+5.7	+1.3	+11.4	C
Lim	BST	10.48	NL	+0.02	+2.6	+0.8	+8.6	D
AIM Funds:								
AdjGv p	BST	9.88	10.19	...	+2.1	+1.1	NS	...
Chart p	G&I	8.93	9.45	+0.06	+4.7	+3.2	+14.2	A
Const p	CAP	15.72	16.63	+0.12	+5.4	+9.0	+19.8	A
Cv Yld p	S&B	15.10	15.85	+0.13	+6.8	+6.9	+14.6	A
HiYld p	BHI	5.82	6.11	+0.01	+7.7	+3.8	+7.8	E
IntlE p	ITL	10.42	11.03	−0.08	+16.3	+13.5	NS	...
LimM	BST	NA	NA	NA	NA	NA	NA	...
Sumit	GRO	9.89	NA	+0.07	+2.6	+3.7	+13.5	B
TF Int	IDM	10.78	11.11	...	+3.8	+0.2	+8.9	C
Weing p	GRO	16.74	17.71	+0.12	−3.4	+1.5	+10.4	D

• • • • • • • • •

price a buyer would have to pay for a load fund's share that day. The price of the no-load fund (identified by NL symbol) is the NAV.

The shortcoming of these prices is that taken by themselves, they do not tell an investor how well or poorly a fund has been performing. Suppose that the NAV of a fund showed no change for a year. This does not mean that it performed poorly. The fund might have distributed income dividends and capital gains during that period. Ironically, a capital gains payout acts to depress the NAV because the fund is actually distributing money that previously was included in its portfolio. Investors cannot get the true measure of a fund's performance unless they take dividends and capital gains payments into account. This is what funds do when they issue their periodic reports to shareholders. For a more meaningful assessment, investors must examine long-term performance.

Reading the Prospectus

Once investors find several funds that meet their criteria and seem equally suitable, they will need to dig a little deeper by examining the **prospectus**. Unlike banks and savings and loan associations, most mutual funds do not have an office on the corner. Investors will need to write or call each fund and ask for a prospectus. It is also essential to request a document called the **statement of additional information**, which includes details of fees and a listing of investments, a copy of the **annual report**, and the most recent **quarterly report**.

The fund's prospectus offers important clues. Reading a fund prospectus is a chore, but from it investors can glean some useful information that will help them make a final choice among several comparable funds. The fund's investment philosophy, the quality of the securities in its portfolio, and the maturities of fixed-income instruments can be determined by reading the prospectus. Investors should also try to determine the fees that the fund charges. Mutual fund companies do not manage your money for free.

Fee Disclosures

The Securities and Exchange Commission adopted regulations in 1988 to standardize and improve advertising and disclosure of fund performance. It also issued rules on **fee disclosure**—how funds must reveal fees and charges in prospectuses. Funds that use 12b-1 have to disclose their use and all other charges in plain English. The rules have two major components. The first requires funds to display sales commissions or "loads," management fees, and other expenses in a standardized fee table near the front of the prospectus. This concise table must list all charges investors pay to buy and sell shares, plus fees for fund operating expenses and total amounts.

The **expense ratio**, found in the condensed financial section of the prospectus, tells how much money the fund is spending to do business in proportion to its assets. The maximum is limited by state statutes and varies from state to state. A ratio of more than 1.5 percent is considered unacceptable. Generally, the larger the fund, the lower will be the ratio.

Beneath this the prospectus must also show how fees and expenses would affect a hypothetical $1,000 invested in the fund with an assumed annual return of 5 percent. The example must show the amount of those fees and expenses if shares are sold at the end of 1, 3, 5, and 10 years.

This page illuminates unusual fees some funds would rather investors never saw, such as a sales fee to reinvest your dividends. Redemption fees, if applicable, are listed next, followed by the cost to shift money from one fund to another. You can see quickly whether a fund assesses both front- and back-end sales charges or whether it describes itself as a no-load fund but takes a cut of all redemptions for five years or so.

Standardized Yield Formula

The SEC rules addressed frequent investor complaints that fee information was often buried in a prospectus or shrouded in legal and technical terminology few investors understand. The second major component of the new rules required all funds to use a **standardized yield formula** if they choose to advertise yields.

Since 1988, any fund that advertises its yield must give equal prominence to **total rate of return,** which is equal to price changes plus dividend distributions for 1, 5, and 10 years, ending with the last calendar quarter. This is intended to discourage funds from doing everything imaginable to boost yields while ignoring risk to principal. Many funds, for example, buy volatile junk bonds because of their higher yields. Yet they often do not offer the best total returns. Since the new rules were adopted, investors can compare fund performance more accurately and easily, and fund sponsors are prevented from boosting their advertised yields by various ploys.

Investment Objectives

A mutual fund's prospectus is required by law to clearly state the fund's objective, including the kinds of investments it makes and the amount of risk it is willing to take to achieve its goal. This usually appears in a section labeled "investment objective" or "investment policy." For example, most funds do not sell short, borrow on margin, or buy options, although some are permitted by state and federal regulators to do so. But these policies must be reported in the prospectus.

Examining the Portfolio

A fund's quarterly report lists the securities contained in its portfolio. In general, the fewer issues an equity fund owns, the better. A stock **fund portfolio** should generally have less than 60 but at least 20 different securities in it. Although many equity funds are broadly diversified in their holdings, investors can get a clue to the manager's investment preferences. Investors should study the portfolio list and concentrate on the funds' 10 largest holdings. There is often a pattern, and if holdings are heavily in stocks of industries with which you feel comfortable, you have probably found the right fund for you. If you feel uncomfortable with the fund's holdings, look for another fund.

By looking at the rating of the bonds in a bond fund's portfolio, investors can tell how much risk a fund is taking with their money. Investors can get a higher return investing in a bond fund that takes big risks than investing in one that takes smaller risks. But with the riskier funds, investors stand more chance of losing part of their initial investment should one or more bond issuers in the portfolio default.

Another major determinant of a bond fund's risk is the **average maturity**—the time remaining until the average bond in its portfolio matures and is redeemed by the issuer. The longer the average maturity, the greater the risk. Lending money for longer terms is inherently riskier than lending for shorter periods. The longer the maturity, the greater the chances for a bond issuer to develop financial difficulties and default.

Diversified or Nondiversified

Most funds are **diversified**, which means they have a restriction that they may not invest more than 5 percent of their assets in a single company's stock or bond. A handful of funds are nondiversified, which means they are exempt from the usual restriction. A nondiversified fund may invest as much as 25 percent of its assets in each of two stocks. It can concentrate the remaining 50 percent among only 10 issues.

Checking the Turnover Rate

The rate at which a fund buys and sells its holdings on an annual basis, or the **turnover rate**, can be located in the condensed financial information on the prospectus' summary page. A turnover factor of 100 percent means that all the fund's securities were replaced in one year; 200 percent indicates that the securities were held on average for six months. A rate as high as 100 percent can indicate that too much churning is going on and consequently too much is being spent on brokerage fees. A turnover rate below 60 is generally good.

Mutual funds are criticized as being too eager to show quarter-by-quarter gains instead of investing for the long term. They do seem to turn over the stocks in their portfolio more rapidly than they did a decade ago. This is evidence of pressure for quick success exerted on fund managers by large investors who switch holdings from one fund to another.

Monitoring a Fund's Batting Average

The process of selecting a fund typically starts and ends with a look at its past performance, on the premise that the past is the best clue to a fund's future. The quarterly and annual statements issued by the fund will show results for the previous year and probably a comparison with the S & P 500. Investors should look at the return for each of the past five years, especially during relatively weak markets.

But extreme caution should be exercised here. Investors need to bear in mind that they are buying future earnings, not history. While a fund's past cannot be ignored, it also cannot be totally relied upon as a future indicator. Many investors choose a fund primarily because it has been one of the leaders in the past. They are often dazzled by spectacular one-year record gains. During 1991, for example, many funds recorded extraordinary gains. Investing in a fund after it has had a successful year is much like expecting to make money this year by buying the stocks that went up the most last year. It sounds foolish, but it is a common fallacy that mutual fund investors want to believe. The public seems to have an insatiable appetite for yesterday's investment heroes.

While chasing last year's best performers is always a suspect strategy, doing so with income funds is perhaps even more dangerous than doing so with growth stock funds. Income funds perform like bonds. A drop in interest rates pulls their prices up. To expect a repeat performance from an income fund next year is to bet on further declines in interest rates.

Over any given period, the market favors certain approaches over others. One year, income-oriented funds may be the big winners. Next year, the rise in stock prices pushes funds that seek capital appreciation into the limelight. Last year's hero can easily become this year's loser. A prudent approach is to use past performance as a starting point. Past performance is not insignificant when choosing a fund, but it is only one factor that needs to be considered, and it is not necessarily the first thing to look at.

Consistency of performance is most important. It is important to search for a fund that has demonstrated good performance in both good and bad cycles over a good stretch of time, such as a 15-year time span. A very large component of the variation among funds in short-term performance is luck, not skill. But a proven track record over a long haul is a much more accurate gauge because it shows how well the fund withstood the bear markets. What determines a fund's long-term performance is its ability to make money in an up market and preserve money in a down market.

In checking the fund's long-term performance, investors should compare the gains and losses of one fund with those of another over the past 5, 10, and 15 years. It would be helpful to consult one of the numerous mutual fund guidebooks. The major reference book on the industry is *The CDA Wiesenberger Mutual Funds Update*, an annual publication which covers more than 1,300 funds, summarizing each one's investment objective, performance data for up to 10 years, and information on how to reach the fund by mail or telephone. Most libraries carry copies of it.

Some other sources of information you might consider in comparing funds are:

1. *Johnson's Charts*

2. *Donahue's Mutual Funds Almanac*

3. *The Handbook for No-Load Fund Investors*

4. *Standard and Poor's/Lipper Mutual Fund Profiles*

5. *The Mutual Fund Encyclopedia*

6. *The Individual Investor's Guide to No-Load Mutual Funds*

7. *Morning Star Mutual Fund Sourcebook*

Mutual fund performance rankings come out regularly, and the results are widely reprinted in a large number of consumer and financial publications. On a periodic basis, trade journals such as *Forbes, Money Magazine, Financial World, Kiplinger's Personal Finance Magazine,* or *Barron's* either comment on or rank the performance of mutual funds overall and also by investment objective. In addition to these popular sources, there are many analytical services that monitor mutual funds, comparing their performance to the popular major stock indices such as the Dow Jones industrials and the S & P 500. To satisfy the enormous demand for fund data, a small industry has emerged to supply this service. Rating services publish performance records of funds over various periods from a few months to 25 years, including the best and worst performers among all funds or among groups. Some publishers maintain lists of recommended funds.

The gyrations of mutual fund gains and losses are brought into sharp focus by performance rankings, which have become a periodic source of edification or embarrassment for their large following of shareholders, portfolio managers, and newsletter publishers. The need for these comparisons is clear. Mutual funds, primarily through diversification and professional management, should produce results that consistently beat the market averages over time.

To improve their odds of success, investors should monitor their fund's performance and be ready to jump off if it does much worse than other funds like it. It should be remembered that no one fund is an investment for all seasons, to be bought and forgotten.

Scrutinize Management It is difficult to escape the conclusion that the most important aspect of the fund's performance is the skill and judgment of the managers who run it. Whether you are interested in a capital appreciation fund, a growth fund, a bond fund, or some other variety, if a fund had a commendable earnings record, it makes sense to check that the managers who achieved these results are still in charge.

Funds Diversification

Investors do not need to find the one perfect fund. One good approach is to assemble a portfolio of funds. These funds can be within a single category, or they can be a variety of funds to make up a balanced portfolio with a number of different investment goals.

Funds should be balanced among different investments that carry varying degrees of risk. A solid base of such relatively secure holdings as money market funds will help investors conserve their savings base. That done, they can consider stock and other funds that will help them boost their capital.

Investors can also diversify their stock and bond fund investment. Suppose that you are conservative but a little worried about inflation. You might put 50 percent of your investment money in an income-oriented stock fund, 10 percent into a specialized fund that buys gold mining shares, and 40 percent in funds that buy fixed-dollar securities such as government securities or corporate bond funds.

Fund Families: All in the Family

Before you get emotionally involved with a fund, check out its family. A **family of funds** is a group of different types of funds offered by one sponsor. Once you find a top-performing fund of the type you want, see if there are enough sister funds in the family to meet your future needs. A fund family should contain at least two bond funds, taxable and tax free, as well as a money fund and several stock funds. Avoid a fund that is too small. If a fund is not part of a family, it may not have enough money to support a large research team. The minimum size of a fund is one that has at least $50 million in assets.

Many funds are structured to let investors ride broad market trends. A typical family might sport a money fund, a handful of stock and bond funds, and perhaps a few specialized funds invested in such narrow categories as foreign stocks and utilities. The companies that manage the big families of mutual funds offer a very tempting proposition, known as "exchange privilege," or **telephone switching.** This entitles shareholders to switch investments almost instantly by telephone from one fund to another within the same family or group of funds at little or no cost. Most funds have toll-free numbers that investors can call to switch or withdraw funds.

At one time investors thought of mutual funds as long-term investments. With the new flexibility offered by computerized exchanges of funds within fund families, investors can essentially trade funds like the stock market does, aggressively switching assets between equity and money market funds, hoping to preserve capital during stock market downswings and to increase their returns during upward moves.

Market Timing

Mutual funds are excellent investment instruments for so-called **market timing.** In a market timing strategy, investors try to move their money into markets when they are rising and to pull it out when they start to fall. There are even advisory services that tell individuals when to be in a particular mutual fund and when to switch out of it and move their money into a money market fund. Market timing in mutual funds revolves around the telephone switch, which allows investors to capitalize on changing investment trends.

Spreading one's assets among several funds in a family is a good way to hedge one's bets about performance of a particular kind of fund. Many investors buy aggressive stock funds when they believe the market is on the rise and switch without much effort or loss of time to the safety of a money market fund when the broad upward cycle shows signs of easing. The catch, naturally, is figuring out when the market is changing directions.

Open- and Closed-End Funds

Open-End Funds

Mutual funds are organized in two different ways. The vast majority are **open-end** companies that continuously issue shares to new investors and buy back from existing investors at net asset value. As a result, an open-end fund's capitalization is always changing. When investors buy in, the fund issues new shares and increases the number of shares. It is committed to redeem or buy back shares from investors whenever the investor wishes to sell. There is no secondary market for the shares of such companies. This means that part of their portfolio must be very liquid, possibly kept in cash accounts at a bank.

Investors can withdraw their money at any time directly from a stock mutual fund without penalty. But the redemption price depends upon the value of the company's portfolio at that time, the net asset value. Whether investors get back more or less than they put in will depend on whether the NAV or the price per share is higher or lower than the price they paid. There may also be redemption charges involved in the sale.

Closed-End Funds

Closed-end funds are a special class of funds. They do not continuously offer to sell their shares as investors send in their money. Closed-end funds usually raise money once, issuing a fixed number of shares when they are set up. After an initial (public offering) sale by the company, the fund is closed. The firm may, for instance, raise $100 million by selling ten million shares for $10 apiece. The shares are then traded in the secondary exchanges like regular shares of common stock. Investors cannot redeem their shares from the fund itself. If they want to get their money out, they must sell their shares on a stock exchange instead of redeeming them with the fund. If investors want to buy in after the fund's initial sale, they likewise would have to buy on the secondary market. A closed-end fund is not technically considered to be a mutual fund.

The closed-end fund managers claim this permits the fund to operate more efficiently, with less overhead and paperwork expenses, enabling all of the fund to be invested in high-yielding investments without having to keep a portion of their

TOTAL

Calculating a Mutual Fund's Total Rate of Return

There is a fairly simple formula for comparing the rates of return for two or more bond funds. To compute the percentage change in a fund's net asset value, or share price, subtract the initial price from its price at the end of a given period. Add all income distributions over that period. Then divide the total by the fund's initial net asset value, and you wind up with a simple rate of return.

For example, assume that a share of a bond fund was worth $30 one year ago and is now worth $36. The fund also paid out $3 in per share income over that period. The $6 share price difference plus the $3 distribution totals $9. Divide $9 by $30 to get the simple total return over the past year: 30 percent.

While knowing total return is obviously important and helpful, one should not automatically choose a bond fund with the very highest past yield or total return. Such a yield could mean the fund is boosting its yield by lowering the qualities of the securities it holds. In general, the lower the quality of the securities held by a fund, the higher will be its yield and the higher the risk. One needs a complete picture before investing.

portfolio in liquid form to handle unexpected redemptions. They do not have to worry about having their strategies disrupted by investors pouring in cash or pulling it out. Closed-end fund managers claim that the performance of open-ended funds is often hindered by their need to maintain liquidity. Closed-end fund managers are free to invest as they see fit, regardless of investor sentiment.

This form of trading, however, divorces the market price of the fund from the market value of the stocks within the fund. When interest is strong, the share price can run higher than the NAV. It is then said to be *trading at a premium*. Typically closed-end mutual funds, in fact, sell at a discount, or less than NAV. The majority of approximately 70 closed-end funds are bought and sold on the NYSE. Their price may fluctuate in response to changes in the value of a company's portfolio and the supply or the demand for its shares.

When investors buy closed-end funds in an initial offering, a portion of the money from the offering, typically 7 percent, goes to the underwriters, reducing the amount of money available for investments. During the first three months, the fund tends to trade at a premium because the issuing brokerage firms support the price. After that, the fund is left to find its own level, usually down. Investors buying in the offering usually watch their closed-end fund fall to a discount after briefly trading at a price above its net asset value.

There are four reasons generally cited by experts as to why closed-end funds tend to trade at a discount:

1. Their lack of "sponsorship" or recommendations by brokerage houses; closed-end funds are rarely promoted after their initial offering, and little information is distributed about them.

2. High management expenses.

3. Refusal by investors to pay net asset value or a premium except in rare cases because they know closed-ends have traditionally sold at a discount.

4. Expectations of larger discounts.

The financial press summarizes activity on closed-end stock funds, usually on Mondays, listed under "Publicly Traded Funds" (see Figure 14–3). This summary reveals that many stock funds trade at deep discounts and some occasionally trade at a premium.

Like other mutual funds, closed-end funds are professionally managed portfolios of stocks and bonds. They may be broadly diversified, focus on special sectors, or be concentrated in foreign securities. Investors can currently choose from approximately 250 closed-end funds in the United States, with a total market value of $60 billion.

Sector Funds

The mutual fund companies continue to crank out specialty or **sector funds**, which allow investors to concentrate on a stock group within an industry or sector such as

FIGURE 14–3 **Publicly Traded Funds**

Friday, March♥ 199♣

Unaudited net asset values per share of publicly traded investment companies (Closed End Funds) as of Friday. Also shown is the closing listed market price of each fund's shares, with the percentage difference between the new asset value and the stock price.

DIVERSIFIED COMMON STOCK FUNDS

	N.A. Value	Stk Price	% Diff
AdmExp	17.61	15 3/4	−10.51
AmsAll**(h)	5.73	4 1/2	−21.4
Baker	23.51	19 3/4	−15.9
Blue Ch Val	7.26	6 5/8	−8.7
Clem-Gl(b)	11.47	9 3/8	−18.2
FrkMIT**(b)	8.63	8 3/8	−2.9
GSOTrust	10.01	9 1/2	−5.0
GemIICap	16.48	13 3/8	−18.8
GemIInc	9.37	12 3/4	+36.0
GenAln	20.27	17 3/8	−16.1
Lehman	14.90	12 3/8	−16.9
LbtyASt	9.21	8	−13.1
NiagSh	16.77	14 1/4	−15.0
NchAGE	10.92	9 3/8	−9.5
QuestValInc	11.68	13	+11.3
QuestValCap	16.82	13 3/4	−18.2
RoyValue	9.96	8 3/4	−12.1
SchfrValu	10.56	9 1/2	−10.0
Source	39.98	39 3/4	−0.5
Tri-Conti	26.48	22 3/4	−14.0
WWVal	18.60	17 1/4	−7.2
Zweig	10.61	11 3/8	+7.2

BOND FUNDS

	N.A. Value	Stk Price	% Diff
ACMMm	11.10	11 3/4	+5.8
ACMGIF	10.19	11 1/4	+10.4
ACMOpp	8.98	9 1/8	+1.6
ACMGSF	10.13	11	+8.5
ACSpc(a)	8.64	9 1/8	+5.6
ACMMinF	8.44	8 1/4	−3.7
Apex	11.17	11 1/2	+2.9
CIMHigh(I)	6.75	6 1/2	−3.7
Comstik	10.03	9 1/2	−5.2
EatonPr	10.00	...	...
FixBdT**	8.43	7 3/8	6.5
FrPMTr(b)	8.03	9	+12.0
FrUnTr(b)	7.89	7 3/8	−6.5
GlobPl	9.20	8 5/8	−6.2
HiYld Inc	n.a.	n.a.	n.a.
HiYld Plus	n.a.	n.a.	n.a.
Hypern	10.77	10 1/2	−2.5
KmpHi	7.63	8 1/4	+8.1
KmplGov	8.70	8 7/8	+2.0
KmpMinc	9.40	9 3/8	−0.2
KmpMunl	11.17	11 1/2	+2.9
KmpSMin	11.40	11 1/8	−2.4
LomasM	11.09	11 1/2	+3.7
MFSChar(b)	10.27	10	−2.6
MFSGv(b)	8.60	9 7/8	+14.8
MFSI&O(b)	8.18	7 7/8	−3.7
MFSIntr(b)	8.56	8 3/8	−2.1
MFSMit(b)	8.10	8 1/4	+1.8
MFSMuni(b)	9.38	9 3/8	+2.6
MFSSpV**(b)	12.95	14 3/8	+11.0
MFSTol(b)	8.61	7 3/4	−9.9
MLPrime	10.00	...	...
MunlEnh	11.24	10 3/4	−4.3
MunlHi	9.47	9 3/8	−1.0
Munilns	9.87	10	+1.3
MuniVest	9.47	9 1/2	−10.3
OppGt	8.91	8 7/8	−0.3
OppMS	10.22	9 7/8	−3.3
PDvPRT	10.70	10 1/4	−4.2
PlIPRT	10.00	...	...
PutC&B	7.29	6 1/2	−10.8
PGrMun	11.12	11	−1.0
PutHyM	9.32	9 1/2	+1.9
PutIntG	8.90	9	+1.1
PutMgMu	9.19	9 1/2	+3.3
PutMsr	8.23	7 3/4	−5.8
PutMsInt	7.84	7 1/8	−9.1
PutPrem	8.04	7 1/2	−6.7
TaurusCa	11.21	12	+7.0
Taurus NY	11.11	12 1/8	+9.1
TmplGl(b)	8.21	8 1/2	+3.5
TemGG(b)	8.57	8 7/8	+3.5
VKMprx	10.02	...	...
WorldIn	8.83	8 1/2	−3.7
ZenixIF	6.26	6 3/8	+1.8
ZwTR**	9.16	9 5/8	+5.0

SPECIALIZED & CONVERTIBLE FUNDS

	N.A. Value	Stk Price	% Diff
AS(b)(c)(g)	67.81	53	−21.8
AmCap	21.79	19 3/8	−11.0
Asia Pac	15.83	16 3/4	+5.8
Austria Fd	15.34	16 1/8	+5.1
Bancrt	20.59	17 3/4	−14.2
Brazil	20.12	13 3/4	−31.6
BrgstmCap	57.41	60 1/4	+4.9
BMtl(b)(e)	12.20	11 1/4	−7.7
CNVHldgCap	9.42	5	−46.9
CNVHtg	9.54	11 3/8	+19.2
Castle	21.48	18 3/8	−14.4
CenFdC(b)	5.29	5 5/8	+6.3
CentS	11.43	9 1/4	−19.0
ChilFd	17.59	19	+8.0
CounsTndm	11.79	10 1/8	−14.1
CypressFd	9.58	9 5/8	+0.4
DufPh Util	8.41	8 1/8	−3.3
Ellswth Cv	8.26	7 1/4	−12.2
Engex	11.31	8 1/2	−24.8
1stAust	9.66	9	−6.8
FstFnFd	7.34	7 1/8	−2.9
1stIbern	9.74	12 5/8	+29.6
FstPhil	11.13	12 1/4	+10.0
Gabelli E	12.26	12 1/4	−0.08
Germany	12.53	16 1/2	+31.6
GlUtFd	10.96	10 1/4	−6.4
H&Q Health	10.67	9 1/4	−13.3
HamCap(b)	11.63	9 7/8	−15.0
HamUP(b)	49.33	48 1/4	−2.1
Helvetia	12.72	13 1/8	+3.1
IndFd(f)	11.90	15 3/4	+32.3
InetMk	11.16	11	−1.4
ItlFd(b)	12.85	13 1/4	+3.2
KoreaFd	17.99	27 3/8	+52.1
MGSmCap	10.36	9 5/8	−7.0
MalaysFd	14.54	18 5/8	+28.0
MesGld	9.26	9 1/4	−0.1
MexFd(b)	13.17	13 1/8	−0.3
NewFer	13.56	16 3/4	+13.5
PDivin	10.91	11 5/8	+6.5
PatPrll	10.70	11 5/8	+6.5
PatPreD	9.38	10 5/8	+13.2
Pete&Res(b)	30.27	27 7/8	−7.9
PllReg	9.83	9	−8.4
PortFd	13.16	13 3/8	+1.6
RESec	7.22	7	−3.0
ROCTwn	16.29	13 5/8	−16.3
RegFnSh	8.77	8 1/2	−3.0
ScudrN A	17.16	13 1/4	−22.7
ScudNEur	11.45	11 3/8	−0.6
SE Sav(b)	8.86	8 3/8	−5.4
SpainFd	12.79	22 3/8	+74.9
TCW Cvt(b)	8.07	8 1/8	+6.5
TwFd(b)	26.46	27 7/8	+6.5
TmpEMk(b)	14.19	14 1/4	−0.4
TmpVal(b)	9.22	8 5/8	−6.4
Thai Fd	17.15	26 1/8	+52.3
Turk Fd	16.65	12 1/4	−26.4
UK Fd	10.54	9 1/2	−12.2
Z-Seven	n.a.	n.a.	n.a.

(a) Ex-dividend
(b) As of Thursday's close
(c) Translated at Commercial Rand exchange rate.
(e) In Canandian dollars
(f) As of Wednesday
(g) Feb ♥, 199♣ NAV:71.94
(h) Feb ♥,199♣ NAV:5.81
(j) Feb ♥,199♣ Fund Ex-Div

technology, energy, health care, high tech, defense, precious metals, aerospace, and so on, instead of being broadly diversified. Sector funds rise and fall with the fortunes of individual industries.

The concept permits investors to focus on an industry where they think there are profits to reap. Needless to say, the main challenge of the sector funds is picking the right sector. Such a fund should not be an investor's only holding since it offers little marketwide diversification. Their volatility makes them best suited for sophisticated investors who can read market signals and are prepared to switch funds often.

Index Funds

There are also stock **index funds**. By buying a portfolio that duplicates the S & P 500 Index, an investor could be assured of never doing worse than the market. The catch, of course, is that the fund would never better it either. This may be considered a fund for the very conservative investor who still wants an equity play.

The index fund concept is based on the premise that managed stock portfolios cannot consistently beat the market averages. The index fund approach may be specifically appropriate for retirement plan accounts (such as IRA and Keoghs discussed in Chapter 18). The longer the period, the more difficult it is to outperform the market consistently.

Tax-Free Bond Funds

Investors can earn tax-free income by purchasing shares in tax-free bond funds. These funds invest in the bonds and note issues of states and municipalities. Dividend income is free of federal income taxes and may be of state and local taxes. Capital gains are subject to taxes.

Money Market Funds (MMFs)

Basically, a **money market fund** is a mutual fund that buys a diversified basket of only short term debt securities, such as Treasury bills and corporate debt obligations known as **commercial paper.** By investing in issues that mature in a few days or months, money funds can be fairly sure that they will not have to sell securities at a loss. It is theoretically possible to lose money in a money market fund. These funds can be vulnerable to unexpected bankruptcies of companies whose debt they own. But the short maturities make it unlikely that a fund will be caught holding the debt of an issuer that gets into financial trouble. As a result, a money fund can nearly guarantee that investors will never lose principal. In more technical terms, the fund asserts that it will hold its net asset value, the price at which investors buy into or redeem from the fund, at $1 a share and no sales charge. Management costs, about three-quarters of 1 percent (0.75 percent) a year, are included in the stated yield.

Investors can withdraw their money from a money market fund at any time without penalty. The fixed-share value, safety, and liquidity are the fund's major attractions for both individual and institutional investors. The development of money market mutual funds has given investors an escape hatch once readily available only to the professionals: being able to switch out of the stock or bond market completely, often with just a phone call, if trouble seems to be looming.

Prior to the creation of money market funds, such money market instruments as Treasury bills or corporate commercial paper came in denominations of $10,000 and up and were out of reach of most households. The money market funds applied mutual fund principals to these instruments, enabling those with $1,000 or more to own a share in a portfolio composed of these high-yielding instruments.

Money market funds flourished in an unstable economic climate during the late seventies and early eighties. Interest rates soared, double-digit inflation raged, and government regulations kept the funds' traditional competitors, banks and small deposits, from offering competitive rates. Many depositors took their money out of their low-yielding savings accounts and put it into one of the hundreds of money market funds that were being formed.

Bank Money Market Deposit Accounts

In order to enable banks to compete with the money market funds, a revolutionary banking bill (discussed in Chapter 2), the **Depository Institutions Act of 1982**, gave banks and thrifts the right to offer their own money market deposit accounts. This permitted banks to compete directly with the money market funds.

Bank money market funds have several attractions. Like other bank deposits, they were usually insured by the federal government up to $100,000. They additionally were more convenient since banks had branches, while money market funds usually only offer post office boxes and toll-free phone numbers.

Bank Money Markets Accounts versus Nonbank MMFs

The nonbank money market funds have demonstrated that they have their own advantages. One is yield. There are greater restrictions on the securities that banks may purchase. Banks, particularly outside the bigger cities, tend to pay interest rates below that of the money market funds. The yield earned on money market accounts can vary considerably from bank to bank. Interest rates generally change weekly and cannot be guaranteed for longer than 30 days.

In addition to yield, nonbank money market funds have other attractions. Money market funds allow an unlimited number of checks to be written against balances. Bank money market accounts permit the writing of only three checks per month. Money market funds also permit wider transfer of funds to designated bank accounts. These funds can be moved overnight by wire and can be drawn against the next day.

By federal regulation, the minimum amount for opening a bank money market account is $2,500. Competitive interest rates apply as long as this minimum sum is maintained on deposit. Each bank can choose the method used to compute the $2,500 minimum balance. Some banks simply reduce the interest rate if the balance falls below $2,500 even one day. Other banks use an average daily balance.

Are All MMFs Alike?

On the surface, the nonbank funds look very much the same. Essentially, a fund collects money from investors and puts it into a variety of short-term credit obligations, which are traded in the billions among such institutions as banks, government bond dealers, and corporations.

Investors should not assume that the more than 300 money funds are all alike. The funds can differ in such things as their minimums for investment and check writing and the ease of getting through to customer service people on the telephone. Perhaps more important, they also vary widely in the types of short-term assets they buy. These differences produce varying yields and levels of risk. Money funds may appear on the surface as a homogeneous, commodity-type product. But when examined closely, one notices real differences in risk and management policy.

Consumers have not had to become aware of the risk differences because the money funds have an excellent safety record. Nevertheless, there conceivably could be principal losses in a money fund, so investors should be aware of how much risk their particular fund is taking. Theoretically, some funds are safer than others. A fund that invests only in Treasury bills, for example, is safer than one investing in commercial paper.

The most common type of money fund is one that invests in a diversified portfolio of short-term government securities, bank certificates of deposit, and corporate commercial paper (see Chapter 13). Other funds stick to the safety of government obligations. There are also big distinctions within each category. Yields generally rise with the risk of the investments. Riskier securities give higher returns. A fund cannot earn as much investing in T-bills as it can from, say, commercial paper.

What the Money Market Funds Buy

The typical money market fund portfolio contains the following securities that mature in as little as one day to as long as one year:

Treasury bills and notes   Sold periodically by the Treasury and backed by the "full faith and credit" of the United States.

Agency securities   Issued by such government agencies as the Government National Mortgage Association (Ginnie Mae) and the Small Business Administration, or by government-sponsored organizations such as the Federal National Mortgage Association (Fannie Mae) and the Federal Home Loan Banks.

Commercial paper   IOUs sold by corporations for day-to-day operating funds.

Certificates of deposit   Large denomination, negotiable CDs sold by domestic and foreign commercial banks and some savings and loans. Very few are in denominations as small as $100,000, the maximum eligible for government deposit insurance.

Eurodollar CDs   Dollar-denominated certificates sold by foreign branches of U.S. banks, usually those in London, or by foreign banks.

Yankee CDs   Certificates issued by U.S. branches of foreign banks, usually New York City branches.

Banker's acceptances   Commercial notes guaranteed by a bank.

Repurchase agreements (Repos)   Buy-sell deals in which the fund buys securities with an agreement that the seller will repurchase them in a short period, ordinarily seven days or before, at a price that includes interest for the period. The fund holds the securities as collateral.

Longer-term securities also pay higher yields but tend to fluctuate more in price than shorter-term issues. A fund with a longer maturity portfolio is more vulnerable to market shifts, for better or for worse. A fund manager anticipating a decline in interest rates can lengthen the portfolio's maturity to lock in the current higher rates for a longer period. A manager who foresees a rate rise can shorten the maturity so that the securities can be replaced sooner with higher-paying issues.

Government securities are the safest investment, followed by top-rated ("prime") obligations of domestic banks and corporations. More risky and higher-yielding investments include Eurodollar certificates of deposit (issued by foreign branches of U.S. banks), Yankee certificates (issued in U.S. dollars by foreign banks), and commercial paper that has received less than top ratings from the independent rating agencies.

The first place to look for information about a particular fund's risk is in the section of the fund prospectus where investment policy is discussed. Individuals should find out what the fund invests in and whether the yield compensates for any added risk. Unfortunately, it is not easy to get up-to-date portfolio information. The funds are required to report their holdings to shareholders only twice a year, and a fund may change the composition of its portfolio substantially after a report. If you are looking for the ultimate in safety, you should look for a fund that only buys Treasuries and holds them directly.

How Safe Is a Nonbank Fund?

Under Securities and Exchange Commission regulations, the average maturity of a money fund may not exceed 120 days. In addition, every security a fund owns must mature within 12 months. The maturities of most funds range from only a few days to several weeks. The average fund's maturity is estimated to be about 50 days. Those figures are regularly included in published tables, or investors can get them by telephoning the funds.

Short maturities protect funds because a bank or company whose securities are sold on money markets is unlikely to default without warning. Moreover, securities maturing within days rarely fluctuate in value, protecting principal. Also, money funds may invest no more than 5 percent of their portfolios in any one corporate issuer of commercial paper or any one bank's certificate of deposit. The only exception is for government and Treasury issues.

If a bank or corporation were to default, a fund might well be able to cover its loss by reducing dividends temporarily. But a gloom and doom scenario for a money market fund collapse is contingent upon some sort of financial catastrophe, perhaps a chain of bank and corporate bankruptcies that would touch off a run on the funds. Such a situation is highly unlikely but in terms of absolute security, it theoretically puts money market funds a notch under FDIC bank accounts.

So far, fund managers have done a commendable job of protecting investors' money. In the entire history of money market funds (since 1972), there have been no disasters or failures. No investor has ever lost any principal in a fund. Neither have there been any runs or panics. They have also been free of fraud.

The only real gamble with a money market fund is in the interest rate. A money market fund's rate usually changes each day along with the rise and fall of interest rates on the investments in the fund's portfolio. The rate that is advertised is the rate for that week, not necessarily for next week or next month. By investing in money market funds, investors are forgoing the opportunity to "lock in" to a high rate of interest through a CD or T-bill or note. Instead they are gambling that interest rates will float higher to their benefit.

There is place in everyone's portfolio for a highly liquid investment, that is, funds investors can have access to at a moment's notice. You should aim (see Chapter 1 on planning) to have three to six months' take-home pay in reserve to see you comfortably through a job change or an unexpected emergency. Money funds have long been recommended as the best place for such emergency funds or cash earmarked for short-term purchases and as a temporary parking place during a downturn in the stock and bond markets.

(You can obtain addresses and telephone numbers of mutual funds as well as MMFs from the Investment Company Institute, 1600 M Street NW, Washington, DC 20036; 202/293-7700. Ask for its *Guide to Mutual Funds* ($2.50), which provides a list of MMFs.)

SUMMARY

A mutual fund is a company formed for the purpose of receiving funds from investors and reinvesting the funds in securities of other firms. Mutual funds cater to small investors by selling shares in conventional installments. They thereby provide small investors who do not have enough money to create their own diversified portfolio with a convenient method of buying into a diversified portfolio containing the added benefit of professional management.

Mutual funds are available in many different forms and with varying objectives. Major types of mutual funds include maximum growth of capital funds, growth funds, growth of capital and income funds, equity funds, balanced funds, corporate bonds funds, municipal bonds funds, and money market funds. Mutual fund shares are priced on the basis of net asset value (NAV) per share. The net asset value can be computed by subtracting the liabilities from assets and dividing by the number of shares outstanding.

Mutual funds are of two basic types—closed-end and open-end funds. Closed-end funds with a fixed number of shares outstanding are sold like those of any other corporation. They often sell at market prices, which are at a discount from their net asset value. Shares of open-end companies are sold and redeemed by the mutual fund and through brokers. An open-end mutual fund issues as many new shares as are demanded and repurchases existing shares at a price equal to the net asset value per share.

Money market funds are mutual funds that buy only short-term debt securities. These funds have an outstanding record for safety although their interest yield is only slightly better than a bank savings account. They can serve as a good store for emergency funds or as a temporary parking place for investment funds during economic turmoil.

There are wide variations in load charges imposed by mutual funds. Some mutual funds charge a commission (load) when the shares are sold; others do not (no load). If a fund is a load fund, a sales commission is added to the NAV to determine the purchase price.

The mutual fund prospectus is required by law to state the fund's investment objectives and how it will attempt to achieve these objectives. With care, diligence, proper research, and an understanding of how mutual funds operate, an investor can select the appropriate funds to meet his or her investment goals.

KEY TERMS

Aggressive growth fund

Annual report

Average maturity

Back-end loads

Balanced fund

Bank money market fund

Closed-end funds

Commercial paper

Contingent deferred sales charges

Corporate bond fund

Depository Institution Act of 1982

Diversified

Equity income

Expense ratio

Fees disclosure

Front-end load

Fund family

Fund portfolio

Fund prospectus

Growth fund

Growth of capital and income fund

Index funds

Investment Company Act of 1940

Load

Low-load fund

Market timing

Maximum capital gains (aggressive growth) fund

Money market fund

Municipal bond fund

Mutual fund

Net asset value (NAV)

No-load

Open-end funds

Portfolio prospectus

Quarterly report

Repurchase agreements (repos)

Sector funds

Standardized yield formula

Statement of additional information

Taxable and tax-free bond funds

Telephone switching

Total rate of return

Turnover rate

12b-1 charge

REVIEW QUESTIONS AND PROBLEMS

1. Briefly define the following terms: (a) NAV, (b) 12b-1 fee, (c) no-load fund, (d) closed-end mutual fund.
2. How should an investor proceed to select the mutual fund most appropriate for his or her investment needs?
3. What are the advantages of investing in a mutual fund family?
4. What are the differences between a money market fund and a bank money market account? Which would be more suitable for your purposes? Explain.
5. Explain why a closed-end mutual fund often sells at a discount from its NAV.
6. Explain the difference between a load fund and a no-load fund. Give reasons why an investor might invest in a load fund even though no-load funds are available.
7. What reasons can you give a small investor to convince him or her to invest in a mutual fund rather than purchasing stocks outright?
8. What information can be derived from a fund prospectus that can be helpful in deciding whether the fund is appropriate for you?
9. What are the most important factors in selecting a mutual fund?
10. How important is the past record of achievement of a fund as an indicator of its future performance?
11. Why would it be unwise for an investor who plans to sell his mutual fund's shares within a year to invest in a front-load fund?
12. What is the main undesirable feature of an open-end fund?
13. How is net asset value (NAV) computed?
14. How safe is a money market fund in regard to mismanagement, embezzlement, and bankruptcy?

15. (LOAD) How much must you invest in an 8.5 percent load fund to achieve a net amount invested of $80,000?

16. (TOTAL) One share in a mutual fund one year ago was worth $1.15. The per share income paid out over that period was $0.12. The simple total return was 19 percent. What is a fund share now worth?

SUGGESTED PROJECTS

1. From your library get the copies of *Forbes, Money, Barron's, Kiplinger's Personal Finance Magazine,* and *U.S. News and World Report* that rate the latest mutual funds.
   A. See if you can find some absolute winners. Trace the record of one or more of these leading funds.
   B. What place were they last year?
   C. Have any funds remained in a leading performance position for the last year, 5 years, 10 years?
   D. Follow your group of leading funds for the next two to three months and see whether or not they continue to outperform the rest.
   E. Try to do some research to find out why these funds are performing above average.
   F. Call or write the fund and request a prospectus. What information can you glean from the prospectus that would explain the firm's extraordinary performance?
2. You are invited to deliver a discourse on mutual funds at an investment seminar.
   A. Visit the library and obtain the most recent copy of *Wiesenberger's Investment Companies.* Read it and other material and prepare a package of recommended mutual funds to your investment seminar (actually your class).
   B. Compare the performance data of your recommended funds to that of one of the stock market indexes.
   C. Be prepared to field questions and to defend your recommendations.

INFORMATION RESOURCES

"Could Your Mutual Fund Go Under, Too?" *Changing Times*, April 1991, 22.

Donnelly, Barbara. "What's in a Name? Some Mutual Funds Make It Difficult for Investors to Judge." *The Wall Street Journal*, May 5, 1992, C-1.

Dorf, Richard. *The New Mutual Fund Investment Advisor.* Chicago: Probus Publishing Co., 1988.

Frailey, Fred W. "Why Fund Expenses Do and Don't Matter." *Kiplinger's Personal Finance Magazine,* June 1992, 93–95.

Gould, Carole. "Mutual Funds—Fees—Front, Back and Sideways." *The New York Times*, March 15, 1992, F-14.

———. "The Feeling is Mutual." *Modern Maturity,* April-May 1993, 55–59.

Hirsch, Michael. *Multifund Investing: How to Build a High Performance Portfolio of Mutual Funds.* Homewood, Ill.: Dow Jones-Irwin, 1987.

Investment Company Institute. Write this institute to obtain the *Guide to Mutual Funds* at 1600 M Street NW, Washington, DC 20036. 202/293-7700. At press time the guide cost $2.50.

"Investors Should Note Funds for Money Market Aren't Equal." *The Wall Street Journal,* February 28, 1991, C-1.

Jacobs, Sheldon. *The Handbook for No-Load Fund Investors.* New York: The No-Load Fund Investor, Inc., 1992.

"Money Market Mutual Funds Still Lure Even As Yields Fall." *The Wall Street Journal,* August 17, 1989, C-1.

"Mutual Funds—An Outbreak of Rights Offerings." *The New York Times,* May 24, 1992, F-13.

"Mutual Funds—How Much Did *You* Make?" *Changing Times,* January 1991, 65-66.

"Never Pay a Load and Other Fund Myths." *Kiplinger's Personal Finance Magazine,* August 1993, 77–81.

The No-Load Mutual Funds Association. Write this organization for information on no-load funds at 11 Penn Plaza, New York, NY 10001.

Perritt, Gerald W. *The Mutual Fund Encyclopedia.* Dearborn Financial Publishing Co., 1992.

"Read the Prospectus." *Newsday,* October 3, 1993, 72.

Renberg, Werner, and J. Blitzer. *Making Money with Mutual Funds.* New York: John Wiley and Sons, 1988.

Rugg, Donald. *New Strategies for Mutual Fund Investing.* Homewood, Ill.: Dow Jones-Irwin, 1988.

Schiffres, Manual. "Good Funds to Buy at a Discount." *Kiplinger's Personal Finance Magazine,* May 1992, 63-66.

"What Net Asset Value Really Means." *Money Magazine,* April 1992, 56.

CHAPTER FIFTEEN

Investing in Real Estate

- To distinguish among different types of real estate investments

- To consider the risks involved in real estate investing

- To describe the advantages and disadvantages of investing in real estate

- To discern between real estate investment trusts (REITs) and real estate limited partnerships and examine how they may be an alternative to direct ownership of real estate

- To examine how to estimate cash flow generated by income property and how to estimate return on real estate investments

- To analyze the risks and rewards of investing in time-shares and undeveloped land

Most college students do not consider investing in real estate during their college years nor even during their first working years. But in a few years, many college graduates find that their income rises considerably. At some point in their working lives they consider various investment options to further their financial aspirations. One of the options available is real estate.

This chapter explores some of the opportunities available in investing in income-earning real estate directly or indirectly. It discusses the advantages and disadvantages of each. Many of the principles that apply to buying a home also apply to commercial real estate. Therefore, the topic of mortgages and financing, which are covered in Chapter 6, are not discussed in this chapter. Any serious investor in real estate would need some courses in that field alone or at least to read several books that specialize in the subject. This chapter is not a real estate investor's guide. It serves only to highlight some approaches to real estate investment and explains how some of these investment vehicles operate.

Direct Ownership

While owning real estate, either commercial or residential, may not guarantee instant fame and fortune, it can be a sound investment. The real estate market has experienced some difficult times in recent years but over the long run, **direct ownership** of property has proved to be a popular as well as profitable investment form. It offers most investors a unique combination of modest income, some tax savings, capital gains, portfolio diversification, and a hedge against inflation. It also offers an attractive middle ground between fixed income securities, such as bonds, and pure inflation hedges, such as gold.

However, investors should not rush out to buy commercial property unless they are suited to this active form of investing. It takes knowledge, time, and energy to locate the right property, arrange financing, make repairs and improvements, find tenants, and collect rent. Most of all, investors need the staying power to weather the market's ups and downs. If, after examining your finances, you decide that being a landlord may be for you, consider the nuisance factor. There are many potential unpleasant experiences that are associated with being a landlord.

Regarding investing in residential real estate, investors have often discovered that rent control imposed by many local municipalities has turned their investment in residential real estate into a loser. Then there are the renters. It is not uncommon for landlords to be summoned at all hours of the day and night by tenants to do battle with floods, fires, stopped-up toilets, bats, rats, bugs, loud stereos, family brawls, unruly pets, tenants trapped in elevators—not to mention the tenants who do not pay rent or chronically pay late. Another factor to consider is the alternative cost. Are you willing to gamble that a well-chosen investment in real estate will outperform alternatives such as stocks, bonds, mutual funds, or even certificates of deposit? If these factors do not daunt or discourage you, then you should start by setting up a financial worksheet.

Cash Flow Factors

Positive cash flow means that an investor's gross income from renting out the property exceeds the gross expenses. The investor has some cash flowing in rather than out as a result of being a landlord. Rental income should at least cover mortgage costs, insurance, and all maintenance costs on the property. Over recent decades, such factors as tax reform, high mortgage interest rates, and high purchase prices have often made being a landlord less attractive. Getting positive cash flow out of rental property is often not easy. Positive cash flow is nevertheless the key to a worthwhile investment, with capital gains potential in second place and tax benefits third.

If you end up with a negative number after you subtract your expenses from your rental income, then you are paying out more each month than you are taking in. This is called **negative cash flow**. For real estate investors who experience negative cash flow, their best hope is to bank on future price appreciation on the property or rising rents to more than outweigh their losses each year and turn them into a profit. But unless there is a boom in real estate prices in their community or a general inflationary spiral, counting on appreciation to salvage a negative cash flow is wishful thinking.

In negotiating the total price, investors' aim should be to avoid properties with a negative cash flow, those on which the mortgage, tax, utilities, and maintenance payments, plus necessary rehab cost, exceed the rentals. Such deals work in times of high inflation when rapid appreciation more than recoups the steady drain of cash needed to hold the property. But they are risky in low inflation periods.

Tax Advantages: Depreciation

Renting out a residence you own still offers some tax breaks due to depreciation. **Depreciation** is a bookkeeping concept. It is an expense to reflect the reduction in the value of an asset that occurs due to time or use. If someone makes a capital investment by purchasing a commercial property or a new piece of machinery, he or she gets to write off a certain percentage of the expenditure each year. The idea is that the money saved by depreciating an asset will be used to pay for eventual replacement when it wears out. But when it comes to investment real estate, the likelihood is that real estate, unlike a machine tool, will gain in value over this span. This makes the ability to deduct depreciation expenses a real bonus for the real estate investor.

Buildings held for business or trade use can be depreciated even while the property itself is increasing in value. The IRS assumes, for tax purposes, that a building will decay and fall down in a certain number of years, and allows owners to depreciate it over that time span. These deductions may offset any cash flow distributions owners may receive.

How to Calculate Depreciation

How is depreciation calculated? First, investors have to figure how much their house is worth for depreciation purposes. This is its so-called tax basis, which may be a lot less than its current market value. The tax basis does not include any appreciation that may have resulted since investors bought their properties.

DEPRECIATION

Depreciation is calculated first by subtracting the original value of the land at the time of purchase from the purchase price. Typically, land accounts for 20 to 25 percent of the total value of a house. For a condominium, the land may be as little as 5 percent of the unit's total value. A fire insurance company's estimate of the building replacement cost may be an indication of the home's value minus the land. Alternatively, the tax assessment may indicate the land's value, or a professional appraiser may provide the breakdown. Investors need these figures because land cannot be depreciated. The IRS does not allow any declining value or depreciation on unimproved land.

After determining the value of the depreciable property, an investor can add to the purchase price the cost of any permanent improvements made since owning the house and thus derive the depreciable basis of the rental property. Once the depreciation has been figured for the year, it is necessary to subtract it from the difference between the rental receipts and the out-of-pocket expenses.

The depreciation schedule under current law is 27.5 years for residential buildings and 31.5 years for commercial property. This means each year investors can deduct 1/27.5, or 3.64 percent, of the value of residential buildings and 1/31.5, or 3.17 percent, of the value of commercial property. The depreciation must be taken steadily over the years and can no longer be accelerated as was possible before tax reform.

Other Tax Write-Offs

The Tax Reform Act sharply restricted the losses from rental real estate that property owners can write off against their regular income. Under the new rules, even if owners actively manage the property, those losses are considered passive and cannot be deducted from regular income. **Passive losses** can be used to offset only **passive income**, such as that from rentals or limited partnerships. However, owners who actively manage their rental properties and whose adjusted gross incomes (AGI) are $100,000 or less can deduct losses of up to $25,000 from regular income.

Landlords can additionally deduct from their rental income a host of other expenses. Some typical landlords' business deductions are fire and liability insurance premiums; expenses for finding, screening, and signing up tenants; commissions paid for collecting rent; expenses for traveling to and from the property to make repairs; the cost of repairs and maintenance; and cash losses from renting.

Real Estate Securities

Partnerships and Trusts

The factors that make owning commercial real estate attractive do not necessarily make it a recommended investment option for most people. Owning investment real estate is often a full-time job. Landlords have to maintain their property, find tenants, and cater to their tenants.

Many investors find owning real estate too cumbersome a form of investment. For those who still want the profit potential and inflation hedge that real estate may

---

Rent, Depreciation, and Taxes

Here is an example of how the numbers might work out on a house which you are considering buying or which you own and are considering renting out instead of selling. Assume you are making payments on a 30-year, fixed-rate $80,000 loan at 12 percent on a house you bought for $100,000. Your mortgage payments (principal and interest) should come to $823 per month. In addition, you incur monthly expenses totaling $277 for property taxes ($120), repairs ($32), insurance ($25), and a property manager ($100) for a total of $1,100 ($823 + $277). Assuming no vacancies, you can also earn monthly rent of $1,100. That seems to leave you with a taxable rental income of zero. If your house is appreciating, you are getting the tenants to pay all the expenses of your house tax free. You could actually earn more than $1,100 a month on this house and still not pay taxes on the rental income because you can deduct depreciation.

In our example, if you estimate that the building without the land is worth $75,000, you can deduct ⅟₃₁.₅ of $75,000 each year from rental income. This comes to $2,380 per year, or $198 per month. You therefore can earn $1,298 ($1,100 + $198) rent each month without paying income tax on it.

In this example, the mortgage interest and property taxes paid shield income and may provide for a positive cash flow, even on a property which is incurring losses.

offer, there are alternatives. Investors can put their money in real estate paper instead of property.

Not long ago any real estate investing other than the purchase of a home was the domain of very wealthy individuals or large corporations. Today, due to the **securitization** of real estate through such mass-marketed investment vehicles, the public can choose from a growing number of securities including partnerships, trusts, and mortgage-backed securities. Investors no longer have to be rich to have an investment in real estate. Let us examine some of the securitized forms of real estate investment.

REITs: Real Estate Investment Trusts

REITs (pronounced "reets"), the acronym for **real estate investment trusts,** were designed for small investors with a yen to own real estate but without sufficient capital to finance large down payments and high mortgage costs. Each REIT pools the money raised from shareholders to invest in a diversified portfolio of real estate assets, much the way a mutual fund pools shareholders' money to invest in stocks and bonds. REITs own property and make mortgage and other loans to developers. They were established as a way for investors to enjoy the capital appreciation and income benefits of real estate ownership without the headaches of property management.

The approximately $40 billion REIT industry operates under special rules. A REIT can be organized as a corporation or as an unincorporated association or trust. It is governed by a board of trustees or directors. The investors, who must number at least 100, are owners of the REIT shares and have limited liability (limited to their investement only) but limited control over management's operation of the REIT. Like the traditional corporation, it goes on indefinitely, or at least as long as it can stay in business or until shareholders, for some reason, decided to dissolve it.

REITs

Liquid Real Estate

REITs sell shares to the public which, like other listed corporations or mutual funds, then trade on a stock exchange. Prices are quoted continuously, and an investor can get in and out at any time. The larger REITs are generally traded on the New York Stock Exchange. Others are listed on the American Stock Exchange or dealt over the counter. A few are traded on regional exchanges. Share prices are published daily.

Many investors are wary of owning a single piece of property which might not do well and might require many months to sell. If a property owner becomes desperate for quick cash, he or she might have to sell at a discounted price. With a REIT, the investor is buying an interest in dozens of pieces of real estate while maintaining **liquidity**. REITs therefore enjoy the not inconsiderable advantage of being a liquid form of investment in a traditionally highly illiquid asset, real estate. When you want to get your money out of a REIT, you just simply call your broker to sell your stock.

Share prices fluctuate with investors' expectations for trust earnings (dividends) and capital gains. For as little as $2,000 to $3,000—the usual price range for 100 shares of a REIT stock plus brokerage commissions—an investor can become part owner of many pieces of prime commercial, industrial, and residential real estate worth hundreds of millions of dollars. As a mark of the growing sophistication within the REIT industry, some sponsors are developing "families" of REITs akin to families of mutual funds, in an attempt to give investors a choice of investment strategies or portfolios under a single management umbrella.

Tax law requires that virtually all (95 percent) operating income be passed directly to shareholders for taxation. REITs therefore are exempt from the double taxation of dividends most corporations face.

Types of REITS

There are four types of trusts: (1) equity REITs, (2) mortgage REITs, (3) hybrid REITs, and (4) self-liquidating REITs.

Equity REITS   **Equity REITs** use shareholders' capital and money they borrow primarily to buy or build rental income–producing real estate such as office buildings, shopping centers, resort hotels, condominiums, restaurants, nursing homes, and industrial plants. They hire a management firm to run the properties. Equity REITs tend to benefit most from the appreciating values of the underlying real estate (capital gain) and rising rents. They are generally considered the safest of the four REIT types. For those investors who believe that a new burst of inflation is likely, REITs that hold property may be a hedge against inflation through rising property values.

Mortgage REITS   **Mortgage REITs** use shareholders' capital and borrowed funds to lend to developers. They provide permanent mortgages and short-term construction loans. Earnings come from the spread between the REIT's cost of funds and its interest income. Mortgage REITs, with more volatile share prices, perform much as bonds do, responding to swings in interest rates. Although broadly speaking, mortgage REITS have less upside potential than equity REITs, they typically pay higher dividends because there is more risk and volatility in making loans than in owning property and usually more current income return on the investment.

Hybrid REITS   **Hybrid REITs** try to create a favorable mix of ownership and mortgage positions. They will take equity positions on some properties and lending positions on others. They both own property and make mortgage loans. Hybrids are designed to get the best of both worlds—more stable stock prices than mortgage REITs and better yields than equity REITs. They also have a greater potential for gain, since their assets could appreciate and rents could be raised.

Finite REITS   The **self-liquidation trust,** which is also known as **finite REIT** or **FREIT,** is basically a newer style REIT. It tells investors at the outset that it will sell off its holdings eventually, usually in 10 years, and pay off its shareholders in what it hopes will be handsome capital gains. Like the conventional REIT, its shares are liquid. Shareholders can buy and sell their shares like ordinary stock.

The Fall and Rise of REITs

REITs, which gained in popularity in the late 1960s and early 1970s, went through a crisis in the mid- and late-70s. In the mid-70s, overbuilding combined with inflation, rising interest rates, and material costs caused a collapse in the real estate market. This crushed REITs' share prices, dividends, and asset values. Risky loans backfired and foreclosures abounded. The many borrowers defaulting on their loans forced REITs to foreclose on properties that they subsequently found nearly impossible to sell. REIT disasters made headlines for months. Of 216 REITs, 9 went bankrupt, dozens teetered on the brink of insolvency, many merged, and most cut or eliminated their dividends. From 1974 to 1976, the REIT industry lost half of its assets, and share prices plunged 70 percent. In 1975, shareholders lost some $3.2 billion when highly leveraged mortgage REITs defaulted on their loans. With the sharp rise in real estate prices in the early 1980s, the public slowly came to view REITS with favor again. REITS again experienced sharp declines with the real estate bust of the late 1980s.

To this day many investors shun REIT shares. Nonetheless, the industry has survived and enjoyed a revival of sorts in recent years as illustrated in Figure 15–1. The industry is much smaller but appears much healthier, too. Currently, there are less than 120 REITs but they seem stronger, of higher quality, and more prudent than before. Most have moved back into more secure types of real estate investing.

FIGURE 15–1	A New Boom Cycle for REITs

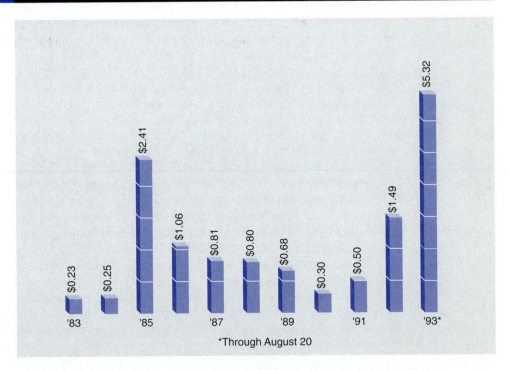

*Through August 20

The data trace the 1980s boom and bust for REITs and the start of remarkable increase for the early 1990s. Amounts show issuance of REIT stock in billions of dollars.

SOURCE: Securities Data Co., 1993.

Instead of relying on risky mortgage lending to build assets, REITs now are buying equity interests in income-producing properties.

Market Price Discounted

Most REITs sell at a perpetual discount to net asset value. Suppose a REIT owns real estate currently appraised at $3 million, with 300,000 shares outstanding. We would expect each share to be worth $10. However, such a REIT might trade as low as $7 a share. The discount could be due to the perpetual nature of the REIT, meaning there is no timetable for selling off all the properties and cashing in the appreciated real estate. Conventional trusts keep buying and selling properties but they never liquidate their portfolios entirely. For that reason, investors treat a trust's appraised value as a promise instead of a reality and refuse to pay face value for the holdings.

Even finite REIT shares sell at some discount from their initial prices since they risk encountering depressed markets when their life is up and may be compelled to sell. Another form of indirect real estate ownership is known as a *limited partnership*.

Real Estate Limited Partnerships (RELPs)

Real estate limited partnerships, or **RELPs**, are organized by so-called **general partners**, who are either individuals, a firm, or a syndicate of real estate professionals. They, like mutual funds, pool large sums of money from the smaller contributions of many limited partners who otherwise could not afford to buy an office building, a group of properties, or a shopping center. The general partners package and manage the venture and arrange to sell partnership shares.

Syndicate offerings are made to investors either by the syndicator directly or through stockbrokers, life insurance companies, financial advisers, and others. The general partner or syndicate receives various fees and a commission (usually 7 to 10 percent) for the service, plus a share of any profits. The investors, who provide most of the capital, are called **limited partners** because their liability for losses is limited to the amount they invest. They are not allowed to participate in the management or decision making of the partnership. The assets are managed by the sponsoring general manager.

Each unit in a partnership represents a share in either a single real estate holding or, more likely, a package of investments. Individuals can commonly buy in for as little as $1,000. This enables people with small sums to share in the large capital gains, tax benefits, and income possible with real estate investments.

The money is used to build everything from apartment buildings, shopping centers, hotels, office and industrial complexes, mobile home parks, or other commercial properties or to acquire other assets, such as short-term mortgages or land.

The limited partners share in proportion to their investment the income from rents, capital gains, interest on mortgages held, or other income. However, the general partners often charge many fees, thereby lowering the actual return on investments. The limited partners also share any profits realized if and when the general partner decides to sell off the holdings and liquidate the partnership, usually 7 to 10 (or even 20) years later.

Before tax reform, RELPs were one of the most popular-selling financial products. Investors nationwide poured billions of dollars a year into RELPs of various kinds.

Guidelines for Selecting the Right REIT

REITs are as safe as the actual real estate they invest your money in. The real estate itself is the ultimate test of your investment. You should be prepared to analyze the economics of each of the properties owned by a REIT just as if you were acquiring it directly.

1. Property Holdings
The first step in selecting a REIT is to get a prospectus from your stockbroker and look at the section that describes what the trust owns and where the property is located. Be on the alert for heavy investment in obsolescent regional shopping centers in well-to-do areas—where merchants can afford to pay higher rents in new malls—as well as aging apartment complexes which are expensive to maintain. Dependence upon a few tenants or exposure to one-industry towns are another warning signal. On the plus side, look for strong investments in recession-resistant industries, a good geographic mix, or a solid position in local markets.

2. Cash Flow
Glean its prospectus for information about the firm's recent earnings and dividend performance and its underlying portfolio of properties. For dividend growth to be sustained, a REIT needs consistently growing cash flow. Calculate the REIT's cash flow per share for the past three years by adding depreciation to net income before capital gains. Divide this sum by the number of shares outstanding. Beware if the REIT's annual dividend per share is higher than its cash flow per share. The dividend may be coming out of borrowings or one-time gains on property sales.

3. Track Record
Scan the prospectus or annual financial statement to see how long the REIT has been in business. Older REITs enable investors to examine their performance records and their history of dividend increases. The key is to look for a REIT that actively tries to improve and add value to the property it buys. Shares in such REITs are likely to out-perform inflation. Check the track record of the individuals running the REIT. Make sure they are more than mere caretakers of property. Good equity REITs tend to be regionalized and to specialize in a particular real estate sector, such as shopping centers or resort hotels. Although specialization does enhance management know-how, it has a drawback of limiting diversification. REITs investing in health care, hospitals, and nursing homes are much less risky than shopping centers, which are more dependent on the economy.

4. Leverage
For safety, REITs that have bought their properties mostly with cash are best. The less debt a REIT carries, the safer it is. It does not have to keep up sizable mortgage payments that could lead to foreclosures during rough times.

5. Fees
Total management fees and other charges should not exceed 1 percent of gross assets a year.

Nearly half of all RELPs were structured as tax shelters. For upper bracket taxpayers, the write-offs were the main attraction.

The limited partners, as owners of commercial real estate, could have claimed tax deductions on their individual returns for their share of depreciation, property taxes, interest on loans, and certain expenses, including some fees paid to the general partner. Depreciation allowances created losses that limited partners could use to offset income from the partner's other income.

The Tax Reform Act of 1986 ended the party for tax avoiders who had flocked to limited partnerships. Their passive losses from write-offs can no longer be offset against earned income but only against passive income. For example, assume you have invested $3,000 in an apartment building, along with several other people. If your share of the tax deductions for the first year is $3,000, you can deduct this only against passive income such as income the RELPs or other trusts earned for you. You cannot deduct it from your earned income.

The Risks   Investors often view RIETs or RELPs as a means of lowering the risk of investing in real estate by spreading it among many investors and often by investing in geographically and economically diverse projects. But although partnerships appear to be a more cautious approach to investing in real estate, investors should be aware of the risks and disadvantages as well. RELPs, like all other investments, contain some risk and it is necessary to approach them with caution.

RELPs additionally require investors to commit their funds until the partnership is liquidated, generally 7 to 10 years after startup. The risk varies widely because each deal is different. The better partnerships are reasonably safe. But any number of things can go wrong. If the deal involves construction, cost overruns are common. It might also be difficult to keep a building rented. High vacancy rates, overbuilding, a recession, or adoption of rent controls could restrict earnings. Incompetent, dishonest, or greedy general partners could create major problems. A badly planned and managed partnership project with no yield and no return on your money may even cause you to lose your original investment. Other risks to be considered are a shift in population or deterioration of the property. Certain pitfalls are inherent in any real estate investment, such as inept management, fluctuating markets, foreclosures, tax audits, skyrocketing loan rates, disallowed deductions, and changes in the law. A lot can happen during the life of a RELP.

Because of the risks involved, most states have enacted laws intended to protect would-be investors from themselves by ensuring that investors have sufficient assets to be able to bear the loss of their entire investment. Most states permit syndicators to sell RELPs only to people who meet certain minimum eligibility requirements. Many states set a minimum of $30,000 of net worth (not counting house, furnishings, etc.) and gross income of at least $30,000, or $75,000 of net income irrespective of assets.

Liquidity   One drawback of RELPs is the lack of an organized resale or secondary market for partnership interests. Limited partnerships are among the least liquid of real estate investments. A partnership is supposed to be a long-term investment. To know the real value, investors must wait until the partnership is dissolved, its assets sold off, and the proceeds divided among the investors. If forced to get out early, investors can lose some of their capital since most RELPs can be sold only at deep discounts under their appraised value. In recent years, a secondary market emerged for some of the larger publicly registered RELPs, providing some liquidity. National Partnership Exchange, or NAPEX, of Tampa, Florida, a national electronic market that lists units for auction, is open to trading by its broker-members.

Blind Pools

One difficulty in assessing risk and forecasting performance of any given offering is that a high percentage of RELPs are **blind pools**, meaning the partnership has not specified what properties it will invest in. Properties are not acquired until after investors buy in. Investors do not know beforehand specifically what will be purchased or how much will be paid for it. Investors in such an arrangement have to rely entirely on the judgment of the general partner.

Professional Advice Required

Because of the very specialized nature of partnerships, it is difficult to assess them without the help of at least one objective expert adviser. Tax attorneys, CPAs, real estate specialists, or financial planners who are familiar with real estate and taxes can offer invaluable advice as long as they are objective. It is well worth the extra expense. Investors should avoid "advisers" who earn a commission on the sale of investments.

Investors, together with their advisers, examine the economic and tax effects thoroughly as well as make certain that the management has the requisite expertise and integrity. The prospectus should describe the prior performance and experience of the general partners.

A limited partnership offered to the public must be registered with the SEC and with the Securities Commission of any state where it is offered. The SEC does not rule on the partnership's merits, but it attempts to ascertain whether the offering prospectus makes full disclosure of all facts that are important to a potential investor.

The extent of the general partners' participation in the project and the amount of the fees payable to them are set forth in the prospectus prepared by the general partners. These documents are required by law to be submitted to the limited partners before they invest. They purport to factually explain what the partners are buying. However, they are often a hundred pages in length and written in technical English.

REITs versus RELPs—How They Square Off

RELPs are substantially different from REITs. Limited partnerships generally dissolve within 10 to 15 years when the properties are sold and the proceeds are distributed. REITs usually have an unlimited life and are actually prohibited from passing along their tax losses on real estate investing to their shareholders.

Partnerships also differ from trusts in their structure and their goals. Partnerships are often established as single project ventures by real estate developers or

Look Before You RELP

f you are considering a RELP, here are some questions that you need to have answered before investing:

1. **Is the general partner betting his or her own money on the deal?** If the general partner, who is much more familiar with the deal than you, does not have confidence enough to invest his or her own money, then you should not either.

2. **How is the deal structured? Does the general partner profit only when the investor does, or does he or she make money regardless?** A reputable general partner should be looking to share risks equitably with the other investors instead of seeking to rake off large up-front fees and leave investors hanging out there for eventual returns.

3. **What is the general partner's reputation, track record, experience, and skill, particularly in this type of project? Has he or she ever constructed a project similar to the one proposed?** A developer of office space may not have the necessary experience to build an apartment complex. If he was a great success in building single-family homes, is he capable of developing a large resort hotel or shopping center?

4. **Does the general partner have the financial muscle to weather a storm? If the market takes a downturn, will he or she be capable of keep the project moving?**

5. **How leveraged is the deal?** The cash down payment should be at least 25 percent, and even more cash would be better.

6. **What is being done to see that a property is well managed?** Most investors in a syndication never see the property in which they own a share. How do they know that the maximum rental income is being obtained from the tenants?

7. **Does the underlying business of the partnership make sense?** If there is a high vacancy rate in the city in which they propose to build, does it make

managers, who then take on limited partners to fund development and construction. Trusts of properties are usually established for ownership rather than development of properties and are often created by companies outside the real estate business, such as brokerage houses.

For smaller investors, REITs are probably a better bet than limited partnerships. With partnerships, minimum investments typically start at $2,000 for just one sponsor's offering. With REITs, investors can get diversification by buying a number of stocks at $3 to $50 a share, offering geographic dispersion and property variations.

Partnerships obviously are not for everyone. There seems to be no persuasive evidence that RELPs or REITs, on the whole, have performed better than, or as well as, less exotic investments, such as money market funds or insured savings certificates.

Mortgage-Backed Securities

Mortgage–backed securities such as Ginnie Maes, Fannie Maes, and Freddie Macs are another form of indirect real estate investments. For a detailed discussion of these, see Chapter 13.

Time-Sharing

Yet another form of indirect property ownership or investment is **time-sharing**. People who tend to vacation at the same kind of facility often may consider vacation time-sharing, the use of a vacation home for a limited, preplanned time.

Despite well-publicized reports of scams and deceiving marketing ploys, time-shares have become an increasingly popular way to take a vacation, and sales keep growing. The general allure is to guarantee yourself prepaid vacation accommodations for a week or more at a resort you would enjoy annually. You can invest anywhere from $2,500 for a winter week in a cramped one–bedroom lakeside condo to $40,000 for Christmas week in a two-story villa in Puerto Vallarta, Mexico, complete with maid service and a private swimming pool. The average condo price, though, is about $9,500 for a two-bedroom unit. Time-share buyers must also pay annual maintenance fees averaging $350 and subject to increase.

Advantages of Time-Sharing
Despite their shortcomings, buying a time-share has several advantages that make this new twist to vacation planning very attractive.

1. Since buyers pay now for future vacations, they are spared the inevitable rising cost of holidays in years to come.

"I find it hard to believe that we've actually won 20 million dollars when they send the letter bulk mail."

SOURCE: "Pepper...and Salt," *The Wall Street Journal,* May 6, 1991, A-17. Reprinted by permission of Cartoon Features Syndicate.

2. Time-share buyers are able to enjoy the feeling of permanence and of having their own place year after year without buying household furnishings or equipment or maintaining a permanent vacation home.

3. Time-sharing can provide an economical resort vacation for the whole family, because many properties offer complete sports and recreational activities. With a fully equipped kitchen, which most units have, vacationers can avoid expensive restaurant meals.

High-Pressure Sales Tactics

You open your mail and read a mailgram: "Congratulations! You are the winner of a brand new stereo set, model no. XL 684J. To claim your prize, you must visit our property within 30 days and receive a free guided tour of Lake Gypum located at the foot of Mount Fraud. Just call Mr. Henry Conjob at the toll-free number below for an appointment to pick up your grand prize plus another bonus surprise gift that is waiting for you. You are under no obligation to buy anything."

Messages like this in the form of telegrams and official-looking notices or letters have no doubt cluttered your mail box and millions of others in the United States. These give-aways and phony sweepstakes promotions are proliferating. Behind this upsurge is the boom in the marketing of resort time-sharing real estate whereby people can spend vacations by buying a fractional ownership interest in some vacation property. Time-sharing facilities can be condominium apartments, townhouses, villa-type buildings, hotels, and motels. Living units vary in style and size, and some shares are even sold on houseboats, yachts, recreational vehicle parks, and campgrounds.

The reason for the lavish gifts offered becomes clear if one examines the enormous potential profitability for time share-sellers. If a developer builds and furnishes 100 apartment units for $60,000 each, including land costs, the outlay is $6 million. If the developer then sells 50 one-week time-shares in each unit for $8,000, the gross income is $40,000,000, or $400,000 per unit. Out of this sum comes marketing and promotional costs, which generally amount to 35 to 40 percent of sales revenue. The net profit is still enormously high.

A typical time-share unit sells for two and one-half times the market price of an equivalent home or condo. For example, a unit that will net $255,000 as a time-share will sell for $100,000 as a regular condo. This explains the very aggressive sales pitches and campaigns.

With markups like those, time-shares should not be bought as real estate investments. Owners who sell their week at time-share auctions often do so at losses as high as 60 percent.

High-intensity selling is commonplace, so brace yourself if you decide to accept an invitation. Solicitation and related expenses can cost a developer $100 for every couple that is lured to the site. Potential buyers are usually taken on a tour and then offered a "today only" special. They are then subjected to a "grind session" in the office with hardball selling techniques.

4. Depending on the resort they choose, time-share owners are usually able to arrange a trade for their time-share when they desire a vacation elsewhere.

Most time-shares offer exchange privileges, which are widely available and enable time-share owners to swap their time slots for one in another resort through an exchange network. State consumer protection laws and computerized exchange networks to make swapping easier have turned time-sharing into a more attractive vacation option. However, the exchange privilege does not guarantee a vacation in another resort. It is based on availability. Time-share owners cannot realistically expect to exchange their February 1–7 week in Hawaii for a Thanksgiving, Easter, or Christmas week in Orlando, Florida.

While some time-share programs are highly regarded, many are simply overpriced, not economical and poor investments. Buyers should carefully consider the risks as well as the benefits of time-sharing before signing any contract. A buyer's total outlay will increase, of course, if the purchase is financed. Most developers offer five- to seven-year loans, and interest rates tend to be higher than regular mortgage rates.

Some other questions to ask yourself before buying time-shares:

TIME

Evaluating a Vacation "Bargain"

Suppose you were offered a time-sharing program at Waikiki Beach in Hawaii for $10,000 for one week each year. If you buy, you would own approximately 1/50th of a room in the Bilk-em-more Hotel. Doing a little bit of financial calculations can put the deal in its proper perspective. If 50 people are paying $10,000 to jointly own your room, then the room is selling for $500,000. Now ask yourself, is that the price of a studio apartment or condo in that area? Or are you paying several times the price for equivalent real estate? A check with a real estate brokerage would provide you with that information.

But suppose for a moment that the price is not inflated. Consider what you are getting for what you are paying. If the bond or money market fund rates are currently yielding 8 percent, then your opportunity cost of owning this time share is $800 of lost interest income annually. If annual maintenance fees of $350 are added, your total cost of your week's vacation is $1,150. Now you need to ask yourself the obvious question. Is $1,150 a week for a room for two in Waikiki Beach, without food, for the week you bought (let's say April 1–8) a fair price? If you booked a room for a week in a regular hotel nearby, would it cost you more or less than $1,150? If you can get a nice room for one week in a comparable hotel for $500, then obviously you are overpaying. The selling pitch that the room is yours free (except for the $350 service charge) for one week each year ignores the loss of income on your initial investment. If, instead of buying into this time-sharing plan, you invested your $10,000 in a safe AAA bond, bank CD, or money market fund and used the earnings (which we assume to be about $800) as your annual one-week vacation fund, would you not be better off?

1. Are you likely to become bored with the development you choose year in and year out?

2. Are you sure you want to and plan to take a vacation every year?

3. What will the place be like in 10 or 20 years? Is it properly maintained?

4. Will annual maintenance fees go up?

5. Is the developer financially sound?

6. What are the prospects for reselling?

The answer to these questions should help you get a better perspective on the time-share offers and enable you to withstand high-pressure sales pitches.

Time-sharing should be regarded as a way possibly to save money on vacation costs, not as a real estate investment. Owners seldom get back their original purchase price in the resale market. A time-sharing purchase is a complex and often risky transaction. Some time-share buyers have been defrauded; others have lost their investment when developers went bankrupt. The federal government does not regulate time-shares as such, but most states have some regulation of them. Alaska, California, Connecticut, Florida, Hawaii, Maine, Nebraska, New Hampshire, New York, Oklahoma, South Carolina, Tennessee, Virginia, and West Virginia all confer **rescission rights** to time-shares. Rescission rights, conferred by the truth-in-lending law, are the right to cancel a purchase contract within a specified time. (To find out about the situation in your state, check with the attorney general's office or the state real estate commission). Most states with regulations require the developer to give at least three days in which buyers can cancel their contracts without penalty. Where laws are in force, marketing abuses have been curbed, though by no means eliminated.

Types of Time-Shares

There are two kinds of time-share plans that are offered for purchase. The most common is a **fee-simple plan**, which gives buyers title to a fraction of the property and ownership of their week. The other kind of time-share, a **right-to-use plan**, grants

Check Out the Developer

Before you do business with a developer, check whether complaints have been filed against the company by contacting the U.S. Department of Housing and Urban Development, Office of Interstate Land Sales Registration Division (OILSR), Room 6266, Washington, DC 20410, 202/755-6716.

If you are buying from a developer who operates across state lines and is selling 100 or more lots, most of what you need to know to protect yourself can be found in the property report required by the OILSR.

buyers occupancy rights for a set number of years. Under the fee-simple plan, a buyer automatically joins an owners' association that will assume control of the resort from the developer once most of the available weeks have been sold. When control is turned over to the association, it may elect to retain the developer as manager or may choose an outside management firm.

This transition can be made smoothly if the developer has been assessing annual maintenance fees that cover day-to-day operating costs and sufficient contributions to a reserve fund for major maintenance. Some developers, however, set annual fees artificially low to encourage sales, thus bequeathing to the new owners a resort with a deficit and insufficient reserves. State regulators have been investigating a growing number of time-share resorts that possibly lack sufficient funds to keep them running after most of the weeks have been sold.

In a disclosure statement and schedule of maintenance fees, check to see whether the developer is setting aside a proportion of your maintenance fee in a reserve fund for major repairs and replacements, or you may face heavy special assessments in later years. Have a real estate attorney who is familiar with time-sharing review all documents before you sign them.

When a time-share project goes bankrupt, your chances of recovering your money depend on which of the two kinds of time-share plans you have purchased. Under a fee-simple plan, if the time-share buyer holds hold clear title, his or her claims cannot be ignored by foreclosing lenders. However, if the buyer has only a right-to-use plan, his or her case is much weaker. In past bankruptcy cases, foreclosing lenders have not been legally obligated to honor these occupancy-only contracts, which lack the force of ownership.

Undeveloped Land: Is Raw Land a Raw Deal?

Buying undeveloped land is especially risky. Investors are gambling on future prospects with no income now and no break for depreciation write-offs. Raw land, however picturesque, scenic, or romantic, ranks among the riskiest of investments, right up there with pork belly futures and oil prospecting.

Raw land comes in all shapes and sizes: urban, rural, residential, recreational, commercial, agricultural. It is important to remember that no raw land has any intrinsic value unless somebody wants it for something. Annual land carrying costs will likely consist of principal and interest, taxes, insurance, maintenance, and professional fees for brokers, lawyers, surveyors, and so on. The cost of planned improvements, such as a road or timber clearing, often needs to be added. Investors should figure the maximum time they will hold the property and then do the calculations and decide if their budget can stand the strain.

Be sure that the property is accessible and that the costs of owning it and building on it are reasonable. Unsuspecting buyers may be stunned to discover that to build on their new lots, they may have to pump sewage uphill through solid rock or face huge bills just to bring in electricity.

Scenic empty land that evokes such inspiration and optimism can tie up investors' money for years until it is parcelled, zoned, cleared, graded, paved, built upon, and rented. While this is happening, investors derive no income from it. And there is always the chance that it may never be developed. Raw land, until it is developed or sold, absorbs money. This absence of current income will also discourage banks from lending an investor money. On the other hand, under the proper circumstances, its value can skyrocket, making its owner very wealthy. The value of raw land tends to fluctuate with the economic fortunes of the region. The point to bear in mind is that this is a highly speculative, nonliquid investment.

SUMMARY

Real estate is a popular tangible asset. After your portfolio contains cash reserves, stocks, and bonds, you may give serious consideration to the inclusion of investment real estate. There are several ways to invest in real estate. These include direct ownership and management of property, indirect ownership through trusts and limited partnerships, time-sharing, and speculating in raw land.

Rental property should generally produce a positive cash flow in order to be considered a worthwhile investment. Cash flow is the yearly earnings after all operating expenses, debt services, and taxes have been deducted. Many people wish to invest in real estate but do not desire to own property directly. They invest in paper real estate such as REITs and RELPs instead. Time-shares and raw land purchases should be considered as highly speculative rather than an investment due to the length of time required to realize any potential profits, the lack of liquidity, the lack of income throughout the time the property is held, and the carrying costs entailed.

KEY TERMS

Blind pools

Depreciation

Direct ownership

Equity REITs

Fee-simple time-share plan

Finite REIT (FREIT)

General partners

Hybrid REITs

Limited partners

Liquidity

Mortgage REITs

Negative cash flow

Passive income

Passive losses

Positive cash flow

REITs (Real estate investment trusts)

RELPs (Real estate limited partnerships)

Rescission rights

Right-to-use time-share plan

Securitizaton

Self-liquidation trust

Time-sharing

REVIEW QUESTIONS AND PROBLEMS

1. Explain the major advantages of investing in real estate.
2. Distinguish between direct ownership and indirect ownership of real estate.
3. What is depreciation and why is it considered a bonus for real estate investors?

4. What does a depreciation schedule of 27.5 years for residential real estate and 31.5 years for commercial property mean? Explain by using an example.
5. Distinguish between positive and negative cash flows when investing in real estate.
6. Compare and contrast REITs and RELPs.
7. What are the differences between equity REITs, mortgage REITs, hybrid REITs, and self-liquidating REITs?
8. What risks are specifically associated with investing in real estate limited partnerships?
9. Present arguments for and against investing money in a vacation time share.
10. Explain why investing in undeveloped land is considered speculative.

11. (DEPRECIATION) You are considering buying a rental property. The worth of the building without land is $250,000. Mortgage payments are $2,500. Taxes are $400, repairs $25, insurance $50, a property manager $110, and the depreciation period is 31.5 years. You would like to earn $1,000 without paying income tax. What monthly rental must you charge?

12. (REITs) A REIT which owns real estate with an appraised value of $10 million and 150,000 shares outstanding has a total market value of $11 million. What is the market price per share?

13. (TIME) You are considering buying into a time-share with 10 other joint owners. You believe a fair price for a room is $85,000. What is the maximum amount each joint owner should pay?

SUGGESTED PROJECTS

Visit a real estate brokerage office and inquire as to the price of a residential three-family apartment house.

A. Find out how much the necessary down payment is.
B. Get a quote on the mortgage interest rate as well as your monthly mortgage payment.
C. Find out the cost of repairs, insurance, and property taxes.
D. Get an estimate as to rents that you can charge and future rent increases.
E. Find out how much depreciation you can write off against earnings.
F. Try now to work through the numbers to determine whether you would have a positive or negative cash flow.
G. Present your figures and proposition to your class and have classmates help you decide whether this building would be a good or bad deal at that price.
H. If it is not a good deal, then decide at what price it would become a good investment.

INFORMATION RESOURCES

Barr, Gary, and Judith H. McGee. *J. K. Lasser's Real Estate Investment Guide*. J. K. Lasser Institute, 1989.

"Faster Ways to Sell Your House." *Changing Times*, April 1991, 28–32.

Giese, William. "Brighter Days Ahead for Real Estate." *Kiplinger's Personal Finance Magazine*, October 1991, 61–63.

Irwin, Robert. *Buy, Rent and Hold: How to Make Money in a "Cold" Real Estate Market*. New York: McGraw-Hill, 1991.

"The Limited Future of Limited Partnerships." *Changing Times*, August 1989, 27–30.

McLean, Andrew. *The Home Equity Kit*. New York: John Wiley & Sons, 1990.

Miller, Peter. *Successful Real Estate Investing*. New York: Harper & Row, 1988.

Nessen, Robert. *The Real Estate Book*. Boston: Little, Brown & Company, 1981.

The New Dow Jones-Irwin Guide to Real Estate Investing Homewood, Ill.: Dow Jones-Irwin, 1989.

Quinn, Jane Bryant. "The Trap in Time-Shares." *Newsweek*, July 12, 1993, 48.

Razzi, Elizabeth. "The Landlord Route to Real Estate Profits." *Kiplinger's Personal Finance Magazine*, April 1993, 89–93.

"Real Estate Partnerships Are Sinking." *Business Week*, July 3, 1989, 74–75.

Shenkman, Martin. *Real Estate after Tax Reform*. New York: John Wiley, 1987.

Slater, Karen. "Central Mart for Partnerships Is Sought." *The Wall Street Journal*, May 1, 1992, C-1.

Sloan, Allan. "Beware These Trusts." *Newsweek*, May 24, 1993, 46.

"Top Yields and Prospects of Gains Make REITs Right." *Money*, June 1989, 159–162.

U. S. Department of Housing and Urban Development, Office of Interstate Land Sales Registration Division (OILSR), Room 6226, Washington, DC 20410. 202/755-6716. Write or call for any history of complaints filed against the intrastate developers with whom you are dealing.

CHAPTER SIXTEEN

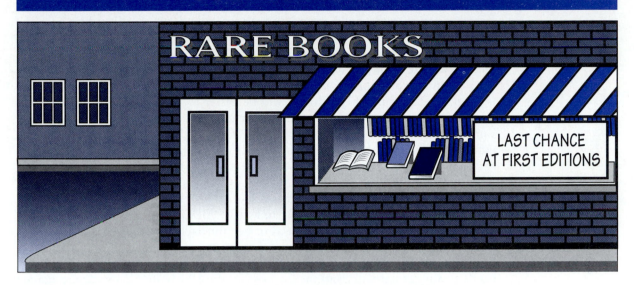

Collectibles and Commodities

- To examine how collectibles can fit into one's overall financial plan

- To differentiate between collectibles as a pure hobby and as an investment

- To evaluate the suitability of collectibles as compared to conventional investments

- To consider the benefits and pitfalls of investing in collectibles and commodity futures

- To evaluate the risk of buying futures contracts and how this risk can be hedged

We have thus far discussed the conventional ways of investing and saving, increasing earnings, and building assets for future needs. However, there are other ways of investing. If you are seeking a sane asylum for your money or a kennel for your homeless savings, then the banks and stock and bond markets need not be your only recourse. This chapter discusses alternate investment forms which could be considered, under certain conditions, by investors. Some of them even may have an added dimension of being enjoyable.

One area of investment is collectibles. Many people start collections of certain items as a hobby or fun activity and carefully develop these collections into a profitable investment or small fortune. Others enter the field of collectibles with the intention mainly of earning profits. The range of collectibles is literally endless. They could be sound investments as long as other people collect the same items and are willing to pay an acceptable price for them. From an investment perspective, the more collectors in a particular market, the more developed that market is. In practical terms, this means it will be easier to buy and sell and establish a price in this market. If there are other people out there who want and collect the same thing you do and are willing to pay for it, then you stand a chance of increasing your wealth besides having fun. If you are the only one who collects old soda bottles, preserved butterflies, or old frisbees, then you may just have fun but are not building an investment.

Other investment alternatives discussed in this chapter are precious metals, the futures markets, options, puts, and calls. All of these are considered risky and speculative investments and need to be approached with great caution, if at all. There are many better investments that are easier to understand and are more liquid and have a higher return and more favorable tax consequences. If inflation's steady retreat will continue throughout the 1990s, it will also argue against collectibles, precious metals, and commodity futures as financial assets. In the inflation of the 1970s and the early 1980s, speculative buying drove prices of tangible assets to impressive heights, but the boom ended with the slowing of inflation. Nevertheless, many sensible people persist in putting their money into antiques, art, and other collectibles. If you are or will ever be interested in any of these, it is worthwhile to know the advantages and pitfalls that are inherent in each of these investment forms.

Collectibles

If the stock market's ups and downs are making you seasick, you can put some money into assets that you can at least have some fun with, like a Shirley Temple doll, comic books, baseball cards, or Star Wars memorabilia. While the idea of sinking investment money into such "kid's stuff" may seem odd, it sometimes turns out to be profitable. These items and many others fall into a category called **collectibles**. Collectibles are objects that are too old to be commonplace but not yet old enough to be antiques. Some of the clutter in attics, basements, and garages starts to become collectible when it is about 30 years old. An **antique** usually predates the turn of the century. A collectible also has to have a certain nostalgic charm that makes people treasure it. That is why the 30 years are important. That amount of time allows children to grow up and become nostalgic for the toys, posters, cars, furniture, clothes, and gadgets of childhood. This engenders a desire to buy these things and pass them along for posterity.

For our purposes, we will consider as a collectible anything that people collect, be it old, new, or antique. The list of items that people collect is almost endless. Some of these categories include the following:

antique fishing lures	medallions
antique furniture	movie posters
antique maps	old cars
antique photographs	old checks
art deco items	old clocks
autographs	old credit cards
Barbie dolls	old furniture
baseball cards	old lunch boxes
Batman dolls	old or rare books
battery-operated toys	old quilts
Beatles memorabilia	orientalia
Beatles wigs	paintings
books	phonograph albums
Chinese ceramics	photographs
coins	political campaign buttons
colored precious stones	rare stamps
comics	rugs
day-glo posters	tools
firearms	toys
fruit crate labels	vintage wines
historic documents	war souvenirs
magazines	

Each of these items constitutes a field of its own, with its own market, collectors, and dealers and usually some literature such as newsletters, catalogues, and so on. Nobody can count on outguessing the market for collectibles.

Investment or Hobby (or Both)?

Collectibles are not investments in the true sense of the word. They generally are not liquid, provide no current income, and take a long time to appreciate in value. However, they can be a reasonable and therapeutic form of savings and investment for those who put a small percentage of their assets (say 5 percent) into these items and who get pleasure and prestige from hanging and displaying or using a collectible with the strong likelihood that in the long run it will appreciate in value. After all, a Hummel or a Chinese rug is much more beautiful than a T-bill or a municipal bond.

A prudent rule of collectibles shopping, therefore, is, Don't buy anything unless you like it enough to use it, wear it, or look at it. Good-quality items will probably increase in value, but nothing is guaranteed. If all you want is to double your money, however, then you should buy a zero-coupon government-backed bond that matures in about 12 years. By contrast, you may have to hold a quality collectible 5 to 10 years to generate any profit at all because most likely you will buy at the marked-up retail price and be forced to sell at the wholesale price, which can be 50 to 85 percent below retail.

Another factor to consider is the opportunity cost. Investors who buy collectibles do not receive any returns on them until they sell. Furthermore, they earn no dividends and no interest, and it often costs money to store and insure these items. The

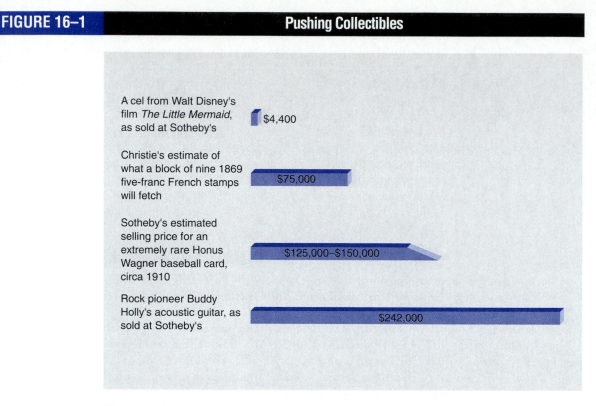

| FIGURE 16–1 | Pushing Collectibles |

A cel from Walt Disney's film *The Little Mermaid*, as sold at Sotheby's — $4,400

Christie's estimate of what a block of nine 1869 five-franc French stamps will fetch — $75,000

Sotheby's estimated selling price for an extremely rare Honus Wagner baseball card, circa 1910 — $125,000–$150,000

Rock pioneer Buddy Holly's acoustic guitar, as sold at Sotheby's — $242,000

Major auction houses such as Sotheby's and Christie's now deal regularly in small-scale items, as shown above.

SOURCE: "Pushing Collectibles," *The Wall Street Journal*, March 1, 1991, C-1.

price will have to rise substantially when they sell just to break even on those costs and to recoup the yield forgone all these years by shunning stocks or bonds.

The chief attraction of many collectibles and memorabilia is nostalgic appeal. There is no guarantee that these items will appreciate in value or that prices in the future will not drop as the nostalgia value wanes. Investors should try to avoid collecting trendy, speculative things which can wither away. It is safest to stick to things that people have collected for years and probably will collect for hundreds of years into the future.

When investing in collectibles, however, you need to amortize your expense in comparison to the pleasure of owning the item. A $400 poster in a $200 frame kept for five years breaks down to a cost of $10 a month. However, if we take into account the opportunity cost of money and assume the $600 could have earned 8 percent a year invested in a CD money market account or other investment form, then the cost of the poster can be derived by multiplying ($600 × 1.08^5), which equals $881.60. Divided by 60 months, this breaks down to a cost of $14.70 a month. If you enjoy looking at the poster, even if it winds up as worthless in terms of significant appreciation, you may consider it a good investment in terms of what you got out of it. If it winds up being worth 10 times what you paid for it, it was a terrific investment.

How to Buy

There could be money in collectibles, but buying wisely and selling later is no easy matter. How can you educate yourself to become a worthwhile collector? To protect themselves, canny collectors specialize in a certain area, learning everything they can about their period, genre, artist, or product process. Although there is no formula for selecting tomorrow's Picasso, collectors can visit museums to train their eye. They can read books, magazines, and newsletters on art, antiques, and collectibles, talk to dealers, and attend art appreciation classes. Above all, a collector studies and compares, developing an eye for style and quality.

Collect Quality   The important factors affecting the value of a work, besides authenticity, are condition, whether the piece needs restoration or has already been heavily restored or repaired, and aesthetic quality. Successful collectors repeat the often cited but often ignored advice to buy the best examples in any collectible category. If a market softens, prices on mediocre pieces will fall more quickly and further, while prices on top-quality items may slip only a little. During market booms, the quality pieces will perform best.

Top grade represents liquidity. When collectors own the finest on the market, they are generally talking about immediate liquidity. For serious investors, condition is critical. No matter how desirable the item, its value plummets if it is not in mint or near mint condition. Next to quality comes rarity. Also, complete sets of a collection can enhance the value of some collectibles.

The best way to avoid buying works that are inferior in condition or quality, or that are not authentic, is to deal only with reputable dealers and auction houses, which are the two major sources of obtaining collectibles. Dealers usually specialize in certain types of collectibles and play a key role in setting prices for the items in which they specialize. One hallmark of a reputable dealer is permanence. The sales receipt should bear the store's name, address, and telephone number. The dealer should write on the receipt exactly what was bought, not just "silver cake basket," for instance, but "English sterling Hester Bateman cake basket, circa 1783." Buying directly from another collector may fetch a better price but can be risky without the advice of an expert. Both dealers and auction houses sift through a multitude of wares and both offer warranties, sometimes limited, that what they sell is as they describe it in their catalogs or bills of sale.

Pricing Collectibles   Once satisfied with authenticity, condition, and quality—the chief components of value—the collector looks at price, which can be the ultimate criterion. More expensive and higher-quality collector items are often sold at public auctions, which are described in greater detail below. The standard measure of worth is the auction-price history of similar works. The presale estimates published in auction catalogs are based largely on past sales. Prices previously paid at auctions are easy to determine. International Auction Records, published annually, records worldwide auction prices. Leonard's Index of Art Auctions, published quarterly, records prices from American auction houses.

Buying at auction requires homework on the buyer's part. One has to study the auction catalog entries, the condition of the item for sale (serious buyers go to previews and examine the items they are considering), and prices from past sales to determine a price that one can work against.

How to Sell

Eventually, most collectors will want to sell all or part of their hoarded treasure. Even noncollectors may wish to unload the garish French clock left to them by dear departed Aunt Tillie. It is often not as simple as they expect.

If you are ready to sell, your first step is to take a comparison shopping trip through the price guides. No two will give exactly the same prices, and indeed you may find only a range in some volumes. Even if a single price is given, do not assume it is the one you will get from a dealer. Because market conditions fluctuate, prices listed are often approximations. Even more important, all guide prices are retail, which means they are prices collectors would pay a dealer.

Something a new collectible investor ought to be aware of is the dealer's markup. It is not exactly modest, and a dealer who sells a $1,000 collectible is not going to buy it back for that amount the next day. Neither will other dealers snap it up for $1,000 unless they have eager buyers willing to pay $1,500 for it. Dealers may buy an "important" and popular high turnover item at 80 percent of its retail value. But for the vast majority of items, when collectors sell to a dealer, they typically get between 15 and 50 percent of the listed price. The difference is the dealer's profit. Collectors are almost certain to lose substantially if they sell to a dealer. They buy at retail and often have to sell at wholesale. Selling collectibles to a dealer is probably the quickest, but least profitable, way to go.

Selling at Auction

If collectors want to sell a unique item and wish to determine its value, then an ancient form of exchange—the auction—may be suitable. Selling via auctions lets collectors reach the largest audience of serious buyers. Many auction houses include pictures of special items in their catalogs. Some may give a free estimate of what an object or entire collection might bring if you send a color photograph and complete description. It is necessary to look for an auction house that has been around for a while and has good references. The sales contract should be in writing and should spell out details of the deal, including the auction house's commission, which may be 10 to 30 percent. Selling at auction carries the risk that an item will either go for a low price or fail to sell at all because the bidding falls short of the owner's minimum price, or "reserve" level.

An alternative way to get higher prices is to sell directly to another collector, usually by placing an ad in a special-interest periodical, such as *Antique Trader Weekly* (Box 1050, Dubuque, Iowa 52001). Many serious collectors belong to clubs. Some clubs are national organizations with local chapters which enable members to contact buyers either at meetings, shows, or conventions or through classified ads in the club publications.

Let us now examine some of the more popular and common collectibles from a personal finance perspective. Each collectible item has its own advantages, rewards, and risks. Although these may be fun, exciting, and educational hobbies, we will examine them as a form of savings or investment. From this perspective they may take on a different complexion. Many people pour lots of money into their collections with the rationale that they are not spending money but investing it for the future. This, as noted previously, may or may not always be true.

How to Handle "Prints Charming"

The stock market may be ailing, bonds could be boring, and precious metals depressing, but the art market may be the rage. Since the 1950s, the art market has run in cycles of about six or seven years. During November 1987, Vincent Van Gogh's "Irises" sold for $53.9 million. At the New York sale room of London-based Sotheby's Holdings, Inc., a major auction firm, bidders spent close to $100 million on impressionist and modern art in less than two hours in May 1988. The average price for an artwork was $1.75 million. In May 1990 another Van Gogh sold for $85 million, also at Sotheby's. Cézanne's painting "Still Life with Apples" sold for $28.6 million during May 1993.

The art market, despite its huge size, is perhaps the largest uncontrolled, unregulated market in the nation. The market for original art masterpieces is obviously limited to the few extremely affluent who can afford to spend $50 million for a single painting. Most readers, especially college students, cannot afford such high-priced luxuries. An art form that is more affordable is the **print** market. Since many recent college graduates often use some of their discretionary income to invest in the print market, let us examine the opportunities and risks inherent in this popular art form.

What Is a Print?   Many people start their art collection with contemporary prints because they are more reasonably priced. But collecting this art form is no guarantee for lucrative profits. The Art Dealers Association of America estimates that less than 2 percent of contemporary art, works done by living artists or some who have died recently, will ever appreciate in value. If, despite these odds, you still want to invest in prints, then your chances of success will be enhanced if you are knowledgeable about the print market.

A fine print literally is a printed picture made by impressing on paper the artist's inked design. This design, which may be engraved or drawn on wood or metal (among other methods), is called the **plate**. The total number of prints made from one plate is called an **edition**. By creating a unique image on a printing surface, multiple identical impressions of that single image are printed so that more than one person can own an original of it.

Artists make prints so that their work is more widely available. While the cost of a painting or sculpture by a known artist would be prohibitive for most buyers, a print by the same artist may be affordable because its multiple nature brings down the price of each impression. A print signed in pencil in the margin by the artist means that the artist has approved its authenticity and the way it was printed. Signed works are more valuable than unsigned ones. Since the mid-19th century, artists have typically signed and numbered each print.

Ideally, the artist should be present during the printing to supervise and to authenticate each print by signing it in pencil and numbering it (for example, "8/40"—the 8th impression in an edition of 40). Defacing or destroying the original printing surface should be witnessed by the artist to guarantee that no more copies will be made.

Prints, which can appreciate in value, are not reproductions of paintings or other fine art but are original works of art produced in multiple. A reproduction may be as beautiful as a print but it is nothing but a printed piece of paper of little worth.

Buying Prints—Don't Get Art Burn   The biggest question for someone who wants to invest in prints is how to tell what a print is worth. Value is established in the marketplace and is what an informed buyer and seller think is a fair exchange. The marketplace is affected by a number of factors. These include the artist, the subject (some subjects are more popular than others), the size of the print (bigger can be more valuable), the quality of the impression (well printed or not, whether it's an impression taken during the artist's lifetime or a restrike), its condition, its age, and the size of the edition.

Collectors have several options. They can buy from a dealer who specializes in the prints for which they are looking, bid at auction, buy directly from the artist, or buy from another collector. Buyers should research print prices before making a major purchase. It is essential to find the right advisers and dealers. Buyers can begin by asking the director or modern art curator of their local museum about the galleries that handle quality artwork. They can also look into museum courses on art appreciation.

Is There a Secondary Market?   We can best determine the value of prints when they have a proven secondary market. A secondary market exists when a print changes hands for the second time. While less-expensive contemporary prints are generally favored by new collectors, there is often no secondary market for them. Thus, when investors want to sell, it could be very difficult to find a buyer at any price. A secondary market exists mainly for the higher-priced prints of well-known artists. Because of multiplicity, these prints have likely turned up at sales in the not-too-distant past and their prices can be followed. All auction houses produce and sell catalogs for their auctions. These catalogs contain descriptions of the prints as well as the auction houses' price estimates and actual prices paid when the prints were sold.

Buying from a Small Edition   The average edition is around 250 to 300 prints. The fewer impressions available, the more valuable each print potentially is. But more important than the number of prints will be the future demand for the artist's works.

The fact that a print was published in a large edition does not necessarily make it a poor investment. Edition size is not by itself a critical factor when one considers the number of collectors in the market. Rarity alone is not important. Rarity, when combined with an artist who is of considerable standing (and has a large following), results in a valuable print.

Who's the Artist?   Investors should buy the work of an up-and-coming artist. This is not an easy task. The investment potential of a print is dependent upon the reputation of the artist. That is why it is important to find out about an artist before buying his or her prints. Where are his or her prints exhibited? Has the artist been awarded any honors or received critical acclaim in major newspapers or art journals? Naturally, the best investment would be to discover artists whose work delights you and whose reputation you believe will grow and to buy their artwork. If prices appreciate, you have made a good investment. If they do not, you have bought art that you have enjoyed and for which you have not paid too much money.

> ## For More Information on Prints
>
> If you have an interest in collecting art prints made with the traditional print-making techniques, write to the International Fine Print Dealers Association for a free directory of their members and their pamphlet "What Is a Print?" (485 Madison Avenue, New York, NY 10022).

Authenticity Checking for authenticity is an essential prerequisite to buying. Buyers should not take the word of the seller as a fact. Check all sources you can. Talk to art professionals and look at art books and magazines. Check the artist's signature and inspect other prints to verify the authenticity of the work of art. You can also get a professional appraisal, if you are willing to pay the extra expense.

Abuses do occur in the print market—forging of artists' signatures on unsigned prints, cutting the words off a poster and selling it as an original, cutting a print out of a large-circulation magazine or book and selling it as a limited edition, selling a restrike as a lifetime impression. To protect yourself, buy from dealers who have been in business for at least five years and get a complete bill of sale with money back guarantees.

Numismatics

The trumpeting of coins as investments is fairly recent. Until the mid-1960s, **numismatics** (the study of coins) was a relatively quiet hobby consisting of a small but dedicated number of collectors. For the most part, they collected coins for enjoyment.

Things began to change when price inflation depressed the stock and bond markets and investors turned to tangible assets. The coin-collecting market then became an arena for devoted collectors as well as fast-buck speculators. The market for American coins is both vast and volatile. Some 1,750 different U.S. issues are considered rare enough to be traded actively, with prices ranging from a few cents over face value for some recent coins to more than $725,000 for a gold doubloon made in New York in 1787. In between are many coins that have become valuable fairly recently.

Those who hope to make a mint in numismatics should not count on a streak of luck discovering a cache of rare coins. They should instead be prepared to devote painstaking attention to the task. The rationale behind investing in rare coins is certainly plausible; growing leisure and rising disposable income should spark interest in coin collecting. The supply of rare coins is fixed. Over the years, the prices of most rare coins have risen quite regularly. Rare coins also offer other advantages over conventional investments. Coins can be stored cheaply and have no significant maintenance costs. They are interesting, historic, and sometimes beautiful pieces of art. New collectors can begin to assemble a worthwhile collection for as little as $2,000.

Investors should not put more than about 5 to 10 percent of their investment portfolio into coins. A coin portfolio should be diversified, containing several kinds of coins. If you buy all gold coins, for example, or all Morgan (1878–1904) silver dollars, you risk big losses if the coins you buy fall out of favor with collectors. To put together an investment-quality portfolio, amateur collectors require the help of an expert. It is almost impossible for an unaided amateur to put together an investment-quality portfolio. Investors should consider coins as long-term investments and plan to hold their portfolio for at least three to five years and often even longer. There usually are from five to eight years between peaks in coin market cycles.

When the time comes to sell, collectors may not find a good price immediately. Coins are not as liquid as other forms of investment. There is no exchange for coins as there is for stocks. It is not a matter of calling up a broker to sell. As with other collectibles, there is a substantial spread between buy and sell prices. Dealers charge a premium of 20 percent or more when they sell coins and may buy them back for 80 percent of their value. This spread (or dealer's fees) can substantially reduce an investor's gains on a coin collection.

The Flip Side of Coins   In a consumer alert issued in 1988, the Federal Trade Commission warned that there is a great deal of risk in coin investments. Those who venture into the field should beware. Among the abuses cited by the FTC were these:

1. Telemarketing fraud, which has grown rapidly. The report warns consumers about committing to any coin purchase over the phone. The accompanying box "Investing in Coins: Guaranteeing a Sure Thing?" shows the script of an actual telemarketing scheme.

2. Fraudulent certification. Fraudulent sellers may use an old certificate to mislead buyers into believing that a coin's grade is accurate.

3. Widespread use of Salomon Brothers Inc.'s index of 20 rare coin prices as evidence of a booming coin market. The compound annual rate of return on coins in the index was 16.3 percent over the past decade. But these 20 coins are very rare and valuable, and the index does not necessarily reflect the performance of the market as a whole.

4. False grading, which has become the "most common form of rare coin fraud."

Failing Grades—A Word about Grading   Experienced dealers examine coins under incandescent light and assign grades to them. The American Numismatic Association has assigned terms for describing a coin's condition. They range from "poor" to "perfect—uncirculated." There are also special gradings for proof and "mint state," or uncirculated coins. Rare coins are typically classified according to their condition on a standard scale that runs from MS-1 to MS-70 (with MS standing for mint state and MS-70 signifying almost unattainable perfection). Investment-grade coins generally are those graded MS-63 or higher. The grading is nevertheless subjective. Unscrupulous dealers frequently take advantage of this by assigning higher than warranted grades to boost the sales price of their merchandise. When these dealers purchase coins, they downgrade them in order to lower the price they have to pay. As a result, rare coin collectors are defrauded out of millions of dollars each year.

The greatest single peril for collectors and investors in the rare coin field is misgrading. With mint-state coins, in particular, small deviations in grade sometimes cause major variations in price. By **overgrading** certain coins only slightly, dealers can inadvertently or perhaps deliberately overcharge customers thousands of dollars per transaction.

Investing in Coins: Guaranteeing a Sure Thing?

Excerpts from a sales script used by A.G. Rothchild & Associates, a company that sold coins from a boiler room in Tukwila, Washington, until authorities closed it down:

Hello (client's name)! HOW ARE YOU? (your name here). HOW ARE THINGS OUT THERE IN (name of city)?

GREAT, LISTEN, AS I SPOKE TO YOU LAST WEEK, I DID NOT HAVE ANYTHING OUTSTANDING TO OFFER YOU ... (Note: Begin escalating voice into an excited fever.) HOWEVER, YOU WOULD NOT BELIEVE WHAT'S GOING ON DOWN HERE ... GRAB A PEN AND A PIECE OF PAPER AND LET ME SHOW YOU WHAT ALL THE EXCITEMENT'S ABOUT. I'LL HOLD ON.

(Name), ONE OF OUR BUYERS JUST GOT BACK FROM AN (estate sale, volume buy, buying trip) AND WE HAVE, IN HOUSE, WE HAVE A COIN. IT'S A (describe coin). NOW, THE GREY SHEET, WHICH IS THE WHOLESALE BIBLE OF THE COIN INDUSTRY, IS LISTING THE COIN AT _____ DOLLARS PER COIN.

(Client's name), THERE ARE 10 BROKERS ON THE FLOOR RIGHT NOW, LITERALLY DIVING FOR THESE COINS.

HEY (name), I'LL TELL YOU WHAT, I'VE GOT TO GO DOWN TO TRADING RIGHT NOW ANYWAY, I'VE GOT TO LOCK UP A COIN POSITION FOR ONE OF MY CLIENTS IN (state). IF I DON'T GET DOWN THERE QUICK THEY'RE ALL GOING TO BE GONE. WHILE I'M THERE, WHY DON'T I GO AHEAD AND LOCK IN A POSITION FOR YOU TOO (AS WELL) ... FAIR ENOUGH?

(Instructions: If client is ready to be closed, then go into trading and close him. If not, proceed ...)

(Name), OUR COINS ARE INDEPENDENTLY GRADED AND CERTIFIED BY THE BEST IN THE BUSINESS ... A COMPANY CALLED NCI. THEY ARE THE CREME DE LA CREME IN OUR INDUSTRY. IN OTHER WORDS, WHEN YOU BUY YOURSELF A CADDILAC *(sic)* YOU WANT A GENERAL MOTORS WARRANTY ... RIGHT? THAT'S WHAT WE GIVE YOU WITH THE COINS, (Name) ... A WARRANTY.

(Optional: THERE'S *(sic)* OVER A HUNDRED DEALERS NATIONWIDE WHO DO A SIGHT UNSEEN, LIVE, TWO-WAY CASH MARKET.)

NOW (name), IF YOU FOLLOW THESE FOUR BASIC RULES, YOU'LL ALWAYS MAKE MONEY IN OUR INDUSTRY. WE GO A STEP FURTHER ... WE GUARANTEE TO BUY THE COINS BACK FROM YOU... AFTER YOU'VE HELD THE COINS FOR A MINIMUM OF SIX MONTHS ... AT THE PUBLISHED BID PRICE.

The Rothchild operation succeeded in taking in about $150,000 during a six-month period last year. Washington's attorney general is currently seeking restitution from the firm.

SOURCE: Reprinted by permission from the February 1989 issue of *Changing Times Magazine.* Copyright © 1989 the *Kiplinger Washington Editors, Inc.*

Unlike stocks or bonds, rare coins are works of art. Numismatics is an art, not a science. There is no definite method of **coin grading,** no authoritative method of evaluating a rare coin. Rare coins are never truly fungible or interchangeable, as are stocks or bonds. The evaluation and grading are to a considerable extent subjective.

The criteria for establishing the quality of an old coin are intricate. Because price depends substantially on grade, the value of a coin may vary from one expert to another. Indeed, experts frequently cannot agree even on matters of attribution or authentication.

Even among brand new coins, slight variations in the detail of striking the grain of the surface and subtle variations of color may cause an authority to value one coin quite differently from another. Any visible flaw, nicks, scratches, or smooth spots caused by wear reduce the value of a coin. Mirror-like coins, known as *proofs,* intended solely for collectors and investors, usually represent perfection. **Proof coins** are specially struck coins that are not meant for circulation. They are stamped twice at the mint for an extra clear image and packaged carefully. Reputable dealers should give buyers a written guarantee stating the numerical grade of the coin they are buying and promise to buy the coin back at that grade, but not necessarily at the same price. The industry is trying to purge itself of the unethical operators and reduce some of the hazards, mainly through new grading levels and certification standards. Since 1986, a few grading services have been encapsulating coins in plastic, a process called *slabbing.* This has led to sight-unseen trading in coins, much the way stocks are traded with "bid" and "asked" prices.

Philately

In many ways, stamp collecting is similar to numismatics and many of the points noted concerning buying and selling coins hold true for stamps as well. Stamp collecting, or **philately**, is said to be the world's most popular hobby, with an estimated 22 million collectors in the United States and 50 million worldwide. Dealers, auction houses, and exhibitors number in the thousands around the country. The true philatelist is well informed about quality, grading, authenticating supply demand ratios, first-day covers, handling, hinging, centering, mounting, gum condition, buying at auctions, doing business with dealers, and much more.

Could philately benefit you? If money is your most important objective, stay away from stamps. Most collectors are in it for fun, not money. If you care to invest time and effort as well as cash in stamps, then you may find philately to be fun and possibly also a lucrative investment. Tens of thousands of different stamps portray this country's past, and thousands more recall the events and people of other lands. Learning the history of a stamp can be interesting as well as profitable, but it can not be done adequately overnight. Rare stamps take time to grow in value, and for those unwilling to take the time to learn the hobby, rare stamps rarely make good investments.

Investment-quality stamps, generally those costing $100 or more, tend to retain their value best and are most likely to increase at least modestly over the long term. The best method to ensure success with stamps, as with nearly any other collectible, is to learn about the market and carefully build a diversified portfolio.

Don't Take a Licking in Stamps   The stamp market can be capricious. Stamps have no intrinsic value. They are worth only what people are willing to pay for them. In 1980 somebody paid $935,000 for a one-cent 1856 British Guiana Stamp, the One Cent Magenta, that had sold for about $45,000 around 1940. In 1968, two 1847 stamps on an envelope from the Island of Mauritius fetched $380,000.

Prices for stamps are generally based on values found in the Scott's catalogs (Scott Publishing Co., 911 Vandermark Road, Sydney, OH 45365), a series of five books, printed annually, that list and provide prices for all stamps. *Scott Standard Postage Stamp Catalog* and *Scott Specialized Catalog of United States Postage Stamps* are among the most widely used. So pervasive are these listings that philatelists identify stamps by their Scott's number. Stamp catalogs are available in most public libraries.

Because of constantly changing market conditions and wide variations in the quality of collections, many of the prices shown may be far out of line with prices that could be obtained. Catalog prices should therefore be used only as a rough guide. While Scott prices are as accurate as any, they generally reflect only what an investor can buy a stamp for retail. Selling is another matter entirely. Prices actually obtained by sellers are generally much lower than those quoted in the catalogs. U.S. stamps customarily trade 50 to 85 percent of catalog value because there is greater demand for them and dealers move the merchandise faster. Some foreign countries' stamps can trade as low as 10 to 15 percent of catalog value.

Perhaps the biggest drawback about investing in stamps has been low liquidity. It can be time consuming and difficult to sell this type of asset. Therefore, investors should consider a stamp collection as an illiquid asset.

Rare stamps in demand can be best sold through private transactions via well-known dealers or at one of the many stamp shows held throughout the country. Once an investor becomes properly educated, auctions tend to be the most popular method for both buying and selling. Bidding at auction requires sufficient knowledge of the market to judge the actual demand for and rarity of a stamp.

Stamp Grading   As with coins, perhaps the most controversial, difficult, and critical element of buying stamps is grading. Various terms are used to grade a stamp, ranging from "mint" to "used." Grading takes into account how well the stamp is centered, perforated, and cut, along with other characteristics. The basic problem is that as with coins, there is no absolute method for determining a grade. Various dealers might easily grade the same stamp differently. Both education and experience are needed.

"This stamp is worth hundreds of thousands of dollars."

SOURCE: Yedioth Ahronoth, September 23, 1988, reprinted by permission.

Investors may discover it is not as easy to sell their stamp collections as they had hoped.

The Funnies Business

Comic book enthusiasts who held onto their treasures while nearly everyone else was throwing theirs away are now possibly enjoying the last laugh. A complete, several-hundred volume collection of Action Comics, the strip that introduced Superman in 1938, sold for close to $60,000 in 1986. The highest price ever paid for a single comic book was $40,000 for an uncirculated 1939 issue of Superman number 1.

The estimated number of active comic book collectors in the United States is 250,000. As with all collectibles, there is great risk in investing in comics. As quickly as prices rise, they have been known to fall. Just like other collectibles, you have to know what you are doing.

Since 1970 there has been an annual guide known as *The Comic Book Price Guide* by Robert M. Overstreet ($10.95), Overstreet Publications, Inc., 780 Hunt Cliff Drive NW, Cleveland, TN 37311. It not only provides an estimate of the value of various comic books but also gives information about other important aspects of investment, such as grading and the history of various comic characters.

Learning how to grade comic books is a critical element in making wise investments. Discovering that you have an item in demand is one thing. Having one in good condition is another. Comic books that are wrinkled, torn, or bound with rusty staples turn off collectors. Overstreet's guide offers general rules for grading quality and lists prices for three categories: good, fine, and mint. Other grading categories include poor, fair, very good, very fine, near mint, and pristine mint. A mint comic would be nearly brand new, with no defect. A fine comic could show a bit of yellowing due to age. The deciding factor, of course, is rarity. Many older comics in top condition are indeed quite rare. An excellent way to buy and sell is to visit comic book conventions usually held in major metropolitan areas.

Vintage Wine Collecting

Some collectors of vintage wines use their specialized knowledge to invest in these wines profitably. Only a few wines, mainly the top vintage French Bordeaux wines, can legitimately be purchased as investments. These wines, such as Chateau Petrus, are in limited supply, compared with world demand. They also improve with age and gain value the longer they are kept. The easiest and most common way to invest in vintage wines is to purchase them by the case from a dealer and put them away for a number of years with the hope of selling them for a profit later.

Collecting vintage wine is not an inexpensive hobby. Adequate storage space to hold a modest wine collection at the proper temperature will run close to $1,000 and can go as high as $4,500. Aging under proper conditions is what makes the wine improve. But a word of caution. You must resist the temptation throughout to dip into or guzzle down this savory and liquid "investment."

Investing in Precious Metals

There are essentially three types of precious metals: gold, platinum, and silver. Gold is the most liquid of the three principal precious metals. Silver is the most speculative because its price moves the fastest, and platinum is the shortest in supply. Gold is by far the most popularly traded metal, and we will therefore concentrate on it. But what holds true for gold to a large extent also holds true for platinum and silver.

Investing in Gold

Gold has traditionally served as an inflation hedge, an asset to own during bad times, such as when the stock and bond markets are falling. It generally had a negative correlation with stocks and bonds. That means that gold prices performed well when those of stocks and bonds do poorly. For example, in 1987, when the stock and bond markets crashed, the average mutual fund that invests in gold was up 34 percent. The yellow metal has traditionally held its value during times of political and economic turmoil. It declines when the world seems peaceful and orderly. When the dollar is strong, gold usually dims and vice versa. Gold's function has served over many years as a defensive investment cushion when other investments performed poorly due to social strife, inflation, fear of or actual monetary collapse, international tensions or war, or generalized unease about the future. Only if you believe that inflation or instability is imminent should you seriously invest in gold, expecting it to increase in value. Since 1987, however, the contrarian investing in gold has been disappointing. Inflation has remained low, and gold does not seem to react to world events like it used to. The Gulf War of 1991 had only a minor impact on gold prices. The general downward trend in gold prices is illustrated in Figure 16–2.

Thus, as a permanent defense against potential inflation, financial advisers recommend that an established investor devote no more than 10 percent of one's portfolio to the precious metal. Investors concerned about serious inflation look upon it as they do insurance policies for fire and accidents, policies on which they hope they will never have to collect. Such investments should be made only with money they can afford to put away and forget.

Gold tempts many first-time investors because it seems uncomplicated. However, it can be volatile and risky. A 50 percent rise or fall in the price of gold in one year is not uncommon. Bear in mind also that gold is not a revenue-producing asset. Unlike a bank account or money market fund, there is no income. Investing in gold coins or **bullion** (as opposed to buying shares in gold mining companies) pays no dividends

FIGURE 16–2   **The Gold Standard?**

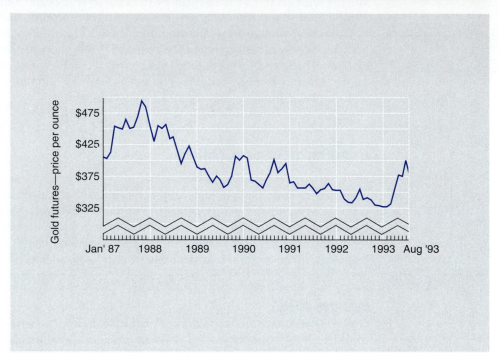

Tracking the nearest futures price of gold over time shows significant fluctuation.

SOURCE: Bridge Information Systems, Inc., 1993.

and no interest while investors hold it. Moreover, investors will have to pay to keep their asset in a safe deposit box or a private vault at a financial institution. And when they sell, if they own the actual metal, they will probably pay assay charges on bullion to verify that they did not tamper with its weight or integrity. Investors will have to pay shipping and insurance costs as well.

Different Forms of Gold Ownership   The major distinction for new investors is between owning the physical metal (coins and bars) and financial instruments backed by or denominated in gold. There are essentially three ways to buy gold:

1. Investing in shares of gold mining companies or the mutual funds that invest in them

2. Buying gold coins, whether they are recently minted or rare old varieties that have numismatic value

3. Buying bullion, the refined metal itself

Gold Shares Of the three, **gold shares** are often regarded as most speculative. Relatively high fixed costs are involved in the mining of gold. When the price of gold rises, mining companies' profit margins grow rapidly. A price decline produces the opposite results. Two advantages of owning gold stocks over owning bullion is not having to pay for physical storage costs and the potential for dividends. The best way to spread risk in gold stocks is to invest in them through gold mutual funds. These are funds that own shares in several different gold mining and refining companies throughout the world.

Gold Coins The easiest and safest way to invest in gold is to acquire recently minted legal tender coins, notably the American Eagle issued by the U.S. mint. While 1 ounce varieties are most popular in the United States, gold coins come in sizes ranging from one-tenth of an ounce to 1.2 ounces. Banks and coin dealers sell standardized and widely accepted 1 ounce coins over the counter. Some popular issues include the Chinese Panda, the Canadian Maple Leaf, the Mexican 50 Peso, and the South African Krugerrand.

Buyers of gold coins pay a considerable price over the value of the coin's gold content. On many coins, the premium, which represents the wholesaler's and dealer's markup, is between 3.5 and 6 percent. On some coins, such as the Chinese Panda, prized by collectors for their artistic qualities, the premium runs as high as 7 to 8 percent. Add to this cost sales tax and you have the makings of an investment that starts with a roughly 15 percent price handicap.

Gold Bullion and Gold Certificates Gold can be bought in bullion (or bar) form. But unless investors derive pleasure from holding and fondling gold, they need not buy gold bullion outright. Instead they can buy certificates of gold ownership. The best way to do that is by opening a metals account, available at most large brokerage houses and metal dealers and at some banks. Basically, certificates signify ownership of a quantity of gold. When you buy gold this way, you will usually get a certificate of ownership stating that the institution is holding in your name in its vaults gold that is insured and guaranteed for quality.

Gold certificates are sold by banks, brokerage firms, and metal dealers, such as Deak-Perera, with offices throughout the United States, and they can even be bought with a credit card through Citibank in New York. Typically, investors have to make a minimum initial purchase of $1,000. Commissions (front-ended) range from about 1 to roughly 3.5 percent when bought, depending upon the quantity. Investors may also pay a 0.5 percent annual storage charge and a 1 percent fee when they sell.

"Good as Gold?" Major brokerage firms and large banks with sizable gold investment services are generally regarded as safe because they fill orders quickly and have a corporate reputation to uphold. It would be prudent to buy only from reputable dealers. Investors should avoid buying a gold certificate from any company whose integrity and long-term solvency is at all doubtful. Investors who are not careful may be exposed to risks they did not count upon. For instance, there is a risk that incompetent, questionable, or fraudulent practices by the firm an investor selected will result in its shutdown. That leaves the investor with nothing to show for his or her investment in gold but a handful of worthless receipts. The New England Rare Coin Galleries, which claimed to be the world's largest rare coin dealer, went bankrupt in 1988, leaving

2,500 clients with undelivered (but fully paid for) coins worth over $30 million. Several other such celebrated cases made headlines during the past few years.

A critical point to investigate before agreeing to a storage contract arranged through a dealer is whether your property and that of all other investors is segregated from the firm's assets. If everything is commingled, refuse to sign. In the event of a bankruptcy proceeding or other legal action, you could lose your investment or end up being a general creditor with lots of company.

Commodity Futures and Options (Are There Futures in Your Future?)

A futures market is an economic institution in which people buy and sell **futures contracts**. These are contracts to buy or sell a specified quantity of a standardized commodity or financial instrument for delivery on a set future date, usually from three months to a year ahead, at an agreed upon fixed (or "quoted") price. Contracts are traded on soybeans, pork bellies, heating oil, coconut oil, alfalfa pellets, rape seed, foreign currencies, or Treasury bills, among other things.

Each futures exchange establishes the ground rules for the contracts it trades. All futures contracts have four standardized terms. They are the:

1. Particular item being traded

2. Amount of that item covered in the contract

3. Method of pricing the item (dollars per ounce, cents per bushel, etc.)

4. Delivery month

Through the means of a central organized marketplace for trading, such as the **Chicago Board of Trade (CBT)** or the **New York Commodity Exchange Center (COMEX)**, futures contracts are standardized. All that buyers and sellers must do is agree upon the price at which the contract will trade for the particular item being traded and the quantity covered by the contract.

Futures trading accounts required for operating in either futures contracts or options on futures are fairly simple to open. Most of the larger brokerage houses have a futures or commodities department with brokers who are licensed to trade futures contracts.

To make a trade in futures, investors place an order with a commodity broker, either at a firm that handles commodity transactions exclusively or at a major stock brokerage house. Contracts usually range in value from $10,000 to $40,000. The broker will ask for a deposit (margin) of 3 to 10 percent of the contract. With a futures contract, you buy or sell the right to have, say, 10,000 bushels of corn delivered on a future date at a fixed price. Futures allow you to capitalize on anticipated price movements in a commodity. If you think corn will rise in value, you buy a contract; to lock into a lower price for the item today. If you think it will drop, you sell one, which allows you to lock into a higher selling price for the commodity today.

Hedging

People who use **hedging** markets are generally classified as either **hedgers** or **commodity speculators**. Hedgers are people who are in businesses using these commodities. They buy and sell futures contracts to avoid the rises or declines associated with price fluctuations.

Let's examine how a farmer and a food processor might use futures contracts to hedge. In April, a Kansas farmer begins planting wheat. His estimated costs are $1 a bushel and current prices for September deliveries are $1.455 a bushel (which are acceptable to the farmer). He believes that his yield will be 200,000 bushels. By locking in the price he will receive at harvest time in September, he can avoid the risk of selling at a low price. He is able to plan and budget his future farming activities. Unless the crop fails, he gets a guaranteed profit. But who may buy this as of yet ungrown wheat crop?

Suppose General Mills will require 200,000 bushels of wheat for its Wheaties cereal production during September and wishes to eliminate the risk that wheat may increase in price by September. The current price (during April) is acceptable to General Mills but the cost of purchasing the wheat and storing it until needed is too high. It therefore would rather buy a futures contract to hedge against a price increase.

Hedging

The farmer, in April, therefore, goes short (sells a futures contract) and General Mills goes long (buys a futures contract) 40 CBT September wheat futures contracts at 145½. The farmer is obligated to deliver and General Mills is obligated to accept 200,000 bushels of wheat, 40 contracts times 5000 bushels per contract at $1.455 per bushel. The total value of the position is ($1.455 × 200,000 =) $291,000. Neither party has to put up that amount of cash when the contract is originated.

Now suppose that in September, just prior to the delivery date, the price of wheat in the (spot) market is $1.9025 per bushel. The farmer must deliver the wheat which is stored at a local grain cooperative to General Mills for $1.455 per bushel, or $291,000. The current market value of the wheat is $380,500 (which we derive by multiplying 200,000 × $1.9025). General Mills, in this case, has gained and the farmer has lost "potential" profit of $89,500. There is always a winner and a loser in a futures contract. But, as stated previously, the price of $1.455 may be sufficient for the farmer to cover his or her costs and provide sufficient profit. The farmer has sold off his or her chance for a potentially greater profit in exchange for eliminating any risk of losses. If the price of wheat had instead fallen to $.60 by September, the farmer would be the winner and General Mills the loser.

Speculation

Unless you are a farmer or manufacturer out to lock in the price of a physical commodity or a currency exchange rate, there are only two reasons to enter the futures markets: speculation and diversification. You do not *invest* in futures; you *speculate* in them.

Speculators are traders who have no use for the commodity in itself. They buy futures contracts (take a long position) when they anticipate a rise in price; they sell futures contracts (take a short position) when they anticipate prices will fall. If the price moves in the direction they anticipated, they make money. The speculator who purchases a contract hopes to sell it and get a higher price before the delivery date, and the speculator who sold a contract hopes to purchase one before the delivery date at a lower price. In this way, the speculator offsets his or her position without taking possession of the commodity. However, when prices move in the opposite direction from that which was anticipated, the speculators will lose money.

Although the contract calls for delivery by a fixed future date, few deliveries are actually made. Speculators and sellers usually take their profits or settle their losses before the contract expires. The contracts are liquidated most often by making the offsetting sales and purchases described above. Before the contract expires, they will sell it to someone else at a profit or loss. Only by accident or negligence would a speculator actually take delivery or be required to supply orange juice, copper, oats, barley, or whatever. Virtually all of these contracts are settled in cash or closed out before they expire, sometimes after just a day or two.

Futures trading volume tends to slump during periods of low inflation and stable prices. The commodities futures markets experienced a marked decline in 1984 to 1985. Since the mid-1980s, the commodities markets have experienced falling prices, heavy discounting on trading fees, bitter competition for institutional accounts, and an exodus of public participants from futures markets into other investments.

An unforeseen renewal of inflation or major crop failures could instantly revive interest in these markets.

Is There a Future for You?   Academic studies stretching back to the 1940s invariably conclude that the majority of individual speculators in the futures markets lose money. In a 1987 study, Michael L. Hartzmark, a University of Michigan professor, concluded after analyzing four and one-half years of futures trading results that an overwhelming number of small speculators, as well as many professional speculators, lost money trading futures. In a follow-up study published in the University of Chicago's *Journal of Political Economy* (January 1990), Professor Hartzmark concluded that "the fortunes of individual futures traders are determined by luck, not forecastability."

Though an estimated 90 percent of individual investors lose money in commodity futures markets, people keep coming back in hope of joining the small group of big winners. Obviously, because of the risks, futures trading is not appropriate for everyone. If you have risk capital which you can afford to lose and want to try it on a small scale, bear in mind that although you can gain large sums by speculating in commodities, the odds are that you will lose. You should speculate in commodities only if you are prepared to lose the total investment and possibly much more.

Futures contracts are a zero-sum game, in which there is a loser for every winner. Every dollar made by the buyer is a dollar lost by the seller or vice versa.

FUTURES

Don't Plunge into the Futures (Unless You Can Afford It)   Most brokerage houses set financial guidelines for would-be investors. They analyze new investors' statements of financial condition in order to set trading and margin limits. If investors do not meet the minimum requirements set by the firm, they are generally denied a commodities account altogether. At Merrill Lynch, futures traders must have easily liquidated assets of at least $40,000 excluding the equity in their homes and cash value on life insurance policies, total net worth of $200,000, and an annual income of at least $50,000. Dean Witter Reynolds, by contrast, requires only a $35,000 annual income, $25,000 in liquid assets, and $100,000 in net worth exclusive of home equity. The minimum requirements vary widely from firm to firm. Minimum requirements are designed to help protect not only the brokerage firm but also the investor.

Back to the Futures

Suppose it is now September and you believe silver prices will soon increase. You can buy (go long) one October silver futures contract traded on the COMEX at 630.0. The amount covered in the contract is 5,000 troy ounces, the price is quoted in cents per ounce (630 cents), and the delivery month is October. The contract stipulates that you must buy 5,000 ounces of silver at \$6.30 an ounce in October. You can also settle your obligation by making an offsetting or reversing trade prior to the delivery month by shorting (selling) a COMEX September silver futures contract, which is what actually happens in more than 95 percent of futures trades.

You will profit if silver is trading at more than \$6.30 an ounce when you close out your position. Your offsetting trade closes out your position with a contract to sell silver at a higher price than you agreed to buy it. Even with a difference of only \$0.50 an ounce, the profit would still be \$2,500 (\$0.50 × 5,000 ounces). If you were wrong and silver declined by \$0.50 an ounce, you would lose \$2,500. In many ways the futures markets are like an elaborate gambling game.

Before deciding to trade in futures contracts, you should ask yourself a few questions to determine whether futures trading is suitable for you.

1. Is futures trading consistent with your overall investment objectives?

2. Do you have the emotional and financial requirements to invest in such high-risk ventures?

3. Can you afford to lose the money without it hurting?

Perhaps the most alluring feature of futures contracts is the possibility that for a relatively small bet, speculators stand to make a big tidy killing in a short period. This can occur because speculators usually place a relatively small amount down on a large investment. But herein also lies the real risk of futures trading.

MARGIN

Hanging by a Margin

The real risk in commodity speculation lies not in price fluctuations of the underlying commodities but in the magnification of those fluctuations by the investor's **leverage,** which involves controlling a large investment position with a small down payment. Futures are said to offer more bang for the buck than just stocks or bonds. Leverage is the double-edged sword of futures trading. Margin provides speculators with that leverage, since futures are traded with small amounts of cash up front called **margins.** Margin is a very small tail wagging a very big dog. Margin requirements vary between 3 and 10 percent of the contract's market value. Low margins in commodities provide the chance to make large gains. Conversely, leverage also makes commodities speculative and risky and can result in large losses.

For example, suppose contracts for 5,000 pounds of coffee to be delivered in three months is trading at $1 per pound, or $5,000. To gain control over one contract, a speculator or trader has to put up only a 5 percent margin, or $250. All it would take to double the contract holder's money would be a 5 cents per pound, or 5 percent increase. A 5 percent drop would wipe out the margin (the figures do not include brokerage commissions). However, if prices plunged 40 percent, the investor would lose the $250 and be in debt for $1,750.

As mentioned, you can also make money if you think the price is going to decline. Simply sell a futures contract instead of buying one. You are selling the promise or commitment to sell someone 5,000 pounds of coffee to be delivered in three months at $1 per pound, or $5,000. Again, you put up only $250, or 5 percent. If the price declines to 90 cents, you could buy coffee at $4,500 (5,000 lbs. × $ .90) and sell it at $5,000 and therefore make a $500, or 100 percent, profit. If the price of coffee rises to $1.10, you lose $500 (or a 200 percent loss). Since you put up only a small fraction of the contract price, futures trading is highly leveraged.

The percentage profit (or loss) on a futures position depends on the amount of margin, or equity, put down. Margin is simply a good faith deposit used to cover possible losses due to adverse market moves. The initial margin is the amount required at the time the futures contract is entered into, and the maintenance margin is the amount of equity that must be kept in the account at all times. The exchanges set minimum margin levels, but individual brokers may require more.

Someone who speculates in the highly leveraged commodity futures markets in the hope of equally handsome returns could instead face multiple margin calls and end up losing more than he or she had initially put up.

In general, when losses exceed some specified amount, brokers ask for more, sometimes much more, margin. If the individual does not provide the money, the broker undertakes an offsetting transaction for his or her client. This, in essence, takes the individual out of the market and protects the brokerage house from having to absorb the potential financial loss.

Options on Futures Contracts

If gambling on futures contracts scares you or appears too risky, there is an alternative, a modified form of investing in futures contracts, known as **futures options**. Buying futures options is an alternative for those who are tempted by the capital growth potential of commodity futures trading but would prefer a limited-risk vehicle.

Futures options give the purchaser the right, but not the obligation, to assume a specified futures contract (either long or short) at an agreed upon price in the underlying futures market. These rights are extended to the option buyer for a specified period of time, and he or she may exercise them at any time during that period.

Futures market investors face unlimited liability, since they are entering into actual contracts to buy or sell the underlying commodity. However, futures option purchasers are subject only to limited liability, since they are not obligated to exercise the option. They are liable only up to the full amount invested. Profit potential, however, is not limited. Thus, buying futures options offers a highly leveraged limited risk investment (as compared with unlimited risk speculation in **commodity futures** contracts) combined with high profit potential.

The difference in risk and opportunities, however, between buying a futures option and selling or writing a futures option is enormous. The seller of an option, also known as the **writer**, is subjected to the unlimited risk associated with direct futures market participation. In exchange, the writer receives as payment the option premium, which is the maximum potential profit he or she may realize. The writer (or seller) faces unlimited risk and limited profit potential while the buyer faces limited risk but unlimited profit potential.

Since buying options gives the holder the "right" rather than the obligation to obtain a futures position, an option holder need only exercise and enter the futures market if such an exercise is economically profitable. If the futures price is below the strike price, at expiration time the option would be worthless and the premium paid would be lost by the investor.

Unlike futures, the option buyer cannot be subject to margin calls of any kind. The full price of the option, which is the premium, represents the buyer's full responsibility.

There are two types of options, known as *puts* and *calls*.

Puts   A **put** option on a futures contract gives the purchaser the right, but not the obligation, to sell (go short) a futures contract at a specified price (the strike price) in the underlying futures market at any time during the life of the option. A speculator would buy a put when he or she expects the price to go down or the market to fall.

Calls   A **call** option on a futures contract gives the purchaser the right, but not the obligation, to buy (go long) a futures contract in the underlying futures market at a specified price (the strike price) at any time during the life of the option. A speculator would buy a call when he or she expects the price to go up or the market to rise.

Futures and options are ephemeral creatures. With a share of stock, investors have bought an interest in a corporation that can usually be held as long as they like. With a bond, investors have bought the right to receive a steady rate of return, often for years or decades. With a future or option, though, investors or speculators have latched on to a perishable commodity that requires constant attention, a steady flow of decisions, and a kind of cool head that the smaller investor is notorious for losing when tensions build. In short, futures and options are probably the most volatile, risky, and complex products that the individual can invest in outside of Las Vegas. The futures market takes no hostages.

Commodity Funds: You Could Always Dive into a Pool

Those who lack the resources or the nerve to trade futures contracts or options on their own can invest in professionally managed futures funds. A growing number of individuals are buying commodities in a way they hope will minimize the risks and maximize the profits. The are buying into **commodity funds**, also called **pools**.

 Commodity funds are large pools of money from as many as several hundred investors. They operate much like stock mutual funds. The commodity funds' large capitalizations and diversified portfolios help them weather day-to-day or even year-to-year losses until markets move in their favor. They have enough money to assemble a diversified range of futures investments, protecting the investor from being wiped out by a precipitous nose dive in one market. The funds usually invest in portfolios of 20 or more commodities, including contracts on gold, grains, foreign

Hedging Your Future Options

Options on futures contracts can be purchased as a hedge to limit the risk of an outright futures position. By purchasing an option, the buyer gains the opportunity to enter or exit the futures markets at a specified price and may utilize such opportunity to attempt to ensure a profit or limit risk of loss on a futures position.

For example, suppose you buy futures contracts in barley. Buying a put option limits the losses you would incur if barley does not rise. Assume barley's current (spot) cash price is $2 a bushel. You purchase a three-month futures contract for 25 cents a bushel, which obligates you to purchase the barley at $1.50 at the expiration date. You believe and hope that barley will rise to $3 a bushel and you will earn huge profits. But just to play it safe, you purchase a put option at $2.75, which entitles you to sell barley at $2.75 at the same expiration date. In the event that barley's market price does not rise above $2.75, you will not lose much money. Suppose barley price remains at $1.50. On the expiration date you must purchase the 5,000 bushels at $2.50 for a total of $12,500. Remember, you additionally paid ($5,000 × $ .25 premium per bushel =) $1,250 as premium to buy the futures contract. Your total cost is $13,750. If on the expiration date the price of barley remains $1.50, you will be compelled to purchase the 5,000 bushels of barley for $13,750 while its market value is only $7,500. You risk losing ($13,750 − 7,500 =) $6,250.

However, if you buy a put option with a strike price of $2.75, you can sell the barley to someone else for (5,000 × $2.75 =) $13,750. You have thereby covered or hedged your trade. Have you not lost anything and effectively eliminated all risk in this venture? Not really. The cost of the put option plus brokerage commissions will in this case be your losses. However, these losses may amount to several hundred dollars instead of $6,250. You have therefore used a futures option to hedge your losses in the commodity futures contract market. Futures options are nevertheless still a speculative gamble but with some built-in safeguards against disaster.

currency, and government securities such as Treasury bills or bonds. As a rule, the more diversified a portfolio, the less the investment risk for shareholders. These pools offer investors a way to dip their toes in the swirling waters of futures trading. It would be wise to check thoroughly the past performance of the fund managers, however. Many have dismal records.

The typical commodity fund is generally organized as a limited partnership in which money put up by individuals is used by a professional trader to speculate in futures. The organizer, a company or individual, becomes the general partner. The other investors are limited partners. Their responsibility for losses is limited to the amount they invest. Partnerships usually start with a minimum of $5,000.

There is virtually no secondary market for these investments. Shares or units can be redeemed only by selling them back to the fund. Because fund values can fluctuate sharply, when investors get into a fund and when they get out can play the key role in whether or not they wind up winners.

As with any mutual fund, carefully reading the prospectus before buying is essential. A prospectus for public offerings of a commodity fund must include the performance records of the pool sponsor and the trading adviser. The prospectus should tell you the following:

1. The types of commodities that will be traded

2. Whether cash distributions will be paid periodically if trading is profitable

3. How redemptions are handled

4. Whether there are any conflicts of interest between the trading adviser and sponsor

5. Whether the fund will be automatically dissolved after a certain period of time

6. The circumstances under which the fund could be dissolved because of declining assets (For example, a pool may liquidate if half of its assets are lost, denying investors a chance to recoup.)

Before opening any account, you should also thoroughly read (and understand) all materials presented by the broker. Risk disclosure statements briefly outline some of the risks of futures trading. Despite the advantage of diversification and professional management, commodity pools are still fairly risky investments. The bottom line is to know what you are getting into before diving into a pool.

Should You Warrant a Warrant?

Another variation of a futures option is a warrant. A **warrant** entitles its owner to buy a specified number of shares of a stock at a stated price until an expiration date, usually several years away. As an added inducement to buy new issues of stocks and bonds, companies sometimes attach warrants to them. This prize is a security with little current value but possibly great potential value. But what exactly are warrants and in what circumstances might they be a good investment?

Suppose that Coca-Cola issued warrants entitling the holder to buy one share of Coke common stock for only $13 until 1997. Since Coke common stock is being traded at around $30, the warrant would sell at around $17. It would appear to make little difference whether an investor bought the stock or paid $17 for the warrants. The prices of warrants move in relation to their underlying shares. That means a warrant is a good buy if the underlying common stock looks likely to go up.

But the consequences could be quite different because the warrants offer leverage since the unit cost of warrants is usually much less than that of the underlying stock shares which they entitle the investor to buy. If an investor thought that Coke shares would go up, he or she might speculate by buying warrants instead of the actual stocks. Because of the conversion feature, the warrants will go up more or less with the stock prices, but warrants would cost $13 less. Thus, if Coke were to rise again to 35, the warrants would go to 22. In this case, stock acquired at today's price at 30 would show a paper gain of nearly 17 percent. But warrants purchased at today's price of 17 might show a gain of 29 percent. If Coke stock were to decline, however, the leverage would work the other way.

There are other speculative elements in owning warrants. They pay no dividends. Furthermore, they usually come into being when a firm is in some kind of financial trouble. Typically, a battered company selling stocks or bonds to raise capital might give prospective buyers warrants as a sweetener on the deal. In the early 1980s, Chrysler gave the U.S. government 14.4 million warrants in return for a guarantee of bailout loans. Warrants are better suited to the long-term investor since, unlike a call option that matures in no longer than nine months, warrants last at least a year and sometimes up to 10 years.

The main point to remember about warrants is that they are more speculative than stocks which, in these days of volatile markets, are fairly speculative themselves.

SUMMARY

There are investment alternatives to the conventional investment methods. We have discussed some of the more common investment alternatives. Investing in collectibles and commodities is no substitute for the traditional investments of stocks, bonds, CDs, and real estate. However, it can be an additional part of one's overall financial plan.

For many people, investing in collectibles is a form of recreation while at the same time providing a means of long-term asset building. Collecting on a serious level requires investment of much time and effort. There are many pitfalls for novices and amateurs. One must develop a certain expertise to discern quality from junk, genuine from fakes, and potential from hype.

On a more speculative level, one can invest in ownership of gold, or buy and sell future commodity contracts. Great fortunes can be made or lost on these markets, which should best be left for those with a thorough familiarity with them. An investor can protect his or her investments in the futures market by hedging. A less-risky method of futures speculation is investing in futures options known as *puts* and *calls* as well as in commodity funds. Speculators can also purchase an option to buy a given stock in the future, known as *warrants*. Futures and rare metals should, if at all, compose a small percent of one's portfolio and should be attempted only by those who can afford to lose the money.

Collectibles, metals, or commodities are not a suitable place for your retirement funds, emergency nest egg, or college fund for your kids.

KEY TERMS

Antiques

Bullion

Calls

Chicago Board of Trade (CBT)

Coin grading

Collectibles

Commodity funds (pools)

Commodity futures

Commodity speculators

Futures Contracts

Futures options

Gold certificates

Gold shares

Hedgers

Hedging

Leverage

Margin

New York Commodity Exchange Center (COMEX)

Numismatics

Options

Overgrading

Philately   Puts

Plate   Warrants

Prints   Writer

Proof coins

REVIEW QUESTIONS AND PROBLEMS

1. Which collectible(s) do you think hold(s) most promise for investors? Explain why.
2. Give some reasons why you would recommend collectibles as an investment form and also present some reasons why you would not recommend it.
3. How much of one's investment portfolio should be in collectibles? Explain why.
4. Why should someone who wants to invest in collectibles buy only top-grade quality?
5. How can you go about determining the value of a collectible?
6. What is an art print? How do you determine its authenticity?
7. What factors will make a print more valuable?
8. How does the grading process of rare coins add to the risk of investing in numismatics?
9. Why should you consider a stamp collection as an illiquid asset?
10. When would you consider it appropriate to invest in precious metals?
11. In what different forms of ownership can gold be acquired?
12. Present some arguments for and against investing in gold.
13. What is the futures market? (a) How does it work? (b) What function does it serve?
14. What is the difference between a speculator and a hedger?
15. How does the power of leverage make the futures market a highly risky investment form?
16. What is an option on a futures contract? Why is it less risky than outright buying of a futures contract?
17. What are puts and calls?
18. What is a commodity fund (pool)? What advantages does it offer the investor over direct investments in commodities?
19. What is the difference between buying a warrant and buying the actual stock outright?

20. (HEDGING) You are setting up a futures position. The price per contract is $225.25. There are 5,000 units per contract. The cost per unit is $2.25. The spot market price per unit is $2.10. You would like to take a long position with a value of $150,000. How many contracts should you buy?

21. (FUTURES) Suppose the amount covered in a contract is 5,000. In order to obtain a total profit of $100,000, given a market price per contract of $8.25, what offsetting trade price is required?

22. (MARGIN) You have purchased at a market price per contract of $12. The margin requirement is 5 percent, with 100 units per contract. After a given price change, the equity in your position is zero. In other words, your position is wiped out. What is the new price?

SUGGESTED PROJECTS

1. Interview someone who is a serious collector of some collectible. Ask him or her to tell you the opportunities and pitfalls the collection presents as an investment vehicle. Make a list of the positive and negative responses and present it to the class.

2. Imagine that you have $5,000 and want to purchase a futures contract. Select a (60-day) commodity contract. Remember, with 5 percent margin you can buy a $100,000 contract with your $5,000. Follow your contract's value for three weeks and then tell the class how much money you would have earned or lost if this were for real.

INFORMATION RESOURCES

"And Now, a Little Fun for Not-So-Serious Investors (Collectibles)." *U. S. News and World Report,* December 4, 1989, 82–84.

Antique Trader Weekly facilitates collector-to-collector sales. Box 1050, Dubuque, IA 52001.

"Art of Investing May Mean Avoiding Art." *The Wall Street Journal,* June 6, 1989, C-1.

"Beating the Odds in Commodity Trading." *The Wall Street Journal,* February 13, 1989, C-1.

Bernstein, Jake. *Facts on Futures.* Chicago: Probus Publishing Co., 1987.

Bodnar, Janet. "Awesome Bucks for Kids' Junk." *Kiplinger's Personal Finance Magazine,* April 1993, 79–83.

"Bogus Brushstroke." *The Wall Street Journal,* May 22, 1989, C-1.

The Comic Book Price Guide, by Robert M. Overstreet, is available for $10.95 from Overstreet Publications, Inc., 780 Hunt Cliff Drive NW, Cleveland, TN 37311.

Giese, William. "Are You Sure That's a Rembrandt?" *Kiplinger's Personal Finance Magazine,* March 1992, 57–60.

"Gold Still Isn't Much of a Prospect." *Business Week,* April 9, 1992, 79.

"Heads You Lose, Tails You Lose: Coins." *Changing Times,* February 1989, 71–76.

International Fine Print Dealers Association, 485 Madison Avenue, New York, NY 10022. Write for free directory of its member and its pamphlet, "What is a Print?"

Kehrer, Daniel. *The Cautious Investor's Guide to Profits in Precious Metals.* New York: Times Books, 1985.

Ketchum, William. *The New and Revised Catalog of American Collectibles.* Gallery Books, 1990.

Lofton, Todd. *Getting Started in Futures.* New York: John Wiley & Sons, 1989.

Moreau, Dan. "Collectibles—Trash or Cash?" *Kiplinger's Personal Finance Magazine,* November 1991, 87–89.

Nichols, Jeffrey. *The Complete Book of Gold Investing.* Homewood, Ill.: Dow Jones-Irwin, 1987.

Peers, Alexandra. "On the Block: Mickey Mantle, Not Matisse." *The Wall Street Journal,* March 1, 1991, C-1.

————."Sotheby's Rare Baseball Card Sale Is a Hit as Childhood Pastime Joins Big Leagues." *The Wall Street Journal,* March 25, 1991, C-1.

Scott's catalog. A series of five books, printed annually, that list and provide prices for all stamps, are available from Scott Publishing Co., 911 Vandermark Road, Sydney, OH 45365.

"Some Appraisers Specialize in the Art of Ripping Off." *The Wall Street Journal,* November 10, 1988, C-1.

"Untarnished Truth About Collectibles." *Changing Times,* October 1988, 79–82.

"When You Should Invest in Gold." *Working Woman,* February 1989, 33.

CHAPTER SEVENTEEN

Marriage and Divorce: Tying and Untying Financial Knots

- To understand the financial aspects of divorce

- To examine the financial issues that arise during divorce proceedings

- To consider how a divorce can be equitably negotiated through the means of mediation

- To study the legal rights of a divorcing spouse in relation to such financial matters as property rights, alimony, taxes, and pensions

Getting married usually is not a problem. But these days, staying married certainly can be.

With a 50 percent divorce rate, twice the number of two decades ago, divorce is no longer something you can afford to remain ignorant about on the assumption that it will not happen to you. If it will not happen to you, then your parents, children, siblings, or friends may be involved in a divorce and you may be asked to advise and help out.

With a bit of luck, you may never need this chapter, but if you should get involved in a divorce, either personally or assisting someone who is in the divorce process, then this chapter may be very helpful.

Young Divorcees Still Are Economic Losers

Young women divorcing today suffer just as much economic loss as those divorcing a quarter of a century ago.

Pamela Smock of Louisiana State University compared two large samples of women, mostly in their 20s; one group separated or divorced between late 1960s and the mid-1970s and the other broke up during the 1980s. More of the later group had been working while married and generally had more job experience than those in the earlier cohort, but the two groups had almost identical declines in economic well-being after divorce or separation.

For example, in the year after marital breakup, white women in the later group who had not remarried or entered into cohabiting relationships typically suffered a 43 percent drop in income, compared with a 46 percent drop for women in the earlier set. For black women, the decline economic well-being produced similar patterns.

Divorcing men continued to fare substantially better. Income of young white men in the 1980s actually rose 7 percent on the average, compared with the women's 43 percent decrease, while those in the earlier cohort showed only an 8 percent drop compared with the women's 46 percent. Young black men showed greater slides in income, especially the more recent group, but still substantially less than those of black women.

"The economic costs of marital disruption for young women are as severe today as they were in the 1960s and 1970s," Dr. Smock concludes.

SOURCE: "Young Divorcees Still Are Economic Losers," reprinted by permission of *The Wall Street Journal,* October 6, 1992, B-1. All Rights Reserved Worldwide.

Divorce is never pleasant, as exemplified in the movie *War of the Roses*. It is certainly difficult, financially as well as emotionally, but if one is not prepared and does not know the rules, one can end up losing more than he or she should. The pain of separation and divorce can be intensified by wrangling over personal finances. With the possible exception of child custody, no issue confronting a divorcing couple is more emotionally charged. The financial aspects alone can be excruciating. It should be noted that in addition to freedom and independence, divorce can bring economic hardship, especially for women and children (see the boxed article above). This chapter will discuss only the financial aspects of a divorce. The psychological, legal, emotional, and social issues will be left to other books and essays dealing with these subjects.

As acrimonious as conflicts over tangible goods such as cars, houses, and furniture can be, they are only part of a tangle of financial questions that must be dealt with. As will be seen further on in this chapter, divorce involves issues of pension rights, tax deductions, and alimony, as well as child support payments. But one should know one's legal marital rights and how to protect his or her assets in event of a divorce before getting married.

Clarifying Property Rights

Whether you are preparing to tie the knot next week or your golden anniversary just passed, the financial assumptions on which your marriage operates need to be examined. You need to have a clear notion of your and your spouse's rights to property brought into the marriage as well as that acquired afterward.

The marriage ceremony itself does not alter the title on property each spouse owns before the wedding. But there is something of a hidden change. In a divorce, a spouse is likely to have some claim on the property you brought into the marriage. Exactly how much will be subject to state law and negotiations. Wives generally have stronger claims on property brought to the marriage by the husband than vice versa.

The precise fate of one's assets in case of divorce may be hard to predict. It will depend upon a number of things: where one lives, the kind of assets at issue and how they were acquired, the temperament of both parties, the lawyers hired, and whether the divorce is settled amicably or goes to court.

Prenuptial Agreements (Signing before Kissing)

Since a marriage is as likely to end these days in a divorce as to continue, it is important to be prepared for that eventuality. If June is the month for weddings, then May might be the month for prenuptial agreements. In order to reduce many of the problems inherent in a divorce, a couple may be wise to negotiate a premarital pact prior to getting married or even living together.

In these days of later first marriages, more second marriages, and the explosion of dual career couples, a wedding can sometimes take on the flavor of a financial merger. The newly formed family unit could have a lengthy inventory of property and debts or may want to deal with assets to be accumulated later. Many marriage contracts are, therefore, rapidly gaining popularity. Being forewarned is forearmed.

A **prenuptial agreement** is a negotiated formal contract that spells out each partner's financial privileges and responsibilities. It is often in the form of a written contract drafted prior to marriage that spells out property rights and financial obligations of each party in the event of divorce, separation, or death. The idea is to forestall legal squabbles by agreeing before marriage how property would be allotted in case of such eventualities. Prenuptial agreements are also designed to establish rules during the marriage, not only after it ends. Financial agreements are most common, but often there are also clauses about such things as children, religion, household duties, job relocation, and death.

Prenuptial agreements are being used most often by persons marrying for the second or third time who want to protect assets they have accumulated over the years, ensuring that they go to their children, rather than to their new spouse, if they die. In most states, without such a prior contract, a spouse has a legal claim to one-third to one-half of the other spouse's estate.

This is often not a matter-of-fact undertaking because people who want a financial understanding worked out before marriage have a specific reason. Parents of newlyweds may want to protect their own assets, often a family business or savings they want their children to inherit, and are sometimes advised to have their children's

Debra Solomon

prospective spouse sign a prenuptial agreement. This may prevent an inheritance received by one spouse from being divided with the other at divorce.

A prenuptial agreement must be meticulously drawn to withstand possible legal challenges later on, and it must be signed before the couple marries.

Playing It Safe

Prenuptial agreements could be a wise move for first-time marriages as well. A couple with a prenuptial agreement may look as if each is eying the back door before reaching the altar. But a prenuptial agreement can make a lot of sense, even for people who are convinced they won't ever need it. Most newlyweds apparently ignore the possible complications for understandable reasons. Writing a prenuptial agreement may not be the most romantic of activities. About the surest way to douse the flames of romance is to have a business discussion on who will own what during the marriage and who will get to keep which assets in event of death, divorce, or separation. If you are about to marry someone, why start off assuming the marriage will fail and stipulating who gets what when the inevitable occurs? However, if this leads to controversy, conflict, or even a breakup before the wedding, it may have served an important purpose. If warning bells go off, maybe wedding bells should not.

Such an approach can save needless wrangling and big legal bills later. Surveys suggest that before the wedding, couples are more likely to discuss openly their feelings about sex than about money. After the marriage, they are more likely to argue about money.

Couples who write a prenuptial agreement themselves risk the chance that it will not hold up in court. It is best to have an attorney prepare it. To make an agreement stick, each partner should be represented by a matrimonial lawyer. The lawyers can assist in negotiating the agreement, offer more specific suggestions about the contract, and advise the couple as to which agreements are binding and will hold up in court.

Complete Financial Disclosure

A segment of prenuptial agreements generally considered essential is **complete financial disclosure,** perhaps with the assets or net worth of the parties listed either in the agreement itself or in an appendix. If one of the prospective spouses is waiving rights to inherit all or part of the estate of the other, then he or she should know exactly what he or she is waiving.

Separate Property versus Marital Property

Each state has its own laws governing prenuptial agreements. Two types of assets, separate property and marital property, are often mentioned in an agreement. **Separate property** is anything owned by either party before the marriage or acquired by one of them through gift or inheritance. **Marital property** is anything acquired during the marriage as well as the increased value of separate property (with the increase due to active management of those assets).

A happy note with such an arrangement is that, while it is legally binding as long as both parties desire, it can be modified periodically if there is a substantial change in financial circumstances or for other reasons. Couples can cancel their prenuptial agreement at any time in the future if they so desire.

Prenuptial contracts are popular enough to have spawned the **Uniform Premarital Agreement Act** drafted by the National Conference of Commissioners on Uniform State Laws and endorsed by the American Bar Association. Since its completion in 1983, it has been adopted by 11 states: Arkansas, California, Hawaii, Maine, Montana, North Carolina, North Dakota, Oregon, Rhode Island, Texas, and Virginia. Although premarital agreements are recognized in most states, this act attempts to make the law uniform. Courts generally uphold such agreements provided they were signed voluntarily and finances were fully disclosed at inception. Courts may ignore them, however, if children are harmed by their terms or if either spouse must apply for public welfare as a consequence.

Oral Prenuptial Agreements

Prenuptial agreements are generally written, as indeed they should be. However, oral prenuptial agreements have recently become more palatable to appeals courts.

When love is blind, some couples make promises without benefit of pen and paper. That was the case when a Colorado couple promised, prior to their 1984 marriage, to put each other through college. They broke up after the husband had received his degree but before the wife had acquired hers. The Colorado Court of Appeals ruled in 1992 that the couple's oral agreement was a "valid and binding contract." The ruling was one of several in recent years giving new weight to oral prenuptial accords. These rulings obviously do not obviate the advisability of written agreements.

POSSLQ Contracts

Single people, too, are adding to the family law burdens of the courts. Approximately 2.6 million couples fit the Census Bureau description of **POSSLQs** (pronounced "possle-kews," **persons of the opposite sex sharing living quarters**). Judges are being asked with growing frequency to resolve "palimony" disputes that erupt when the relationship ends.

More than a dozen states have adopted a 1976 California Supreme Court ruling that upheld the right of singer Michelle Triola, who lived with actor Lee Marvin for more than six years, to sue for a share of the property the two obtained, even though no written contract existed. Actor Trevor Hook in 1983 was awarded $125,000 from the estate of a woman with whom he lived for 17 years. But because oral agreements can be difficult to prove, unmarried couples with valuable property are best advised to draw up contracts.

Although sheer numbers have helped render unconventional relationships more socially acceptable, unmarried couples still live in a cloudy and unpredictable legal climate. Unmarried partners do not have the same legal rights as spouses to share property. That can make a dispute more unpleasant and expensive than a divorce. Among the major problems are these:

1. *Inheritance* When a married person dies without a will, state laws typically ensure that the bulk of the person's property will pass to the surviving spouse. But when an unmarried person leaves no will, all of his or her earthly goods can be claimed by the next of kin, with the POSSLQ often having no rights.

2. *Health insurance* Health insurance plans through an employer that cover a spouse almost never extend to an unmarried live-in partner.

3. *Legal status* The couple is faced with a wide disparity of state laws ranging from outright bans on cohabitation to various shades of permissiveness. (Cohabitation is still illegal in a few states—including Arizona, Georgia, Mississippi, North Carolina, and Virginia, but the laws are rarely enforced.) In Georgia, unwed cohabitants risk a $1,000 fine and a year in jail. In a court dispute with a landlord, such a couple with an entirely justified claim may find themselves out on the sidewalk because their living arrangement is against the law.

It is usually possible for unmarried couples to plug the holes in a legal system that predates POSSLQs and gay rights by drawing up **cohabitation contracts**. Similar to prenuptial agreements, these documents spell out precisely who gets what in the event of a separation. Young couples with few assets and little income probably don't need a written cohabitation contract. However, they probably do need one if they believe their relationship will be long-term or if they buy major assets together, especially real estate. They also need a contract if they have children, either together or from a prior relationship. The POSSLQ contracts do not have to be complicated. In one common type of agreement, couples simply waive all financial claims on each other. What is his remains his and what is hers is hers, period. Without written contracts, unmarried couples often forfeit the legal protections of married couples and leave the door wide open for spurned lovers to initiate palimony suits. The laws protect the institution of marriage. Unmarried people living together need to understand how different their rights are legally and to protect their interests.

Gay couples are at particular risk. The laws in virtually all the states are designed to protect heterosexual families. All 50 states currently prohibit gay marriages. To achieve an equal legal footing, gay couples have to draw up such legal documents as wills, powers of attorney, joint leases on homes, and cohabitation contracts. The best approach, therefore, is to consult an attorney before deciding to live together to clarify the legal and financial ramifications.

The Divorce Process

Separating Physically and Fiscally (Cutting up the Wedding Cake)

Marriages may be made in heaven, but divorces should be negotiated in lawyers' and accountants' offices. The first thing to do if you want a divorce is to consult an attorney. Obviously, when you are uncertain about property, custody, and various financial arrangements, it pays to hire an expert to represent you.

No-Fault Divorce

Attitudes toward divorce have changed radically in recent years. So have the divorce laws. Since 1970 all states have authorized some form of **"no-fault" divorce,** which means it is not necessary to establish that one party "sinned" or is to blame for the marriage failure. Consequently, the procedures for getting a divorce are much simpler than they used to be. You no longer have to hire a private detective to prove in court that your spouse is committing adultery or is a demented sadist.

Although getting a divorce may be less problematic than in the past, it is not necessarily easier. The emphasis has changed from litigation over fault to negotiation over assets. The divorce process no longer focuses on "who did what" so much as "who gets what."

With the spread of no-fault divorce and the rise of state laws requiring that a couple's assets be divided equitably between them, divorce—if both sides are mature about it—can be done in a businesslike and respectable, neat and efficient manner, with no loose ends untied, much like the dissolution of a business partnership.

Contested and Uncontested Divorces

The range of legal costs involved in a divorce is wide. If a lawyer specializing in divorce cases is hired, the fee may amount to several thousands of dollars or more.

It is also possible to buy a do-it-yourself kit or book for a few dollars. The question is how much and what kind of legal help you need. The answer to that depends on whether the divorce is **contested** or **uncontested**. In a contested divorce, the parties have serious differences that they cannot settle amicably, and they are willing to go to court to have a judge settle them. This usually involves several thousands of dollars of legal fees.

Fewer than 10 percent of all divorces are contested. However, divorce litigation now constitutes almost 50 percent of civil filings in the United States and has become as complicated and as commercial as corporate cases.

Uncontested divorce actions are settled amicably out of court either through negotiations by the attorneys for both sides or by using a professional mediator. If both parties want a divorce and are willing to negotiate a fair settlement, they can arrive at an out-of-court settlement. This saves thousands of dollars of legal fees which would otherwise be incurred if they have a contested divorce court battle. Like other contracts, divorce settlements can be designed to benefit both parties if good will exists.

Mediation   Dividing a divorcing couple's assets may be the most contentious and complicated issue in the family legal strife. Sometimes each member hires an attorney and lets the attorneys negotiate. Others agree to hire a **mediator** who will supervise and direct negotiations between the two sides. Increasingly, people are turning to mediators to work out settlements without trials. (A mediator can be found by contacting the Academy of Family Mediators, P. O. Box 10501, Eugene, OR 97440, 503/345-1205.) Mediating couples generally recognize that they have common objectives:

1. To terminate the marriage

2. To minimize the fees and costs involved

3. To reduce their tax consequences

4. To begin their new lives in financial security

Several states require that mediation be attempted before going to a judge. During the mediated divorce, couples are separated from the problem. The focus is kept upon their interests, rather than their respective positions. The mediator stops the process of assigning blame and assists the couple in making the best of their situation.

The Advantages of Mediation   As stated, mediation is much less expensive than a litigated divorce in court. A mediator's fee can amount to a considerable savings over the cost of hiring two lawyers. Mediators do not entirely eliminate the need for attorneys. But they do reduce the time that each partner spends with his or her lawyer. If lawyers were to be actively involved in the often protracted negotiations between husband and wife over the nitty gritty of who gets to keep their pet dog, the gold fish, or the family album, then both spouses may end up with astronomical lawyers' bills. Moreover, mediation often reduces much of the bitterness and divisiveness of adversarial divorces.

Full Disclosure of Assets   Couples need to present an itemized list of all their assets when they meet with the mediator. Most states require that both parties make full financial disclosure to each other. If a divorcing spouse suspects that a partner is concealing something, a judge may authorize hiring an **investigative accountant** to look into the records.

A couple's property may include not only such obvious things as houses, cars, and cash, but also financial property or "intangibles." In addition to bank accounts, investments, and real estate, the couple must include credit union accounts; pensions, profit-sharing plans; the cash value in life insurance policies, IRAs, KEOGHs, royalties, tax shelters, income tax refunds, stock options, and any other pools of income the family has had. The couple must also include nonliquid assets, jewelry, art, cars, boats, vacation time-shares, and collectibles, as well as business interests. Even the value of a professional license or practice may have to be included as part of the assets subject to division, or an intangible such as good customer or client relations that one spouse has built up in his or her business.

Once the parties have determined what they have and where it came from and have drawn up an accurate list of the family's assets, they have to assign value to them. They may need professional help in figuring their worth. Appraising a pension's current value or the value of a tax shelter or an ongoing business generally requires the help of an accountant, actuary, or investment banker.

The designated value of each asset will help determine which asset each party gets. The appraisals of each other's assets can often be subject to negotiation and controversy. It is most often settled by a mediator getting the parties to rely on a mutually agreed upon professional appraisal. The problem can be compounded if some of the property is not easily evaluated or divided, such as a business.

The value of a spouse's share of a family business must be assessed, often a difficult task. A divorcing woman who had worked as a secretary in her husband's insurance agency office may claim to be entitled to part of the "good will" that constitutes a large part of the business value. If both spouses are employed, each may hire an accountant to appraise the other's fringe benefits. Once the appraisals are agreed upon, a mediated out-of-court settlement can be attained.

At mediation, couples generally also work out their custody and child and spouse support problems. The mediator may be a counselor trained in family therapy or a lawyer who has given up the adversarial approach to divorce.

The couple usually decides how their property is to be divided prior to the divorce, but the actual division may occur much later. For example, if they own a house and there are minor children in the family, the couple might agree that whoever has custody of the children may live in the house until the children are grown and independent. Then the house can be sold and the proceeds divided according to a formula specified at the time of the divorce. Alternatively, the couple can decide to maintain joint ownership, so that both parties maintain their investment, or turn over the house to one spouse and compensate the other with assets equal in value to the forfeited share of the house.

Often a jointly owned house is transferred to the wife as part of her share of the settlement. But some mortgages contain clauses that require the loan to be repaid if the ownership changes. In the case of an old low-interest mortgage, the wife can suffer great hardship, since she may have to refinance the house at a much higher rate and also might not qualify for a new mortgage on her income alone.

The Separation Agreement

After all the issues have been resolved, the mediator typically has the couple sit down, usually with one lawyer, who draws up a formal **separation agreement,** covering the property settlement and spelling out the details of such subjects as how the two will file their tax returns and how they will share the college costs for their children and how and when they will sell jointly owned property. The actual mediated settlement agreements should be carefully reviewed by lawyers for both husband and wife before either signs. The signed agreement can then be submitted to a court for incorporation into the final divorce decree.

When a separation agreement is submitted to the court, the judge will usually accept it as written unless the terms are clearly unfair to one of the parties. In most states, judges have the power to modify those terms that create hardship. In other states, judges are empowered to change only those terms that apply to the couple's children. The children are considered wards of the state, so it is up to the judge to see that their rights are protected. If everything appears fair and voluntary, the couple, in most cases, will get their divorce decree 30 to 90 days later.

Contested Divorces: Litigation

Couples who cannot reach an accord outside the courtroom need to be prepared for a slow and costly process of litigation. There is no special preference for divorce cases on the civil court calendar, so the wait to begin the trial can be as long as two to three years in some districts. The legal cost of even a simple case can exceed $15,000 for each side.* When a married couple goes to court, they hand over the decision making to a judge, who will issue a binding decision.

Knowing Your Legal Rights

In both contested and uncontested divorces, both parties should know their legal rights before the main issues are stated. These issues are usually property rights, alimony, child support, and possible tax implications of divorce. Let's briefly examine some legal aspects of these issues.

Equitable Distribution Laws versus Community Property Laws

Not long ago, it was considered an ex-husband's obligation to support his wife until she remarried, if ever, and his children until they were grown. He held most of the assets in his name and gave his wife an allowance, called *alimony* or *maintenance,* after they were divorced. In recent years, however, state legislatures and courts across the country have acknowledged that both parties put effort into a marriage, so both are entitled to their fair share of the assets if they divorce. Almost every state has adopted some form of **equitable distribution divorce laws**. These laws treat a marriage as an economic partnership and require judges to exercise their discretion in fairly dividing assets accumulated during a marriage. The only exception is anything that a spouse owned before marriage or received as an inheritance or a gift during the marriage. In

---

*A marital law specialist can be found by contacting the American Academy of Matrimonial Lawyers, 150 N. Michigan Avenue, Suite 2040, Chicago, IL 60601, (312/263-6477).

"First let me read you your rights!"

SOURCE: "Pepper…and Salt," *The Wall Street Journal*, May 30, 1991, A-15. Reprinted by permission of Cartoon Features Syndicate.

most states, such **separate property** continues to belong to that spouse. The balance, as previously mentioned, is **marital** or **community property.**

Most states define *marital property* very broadly as all property acquired by either or both spouses during their marriage. This marital property is what is subject to division of some kind. Forty-one states follow equitable division under which courts exercise wide discretion in apportioning holdings. In order to avoid potential problems in the event of a divorce, couples should, whenever possible, segregate premarital and inherited property from property bought with earnings during the marriage. For example, a wife might put money brought into a marriage into a mutual fund and reinvest all dividends. Keeping investments separate and in one's own name will not guarantee that one will still own them after a divorce. But if they are kept separately, it becomes much easier to claim as "separate property."

The courts have the power to require equitable distribution of marital property in divorces, without regard to who actually holds title to the property. That does not necessarily mean a 50–50 split. The division may favor one spouse or the other, depending upon the circumstances.

Equitable distribution is based upon such factors as the length of the marriage; how employable each spouse is; each spouse's age, needs, health, income capacity, wealth, liabilities, and accustomed standard of living; as well as how much each spouse contributed by taking care of the home and children, for example, or by holding a job while the other attended school or college. A critical factor influencing how such issues are decided is the state in which the divorcing couple resides.

About 25 percent of the population lives in nine states governed by **community property laws:** Arizona, California, Idaho, Louisiana, Nevada, New Mexico, Texas, Washington, and Wisconsin. The primary characteristic of property laws in these states is that marriage is a 50–50 deal financially. Community property along with community debts is divided equally between the spouses. Basically, this means half of what one spouse earns and half of what that spouse buys with his or her earnings belong to the other spouse and vice versa. Assets a spouse brings to the marriage and those earned during the marriage are generally community property.

In October 1988, Mike Tyson, who grossed about $40 million in the ring, filed for divorce in New Jersey allegedly because that state uses equitable distribution, which takes into account individual assets and length of the marriage. His wife, Robin Givens, filed for divorce in California. That state's community property law, as mentioned above, divides assets 50–50.

Common Law

Some states use common law in divorce cases. In states adhering to common law or **separate property laws (common law)**, what you earn is yours and what your spouse earns is his or hers. And what you buy with separate funds is separately owned.

Three states, Mississippi, Virginia, and West Virginia, follow common law, a collection of rules and principles based upon custom and precedent rather than statutes. In those states, the spouse who holds title to the property is generally allowed to keep it.

Since the divorce and marital property laws are not uniform and vary from state to state, this is yet another reason that an attorney must be consulted to clearly delineate your rights and obligations under your state's law.

Alimony—It Ain't What It Used to Be

Alimony is from the Latin "alimonia," meaning nourishment or sustenance. The term is linked to the ancient idea that, in return for her services in the home, a wife is entitled to be supported by her husband. Traditionally, alimony has been awarded only to wives, but the U.S. Supreme Court ruled that alimony statutes have to be gender neutral. Therefore, the courts can award a husband alimony if the wife's salary is much greater than his or if he is unemployed or disabled and she has a job.

Moreover, family law now mirrors the increasingly unisex character of the roles played by marriage partners. In the past, as stated, a husband usually earned the family income while his wife managed the household. When a divorce was granted, the man's obligation to support his nonworking ex-wife might be lifelong.

Today, with more women in the workforce and both sexes demanding equal treatment, support orders from courts are being trimmed or eliminated altogether. Alimony is far from automatic. In a no-fault divorce between two career people with no children, for example, alimony is not likely to be awarded. Courts are less paternalistic of women and expect them to work and be self-supportive. Alimony is no longer intended as an indefinite means of support. In many states, the concept of long-term alimony has almost completely gone by the wayside, except for marriages of two decades or more in which one spouse has no employment skills or is physically or mentally unable to enter the labor force.

Courts no longer are burdening a husband with an ex-wife's maintenance for years and years. Instead, courts provide dependent spouses with short-term payments that rarely last longer than five years. As women become more financially independent and as the equitable distribution rules spread, alimony is becoming a less important element in divorce settlement.

In many states, alimony has come to be known as **maintenance payments** or **rehabilitative alimony.** The general idea is for the former spouse to help pay for the further education or training that the other ex-spouse needs to get a job. Its function, thereby, is to give the dependent partner a kind of unemployment compensation until he or she may be self-supporting and then scale down the support as the dependent's former partner's earning power grows. This type of arrangement, a temporary boost for the nonworking spouse into the job market, has become increasingly popular among divorcing couples. Although the premise of this arrangement *seems* fair, it is often an injustice to the women who must try to find an entry-level position after being out of the workforce for many years (especially older women who have raised children). Their salary is often low compared to what they could have earned had they been in the job market during all the years of their marriage.

Support of the children is now likewise considered both parents' responsibility.

Alimony, Child Support, and the IRS

The law requires parents to support their children, and that obligation does not end with divorce. The judge will expect to see provisions of **child support** in any

| FIGURE 17–1 | How Families Are Changing |

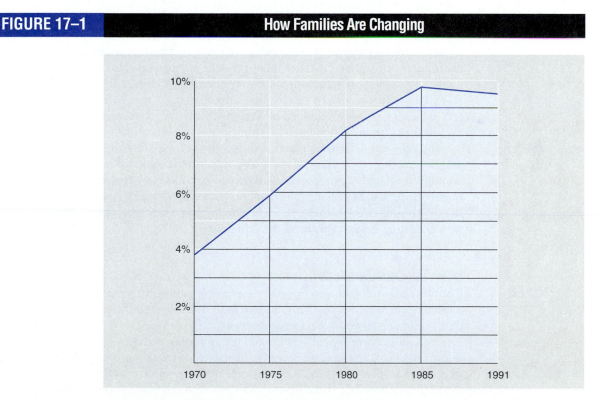

The percentage of children in the United States (under the age of 18) living with a divorced parent has increased markedly.

SOURCE: U.S. Census Bureau.

agreement submitted. Support obligations vary from state to state. All states have guidelines that factor in things such as parental income and children's expenses.

The fact that alimony and child support are treated differently for tax purposes provides divorcing couples with another strategy for saving money in their settlement. Alimony payments are tax deductible, but child support payments are not.

Child support is treated as part of the taxable income of the one who earns it, not for the one who receives it, but alimony is a tax deduction for the one who earns it but must be reported as taxable income for the one who receives it. Under the old system, partners could choose to what extent they could treat payments as child support and to what extent they could treat payments as spousal support. This usually was part of the separation agreement worked out between husband and wife.

The payer usually needs a tax deduction, since a divorce transforms him or her into the higher tax bracket of a single person. With, for example, 28 percent of alimony payments recouped as tax savings, the payer can afford to pay more to his or her former spouse until he or she becomes self-supporting.

The Tax Equity and Fiscal Responsibility Act (TEFRA) of 1984, which became effective January 1, 1985, redefined what constitutes tax-deductible alimony far more narrowly than the term had come to be interpreted by state laws and courts. This applies only for divorce agreements signed after January 1, 1985.

Under TEFRA, alimony continued to be tax deductible for the spouse who pays it and taxable income for the spouse who receives it. The 1984 law defined alimony as any monetary payment from one ex-spouse to another under a divorce or separation agreement. Excluded are other types of payments such as money that changes hands between former spouses for the upbringing of children.

TEFRA's intent was to ensure that alimony could not be a substitute for property transfers and was intended to keep people from trying to fudge a deduction by disguising a property settlement as alimony.

The 1984 tax bill also cleared up a matter of long-standing controversy, namely which parent gets to claim a child as a dependent and thus claim the exemption. Couples frequently argued over who provided what support for the dependent, ultimately bringing the IRS into the dispute. Under current tax law, the parent the child lives with is entitled to the dependency deduction unless the custodial parent signs a waiver giving the exemption to the other parent.

Other Tax Considerations

Couples undergoing the emotional trauma of breaking apart often become victims of a tax system they did not fully understand. The average person is largely unaware that divorce itself could be a taxable event.

The Tax Reform Act of 1984 made the sweeping change of also completely eliminating taxes on appreciated property transferred from one spouse to another as part of a divorce. This nullifies a court decision that property settlements involving the transfer of a house or some other asset can create an immediate taxable capital gain for the spouse who gives up the asset. The IRS now views such transfers as untaxable gifts rather than as taxable sales.

But it is not always so equitable for both sides. Suppose that in a divorce settlement, a husband transfers to his wife stock that he bought for $10,000 in his own name and is now worth $100,000. The new law relieves him of the capital gains tax and gives it instead to his new wife. Should she sell the stock, she becomes

What Is Considered Alimony?

I f a husband pays $240,000 to his wife in settlement for her marital claims, for example, this is not alimony and hence is neither deductible by him nor taxable to her. But if these payments are spread over a period of years, say $40,000 for six years, they take on the appearance of alimony.

The payments cannot, however, fluctuate in relation to a child's age, school, or matrimonial status. This is meant to prevent child support (which is not deductible), camouflaged as alimony, from being cut as the child gets older. Any divorce settlement that schedules a reduction of payments coinciding with a child's coming of age will be a signal to the IRS of just how much is for child support and therefore taxable to the spouse providing it.

In addition, the new law requires that the divorce agreement specifically state that there is no liability for payments after the death of the recipient. The rationale here is that alimony is intended just to meet the support needs of the recipient. If payments are to continue beyond death, the payments are more in the nature of a property settlement than for support.

Tax-Free

liable for the tax on the $90,000 that the stock appreciated since her husband bought it.

Therefore, a spouse who transfers property incident to a divorce is relieved of the tax on the gain. But the trade-off is that when the spouse who receives the property sells it, he or she will have to pay tax on the full appreciation. If the wife accepts the $100,000 stock as part of a settlement and in exchange gives the husband a $100,000 bank certificate, she is being shortchanged. The net after-tax value of the stock to her is far less than $100,000. She needs to calculate its after-tax value, not its face value. Before accepting any assets as part of a divorce settlement, an attorney or CPA should be consulted as to the future tax liabilities when the asset will be sold.

Cutting up the Pension Pie

Normally, after the marital home, the most valuable asset that a husband or wife owns is an interest in an employer's retirement plan. Yet in many divorce cases, pension rights may be overlooked in the property settlement.

As a result of the Retirement Equity Act of 1984, couples who are splitting up can put a new item on the bargaining table—the spouse's pension. The value of one spouse's right to a future pension earned during the marriage is generally considered by the courts to be marital property and should be divided equitably between the spouses. Under this law, an ex-housewife can be assured of collecting on her former husband's pension, if a judge has awarded her that right. Additionally, a nonworking spouse is entitled to part of his or her ex-spouse's social security benefits.

The Retirement Equity Act of 1984 makes it easier to claim a share of a former spouse's pension. A vehicle known as a **qualified domestic relations order (QDRO)** allows pension plan administrators to comply with state court orders. Pension plan administrators can partition a portion of a qualified pension plan to a divorcing spouse. In the past, some states did not allow courts to divide retirement benefits.

The law is expressed in unisex language but was designed primarily to strengthen the claims of nonworking divorced wives to pensions earned by their ex-husbands during the marriage. The new law also permits a wife to begin collecting her share of her ex-husband's retirement benefits even if he is still working, once he qualifies for early retirement, normally at 55. Or she can demand her share in a lump sum if the company pension plan allows it and postpone paying taxes on the sum by rolling it over into an IRA. However, the ex-wife's choices are limited to what is offered by the particular plan. Basically, an ex-wife is now treated as a separate participant in the company pension plan.

Another option available to the wife is to relinquish her share in her husband's pension in exchange for some other property. She may allow him to keep his entire pension in exchange for the entire family home. The pension can therefore be used as another bargaining asset to be swapped for something else.

In order to determine how much a pension is currently worth in a trade, its "current or present value" must first be established. A pension actuary can help to calculate the value, in today's dollars, of a company pension that may not be paid out to the worker-spouse for another 10 or 15 years.

A pension to be paid out over a period of years, starting at some date in the future, is simply not worth the sum of those future payments. Since the payments will be made in the future, the money cannot be invested in the meantime. The further the point when the money will be paid out, the less the pension is worth right now.

Finally, divorcing individuals should not overlook routine paperwork, such as changing beneficiaries named on their accounts at banks, brokerage firms, and mutual funds, and on insurance policies. They need to close all joint credit cards as well as update wills and powers of attorney.

SUMMARY

Divorce is unpleasant, difficult, and often emotionally traumatic. However, it is a widespread phenomenon and therefore both parties to a marriage should be knowledgeable of their rights and the divorce process. Most of the issues in contention at divorce proceedings are financial. Divorce can be seen from a financial perspective as a dissolution of a partnership. This should be negotiated in a fashion that is as neat, businesslike, and equitable as possible.

Divorces can be contested or uncontested. Contested divorces include litigation, expensive legal fees, and long waits for trial dates. Such divorces leave the final terms of the divorce and division of assets to a judge. Uncontested divorces could be negotiated by mediation. A mediator will try to get the couple to resolve the issues by mutual consent and sign a separation agreement. This agreement is submitted to the court and becomes part of the divorce decree.

Couples need to know their rights to property, alimony, and child support prior to entering divorce negotiations. Property laws vary among the states. Most states have equitable distribution of property laws, while some states follow separate property laws. Alimony has changed from a lifetime payment to a temporary stipend to enable the unemployed spouse to become self-sufficient. Tax consequences of divorce and division of any future pension rights are additional items that need to be negotiated by a divorcing couple.

KEY TERMS

Alimony

Child support

Cohabitation contracts

Community property laws

Complete financial disclosure

Contested divorce

Equitable distribution laws

Investigative accountant

Maintenance payments

Marital property

Mediator

No-fault divorce

POSSLQs

Prenuptial agreements

Qualified domestic relations order (QDRO)

Rehabilitative alimony

Separate property

Separate property laws (common law)

Separation agreement

Uncontested divorce

Uniform Premarital Agreement Act

REVIEW QUESTIONS AND PROBLEMS

1. Do you think prenuptial agreements are a good idea? Present arguments for and against.
2. Why would POSSLQs need a cohabitation agreement? What protection does it provide them? What should typically be included in such an agreement?
3. What is the difference between equitable distribution laws and community property laws?
4. Explain why one spouse may file for divorce in one state while the other spouse may file in another state. What reasons would motivate them to do this?
5. Identify and define the following: (a) marital property, (b) separate property, (c) qualified domestic relations order (QDRO), (d) no-fault divorce.
6. Why is alimony no longer a lifetime payment made by a working spouse to the unemployed spouse? What sociological changes have influenced the definition of alimony?
7. Give examples of how tax implications can affect divorce negotiations.
8. What are the advantages of an uncontested and mediated divorce?
9. (TAX-FREE) You own an asset with a cost basis of $50,000. The capital gain tax rate is 34 percent. You wish to limit your capital gains tax to no more than $10,000. The value of the asset has fallen recently and you are considering selling it. What is the highest price you should sell it for? (Ignore "per unit" amounts.)

SUGGESTED PROJECTS

Try to find three people who are divorced and who agree to be interviewed by you (in complete anonymity). Ask each person to outline for you the following: 1. What were the main financial issues negotiated at their divorce proceedings? 2. How were these financial matters resolved? 3. How has the divorce affected their tax situation? 4. What costs were incurred in the divorce proceedings? 5. Do they consider their divorce settlement to be fair? Why or why not? 6. What advice could they offer to someone undergoing a divorce currently?

Assign each case a number (1, 2, and 3). Present your findings to the class showing the similarities and differences in each case and what can be learned from each.

INFORMATION RESOURCES

Academy of Family Mediators can help you find a mediator. Write or call the academy at P.O. Box 10501, Eugene, OR 97440, 503/345-1205.

American Academy of Matrimonial Lawyers can help you locate a marital law specialist. Write or call the academy at 150 N. Michigan Avenue, Suite 2040, Chicago, IL 60601, 312/263-6477.

"The Delicate Balances of Living Together." *Money,* March 1989, 88–90.

"Differences in Divorce Laws." *The Wall Street Journal,* April 14, 1988, A-33.

"Dividing the Spoils in Divorce." *U.S. News and World Report,* April 7, 1986, 57–58.

"The Dollar Side of Divorce." *Changing Times,* May 1987, 94–100.

"A Fresh Look at Divorce Settlements." *Sylvia Porter's Personal Finance,* August 1985, 72–79.

Holden, K. C., and P. J. Smock. "The Economic Costs of Marital Dissolution: Why Do Women Bear a Disproportionate Cost?" *Annual Review of Sociology 1991,* 51–78.

"I Get Half of Everything ... and Other Expensive Myths about Divorce." *Changing Times,* January 1991, 61–63.

"Just Living Together." *Money,* January 1989, 107–112.

Moreau, Dan. "Yours, Mine, and Ours." *Kiplinger's Personal Finance Magazine,* August 1993, 71–75.

"The New Economics of Custody Suits." *The New York Times,* April 6, 1986, F-11.

"New Pension Rights for Former Spouses." *The New York Times,* March 31, 1985, D-2.

"Prenuptial Contracts." *The New York Times,* June 13, 1987, 34.

Rowland, Mary. "A Child's Medical Care after Divorce." *The New York Times,* October 3, 1993, F-13.

"Some Financial Answers, When It Comes to Divorce." *The Wall Street Journal,* April 2, 1991, C-1.

"Some Second Thoughts about No-Fault Divorce." *The New York Times,* August 17, 1986, E-24.

Teachman, J. D. "Who Pays? Receipt of Child Support in the U.S." *Journal of Marriage and the Family,* August 1991, 759–772.

Your Pension Rights at Divorce: What Women Need to Know. (For a copy, send $14.50 to the Pension Rights Center, 918 16th Street NW, Suite 704, Dept. A, Washington, DC 20006.)

CHAPTER EIGHTEEN

Preparing for Retirement

- To understand the necessity for and the importance of planning for retirement

- To estimate our planned retirement needs

- To identify what benefits are available under Social Security

- To discuss how Social Security fits into our overall retirement plan

- To review the status of the Social Security system today

- To examine the characteristics and the features of employer-sponsored pension plans

- To explore tax sheltered private retirement plans, such as Keoghs and IRAs

- To analyze the basic principle underlying annuities, different annuity classifications, and factors to consider when purchasing annuities

For most students, retirement is 30 to 40 years down the road and not considered as a very urgent topic. Turning 65 can seem as distant to most students as winning the Irish sweepstakes. Students generally have plenty of other things that are of more immediate concern. But those pension and Social Security dollars that often mysteriously disappear from our paycheck represent a substantial, long-term investment in our personal financial future. Retirement is an inevitable but important part of our lives that cannot be left to chance and must be planned for with careful consideration and strategy. It requires discipline and a methodical approach. Retirement planning also requires taking some risk, which will be discussed further in this chapter.

All working people, young and old, face a changing and uncertain world that threatens our retirement years. The trend toward later marriage and childbearing means that when today's 35-year-olds get around to seriously saving, the bulk of their resources could be consumed by their children's college bills. As discussed in Chapter 4, in 20 years, the average cost of a private, four-year college education is projected to exceed $180,000. Unless planned for properly, retirement in the next century could be a luxury affordable only by the wealthy and by those who started saving in early years.

This chapter provides information that may help you, whether you are 18, 35, or 50 years old, to start making the right decisions and examine options for the "golden years" which we all aspire to reach. If you have some foresight and a financial plan, aging should not present you with a financial crisis. The term "aging gracefully and intelligently" should apply to our financial life as well. This chapter therefore explores various pension programs, both employer and employee funded, as well as Social Security. Recent pension legislation and tax reform as well as Social Security revamping have drastically altered retirement planning. These are explored in order to enable us to organize and plan our future retirement needs based on these changes.

ONLY 22,463 DAYS UNTIL RETIREMENT.

We Probably Cannot Afford to Ignore Retirement

Consider some important facts about our financial lives. Most people have an average of 44 "earning" years and will probably live 13 to 20 retirement years after age 65. Very few people have so much money that they can afford to ignore the fundamentals of retirement planning. Only 2 percent of all Americans who reach age 65 are financially independent; the rest must either continue to work or to rely on pensions, Social Security benefits, and savings accumulated during their working years.

The Shaky Three-Legged Stool

The secret of retirement security is discipline. Discipline to save a part of our earnings and put it to work for us is essential to retirement planning. Retirement security is often described as the **three-legged stool** of Social Security, private pensions, and personal savings. For many people, the balance is precarious because at least one leg (either pensions or savings) is missing.

Millions of people are counting on company pension plans to provide a good part of their retirement income. However, despite the apparently strict regulations by the government and despite the tax incentives held out to industry, the current pension system still has some glaring weaknesses. (This will be discussed further in this chapter.) Roughly half the private workforce has no pension coverage. Many of those who are covered will never receive benefits, and many of those who do receive benefits will find them inadequate.

We used to believe that Social Security would take care of us in our old age, but rising inflation and the aging of America have made this a doubtful factor in retirement planning. Although Social Security will certainly survive in one form or another, major changes lie ahead in the type and level of benefits that are provided as well as the way they are financed. Most potential retirees can look forward to Social Security income. But will that be enough for the lifestyle we want? The burden of responsibility for our financial future is rapidly shifting to us.

Statistically, we are likely to live longer and thus need more money than our parents did. That means we need alternative sources of income, such as private savings, IRAs, Keoghs, life insurance, and other investments, in addition to a good private or company pension.

Retirement Planning: An Ongoing Process

Retirement planning should therefore be an ongoing process. It should be a financial priority beginning during working people's early years and continuing throughout their entire earning lifetime. There is no specific age that marks the proper time to begin a retirement plan. The time to start planning for retirement is the day you collect your first paycheck.

How much should you save each month or each year? That depends upon the kind of retirement living you have in mind, how much money you already have and a lot of unpredictable factors, such as inflation, investment conditions, Social Security legislation, and the type of company pension plans you have. As a rule of thumb, most young people should try to set aside at least 5 to 10 percent of their gross income for retirement each year. While people may not have much say about the way they collect a company pension or Social Security, it is how safely and diligently they deploy the third leg of the above mentioned stool that can spell the difference between basking on Golden Pond and being up the creek.

Table 18–1 shows how much must be saved each year until age 65 to generate various levels of annual retirement income. (These figures assume an 8 percent tax-free yield on investments.)

How Much Will You Need?

RETIREMENT

How much money will be required to live comfortably in retirement? Fortunately, your expenses will probably be lower after you retire. Daily outlays for food, transportation, and clothing tend to diminish, as do taxes, so less may be needed when you retire, but not a lot less. Retirement income should generally be no less than income before retirement, less taxes, work expenses, and savings. The American Council of Life Insurance estimates that for the average income household, it will take 75 to 80 percent of its gross preretirement income to maintain an equivalent retirement lifestyle.

People whose preretirement income is higher than average, say, over $100,000, may need only somewhat more than half of it after retirement. With a calculator, we can adjust that result for inflation (it is recommended to use the historically weighted average of 5 percent) to calculate the dollar amount equal to today's purchasing power. For example, if you estimate that you need $30,000 for living expenses, you will need approximately $80,000 annually if you retire in 20 years.

Continuing this illustration, to earn $80,000 a year, you will need to have $1 million of principal, assuming an 8 percent return. Subtracting pension benefits, say $40,000 annually, and Social Security of $700 monthly (or $8,400 annually), you will need to provide an additional $32,000 annually. For the required principal sum of $400,000 needed to generate $32,000, you must save $9,000 annually for those 20 years, still assuming an 8 percent return.

The above example assumes that interest, not principal, is used for retirement income. Less needs to be saved if principal is consumed. This is best done through the purchase of an annuity, discussed further on.

Periodically, throughout their working lives, people should take inventory of their current financial situation and ask themselves: "If I retire tomorrow, would my

TABLE 18–1	Yearly Retirement—Income Goal			
	$20,000	**$30,000**	**$40,000**	**$60,000**
Present Age	**Annual Savings Required**			
30	$ 1,022	$ 1,534	$ 2,044	$ 3,066
35	1,552	2,332	3,109	4,665
40	2,409	3,614	4,818	7,227
45	3,849	5,773	7,697	11,546
Total Saved	$176,126	$264,190	$352,253	$528,379

income from Social Security, employer's pension plan, real estate, stocks, and annuities, replace 75 to 80 percent of my annual income?" Individuals' very first investment, if they plan to put away significant sums, should probably be on the advice of an accountant, lawyer, or financial planner who knows his or her way in the labyrinths of tax law. Retirement planning obliges individuals to invest more money and deal with more tax ramifications than they have ever had to before.

The Problem of Future Inflation

Inflation erodes the value of our savings as well as our private pensions. A pensioner who retires on $10,000 will need $14,802 a year 10 years later just to have the same buying power. In 25 years, he or she will need $26,658 a year to stay even, assuming an historical inflation rate of 4 percent.

Table 18–2 illustrates the impact of inflation on retirement plans.

Private pensions rarely provide for automatic inflation protection after an employee retires. Retirees usually find the value of their pensions shrinking each year. Companies argue that providing automatic **cost of living adjustments (COLAs)** would be expensive. Instead of automatic increases, some companies, primarily large ones, give occasional cost of living increases to their retired employees. Such increases, however, generally fail to keep up with inflation. Some companies offer their employees a smaller benefit at retirement, with the rest of the benefits coming in the form of cost of living raises during retirement.

Social Security

Let us first examine what you can expect from Social Security. **Social Security** is the only public retirement program. It is actually much more than a retirement program available to workers today. Social Security is a package of insurances, known as OASDHI, which stands for Old-Age, Survivors, Disability, and Health (Medicare) Insurance. This package protects workers and their families while they work as well

TABLE 18–2　　Spendable Income Needed during Retirement

Spendable Income Needed during Retirement to Buy What $10,000 Buys at the Start of Retirement

Number of Years after the Start of Retirement	Inflation Rate 2%	4%	6%	8%
5	$11,041	$12,167	$13,382	$14,693
10	12,190	14,802	17,908	21,589
15	13,459	18,009	23,966	31,722
20	14,859	21,911	32,071	46,610
25	16,406	26,658	42,919	68,485

as after they retire. In addition to a retirement pension, a worker's Social Security deductions pay for disability and survivors insurance. Part of the deductions also pay for health and hospital (Medicare) insurance protection.

Workers cannot count on Social Security alone to retire comfortably, but it will help. It will also not replace all earnings lost because of disability or death. Social Security was designed to provide workers and retirees with only a floor of protection. It was never intended to meet all such needs, and it never will so long as our society maintains an important element of free enterprise and individual responsibility. But it does provide a good, solid base of income that people can build upon with other pensions; life, disability, and medical insurance; savings; or investments. Social Security, therefore, is a basic benefit to be supplemented by other income.

People in practically all lines of work, including members of Congress, the president, newly hired federal workers, and the self-employed are covered. More than 126 million people contribute to Social Security through payroll taxes on wages, salaries, commissions, and tips. Social Security is not voluntary. It is a mandatory program. Approximately one of every six persons in the United States now gets a monthly Social Security check. These 41.9 million beneficiaries include 28 million retirees, 3.8 million disabled workers and their spouses, 3.3 million children of deceased or disabled workers, and 5.4 million spouses of deceased workers (mostly widows).

Despite all the criticisms, Social Security remains a good deal. It is estimated that workers paying in now and retiring 25 to 30 years later can expect to get at least what they paid in with interest. In effect, it enables workers to take out a pension on their very first job and continue contributing to it throughout their working life regardless of how often they switch jobs. They can also participate in a private pension plan without losing any of their Social Security retirement benefits.

Every American has an enormous stake in the future of Social Security, directly as a taxpayer and beneficiary and indirectly because the system has a substantial impact on the economy (see Figure 18–1). The federal government now spends more on Social Security and Medicare than it does on defense. Most people pay more in Social Security taxes (including the employer contribution) than they do in income taxes.

How Secure Is Social Security?

The basic idea of Social Security, set up in 1934 under the Roosevelt administration, was simple: During working years, employees, their employers, and self-employed people pay Social Security taxes. These payroll taxes, paid by current employees, provide benefits only for current retirees. The money paid in is not an annuity invested at interest for the employees' own future benefit as in private pension funds. Instead, Social Security is a pay-as-you-go, or a cash in–cash out system. That is, the money paid in currently is used only to pay benefits to the 41.9 million people receiving benefits and to pay administrative costs of the program. The money paid in this month is used this same month to pay out benefits to recipients. Then, when today's workers become eligible for benefits, the money they will be receiving will not be the funds they paid in but rather the money that the workers will pay in at that time. Surplus funds not required for current benefit payments and expenses are invested in interest-bearing U.S. government securities.

In the early 1980s, Social Security began to incur deficits and had to receive help from the Treasury. Actuarial projections at the time indicated that the situation

FIGURE 18–1   Fate of the Retirement Kitty

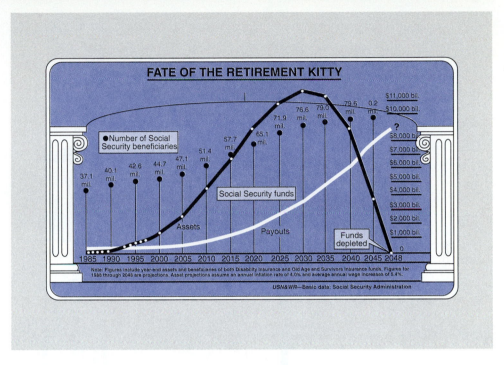

SOURCE: *U.S. News & World Report,* June 13, 1988, 71. Chart by Richard Gage and James Trautman.

would go from bad to worse. They showed that Social Security was heading for bankruptcy in the 21st century, as indicated in Figure 18–1. This was due to:

1. The projected retirement of the baby boom generation of the 1940s and 1950s

2. Increased life expectancy of retirees

3. A decline of new younger entrants into the labor market

Figure 18–2 clearly shows the magnitude of this problem.

During the early 1980s, these projections caused concern and social insecurity throughout the working and retired population. Many younger people began to doubt whether they would ever collect any benefits when they become eligible. Older people were fearful of losing all or part of their pensions. The 1983 reform of Social Security financing rescued it by establishing higher Social Security taxes and a long-term rise in the retirement age and implementing cuts in other benefits. In repairing Social Security, lawmakers changed the rules so that you will likely receive less income during your retirement than do today's elderly, taking inflation into account.

Congress deliberately created a built-in annual surplus. While baby boomers are in their prime earning years, Social Security takes in substantially more than it pays

FIGURE 18–2   **Fewer Workers to Shoulder the Load**

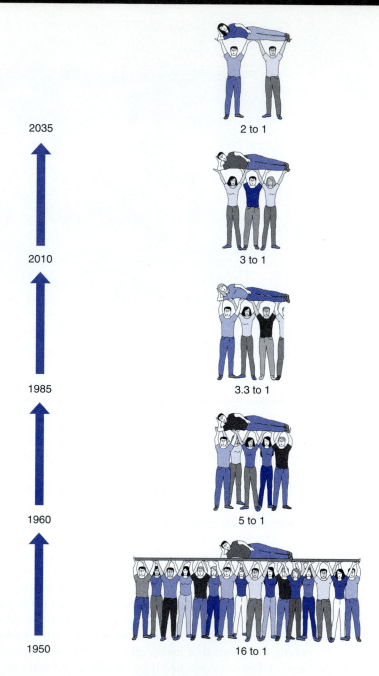

2035

2010

1985

1960

1950

In 1950 there were 16 workers paying in to Social Security for each beneficiary. That ratio shrinks to 2 to 1 in 2035.

SOURCE: 1984 Report of the Board of Trustees of Social Security Trust Funds.

out. In 1987 it ran a $21.9 billion surplus. By 1993 the annual surplus was about $53 billion. By 2030, the Social Security trust funds are slated to grow to $11.8 trillion, enough to cover the national debt. This surplus ought to ease the fears of the baby boomers that Social Security might not exist when they retire. The surplus is intended to offset the additional claims on Social Security early in the next century when the baby boom generation begins retiring. Without these surpluses, which are placed in trust funds, the baby boomers' children and grandchildren would have to pay punishingly high payroll taxes.

Let us now move from these broader issues to the narrower focus of what Social Security offers you and how it fits into your financial life.

How to Qualify for Coverage: Eligibility Requirements

To qualify for benefits, workers must earn **work credits** known as quarters of coverage on their Social Security account. A work credit is simply a unit that stands for a specific amount of money that a worker earned during a certain period. A worker in 1993 received one credit for $590 of earned income covered by Social Security. Only four work credits can be earned in one year, regardless of how much the worker earned in dollars. A worker in 1993 earned four credits if his or her covered annual earnings are $2,360 or more. As of 1991, at least 40 work credits or 10 years was needed to be fully insured. The amount of earnings needed to get a work credit, or quarter of coverage, will increase automatically in the future to keep pace with average wages.

FICA: Social Security Taxes

FICA

If you are employed, your Social Security tax is deducted from your wages each payday. Your employer matches your payment and sends the combined amount to the Internal Revenue Service. Your paycheck stub or payroll document may list Social Security deductions as **FICA (Federal Insurance Contributions Act)**. As of 1990, employees and employers each contribute 7.65 percent on the first $51,600 of a worker's income. The maximum an employee paid therefore was ($51,600 × .0765 =) $3,947.45. A change in the law for 1991 divided Social Security and Medicare taxes into separate categories. While the total tax remained at 7.65 percent, the Social Security tax rate of 6.2 percent was withheld on the first $53,400 and the 1.45 percent of Medicare tax was withheld on the first $125,000 of wages. The maximum tax for a wage earner earning $125,000 a year was .062($53,400) + .0145($125,000) = $5,123.30.

In 1994 the amount of earnings subject to the 6.2 percent rate increased to $60,600, and the amount of earnings subject to the 1.45 percent rate increased to $145,000. These amounts are adjusted periodically to keep up with inflation.

Self-employed persons bear the burden of paying both the employee and employer contributions for a total of 15.3 percent, or double that for an employee. Nearly all self-employment is covered by Social Security. Earnings for Social Security are reported at the same time as federal income tax returns are filed.

Employees who work for more than one employer in a year and pay Social Security taxes on wages over the maximum amount may claim a refund of the excess amount on their income tax return for that year. As long as workers have earnings

TABLE 18–3	Annual Benefits from Maximum Salary	
If you retire in...	**You can expect payments of**	
1990	$ 9,867	
1995	$10,708	
2000	$11,923	
2005	$13,257	
2010	$14,645	
2015	$16,014	
2020	$17,261	
2025	$18,550	

SOURCE: Social Security Administration.

that are covered by the law, they continue to pay Social Security taxes regardless of their age and even if they are receiving Social Security benefits.

Retirement Benefits: How Much Can You Expect to Get?

After workers reach age 60½, the Social Security Administration will estimate their benefits based upon their full work history, assuming they retire at 65. Exactly how much they receive depends on how long they have worked, their age at retirement, and how much their spouse earned. Benefits generally are based on workers' earnings over most of their career, not their salary the last year they worked. Workers cannot pay in more to increase their benefits. The Social Security Administration averages a

LET ME SEE IF I UNDERSTAND THIS--IN SPITE OF ALL THE WARNINGS, IN SPITE OF ALL THE EFFORTS OF OUR PRESIDENT, KNOWING FULL WELL HOW MUCH FINANCIAL TROUBLE WE'RE IN, YOU WENT RIGHT AHEAD AND GOT OLD!

SOCIAL SECURITY
TAKE A NUMBER AND HAVE A SEAT

SOURCE: Reprinted by permission of Tribune Media Services.

worker's income from age 22 to 62, not counting his or her lowest five years of income.

Table 18–4 shows how much retirees can expect to receive from Social Security each year if they have made the maximum contribution during most of their working years. You will note that the payments increase over time. This happens because Social Security currently guarantees that benefits in succeeding years will be essentially "inflation proof" by raising them annually to match increases in the consumer price index.

Unless you happen to be on the brink of retirement, it is very difficult to get an accurate estimate of your Social Security benefits. From time to time, you may see charts and tables, like the one in Table 18–4, that purport to give an estimate of how much money you can expect upon retirement. These calculations are hit-or-miss propositions at best. They make certain assumptions that may not apply to you, such as that you will stay healthy, work continuously, receive average pay increases, and that the rate of inflation is fixed. A more useful way to estimate your benefits is to look at what percentage of your annual earnings Social Security is likely to replace. Right now, if you earn at or slightly above the maximum taxable amount, you can count on Social Security to replace approximately 20 percent of your current earnings. Clearly, these funds are not designed to be your main source of income upon retirement.

Retirement Age

The older you are when you retire, the higher your Social Security benefit will be. If you retire early, you will receive less. Currently if you begin tapping your benefits at age 62, your monthly checks will be 20.8 percent less for life than if you wait until the traditional retirement age of 65 (see Table 18–4). The current reduction is

TABLE 18–4	Your Eligibility Age for Retirement			
Year of Birth	Full Retirement Age (Years/Months)	Credit for Each Year of Delayed Retirement	Attainment of Age 62	Benefit Reduction for Choosing Early Retirement at Age 62
1938	65/2	6.5%	2000	20.8%
1939	65/4	7.0%	2001	21.7%
1940	65/6	7.0%	2002	22.5%
1941	65/8	7.5%	2003	23.3%
1942	65/10	7.5%	2004	24.2%
1943–1954	66/0	8.0%	2005–16	25.0%
1955	66/2	8.0%	2017	25.8%
1956	66/4	8.0%	2018	26.7%
1957	66/6	8.0%	2019	27.5%
1958	66/8	8.0%	2020	28.3%
1959	66/10	8.0%	2021	29.2%
1960 and after	67/0	8.0%	2022+	30.0%

SOURCE: Social Security Amendment of 1983.

⅚ of 1 percent per month for each month you retire before age 65. For example, if you retire at age 63½ (18 months before age 65), your monthly benefit would be reduced by (⅚ × 18 =) 10 percent. But that percentage will gradually increase after the year 2000. Those who will retire at 62 after 2022 will get 30 percent less. Only people born before 1938 can get 100 percent of their retirement benefit at the traditional age of 65.

Starting in the year 2000, the age at which full benefits are payable will be increased in gradual steps until it reaches 67. This will affect people born in 1938 and later. The minimum age for getting the most you are entitled to, as shown in Table 18–4, will increase by two months a year, reaching 66 in 2005. From 2006 through 2016, the minimum age will stay at 66. After that, it will go up by one month a year until it reaches 67 in 2027. Therefore, for anyone born in 1960 or after, 67 is the earliest age at which he or she can receive full benefits. Early retirees will be penalized, but late retirees will benefit.

Does Early Retirement Pay?

Currently, if you have a good income from investments, rents, royalties, or other nonemployment sources, enough so you can save and invest all or part of your Social Security pension, collecting at 62 will financially be profitable. Permanently forfeiting 20 percent appears at first to be a major deterrent to retiring early. But the money you would collect during the three years between ages 62 to 65 will put you ahead for quite a while. If you wait until you are 65 to start receiving benefits, it will take you 12 years to break even, that is, to collect the money you passed up by not retiring at 62. If you did not use your early pension but invested it or put it in the bank, the earnings on it may more than make up the reduction in pension when you reach 65 years of age. Many 62-year-olds apparently came to the same conclusion since each year about half of the applicants for benefits sign up at age 62 for the smaller check.

Delayed Retirement

Older employees have an incentive to work in the form of a delayed retirement credit. Social Security benefits increased by 3.5 percent each year for those who reached 65 during 1990 and 1991 and who delayed collecting benefits. As shown in Table 18–4, the credit will rise .5 percent every other year until it reaches 8 percent in 2005. In other words, after the year 2005, if workers postpone collecting benefits until the age of 70, they will receive 40 percent more monthly than if they had retired at 65.

Partial Retirement: The Earnings Test

Another option besides early retirement or delayed retirement available to workers is partial retirement. Workers do not have to retire completely to get Social Security checks. But their earnings from work will affect their Social Security benefits. Social Security laws set up stumbling blocks to work. Monthly payments generally are reduced if earnings go above a certain level. The measure used to decide whether benefits must be reduced or stopped is called the **earnings test**. The earnings test

The Early Retirement Calculation

Harry Henderson is entitled to $750 at age 65 but decides to retire at 62 with the maximum 20 percent reduction in benefits. Harry receives 80 percent of $750, or $600 monthly. He sacrifices $150 a month in order to retire three years early. If we ignore the time value of money concepts for simplicity, during these three years he receives 36 checks for $600, totaling $21,600. Had Harry waited until 65, it would take him 144 months, or 12 years, to retrieve the $21,600 lost (since $150 × 144 = $21,600). He would be 77 before the extra $150 a month added up to $21,600 (again ignoring the opportunity cost). The case for taking early retirement may be even stronger if Harry does not need the money and can afford to save it all. If he did not spend the monthly benefit (assuming he has other income) but invested or banked it and received an average return of say 8.5 percent, his savings plus compound interest after the three years would equal approximately to $25,000. After the three years, he would receive $2,210 interest annually, or $184 monthly. Therefore, at 65, Harry will have the extra monthly income of $184 to compensate the $150 reduction in monthly benefits, plus he has the added advantage of having the $26,000 in the bank or in an investment portfolio.

sets a limit on the amount workers can earn without losing any of their retirement benefits. It applies to everyone who gets Social Security retirement checks except those who are 70 or older. At age 70, the work penalty is dropped. Different rules, which include medical considerations, also apply to work performed by people receiving checks because of disability.

Unearned incomes from sources such as dividends, interest, insurance, or rent are not included in the earnings test calculations. In general, workers can receive all benefits due them for the year if their earnings do not exceed the annual exempt amount. This limit changes periodically. As of 1990, if workers' earnings go over the annual limit, then $1 will be deducted from their benefits for each $3 they earn above the exempt amount, between age 65 and 70 ($1 per each $2 if under age 65).

Are Benefits Taxable?

Up to one-half of Social Security benefits may be subject to federal income taxes. Social Security laws set up stumbling blocks to work. Benefits become taxable once the total of a worker's adjusted gross income, tax-exempt interest income, and one-half of his or her Social Security benefits exceeds a base amount. For 1993 the base amount was $32,000 for couples, or $25,000 for individuals.

Cost of Living Adjustment

You may worry that, because of price inflation, the dollars you receive in future years will have less and less purchasing power. Under current law, Social Security benefits are increased when living costs rise 3 percent over a given period. That provision seems to be perennially under attack in Congress and there is no telling how the cost of living adjustment will work or whether it will be in effect at all years down the road.

Survivors Benefits

A monthly benefit plus a lump-sum death (or burial) benefit is paid to the eligible surviving spouse or children of a worker who dies. Survivors benefits are not automatically paid to the surviving children or spouse of a deceased. If, for example, a man dies and is survived by a working wife under 60 without minor children, then she is not qualified to collect survivors benefits. Neither will surviving children over age 18 be eligible. In order to qualify for benefits, the surviving relatives must match one of the following categories:

1. Unmarried children under 18, or children under 19 attending high school full-time

2. Unmarried children who were severely disabled before age 22 and continue to be disabled

3. A widow or widower age 60 or over

4. A widow or widower or surviving divorced mother or father if the person is caring for the worker's child under age 16 who is getting a benefit based on the worker's earnings

5. A widow or widower age 50 or older who is disabled or later becomes so

6. Dependent parents age 62 or older

7. A divorced spouse aged 62 or older

Disability Insurance

Nearly 3 million American workers are now receiving Social Security benefits because they have been disabled. Under Social Security rules, as discussed in Chapter 7, workers are considered disabled if they cannot engage in any substantial gainful activity because of a medically determined physical or mental impairment that can be expected to end in death or last for a continuous period of at least a year. If a worker meets these requirements and has worked long enough to be covered under Social Security, the worker and his or her dependents will be entitled to Social Security checks and, after two years, Medicare health insurance.

There is a five-month waiting period before disability payments begin. Once they do, they continue as long as the beneficiary is unable to perform "substantial gainful work."

Rules governing eligibility for Social Security disability benefits are complicated and have been significantly tightened in recent years. A key point is that you must be able to prove not merely that you are unable to do your previous kind of work but that you are now physically or mentally unable to do any other kind of gainful work.

Medicare Insurance

Medicare comes in two parts—hospital and medical insurance—which help protect people 65 and over from the high costs of health care. Disabled people under 65 who

Supplemental Security Income

Supplemental security income (SSI) is a federal program designed to provide financial assistance to specific people with very low incomes, people over 65, the blind, and the disabled. The program is administered by Social Security, but it is financed through general revenues, not through the taxes you pay into Social Security. In order to be eligible, an individual must prove to Social Security that he or she had less than $2,000 in assets (in 1990). For a couple, the 1990 figure is $3,000.

have been entitled to Social Security disability benefits for 24 or more months are also eligible for Medicare. Medicare is handled by the Health Care Financing Administration, not by Social Security. But the people at Social Security offices will help those eligible apply for Medicare and process claim forms.

People pay for Medicare insurance during their working years. It is part of the Social Security taxes each worker, employer, and self-employed person pays. But more than two-thirds of the costs of the medical insurance premium is paid from general revenues of the federal government. For further discussion of disability insurance and Medicare see, Chapter 7, Health and Disability Insurance.

Checking Your Social Security Records

Your wages and self-employment income are entered on your Social Security record throughout your working years. The amount of Social Security benefits you will receive from Social Security during your retirement years is based on how much money you have earned, up to a maximum, not on what you paid into the system. You cannot check on how much you have paid in, but you can check on the amount of earnings the Social Security Administration (SSA) has on record for you.

The Social Security Administration itself urges everyone to run a check on a regular basis, every three years or so, of his or her Social Security records. To check up on your record, call 800/772-1213 or visit or write to the nearest Social Security office and ask for **Form SSA-7004**, "Request for Personal Earnings and Benefit Estimate Statement" (see Figure 18–3). This is a questionnaire requesting a number of facts, including your name, Social Security number, date of birth, previous year's earnings, the age at which you plan to retire, and your projected earnings from now to retirement. About four to six weeks after mailing in the form, you can expect to receive an eight-page document called a Personal Earnings and Benefit Estimate Statement. It will contain this list of estimated benefits:

1. Your monthly retirement check from Social Security in today's dollars at your stated retirement age

2. The full benefit you could get by waiting until you are age 65 to retire

3. Your benefit if you continue working until age 70

4. Your survivor's monthly benefit if you die during the current calendar year

FIGURE 18–3 **Form SSA-7004**

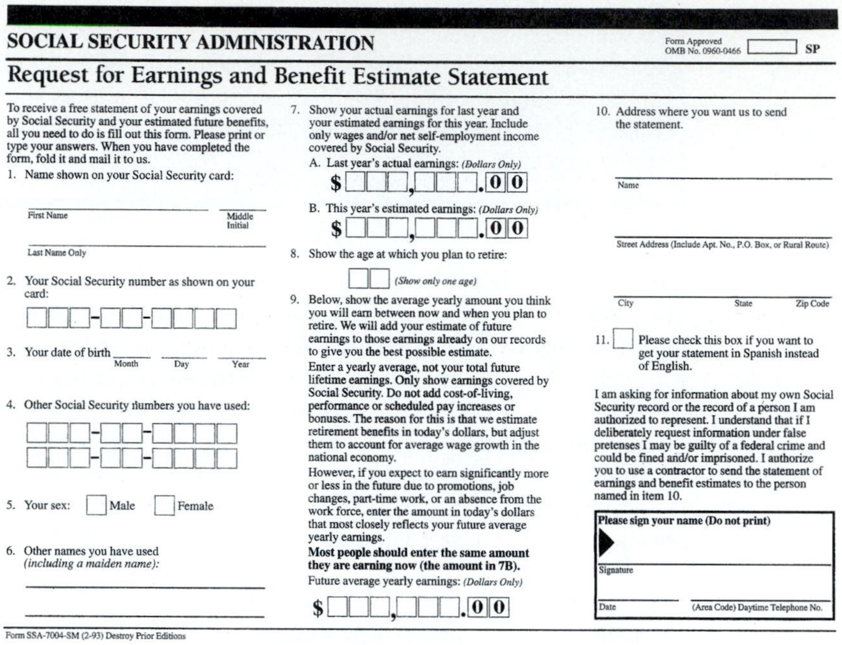

SOCIAL SECURITY ADMINISTRATION Form Approved OMB No. 0960-0466 SP

Request for Earnings and Benefit Estimate Statement

To receive a free statement of your earnings covered by Social Security and your estimated future benefits, all you need to do is fill out this form. Please print or type your answers. When you have completed the form, fold it and mail it to us.

1. Name shown on your Social Security card:
   First Name / Middle Initial
   Last Name Only
2. Your Social Security number as shown on your card:
3. Your date of birth Month Day Year
4. Other Social Security numbers you have used:
5. Your sex: Male Female
6. Other names you have used *(including a maiden name)*:
7. Show your actual earnings for last year and your estimated earnings for this year. Include only wages and/or net self-employment income covered by Social Security.
   A. Last year's actual earnings: *(Dollars Only)* $, .00
   B. This year's estimated earnings: *(Dollars Only)* $, .00
8. Show the age at which you plan to retire: *(Show only one age)*
9. Below, show the average yearly amount you think you will earn between now and when you plan to retire. We will add your estimate of future earnings to those earnings already on our records to give you the best possible estimate.
   Enter a yearly average, not your total future lifetime earnings. Only show earnings covered by Social Security. Do not add cost-of-living, performance or scheduled pay increases or bonuses. The reason for this is that we estimate retirement benefits in today's dollars, but adjust them to account for average wage growth in the national economy.
   However, if you expect to earn significantly more or less in the future due to promotions, job changes, part-time work, or an absence from the work force, enter the amount in today's dollars that most closely reflects your future average yearly earnings.
   Most people should enter the same amount they are earning now (the amount in 7B).
   Future average yearly earnings: *(Dollars Only)* $, .00
10. Address where you want us to send the statement.
   Name
   Street Address (Include Apt. No., P.O. Box, or Rural Route)
   City State Zip Code
11. Please check this box if you want to get your statement in Spanish instead of English.

I am asking for information about my own Social Security record or the record of a person I am authorized to represent. I understand that if I deliberately request information under false pretenses I may be guilty of a federal crime and could be fined and/or imprisoned. I authorize you to use a contractor to send the statement of earnings and benefit estimates to the person named in item 10.

Please sign your name (Do not print)
Signature
Date (Area Code) Daytime Telephone No.

Form SSA-7004-SM (2-93) Destroy Prior Editions

SOURCE: Social Security Administration.

5. Your disability benefits if you will be unable to work for at least a year or if you are terminally ill or disabled

6. A year-by-year statement of your earnings that were subject to Social Security taxes and of the Social Security taxes that you paid

The Personal Earnings and Benefits Estimate Statement will also tell you whether you are a victim of the most common error, having zero earnings posted for a year that you were working. That happens when an employer reports your wages under an incorrect Social Security number.

Maximum amounts of employment earnings that can count for Social Security are shown in the accompanying table. No matter how much you earned, you are credited only up to a certain maximum amount. The SSA cares only about what you earn up to the maximum taxable earnings per year and does not record anything above that level.

For more detailed information, including the names of everyone you ever worked for starting with your first job, you have to visit the Social Security office in person.

There is no cause for panic if you find that your records are not accurate. It is up to you to find out if errors have been made and to see that they are corrected. The best protection is through maintaining your own Social Security file. If you are employed, keep all pay slips, check stubs, W-2 forms and the statements of amounts withheld from your pay check each year for income taxes and Social Security taxes. If you are self-employed, keep copies of all your Social Security tax reports and the addresses of the IRS offices to which they were sent.

A change in the law in 1990 required the Social Security Administration to correct your record, no matter how long ago the error occurred. Before 1990, most errors that occurred more than three years earlier could not be corrected.

TABLE 18–5	Maximum Annual Earnings Subject to Social Security Tax
Year	**Maximum Annual Earnings Subject to Social Security Tax**
1937–50	$ 3,000
1951–54	3,600
1955–58	4,200
1959–65	4,800
1966–67	6,600
1968–71	7,800
1972	9,000
1973	10,800
1974	13,200
1975	14,100
1976	15,300
1977	16,500
1978	17,700
1979	22,900
1980	25,900
1981	29,700
1982	32,400
1983	35,700
1984	37,800
1985	39,600
1986	42,000
1987	43,800
1988	45,000
1989	48,000
1990	51,600
1991	53,400
1992	55,500
1993	57,600

SOURCE: Social Security Administration.

Private Retirement Programs: Company Pension Plans

It has been an American tradition for employees to devote their working lives to a company with the promise that their loyalty will be repaid with a pension that provides a decent standard of living. Unfortunately, this promise is not always honored.

An employee's first step in retirement planning should be to become familiar with the company's retirement benefit program. Federal law requires pension plan administrators to give participants understandable information about the plans, including details about the requirements for receiving the benefits and any conditions that might prevent someone from receiving them.

Most companies provide some private retirement programs either in the form of a pension annuity or savings program. Employees who retire after working 25 years at a company with a good pension plan often can expect to receive about 70 percent of their salary. Less generous plans may pay only 40 percent.

The Tax Incentive

Typically, pension funds are set aside and managed by trustees or outside financial institutions, frequently insurance companies. As an incentive to employers to begin and maintain plans, the government defers taxes on the pension contributions and their earnings.

Retirement money can therefore be saved only through a qualified pension plan or tax sheltered account such as individual retirement accounts (IRAs) or Keoghs (explained further on). Once money qualifies as retirement savings, it remains free of taxes until withdrawn. This does not mean that it is frozen. Often it can be moved from one financial instrument to another. Retirees pay income taxes on the money as they receive it.

To evaluate a pension program, employees have to carefully examine the features of the plan. This is not an easy task. Designed by actuaries and written by lawyers, pension plans are loaded with perplexing formulas and terminology.

Before workers can dissect their plans, they will need to differentiate between the various types of plans. Let us survey the most common company pension plans available.

Defined Benefit Plans

Most companies offer **defined benefit plans**. Defined benefit plans provide workers, upon retirement, with a fixed sum that is paid at regular intervals (usually monthly) for the rest of their lives. Employees receive a yearly statement that shows how much they have accumulated so far. Projecting ahead from these figures (assuming continued employment with the company and calculation of expected salary increases and projected inflation rates) can provide an approximate estimation of benefits upon retirement.

The company sets up a fund to which it makes annual contributions that the actuaries (professional mathematicians who specialize in pension and insurance fund planning) estimate are required to pay for retirement and other benefits when they fall due. The company then pays into the fund each year whatever is needed to cover expected benefit payments. Thus, the contribution a company makes is not fixed. It is determined actuarially, based upon projections of how many employees will receive benefits and how much the benefits will amount to. Those benefits are predetermined according to formulas laid out in the pension plan's charter. Contributions to the fund are invested in stocks, bonds, mortgages and other assets, and the income they generate helps pay for future benefits.

The more the fund's assets earn, the less the employer needs to contribute. But regardless of how much or little the fund earns, the company remains responsible for covering "funding" of the promised benefits. In other words, if the plan says you will get $500 a month starting at age 65, the pension fund will need to have enough to pay you $500 a month.

Most companies base their pensions on the average of an employee's last five years' salary at work or longer. The better plans average the last three years. Formulas that base the pension on employees' salaries during their final few years of service usually provide the most inflation protection because salaries normally increase over the years along with the cost of living. Some plans use employees' career average salary, which includes their early low-earning years. This works to an employee's disadvantage.

Companies typically calculate benefits by multiplying the number of years an employee participated in the plan times 1.4 to 1.7 percent of his or her average salary during the last years at work. For example, a worker covered by his pension for 20 years, whose final salary is $40,000, might get an $11,200 annual pension. The $11,200 is derived by multiplying 20 years $\times$ 1.4 percent $\times$ $40,000, or $40,000 $\times$ .28 = $11,200.

The number of defined benefit plans has been declining since 1983 as shown in Figure 18–4.

Defined Contribution Plans

A **defined contribution plan** stipulates a formula for annual employer payments into the pension fund. Such plans may be set up in a variety of ways. One method is where the contributions are fixed.

A typical formula, for example, might require an employer to make an annual contribution of 6 percent of each employee's salary. The benefits paid at retirement are not determined beforehand but depend on the amount that has accumulated in an employee's account. That account will be used to buy an annuity (discussed further on) or will be given to the employee in a lump sum. This arrangement fixes a rate for employer contributions to the fund. Future retirement benefits depend on how fast the fund grows. Thus, companies have a good idea of what their pension costs will be, but employees cannot be sure of the size of their retirement checks.

In defined contribution plans, employees have an individual account in which are accumulated the contributions made for them plus their share of the plan's investment earnings. An employee's account balance is his or her **accrued benefit**. Upon retirement, the employee receives whatever benefits the money will provide at the time. If the trustees do not invest the fund's assets wisely, the worker comes out with less than he or she might have anticipated. In other words, employees, not the fund, bear the investment risk. Pension benefits are not guaranteed ahead of time. Ideally to prepare for a financially secure retirement, a typical worker needs to contribute 15 percent of his or her salary over a career of 35 years. This amount is several times higher than companies usually set aside today.

FIGURE 18–4	A Decline in Defined Benefits Plans

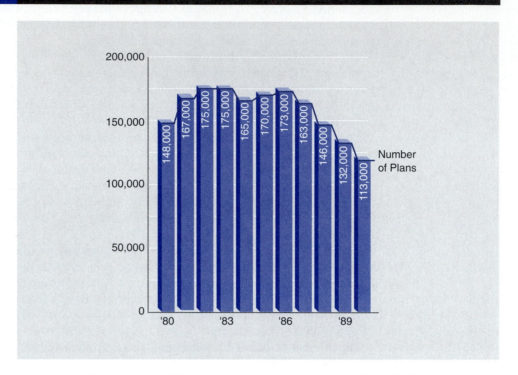

According to the most recent figures available, we are experiencing a decline in the number of defined benefits plans in effect at U.S. companies.

SOURCE: Employee Benefits Research Institute.

Among the more common defined contribution plans are the following:

1. Simplified employee pension plans (SEP)

2. 401(K)

3. Profit sharing

4. Keoghs

5. ESOPs

Let us now examine each one.

Simplified Employee Pension (SEP)

A **simplified employee pension,** nicknamed **SEP,** is a pension plan that may indeed be true to its name in that it is simple to set up and administer. Congress created SEPs under the Revenue Act of 1978 to provide a simple, inexpensive, and tax-advantaged pension vehicle.

SEPs are a way for owners of small incorporated or unincorporated businesses, consultants, and free lancers to provide themselves as well as their employees with pension and tax benefits without the complicated paperwork of qualified pension and Keogh plans.

To establish a SEP, an employer can simply complete a half page IRS form, 5305-SEP, and distribute copies to the employees. The employer then makes a "written allocation formula" that details the percentage of salary used for making contributions. Often the financial institution where the funds are deposited supplies the requisite forms and takes care of reporting the details of the plan to the employees. The employer does not have to file detailed annual reports with the Department of Labor or IRS. The employer is required only to include the amount contributed to a SEP on the employees' W-2 form.

Though SEPs are designed to encourage small firms without pension plans to set up retirement programs, self-employed people who do not have Keoghs (which are described later) may also find SEPs appealing. They permit small businesses and people who work for themselves to contribute up to $30,000 per year, depending upon the profits, to their own IRA (described later) accounts and those of eligible employees. All contributions are deductible from self-employment income and earnings accumulate tax free. Employers can establish a SEP at banks, insurance companies, mutual funds, brokerage firms, and just about anywhere that a Keogh plan, 401(K), or IRA is sponsored.

When an employer establishes an SEP, the employee opens an individual retirement account (IRA) at a bank or other financial institution. The employer then contributes directly to that IRA. The employer gets a business deduction for the amount put in. The employee pays no taxes on the deposit or on earnings on the account until withdrawals occur. While a SEP works just like an individual retirement account, there is one big difference. Only $2,000 a year can be deposited into an IRA but as much as $30,000 a year can go into a SEP–IRA.

An employer, however, cannot put in more than 15 percent of an employee's annual earnings. For example, if an employee earns $50,000, the employer contribution cannot exceed $7,500. Deposits need not hit the same percentage each year, nor do they have to be made every year.

All corporate contributions are fully vested immediately, which means you own 100 percent of your pension plan and can collect it even if you leave the company before you retire. (Vesting is discussed more fully later in this chapter.) Your use of the SEP account is restricted by the IRS. If you withdraw money before age 59½, you'll pay a 10 percent penalty.

SEPs have increasingly become more popular as the rules of other retirement plans have grown more complex.

401(K) Salary Reduction Plans

Growing numbers of people have been offered another choice for their retirement savings—a tax-deferred salary reduction plan bearing the uninviting title of **401(K)**, named for the section of the Internal Revenue Service code that authorized them.

This popular program (see Figure 18–5) has since 1981 allowed employees to contribute pre-tax salary dollars into a retirement plan administered by their employer. Although 401(K)s are employer sponsored, employees can usually select the way their money is invested from a menu of choices. Typical options include a money

FIGURE 18–5   **A Rise in 401(K) Plans**

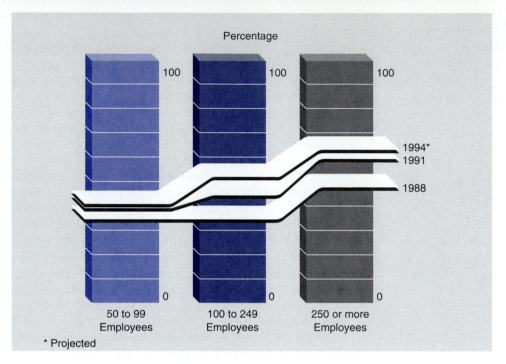

The percentage of U.S. companies offering 401(K) plans has increased dramatically over the last several years, with the greatest percentage among large companies.

SOURCE: Gallup and publisher estimates.

market mutual fund and portfolios of stocks and bonds. The 401(K) is like a glorified IRA in that it lets employees shelter part of their pre-tax income and watch the earnings accumulate tax free until they make withdrawals. But unlike an IRA, 401(K) plans can be set up only by an employer's company. Individuals cannot set one up on their own.

Many firms match all or part of employee contributions to a 401(K), which greatly enhances the tax-deferred return on their principal. All employee, as well as employer, contributions to a 401(K) are considered "deferred compensation" and are not taxed as part of an employee's annual income. The money is deductible from employees' paychecks and does not even appear on their W-2 form. That is, employees pay no tax on it until they take it out, usually at retirement, at which time they are likely to be in a bracket considerably lower than their present one. In addition, the amount set aside reduces their current gross income. An individual electing this plan would thus be taxed on his or her earnings minus the amount deferred.

For example, if you earn $40,000 and you put $5,000 into a 401(K), your taxable income is only $35,000. So you may well slip into a lower tax bracket when you file your 1040.

Maximum employee contributions to 401(K) plans were $8,994 annually in 1993, less any amounts contributed to an IRA. This limit does not include employer matching contributions. The $8,994 ceiling is increased annually with the consumer price index. The maximum amount that can go into a 401(K), including employee and employer contributions, is the lesser of $30,000, or 25 percent of annual salary. A 10 percent penalty plus a 20 percent withholding tax generally applies to early withdrawals. After age 59½, employees can withdraw the principal and interest in a lump sum.

Although contributions are locked up until an employee reaches age 59½, they can be withdrawn under certain circumstances. Employees can take their money out without penalty only if they become disabled, unemployed, or encounter an immediate and heavy financial hardship. The IRS has defined an "immediate and heavy financial hardship" to be such things as needing cash to pay funeral expenses, tuition, or medical bills for a family member, or to make a down payment on a home that will be an employee's main residence. Upon leaving a company, employees can also take their savings with them. But if they keep the money, it becomes taxable as current income. They can avoid current taxes by having the former employer roll it over into their new employer's pension plan or in an IRA, if that plan allows it.

If employees plead hardship, they are permitted to withdraw only their own money (not the employer contribution) and still have to pay a 10 percent penalty as well as income tax on the sum. The penalty is waived if they use the money to pay medical expenses that exceed 7.5 percent of their adjusted gross income.

When a plan is set up, it specifies how the money is to be invested. Usually the employer selects an investment adviser and offers employees a choice of investments, such as a common stock fund, a money market fund, a guaranteed interest contract, or an annuity. Employees can often split contributions between the choices the company offers.

The responsibility for investment selection falls squarely upon the employee, who is usually given the opportunity to switch assets in and out of funds on a quarterly basis. The plan usually supplements an employer's primary pension plan.

As employers are slashing their benefits budgets, many workers have come to realize that 401(K) retirement plans are the wave of the future rather than the more traditional defined benefit plans.

Profit-Sharing Plans

Another arrangement takes the form of a **profit-sharing** program. The employer contributes a certain percentage of the company's profits each year to the retirement fund. The employee's eventual benefits depend upon the size of these contributions and their accrued investment earnings. In this system, the company contributes more to a pension plan in profitable years and less in lean years. In most cases, the company contributes up to 15 percent of employees' salaries while employees contribute up to 10 percent. The interest in workers' accounts accumulates tax free until withdrawn.

Integrated Plans

Many plans take into account the benefits workers are to receive from Social Security and adjust the plan's benefits accordingly. These are known as **integrated plans.**

Looking to the Future of Your 401(K)

The benefits of a 401(K) plan include tax-deferred compounding of interest in addition to the continuing contributions of the employee. When those benefits are boosted by matching contributions from the employer, the 401(K) could provide huge benefits at retirement. The figures shown below are based on the following assumptions: The plan earns 8 percent a year, the employee's salary grows 4 percent annually, and the employer matches 50 cents on the dollar for every contribution up to 6 percent of the employee's salary.

VALUE OF PLAN UPON RETIREMENT AT AGE 62

	Annual Contribution	
	6 percent	**10 percent**
25-year-old earning $25,000	$797,788	$1,152,650
35-year-old earning $40,000	506,556	731,692
42-year-old earning $70,000	433,923	626,777
53-year-old earning $80,000	122,163	176,457

The company must deduct Social Security benefits directly or may integrate them in certain specified ways. Many such plans are designed so that the Social Security benefit plus the pension benefit will replace a certain percentage of preretirement income.

The results of integration, however, sometimes mean that low-paid employees receive a very small company pension or none at all. This is due to the fact that the Social Security benefit formula gives low-paid employees a higher percentage of their preretirement income than it gives high-paid employees. If an employer designs a pension plan that, when integrated into Social Security, replaces the same percentages of preretirement income for all employees, it is obvious that the employer's plan will be tilted toward high-paid employees.

Keogh Plan

Another retirement program, designed for people who are self-employed, is the **Keogh plan**. This plan, favored by doctors, dentists, attorneys, and other professionals, permits self-employed people to set aside money, deduct the investment from taxable income, and defer tax on earnings from the investment until age 59½ or later, the retirement years when income and tax rates typically drop. The contribution limit is 20 percent of earned income, to a maximum nontaxable contribution of $30,000 annually. Dividends, interest, and other gains made by Keogh investments accumulate tax free. Neither the contributions nor earnings are subject to tax until the money is withdrawn at retirement.

Self-employed people can open a Keogh at most banks, brokerage houses, insurance companies, and mutual funds. And they can set up as many Keoghs as they want as long as the combined totals do not exceed the legal ceiling.

The major disadvantage of Keogh plans is the onerous disclosure forms that account owners must file annually with the IRS, which may cost several hundred dollars in accountant fees.

ESOP: Employee Stock Ownership Plan

Employee participation in company ownership has long been a popular idea, envisioned as a way to give the nation's workforce a stake in American business and a direct interest in their company's success.

A fast growing program for employee ownership today is the **employee stock ownership plan** (or stock option plan) or **ESOP**. An ESOP is customarily structured as a retirement fund to which the company makes regular contributions on behalf of its participating workers. ESOPS may also take the form of incentive plans for workers. The fund is required to invest this money primarily in the company's own stock and bonds. The ESOP is a defined contribution pension plan. Some 8,000 companies with more than 8 million employees have ESOPs or similar plans. The most popular ESOP is incorporated with the above mentioned 401(K) plan, a tax-sheltered account that lets employees set aside a percentage of their pre-tax salary into the firm's shares with the employer matching the worker's contribution.

The tax advantages are considerable. The company's contributions are generally tax deductible. Employees pay taxes on their shares only when they receive them after retiring or leaving the company.

ESOP's Foibles

Putting all retirement funds into the company's own stock could be risky and denies employees the benefits of diversification. The ESOP movement is making the fates of companies and their employees more intertwined than ever. Bankruptcy of the firm could wipe out the retirement benefits of all concerned. Employees get a double blow if the employer goes bankrupt. They lose their jobs and could lose their pensions.

Pension Vesting (You *Can* Take Your Pension Plan with You)

While the mechanics of the defined benefit and defined contribution plans may differ, they both share a common element: **vesting**. Vesting means that employees are entitled to the money held in their account by the employer when they retire or leave, after having completed a certain number of years of service.

Just because employees are covered by a pension plan does not mean they will actually receive benefits. If employees do not stay at the job long enough to satisfy their plan's vesting requirements, they have no legal rights to any accrued pension benefits, except portions which are self-funded. Statistics show that the average male worker switches jobs every four and a half years; the average female worker switches every two and a half. Yet most plans, until 1987, required an employee to work for at least 10 years to receive any benefit. If job changing is your style, you should know how pension vesting works and how you can work it to your benefit.

The 1986 Tax Reform Act required corporate pension plans either to vest employees fully after five years of service or stretch the process out to seven years by vesting them with 20 percent of their pension benefits after three years, plus 20 percent in each one of the next four years. This is known as **partial vesting**. The rule went into effect in 1989, but the years that one worked for a company by then count. The 1986 rule does not apply for public sector employees.

Many young workers look askance at the length of time they must work until they are vested in their pension plans. But only employee contributions to a pension plan are returned to a worker if he or she leaves before vesting. The employer contributions are forfeited. Most likely, you will have to participate in a pension plan five to seven years before becoming vested, that is, before your employer's contributions belong to you. Not until you are vested can you take with you the right to a specified amount of income when you retire.

Companies do not want to liberalize vesting provisions, partly because they fear it will increase costs and partly because they have used pensions as inducements to keep employees on the job, thereby reducing the costs of employee turnover.

The Quest to Vest—Employee Retirement Income Security Act (ERISA)

In 1974, after a decade of hearings and debate over pension plan abuses and how to deal with them, Congress passed the **Employee Retirement Income Security Act**, better known as **ERISA**. ERISA spelled out the rights of pension plan participants. Though the act neither required a company to offer pensions nor specified the amount of a pension when voluntarily provided, it did set minimum standards for vesting, participation, and accrual of benefits.

ERISA also set minimum funding and fiduciary standards that required companies to finance retirement benefits in a systematic way and to give greater assurance that there would be enough money on hand to pay promised benefits. Under ERISA American companies have to prudently invest pension money in diversified instruments, mostly stocks and bonds; it is almost impossible for them to lend themselves money in their pension plans or invest in their own businesses. ERISA provided a guarantee that once an employee becomes vested and earns any pension benefits with an employer, he or she is entitled to some portion of them. However, these pensions are not transferable and do not necessarily build toward one big pension. With the exception of some multiemployer plans involving union pensions where credit can be built up and transferred from job to job, what they have earned with one employer is good only with that employer. Workers begin the vesting process anew each time they change jobs. And with each job switch, if they are vested, they acquire slices or slivers of a pension pie. The value of each slice depends upon how long they worked for each employer and their average salary during their employment.

ERISA also created the **Pension Benefit Guaranty Corporation** (PBGC), known (believe it or not) as Penny Benny. This wholly owned independent federal insurance agency guarantees the benefits of employees who participate in certain types of pension plans. It is empowered to insure the 85,000 private defined benefit plans and take over those that terminate without sufficient assets to pay off their guaranteed, vested benefits. It does not insure any defined contribution plans such as 401(K)s or profit-sharing programs. PBGC levies a flat rate premium per participant in each pension plan, with the rates set by Congress.

If the plan's assets are insufficient to cover all the vested benefits, the Pension Benefit Guarantee Corporation becomes the trustee of the plan, assuming its assets and liabilities and guaranteeing payments of all or some of those benefits. In 1993 PBGC guaranteed pensions of up to $29,250 a year for a 65-year-old. Nearly 41 million Americans, about one-third of the labor force, have private, employer-sponsored pensions that are insured by PBGC. PBGC assumed pension obligations of $1.2 billion in 1991 when bankruptcy permanently grounded Pan Am and Eastern Airlines.

Although it is certainly comforting to have government insurance available, PBGC's payout might fall short of what a pensioner expects. PBGC covers only vested benefits. If a plan terminated before an employee had enough service to become vested, PBGC is not obligated to pay him or her for the prevesting years of service.

Checking Out a Private Pension Program

The rules of each pension must by law be spelled out in a **trust agreement,** a highly technical instrument. ERISA requires that employers offering a pension plan provide employees with a simplified version of the plan's trust agreement, known as a **summary plan description,** which highlights basic information about the plan. You will probably need both documents and some help from the company's personnel office as well as your attorney to fully understand the plan.

A pension plan, just like an insurance policy or any other contract, must be studied and analyzed to fully understand its terms and conditions. This should be a major consideration when negotiating the terms of a new job. Your analysis should split into two questions: Will you work for the company long enough to vest? Will there actually be a company pension when you retire?

Here are some key points to investigate before accepting a job. Most of the questions below should be answered in the aforementioned documents.

1. Is the job covered by the company's pension plan? What are the requirements to be covered (age, rank, longevity)?

   The fact that a company has a pension plan does not always mean that everyone is eligible to join. Some companies have several different pension plans for different categories of employees. Others have what is known as "cafeteria" pension programs in which employees can choose the plans they want.

2. Is the plan a defined benefit or a defined contribution plan?

3. When will I become eligible for membership?

4. What is the formula for determining my benefits or, in a defined contribution plan, the employer's contribution?

   The formula will give you a rough idea of how much you may be entitled to at retirement so you can plan your savings and investments accordingly.

5. How long must I work before my benefits are vested?

   This is probably the plan's most important provision. Many plans do not fully vest until you have seven years of credited service. If you leave or are fired before then, you may in some instances come away with nothing. As mentioned, some plans vest in stages. Here again, you lose benefits if you leave before one of the scheduled vesting installments.

6. How are benefits finally figured?

7. Are the benefits integrated with Social Security?

8. What are the payout options?

9. How do I check benefits?

10. How are service years counted, by hours worked, months, weeks?

11. How many hours must I work during the year to remain in the plan and accrue benefits?
    Naturally, you want to satisfy the minimum if you have a choice. But the employer may specifically limit you to fewer hours so you do not qualify for a pension.

12. What would happen to my status in the plan and my pension credits if I took a leave of absence?

13. What is the earliest age or combination of age and years of service at which I may retire?

14. By how much will my retirement benefits be reduced if I retire early?

15. How much will my retirement benefit be increased if I work beyond age 65?

16. What will happen to my pension when I die?

17. Can I take money out of my savings plan before retirement?

18. Will my employer contribute to my savings plan if I do not?

19. How have the company's pension plans' investments performed?

20. What if the plan ends?

The Ins and Outs of Annuities

Another way to build your own portable pension is through a tax-deferred **annuity**. An annuity is a written contract between an individual and an insurance company. The company guarantees you, upon your retirement, a regular benefit for a specified period of time, up to as long as your lifetime. It is basically a sort of savings account in which you deposit a sum of money and from which you are paid regular, periodic (usually monthly) sums for the rest or your life, or your survivors' life or for a selected period of time. They are therefore a combination of insurance and savings program. You enjoy the rate of interest and the income specified for as long as you live. You are gambling that you will live a long time. The insurance company is betting against you.

"We're your parents Timothy—we're here to help you. So if you do have any questions about early retirement, please feel free to ask them."

SOURCE: *Changing Times*, September 1988, 108. © Michael Maslin 1988.

The basic appeal of annuities is the same as many life insurance products: Put away money now regularly, and it will come back to you regularly later in life. The chief value of annuities, whether purchased at retirement or earlier, is that they guarantee the holder a check in the mail no matter how long he or she lives, even if those payments ultimately total more than their investments. By contrast, when an IRA, Keogh, or other savings nest egg is depleted, the payouts from it end. Another main attraction of annuities is the tax-free accumulation of investment earnings. Unlike IRAs, the investment is not limited to $2,000 a year.

Annuities are issued by life insurance companies and are sold by their traditional agents or brokerage firms acting as agents. Annuity contracts have two phases, an **accumulation phase**, during which the account is built up by deposits and investment returns, and a **payout phase**, during which investors receive payments under the contract. Although they typically include a death benefit, annuity contracts, unlike life insurance policies, are geared to provide income after retirement rather than for heirs.

Although annuity contributions are not tax deductible, they offer the investor the benefit of deferring taxes on all interest earned until it is withdrawn. Because earnings in an annuity are not taxed until removed, assets build up more quickly than in conventional savings vehicles.

The following example (see also Table 18–6) illustrates the advantage of tax-deferred compounding: Assume that two investors, each in the 28 percent tax bracket, invest $100,000. Each earns the same return of 8 percent. One pays taxes on earnings before reinvesting, but the other's investment compounds tax deferred in an annuity. The cash value of the tax-deferred annuity grows to more than $466,000 in 20 years while the taxed investment grows to less than $306,500.

There are basically two types of annuities: fixed and variable.

Fixed Annuity

A **fixed annuity** promises a stated rate of return for at least a minimum period of time and guarantees the return of the investor's principal. Money deposited in a fixed

TABLE 18–6	The Advantage of Tax-Deferred Compounding	
End of Year	**Taxable Account Value**	**Tax-Deferred Account Value**
1	$105,760	$108,000
2	111,851	116,640
3	118,294	125,971
4	125,108	136,048
5	132,314	146,932
10	175,071	215,892
15	231,644	317,216
20	306,498	466,095

annuity goes into the insurance company's general account. Investors' deposits, less any expense charges, are held in an account for them and credited with interest. The interest rate paid on the deposits may be based on the earnings of a variety of investments in the general account less a deduction for expenses and profits. The funds are generally invested in long-term secured bonds or commercial mortgages. Their stability of principal and fixed rates of return give annuities an edge over variable investments such as stocks and mutual funds.

Many annuities are designed to provide payouts to the holder at a future date. They are known as *deferred annuities* used to supplement retirement income. At a certain point, investors "annuitize" their contract; that is, they stop paying in and start taking out. Investors may take a lump sum and pay all the deferred taxes at once. Or they may elect to receive periodic payments, perhaps for the rest of their lives.

Companies may declare new rates every year or at more frequent intervals. Most contracts guarantee that the rate will not fall below a minimum rate, but this rate is quite low, usually 3.5 to 6 percent. The actual rate is usually much higher but varies greatly from company to company.

Variable Annuities

High inflation in the 1970s made investors leery of fixed returns, so annuity marketers came up with the variable twist. Instead of leaving investment decisions to the insurance company, the customers could switch their money back and forth among a small set of managed funds. With a **variable annuity**, also called **wraparounds**, investors give up the guaranteed rate in exchange for a chance to earn higher rates (and, of course, the risk of losses). The money accumulates in a separate account, not the company's general account. It is invested in assets such as stocks that fluctuate in value. A company may offer investors a choice of a stock, bond, or money market fund, usually managed by the insurer. As a rule, investors elect the type of fund or funds their money goes into. Sometimes investors can allocate their deposits among several accounts or switch at will from one account to another.

Investors can invest a lump sum and add to it as they wish. Their deposits, less any expense charges, purchase **units** in the account or accounts. A unit's value (like stock shares) varies with the performance of the underlying investments in the account. If those values rise, investors have an opportunity for capital appreciation. If they decline, they take a loss. Thus, the risk with a variable annuity is the same as the risk of the underlying investment. Investors' returns are directly tied to the fund's performance.

Variable annuities provide a convenient way of investing in a mutual fund while lowering one's tax bill.

Paying for an Annuity

Flexible Premium Annuity

There are different ways of paying for an annuity. If payments or deposits are accumulated over a period of time in monthly installments, these are known as a **flexible premium annuity**.

Single Premium Deferred Annuity (SPDA)

Single premium deferred annuities (SPDA) are similar to a pension plan, but with only one payment into the plan. Investors deposit a one-time lump sum, the "single" premium, and the money compounds untaxed until withdrawn. An insurance company invests the money in its portfolio of bonds, mortgages, stocks, and real estate and assumes full market risk. Investors are guaranteed a set rate of return for a specific period, usually one year. After that, the company declares a new interest rate each year. Some SPDAs also provide for variable returns.

When investors are ready to start drawing on the account, they can take the whole amount out at once when they reach age 59½ or can postpone the tax bite by annuitizing, which means converting the balance into monthly annuity payments. At that point, the portion of payout which represents the growth of the original investment is taxable. Ideally, investors are in a lower tax bracket at that point. They can select an option to have their SPDA pay them monthly payments over a fixed period of years or a life annuity guaranteed to continue as long as they live. This alternative requires the annuitant to start with a fairly large lump-sum investment. Sometimes life insurance cash values are used as a funding mechanism for SPDAs.

Since annuity rates are based on mortality tables, they may vary with the age of the annuitant. The older the annuitant at the time the accumulation is converted to an annuity payment, the more likely the monthly annuity will be larger because of the shorter life expectancy.

The Drawbacks of Annuities

Poor Rates of Return Annuities guarantee a certain return on a regularized basis, which is a comforting thought to many people. Annuities, however, have some decided disadvantages. They are not always the best form for accumulating capital. Even taking into account tax benefits, investors often can earn higher yields managing their own money. Annuities frequently have produced underwhelming returns.

Penalties and Surrender Charges One of the things to watch for in buying either a fixed or variable annuity is the surrender penalty. How much do they charge if you want to get your money back? Annuities are relatively illiquid investments intended for long-term investing. They come with a crushing load of fees, stiff tax penalties, and early withdrawal charges that could devour a big portion of your earnings. There are severe penalties for cashing in or transferring an annuity, particularly in the first few years. Although these are slowly phased out, there can still be problems. Many annuities have "surrender" charges that start at 7 percent in the early years, phasing out over seven years if you want to withdraw or transfer your money to another institution. In some cases you forfeit interest as well.

Hidden Charges Annuities additionally bristle with hidden and undisclosed costs that make comparison shopping a bit like a trip through a mine field. These costs can change this vehicle from an attractive investment to a rather poor one. In addition, each year you may pay an administrative charge, usually $20 to $50, a management fee (approximately .5 percent), and a 1 to 2 percent fee for what is called mortality expense—a reserve the company sets aside to pay annuitants who live beyond their group's average life expectancy. Moreover, the 1986 tax reform bill imposed a 10 percent penalty on money withdrawn from annuities before age 59½. (There is one exception: If a person under age 59½ elects to "annuitize," that is, agrees to have the money accumulated in the annuity paid out in equal monthly payments for a certain number of years, or until the investor dies, the 10 percent penalty does not apply.)

No Inflation Protection Annuities have another major drawback. Your monthly payment on a fixed annuity does not increase with inflation. It would not be prudent to put all your money into an immediate annuity. If you have assets to spare, you might buy one for steady income and invest the rest to keep pace with inflation.

Uncertain "Fixed" Rates When shopping for a fixed-rate annuity, you may be tempted to buy one that promised the highest interest. Some of the highly advertised claims of secure high rates of return are about as reliable as campaign promises. Insurers are free to pay any rate they want. The "fixed" high rates often vanish after only a few months or a year. A company guaranteeing 10 percent this year can easily declare 5 percent next year. Then you are at the firm's mercy because a high surrender charge may make it forbiddingly expensive to get out.

Investors should also note that some companies quote gross interest rates (before fees and mortality charges have been deducted), while others quote net rates. Investors should make sure that any annuity contract they sign contains an escape clause that allows them to withdraw monies should interest rates go down. A contract should provide for a penalty-free withdrawal if interest rates move down more than a certain percentage.

These practices vary widely and should be fully investigated. Before buying an annuity, check the minimum rate guaranteed and compare this with other forms of investment. Also look first for an escape clause rather than for an extraordinary rate. A policy that pays a lower rate but has a more liberal surrender clause might be a better deal in the end. Investors should also ask for data on past performance and previous fees. Performance data for annuities are scarcer and harder to evaluate than those for mutual funds.

Risk of Default   While annuities are considered safe in the world of investments and fixed annuities guarantee your principal and a small return, the guarantee is only as good as the company behind it. The 1991 bankruptcies of Executive Life of California ($10.1 billion) and Mutual Benefit Life of Newark, New Jersey ($13.8 billion), are cases in point. They were the largest insurance company failures in U.S. history and shook the security of the American pension system. An estimated 370,000 people found the cash value of their tax-deferred annuities frozen or their monthly pension checks cut back as much as 30 percent.

If an insurance company files for bankruptcy, annuity owners may have to wait years before they can withdraw their contributions. Forty-five states have guaranty arrangements for paying off annuity buyers in the event of an insurance company's default. Only Alaska, California, Colorado, Louisiana, and New Jersey do not provide such protection. To insulate themselves from shaky insurers, investors should buy annuities only from companies that receive top safety rankings from major rating firms. One of the best sources for checking the financial condition of companies issuing annuities is *Best's Insurance Reports,* which is found in many public libraries. Another effective strategy is to diversify. Instead of buying a single large annuity, investors can buy several smaller ones from different insurers.

Annuities are not for people seeking a convenient place to park their short-term spending money. They are also not for young people who cannot afford to tie up their capital. They are best suited for disciplined savers in their 40s or older who need tax relief.

Should you buy an annuity at all? Some financial advisers say no, because you can potentially do better with a well-selected mutual fund and have constant access to your money and the risk is tolerable. You may also be better off taking advantage of a 401(K) salary reduction plan if your employer offers one, or you may consider an IRA, which is discussed further on.

Choosing an Income Option

When the time comes to retire and you are ready to receive income from your private pension or annuity, you will be faced with several payout options. There is no ideal option. You will have to decide which option fits your circumstances and needs.

Here are some options you will need to consider.

Lump-Sum Payout

Some plans, particularly annuities used as defined contribution plans, give benefits in a single payment. Retirees who choose the **lump-sum payout** option may likely have a tax problem since the payout will be taxed as current income. Retirees will need to reinvest the money so that it continues to provide a steady stream of income.

Straight Life or Lifetime Only Annuity

Under a **straight life annuity,** the pension benefits are paid as a stream of monthly payments, guaranteed to continue only for the life of the retiree. The annuity pays the retiree until he or she dies whether he or she lives to 120 years or dies shortly after signing the contract. No payment is made to any beneficiary after the retiree dies. Since straight life contracts are risky, they usually offer the highest monthly payments. They are suitable for people who need maximum income and lack dependents to whom they wish to leave an inheritance.

Life Annuity with Period Certain and Continuous

As with a lifetime only annuity, payments are made as long as the retiree lives. But if the retiree dies within a stated period, generally 5, 10, 15, or 20 years, payments will continue to the retiree's beneficiary for the remainder of the 5-, 10-, 15-, or 20-year period. The amount of the monthly payment under this annuity is less than under a lifetime only annuity.

Joint and Survivor Life Annuity

This annuity, also known as a **contingent annuity**, pays a benefit as long as the retired employee lives. If the retiree dies and his or her spouse is still living, payments continue to the spouse. Payments to the spouse will usually be 50 percent of those received by the retiree, although, depending upon the plan, they could be as much as 100 percent. Under the **joint and survivor life annuity,** the benefit at retirement is somewhat reduced to make up for the amount that will be paid to the spouse for married employees. The amount of the monthly check is based on the retiree's age as well as the spouse's.

Installment Refund Life Annuity

Monthly payments are made for life, until the total amount paid out equals the initial fund at retirement. If the retiree dies before that, the **installment refund life annuity** pays back the balance of the original investment to the beneficiaries. Installment refund annuities usually pay 4 to 5 percent less than the straight life variety.

Pension Maximization

A **pension maximization** program may combine a higher payment with a life insurance policy. Some retirees chose the higher-paying straight life plan, which results in as much as 20 percent higher benefits than the joint and survivor life option. Part of the extra income (the difference between the straight life and joint and survivors payments) provides a lifetime income for the spouse upon the retiree's death. The advantage is that insured parties have the higher straight life payout, their spouse is protected, and they can cancel the life insurance policy in the event of the spouse's death. A pension maximization option transfers the financial risk to the retiree and the spouse. If the retiree becomes ill or for some other reason does not keep up with premium payments, the spouse could be left with nothing. Such an option needs to be carefully considered and by law requires the written consent of the spouse.

Other options and some variations of those above are also offered by insurers.

IRAs: The Tarnished Financial Hero

When **individual retirement accounts (IRAs)** were first made available to all workers in January 1982, the word *millionaire* popped up in quite a few ads for IRA contributions. Banks, savings and loans, credit unions, and even brokerage houses published neat little charts showing how young investors could save $2,000 a year for 30 to 40 years and watch their net worth climb to seven digits. The American dream seemed within reach, thanks to the magic of tax-deferred compounding and double-digit interest rates.

But in recent years there have been no references to millionaires in IRA promotions. That is because several key variables in the IRA equation have changed. Interest rates since then have sharply declined. Additionally, what the government giveth the government taketh away. Since January 1, 1987, contributions to an IRA are not tax deductible for most people. For taxpayers who lost the deduction entirely, the IRA was severely tarnished. The reduction in tax rates as of 1987 further diminished the value of the IRA.

Nevertheless, the IRA still remains a valuable retirement option. The basic tenets of IRA investing (except for the right to deduct the $2,000 contribution from taxes) remain as they have been since 1982. Any working taxpayer under age 70½, no matter how high his or her income, can invest up to $2,000 a year in an IRA at a banking institution, brokerage house, mutual fund, or insurance company and benefit from tax deferral of all their earnings, either capital gains, dividends or interest until the funds are withdrawn for retirement. Nonworking spouses can contribute up to $250 per year.

Although the contributions themselves are no longer automatically tax deductible, the ability to defer taxes on earnings is still a significant advantage because the base on which the yield is compounded is not reduced over the years by any taxes. This permits more rapid compounding than if taxes were paid each year, and since most people are in a lower income tax bracket after retirement, the tax advantages of an IRA can be considerable.

If you started the same IRA at age 40, earning average annual rate of 8 percent return, by the time you are 70½ and have to start drawing money out, you will have accumulated about $245,000. The nondeductible IRA is actually very similar to a tax-deferred annuity.

Qualifying for the Annual $2,000 Deduction

Some people are still eligible to deduct the actual $2,000 investment from their taxes. If neither you or your spouse is covered by a retirement plan at work, such as a corporate pension, profit-sharing plan, or a Keogh or 401(K) plan, you continue to qualify for the $2,000 per worker or $2,250 one-income couple deduction regardless of your income.

A married couple falls under the income restriction if one spouse is covered by a pension plan. A single person in a corporate plan can take the full deduction only if he or she earns $25,000 or less annually in adjusted gross income. Above that, the amount that can be deducted drops in steps, $200 for each $1,000 income until the deduction is fully phased out at incomes of $35,000 and above. Married couples

IRA

The Tax Advantage of an IRA

If you invest $2,000 a year in a taxable account earning 8 percent and pay taxes on the earnings at the 28 percent rate, at the end of 20 years you will have $75,831. Put those $2,000 deposits in a tax-deferred IRA and at the end of that time, you will have $98,846. If you withdrew it all and paid the deferred tax bill on the earnings ($58,846), you would wind up with just $82,370. That is, if you are in the 28 percent bracket, you keep 72 percent of your earnings plus your original $40,000 principal. This comes to $40,000 + .72 ($58,846), which equals $82,370. The longer you contribute to an IRA or the higher your rate of return, the greater the advantage of tax-sheltered earnings.

filing jointly keep the deduction if their combined income is under $40,000, but as with singles, the deduction tapers off if either spouse is in a corporate plan.

If an individual's income is between $25,000 and $35,000 (or $40,000 to $50,000 for a married couple), then for every $100 in adjusted gross income above $40,000 (married) or $25,000 (single), the IRA deduction is reduced by $20. The deduction vanishes altogether when adjusted gross income topped $50,000 for a married couple and $35,000 for a single.

The Rules

An IRA is nothing more than a program with special rules. Precisely how and where you invest the money in it is up to you. IRAs have almost boundless flexibility. IRA money, however, cannot be kept under the mattress; it must be deposited in or invested through an institution qualified by the IRS to act as an IRA custodian or trustee, such as a bank, S&L, insurance company, stock brokerage firm, mutual fund company, or credit union.

Investors are often unaware of the variety of financial instruments that can be purchased by an IRA plan. They are allowed to buy certificates of deposit, stocks, bonds, options, futures, government securities, mutual funds (including money market funds), limited partnerships, annuities, and real estate. Investors can have as many IRA accounts as they wish, using a different sponsor each year, for example, or dividing their money among several investments. An IRA, therefore, is not one particular kind of investment like a CD or a mutual fund but an overall investment plan that can include almost the entire investment gamut.

Withdrawals

All funds withdrawn from an IRA are taxed as ordinary income. If investors withdraw from an IRA before age 59½, they owe the tax as well as a 10 percent penalty. Exceptions to the penalty are made in cases of death or disability. After age 59½, those who were eligible to deduct contributions from taxes are subject to pay taxes on all withdrawals from their IRA. Those who did not write off contributions have only to pay income tax on the portion of withdrawals that represent their investment earnings, not on contributions.

Record Keeping

To protect themselves from overpaying their taxes later on, IRA investors should keep detailed records of their IRA accounts. Otherwise, many years down the road, after several rollovers and consolidations, it might be impossible to reconstruct what part of an account represents the investor's contribution and what part earnings. This is one of the drawbacks of an IRA. The 1986 tax reform law burdened people who make contributions to nondeductible IRAs with a lifelong snarl of paperwork. Each year investors must fill out a new IRS tax form—number 8606—to keep track of their deductible and nondeductible contributions. These forms must be saved for the life of each IRA. The information on them will determine the tax on any withdrawals when investors begin taking money out of their account.

Managing Your IRA

IRAs are a long-term investment commitment. Investors have to manage these accounts for decades, both for the years they make contributions and also over the withdrawal period. The challenge is considerable. If you have opened an IRA and are not close to retirement, you face years of coming up with voluntary annual contributions. You will have to decide where to put your money initially, and as the account grows in size, you must be able to manage it successfully. As your needs and goals change, so must your IRA portfolio. In a sense, you have to be both a portfolio manager, trying to maximize your returns, and the fiduciary, prudently watching to see that the account is properly handled.

The IRA Installment Plan

It is not necessary to make an entire IRA contribution at one time, nor are investors required to put in the full $2,000. Married persons and their spouses could each, for instance, put $166.67 away each month into their IRA bank money market account or brokerage account. That comes to $2,000 for the year for each. This is far less painful than coming up with one big chunk at once. Although they will not earn as much as if they deposit the entire amount on January 1, they would earn substantially more over the years than if they waited for April 15 of the following year.

Rollovers and Transfers

Although the IRS extracts a penalty if funds are withdrawn from an IRA early, investors can move that money around among different accounts, mutual funds, stocks, and other investments, whenever and as often as they want as long as they do not actually receive the money. **Direct transfer** involves telling the current IRA sponsor to transfer the funds to a new account. Investors can use the direct transfer method as often as they wish, and it is usually the most convenient method of transferring. However, it may be quicker to use a rollover, especially if timing is important, to lock in a certain investment.

In an **IRA rollover,** investors actually cash in one account and personally serve as the intermediary, escorting the funds to the new IRA account. As of 1992, new tax guidelines preclude tax-free rollovers without a 20 percent withholding up front. Within 60 days of the date the money was withdrawn, it has to be reinvested in an IRA. Investors who miss the 60-day deadline forfeit the right to a rollover and are considered to have cashed in the IRA. The full amount is then added to their current taxable income, and if they are under 59½, a 10 percent penalty is imposed. Unless an investor informs the sponsor of rolling the money into another IRA, it is required to deduct 10 percent as penalty and send it to the IRS. The rollover method can be used only once every 12 months per IRA account.

Investors cannot borrow from their IRA or take out loans against it. However, in a pinch, they can use their IRA money as a substitute short-term loan by taking advantage of the 60-day withdrawal provision. There is no rule saying they cannot use the money as long as they return it to an IRA account within 60 days.

Withdrawals upon Retirement

Though young people today concentrate on putting money into their IRAs, there comes a time to start pulling out cash. Since the money they will take out will be taxed as regular income, the best time to make withdrawals is when their other taxable income is modest and they are in a relatively low tax bracket. That is often the case when people retire.

Funds can be legally withdrawn from an IRA without penalty upon reaching age 59½. Investors (59½ and older) do not have to withdraw their IRA money in one lump sum. Until they reach 70½, they can take out as little or as much as they want, or leave everything in their tax sheltered account and let it keep compounding.

However, the IRA tax shelter does not last forever. After age 70½, tax rules require retirees to start withdrawing a minimum of funds each year. They have to start withdrawing funds and paying taxes on it by April 1 following the year in which they reach 70½. The IRS imposes a 50 percent penalty on any funds that should have been, but were not, withdrawn. The minimum withdrawal is based on the retiree's life expectancy or, if the retiree named a beneficiary for the IRA, the joint life expectancy of the retiree and the beneficiary. A 70-year-old has a life expectancy of 16 years, for example, so the first required payment would be one-sixteenth, or 6.25 percent, of the account balance.

Is an IRA for You?

Appealing as they are, IRAs are not for everyone. If you are just getting started, accumulate at least a three-month emergency fund and establish credit first. Financial planners disagree about whether young people should put the maximum $2,000 a year into an IRA account. Some recommend a more liquid investment for those who may need to tap their savings to make a down payment on a home, for instance. Given a choice, young people may be better off purchasing a home before purchasing an IRA. The mortgage interest deduction on a home is worth as much as, if not more than, the tax benefits of an IRA.

It would be unwise to invest money in an IRA that you are sure you will need in the next few years for a house, a car, or more schooling. An IRA can be appropriate if you are 50 and only locking in your money for nine years. But what if you are

29 and it is another 30 years before you can get the money without paying a penalty? For younger wage earners, it might not be prudent to tie up money for 30 years.

While IRAs still have their merits, without their previous tax deduction on contributions, they have lost their absolute edge over a number of investments that also offer tax breaks.

There are other attractive and competitive tax advantaged savings vehicles available besides IRAs: 401(K)s, SEPs, and Keoghs, as discussed earlier, seem more attractive, if available. With municipal bonds, for example, investors are not subject to federal taxes on the interest, nor are they subject to a withdrawal penalty. Variable universal life insurance and other permanent insurance products offer tax exemption as well. Even annuities, although not always recommended as the most profitable and flexible investment for young people, offer the same tax deferral and profit potential as an IRA, and there is no limitation on the amount that can be invested. Each IRA investment should therefore be compared with other investments that offer tax advantages.

SUMMARY

Financial planning involves a careful analysis of present and future needs and an examination of how present and future resources may be allocated to meet those needs. The process involves setting retirement goals, determining needs, and preparing adequately to meet those needs.

The basic foundation of a retirement program for most people is Social Security. Social Security, composed of several types of insurances, provides important but limited income security. Social Security must be coordinated with individual and private insurance policies. Private insurance benefits must supplement and complement Social Security benefits.

Employer pension plans constitute an important source of retirement income for about half the working population. Savings may also be channeled through non-company-sponsored private plans, such as IRAs, Keoghs, and annuities. An annuity offers an arrangement under which you can receive benefits from retirement savings for as long as you live.

In conclusion, there is a wide variety of financial vehicles available to plan and prepare for your eventual retirement. You obviously need not avail yourself of all the instruments discussed in this chapter. What you need to do is to select those that are more appropriate to your specific needs and circumstances, and to make sure that these plans will adequately provide for your retirement needs. The sooner you get started, the easier it will be to meet your future retirement goals.

KEY TERMS

Accrued benefit	Earnings Test
Accumulation phase	ESOP
Annuity	ERISA
COLAs	Flexible premium annuity
Defined benefit plan	FICA
Defined contribution plan	Fixed annuity
Direct transfer	Form SSA-7004

401(K)

Integrated plans

IRA

IRA rollovers

Joint and survivor life annuity

Keogh plan

Lump-sum payout

Partial vesting

Payout phase

Pension Benefit Guaranty Corporation (PBGC)

Pension maximization

Profit-sharing plans

Simplified employee pension (SEP)

Single premium deferred annuity (SPDA)

Social Security

SSI

Straight life annuity

Survivors benefits

Three-legged stool

Units

Variable annuity

Vesting

Work credit

Wraparounds

REVIEW QUESTIONS AND PROBLEMS

1. Describe the "package" of benefits available under the OASDHI Social Security System. Who else, besides the insured worker, can receive Social Security benefits?
2. What are the eligibility requirements for Social Security?
3. How much Social Security tax does someone earning $40,000 a year pay?
4. Do you think Social Security is a good deal?
5. What fiscal problems has Social Security faced in recent years and what steps has it taken to deal with these problems?
6. What are the differences between defined benefits and defined contribution plans?
7. Explain what is meant by the term *vesting*. How can vesting provisions deny workers their benefits from employer-funded retirement plans?
8. How has the 1986 Tax Reform Act improved workers' vesting rights?
9. What factors regarding a company's pension plan should be checked by an employee before enrolling in the plan?
10. Discuss ERISA and explain its impact on pensions.
11. Explain what a Keogh Plan is and for which group of people it is best suited.
12. Who is eligible to establish a 401(K) and what are its characteristics?
13. What are the main advantages and disadvantages of an ESOP?
14. What is the function of the PBGC? Which pensions does it and does it not cover?
15. What is an annuity? What is the difference between fixed and variable annuities? Which would you prefer? Explain.
16. Explain the different payout options of annuities and pensions: (a) lump sum, (b) straight life, (c) life annuity with period certain, (d) joint and survivor life annuity, (e) installment refund life annuity.
17. What are the financial arguments for taking an early retirement option under Social Security?

18. (RETIREMENT) Suppose Social Security will pay you $800 monthly. You think you can earn a return of 7 percent. Your pension benefits are $48,000. You have 11 years until retirement. If your desired retirement is $65,000, how much must you save annually to meet your goal?

19. (IRA) You are in the 28 percent tax bracket with an annual income of $25,000. Assume an IRA lower limit of $25,000 and a higher limit of $35,000. Assume that the step increment over the limit is $100 amd that the deduction is reduced by $20 for each step increment over the limit. What are your tax savings with an annual IRA deduction of $2,000.

SUGGESTED PROJECTS

1. Talk with your grandparents or a couple in retirement and discuss with them the following:
   A. What pre-retirement planning have they made?
   B. What are their sources of income?
   C. What financial concerns, if any, do they have?
   D. If they had to do it over again, how would they prepare differently for retirement? Present your findings to your class.

2. Visit a senior citizen center and conduct an opinion poll. Ask the senior citizens for their advice on what is the most important thing young people today can do in order to retire comfortably.

INFORMATION RESOURCES

Ansberry, Clare. "Autumn Years—The Rising Prosperity of America's Retirees Is Unevenly Spread." *The Wall Street Journal,* November 30, 1990, A-1.

Castro, Janice. "Is Your Pension Safe?" *Time,* June 3, 1991, 42–44.

"Early Retirement: It Pays to Plan Early." *Business Week,* February 27, 1989, 134–135.

Eisenberg, Richard. *How to Avoid a Mid-Life Financial Crisis.* New York: Penguin, 1988.

Hardy, C. Colburn. *How to Retire Prosperously and Gracefully: The Comprehensive Guide to Retirement Planning and Living.* Englewood Cliffs, NJ: Prentice-Hall, 1989.

"Is Your Pension Safe?" *Time,* June 3, 1991, 42–44.

"Job Buyout: Take It and Leave." *Changing Times,* January 1991, 45–51.

Kirkpatrick, David. "Retirement: Save until It's Painful." *Fortune,* February 25, 1991, 121–126.

McGee, Judith Headington. *J.K. Lasser's Guide to Planning Your Successful Retirement.* New York: Simon & Schuster, 1989.

Martindale, Judith, and Mary Moses. *Creating Your Own Future: A Woman's Guide to Retirement Planning.* Source Books, 1992.

Mayer, Martin, "Pensions: The Naked Truth," *Modern Maturity,* February–March 1993, 40–44.

Micheli, Robin. "Social Security Explained." *Money,* September 1988, 107–110.

Morse, David Evan. *Retire Rich! How to Plan a Secure Financial Future.* New York: Simon & Schuster, 1988.

"The Power of the Pension Funds." *Business Week,* November 6, 1989, 58–72.

Rowland, Mary. "Getting the Most out of a Pension." *The New York Times,* April 26, 1992, F-16.

———. "Picking Through the Annuity Tangle." *The New York Times,* February 16, 1992, F-12.

———. "When Working Isn't Worth It." *The New York Times,* September 26, 1993, F-13.

"The Rush to ESOP's." *Business Week,* May 15, 1989, 56–63.

Schultz, Ellen. "Big Fees Can Tarnish Variable Annuities." *The Wall Street Journal,* March 26, 1991, C-1.

Sloane, Leonard. "Going Beyond Social Security." *The New York Times,* March 9, 1991, L-28.

Smalhout, James. "The Coming Pension Bailout." *The Wall Street Journal,* June 10, 1992, A-14.

Social Security Administration. Dial 800/772-1213 to reach one of the 4,200 Social Security representatives who assist the public.

Stern, Linda "Nothing Ventured." *Modern Maturity*, February–March 1993, 52–83.

"Stuffing Nest Eggs with ESOPs." *Business Week,* April 24, 1989, 38.

Updegrave, Walter L. "Getting Past the Hype of Annuities." *Money,* September 1991, 118–122.

"Wiener, Leonard. "How You Can Afford to Retire." *U.S. News and World Report,* October 21, 1991, 86–91.

Wilcox, M.D. "Closing In on Retirement." *Kiplinger's Personal Finance Magazine,* July 1993, 57-61.

———. "Retiring in Style." *Kiplinger's Personal Finance Magazine,* May 1992, 75–80.

"Your IRA Money: What to Take and When to Take It." *Kiplinger's Personal Finance Magazine,* April 1992, 105-107.

The Retirement Equity Act (1984) and Women's Rights

Estimates are that fewer than 11 percent of the country's 15 million women over the age of 65 collect private pensions, compared to 29 percent of men in that age group. The reason is that until 1984, most plans were not required to provide automatic survivor benefits, even though the average age of widowhood in the U.S. is a surprisingly young 56 years. The special life patterns women share militate against winning pensions. Often they work part-time, pause to rear children, and jump from job to job as they or their spouses advance. In the past, many women had not been employed outside the home and did not earn their own benefits.

The Retirement Equity Act of 1984 was drafted mainly to eliminate some obvious inequities in the pension system that had primarily affected some women. It has been widely hailed as a women's bill. The bill is an acknowledged attempt to provide some retirement income for widowed women who were homemakers and never part of the paid labor force. The bill, however, benefits both sexes since it is couched in unisex language.

Surviving Spouses' Pension Rights

The law benefits older people who find themselves without a pension when their spouse dies. Until 1984, wives (or husbands) of employees who died before retirement often did not receive vested pension benefits unless the spouse had elected preretirement **survivors benefits** and had reached the company's earliest retirement age, usually 55. Now, however, companies have to offer preretirement survivor benefits to all vested workers. The surviving spouse is entitled to receive a benefit beginning when the deceased employee would have become eligible for early retirement.

The 1984 act demands that preretirement and retirement survivor benefits be included in all retirement plans that qualify for tax exemptions under the Internal Revenue Code. The law also allows one to know whether their spouse has provided for survivor benefits in his or her pension plan. In the past, workers sometimes rejected the joint and survivor option that provided the spouse with a pension after the worker's death, without notifying or consulting the spouse. Now, before an employee can choose to opt out of survivor benefits in his or her pension plan, the spouse must provide his or her employer with written permission, a notarized waiver that has been signed by both the employee and the spouse. This ruling is especially beneficial to nonworking women, who may be entirely dependent on their husband's pension. No longer does a married employee have a unilateral right to decide the form in which his or her pension will be paid and who his or her beneficiary will be. A married worker can no longer secretly bequeath his or her pension benefits to someone other than the spouse.

Divorced Spouses' Pension Rights

This law also provides that a divorced spouse can begin collecting a share of the working employee's pension at the early retirement age, even if the employee has not retired. Suppose a man is 55 years old and eligible for early retirement under his employer's plan. He, however, does not retire and continues working. His divorced wife, however, wants to receive her portion of his pension right now. The company must honor her request. It pays her half of the pension benefits even though the man may not be entitled to any pension benefits until his actual retirement.

Lower Minimum Eligibility Age

The law has lowered the minimum age at which employees can join a pension plan from 25 to 21 years. The old requirement penalized many women, since women between 20 and 24 were more likely to be employed than women of other ages. Women lost again when it came to vesting. Pension plans sometimes did not start to count years of service for vesting purposes until an employee reached 22. Now vesting credits begin at 18.

The Retirement Equity Act also changed the rules governing pensions for employees who leave a company and then return months or years later. If employees without vested benefits left for at least one year and the first period of their employment was shorter than the time they were out of the workforce, their employers did not have to count the first years of service for vesting purposes. An employer can disregard the service before the break only if the break is for at least five years.

An Example: Fred Gets His Vest

Fred Clark, a 20-year-old man, goes to work as a salesman for a chain of hardware stores. He works three years and then resigns and works somewhere else for four years. Afterward, he returns to his old job. It comes time to compute his years of service for vesting purposes. Does the company have to give him credit for those first three years he worked?

The answer is yes. The act says that if an employee leaves a job and returns, he or she must receive credit for that earlier period, unless the number of consecutive one-year breaks in service equals or exceeds five years, or the number of prebreak years of service, whichever is greater.

FIGURE 18–6	Planning Bonus: A Retirement Worksheet

Where do you stand?

Use this work sheet to get an idea of how much you'll need to retire in style.

1. TARGET INCOME

Assemble these numbers in today's dollars. The accompanying article tells how to get social security and pension projections.

Estimated annual social security benefit: $ _____

Estimated annual pension benefit: $ _____

Retirement savings to date: $ _____

Proportion of current income (70% or more) you would like to replace in retirement

$ _____ × _____% = $ _____
(current income)   (target Income)

2. TARGET INCOME AFTER INFLATION

Use these numbers to project what your target income, social security and pension will be when you retire, assuming 4% inflation.

YEARS TO RETIREMENT	10	15	20	25
Inflation factor	1.48	1.80	2.19	2.67

$ _____ × _____ = $ _____
(target income)   (factor)   (adjusted target income)
$ _____ × _____ = $ _____
(social security) (factor) (adjusted social security)
$ _____ × _____ = $ _____
(pension)   (factor)   (adjusted pension)

3. SHORTFALL

Subtract the sum of adjusted social security and pension income from adjusted target income to find the annual shortfall.

$ _____ – $ _____ = $ _____
(adjusted target   (adjusted social security   (annual shortfall)
income)   + adjusted pension)
Annual shortfall divided by 12 = $ _____
                                    (monthly shortfall)

4. PRELIMINARY GOAL

The following table shows how much you'll need when you retire to produce $100 of income each month over various lengths of time. Assume, for example, that your monthly shortfall is $2,700 and you want your nest egg to last for 25 years. If you anticipate a 10% rate of return, find where the 10% and 25-year columns intersect and multiply the amount there ($11,474) by 27 (your shortfall divided by 100). The result, approximately $310,000, is your preliminary retirement goal.

AMOUNT NEEDED TO GENERATE $100 PER MONTH

YEARS IN RETIREMENT	ANNUAL RATE OF RETURN		
	8%	10%	12%
10 years	$8,397	$7,767	$7,213
15 years	10,711	9,614	8,695
20 years	12,286	10,762	9,536
25 years	13,358	11,474	10,013

$ _____ × $ _____ = $ _____
(amount from table) (shortfall divided by 100) (preliminary goal)

5. RETIREMENT GOAL

The preliminary retirement goal must be increased to account for inflation after you retire. For a rough estimate, increase this figure by 50%.

$ _____ × 1.5 = $ _____
(preliminary goal)   (retirement goal)

6. PROJECTED SAVINGS

Estimate how much your current savings will be worth at retirement. If you plan to retire in 20 years and you expect your investments to grow by 10% a year, for instance, find the multiplier where the 20-year and 10% columns intersect: $1,000 in your retirement account today will grow to $6,730 in 2012.

YEARS TO RETIREMENT	ANNUAL RATE OF RETURN		
	8%	10%	12%
FACTOR FOR ESTIMATING PROJECTED SAVINGS			
10 years	2.16	2.59	3.11
15 years	3.17	4.18	5.47
20 years	4.66	6.73	9.65
25 years	6.85	10.83	17.00

$ _____ × _____ = $ _____
(savings)   (factor)   (projected savings)

7. RETIREMENT GAP

Subtract from your retirement goal the projected value of your savings calculated in step six. The result is what you still need to come up with before you retire (the retirement gap). A negative number means that you're poised to meet your goal.

$ _____ – $ _____ = $ _____
(retirement goal)   (projected savings)   (retirement goal)

8. WHAT YOU NEED TO SAVE

Say you have a retirement gap of $275,000 and you have 20 years to fill it. Assume, too, that you can earn 10% on your retirement savings. Find the factor where the 10% and 20-year columns intersect in the table and multiply that number (0.0175) by your retirement gap ($275,000). The result tells you that you need to save $4,813 a year, or roughly $400 a month.

YEARS TO RETIREMENT	ANNUAL RATE OF RETURN		
	8%	10%	12%
FACTOR FOR CALCULATING A SAVINGS TARGET			
10 years	0.0690	0.0627	0.0570
15 years	0.0368	0.0315	0.0268
20 years	0.0219	0.0175	0.0139
25 years	0.0137	0.0102	0.0075

$ _____ × _____ = $ _____
(retirement gap) (factor)   (annual savings needed)

For a more precise estimate of what you'll need, get the T. Rowe Price Retirement Planning Kit, available for free by calling 800-541-02295. A software version of the kit costs $15 (call 800-541-4041). You'll need an IBM-compatible PC with graphics capability to run the software.

SOURCE: Reprinted by permission from the May 1992 issue of Kiplinger's Personal Finance Magazine. Copyright © 1992 the Kiplinger Washington Editors, Inc.

Break In Service Rule for New Parents

The law liberalized the **break in service** rule, which used to hurt women who left the work place for a while to raise children. Maternity and paternity leaves up to one year are not counted as a break in service. The law therefore allows new parents to take a full year parental leave. That time can then be added to the five years allowed other workers, for a total of six years, or until the child is old enough for first grade.

CHAPTER NINETEEN

Estate Planning and Writing a Will: You Can't Take It with You

- To consider the meaning, importance, and objectives of estate planning
- To explore the basic steps involved in estate planning
- To examine the various ways to transfer property at death
- To discuss the importance of writing a will and what provisions to include in it
- To outline the function of trusts and how they can be used to accomplish estate planning goals
- To investigate the methods of legally bypassing or reducing estate taxes

A **will** is a legal document that transfers assets to a person's heirs at his or her death. It is the most basic estate planning tool and should be the cornerstone of every financial plan. Nearly every adult needs a will. Yet only a third of all adults have wills, and it is impossible to guess how many of them have never updated the documents to reflect changes in their lives or in the law.

The hardest part of drawing up a will is psychological, accepting that one will die and planning for that eventuality. However, we all need to anticipate how our death will affect our assets. Most people would probably rather ignore the whole subject of who is going to get their assets after their demise. Pondering one's mortality is not

657

a very pleasant pastime. Nonetheless, "you can't take it with you," and what you do leave behind if you do nothing is a mess that will haunt your survivors. People who fail to make such provisions do not suffer; their heirs do.

"What you leave at your death," wrote Sir Thomas Browne, a 17th century physician, "let it be without controversy, else the lawyers will be your heirs." His advice is as true today as it was then. A person's **estate** is essentially his or her net worth at death. **Estate planning** means taking steps to ensure that in the event of death, the surviving spouse, children, and other loved ones are provided for. Young people need estate planning also and have to look at it as family funding. Clearly, the more thought people put into estate planning, the better off their heirs will be. Estate planning can therefore be considered another act of love.

This chapter examines the entire subject of estate planning. Writing a will, the probate process, appointing executors and guardians, setting up trust funds, and avoiding estate taxes are all basic tools used in crafting a solid estate plan.

The Need for a Will

A person who writes a will is known as a **benefactor** (or testator). The person (or persons) named in the will to inherit property is known as a **beneficiary**. The main purpose of a will is to make sure the benefactor's property is distributed within limits the way he or she wants, with a minimum of delay and expense. It also specifies who the benefactor wants to handle his or her financial and personal affairs. President Calvin Coolidge squeezed his will into a single sentence: "I leave my entire estate to my wife, Grace, and request that she be appointed executrix without bond." But chances are that a benefactor will have more than one beneficiary and will want to be more specific as to who gets what, when, and under which circumstances.

A simple will for most people ensures that their assets pass to their desired beneficiaries. A will can apportion people's assets according to what they see as their heirs' needs or merits instead of following a rigid legal formula. It can bestow gifts on friends, relatives, lovers, charities, stepchildren, or grandchildren or put money into trusts. If you die without leaving a will, such people or institutions will receive nothing.

The time to prepare your first will is when you have acquired assets that can be passed on to someone else or when you have acquired minor dependents. Wealth alone, however, does not determine the need for estate planning. The person who leaves only $20,000 has as much interest as someone leaving $2,000,000 in making sure that those assets go to the right people. However, a larger and more complicated estate will probably require a more elaborate plan. In life, a millionaire may have less to worry about, but in death, the tables are turned. For larger estates (over $600,000), wills are indispensable to ensure the distribution of a person's possessions in a way that will minimize estate taxes.

How to Write a Will

Once a benefactor has decided to write a will, it is rather simple, involves generally one or two visits with an attorney, and does not cost very much. There are few eligibility requirements to writing a will. The benefactor must be above a certain age (the minimum varies from state to state, from 14 to 21), must be fully aware of the consequences of making a will, and must be acting voluntarily.

Once the will is typed, there should be no insertions or corrections and no room for insertions. Pages should be numbered to indicate the sequence and the total number of pages. Example: Page one of five. All references to fractions, ages, and dollar amounts should be expressed both in words and numbers to avoid confusion. Example: Ten thousand dollars ($10,000). Since the benefactor's signature must appear right after the final sentence of the will, the will should be typed so at least the final sentence appears on the same page as the signature. When you have worked out the will as you want it, have the final draft typed perfectly. Typed wills are preferable to handwritten ones. They are much easier to read and therefore less likely to be misinterpreted. It is all right to make extra copies of the will, but only one should be "executed"—signed, dated, and witnessed. Wills should be stored in your lawyer's custody with a copy kept at home. It is not advisable to keep a will in your safe deposit box because the box may be sealed at your death and require court approval to be opened.

Don't Be Mean or Nasty

Although the law generally allows benefactors to distribute their property any way they want, it is hard, but not impossible, to cut out of a benefactor's estate people who would normally be considered his or her natural heirs. Every state has statutes that do not allow a married person to disinherit a spouse. A surviving spouse is usually entitled to a minimum share, typically one-third to one-half of the deceased spouse's estate, unless a prenuptial agreement exists which specifies otherwise. A benefactor cannot disinherit a spouse without his or her written consent. Disinheriting a spouse will most likely result in the court having a will overturned.

Whether or not you have children, common law states usually give a spouse one-third or one-half of an estate. If you have no children, your parents or siblings would get the rest. To bequeath all of your property to your spouse requires a will. In community property states (Arizona, California, Idaho, Louisiana, Nevada, New Mexico, Texas, Washington, and Wisconsin), each spouse automatically owns one-half of all (community) property acquired during the marriage by means other than inheritance or gifts. You can leave your half of the property to anyone you want, including your spouse.

For example, suppose your will awards your spouse 25 percent of your property. Suppose, too, that the common law in your state would award your spouse 50 percent of your property if you had died without a will. In that case, if your spouse requests, the probate court must override your will and give him or her 50 rather than 25 percent.

If one is dead set on leaving a spouse as little as possible, he or she can also do so outside the will. The best approach is to reduce one's estate by gradually moving assets out of it in the form of trusts and gifts (discussed further on) to other relatives, friends, and charities. Generally, if a will contains any instructions that might be construed as out of the ordinary, the benefactor should explain them thoroughly to forestall attempts to overturn the document on the grounds that he or she did not realize what they were doing.

Individuals who want to leave the bulk of their estate to a child or someone else when there are other heirs to press equally strong claims should write a letter in their own hand to their lawyer explaining the reasons for the unequal disposition.

The lawyer should reply to the letter, pointing out the inequity and asking the benefactor to respond to it. The benefactor should mention his or her children by name in the will but is not obligated to leave them anything (except in Louisiana). If a benefactor wants to cut a child out of his or her will, the safest way is to name the child and make some tactful statement such as: "I realize I have not provided for my sons, Henry and Peter. Their omission is not the result of inadvertence or mistake." Or "For personal reasons, I do not choose to leave any money or property to my daughter, Betty Ann." Such wording can forestall a challenge to the will. This should all be done in consultation with an attorney.

Don't Rule from the Grave

A will can be left open to contest if benefactors try to rule their beneficiaries from the grave. Most vulnerable to attack are clauses that make a legacy conditional upon something that might reasonably destroy an heir's health, wealth, or happiness. You can, however, dictate in your will the conditions under which your heirs can inherit. You can set up a trust and stipulate that your children cannot get their money outright until they are 30 or married or that your 150-pound daughter can get hers only if she weighs in at 110 pounds. You can also leave your nephew $10,000 upon his finishing college but not for marrying a particular woman or on condition he climb Mt. Everest or pass a course in free-fall parachuting.

Moreover, a benefactor should not leave any parting shots or demeaning remarks. Wills are public documents and indiscretion could be embarrassing and costly. If you additionally bequeath your exercise equipment to your 150-pound daughter "in the hope that she cease looking like an overgrown elephant (or pumpkin)," the injured party may be able to sue your estate for defamation and get a fat check from your estate to pay legal expenses.

Dividing an Estate: Specific and General Gifts

The property covered by a will can be left in various ways. You can leave property as **specific gifts** (known as legacies or bequests) such as your grandmother's diamond earrings or your grandfather's gold watch or any other jewelry, cars, artwork, or antiques to your sister, Henrietta, or as **general gifts**, such as $3,000 to your Aunt Millie. Specific gifts come from the property of the estate, while general gifts are gifts to particular people, taken out of the general assets of the estate. Each specific gift should be described in detail to avoid ambiguity and potential bickering later on. When specific or general gifts are left, there should be instructions indicating what is to happen to that property if the beneficiary does not outlive the benefactor.

Residuary Estate

It is important for a benefactor to include a catch-all statement about how to distribute his or her residuary estate. That will take care of any property not specifically mentioned in the will. The **residuary estate** is what is left after the deceased's debts, funeral expenses, administrative expenses, and taxes have been paid, and after all specific and general gifts have been passed on.

Since individuals cannot determine what their estate will be worth when they die, it is best to divide the residuary estate as fractions or percentages of the estate rather than as specific sums. If your $200,000 estate grows to $600,000 by your death, your kids will thank you thrice as much for the 10 percent share you left each of them instead of the $20,000. Conversely, if your $200,000 dwindles to $100,000 at your death, that $20,000 you left to charity is 20 percent of your estate, not the 10 percent it represented when you wrote the bequest.

Most wills include instructions about where the money for taxes and other expenses is to come from. Benefactors who have any preferences about this should state specifically what they have in mind. For example, if you prefer that your stocks rather than your jewelry or home be sold to pay taxes and expenses, this is the place to say so. In addition to leaving gifts of property or cash, a will can also be used to forgive debts. For example, you may write that your brother upon your death need not repay the money you loaned him for the down payment on his home. Your estate therefore will not have a claim against him upon your demise.

Witnesses

A will must be signed in the presence of witnesses who are not beneficiaries to the will and have no interest in it. This is known as **attestation.** If witnesses are beneficiaries, the entire will may be invalidated. Witnesses should be adults, preferably people who have known the benefactor well for some time. The witnesses do not have to read the will or even know what is in it but they should know that they are witnessing one. Each of the witnesses must sign his or her name and address in the presence of the others. It is best to have witnesses who are younger than the benefactor since they are more likely to be available if there is a question about the will after the benefactor's death.

Electronic Wills

Tape recordings or videotapes of benefactors reciting how they want their property divided after death may appear to be an up-to-date way to make a will. But **electronic wills** should not be counted upon as a substitute for a written one. Several courts have rejected them on the ground that the traditional definition of "writing" does not include tape or video recordings. In the expectation that a written will might be contested, some lawyers have been videotaping the will signing and witnessing as evidence proving proper execution of wills. A discussion on film between the benefactor and his or her attorney of the reasons for the bequests can help thwart future challenges by slighted heirs in which it is argued that the benefactor was incompetent or of unsound mind.

Do-It-Yourself Wills

Standard will forms and computer software for writing a will can be bought inexpensively and completed without using a lawyer. A do-it-yourself will may appear inviting for being simple and cheap, but most people should turn down the invitation. Although it is possible to write a will by oneself, a mistake or oversight can prove costly. The do-it-yourself standard form wills are designed for people with relatively small, uncomplicated estates. For many people, they are too standard and do not provide enough room for comfortable maneuvering. If an individualized will with special requests and conditions is required, then it is recommended that a lawyer draft it.

"Being of sound mind, I videotaped my will instead of hiring a lawyer."

SOURCE: "Pepper...and Salt," *The Wall Street Journal*, April 28, 1990, A-21. Reprinted by permission of Cartoon Features Syndicate.

Using Professional Assistance

For most people, the main objective of estate planning is making sure that they transfer their assets intact to their heirs. People with considerable assets can construct a complex strategy that includes trusts, annual gifts to children, and a life insurance policy to pay any estate taxes. Such an estate plan generally requires the assistance of four specialists—an attorney, a financial planner, a CPA, and a bank trust officer.

Not everyone needs the assistance of specialists. An estate plan requiring professional assistance is in order if at least one of these situations applies to you:

1. You have minor children.

2. You want to shield your survivors from the delay, expense, and public disclosure of probate (discussed further on), the process that proves a will is valid.

3. Your estate is large enough to be subject to estate taxes.

If you decide to draw up a very special will listing all your wishes, you may be able to hold down the legal costs by doing some homework before visiting an attorney. The lawyer should be presented with a complete list or inventory of your assets, including bank accounts, investments, real estate, life insurance, IRA accounts and

---

A Living Will

A **living will** instructs others of your wishes about medical care if you become terminally ill or mentally incapacitated. Your agent, under durable power of attorney for health care, can usually legally make all health care decisions anytime you cannot. This kind of will has gained in popularity in recent years, since the cost of keeping terminally ill or brain-dead patients alive is often financially devastating to the immediate family members and relatives.

pension funds, jewelry, and other valuables. It is also helpful to prepare an estimate of your net worth as well as to bring any important documents and records for any property you own jointly.

The cost of lawyers' services will vary with the complexity of the will. The fee may run anywhere from less than $100 for a simple will to several thousand dollars for a complete estate plan package.

Changes and Codicils: Revising and Updating a Will

A will can be just as mortal as a person. Once written, a will is not set in stone. Even the best-drawn wills can grow stale if left without periodic monitoring. Estate plan arrangements made only a few years ago may be so outdated that many of a person's assets could go to the wrong people or in the wrong amounts. Therefore, a will should be reviewed every few years to make sure it still does what the benefactor currently wants it to.

If you change your mind about what is in your will, you can revoke it at any time simply by writing a new will. The new will should state that all previous wills are revoked. If you want to add to or change only a portion of the will, you can add a **codicil**, a written amendment. There is no limit to the number of changes that can be made. Codicils should, however, be carefully constructed not to conflict with certain terms still to remain in effect in the will.

There are certain telltale signs that a will may have developed some weak spots that need updating. They are possible to detect if the benefactor asks himself or herself the right questions:

1. Have I had any more children?

2. Have any of my children for which I established trust funds grown up?

3. Are my appointed guardians or trustees still the best choice?

4. Have I married, divorced, or remarried?

5. Has my net worth increased a lot more?

6. Have I moved to another state?

7. Have the tax laws changed?

8. Has my health or spouse's health deteriorated?

9. Has anyone mentioned in my will died?

10. Have I acquired or disposed of major assets?

11. Have I changed my mind about when or if an heir should inherit?

12. Has my net worth increased dramatically?

Without a periodic review of a will's arrangements, changes over time could cause serious problems after the benefactor is gone. A divorce or a remarriage can obviously create the need for an estate plan overhaul. In divorces, the changes might stem from court orders affecting the parties' rights in property, such as a home. Or the court may order a spouse to maintain his or her ex-spouse on a life insurance policy. An ex-spouse may want to make his or her new spouse the trustee of the trust set up to pay for his or her child's college education.

Do It for the Kids' Sake

If there are minor children, a will is crucial. The biggest problems occur when there are young children. Most significant, in the event the parents die simultaneously, they give up their say in who will bring up their minor children. The courts could designate someone as guardian to bring up the children whom the parents would not have selected. Therefore, even those who hardly have any assets should still have a will to select who would be guardian of their minor children. The courts might, for instance, have the children live with relatives in a distant state, while the parents would prefer they be raised by friends in their community. In addition, the costly court fees can quickly erode the estate the children might have gotten.

The Probate Process

The word *probate* has come to be used to mean the process by which a will is validated and the court supervises the transfer of the deceased's wealth. *Probate* literally means "proving the validity of will." A **probate court** (called **surrogate's court** or **chancery court** in some states) is the court that supervises the passing on of deceased persons' estates after they die, whether they leave a will or not.

In his 1853 novel, *Bleak House*, Charles Dickens vehemently criticizes the procedure for settling estates in Britain as a hopeless morass. Probate is not quite as bad today. It can take about two months to two or more years, depending upon the efficiency of the attorney as well as the court in the particular jurisdiction. A study in 1990 found that probate of estates under $100,000 took, on average, well over a year.* During that time, the heirs may not have access to their inheritance. Consequently, it is to any heir's advantage to have as much of an estate as possible pass to him or her directly, without passing through the lengthy probate procedure. In addition, court expenses can consume a chunk of the bequeathed estate. Courts commonly charge the estate a fee.

It is unlikely that a person can avoid probate altogether. What can be done is to minimize the share of one's assets that passes through probate. Not all assets are subject to probate. The probate process covers only these assets which are owned entirely by a deceased person and pass through the estate's executor (explained further on) and the courts. People may get some property transferred to their heirs without delay because it passes outside of probate.

---

*American Association of Retired Persons, *A Report on Probate: Consumer Perspectives and Concerns* (AARP, 1990).

An asset not included in the probate process is known as a **nonprobate asset**. Nonprobate assets pass directly to their named beneficiary. They include assets for which beneficiaries are named, such as pension plans, IRAs, and proceeds of life insurance policies owned by the deceased and payable to a named beneficiary other than the deceased's own estate. Assets and property owned with the deceased person as joint tenants with the right of survivorship and assets of certain kinds of trusts also automatically bypass probate. (This is discussed further on.)

How probate is handled usually depends upon the nature and size of the estate and, in some cases, the wishes of the heirs. Most states have a streamlined procedure for certain small estates, often between $5,000 and $10,000. Many states have informal probate procedures requiring little court supervision for small estates. Sometimes all that is necessary is for the appropriate person to file an affidavit with the court and have relevant records, such as title to property, changed. Formal probate, where major steps along the way are supervised by the court, is commonly used for larger estates.

Every state allows a certain period, usually between four to six weeks, for creditors to file claims for payment against the estate. This notice period, plus a certain period in advance to organize and after to wind things up—usually a month on either end—is probably the minimum length of a regular probate.

The due dates of tax returns can also affect the length of a probate. If the estate is large enough to require a federal estate tax return, which is due nine months after death, the estate will probably be open at least that long. Sometimes estates are kept open for the three-year federal audit period for the estate tax return. The kinds of property in an estate can also affect how quickly distribution can take place. One of the slowest processes is having a name changed officially on a stock certificate.

Executing the Will

A major decision involved in writing a will is to select the appropriate person to serve as the **executor** (or if it is a woman, she may be called **executrix**). The executor's job is to wrap up the deceased benefactor's financial affairs. He or she must first assemble and identify the benefactor's property, inventory it, and determine its value, collect any money due the benefactor, pay his or her debts and funeral expenses, file estate and income tax returns, and pay any taxes due. The executor must also make sure that all estate and inheritance taxes are paid and may sell the deceased benefactor's property, if necessary, to meet the benefactor's obligations. The executor will then distribute whatever is left of the estate to the heirs according to the instructions in the will and submit a final accounting to them. He or she must also make sure that the affairs of the estate are formally settled to the satisfaction of the court supervising the estate.

An executor can be held liable for making imprudent decisions or even failing to take timely and judicious action. For example, an executor may have to pay penalties and interest out of his or her own pocket if an accountant the executor hires fails to pay the estate's taxes on time. Throughout, the executor must keep careful records. Most probate courts will demand a detailed account of all money received, spent, and held by the estate. This often requires hiring appraisers whose fees come out of the deceased's estate, as do expenses for lawyers, accountants, and other professionals.

It is important to appoint someone who will be willing and able to handle these transactions with good judgment and discretion. Almost any person you trust can be your executor. For most people, the best choice is their spouse or best friend, who may also be a beneficiary. Large estates may need two executors—one person to interpret and carry out the deceased's wishes and another person or institution, such as a bank, to make business or investment decisions, pay taxes, and keep records.

Letters of Testamentary

The executor-to-be files a petition for probate in the appropriate court, submitting a death certificate and the original of the will. One cannot exercise the official powers of an executor until a court establishes that the deceased left a valid will and issues **letters of testamentary** formally designating the executor. Before receiving these letters, the executor must notify all creditors and everyone named in the will. The purpose of this notification is to give potential beneficiaries a chance to object by claiming that the alleged will is invalid. The executor must also place a notice in a newspaper published in the county where the deceased lived. If no one complains, probate will be granted and the executor will be issued the letters.

Reluctant to dwell on the subject of death, many people have a will drawn up and name an executor without telling the relative or friend about the task that lies ahead. The person you choose should have a clear idea on how best to work things out to make sure that your heirs and beneficiaries get the most out of what you leave for them. Be sure to discuss the executor's job with the person you're planning to appoint. It's also important to nominate a substitute in case the original executor isn't able to handle the job, chooses to resign, or dies before the work is completed.

The executor is usually required by law to post a bond as insurance to protect your heirs against the executor's absconding with money or property. This bond requirement can be waived if the waiver is explicitly stated in the will.

Intestacy: The No-Will Way

Dying **intestate** means without a will. Presidents Abraham Lincoln, Andrew Johnson, U.S. Grant, and James Garfield as well as billionaire Howard Hughes each died

"Maybe the meek will inherit the Earth, but they'll need tough guys like me for executors!"

SOURCE: "Pepper...and Salt," *The Wall Street Journal*, May 4, 1991, A-15. Reprinted by permission of Cartoon Features Syndicate.

intestate. In fact, more than two-thirds of all adult Americans die without wills. By so doing, they abdicate to the state the right to make decisions about how their property is to be divided, inviting government intrusion into the administration of their estate.

Dying intestate is not necessarily a catastrophe. All states have a ready-made will waiting for people who die without one of their own. Each state has laws detailing how an estate is to be distributed among the heirs if there is no will. The proportion each family member gets varies widely from state to state. Therefore, those who die intestate let the state law parcel out their belongings. The distribution of the estate is supervised by a probate or surrogate court.

The probate court also appoints people to handle deceased persons' affairs, a guardian for their children, and an administrator to pay their debts and taxes and to turn over the remainder to their heirs. In the absence of a will, the executor's functions are performed by a **court-appointed administrator.** The administrator distributes property according to the state's laws of intestacy instead of according to a will. Without a will, the court is quite unlikely to appoint the people that the deceased would have preferred. In such an instance, the presumed heir, often a surviving spouse, should go to probate court and ask to be named administrator of the estate. When no relative or beneficiary can take the job, the appointee is likely to be a civil servant or even a creditor.

Dying intestate is often an expensive proposition. Heirs may face cumbersome proceedings and added legal expenses. The above mentioned administrators receive fees normally equal to 3 to 5 percent of an estate and must post a bond, the cost of which comes out of the estate and usually comes to several hundred dollars. The worst part of dying intestate, however, is that the state's method of dividing the assets of the estate might not suit the deceased and might be unfortunate for the beneficiaries.

Although they vary from state to state, intestacy rules are always impersonal and inflexible. Most states set up a chain of priority for inheritance. While state formulas for distributing a person's assets favor close relatives, the particulars are often quite different from those that people want. The laws generally place the surviving spouse and children first, then the deceased's parents, then brothers and sisters, and then nieces and nephews.

There is a good chance that the law calls for a significantly different distribution of your property than you ever imagined. Do not assume, for example, that your surviving spouse will automatically get the bulk of your estate. Consider, for instance, a man with a wife and two adult children—most states would give his spouse only one-third to one-half of his estate. The law may give half or more to his children. In many states, if a childless married person dies intestate, the state would give parents or siblings of the deceased as much as half of the estate.

How badly a surviving widow or widower needs the property will have no impact on the state's decision. The law also makes no provision for anyone who is not related to the deceased or for the distribution of any specific property.

Appointing a Guardian

Providing for the upbringing of your children is one of the will's most important functions. Even if you have a spouse, you should appoint a **guardian** and a substitute to care for any minor children in your family, just in case you and your spouse die simultaneously. Do not assume your spouse will survive you to care for the children. A will is a form of planning for the worst eventuality, such as husband and wife both getting killed instantly in a car crash.

Chances are your children will never need a guardian. It is extremely rare for both parents to die. But it is possible. If you and your spouse die without appointing a guardian in your wills, the court may appoint someone whom your children dislike or whose views and values are disturbingly different from your own. Suppose your sister thinks she is the best candidate and your spouse's brother thinks that he is. The cost of the ensuing court fight will come out of your estate, thereby diminishing your children's inheritance.

Naming a guardian means you just nominate someone in your will. Although the court actually appoints the guardian, the judge usually follows the will's instructions. The court's first choice is usually a family member, but it can technically appoint anyone as your child's legal guardian. If you name a friend over a close relative, you should spell out your reasons. Make sure to ask the people you appoint as guardians whether they would be willing to take on the responsibilities of guardianship. A guardian named in the will is under no legal obligation to accept the responsibility and can refuse it. Therefore, discuss the task with the person or persons you appoint as guardian to get their reaction and consent.

Any number of things could happen to make your original selection of guardians or trustees for your estate inappropriate. They may have moved to some distant city or become too sick or old to shoulder the care of your teenagers. Your relationship with an appointed trustee may have gone sour, or one of the trustees may have died. In that event, the court will have to find another person who may not be someone to your liking. For that reason, it would be prudent to name an alternative in your will in case your first choice cannot or will not serve.

The guardian, like the executor, must post a bond to protect the estate in case he or she absconds with the money. Bonds are expensive, about one-third of 1 percent of estate value, or about $850 a year on a $250,000 estate, and the estate pays for it.

Types of Guardians

There are two kinds of guardians: of the person and of the property or the estate. A **guardian of the person** handles the children's day-to-day upbringing, while a **guardian of the inheritance property** manages whatever money was left for the children.

A guardian of the inheritance property, either named in a will or appointed by the court, must annually report his or her major expenditures and investments on the children's behalf to a judge. He or she also must often request court permission to pay the children's expenses from their legacy. That seems like an excellent way to ensure that a guardian does not steal or squander an orphan's inheritance, but it requires cumbersome paperwork and gives a judge who is unfamiliar with a family power over how their legacy is invested and spent.

Another limitation of the guardianship system is that a guardian and the court can control a child's money only until the child reaches the age of majority, 18 in most states. At that time, the beneficiary is free to spend the inheritance as he or she pleases, on a college education or at the race track.

A Simple Will (Sample)

Last Will of Nancy Brown

I, Nancy Brown, of 458 W. 5th Street, Houston, Texas, state that this is my last will, revoking all previous wills.

1. *Executors* I appoint my husband, Hank Brown, executor of this will. I also appoint my friend, Sally White, substitute, in case Hank is unable or unwilling to act as executor, or ceases to do so. The executor does not have to be bonded.

2. *Guardians* If Hank dies before I do, or at the same time, I appoint my brother, Bill Green, guardian of the person and property of my children until they are eighteen (18) years old. I also appoint my sister, Mary Grey, guardian, in case Bill is unable or unwilling to act as guardian, or ceases to do so. The guardian does not have to be bonded.

3. *Specific Gifts* I give my 1993 Toyota Celica car to my son, Gary Brown. If he dies before I do, or at the same time, this car is to be considered part of my residuary estate. I give my Renoir etching to my daughter, Gertrude Brown. If she dies before I do, or at the same time, this etching is to be considered part of my residuary estate.

4. *General Gifts* I give my children, Gary and Gertrude, ten thousand dollars ($10,000) each. If either dies before I do, or at the same time, his or her gift is to become part of my residuary estate.

5. *Residuary Estate* I give all the rest of my property to my husband, Hank. If he dies before I do, or at the same time, I give all of this property to my children, Gary and Gertrude, in equal parts. If all three of these people die before I do, or at the same time, all my property is to go to my sister, Mary, and to my brother, Bill, in equal parts, or entirely to the sole survivor if only one outlives me.

6. *Taxes* All taxes and government fees associated with the transfer of my property are to be paid out of the residuary estate.

7. *Executor's Options* In order to carry out the distribution of my estate, I give my executor full power to sell, lease, mortgage, reinvest, or otherwise dispose of the assets in my estate.

Signed: _____

Date: _____

Witnesses At Nancy Brown's request, we met on the date inserted above to witness her signing of this will. With all of us present at the same time, she signed it and stated it was her last will.

Signed: _____ Address: _____
Signed: _____ Address: _____
Signed: _____ Address: _____

Estate Taxes: Postmortem Estate Tax Planning

Estate planning is an important part of personal financial management because death taxes can take a huge bite out of the assets people struggle all their lives to accumulate. The maxim about death and taxes should include a warning that the former, inevitable though it may be, does not mean the end of the latter. Many people need something called **postmortem estate tax planning** to keep the tax collector from sharing in the wealth they leave to their heirs.

Federal Estate Taxes

The federal government imposes a tax on residuary estates, after all debts and expenses, funeral costs, charitable contributions, and administrative legal fees are paid and certain exemptions and deductions have been made. Marginal rates start at 18 percent and rise to 50 percent for estates valued at more than $2.5 million.

State Estate Taxes

Thirty states and the District of Columbia collect death taxes independently of the federal government, a few of them on estates as modest as $100. State death taxes vary significantly. Many states impose either an estate tax or an inheritance tax but not both. **Estate taxes** are paid by the executor out of the entire value of the estate. **Inheritance taxes** are generally paid by those who inherit the estate. Both kinds of taxes are collected by the state in which the deceased was a legal resident at the time of death.

Unlimited Marital Deduction

The federal tax code contains an assortment of opportunities for people to protect their estate from estate taxes. The most generous is the so-called **marital deduction**. This federal law enables a person to give all of the estate to the surviving spouse without having to pay any federal taxes. In addition, each married person can pass to other heirs a total of as much as $600,000 in assets. Federal tax brackets start at 37 percent on estates above $600,000 and top out at 55 percent on estates valued over $10,000,000. Any amount in excess of $600,000 is subject to the tax schedule reported in Table 19–1.

GIFTS

In addition, federal law permits an individual to give $10,000 a year, and a couple $20,000, to any one person free of gift tax. A couple with three children and five grandchildren, for instance, could give them a total of $160,000 a year. If all three children are married and the spouses are included, the amount would rise to $220,000. As long as the gifts to any one individual from any one donor do not exceed $10,000 a year, they do not affect the $600,000 exclusion from estate taxes.

However, a good estate plan should not involve just your own estate. The unlimited marital deduction doesn't take into consideration the consequences when the surviving spouse eventually dies. An important goal of estate tax planning is to arrange one's assets so that, if possible, the spouse who dies first will not leave the survivor with a taxable estate of more than $600,000. That way, the second spouse's estate will not be taxed later because it will be smaller than the exemption.

TABLE 19–1	Federal Estate Rate Table

ESTATE

No federal taxes are owed on the first $600,000 of an estate. The tax rate on the remainder is as follows:

Amount	Tax Rate
$600,001 to $750,000	37%
$750,001 to $1,000,000	39%
$1,000,001 to $1,250,000	41%
$1,250,001 to $1,500,000	43%
$1,500,001 to $2,000,000	45%
$2,000,001 to $2,500,000	49%
$2,500,001 to $10,000,000	50%
$10,000,001 to $18,340,000	55%*
$18,340,001 and above	50%

*Includes a 5 percent surcharge which results in an overall rate of 50 percent

SOURCE: Internal Revenue Service (1993).

Setting Up a Trust: In Trusts We Trust

While there is no alternative to appointing a legal guardian of the person to raise your children, there is an alternative to appointing a guardian of your estate which you will leave to your children. The wisest strategy is for parents to write wills in which a trust is created to hold their children's inheritances.

A **trust** is a legal arrangement, actually a contract between one person with property called the **grantor, settlor,** or **trustor** and another person, called the **trustee.** Basically, the grantor turns over money or property to another person or organization (the trustee). Almost anything can be placed in a trust: bank accounts, stocks, bonds, real estate, personal property, and life insurance. The trustee who receives legal title to the trust property then invests the trust principal, known as the **trust corpus.** The property placed in trust by the grantor is managed by the trustee for the benefit of a third person, called the **beneficiary.** The grantor sets down instructions for the management of the trust and the disbursement of its income and principal. This is done in the document called a **trust agreement** that is drawn up by an attorney. It is necessary to work with a lawyer to establish a trust because the documents are often complex.

Trusts can be used to achieve numerous goals. They can safeguard property until a child is old enough to handle it and provide professional management and investment services. They can also be used as a legal means to avoid estate taxes (explained further on).

One common problem arises when the person writing the will lacks the confidence in the surviving spouse's (or children's) ability to manage the estate. Through a trust, professionals can manage the estate, thereby removing the burden from the survivor.

If a grantor establishes a minor's trust, the trustee is obligated to follow the rules and instructions set down by the grantor in the trust agreement without interference from a court. A trustee has a legal duty to use a high degree of care and good faith in handling a trust. If this fiduciary duty is violated, the beneficiaries can go to court for help. Therefore, a trust negates the need for one to name a guardian for his or her children's property.

A trust lets parents specify when their children will get their legacy. Parents can keep the trust principal out of their kids' hands until they are older and presumably more mature. Parents often stipulate that a part of a trust's assets should go to a child at age 21 and the rest at age 30.

Depending upon the terms in the trust agreement and the trustee's discretion, the income is either distributed to people named by the grantor known as **income beneficiaries** or **life tenants** or accumulated in the trust. Some trusts also let the trustees give part of the trust principal to the income beneficiaries, in case of an emergency.

When the trust ends, the trustee turns over the trust assets to the **remainderman** (recipient) chosen by the grantor. The remainderman need not be the same person as the beneficiary. For example, a husband may establish a trust for his wife whereby she as beneficiary receives the income from the trust but upon her death, the trust dissolves and the husband's children are the remaindermen and receive the trust assets. The income beneficiaries and remaindermen can be grantors, children, spouse, friends, or a charitable institution. Some trusts even allow the grantor to get the property back after a period of time.

Selecting a Trustee

No matter how carefully a trust agreement is written, it takes people to make it work. Therefore, choosing a trustee, someone who will be responsible for seeing that the terms of the trust are carried out, is among the most important steps in the estate planning process. The toughest part of establishing a trust is likely to be searching for someone who is both financially astute and sensitive to the needs of the beneficiaries.

Before you consider possible candidates for the job, you have to decide exactly what you expect the trustee to do. Do you want someone just to disburse the proceeds honestly to your beneficiaries? Will the person you choose be expected to manage assets as well? Do you need someone who can help guide your children or who will supervise the money for someone unable to manage his or her finances?

The trustee(s) may be family members, a spouse, relatives, friends, a financial institution, or sometimes even the grantor. Attorneys, accountants, financial planners, and other professionals may also be suitable as trustees. It is important to consider a potential trustee's competence, integrity, and compassion, as well as skills at

Parent's College Trust

Ben Foster, 29, and his wife Rochelle, 27, want to ensure that their children, Michelle, 3, and Jason, 6 months, can afford to go to college in the event that the children become orphaned. The Fosters establish a trust that takes effect upon their deaths according to instructions in their wills. The agreements remain in force until their youngest child reaches age 22 and has presumably finished college. At that time, the children receive equal inheritances.

money management, record keeping, and general administration. Fee arrangement with a trustee should be discussed and put in writing.

Banks and trust companies are another choice. These institutions are staffed to do the tax accounting, portfolio management, legal procedures, and other paperwork. If the management of the trust is complicated and an appropriate family member is not available, a professional trustee such as a financial institution would be appropriate. People with modest and simple trusts should probably select a relative or friend as trustee. Unlike professional trustees whose fees usually are determined by state law, friends and relatives may agree to serve without compensation. Professional trustees, such as banks, trust companies, brokerage firms, attorneys, and accountants charge annual fees usually equal to 1 to 1.5 percent of a trust's assets. Not surprisingly, professional trustees reserve the right to reject trusts that would earn them paltry fees. Large banks and trust companies generally would reject trusts worth less than $200,000 or $300,000.

Types of Trusts

A trust is a simple concept capable of scores of variations. There are two main basic types of trusts—testamentary and living (also called *inter vivos*) trusts.

Testamentary Trust   A **testamentary trust** is created in the grantor's will and takes effect upon his or her death. Such trusts are often used to manage money for heirs who lack financial know-how, such as minor children or sick relatives. The trust becomes irrevocable upon the grantor's death. The assets in a testamentary trust are included in probate because such trusts are created in wills which are public records.

Living Trusts   Some trusts are set up by a contract between living people. They go into effect during the grantor's lifetime. These are called **inter vivos** or **living trusts**. Their advantage is that assets placed in living trusts are not subject to probate. Upon the grantor's death, trust assets automatically pass to the chosen heirs or remain in trust for their benefit because a living trust is a private legal agreement between a grantor and his trustee.

A living trust may be **revocable** or **irrevocable**. With a revocable trust, a grantor continues to enjoy complete control of the property and can even act as trustee during his or her lifetime. Some states do not allow this. The grantor retains the right to terminate the trust, or change its provisions. Upon the grantor's death, the person named successor trustee takes over. An irrevocable trust cannot be changed. Testamentary trusts are always revocable as long as the grantor is alive and legally competent.

Probate costs can be expensive and time consuming. Grantors can spare their beneficiaries the costs and delays associated with probate by transferring all of their assets to a revocable living trust during their lifetime. Assets in living trust avoid probate because the grantor does not own them anymore; the trust does. Only property a person owns in his or her name at death has to go through probate. A living trust is settled without a court proceeding. A successor trustee simply distributes assets according to the trust's instructions with an accountant, notary public, or lawyer certifying any transfer or title.

Finally, privacy may be the most valuable feature of the trust. The trust can keep the details of a grantor's financial affairs under wraps by taking his or her assets out of the public record and putting them into a private contract. Probate court records are open to anyone who cares to look at them, from nosy neighbors, to relatives receiving no inheritance, to newspaper reporters. The living trust process is thus much quicker, cheaper, and more private than settling a will.

Other Trusts   There are many other kinds of trusts, and they can be established simply by adding a few paragraphs to a will. For example, suppose you want to make sure your children will not spend all their inherited money before they reach the age of 30. Instead of leaving them sums outright, you can arrange to have a trustee dispense a certain amount to them annually. You can also give the trustee the power to transfer all the remaining money to your children before they reach 30 for a compelling reason, such as a medical emergency or if the trustee thinks they are mature enough to handle the money. The wording in establishing a trust needs to be chosen very carefully. Experienced counsel should be consulted for this purpose.

A trust with two or more children as beneficiaries can also include a so-called **sprinkling provision**, which allows the trustee to allocate income and principal to beneficiaries based upon their changing needs.

Joint Ownership

Another aspect of estate planning is figuring out how best to jointly own assets. People choose joint ownership for emotional and economic reasons. Married couples, for instance, usually consider themselves an economic unit and get a sense of security from sharing possessions. Relatives and friends buy big-ticket items jointly because they cannot afford them on their own. Joint ownership may simplify estate planning and the eventual disposition of valuable property. Jointly owned property gets excluded from the probate process and is passed immediately to the other owner(s) without review by the courts. In some cases, however, it can also produce undesirable results.

Generally, any number of people can own property jointly. There are three main forms of joint ownership:

1.   **Joint ownership**, also known as **joint tenancy with the right of survivorship**, is a quick and inexpensive way to hold assets. This form is most common between spouses but can be set up by any two or more persons. Each owner is known as a *joint tenant* and possesses an equal share of the property. Each of 2 owners has a one-half interest, each of 3 owners a one-third interest, each of 10 owners a one-tenth interest, and so forth. When one tenant dies, ownership of the deceased's share automatically passes to the surviving joint tenant or tenants. In the most common case of husband and wife being joint tenants, the surviving spouse automatically acquires the entire property, bypassing the time-consuming and expensive probate proceedings. Any property owned as a joint tenant with the right of survivorship will pass to the surviving owner, regardless of a will.

     For example, if you and your spouse are joint tenants (owners) of a piece of property, a bank account, bond, or stock certificate, your spouse becomes the sole owner when you die. The property should not be included in your will since it is outside any will left by you. Joint ownership with the right of survivorship is not considered part of a deceased's estate. It is generally appropriate for passing title of a residence, brokerage, savings or checking accounts, or U.S. savings bonds.

2. **Tenancy in common** is a form of joint ownership that permits two or more persons to own undivided shares in real or personal property without right of survivorship. Under this rarer type of ownership, when a co-owner dies, his or her share passes not to the surviving partner(s) but rather to heirs named in his or her will or if there is no will, to the next of kin under the statutes known as law of intestacy.

   For example, suppose you and three friends own 25 percent of a sailboat as tenants in common. When you die, your share will go to your family or whomever you designate in your will. This form of joint ownership is best for unmarried people and may also serve the needs of a couple, both of whom have children from a previous marriage. Each spouse would like to jointly own the property but upon his or her death, each spouse wants his or her own children to inherit his or her share. People who hold property as tenants in common can own equal or unequal shares. They can sell their interest without consulting the other tenants and decide who gets their share when they die.

3. **Tenancy by the entirety** can be established only by married couples and in many states is limited only to real estate. As in a joint tenancy with the right of survivorship, each spouse owns an equal share of the asset. On the death of one spouse, the survivor gets the deceased partner's share. Tenancy by the entirety has three main advantages:
   a. One spouse cannot sell or give away his or her interest without the other's consent.
   b. One spouse cannot terminate the other's rights except by divorce or consent of the other spouse.
   c. Assets of one spouse are protected from the creditors of the other.

Many people who lack wills rationalize that joint ownership can take the place of a will. Joint ownership should never be considered as a substitute for a will. There are bound to be assets not owned jointly. Both joint owners could die simultaneously, or there could be a last-minute asset acquisition, such as an inheritance that would not be covered by a joint ownership arrangement. In any of these circumstances, the law would distribute the property in a manner the co-owners might not have wanted.

Consider what would happen if a childless married couple who owned all of their major assets jointly were involved in an accident in which the husband was killed instantly and the wife died a day later. The husband's half of the couple's joint property would automatically pass to his wife upon his death. Unless she managed to write a will on her deathbed, all of the couple's assets would go to her relatives after her death, leaving his family without a legacy. A will could ensure that the assets will be split between both their families if they both die within a short time of each other.

A well-crafted estate plan can reduce or eliminate the tax on the transfer of assets from one spouse to another and then to children and grandchildren. This can be achieved by means of a trust.

Irrevocable Bypass Trust The first type of trust people need to include in their will is a trust equal to the amount of the federal exemption known as an **irrevocable bypass trust** or an **exemption equivalent**. With such a trust, a married person and his or her spouse can pass up to $1.2 million in assets to their children or other beneficiaries, free of federal estate tax. The box "A Postmortem Bypass Operation" shows how it is done.

There are, of course, many variations of the scenario described for Robert and Betty Smith. Each family's situation, if the assets exceed $600,000, requires a slightly different approach.

Take, for example, the situation of Mrs. Sally Richman, who is a millionairess and who dies leaving her entire $1,000,000 estate to her husband, Fred. No federal tax is paid because the bequest is from one spouse to another. But when Fred dies, only $600,000 will be exempt from federal tax; the remaining $400,000 will not.

However, if Sally had created a $600,000 irrevocable bypass trust for her children, giving income to Fred during his life, and had bequeathed the remaining $400,000 to him outright, there would be no federal estate tax on his estate either. This is because the $600,000 trust that Sally established is not part of the surviving

A Postmortem Bypass Operation

Let us assume that Robert and Betty Smith each has an estate valued at $600,000. Their combined estate of $1.2 million can effectively escape taxation if divided evenly between husband and wife. If one of them dies, it would make no sense to increase the survivor's estate. As Table 19–1 indicates, an estate of $1.2 million (minus the $600,000 exemption) would pay $155,800 in federal estate taxes. In other words, if, say, Robert dies and leaves his $600,000 to Betty, she will have an estate of $1.2 million. When she dies her estate will be taxed.

One way to avoid that tax is for Robert to leave his $600,000 estate in the form of an irrevocable bypass trust for his children (as remaindermen) with Betty being the beneficiary during her lifetime. Robert might appoint a friend as trustee. The trustee would invest that $600,000 in government bonds perhaps, and only the income would be turned over to Betty at least once a year. The wife would receive the trust income, but the money in the trust (principal) would never become her property. When Betty dies, Robert's $600,000 trust would not be included in her estate and subject to tax. The trust assets legally belong to the children who inherited it in trust, tax free, under the $600,000 personal exemption deduction. The trust money would remain in a kind of taxation limbo until Betty dies. Upon Betty's demise, the trust ends and the money is passed on to the children without being subject to estate tax.

Betty's estate is therefore able to use her personal exemption to transfer up to $600,000 of her estate tax free to her children. The underlying principle at work here is that by taking advantage of each spouse's $600,000 exemption allowance, a couple can transfer combined assets of $1.2 million tax free to their children or other beneficiaries.

husband's estate and the $400,000 remainder is less than the $600,000 exemption threshold.

Q–Tip Trusts   Another variation of these trusts is the **Q-TIP trust** (short for **qualified terminable interest property trust**), which could be established in a will. A Q-TIP trust allows one spouse to direct income from an estate to the surviving spouse but to keep the estate out of the hand of the spouse's future mate should there be one. Your spouse gets lifetime income from the trust, but the principal goes to your choice of heirs after your spouse dies. Q-TIPs can be used to ensure that children from a previous marriage eventually receive a bequest or to prevent a surviving spouse from turning over assets to a new marriage partner.

Grantor Retained Income Trusts (GRITs)   Millionaires who want to make gifts to family members or friends rather than charities may want to consider opening a **GRIT** (or **grantor retained income trust**). A GRIT is a trust opened during a grantor's lifetime, thereby enabling the grantor to continue to receive income from it for a specified period. After the trust's term elapses, ownership of the property goes to the beneficiary, removing it from the grantor's estate. GRITs are most attractive to very wealthy people who can contribute much more than the $600,000 exclusion to the trust and still avoid estate and gift taxes.

Irrevocable Life Insurance Trust   An **irrevocable life insurance trust** combines a life insurance policy with an irrevocable trust. One common estate tax planning device is life insurance. People regularly buy policies naming a child or spouse as beneficiary to provide future income (discussed in Chapter 9). Although death benefits from life insurance policies are not subject to income tax, they are considered part of the dead person's estate. Insurance can therefore increase the federal estate tax bill. To avoid estate tax on the payment, it is necessary to ensure that life insurance death benefits are not included in your estate. This can be done by setting up an irrevocable life insurance trust to own the policy, with the proceeds going to your beneficiaries.

Upon your death, the policy avoids estate taxes because it is owned by the trust, not by your estate. The proceeds are then paid into the trust. The trustee collects the death benefits and distributes them to your beneficiaries according to the directions in the trust.

GRITs Are Healthy for Children

Brian Phillips puts real estate valued at $1.5 million into a GRIT for his son, Jason, who gets the property when the trust terminates in 10 years. Brian receives any income the trust produces during that period while Jason will get the real estate in a decade. But because the IRS assumes that assets placed in a GRIT earn 10 percent annual return, they view property that will be valued at $1.5 million in 10 years to be worth (or have a present value of) only $577,000 today, which is less than the $600,000 exclusion.

A Trustworthy Widow

Suppose a widow dies, leaving an estate of $5.5 million, including a $1 million insurance policy she had owned, with her children as beneficiaries. The children would not pay any income taxes on the $1 million death benefit, but they would have to pay 55 percent (or $550,000) in federal estate tax because the policy would be part of her estate. The woman's estate would be taxed at a 55 percent rate. If she had placed the policy in an irrevocable life insurance trust, the children would not have to pay any estate tax on the policy's death benefits.

SUMMARY

Estate planning is not a pastime just for the morbid, depressed, elderly, or chronically ill. It is an integral part of financial planning for all adults, young and old. The purpose of estate planning is to see that the maximum amount of a person's wealth will be transferred to the people or organization(s) that he or she desires. The methods that exist for transferring property at death are wills, intestacy, joint ownership, trusts, and beneficiary designation in life insurance.

Wills are processed through a court system known as *probate* to ensure that a person's estate is transferred in the manner(s) he or she specified. A person who dies without a valid will is referred to as being *intestate*. In such a case, the law, not the deceased, determines the disposition of the deceased's property.

Many people use trusts in their estate planning. Trusts are a legal format by which a trustee holds and disburses funds on behalf of a grantor's beneficiaries. This device has many uses, particularly for planning larger estates. Trusts are revocable or irrevocable. They can also be living trusts or testamentary trusts.

Through postmortem estate tax planning, people can transfer their assets to their heirs in a fashion that would minimize federal and state taxes.

KEY TERMS

Benefactor	Grantor retained income trust (GRIT)
Beneficiary	Guardian
Chancery court	Guardian of the inheritance property
Codicil	Guardian of the person
Electronic will	Inheritance tax
Estate	*Inter vivos* trust
Estate planning	Intestate
Estate tax	Irrevocable bypass trust
Executor/Executrix	Irrevocable life insurance trust
Exemption equivalent	Irrevocable trust
General gifts	Joint ownership
Grantor	Joint tenancy with right of survivorship

Letters of testamentary

Living trust

Living will

Marital deduction

Nonprobate asset

Probate process

Postmortem estate tax planning

Probate court

Qualified terminable interest property trust (Q-TIP)

Remainderman

Residuary estate

Revocable trust

Specific gifts

Sprinkling provision

Surrogate's court

Tenancy by the entirety

Tenancy in common

Testamentary trust

Trust

Trust agreement

Trust corpus

Trustee

Trustor

Will

REVIEW QUESTIONS AND PROBLEMS

1. Discuss the importance and advantages of estate planning.
2. What is the main purpose of having a will?
3. What should be included in a will?
4. What circumstances might prompt you to update or change a will?
5. What are the consequences of dying intestate?
6. How does the probate process work? Explain how the probate process can be avoided.
7. What function does the executor or executrix perform in the probate process?
8. What are the different forms of joint ownership? How do they differ from each other? Is one form of ownership better than others?
9. Explain how and why trusts are often used in estate planning.
10. What is the difference between an *inter vivos* (living) trust and a testamentary trust?
11. What is the difference between an inheritance tax and an estate tax?
12. John and Betty Finch have a combined net worth of $1,100,000. They consult you on estate planning. They would like to arrange things in such a manner that when either dies, each can leave the entire estate to the other and when both die, the estate should be transferred to their children. What advice can you offer them to implement their plans without paying estate taxes?
13. Define each of the following: (a) intestacy, (b) remainderman, (c) grantor, (d) residuary estate, (e) codicil, (f) beneficiary.
14. What are letters of testamentary?

15. (ESTATE) Your rich aunt died and her estate paid $1,000,000 in taxes. What was the size of her estate?
16. (GIFTS) You are a single giver facing an estate tax rate of 55 percent. You have two married children, three single children, and four grandchildren. You would like to save $20,000 in estate taxes. How can you use the gift tax law to reach your goal?

SUGGESTED PROJECTS

Do you know where your parents' wills are? Or for that matter, do your children know where your will is? Or the bank accounts? Or the attorney's name and phone number? If the answer to any of these questions is "no," you need to prepare what financial planners call a *document locator*. It is a detailed list of everything a survivor needs to know but is too polite to ask. Prepare the following document locator for yourself or help your parents prepare one for themselves. Use the family financial statement in Chapter 1 (Figure1–1) as your guide. Be certain to record the name, address, and phone number of such people as:

Tax preparer
Insurance agent
Stockbroker
Attorney
Financial planner
Employee benefits counselor
Executor
Potential guardian of minor children

Record the policy numbers, name, and address of financial institutions for such items as:

1. Insurance policies

2. Bank accounts

3. Stock brokerage accounts

4. Mutual funds

5. Mortgages

6. Auto and personal loans

7. Safe deposit box (location of keys)

INFORMATION RESOURCES

Abts, Henry W. *The Living Trust*. Chicago: Contemporary Books, 1989.

Asinof, Lynn. "The Talk You Must Have with Your Parents" *The Wall Street Journal*, March 26, 1993, C-1.

Belin, David W. *Leaving Money Wisely: Creative Estate Planning for Middle- and Upper-Income Americans for the 1990's*. New York: W. Scribners/Macmillan, 1990.

Bove, Alexander A., Jr. *The Complete Book of Wills and Estates*. New York: Henry Holt & Co., 1990.

Budish, Armond D. "The Multipurpose Trust." *Money*, September 1991, 44–80.

Clifford, Denis. *Plan Your Estate*. Nolo Press, 1990.

Dacey, Norman F. *How to Avoid Probate.* New York: Collier/Macmillan, 1990.

Davis, Kristin. "Who Will Raise the Kids If You Can't?" *Kiplinger's Personal Finance Magazine,* June 1992, 77–81.

Dunn, Don. "The Delicate Task of Being an Executor." *Business Week,* June 27, 1988, 106.

Esperti, Robert A., and Renno L Peterson. *The Handbook of Estate Planning.* New York: McGraw-Hill, 1991.

"Estate Planning." *Money,* February 1989, 84–87.

Faltermayer, Edmund. "The (Financially) Perfect Death." *Fortune,* February 25, 1991, 131–136.

"Financial Matters Besides a Will Are Crucial, Often Overlooked." *The Wall Street Journal,* January 3, 1991, C-1.

"Give It Away While You're Alive ... Just Don't Give It 'Til It Hurts." *The Wall Street Journal*, April 22, 1991, C-1.

Hughes, Theodore E., and David Klein. *A Family Guide to Wills, Funerals and Probate: How to Protect Yourself and Your Survivors.* New York: Scribner's, 1987.

Ostberg, Kay. *Probate.* New York: Random House, 1990.

"A Parents' First Duty—Estate Planning." *Working Woman,* December, 1988, 55–57.

"Passing Wealth On Intact Takes a Will and a Way." *U.S. News & World Report,* July 17, 1989, 60–66.

Plotnick, Charles K., and Stephen R. Leimberg. *Keeping Your Money: How to Avoid Taxes and Probate Through Estate Planning.* New York: Wiley, 1987.

Roha, R. R. "Seven Reasons to Change Your Will." *Kiplinger's Personal Finance Magazine,* February 1992, 61–63.

Rowland, Mary. "Estate Planning in an Era of Change." *The New York Times,* February 7, 1993, F-17.

Schulman, Margaret B. *The Dow Jones-Irwin Guide to Property Ownership.* Homewood, Ill.: Dow Jones-Irwin, 1986.

Sloane, Leonard. "Who Needs a Will? Just About Everyone." *The New York Times,* May 1, 1993, A-37.

"When You're Asked to Be an Executor." *Changing Times,* April 1989, 87–92.

Accelerated depreciation   A method of depreciation that charges more of the original cost of fixed assets in the earlier year of the new service life than in the later years. Some companies use straight-line depreciation for financial reporting and accelerated depreciation for income tax purposes to improve their cash flow position.

Accidental death benefit   A provision added to a life insurance policy for payment of an additional benefit of double (or triple) the face amount in case of accidental death. This is often called double indemnity.

Actuary   A person professionally trained in the technical aspects of insurance and related fields, particularly in the mathematics of insurance, such as the calculation of premiums, reserves, and other values.

Adjustable rate mortgages   See *ARMs*.

Alternative minimum tax (AMT)   A tax law that requires upper income taxpayers who benefit from many deductions and credits to pay at least a minimum amount of tax through a special tax.

Amortization   The gradual reduction of debt by making regular periodic principal and interest payments.

Annual percentage rate (APR)   The cost of credit at a yearly rate expressed as a percentage. The APR is based on the interest charges for the life of the loan at the note rate plus all prepaid finance charges.

Annual report   The annual statement by a corporation after the close of its fiscal year. The report includes the balance sheet and profit and loss statements of the preceding and current years.

Annuity   A contract that provides an income for a specified period of time, such as for a number of years or for a person's lifetime. Annuities can be purchased separately from a life insurance contract and are often used to provide retirement income.

Arbitrage   A low-risk transaction to profit from price differences in two markets, buying ABC shares of a low price on the New York Stock Exchange and selling ABC at a higher price on the Pacific Stock Exchange.

ARMs (adjustable rate mortgages)   A mortgage on which the interest rate paid moves up and down at regular stated intervals (often yearly), depending on changing market conditions. They have become very popular with homeowners and lending institutions because their rates are lower than usual mortgages during high interest rate periods.

Assets   Anything owned that has monetary value.

Assumable loan   A loan that can be transferred from the previous owner to a new owner. See *assumable mortgage*.

Assumable mortgage   A mortgage that is assumed by the buyer of mortgaged property, whereby the buyer accepts liability for the debt that continues to exist. The seller remains liable to the lender unless the lender agrees to release him or her.

At the money   Describes a call or put with a strike price equal to the current value of the index that underlies the contract.

Automated teller machines (ATM)   Computer-controlled terminals located on the premises of fiscal institutions or elsewhere through which customers may make deposits, withdrawals, or other transactions as they would through a bank teller.

Automatic premium loan   A provision in a life insurance policy that any premium not paid by the end of the grace period (usually 31 days) be automatically paid by a policy loan if there is sufficient cash value.

Automatic transfer service account (ATS)   A depositor's savings account from which funds may be transferred automatically to the same depositor's checking account to cover a check written or to maintain a minimum balance.

Baby bond   A bond sold in denominations of less than $1,000.

Balanced fund   A mutual fund with the policy of investing its assets proportionately in high-yielding bonds, preferred stocks (for growth), and common stocks (for income). The proportions vary, depending on market conditions for stocks and bonds. Such funds are generally conservative in investment policy, choosing less volatile securities and providing a high quarterly income.

Balance sheet   A financial statement of a company's financial situation that includes a company's assets, liabilities, and stockholders' equity on a given date, usually the last day of its fiscal year.

Balloon payment   A large extra payment that may be charged at the end of a loan or lease.

Bankers' acceptances   Negotiable interest-bearing documents by which a seller of merchandise gets money before the buyer is ready to pay. The seller receives the buyer's promise to pay the amount involved on a specified date. The buyer's bank stamps the draft "accepted," guaranteeing the payment. Accepted drafts have a ready sale to banks and others.

Bearish   An opinion or trading strategy that anticipates falling prices.

Bear market   A stock market in which prices are falling for at least two consecutive months and in which the fall wipes at least 20 percent off the market value of share price.

Beneficiary   The person (or institution) named to receive a life insurance policy's death benefits when the insured person dies. There may be one or more beneficiaries.

Beta   A measure of the extent to which a stock's price moves in tandem with the market as a whole. Beta illustrates the volatility of the asset relative to the market as a whole (usually S&P 500). Any issue that tends to rise and fall at the same rate as the market is assigned a beta of 1. A stock that moves up and down 50 percent more than the market has a 1.5 beta; it is said to be highly volatile or aggressive while a stock with a beta less than 1 is considered to be defensive.

Bid or redemption price   The price at which a mutual fund's shares are redeemed (bought back) by the fund. The bid or redemption price usually means the current net asset value per share.

Blue chip company   A nationally known and highly esteemed company noted for the quality and wide acceptance of its products and services and for its consistent record of making profits and paying dividends.

Bond   An IOU certificate in which the issuing corporation or government promises to repay a loan at a certain time and pay a specified amount of interest over that period. It is a debt instrument provided by the issuer to formalize an obligation of the issuer to the bond holder. Repayment generally is not due for a long period, usually 10 years or more. Bond holders have no ownership rights as stockholders do.

Bond discount The amount by which a bond sells below par value.

Bond fund Investment companies that hold corporate, municipal, or U.S. Treasury bonds. Such companies concentrate variously on high-grade bonds, medium-grade bonds, convertible bonds, or a combination of bonds and preferred stocks. Their main objective is the security of principal with as much income as possible.

Bond Indenture The contract describing the interest rate, maturity date, and other terms under which bonds are issued.

Bond premium The amount by which a bond sells above par value.

Bond rating An assessment of a bond's credit risk by an independent agency. The most popular are prepared by Moody's Investors Service, Inc., and Standard & Poor's Corp.

Book value per share Sum of common stock at nominal balance sheet value, capital surplus, and retained earnings as shown in company accounts, divided by number of shares outstanding.

Broker A sales and service representative who handles insurance for his or her clients, generally selling insurance of various kinds and for several companies.

Broker call rate The interest rate brokerage firms pay when they borrow from banks.

Budget A detailed plan of financial operation embodying an estimate of proposed expenditures and income for a given period or purpose.

Bullish An opinion or trading strategy that anticipates rising prices.

Bull market A market in which prices are rising.

Call feature The right of a bond issuer to call bonds for payments before they are due.

Call option A contract giving the buyer the right, but not the obligation, to purchase a specified amount of an underlying security at a predetermined strike price any time prior to expiration.

Call provision The right of the issuer of a bond to redeem the bond prior to maturity by paying the holder a call premium, usually stated as a percentage over par value. The call provision may also provide for a certain period of time immediately following issuance during which the bond may not be called.

Cap A ceiling or maximum rate increase for adjustable rate mortgages. Caps can be applied to yearly increases or increases over the life of the loan.

Capital gain or capital loss Profit or loss realized from the sale or exchange of an asset, such as securities or real estate. Under the current tax law, this can be either short term—if the asset is held one year or less—or long term—if the asset is held more than one year.

Capital gains distribution Payments to mutual fund shareholders that consist of the realized gains on the assets sold by the fund. These gains are usually paid once a year and are usually long term in nature.

Capitalization How a company is funded, including ownership capital (shareholder equity) and borrowed capital (debt).

Cash flow A gauge of a company's ability to generate cash, including income and depreciation to service debt, invest in equipment, and pay dividends.

Cash surrender value   The amount of money payable to an investor in exchange for a life insurance policy or annuity that has not yet matured.

Cash value (cash surrender value)   The tax-deferred savings component of a whole life policy. Part of the premium pays for insurance, and part goes to cash value. It is the money available upon surrender of certain life insurance policies before death or maturity. It also can be borrowed against by the policy holder. See also *loan value and policy loan.*

Certificate of deposit (CD)   A form of time deposit at a bank or savings institution, earning a specified rate of interest over a given time.

Charge card   A bank card that requires payment for purchases at fixed intervals. Normally, no interest is charged on the balance because no credit is extended. Charge cards tied to central asset accounts have a credit line based on the value of marginable securities in the account.

Chartered Life Underwriter (CLU)   A designation awarded by the American College of Life Underwriters following successful completion of an intensive college-level course of study.

Check clearing   The movement of checks from the banks or other depository institutions where they are deposited back to those on which they are written, and funds movement in the opposite direction. This process results in credits to the accounts of the institutions of deposit and corresponding debits to the accounts of the paying institutions. The Federal Reserve operates a nationwide check-clearing system, though many checks are cleared by private sector arrangements.

Claim   A notice filed with an insurance company that payment is due under the terms of the policy.

Closed-end investment company   Unlike mutual funds (known as open-end funds), a closed-end company is a type of fund that issues only a set or limited number of shares and does not redeem them (buy them back). Investors must trade their shares on the securities exchange markets, with supply and demand determining the price.

Closing   Also called *settlement.* The final home-buying step. At the closing you sign for the loan, make a down payment, and take title to your house. Closing costs, such as attorney fees, title search, and inspection, can run roughly 3 percent of the home price.

COLA   Cost of living adjustment clause, included in many labor contracts, that requires periodic adjustments of wages as to maintain constant purchasing power.

Collateral   Property offered to support a loan or credit and subject to seizure on default.

Collateralized mortgage obligations (CMOs)   Securities, such as those issued by Freddie Mac, in which the underlying mortgage pools are divided into packages with short-, medium-, and long-term maturities.

Commercial paper   Short-term unsecured notes of businesses.

Commission   The fee charged by a broker/dealer for services performed in buying or selling securities on behalf of a customer.

Common stock   Represents an ownership share in a corporation. Common stock may be of several classes, all usually combined with voting rights as to the corporation issuing such stock. It does not entitle its holders to preferential treatment for dividends or distribution of assets in the event of liquidation. Common stockholders are not guaranteed any set amount of dividends and receive dividends only if the company decides to issue them.

Condominium   Home ownership in a multiunit project. Each person owns his or her unit plus an interest in the overall land and common areas such as the lobby.

Consumer price index Commonly known as the *CPI,* is a statistical measure of the average of prices of a specified set of goods and services purchased by wage earners. The CPI, published by the Bureau of Labor Statistics of the U.S. Department of Labor, measures increases in consumer prices from the base of 100 established in 1972.

Contestability clause A clause included in most life and health insurance policies that allows the insurance company to contest payment of claims for a designated period (usually two years). It could be exercised, for example, if, prior to the second policy anniversary, the insured died from a medical condition intentionally concealed from the insurance company upon application for insurance. The policy becomes incontestable after the designated period.

Convertible bonds Debt issues that can be exchanged for a predetermined number of common shares once a company's stock appreciates to a certain level.

Cooperative (co-op) An apartment project directly owned by a corporation and indirectly owned by the residents. Each resident owns shares of stock in the corporation and holds a "proprietary lease" on his or her apartment unit.

Cost index method A means of comparing life insurance policies with the objective of identifying the most cost-effective policy.

Coupon rate The interest payment, stated as a percentage of par value, that is paid annually to the bondholder.

Coupon yield See *current (coupon) yield.*

Credit card A card that extends bank credit for purchases. Charges carry over to succeeding payment periods, and interest accrues.

Credit history The record of how a person has borrowed and repaid debts.

Credit scoring system A statistical system used to rate credit applications according to various characteristics related to creditworthiness.

Credit unions Financial cooperative organizations of individuals with a common affiliation (such as employment, labor union membership, or residence in the same neighborhood). Credit unions accept deposits of members in the form of share purchases, pay interest (dividends) on them out of earnings, and primarily provide consumer installment credit to members.

Creditworthiness Past and future ability to repay debts.

Current (coupon) yield The payments to investors expressed as a percentage of current asset price. The payments can be in the form of dividends or capital gain distributions.

Custodian For mutual funds, a qualified bank otherwise unconnected with the fund. It holds the cash and securities of the fund and performs a variety of clerical services for the fund related to the securities held.

Death benefit Total proceeds payable to the beneficiary of a life insurance policy after the policyholder's death.

Debenture A certificate stating the amount of a loan, the interest to be paid, and the time for repayment but not providing collateral. It is backed only by the corporation's reputation and promise to pay.

Debit A debt or negative balance.

Debit card A card that customers may use to make purchases through a point-of-sale terminal. The card allows electronic transfer of funds from the customer's checking or savings account to the merchant's account. Because payment is made automatically, interest is not normally charged or credit extended.

Debt-to-equity ratio Obtained by dividing a company's total liabilities (debt) by its shareholders' equity. The lower the debt-equity ratio, the healthier a company's financial condition is considered to be.

Deductible The amount of expense a policyholder must first incur before the insurer begins payment for a claim.

Defined benefit plan A retirement plan that calculates a pension by fixing the level of retirement benefits based on the years of employment or income of the worker.

Defined contribution plan A retirement plan that calculates retirement benefits by clearly specifying the amounts contributed to the plan by the employer and the employee. The actual amount of the pension is known only upon the worker's retirement.

Default The failure to meet the terms for repayment. It can apply to a person, corporation, or government.

Demand deposit A deposit payable on demand, which commonly takes the form of a checking account.

Depository Institutions Deregulation and Monetary Control Act One of a series of deregulation actions to reduce government control of the banking system and the economy. Starting in 1980, this legislation provided for abolition of interest rate ceilings on time and savings deposits. It also phased in uniform reserve requirements at all deposition institutions.

Depreciation Reduction in the value of capital goods due to wear and tear or obsolescence. Estimated depreciation may be deducted from income each year as a cost of doing business.

Discount rate The interest rate at which eligible depository institutions may borrow funds for short periods directly from the Federal Reserve banks. The law requires the board of directors of each Reserve Bank to establish the discount rate every 14 days subject to the approval of the Board of Governors in Washington.

Distributions Payments made to shareholders. These may be dividends, capital gains, or return of shareholders' capital.

Diversified investment company A company defined by the Investment Company Act of 1940 as one that invests at least 75 percent of its funds in a diversified manner with the limit that no more than 5 percent of the company's assets can be in a single issuer's securities nor can that investment amount to more than 10 percent of the issuer's outstanding securities.

Dividend The distribution of a portion of net earnings paid to its stockholders by a corporation, usually quarterly. In preferred stock, dividends are usually fixed; with common shares, dividends vary with the fortunes of the company.

Dividend rate Indicated annual payment rate based on the latest quarterly dividend plus any recurring extra or special year-end dividends.

Dollar-cost averaging Investing equal amounts of money at regular intervals regardless of whether the stock market is moving upward or downward. This reduces average share costs to the investor who acquired more shares in periods of lower securities prices and fewer shares in periods of higher prices.

Dow Jones averages The averages of industrials, transportation, and utilities that are published daily. They are the most commonly referred to averages of Wall Street's stock exchange share prices.

Earnings Profits a company generates from its operations, investments, or sale of assets. Dividends are paid out of earnings after a company has first paid taxes and interest to bondholders and has plowed any money needed for expansion back into the business.

Earnings per share   Primary earnings per share, the net income (including proceeds from certain convertible securities, warrants, and options that are common stock equivalents, but excluding extraordinary profit or loss items) divided by number of common and common-equivalent shares.

Electronic funds transfer (EFT)   Movement of bank funds initiated other than by check. Withdrawals or transfers at automated teller machines and debits to accounts at point of sale are EFTs.

Equity   In a financial sense, the value of a person's ownership in real property or securities beyond the amount that is owed on it. A stockholder's equity in a corporation is the value of the shares he or she holds. A homeowner's equity is the difference between the current market value of the house minus the balance due on any mortgages.

Equity income   A firm's net operating income less loan interest.

Escrow (or trust) account   Depositing money or documents with a neutral third party until the actual sale. For example, a seller might put a deed in escrow and a buyer a down payment, both to be held until the closing. Escrow can also refer to the tax and insurance money paid out at settlement and held by the lender until both come due.

Estate planning   Establishing during one's lifetime a definite plan for the administration and disposition of one's property at one's death. This is usually set forth in a will and in trust agreements.

Estate taxes   Taxes imposed by the federal government (and by some state governments) on the taxable estate of a person who has died.

Eurodollars   Deposits denominated in U.S. dollars at banks and other financial institutions outside the United States. Although this name originated because of the large amounts of such deposits held at banks in Western Europe, sim-

ilar deposits in other parts of the world are also called *Eurodollars*.

Ex-dividend date   The beginning of a period during which purchasers of a stock do not qualify to receive the next quarterly dividend, typically paid three to four weeks later.

Executor (Executrix)   The person named in a will to manage the estate of a deceased person according to the terms of the will and subject to the rules of law and the supervision of a surrogate court judge.

Exercise period   The time period that an option can be executed. Options are generally written for three-, six-, and nine- month periods.

Exercise price   The price at which an option can be executed.

Face value   The amount stated on the face of a policy that will be paid in case of death or at maturity. It does not include dividend additions or amounts payable under accidental death or other special provisions.

Family of funds   A group of mutual funds under a single management group. Investors can switch from one fund to another free or at a minimal charge, often via telephone.

Fannie Mae   (Federal National Mortgage Association). Congressionally chartered, shareholder-owned mortgages. Fannie Mae holds a large "portfolio" of mortgages, but it is not a direct lender. Fannie Mae is the largest single supplier of home mortgage funds in the nation.

Fannie Mae securities   Mortgage securities sold by the Federal National Mortgage Association (FNMA) and backed, as to timely interest and principal payments, by the Federal Housing Administration.

Federal Deposit Insurance Corporation (FDIC) Agency of the federal government that insures accounts at most commercial banks and mutual savings banks. The FDIC also has primary federal supervisory authority over insured state banks that are not members of the Federal Reserve System.

Federal funds   Reserve balances that depository institutions lend each other, usually on an overnight basis. In addition, federal funds include certain other kinds of borrowings by depository institutions from each other and from federal agencies.

Federal Reserve   The U.S. Central Bank often referred to as *The Fed*. Its chief responsibility is to regulate the flow of money and credit in order to promote economic stability and growth. It also performs many service functions for banks, the Treasury, and the public.

FHA loan   Short for the Federal Housing Administration, which insures this type of loan. An FHA loan allows borrowers to make as little as a 3 percent down payment on a home.

Finance charge   The total cost of a loan in dollars as required by the Truth in Lending Act.

Financial Accounting Standards Board (FASB)   An organization independent of other businesses that is responsible for establishing standards for financial accounting and reporting. These standards are the generally accepted accounting principles (GAAP) used by auditors and accountants.

Financial planning   The analysis and coordination of one's long-term personal finances in order to achieve personal financial objectives successfully.

Financial statement   A report summarizing the financial condition of an organization on a specific date or for a specific period.

First mortgage   A legal instrument that creates or conveys a lien on or a claim against an owner's rights in property prior to a lien created by any other mortgage or bond.

Fiscal policy   Government policy regarding taxation and spending. Fiscal policy is made by Congress and the administration.

Fiscal year   A period of 12 consecutive months chosen by a business as the accounting period for annual reports.

Fixed-income fund   A mutual fund that invests in corporate, government, or other issuer bonds. Despite the name, annual income is rarely fixed or guaranteed.

Fixed-rate mortgage   A loan, secured against the value of a home, made for a specific number of years. Monthly payments, interest rates, and loan term are fixed for 25 to 30 years and may not be changed.

Float   Checkbook money that, for a period of time, appears on the books of both the check writer and the check receiver due to a lag in the check collection process.

Floater policy   An insurance policy covering property for all risks without regard to its location at the time of loss.

Foreclosure   A proceeding that terminates or closes out all interests in real estate inferior to the interest of the mortgage being foreclosed.

Freddie Mac   (Federal Home Loan Mortgage Corporation). Buys conventional mortgages from mortgage lenders, packages them into pools of mortgage pass-through securities, and sells them through dealers to institutions such as thrifts, insurance companies, and pension funds.

Freddie Mac securities   Mortgage securities issued and guaranteed, as to timely interest payments and eventual principal payments, by the Federal Home Loan Mortgage Corp.

Front-end load fees   Common jargon for fees charged by a syndicator in developing, administrating, and closing a real estate limited partnership offering. These fees include expenses of the offering together with all fees charged by the syndicator.

Full-faith-and-credit bond   An alternative term for a general obligation bond, often used to contrast such a bond with a moral-obligation bond or revenue bond.

Fundamental analysis   Price forecasting based on evaluation of supply and demand in a particular market.

Future value   The amount that an investment will be worth at some future time if invested at a constant rate of interest.

Futures contract   A standardized exchange-traded contract in which the buyer agrees to take, or seller agrees to deliver, a fixed amount of a particular commodity on a specified future date at a locked-in price.

Futures exchange   An organization licensed and regulated by the Commodity Futures Trading Commission and that operates a market in which goods are bought and sold for delivery at a specified future date but at a price agreed upon at the present.

Futures options   Contracts on futures of commodities such as agricultural products, grain, currency, and precious metals, or of cash-settled instruments such as options on Treasury bond futures. These are synthetic options, which are settled in cash.

Futures price   The price at which a future commitment is traded.

Garnishment   The court-sanctioned procedure by which a portion of a debtor's wages is set aside to repay creditors.

GEMs   (growing equity mortgages). Mortgages for which the repayment schedule is higher at first then decreases. They are most attractive to home buyers earning high taxable incomes that they expect to decline in the future. In many respects, these are the opposite of GPMs.

General obligation bond   A bond that has had the formal approval of either the voters or their legislature. The government's promise to repay the principal and pay the interest is constitutionally guaranteed to on the strength of its ability to tax the population.

Ginnie Mae   (Government National Mortgage Association). An agency within the U. S. Department of Housing and Urban Development. Also refers to mortgages backed by Ginnie Mae, one of the federal entities created to encourage lending to home buyers, and guaranteed as to timely interest and principal payments.

Going naked   Selling an option without owning the underlying security.

Government obligations   Instruments of the U.S. government's public debt, such as Treasury bills, notes, bonds, savings bonds, and retirement plan bonds. These are fully backed by the government, as opposed to U.S. government agency securities.

GPMs   (graduated payment mortgages) Mortgages with fixed rates, but graduated repayment schedules. Repayments are lower in the first five to seven years and higher thereafter. This is most attractive to young prospective homeowners who expect to be earning more money in the coming years but want to move in now.

Grace period   A period (usually 31 days) of time after a payment due date not subject to late charges.

Graduated payment mortgage   Initial monthly payments are low and increase over a 5- to 10-year period. They are appropriate for home buyers who expect their income to increase over a period of years. The term of loan can be fixed for 25 to 30 years. Interest rate can be fixed or adjustable.

Gross income Total earnings prior to deductions for taxes, health insurance, employee benefit plans, and so on.

Gross national product (GNP) The total value of a nation's output of goods and services.

Growing equity mortgage Monthly payments that are usually fixed for a 25- to 30-year term but increase 3 to 7 percent a year after the third year. Additional payment goes toward principal. Loan is paid off in 12 to 18 years.

Growth Fund A mutual fund that seeks growth of capital as its primary objective. The fund usually invests in common stocks and securities convertible into common stock. Income usually plays a minor role in asset selection.

Growth-income funds A mutual fund that seeks both capital growth and current income. The assets of these funds may be balanced (consist of both equities and bonds) or stock funds whose assets are invested in high-yielding common stocks.

Growth stock A stock whose return to investors comes primarily from increases in share price. Such stocks may pay little or no dividends because much of their earnings is used to keep the company growing.

Guaranteed insurability An option or rider often available with cash value policies that permits the policyholder to buy additional amounts of life insurance at stated times without evidence of insurability.

Health maintenance organization (HMO) A prepayment health care plan that provides complete medical coverage for a flat premium.

Hedge The implementation of strategies designed to reduce or eliminate the risk of certain investments. A hedge often involves buying or selling options and futures contracts as a temporary substitute in order to fix the price of an intended cash market transaction.

High-yield stock A stock whose yield is above the average yield for Standard & Poor's index of 500 stocks, recently 3.8 percent. Also sometimes called an *income stock*.

Homeowner insurance Protection for both real and personal property. Most homeowner policies also provide coverage for miscellaneous costs resulting from an insured loss such as *liability coverage*, which protects you against lawsuits resulting from bodily injury or property damage you caused, and *nonliability coverage*, for injury or property damage for which you are morally, but not legally, responsible.

Income dividends Payments to mutual fund shareholders of dividends, interest, and short-term capital gains earned on the fund's portfolio securities after deducting fund operating expenses. They are taxable at ordinary rates.

Income fund A mutual fund whose primary objective is current income. Such funds generally invest their assets in corporate or other bonds. Some income funds may include high-yielding common stocks in their portfolios.

Income statement A statement of revenues and earnings for a given period of time, usually one year.

Index fund A mutual fund designed to follow market indicators, such as S&P's 500 stock index. They are intended to serve as surrogates for a portion of the overall market portfolio.

Index of leading economic indicators A composite of 12 economic measurements that was developed to help forecast likely changes in the economy as a whole. It is compiled by the Commerce Department.

Index options A put or a call on an actual index of prices like the Standard & Poor's 100. Unlike options on individual stocks, index options are settled by the exchange of money, not the delivery of stock.

Individual retirement account (IRA) A provision of U.S. tax law that allows individuals not covered by group retirement plans to deposit up to 15 percent of their income a year into a special tax-exempt fund.

Insured The person covered by a life insurance policy.

Intangible assets Those company-owned items that have no physical existence but have real value because they can help a company generate cash. Examples are patents and brand names.

Internal rate of return (IRR) Equates the value of cash returns with cash invested over a specific period of time and represents the true annual rate of earnings on an investment.

Intestate A person who dies without disposing of his or her property by a valid will.

Intrinsic risk The risk directly related to a specific company's stock price; also called *unsystematic risk*.

Investment company A firm that reinvests money obtained through the issuance of its own securities. Generally called *mutual funds* or *investment trusts*, these companies invest in various types of stocks and bonds and redeem their shares on demand.

Investment Company Act Federal statute enacted in 1940 for the registration and regulation of investment companies.

Investment grade A bond with relatively low credit risk suitable for purchase by institutional investors.

Investment objective The goal (e.g., long-term capital growth, current income) that an investor or a mutual fund pursues.

Issuer A corporation or municipality that raises cash through the public sale of bonds or stocks.

Joint account A credit arrangement for two or more persons, enabling all to use an account and assume liability to repay.

Junk bond A high-yield, high-risk bond, rated below BBB by a bond-rating agency.

Kiddie tax The part of the 1986 Tax Reform Act that requires that part of some children's income be taxed at their parents' tax rate. This tax has largely eliminated the use of children by their parents as a tax shelter.

Lessee One who rents real or personal property from a lessor for a fee, called *rent*.

Lessor One who owns real or personal property that is leased.

Level premium insurance Insurance whose cost is spread evenly over the premium payment period. The premium remains unchanged from year to year and is more than the actual cost of protection in the earlier years of the policy and less in the later years.

Leverage The unequal relationship between a market value price change, as a percentage, and the result this amount has on money expressed as a percentage, such as a 10 percent market value change resulting in a 100 percent return on, or loss of, investment. This is made possible through the use of borrowed funds for investment purposes. You can do it in commodity futures and in options that require a fraction of the stock price or in a margin account, entitling you to buy shares on credit. Leverage is also possible in real estate transactions. Positive leverage occurs when investment returns are greater than the cost of borrowed funds. The result is greater return on equity. The reverse (negative leverage) occurs when the cost of borrowed funds exceeds investment returns.

Liability Legal responsibility to repay debt.

Lien A recorded or filed claim one person has against the property of another person as security for payment of a debt.

Limited partnership   A partnership wherein the losses as to the limited partners are limited to the amount invested by such limited partner. Limited partners usually exercise no influence in making investments or in management decisions.

Line of credit   The dollar amount a lender is making available to a borrower, which may or may not be borrowed.

Liquidity   Easy access to your own money. The most liquid investments—money market funds, for one—give you back your capital quickly and intact. Most stocks and many bonds can be sold easily but always at uncertain prices. Examples of illiquid investments are real estate and tax shelters.

Load fund   A mutual fund that imposes a charge made at the time of purchase or sale to cover overhead, such as sales commissions and distribution fees. A front-end load is the fee paid when buying into a fund. A back-end load is the fee paid when selling it.

Loan value   The amount that can be borrowed at a specified rate of interest from the issuing insurance company by the policy owner, using the value of the policy as collateral. If the policyholder dies with the debt partially or fully unpaid, then the amount borrowed, plus any accrued interest, is deducted from the amount payable. See also *cash value* and *policy loan*.

Long position   Owning or contracting to purchase an underlying security.

Loss assessment endorsement   A feature of condominium owners' insurance that protects the unit owner from inadequacies in the association's coverage.

Management company   The business entity that begins, promotes, and manages a fund or group of mutual funds, each of which is a separate corporation with its own board of directors.

Margin   The amount of cash that must be put up as collateral by a customer when he or she uses a broker's credit to purchase a security. When trading on margin, investors must borrow to finance the leveraged part of their portfolios. Margin requirement set by the Federal Reserve is currently 50 percent. That is the percentage of the purchase price the buyer must put up; he or she can borrow the rest.

Margin call   A broker's demand for more cash or marginable securities to maintain minimum margin requirements.

Marginable securities   Stocks, mutual funds, or bonds that, according to Federal Reserve guidelines, can be used as collateral for loans.

Market capitalization or market value   Interchangeably used terms referring to the number of shares outstanding, multiplied by the current share price. This is how the stock market values a company. For example, if the current share price is $4 and the number of shares outstanding is 5,000,000, market capitalization $4 \times 5,000,000 = \$20,000,000$.

Market maker   Securities firms that buy, sell, and maintain inventories of a specific stock in order that other securities firms can buy or sell shares of that stock. Market makers for stocks that trade on stock exchanges are called *specialists*. They do their actual market trading from the floor of the exchanges upon which the stock trades.

Market volume   The number of shares traded on a given day is known as *market volume* and indicates the mood of investors. If stock prices decline in a market where trading is high, this indicates a bearish, downward trend. Consistently high volume trading in a rising market usually signals investor optimism and a bullish trend.

Maturity date   The date on which final payment is due.

Medigap Private health insurance designed to supplement Medicare.

Monetary policy Federal Reserve actions to influence the cost and availability of money and credit, as a means of helping to promote high employment, economic growth, price stability, and a stability in international transactions. Tools of monetary policy include open market operations, discount rate changes, and reserve requirements.

Money market mutual fund A mutual fund that invests in short-term securities. It seeks maximum current income through investment in securities whose maturities are less than one year. Such securities may include bank CDs, bankers' acceptances, T-bills, repurchase agreements (repos), and commercial paper.

Money markets Markets where short-term securities are traded.

Moral obligation bond A government bond that has not had the formal approval of either the voters or their legislature. It is backed only by the government's "moral obligation" to repay the principal and interest on time.

Mortality table A statistical table showing the probability of death at each age.

Mortgage A loan backed by real estate; a legal instrument by which a borrower gives a creditor a lien on property as security for a loan.

Mortgage-backed securities Investments such as Ginnie Maes, Fannie Maes, and Freddie Macs that are based on a pooling of home loans.

Mortgage bonds Bonds that are backed by real property of the issuing corporation, such as land or buildings, or both.

Mortgage insurance Coverage that guarantees that your home loan will be paid in the event of your death or disability. The lender is the beneficiary.

Mortgagee A lender of money on the security of a mortgage (e.g., a bank).

Mortgagor An owner of property who executes a mortgage covering property as security for a loan.

Municipal bond A general obligation bond issued by a state, county, city, town, or village; or a bond issued by an agency or authority set up by one of these governmental units. In general, interest paid on municipal bonds is exempt from federal income taxes. These bonds are also known as *tax-exempts*. There are both general obligation bonds and revenue bonds.

Municipal bond fund A mutual fund that specializes in investing in municipal bonds. Investors in municipal funds may also enjoy federal income tax exemptions on their dividends.

Mutual fund A fund operated by an investment company that pools the money of many investors to purchase securities or other investments. The primary advantages of a mutual fund are diversification and professional management. Mutual funds differ in their orientation toward growth and income in order to meet the diverse needs of investors. Mutual funds ordinarily stand ready to buy back (redeem) shares at their current net asset value. The value of the shares depends on the market value of the fund's portfolio securities at the time. Also, most mutual funds continuously offer new shares to investors.

Mutual fund families A mutual fund sponsor usually offers a number of funds with different investment objectives within its fund family.

Mutual savings banks Accept deposits primarily from individuals and place most of their funds into mortgage loans. These institutions are prominent in many of the northeastern states. Savings banks generally have broader asset and liability powers than savings and loan associations but narrower powers than commercial banks. Most savings banks are authorized to offer checking-type accounts.

National Credit Union Administration (NCUA) The federal government agency that supervises, charters, and insures federal credit unions. NCUA also insures state-chartered credit unions that apply and qualify for insurance. NCUA also operates a credit facility for member credit unions.

Negative amortization Amount of principal balance owed by the buyer increases because lower interest rate-based payments do not cover interest due.

Negotiable order of withdrawal (NOW) account An interest-earning account on which checks may be drawn. Withdrawals from NOW accounts may be subject to a 14-day or more notice requirement, although such is rarely imposed. NOW accounts may be offered by commercial banks, mutual savings banks, and savings and loan associations and may be owned only by individuals and certain nonprofit organizations.

Net asset value (NAV) More precisely *net asset value per share*. The daily closing price used by investment companies for a mutual funds portfolio's securities. It is calculated at least daily by totaling the market value of all securities owned by the company divided by the total number of shares outstanding.

Net earnings, net income, net profits The "bottom line" of an income statement, or the amount by which total revenues exceed total expenses for a given period. The opposite is *net losses*.

Net realized capital gains The net difference between gains and losses on the sale of securities by a mutual fund. Generally, only those securities that have been held for a period longer than one year are included in the computation.

Net worth statement A statement showing the total assets of a person or business less the total liabilities.

No-load fund A mutual fund selling its shares at net asset value without the addition of sales charges. In a purchase of a no-load investment instrument, the investor pays only the face value of the instrument purchased and pays no commissions or other costs associated with the sale of such instrument.

Nonparticipating life insurance Life insurance in which the premium is calculated to cover as closely as possible the anticipated costs of insurance protection. No dividends are payable.

Note A certificate issued by a corporation or government stating the amount of a loan, the interest to be paid, and the collateral pledged in the event payment cannot be made. The date for repayment is generally more than a year after issue but not more than seven or eight years later. The shorter interval for repayment is the principal difference between a note and a bond.

Offset A previously bought (sold) futures contract is offset, or closed, when an order to sell (buy) the same contract is executed on the same exchange.

Odd lotter An investor who buys or sells stocks in less than a round lot of 100 shares. Investors pay extra to be an odd lotter, typically 12.5 cents a share plus the highest brokerage fee.

Open-end investment company An investment company (mutual fund) that continually issues shares of stock. Such shares are usually sold and redeemed on the basis of the net asset value that is computed at the market close each day. It has no set number of shares but accepts deposits from as many investors as are interested in participating.

Open-end lease Lease that may involve an additional payment based on the value of property when returned.

Open market operations Purchases and sales of government and certain other securities in the open market by the New York Federal Reserve Bank as directed by the FOMC in order to influence the volume of money and credit in the economy. Purchases inject reserves into the depository system and lead to expansion in money and credit; sales have the opposite effect. Open market operations are the Federal Reserve's most important and most flexible monetary policy tool. They are used both to raise or lower growth in money and credit and to offset the impact of other factors on the reserve positions of depository institutions.

Option An investment instrument that gives the purchaser the right, but not the obligation, to buy or sell either individual stocks or an index of stocks at a particular fixed price, called the *exercise price*, within a specified time period.

Ordinary life insurance Life insurance usually issued in amounts of $1,000 or more with premiums payable on an annual, semiannual, quarterly, or monthly basis. The term is also used to mean straight life insurance.

Origination fee A fee charged by the lender to the borrower for making a mortgage or cooperative loan. It is also referred to as *points*.

Out of the money Describes a call option whose strike exceeds the price of the underlying index or a put option whose strike price is lower than the price of the underlying index.

Outstanding Unpaid.

Over the counter Any trading of securities apart from trading on an exchange. Over-the-counter stocks and bonds are bought and sold primarily over the telephone. Dealers do not have to be members of an exchange. Securities of smaller companies are frequently bought and sold in this market. Over-the-counter quotations are supplied by the National Association of Securities Dealers' Automated Quotations (NASDAQ) system.

Overdraft checking account A line of credit permitting a person to write checks for more than the actual account balance, with interest charged on the amount borrowed.

Par value Also called *face value*. The amount returned to bond holders at maturity—$1,000 for most corporate bonds, $5,000 for most municipal bonds. In the case of a stock, the amount listed on the company's balance sheet, which usually has no relation to the stock's market value.

Pass-through certificates Securities in which principal and interest payments are passed on to investors by intermediary agencies, that pool and package the underlying loans.

Payout ratio The percentage of a company's profits paid out to shareholders in dividends. The lower the payout ratio, the greater the odds that the firm's earnings will sustain future dividend payments.

P/E ratio See *price-earnings ratio*.

Penny stocks Low-priced stocks, often highly speculative, usually selling at less than $1 a share.

PITI Shorthand for a homeowner's monthly payment to the mortgage lender consisting of principal, interest, (real estate) taxes, and insurance.

Plan See *financial planning*.

Point 1. Unit of measure in reporting security prices. When referring to share prices of stock, a point is $1. For bonds, a point represents $10. 2. A one-time up-front finance fee charged borrowers by lenders, included as part of a first mortgage loan. This is in addition to monthly interest. Each point equals 1 percent of the loan amount.

Point of sale (POS) Systems that allow for transfer of funds between accounts, authorization for credit, verification of checks, and provision of related services at the time of purchase. POS terminals are located in many shopping areas and allow customers or participating financial institutions to effect transactions through the use of machine-readable debit cards.

Policy loan The withdrawal of cash value by the owner from the insurance company. This borrowing is considered a loan because, technically, the cash value of the policy belongs to the insurer. Interest sometimes is not charged, but when it is, the rate is usually below market. See also *cash value* and *loan value*.

Prenuptial agreement A legal contract written by a couple before marriage, specifying the terms of their marriage and the right of each partner, pertaining to such matters as assets, survivorship, and custody of children in the event of death or divorce.

Prepayment penalty Assessed by loan company or originator to borrower who pays off a loan before the term is finished.

Present value The amount that, if invested today at a constant rate of interest, will grow to a specified future amount.

Price-earnings (P/E) ratio The price (P) of a share of stock divided by the earnings per share (E) for a 12-month period. For example, a stock selling for $60 a share and earning $6 a share would be selling at a price-earnings ratio of 10 to 1.

Price index A device to show the relative change in the average of the prices of a number of selected goods over time. The U.S. government compiles many price indexes.

Prime rate The base interest rate that commercial banks charge on loans to their biggest borrowers with the best credit ratings. Fluctuations in the prime rate seldom have an immediate impact on consumer loan rates. Over the long term, however, consistent increases (or decreases) in the prime rate can lead to increases (or decreases) in the interest rates for mortgages and all types of personal loans.

Principal The actual amount of a loan before finance charges and other charges are added or deducted.

Private placement Generally, an investment in real estate offered for sale to a small group of investors, usually under exemptions to registration allowed under the Securities and Exchange Act and state securities laws.

Probate process The legal act of admitting a will before a court of law to establish official proof of its validity.

Producer-price index Actually three indexes. The index for finished goods represents "commodities that will not undergo further processing and are ready for sale to the ultimate user," either an individual or business. The other two indexes are for intermediate materials and for crude materials. All three replaced the wholesale price index, which wholesalers claimed was misleading.

Prospectus The document that formally offers a new issue of securities to the public and describes the issuing organization in detail. The prospectus contains per share growth, capital changes over the years, and an auditor's report.

Put An option that gives the buyer the right, but not the obligation, to sell shares of stock at a selected price within a specified period.

Real estate investment trust (REIT) A type of company in which investors pool their funds to buy and manage real estate or to finance real estate construction or purchases.

Real rate of return The stated rate of return less both the inflation rate and the risk premium.

Realtor Real estate agent who is a member of the National Association of Realtors.

Recording fee Cost of recording necessary documents with the appropriate state or county administrative office.

Red herring The mandatory disclosure document (known formally as a *preliminary prospectus*) that companies provide before they issue new securities. It not only spells out how the proceeds will be used but also discusses candidly such sensitive matters as the strength of the competition and management's background.

Redemption price The amount per share the mutual fund shareholder receives when he or she cashes in shares (also known as *bid price*). The value of the share depends on the market value of the fund's portfolio securities at the time.

Refinance To revise the payment schedule of existing debt.

Regulation Q A regulation giving the Federal Reserve Board the power to set the maximum interest rates that S&Ls and banks could pay on savings deposits. It was phased out in 1986.

Reinvestment privilege A service provided by most mutual funds for the automatic reinvestment of dividends and capital gains or interest distributions into additional fund shares.

REIT See *real estate investment trust.*

Renewable term insurance Term insurance that can be renewed at the end of the term, at the policyholder's option, and without evidence of insurability, for a limited number of successive terms. The rates increase at each renewal as the age of the insured increases.

Repurchase agreement (repo) An arrangement with a bank in which the investor acquires certain short-term securities subject to a commitment from the bank to repurchase the securities on a specified date.

Rescission rights A clause in a contract that grants the buyers the right to cancel the contract and return to the position they would have occupied if the contract had not been made.

Reserve requirement The proportion of their customers' deposits that commercial banks must keep in cash or on deposit with the Reserve System, by order of the Federal Reserve Board, to protect the deposits.

Return to shareholders The net earnings after taxes divided by the shareholders, equity. It is a good measure for comparing the performance of different companies. For example, $2,000,000 (Net Earnings)/5,000,000 (Shareholders, Equity) = 40%.

Revenue bond A bond backed only by the revenue of the airport, turnpike, or other facility that was built with the money it raised.

Revolving account A line of credit that may be used repeatedly up to a certain specified limit.

Rider An amendment to a policy that modifies it by expanding or restricting benefits or excluding certain conditions from coverage.

Risk The possibility or chance of gain or loss.

Risk capital Funds used for risky investments; the amount of money that could be lost completely without significantly changing the trader's overall financial condition.

Sallie Maes Poolings of student loans guaranteed by the Student Loan Marketing Association (SLMA) to increase the availability of education loans. Sallie Mae packages the loans after buying them on the secondary market from lenders. Sallie Mae stock is publicly traded.

Savings and loan associations Also sometimes called *building and loan associations, cooperative banks*, or *homestead associations*. They accept deposits primarily from individuals and channel their funds primarily into residential mortgage loans. Most savings and loan associations are technically owned by the depositors, who receive shares in the association for their deposits.

Selling short To sell a company's stock (borrowed from a broker) in the hope that a price drop will allow the investor to repurchase the stock later at a lower price. The subsequent repurchase is called *covering the short position*.

Shareholders' equity The portion of a company's balance sheet made up of the stock owned by its shareholders.

Shares fully diluted The number of common shares that would be outstanding if all options and warrants to buy common stock were exercised and all preferred stock with conversion privileges were converted.

Shares outstanding The number of common shares actually issued (thus outstanding) as of a company's latest available financial report, excluding treasury shares.

Short position Borrowing or contracting to sell an underlying security.

Simple interest A method of calculating interest on an outstanding balance that produces a declining finance charge with each payment of the installment loan.

Single-premium life A life insurance policy that requires just one initial payment. These policies are usually geared toward investors who want high cash value more than insurance coverage.

Sinking fund Segregated assets that are accumulated for the retirement of bonds.

Social Security A government-sponsored compulsory insurance program for workers in the United States against the risks of death, disability, and old age.

Special situation fund A mutual fund that specializes in the securities of certain industries, special types of securities, or regionally issued assets.

Specialist On the stock exchanges, an exchange member who is designated to maintain a fair and orderly market in a specified stock.

Speculation A highly risky investment; the commitment of risk capital in order to realize a profit from expected price changes; usually characterized by leverage.

Split The division of a company's outstanding shares of stock into a larger number of shares. A 2-for-1 split with 1 million shares outstanding would produce 2 million like shares of stock. A person formerly owning 100 shares would now own 200 shares.

Sponsor The originator of a unit trust, usually a brokerage or investment banking firm.

Statement of financial position A statement outlining how a company's funds were obtained and spent during the past year, including changes in depreciation and debt.

Stock-for-debt exchange The process by which a company issues additional stock to a creditor, paying off debt and lowering its debt-to-equity ratio.

Stock index futures Futures contracts with a value linked directly to broad measure indexes or averages of common stock prices.

Stop order Standing instructions to one's broker to sell designated securities if the price falls below a given point. Think of it as a kind of preprogrammed panic button. Stop orders, however, are not fool-proof. If stock falls too fast, the stockholder may get less than his or her trigger price. With other types of orders the stockholder can arrange to sell when their stocks reach the profit target.

Straight life insurance See *whole life insurance*.

Strike price The price at which a futures option gives you the right to buy or sell a futures contract.

Stripped treasuries U.S. Treasury debt obligations in which coupons are removed by brokerage houses, creating zero-coupon bonds.

Sweep The automatic deposit of cash into a money market fund.

Tax-exempt bonds Bonds whose earnings are not subject to income tax. U.S. federal income tax is not taken from interest paid on bonds issued by state, country, and local governments.

Tax-free income fund A type of fund that invests solely in tax-free securities, notably municipal bonds. Some funds specialize further, buying bonds of only one state and selling shares in that state. These are referred to as *double tax-free funds*, since neither federal nor state taxes are assessed.

Tax shelter An investment that produces tax-free cash flow while generating losses to shield from taxation income from sources outside the investment as well as income within the investment.

Taxable-equivalent yield The yield an investor has to get on a taxable investment to equal a tax-free yield, taking the investor's tax rate into account.

Technical analysis Price forecasting based on interpretation of chart patterns of historical prices in a particular market.

Tender offer A request by one company to the shareholders of another to sell, or tender, their shares. The object is a takeover, often a hostile one. With tender offers lately averaging 50 percent above the price before investors got wind of merger plans, lucky shareholders are cashing in handsomely.

10-K A detailed financial statement that companies must file each year with the Securities and Exchange Commission. The 10-K is a fount of data unavailable elsewhere on such pertinent matters as principal shareholders and earnings of subsidiaries. Companies must send this document to shareholders who request it. If you are not a shareholder, you can get a copy from the SEC (Public Reference Room, Washington, DC 20549). It will cost at least $5.

Term life insurance The most basic type of life insurance and often the least expensive. It covers a policyholder for only a certain period of time (the term), not his or her entire life. It pays death benefits to beneficiaries only if death occurs during the term of the policy.

Term rider Term insurance added to a "whole life" policy when purchased or at a later date.

Thrift A financial intermediary that takes deposits and makes loans for the purchase of homes and other durable goods.

Title search A check of public records to determine current ownership of a parcel of real estate.

Total return The percentage return received on an investment, taking into account both price increases and income-dividends in the case of stock.

Transfer agent A bank or some other entity that facilitates the transfer of mutual fund shares and disbursement of dividends and maintains shareholder records. It is reimbursed for services by both the investment adviser and the fund.

Treasuries   See *Treasury securities*.

Treasury bills   Interest-bearing obligations of the U.S. government issued by the Treasury, maturing in a year or less. The buyer's income is determined by the discount below par when the bills are sold by the Treasury at auctions.

Treasury bonds   Interest-bearing obligations of the U.S. government issued by the Treasury that come due in 10 years or more.

Treasury notes   Interest-bearing obligations of the U.S. government issued by the Treasury that come due in 1 to 10 years.

Treasury securities   Interest-bearing obligations of the U.S. government issued by the Treasury as a means of borrowing money to meet government expenditures not covered by tax revenues. Marketable Treasury securities fall into three categories: bills, notes, and bonds. The Federal Reserve System holds more than $100 billion of these obligations, acquired through open market operations.

Trust   A property interest held by one person for the benefit of another, usually under conditional terms such as that ownership transfers to a trustee until an heir becomes of legal age.

Turnover rate   The frequency with which a mutual fund replaces its portfolio, based on total sales and purchases. This can be used to measure a fund's stability and market activity. A portfolio turnover of 100 percent implies a complete turnover of fund assets within one year.

12b-1 plan   Named for an SEC ruling, provides that a mutual fund may assess a fee against the assets of the fund to cover marketing and distribution expenses. This plan is in addition to the adviser's management fee agreement (which is not allowed to include fees for these purposes). The information must be provided in the prospectus.

Underwriter   A company that provides consulting and marketing services to corporations and municipalities selling bonds to the public. With respect to mortgage lending, an underwriter is a proposed lender who reviews a loan application and approves or denies such application based upon the data before him or her. In the offering of securities, underwriting is the process through which the investment or brokerage firm sells the issue and, unless sold on a "best-effort basis," agrees to purchase the shares not bought by the public.

Unemployment rate   As compiled by the Labor Department, the percentage of the civilian workforce that is looking for jobs, adjusted for seasonal variations.

Unit investment trusts (UITs)   A limited portfolio of diversified bonds or other securities in which investors may purchase shares. Unlike a mutual fund, no new securities will be added to the portfolio.

Universal life insurance   Life insurance that combines term life insurance and a money market investment fund in one policy. Under most policies, policyholders receive both the face amount of the policy and the cash value of the investment fund as a death benefit.

VA loan   Veterans Administration backing of home loans for veterans that can mean a low down payment or none at all.

Variable life insurance   Whole life policies that invest the cash value portion in stock, bond, and money market mutual funds. The death benefit is guaranteed never to fall below the face value, but it could increase if the value of the securities increases. There may be no guaranteed cash surrender value under this kind of policy. Variable life comes in both universal and single premium forms.

Variable rate mortgage   A home mortgage with an interest rate that fluctuates during the life of the mortgage, usually in accordance with a specified market rate or index. The maximum permissible increase in the mortgage interest rate and monthly payment is limited by law and regulation and must be disclosed at the time the mortgage loan is made.

Vesting   Making an employee pension irrevocable by the employer. When an employee is vested in a pension plan, he or she can draw the expected benefits at retirement age, even if that employment was terminated earlier.

Waiver of premium   A provision that under certain conditions an insurance policy will be kept in full force without the payment of premiums. It usually serves as a total and permanent disability benefit.

Warrant   The right to purchase securities at a stated price within a specified time.

Whole life (straight life) insurance   The most basic type of cash value insurance. A plan of insurance for the whole of life, with premiums payable for life. Whole life insurance policies provide both life insurance and cash value. The cash value results from a deliberate premium overcharge in the early years of the policy.

Working capital   The difference between current assets and current liabilities on the balance sheet, which indicates whether or not a company is solvent. The statement of changes in financial position shows how working capital occurred and breaks it down into component parts useful in calculating cash flow.

Wraparound mortgage   A second mortgage on a property that includes the balance due under the first mortgage as well as additional financing. The wraparound lender collects payments based on the full amount of the second mortgage and from the amount of these mortgage payments, continues to make payments on the first mortgage, which is kept in place.

Yield   The annual rate of return on an investment, as paid in dividends or interest. It is calculated as a percentage of the amount invested. It is expressed as the interest or dividend payments generated by a bond or stock divided by its current price. A decline in a stock's or bond's price boosts its yield even though the dividend or interest payment remains unchanged.

Yield curve   A line charting the relationship between bond yields and bond maturities.

Yield to maturity (YTM)   An important indicator of rates of return on interest rate-sensitive investments. Securities are assumed held until the date principal is repaid, and interest payments are assumed to be reinvested at the YTM rate.

Zero-coupon bonds   Securities that do not pay interest but are instead sold at a deep discount from face value. They rise in price as the maturity date nears and are redeemed at face value upon maturity.

Annual Compound Interest Rate (Future Value)

Future Value of $1—Principal Plus Accumulated Interests Compounded Annually

Number of Years	1.00%	1.50%	2.00%	2.50%	3.00%	3.50%	4.00%	4.50%	5.00%	5.50%	6.00%	6.50%	7.00%	7.50%	8.00%	8.50%	9.00%	9.50%
1	1.010	1.015	1.020	1.025	1.030	1.035	1.040	1.045	1.050	1.055	1.060	1.065	1.070	1.075	1.080	1.085	1.090	1.095
2	1.020	1.030	1.040	1.051	1.061	1.071	1.082	1.092	1.103	1.113	1.124	1.134	1.145	1.156	1.166	1.177	1.188	1.199
3	1.030	1.046	1.061	1.077	1.093	1.109	1.125	1.141	1.158	1.174	1.191	1.208	1.225	1.242	1.260	1.277	1.295	1.313
4	1.041	1.061	1.082	1.104	1.126	1.148	1.170	1.193	1.216	1.239	1.262	1.286	1.311	1.335	1.360	1.386	1.412	1.438
5	1.051	1.077	1.104	1.131	1.159	1.188	1.217	1.246	1.276	1.307	1.338	1.370	1.403	1.436	1.469	1.504	1.539	1.574
6	1.062	1.093	1.126	1.160	1.194	1.229	1.265	1.302	1.340	1.379	1.419	1.459	1.501	1.543	1.587	1.631	1.677	1.724
7	1.072	1.110	1.149	1.189	1.230	1.272	1.316	1.361	1.407	1.455	1.504	1.554	1.606	1.659	1.714	1.770	1.828	1.888
8	1.083	1.126	1.172	1.218	1.267	1.317	1.369	1.422	1.477	1.535	1.594	1.655	1.718	1.783	1.851	1.921	1.993	2.067
9	1.094	1.143	1.195	1.249	1.305	1.363	1.423	1.486	1.551	1.619	1.689	1.763	1.838	1.917	1.999	2.084	2.172	2.263
10	1.105	1.161	1.219	1.280	1.344	1.411	1.480	1.553	1.629	1.708	1.791	1.877	1.967	2.061	2.159	2.261	2.367	2.478
11	1.116	1.178	1.243	1.312	1.384	1.460	1.539	1.623	1.710	1.802	1.898	1.999	2.105	2.216	2.332	2.453	2.580	2.714
12	1.127	1.196	1.268	1.345	1.426	1.511	1.601	1.696	1.796	1.901	2.012	2.129	2.252	2.382	2.518	2.662	2.813	2.971
13	1.138	1.214	1.294	1.379	1.469	1.564	1.665	1.772	1.886	2.006	2.133	2.267	2.410	2.560	2.720	2.888	3.066	3.254
14	1.149	1.232	1.319	1.413	1.513	1.619	1.732	1.852	1.980	2.116	2.261	2.415	2.579	2.752	2.937	3.133	3.342	3.563
15	1.161	1.250	1.346	1.448	1.558	1.675	1.801	1.935	2.079	2.232	2.397	2.572	2.759	2.959	3.172	3.400	3.642	3.901
16	1.173	1.269	1.373	1.485	1.605	1.734	1.873	2.022	2.183	2.355	2.540	2.739	2.952	3.181	3.426	3.689	3.970	4.272
17	1.184	1.288	1.400	1.522	1.653	1.795	1.948	2.113	2.292	2.485	2.693	2.917	3.159	3.419	3.700	4.002	4.328	4.678
18	1.196	1.307	1.428	1.560	1.702	1.857	2.026	2.208	2.407	2.621	2.854	3.107	3.380	3.676	3.996	4.342	4.717	5.122
19	1.208	1.327	1.457	1.599	1.754	1.923	2.107	2.308	2.527	2.766	3.026	3.309	3.617	3.951	4.316	4.712	5.142	5.609
20	1.220	1.347	1.486	1.639	1.806	1.990	2.191	2.412	2.653	2.918	3.207	3.524	3.870	4.248	4.661	5.112	5.604	6.142
21	1.232	1.367	1.516	1.680	1.860	2.059	2.279	2.520	2.786	3.078	3.400	3.753	4.141	4.566	5.034	5.547	6.109	6.725
22	1.245	1.388	1.546	1.722	1.916	2.132	2.370	2.634	2.925	3.248	3.604	3.997	4.430	4.909	5.437	6.018	6.659	7.364
23	1.257	1.408	1.577	1.765	1.974	2.206	2.465	2.752	3.072	3.426	3.820	4.256	4.741	5.277	5.871	6.530	7.258	8.064
24	1.270	1.430	1.608	1.809	2.033	2.283	2.563	2.876	3.225	3.615	4.049	4.533	5.072	5.673	6.341	7.085	7.911	8.830
25	1.282	1.451	1.641	1.854	2.094	2.363	2.666	3.005	3.386	3.813	4.292	4.828	5.427	6.098	6.848	7.687	8.623	9.668
26	1.295	1.473	1.673	1.900	2.157	2.446	2.772	3.141	3.556	4.023	4.549	5.141	5.807	6.556	7.396	8.340	9.399	10.587
27	1.308	1.495	1.707	1.948	2.221	2.532	2.883	3.282	3.733	4.244	4.822	5.476	6.214	7.047	7.988	9.049	10.245	11.593
28	1.321	1.517	1.741	1.996	2.288	2.620	2.999	3.430	3.920	4.478	5.112	5.832	6.649	7.576	8.627	9.818	11.167	12.694
29	1.335	1.540	1.776	2.046	2.357	2.712	3.119	3.584	4.116	4.724	5.418	6.211	7.114	8.144	9.317	10.653	12.172	13.900
30	1.348	1.563	1.811	2.098	2.427	2.807	3.243	3.745	4.322	4.984	5.743	6.614	7.612	8.755	10.063	11.558	13.268	15.220

Number of Years	10.00%	10.50%	11.00%	11.50%	12.00%	12.50%	13.00%	13.50%	14.00%	14.50%	15.00%	15.50%	16.00%	16.50%	17.00%	17.50%	18.00%
1	1.100	1.105	1.110	1.115	1.120	1.125	1.130	1.135	1.140	1.145	1.150	1.155	1.160	1.165	1.170	1.175	1.180
2	1.210	1.221	1.232	1.243	1.254	1.266	1.277	1.288	1.300	1.311	1.323	1.334	1.346	1.357	1.369	1.381	1.392
3	1.331	1.349	1.368	1.386	1.405	1.424	1.443	1.462	1.482	1.501	1.521	1.541	1.561	1.581	1.602	1.622	1.643
4	1.464	1.491	1.518	1.546	1.574	1.602	1.630	1.660	1.689	1.719	1.749	1.780	1.811	1.842	1.874	1.906	1.939
5	1.611	1.647	1.685	1.723	1.762	1.802	1.842	1.884	1.925	1.968	2.011	2.055	2.100	2.146	2.192	2.240	2.288
6	1.772	1.820	1.870	1.922	1.974	2.027	2.082	2.138	2.195	2.253	2.313	2.374	2.436	2.500	2.565	2.632	2.700
7	1.949	2.012	2.076	2.143	2.211	2.281	2.353	2.426	2.502	2.580	2.660	2.742	2.826	2.913	3.001	3.092	3.185
8	2.144	2.223	2.305	2.389	2.476	2.566	2.658	2.754	2.853	2.954	3.059	3.167	3.278	3.393	3.511	3.633	3.759
9	2.358	2.456	2.558	2.664	2.773	2.887	3.004	3.126	3.252	3.383	3.518	3.658	3.803	3.953	4.108	4.269	4.435
10	2.594	2.714	2.839	2.970	3.106	3.247	3.395	3.548	3.707	3.873	4.046	4.225	4.411	4.605	4.807	5.016	5.234
11	2.853	2.999	3.152	3.311	3.479	3.653	3.836	4.027	4.226	4.435	4.652	4.880	5.117	5.365	5.624	5.894	6.176
12	3.138	3.314	3.498	3.692	3.896	4.110	4.335	4.570	4.818	5.078	5.350	5.636	5.936	6.250	6.580	6.926	7.288
13	3.452	3.662	3.883	4.117	4.363	4.624	4.898	5.187	5.492	5.814	6.153	6.510	6.886	7.282	7.699	8.138	8.599
14	3.797	4.046	4.310	4.590	4.887	5.202	5.535	5.888	6.261	6.657	7.076	7.519	7.988	8.483	9.007	9.562	10.147
15	4.177	4.471	4.785	5.118	5.474	5.852	6.254	6.682	7.138	7.622	8.137	8.684	9.266	9.883	10.539	11.235	11.974
16	4.595	4.941	5.311	5.707	6.130	6.583	7.067	7.585	8.137	8.727	9.358	10.030	10.748	11.514	12.330	13.201	14.129
17	5.054	5.460	5.895	6.363	6.866	7.406	7.986	8.609	9.276	9.993	10.761	11.585	12.468	13.413	14.426	15.511	16.672
18	5.560	6.033	6.544	7.095	7.690	8.332	9.024	9.771	10.575	11.442	12.375	13.381	14.463	15.627	16.879	18.226	19.673
19	6.116	6.666	7.263	7.911	8.613	9.373	10.197	11.090	12.056	13.101	14.232	15.455	16.777	18.205	19.748	21.415	23.214
20	6.727	7.366	8.062	8.821	9.646	10.545	11.523	12.587	13.743	15.001	16.367	17.850	19.461	21.209	23.106	25.163	27.393
21	7.400	8.140	8.949	9.835	10.804	11.863	13.021	14.286	15.668	17.176	18.822	20.617	22.574	24.708	27.034	29.566	32.324
22	8.140	8.994	9.934	10.966	12.100	13.346	14.714	16.215	17.861	19.666	21.645	23.812	26.186	28.785	31.629	34.740	38.142
23	8.954	9.939	11.026	12.227	13.552	15.014	16.627	18.404	20.362	22.518	24.891	27.503	30.376	33.535	37.006	40.820	45.008
24	9.850	10.982	12.239	13.633	15.179	16.891	18.788	20.888	23.212	25.783	28.625	31.766	35.236	39.068	43.297	47.963	53.109
25	10.835	12.135	13.585	15.201	17.000	19.003	21.231	23.708	26.462	29.521	32.919	36.690	40.874	45.514	50.658	56.357	62.669
26	11.918	13.410	15.080	16.949	19.040	21.378	23.991	26.909	30.167	33.802	37.857	42.377	47.414	53.024	59.270	66.219	73.949
27	13.110	14.818	16.739	18.898	21.325	24.050	27.109	30.541	34.390	38.703	43.535	48.946	55.000	61.773	69.345	77.808	87.260
28	14.421	16.374	18.580	21.072	23.884	27.056	30.633	34.664	39.204	44.315	50.066	56.532	63.800	71.966	81.134	91.424	102.967
29	15.863	18.093	20.624	23.495	26.750	30.438	34.616	39.344	44.693	50.741	57.575	65.295	74.009	83.840	94.927	107.423	121.501
30	17.449	19.993	22.892	26.197	29.960	34.243	39.116	44.656	50.950	58.098	66.212	75.415	85.850	97.674	111.065	126.222	143.371

Monthly Compound Interest Rate (Future Value)
Future Value of $1—Principal Plus Accumulated Interests

Number of Months	1.00%	1.50%	2.00%	2.50%	3.00%	3.50%	4.00%	4.50%	5.00%	5.50%	6.00%	6.50%	7.00%	7.50%	8.00%	8.50%	9.00%	9.50%
1	1.001	1.001	1.002	1.002	1.003	1.003	1.003	1.004	1.004	1.005	1.005	1.005	1.006	1.006	1.007	1.007	1.008	1.008
2	1.002	1.003	1.003	1.004	1.005	1.006	1.007	1.008	1.008	1.009	1.010	1.011	1.012	1.013	1.013	1.014	1.015	1.016
3	1.003	1.004	1.005	1.006	1.008	1.009	1.010	1.011	1.013	1.014	1.015	1.016	1.018	1.019	1.020	1.021	1.023	1.024
4	1.003	1.005	1.007	1.008	1.010	1.012	1.013	1.015	1.017	1.018	1.020	1.022	1.024	1.025	1.027	1.029	1.030	1.032
5	1.004	1.006	1.008	1.010	1.013	1.015	1.017	1.019	1.021	1.023	1.025	1.027	1.030	1.032	1.034	1.036	1.038	1.040
6	1.005	1.008	1.010	1.013	1.015	1.018	1.020	1.023	1.025	1.028	1.030	1.033	1.036	1.038	1.041	1.043	1.046	1.048
7	1.006	1.009	1.012	1.015	1.018	1.021	1.024	1.027	1.030	1.033	1.036	1.039	1.042	1.045	1.048	1.051	1.054	1.057
8	1.007	1.010	1.013	1.017	1.020	1.024	1.027	1.030	1.034	1.037	1.041	1.044	1.048	1.051	1.055	1.058	1.062	1.065
9	1.008	1.011	1.015	1.019	1.023	1.027	1.030	1.034	1.038	1.042	1.046	1.050	1.054	1.058	1.062	1.066	1.070	1.074
10	1.008	1.013	1.017	1.021	1.025	1.030	1.034	1.038	1.042	1.047	1.051	1.056	1.060	1.064	1.069	1.073	1.078	1.082
11	1.009	1.014	1.018	1.023	1.028	1.033	1.037	1.042	1.047	1.052	1.056	1.061	1.066	1.071	1.076	1.081	1.086	1.091
12	1.010	1.015	1.020	1.025	1.030	1.036	1.041	1.046	1.051	1.056	1.062	1.067	1.072	1.078	1.083	1.088	1.094	1.099
24	1.020	1.030	1.041	1.051	1.062	1.072	1.083	1.094	1.105	1.116	1.127	1.138	1.150	1.161	1.173	1.185	1.196	1.208
36	1.030	1.046	1.062	1.078	1.094	1.111	1.127	1.144	1.161	1.179	1.197	1.215	1.233	1.251	1.270	1.289	1.309	1.328
48	1.041	1.062	1.083	1.105	1.127	1.150	1.173	1.197	1.221	1.245	1.270	1.296	1.322	1.349	1.376	1.403	1.431	1.460
60	1.051	1.078	1.105	1.133	1.162	1.191	1.221	1.252	1.283	1.316	1.349	1.383	1.418	1.453	1.490	1.527	1.566	1.605
84	1.072	1.111	1.150	1.191	1.233	1.277	1.323	1.369	1.418	1.468	1.520	1.574	1.630	1.688	1.747	1.809	1.873	1.939
120	1.105	1.162	1.221	1.284	1.349	1.418	1.491	1.567	1.647	1.731	1.819	1.912	2.010	2.112	2.220	2.333	2.451	2.576
240	1.221	1.350	1.491	1.648	1.821	2.012	2.223	2.455	2.713	2.997	3.310	3.656	4.039	4.461	4.927	5.441	6.009	6.636
360	1.350	1.568	1.821	2.115	2.457	2.853	3.313	3.848	4.468	5.187	6.023	6.992	8.116	9.422	10.936	12.692	14.731	17.095

Number of Months	10.00%	10.50%	11.00%	11.50%	12.00%	12.50%	13.00%	13.50%	14.00%	14.50%	15.00%	15.50%	16.00%	16.50%	17.00%	17.50%	18.00%
1	1.008	1.009	1.009	1.010	1.010	1.010	1.011	1.011	1.012	1.012	1.013	1.013	1.013	1.014	1.014	1.015	1.015
2	1.017	1.018	1.018	1.019	1.020	1.021	1.022	1.023	1.023	1.024	1.025	1.026	1.027	1.028	1.029	1.029	1.030
3	1.025	1.026	1.028	1.029	1.030	1.032	1.033	1.034	1.035	1.037	1.038	1.039	1.041	1.042	1.043	1.044	1.046
4	1.034	1.035	1.037	1.039	1.041	1.042	1.044	1.046	1.047	1.049	1.051	1.053	1.054	1.056	1.058	1.060	1.061
5	1.042	1.045	1.047	1.049	1.051	1.053	1.055	1.058	1.060	1.062	1.064	1.066	1.068	1.071	1.073	1.075	1.077
6	1.051	1.054	1.056	1.059	1.062	1.064	1.067	1.069	1.072	1.075	1.077	1.080	1.083	1.085	1.088	1.091	1.093
7	1.060	1.063	1.066	1.069	1.072	1.075	1.078	1.081	1.085	1.088	1.091	1.094	1.097	1.100	1.103	1.107	1.110
8	1.069	1.072	1.076	1.079	1.083	1.086	1.090	1.094	1.097	1.101	1.104	1.108	1.112	1.115	1.119	1.123	1.126
9	1.078	1.082	1.086	1.090	1.094	1.098	1.102	1.106	1.110	1.114	1.118	1.122	1.127	1.131	1.135	1.139	1.143
10	1.087	1.091	1.096	1.100	1.105	1.109	1.114	1.118	1.123	1.128	1.132	1.137	1.142	1.146	1.151	1.156	1.161
11	1.096	1.101	1.106	1.111	1.116	1.121	1.126	1.131	1.136	1.141	1.146	1.152	1.157	1.162	1.167	1.173	1.178
12	1.105	1.110	1.116	1.121	1.127	1.132	1.138	1.144	1.149	1.155	1.161	1.166	1.172	1.178	1.184	1.190	1.196
24	1.220	1.233	1.245	1.257	1.270	1.282	1.295	1.308	1.321	1.334	1.347	1.361	1.374	1.388	1.402	1.415	1.430
36	1.348	1.368	1.389	1.410	1.431	1.452	1.474	1.496	1.518	1.541	1.564	1.587	1.611	1.635	1.659	1.684	1.709
48	1.489	1.519	1.550	1.581	1.612	1.644	1.677	1.711	1.745	1.780	1.815	1.852	1.888	1.926	1.964	2.004	2.043
60	1.645	1.687	1.729	1.772	1.817	1.862	1.909	1.957	2.006	2.056	2.107	2.160	2.214	2.269	2.326	2.384	2.443
84	2.008	2.079	2.152	2.228	2.307	2.388	2.472	2.559	2.649	2.743	2.839	2.939	3.042	3.149	3.260	3.374	3.493
120	2.707	2.845	2.989	3.141	3.300	3.468	3.644	3.828	4.022	4.226	4.440	4.665	4.901	5.149	5.409	5.682	5.969
240	7.328	8.092	8.935	9.866	10.893	12.026	13.277	14.657	16.180	17.861	19.715	21.762	24.019	26.510	29.258	32.289	35.633
360	19.837	23.019	26.708	30.987	35.950	41.704	48.377	56.114	65.085	75.485	87.541	101.517	117.717	136.494	158.256	183.477	212.704

Annual Present Value Factors

Present Value of $1 After Accumulated Interest Compounded Annually

Number of Years	1.00%	1.50%	2.00%	2.50%	3.00%	3.50%	4.00%	4.50%	5.00%	5.50%	6.00%	6.50%	7.00%	7.50%	8.00%	8.50%	9.00%	9.50%
1	0.990	0.985	0.980	0.976	0.971	0.966	0.962	0.957	0.952	0.948	0.943	0.939	0.935	0.930	0.926	0.922	0.917	0.913
2	0.980	0.971	0.961	0.952	0.943	0.934	0.925	0.916	0.907	0.898	0.890	0.882	0.873	0.865	0.857	0.849	0.842	0.834
3	0.971	0.956	0.942	0.929	0.915	0.902	0.889	0.876	0.864	0.852	0.840	0.828	0.816	0.805	0.794	0.783	0.772	0.762
4	0.961	0.942	0.924	0.906	0.888	0.871	0.855	0.839	0.823	0.807	0.792	0.777	0.763	0.749	0.735	0.722	0.708	0.696
5	0.951	0.928	0.906	0.884	0.863	0.842	0.822	0.802	0.784	0.765	0.747	0.730	0.713	0.697	0.681	0.665	0.650	0.635
6	0.942	0.915	0.888	0.862	0.837	0.814	0.790	0.768	0.746	0.725	0.705	0.685	0.666	0.648	0.630	0.613	0.596	0.580
7	0.933	0.901	0.871	0.841	0.813	0.786	0.760	0.735	0.711	0.687	0.665	0.644	0.623	0.603	0.583	0.565	0.547	0.530
8	0.923	0.888	0.853	0.821	0.789	0.759	0.731	0.703	0.677	0.652	0.627	0.604	0.582	0.561	0.540	0.521	0.502	0.484
9	0.914	0.875	0.837	0.801	0.766	0.734	0.703	0.673	0.645	0.618	0.592	0.567	0.544	0.522	0.500	0.480	0.460	0.442
10	0.905	0.862	0.820	0.781	0.744	0.709	0.676	0.644	0.614	0.585	0.558	0.533	0.508	0.485	0.463	0.442	0.422	0.404
11	0.896	0.849	0.804	0.762	0.722	0.685	0.650	0.616	0.585	0.555	0.527	0.500	0.475	0.451	0.429	0.408	0.388	0.369
12	0.887	0.836	0.788	0.744	0.701	0.662	0.625	0.590	0.557	0.526	0.497	0.470	0.444	0.420	0.397	0.376	0.356	0.337
13	0.879	0.824	0.773	0.725	0.681	0.639	0.601	0.564	0.530	0.499	0.469	0.441	0.415	0.391	0.368	0.346	0.326	0.307
14	0.870	0.812	0.758	0.708	0.661	0.618	0.577	0.540	0.505	0.473	0.442	0.414	0.388	0.363	0.340	0.319	0.299	0.281
15	0.861	0.800	0.743	0.690	0.642	0.597	0.555	0.517	0.481	0.448	0.417	0.389	0.362	0.338	0.315	0.294	0.275	0.256
16	0.853	0.788	0.728	0.674	0.623	0.577	0.534	0.494	0.458	0.425	0.394	0.365	0.339	0.314	0.292	0.271	0.252	0.234
17	0.844	0.776	0.714	0.657	0.605	0.557	0.513	0.473	0.436	0.402	0.371	0.343	0.317	0.292	0.270	0.250	0.231	0.214
18	0.836	0.765	0.700	0.641	0.587	0.538	0.494	0.453	0.416	0.381	0.350	0.322	0.296	0.272	0.250	0.230	0.212	0.195
19	0.828	0.754	0.686	0.626	0.570	0.520	0.475	0.433	0.396	0.362	0.331	0.302	0.277	0.253	0.232	0.212	0.194	0.178
20	0.820	0.742	0.673	0.610	0.554	0.503	0.456	0.415	0.377	0.343	0.312	0.284	0.258	0.235	0.215	0.196	0.178	0.163
21	0.811	0.731	0.660	0.595	0.538	0.486	0.439	0.397	0.359	0.325	0.294	0.266	0.242	0.219	0.199	0.180	0.164	0.149
22	0.803	0.721	0.647	0.581	0.522	0.469	0.422	0.380	0.342	0.308	0.278	0.250	0.226	0.204	0.184	0.166	0.150	0.136
23	0.795	0.710	0.634	0.567	0.507	0.453	0.406	0.363	0.326	0.292	0.262	0.235	0.211	0.189	0.170	0.153	0.138	0.124
24	0.788	0.700	0.622	0.553	0.492	0.438	0.390	0.348	0.310	0.277	0.247	0.221	0.197	0.176	0.158	0.141	0.126	0.113
25	0.780	0.689	0.610	0.539	0.478	0.423	0.375	0.333	0.295	0.262	0.233	0.207	0.184	0.164	0.146	0.130	0.116	0.103
26	0.772	0.679	0.598	0.526	0.464	0.409	0.361	0.318	0.281	0.249	0.220	0.194	0.172	0.153	0.135	0.120	0.106	0.094
27	0.764	0.669	0.586	0.513	0.450	0.395	0.347	0.305	0.268	0.236	0.207	0.183	0.161	0.142	0.125	0.111	0.098	0.086
28	0.757	0.659	0.574	0.501	0.437	0.382	0.333	0.292	0.255	0.223	0.196	0.171	0.150	0.132	0.116	0.102	0.090	0.079
29	0.749	0.649	0.563	0.489	0.424	0.369	0.321	0.279	0.243	0.212	0.185	0.161	0.141	0.123	0.107	0.094	0.082	0.072
30	0.742	0.640	0.552	0.477	0.412	0.356	0.308	0.267	0.231	0.201	0.174	0.151	0.131	0.114	0.099	0.087	0.075	0.066

Number of Years	10.00%	10.50%	11.00%	11.50%	12.00%	12.50%	13.00%	13.50%	14.00%	14.50%	15.00%	15.50%	16.00%	16.50%	17.00%	17.50%	18.00%
1	0.909	0.905	0.901	0.897	0.893	0.889	0.885	0.881	0.877	0.873	0.870	0.866	0.862	0.858	0.855	0.851	0.847
2	0.826	0.819	0.812	0.804	0.797	0.790	0.783	0.776	0.769	0.763	0.756	0.750	0.743	0.737	0.731	0.724	0.718
3	0.751	0.741	0.731	0.721	0.712	0.702	0.693	0.684	0.675	0.666	0.658	0.649	0.641	0.632	0.624	0.616	0.609
4	0.683	0.671	0.659	0.647	0.636	0.624	0.613	0.603	0.592	0.582	0.572	0.562	0.552	0.543	0.534	0.525	0.516
5	0.621	0.607	0.593	0.580	0.567	0.555	0.543	0.531	0.519	0.508	0.497	0.487	0.476	0.466	0.456	0.446	0.437
6	0.564	0.549	0.535	0.520	0.507	0.493	0.480	0.468	0.456	0.444	0.432	0.421	0.410	0.400	0.390	0.380	0.370
7	0.513	0.497	0.482	0.467	0.452	0.438	0.425	0.412	0.400	0.388	0.376	0.365	0.354	0.343	0.333	0.323	0.314
8	0.467	0.450	0.434	0.419	0.404	0.390	0.376	0.363	0.351	0.338	0.327	0.316	0.305	0.295	0.285	0.275	0.266
9	0.424	0.407	0.391	0.375	0.361	0.346	0.333	0.320	0.308	0.296	0.284	0.273	0.263	0.253	0.243	0.234	0.225
10	0.386	0.368	0.352	0.337	0.322	0.308	0.295	0.282	0.270	0.258	0.247	0.237	0.227	0.217	0.208	0.199	0.191
11	0.350	0.333	0.317	0.302	0.287	0.274	0.261	0.248	0.237	0.225	0.215	0.205	0.195	0.186	0.178	0.170	0.162
12	0.319	0.302	0.286	0.271	0.257	0.243	0.231	0.219	0.208	0.197	0.187	0.177	0.168	0.160	0.152	0.144	0.137
13	0.290	0.273	0.258	0.243	0.229	0.216	0.204	0.193	0.182	0.172	0.163	0.154	0.145	0.137	0.130	0.123	0.116
14	0.263	0.247	0.232	0.218	0.205	0.192	0.181	0.170	0.160	0.150	0.141	0.133	0.125	0.118	0.111	0.105	0.099
15	0.239	0.224	0.209	0.195	0.183	0.171	0.160	0.150	0.140	0.131	0.123	0.115	0.108	0.101	0.095	0.089	0.084
16	0.218	0.202	0.188	0.175	0.163	0.152	0.141	0.132	0.123	0.115	0.107	0.100	0.093	0.087	0.081	0.076	0.071
17	0.198	0.183	0.170	0.157	0.146	0.135	0.125	0.116	0.108	0.100	0.093	0.086	0.080	0.075	0.069	0.064	0.060
18	0.180	0.166	0.153	0.141	0.130	0.120	0.111	0.102	0.095	0.087	0.081	0.075	0.069	0.064	0.059	0.055	0.051
19	0.164	0.150	0.138	0.126	0.116	0.107	0.098	0.090	0.083	0.076	0.070	0.065	0.060	0.055	0.051	0.047	0.043
20	0.149	0.136	0.124	0.113	0.104	0.095	0.087	0.079	0.073	0.067	0.061	0.056	0.051	0.047	0.043	0.040	0.037
21	0.135	0.123	0.112	0.102	0.093	0.084	0.077	0.070	0.064	0.058	0.053	0.049	0.044	0.040	0.037	0.034	0.031
22	0.123	0.111	0.101	0.091	0.083	0.075	0.068	0.062	0.056	0.051	0.046	0.042	0.038	0.035	0.032	0.029	0.026
23	0.112	0.101	0.091	0.082	0.074	0.067	0.060	0.054	0.049	0.044	0.040	0.036	0.033	0.030	0.027	0.024	0.022
24	0.102	0.091	0.082	0.073	0.066	0.059	0.053	0.048	0.043	0.039	0.035	0.031	0.028	0.026	0.023	0.021	0.019
25	0.092	0.082	0.074	0.066	0.059	0.053	0.047	0.042	0.038	0.034	0.030	0.027	0.024	0.022	0.020	0.018	0.016
26	0.084	0.075	0.066	0.059	0.053	0.047	0.042	0.037	0.033	0.030	0.026	0.024	0.021	0.019	0.017	0.015	0.014
27	0.076	0.067	0.060	0.053	0.047	0.042	0.037	0.033	0.029	0.026	0.023	0.020	0.018	0.016	0.014	0.013	0.011
28	0.069	0.061	0.054	0.047	0.042	0.037	0.033	0.029	0.026	0.023	0.020	0.018	0.016	0.014	0.012	0.011	0.010
29	0.063	0.055	0.048	0.043	0.037	0.033	0.029	0.025	0.022	0.020	0.017	0.015	0.014	0.012	0.011	0.009	0.008
30	0.057	0.050	0.044	0.038	0.033	0.029	0.026	0.022	0.020	0.017	0.015	0.013	0.012	0.010	0.009	0.008	0.007

Monthly Present Value Factors

Present Value of $1 After Accumulated Interest Compounded Monthly

Number of Months	1.00%	2.00%	3.00%	4.00%	5.00%	7.00%	7.00%	7.50%	8.00%	8.50%	9.00%	9.50%	10.00%	10.50%	11.00%
1	0.999	0.998	0.998	0.997	0.996	0.994	0.994	0.994	0.993	0.993	0.993	0.992	0.992	0.991	0.991
2	0.998	0.997	0.995	0.993	0.992	0.988	0.988	0.988	0.987	0.986	0.985	0.984	0.984	0.983	0.982
3	0.998	0.995	0.993	0.990	0.988	0.983	0.983	0.981	0.980	0.979	0.978	0.977	0.975	0.974	0.973
4	0.997	0.993	0.990	0.987	0.984	0.977	0.977	0.975	0.974	0.972	0.971	0.969	0.967	0.966	0.964
5	0.996	0.992	0.988	0.983	0.979	0.971	0.971	0.969	0.967	0.965	0.963	0.961	0.959	0.957	0.955
6	0.995	0.990	0.985	0.980	0.975	0.966	0.966	0.963	0.961	0.959	0.956	0.954	0.951	0.949	0.947
7	0.994	0.988	0.983	0.977	0.971	0.960	0.960	0.957	0.955	0.952	0.949	0.946	0.944	0.941	0.938
8	0.993	0.987	0.980	0.974	0.967	0.955	0.955	0.951	0.948	0.945	0.942	0.939	0.936	0.933	0.930
9	0.993	0.985	0.978	0.970	0.963	0.949	0.949	0.945	0.942	0.938	0.935	0.931	0.928	0.925	0.921
10	0.992	0.983	0.975	0.967	0.959	0.943	0.943	0.940	0.936	0.932	0.928	0.924	0.920	0.917	0.913
11	0.991	0.982	0.973	0.964	0.955	0.938	0.938	0.934	0.930	0.925	0.921	0.917	0.913	0.909	0.904
12	0.990	0.980	0.970	0.961	0.951	0.933	0.933	0.928	0.923	0.919	0.914	0.910	0.905	0.901	0.896
24	0.980	0.961	0.942	0.923	0.905	0.870	0.870	0.861	0.853	0.844	0.836	0.828	0.819	0.811	0.803
36	0.970	0.942	0.914	0.887	0.861	0.811	0.811	0.799	0.787	0.776	0.764	0.753	0.742	0.731	0.720
48	0.961	0.923	0.887	0.852	0.819	0.756	0.756	0.742	0.727	0.713	0.699	0.685	0.671	0.658	0.645
60	0.951	0.905	0.861	0.819	0.779	0.705	0.705	0.688	0.671	0.655	0.639	0.623	0.608	0.593	0.578
84	0.932	0.869	0.811	0.756	0.705	0.613	0.613	0.593	0.572	0.553	0.534	0.516	0.498	0.481	0.465
120	0.905	0.819	0.741	0.671	0.607	0.498	0.498	0.473	0.451	0.429	0.408	0.388	0.369	0.352	0.335
240	0.819	0.671	0.549	0.450	0.369	0.248	0.248	0.224	0.203	0.184	0.166	0.151	0.136	0.124	0.112
360	0.741	0.549	0.407	0.302	0.224	0.123	0.123	0.106	0.091	0.079	0.068	0.058	0.050	0.043	0.037

Number of Months	11.50%	12.00%	12.50%	13.00%	13.50%	14.00%	14.50%	15.00%	15.50%	16.00%	16.50%	17.00%	17.50%	18.00%
1	0.991	0.990	0.990	0.989	0.989	0.988	0.988	0.988	0.987	0.987	0.986	0.986	0.986	0.985
2	0.981	0.980	0.979	0.979	0.978	0.977	0.976	0.975	0.975	0.974	0.973	0.972	0.971	0.971
3	0.972	0.971	0.969	0.968	0.967	0.966	0.965	0.963	0.962	0.961	0.960	0.959	0.957	0.956
4	0.963	0.961	0.959	0.958	0.956	0.955	0.953	0.952	0.950	0.948	0.947	0.945	0.944	0.942
5	0.953	0.951	0.950	0.948	0.946	0.944	0.942	0.940	0.938	0.936	0.934	0.932	0.930	0.928
6	0.944	0.942	0.940	0.937	0.935	0.933	0.930	0.928	0.926	0.924	0.921	0.919	0.917	0.915
7	0.935	0.933	0.930	0.927	0.925	0.922	0.919	0.917	0.914	0.911	0.909	0.906	0.904	0.901
8	0.927	0.923	0.920	0.917	0.914	0.911	0.908	0.905	0.902	0.899	0.897	0.894	0.891	0.888
9	0.918	0.914	0.911	0.908	0.904	0.901	0.898	0.894	0.891	0.888	0.884	0.881	0.878	0.875
10	0.909	0.905	0.902	0.898	0.894	0.890	0.887	0.883	0.880	0.876	0.872	0.869	0.865	0.862
11	0.900	0.896	0.892	0.888	0.884	0.880	0.876	0.872	0.868	0.864	0.861	0.857	0.853	0.849
12	0.892	0.887	0.883	0.879	0.874	0.870	0.866	0.862	0.857	0.853	0.849	0.845	0.841	0.836
24	0.795	0.788	0.780	0.772	0.765	0.757	0.750	0.742	0.735	0.728	0.721	0.713	0.706	0.700
36	0.709	0.699	0.689	0.678	0.668	0.659	0.649	0.639	0.630	0.621	0.612	0.603	0.594	0.585
48	0.633	0.620	0.608	0.596	0.585	0.573	0.562	0.551	0.540	0.530	0.519	0.509	0.499	0.489
60	0.564	0.550	0.537	0.524	0.511	0.499	0.486	0.475	0.463	0.452	0.441	0.430	0.420	0.409
84	0.449	0.434	0.419	0.404	0.391	0.377	0.365	0.352	0.340	0.329	0.318	0.307	0.296	0.286
120	0.318	0.303	0.288	0.274	0.261	0.249	0.237	0.225	0.214	0.204	0.194	0.185	0.176	0.168
240	0.101	0.092	0.083	0.075	0.068	0.062	0.056	0.051	0.046	0.042	0.038	0.034	0.031	0.028
360	0.032	0.028	0.024	0.021	0.018	0.015	0.013	0.011	0.010	0.008	0.007	0.006	0.005	0.005